T0217242

# Communications
# in Computer and Information Science 710

*Commenced Publication in 2007*
Founding and Former Series Editors:
Alfredo Cuzzocrea, Dominik Ślęzak, and Xiaokang Yang

More information about this series at http://www.springer.com/series/7899

Fuchun Sun · Huaping Liu
Dewen Hu (Eds.)

# Cognitive Systems and Signal Processing

Third International Conference, ICCSIP 2016
Beijing, China, November 19–23, 2016
Revised Selected Papers

 Springer

*Editors*
Fuchun Sun ⓘ
Department of Computer Science
  and Technology
Tsinghua University
Beijing
China

Dewen Hu ⓘ
College of Mechatronics and Automation
National University of Defense Technology
Changsha
China

Huaping Liu ⓘ
Department of Computer Science and
  Technology
Tsinghua University
Beijing
China

ISSN 1865-0929          ISSN 1865-0937 (electronic)
Communications in Computer and Information Science
ISBN 978-981-10-5229-3          ISBN 978-981-10-5230-9 (eBook)
DOI 10.1007/978-981-10-5230-9

Library of Congress Control Number: 2017945729

Printed on acid-free paper

This Springer imprint is published by Springer Nature
The registered company is Springer Nature Singapore Pte Ltd.
The registered company address is: 152 Beach Road, #21-01/04 Gateway East, Singapore 189721, Singapore

# Preface

Welcome to the proceedings of the Third International Conference on Cognitive Systems and Information Processing (ICCSIP 2016), which was held in Beijing, the capital of China, during November 19–23, 2016. ICCSIP is the prestigious biennial conference on Cognitive Systems and Information Processing with past events held in Beijing (2012, 2014). Over the past few years, ICCSIP has matured into a well-established series of international conference on cognitive information processing and related fields over the world. Similar to the previous one, ICCSIP 2016 provided an academic forum for the participants to share their new research findings and discuss emerging areas of research. It also established a stimulating environment for the participants to exchange ideas on future trends and opportunities of cognitive information processing research.

Currently, cognitive systems and information processing are applied in an increasing number of research domains such as cognitive sciences and technology, visual cognition and computation, big data and intelligent information processing, bioinformatics and applications. We believe that cognitive systems and information processing will certainly exhibit greater-than-ever advances in the near future. With the aim of promoting the research and technical innovation in relevant fields domestically and internationally, the fundamental objective of ICCSIP is defined as providing a premier forum for researchers and practitioners from academia, industry, and government to share their ideas, research results, and experiences. This year, ICCSIP received 171 submissions, all of which are written in English. After a thorough reviewing process, 59 papers were selected for presentation as full papers, resulting in an acceptance rate of 34.5%. The selected papers included in the proceedings not only address challenging issues in various aspects of cognitive systems and information processing but also showcase contributions from related disciplines that illuminate the state of the art. In addition to the contributed papers, the ICCSIP 2016 technical program included three plenary speeches by C. L. Philip Chen (University of Macau), Hong Cheng (University of Electronic Science and Technology of China), and David Yuan.

We would also like to thank the members of the Advisory Committee for their guidance, the members of the International Program Committee and additional reviewers for reviewing the papers, and members of the Publications Committee for checking the accepted papers in a short period of time. In particular, we are grateful to Springer for publishing the proceedings in the prestigious series of *Communications in Computer and Information Science*. Moreover, we wish to express our heartfelt appreciation to the plenary and panel speakers, session chairs, reviewers, and student volunteers. In addition, there are still many more colleagues, associates, friends, and supporters who helped us in immeasurable ways; we express our sincere gratitude to them all. Last but not the least, we would like to thank all the speakers and authors as well as the participants for their great contributions that made ICCSIP2016 successful and all the hard work worthwhile.

November 2016                                                    Fuchun Sun
                                                                Huaping Liu
                                                                Dewen Hu

# Organization

## Honorary Chairs

Bo Zhang                Tsinghua University, China
Deyi Li                  Chinese Academy of Engineering, China

## Advisory Committee Chairs

Nanning Zheng       Xi'an Jiaotong University, China
Wei Li                  Beihang University, China
Lin Chen              Chinese Academy of Sciences, China
Ning Xi               Michigan State University, USA
Yoshikazu Hayakawa    Nagoya University, Japan
Yinxu Wang          University of Calgary, Canada

## General Chairs

Fuchun Sun          Tsinghua University, China
Jianwei Zhang       Universität Hamburg, Germany

## Program Committee Chairs

Dewen Hu          National University of Defense Technology, China
Stefan Wermter      University of Hamburg, Germany
Jennie Si            Arizona State University, USA
Jinglong Wu        Beijing Institute of Technology, China

## Organizing Committee Chairs

Guangbin Huang      Nanyang Technological University, Singapore
Huaping Liu          Tsinghua University, China
Guojun Dai          Hangzhou Dianzi University, China

## Plenary Sessions Chair

Chenglin Wen        Hangzhou Dianzi University, China

## Special Sessions Chairs

Haibo He           University of Rhode Island, USA
Fei Song            Science China Press, China

## Publications Chair

Wei Li                        California State University, USA

## Publicity Chair

Jianmin Li                    Tsinghua University, China

## Finance Chair

Chunfang Liu                  Tsinghua University, China

## Registration Chairs

Chunle Gao                    Tsinghua University, China
Chao Yang                     Tsinghua University, China

## Local Arrangements Chairs

Hongbo Li                     Tsinghua University, China
Zhongyi Chu                   Beihang University, China

## Electronic Review Chair

Xiaolin Hu                    Tsinghua University, China

## Committees

Fuchun Sun                    Tsinghua University, China
Dewen Hu                      National University of Defense Technology, China
Guojun Dai                    Hangzhou Dianzi University, China
Zhiguang Qin                  University of Electronic Science and Technology,
                                China
Jingmin Xin                   Xi'an Jiaotong University, China
Huaping Liu                   Tsinghua University, China
Wanzeng Kong                  Hangzhou Dianzi University, China
Yuanlong Yu                   Fuzhou University, China
Chenglin Wen                  Hangzhou Dianzi University, China
Zhiquan Feng                  University of Jinan, China
Yi Ning                       Henan University of Technology, China
Rui Nian                      Ocean University of China, China
Fang Liu                      Shenyang Ligong University, China
Meiqin Liu                    Zhejiang University, China
Bin Xu                        Northwestern Polytechnical University, China
Weihua Su                     Academy of Military Medical Sciences, China
Yujian Li                     Beijing University of Technology, China

| Ke Li | Beihang University, China |
|---|---|
| Yongming Li | Shaanxi Normal University, China |
| Shunli Li | Harbin Institute of Technology, China |
| Hongbo Li | Tsinghua University, China |
| Li Li | Tianjin Normal University, China |
| Tieshan Li | Dalian Maritime University, China |
| Zhijun Li | South China University of Technology, China |
| Xia Li | Shenzhen University, China |
| Dongfang Yang | Rocket Force University of Engineering, China |
| Ming Yang | Shanghai Jiao Tong University, China |
| Jian Yang | Nanjing University of Science and Technology, China |
| Fengge Wu | Chinese Academy of Sciences, China |
| Licheng Wu | Minzu University of China, China |
| Jian He | Beijing University of Technology, China |
| Haibo Min | Rocket Force University of Engineering, China |
| Hongqiao Wang | Rocket Force University of Engineering, China |
| Liejun Wang | Xinjiang University, China |
| Hui Shen | National University of Defense Technology, China |
| Pengfei Zhang | China North Vehicle Research Institute, China |
| Jianhai Zhang | Hangzhou Dianzi University, China |
| Chun Zhang | Tsinghua University, China |
| Jinxiang Chen | China Iron & Steel Research Institute Group, China |
| Liang Chen | Shenzhen University, China |
| Minnan Luo | Xi'an Jiaotong University, China |
| Xiong Luo | University of Science & Technology Beijing, China |
| Fan Zhou | Shenyang Ligong University, China |
| Erqiang Zhou | University of Electronic Science and Technology, China |
| Yucai Zhou | Changsha University of Science & Technology, China |
| Dongbin Zhao | Chinese Academy of Sciences, China |
| Yuntao Zhao | Shenyang Ligong University, China |
| Qingjie Zhao | Beijing Institute of Technology, China |
| Huijing Zhao | Peking University, China |
| Shiqiang Hu | Shanghai Jiao Tong University, China |
| Laihong Hu | Rocket Force University of Engineering, China |
| Ying Hu | Chinese Academy of Sciences, China |
| Zhansheng Duan | Xi'an Jiaotong University, China |
| Peijiang Yuan | Beihang University, China |
| Chen Guo | Dalian Maritime University, China |
| Deshuang Huang | Tongji University, China |
| Panfeng Huang | Northwestern Polytechnical University, China |
| Yongzhi Cao | Peking University, China |
| Rongxin Cui | Northwestern Polytechnical University, China |
| Quanbo Ge | Hangzhou Dianzi University, China |
| Hong Cheng | University of Electronic Science and Technology, China |

# Contents

## Machine Learning

**Robotics**

**Cognitive System**

# Cognitive Signal Processing

# Control and Decision

# A Novel Pulsar Navigation Method Based on an Asynchronous Observation Model

Pengbin Guo, Jian Sun[(⊠)], Shuling Hu, and Ju Xue

State Key Laboratory for Strength and Vibration, School of Aerospace,
Xi'an Jiaotong University, Xi'an 710049, People's Republic of China
sunjian10@xjtu.edu.cn

**Abstract.** Pulsar navigation has been a potential navigation method for high-orbit satellites or deep space exploration. One of the main problems is that the update rate of measurements are too slow that results in the low navigation accuracy. To solve this problem, an asynchronous model together with a corresponding Kalman filter is proposed. The simulations show that the proposed model has better performance than that of the synchronous model which is widely used in lots of previous literatures.

**Keywords:** Pulsar navigation · Asynchronous observation model · Kalman filtering

## 1 Introduction

Pulsars are rapidly rotating neutron stars. They produce highly regular and very stable pulses that can be predicted accurately which can be utilized in a navigation system [1]. After a period of observation, the stable X-ray pulse profile is acquired through the epoch folding (EF) procedure [2]. By observing stellar emissions in X wavelengths, the orientation, position and time of spacecraft can be determined. There are already over 1800 known pulsars in the celestial sphere, makes pulsars a very firm base for suitable for a variety of tasks in low orbit to spacecraft on interplanetary missions [3].

Unlike man-made navigation satellites, pulsars, are immune to solar flares or hostile attempts at disabling them [4]; Compared with DSN(Deep Space Network), the main advantage of pulsar navigation is that DSN needs extensive ground operations and scheduling while pulsar navigation does not because it is an autonomous navigation [3].

Currently, some literatures use one detector to observe pulsars [3, 5], but Wang Y. D [6] has proven that the navigation accuracy of using multi detectors in the case of the same total areas with one detector is better. However, the literatures of adopting multi detectors [6–11] used one integration time for different pulsars, and to make sure that the profile had a high TOA accuracy for all selected pulsars, the integration time had to been set very long which resulted in the slow update rate of the measurements.

In fact, the key issue of pulsar navigation is measuring the TOA between spacecraft and solar system barycenter (SSB), and the TOA accuracy has a direct impact on the final accuracy of the navigation. According to [3], TOA accuracy is related to the integration time and the features of pulsars which are quite different for different

© Springer Nature Singapore Pte Ltd. 2017
F. Sun et al. (Eds.): ICCSIP 2016, CCIS 710, pp. 3–12, 2017.
DOI: 10.1007/978-981-10-5230-9_1

pulsars. Therefore, different pulsars should take different integration times to get the same TOA accuracy.

An asynchronous observation model is proposed, and a Kalman filter algorithm is also designed for this model in the article. This paper is organized as follows: the filter algorithm of the asynchronous observation model is presented in Sect. 2. The pulsar navigation model is proposed in Sect. 3. Some simulations are done in Sect. 4. The conclusion are drawn in Sect. 5.

## 2   Filter Algorithm of the Asynchronous Observation Model

The system equation can be represented as:

$$x_{t_k} = f(x_{t_{k-1}}) + w_{t_{k-1}} \tag{1}$$

where $x_{t_k}$ is the state vector. $w_{t_{k-1}}$ is white noise sequence with zero mean and its covariance is $Q_k$.

Equation (1) can be written in a form of linearization:

$$x_{t_k} = \Phi_{t_{k-1}} x_{t_{k-1}} + w_{t_{k-1}} \tag{2}$$

where: $\Phi_{t_{k-1}}$ is the state-transition matrix after linearization.

Suppose there are N sensors measuring the state independently, $T$ is the sampling period. $n_k^i$ is the number of the measurement during the time $(t_{k-1}, t_k]$ of sensor $i$. So the total numbers of measured values are:

$$N_k = \sum_{i=1}^{N} n_k^i \tag{3}$$

It should be noted that during the sampling time $T$, some sensors may have a plurality of measured values, and others may not have any measured values. If there are no values measured, $n_k^i$ can be set as 0.

Define $\lambda_k^i$ as the time interval between $t_k$ and the measurement i ($i = 1, 2, \cdots N_k$), in the time interval $(t_{k-1}, t_k]$, all measurements are sorted in chronological order of measured time and it can be seen in Fig. 1.

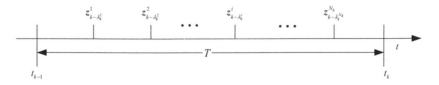

**Fig. 1.** All measurements sorted in chronological order in $(t_{k-1}, t_k]$

The measurement $i$ can be expressed as:

$$z^i_{t_k - \lambda^i_k} = h^i \left( x_{t_k - \lambda^i_k} \right) + v^i_{t_k - \lambda^i_k} \quad i = 1, 2, 3, \cdots, N_k \tag{4}$$

We write Eq. (4) into a linear form:

$$z^i_{t_k - \lambda^i_k} = H^i_{t_k - \lambda^i_k} x_{t_k - \lambda^i_k} + v^i_{t_k - \lambda^i_k} \quad i = 1, 2, 3, \cdots, N_k \tag{5}$$

where: $H^i$ is the measurement matrix. $v^i$ is white noise sequence with zero mean and the covariance $R^i$.

According to Eq. (2), we can obtain:

$$x_{t_k} = \Phi_{t_k - \lambda^i_k} x_{t_k - \lambda^i_k} + w_{t_k - \lambda^i_k} \tag{6}$$

It can be obtained from Eq. (6):

$$x_{t_k - \lambda^i_k} = \Phi^{-1}_{t_k - \lambda^i_k} x_{t_k} - \Phi^{-1}_{t_k - \lambda^i_k} w_{t_k - \lambda^i_k} \tag{7}$$

Substituting Eq. (7) into Eq. (5)

$$\begin{aligned} z^i_{t_k - \lambda^i_k} &= H^i_{k - \lambda^i_k} \Phi^{-1}_{t_k - \lambda^i_k} \left( x_{t_k} - w_{t_k - \lambda^i_k} \right) + v_{t_k - \lambda^i_k} \\ &= H^i_{t_k - \lambda^i_k} \Phi^{-1}_{t_k - \lambda^i_k} x_{t_k} - H^i_{t_k - \lambda^i_k} \Phi^{-1}_{t_k - \lambda^i_k} w_{t_k - \lambda^i_k} + v^i_{t_k - \lambda^i_k} \end{aligned} \tag{8}$$

Define:

$$\bar{H}^i_k = H^i_{t_k - \lambda^i_k} \Phi^{-1}_{t_k - \lambda^i_k} \tag{9}$$

$$\bar{v}^i_k = -H^i_{t_k - \lambda^i_k} \Phi^{-1}_{t_k - \lambda^i_k} w_{t_k - \lambda^i_k} + v^i_{t_k - \lambda^i_k} \tag{10}$$

$$\bar{z}^i_k = z^i_{t_k - \lambda^i_k} \tag{11}$$

So Eq. (8) goes into:

$$\bar{z}^i_k = \bar{H}^i_k x_{t_k} + \bar{v}^i_k \tag{12}$$

If we define:

$$z_k = \left[ \left( \bar{z}^1_k \right)^T \quad \left( \bar{z}^2_k \right)^T \quad \cdots \quad \left( \bar{z}^{N_k}_k \right)^T \right]^{\mathbf{T}} \tag{13}$$

$$\mathbf{H}_k = \left[ \left( \bar{\mathbf{H}}^1_k \right)^T \quad \left( \bar{\mathbf{H}}^2_k \right)^T \quad \cdots \quad \left( \bar{\mathbf{H}}^{N_k}_k \right)^T \right]^{\mathbf{T}} \tag{14}$$

$$\mathbf{v}_k = \left[ \left(\bar{\mathbf{v}}_k^1\right)^T \quad \left(\bar{\mathbf{v}}_k^2\right)^T \quad \cdots \quad \left(\bar{\mathbf{v}}_k^{N_k}\right)^T \right]^{\mathbf{T}} \tag{15}$$

The measurement equation can be written as:

$$z_k = H_k x_{t_k} + v_k \tag{16}$$

and the covariance of the measurement noise can be calculated as follow:

$$R_k = \mathrm{cov}[\bar{v}(k), \bar{v}(k)] = \begin{bmatrix} \bar{\mathbf{H}}_k^1 \mathbf{Q}_{t_k - \lambda_k^1} \left(\bar{\mathbf{H}}_k^1\right)^T & \bar{\mathbf{H}}_k^1 \mathbf{Q}_{t_k - \lambda_k^2} \left(\bar{\mathbf{H}}_k^2\right)^T & \cdots & \bar{\mathbf{H}}_k^1 \mathbf{Q}_{t_k - \lambda_k^{N_k}} \left(\bar{\mathbf{H}}_k^{N_k}\right)^T \\ \bar{\mathbf{H}}_k^2 \mathbf{Q}_{t_k - \lambda_k^2} \left(\bar{\mathbf{H}}_k^1\right)^T & \bar{\mathbf{H}}_k^2 \mathbf{Q}_{t_k - \lambda_k^2} \left(\bar{\mathbf{H}}_k^2\right)^T & \cdots & \bar{\mathbf{H}}_k^2 \mathbf{Q}_{t_k - \lambda_k^{N_k}} \left(\bar{\mathbf{H}}_k^{N_k}\right)^T \\ \vdots & \vdots & \ddots & \vdots \\ \bar{\mathbf{H}}_k^{N_k} \mathbf{Q}_{t_k - \lambda_k^{N_k}} \left(\bar{\mathbf{H}}_k^1\right)^T & \bar{\mathbf{H}}_k^{N_k} \mathbf{Q}_{t_k - \lambda_k^{N_k}} \left(\bar{\mathbf{H}}_k^2\right)^T & \cdots & \bar{\mathbf{H}}_k^{N_k} \mathbf{Q}_{t_k - \lambda_k^{N_k}} \left(\bar{\mathbf{H}}_k^{N_k}\right)^T \end{bmatrix}$$
$$+ \begin{bmatrix} \mathbf{R}_{t_k - \lambda_k^1}^1 & \mathbf{0} & \cdots & \mathbf{0} \\ \mathbf{0} & \mathbf{R}_{t_k - \lambda_k^2}^2 & \cdots & \mathbf{0} \\ \vdots & \vdots & \ddots & \vdots \\ \mathbf{0} & \mathbf{0} & \cdots & \mathbf{R}_{t_k - \lambda_k^{N_k}}^{N_k} \end{bmatrix} \tag{17}$$

Where: $\mathbf{Q}_{t_k - \lambda_k^i} = E\left( \mathbf{w}_{t_k - \lambda_k^i} \mathbf{w}_{t_k - \lambda_k^i}^T \right)$

The covariance of the state noise and measurement noise can be expressed as:

$$W_k = \mathrm{cov}[\mathbf{w}_{t_{k-1}}, \bar{\mathbf{v}}_k] = \left[ -\mathbf{Q}_{t_k - \lambda_k^1}\left(\bar{H}_k^1\right) \quad -\mathbf{Q}_{t_k - \lambda_k^2}\left(\bar{H}_k^2\right)^T \quad \cdots \quad -\mathbf{Q}_{t_k - \lambda_k^{N_k}}\left(\bar{H}_k^{N_k}\right)^T \right] \tag{18}$$

From Eq. (18), it can be seen that the state noise is related to the measurement noise. The Kaman filter of which the process noise is related to the measurement can be written as [12]:

$$\hat{x}_{k|k-1} = f(\hat{x}_{k-1}) \tag{19}$$

$$\hat{x}_{k|k} = \hat{x}_{k|k-1} + K_k\left(z_k - H_k \hat{x}_{k|k-1}\right) \tag{20}$$

$$P_{k,k-1} = \Phi_{k-1} P_{k-1} \Phi_{k-1} + Q_k \tag{21}$$

$$P_{(x,z)_k} = P_{k,k-1} H_k^T + W_k \tag{22}$$

$$P_{z_k} = H_k P_{k|k-1} H_k^T + H_k W_k + W_k^{\mathrm{T}} H_k^{\mathrm{T}} + R_k \tag{23}$$

$$K_k = P_{(x,z)_k} P_{z_k}^{-1} \tag{24}$$

$$P_k = P_{k,k-1} - P_{(x,z)_k} P_{z_k} P_{(x,z)_k}^{T^T} \tag{25}$$

## 3  The Asynchronous Observation Model of Pulsar Navigation

The dynamic model of pulsar navigation is described as:

$$f(\mathbf{x}(k-1)) = \mathbf{x}(k-1) + \begin{bmatrix} v_x \\ v_y \\ v_z \\ -\frac{\mu r_x}{r^3}\left[1+\frac{3}{2}J_2\left(\frac{\mathrm{Re}}{r}\right)^2\left(1-5\frac{r_z^2}{r^2}\right)\right] \\ -\frac{\mu r_y}{r^3}\left[1+\frac{3}{2}J_2\left(\frac{\mathrm{Re}}{r}\right)^2\left(1-5\frac{r_z^2}{r^2}\right)\right] \\ -\frac{\mu r_z}{r^3}\left[1+\frac{3}{2}J_2\left(\frac{\mathrm{Re}}{r}\right)^2\left(1-5\frac{r_z^2}{r^2}\right)\right] \end{bmatrix} \tau \tag{26}$$

where: $J_2$ is the coefficient of the Earth gravitational zonal term. Re is the radius of Earth, $r = \sqrt{r_x^2 + r_y^2 + r_z^2}$ is the distance of the satellite from Earth's center, $\tau$ is the step size and in this article is set as 1 s. We assume that the time has been converted into coordinate time. $\mathbf{r} = \begin{bmatrix} r_x & r_y & r_z \end{bmatrix}^T$ and $\mathbf{v} = \begin{bmatrix} v_x & v_y & v_z \end{bmatrix}^T$ are position and velocity vectors of the satellite in the Earth-centered inertial coordinate system.

The pulsar observation model is the time difference between the TOA of the pulsar at the spacecraft $t_{obs}^i$ and the TOA of the same pulse at the SSB $t_b^i$. $t_{obs}^i$ is obtained from the x-ray detector, while $t_b^i$ is predicted through the pulsar phase model. The pulsar observation model can be written as [5]:

$$t_b^i - t_{obs}^i = \frac{1}{c}\mathbf{n}_i \cdot \mathbf{r}_{SC} + \frac{1}{2cD_i}\left[(\mathbf{n}_i \cdot \mathbf{r}_{SC})^2 - r_{SC}^2 + 2(\mathbf{n}_i \cdot \mathbf{b})(\mathbf{n}_i \cdot \mathbf{r}_{SC}) - 2(\mathbf{b} \cdot \mathbf{r}_{SC})\right] + \frac{2\mu_s}{c^3}\ln\left|\frac{\mathbf{n}_i \cdot \mathbf{r}_{SC} + r_{SC}}{\mathbf{n}_i \cdot \mathbf{b} + b} + 1\right| \tag{27}$$

where: $\mathbf{n}_i = \left[\cos(\theta_i)\cos(\varphi_i), \cos(\theta_i)\sin(\varphi_i), \sin(\theta_i)\right]^T$ is the unit vector in the direction of the pulsar $i$, and $\varphi_i$ and $\theta_i$ denote the measured ascension angle and declination angle respectively. c is the speed of the light, $\mathbf{r}_{SC} = \mathbf{r}_E + \mathbf{r}$ denotes the position vector of the satellite with respect to the SSB. $\mathbf{r}_E$ is the position vector of Earth's center and can be obtained from ephemeris, $D_i$ denotes the distance between the i-th pulsar and the SSB(Solar System Barycenter). $\mu_s$ is the gravitational constant of the sun. $\mathbf{b}$ is the position of the SSB relative to the sun's center.

From Eq. (27), it can be seen that the key issue of pulsar navigation is to obtain the TOA. As the signals are very weak it usually takes some time (i.e. integration time) to obtain the TOA with some precision. That is to say that the integration time decides the update rate of measurement. According to [3], we can derive the relation between TOA and the integration time:

$$\sigma_{TOA} = \frac{1}{2} \frac{W \sqrt{[B_X + F_X(1 - p_f)](At_{obs}W/P) + F_X A p_f t_{obs}}}{F_X A p_f t_{obs}} \tag{28}$$

In which A is the area of the detector, $p_f$ is the pulsed fraction, $B_X$ is the background radiation, $t_{obs}$ is the observation time, in this paper also called integration time or update time. $F_X$ is the photon flux.

It can be seen from Eq. (28) that the TOA accuracy is related to the probe area, pulse integration time, the pulse period of the pulsar, the duty ratio of the pulse signal and radiation flux which are quite different for different pulsars. Table 1 shows parameters of some common pulsars.

**Table 1.** Pulsar parameters table adapted from [3, 7]

| Name | Galactic longitude | Galactic latitude | P(s) | W(s) | $F_x$(photons/cm$^2$/s) | $P_f$(%) |
|------|------|------|------|------|------|------|
| B0531 +21 | 184.56 | −5.78 | 0.334 | $1.7 \times 10^{-3}$ | 1.54 | 70 |
| B1937 +21 | 57.51 | −0.29 | 0.00156 | $2.1 \times 10^{-5}$ | $4.99 \times 10^{-5}$ | 86 |
| B1821 −24 | 7.8 | −5.58 | 0.00305 | $5.5 \times 10^{-5}$ | $1.93 \times 10^{-4}$ | 98 |
| J1808 −3658 | 355.39 | −8.15 | 0.00249 | $6.2 \times 10^{-4}$ | 0.329 | 4.1 |
| B0540 −69 | 279.72 | −31.52 | 0.0504 | $2.5 \times 10^{-3}$ | $5.15 \times 10^{-3}$ | 67 |

With the parameters and Eq. (28), it can be obtained the relationship between the TOA accuracy and the integration time in the case of A = 1m$^2$ and $B_X$ = 0.005 photons/cm$^2$/s as shown in Fig. 2.

From Fig. 2, we can see that different pulsars have different integration times to get the same TOA accuracy and the integration times are quite different. Also we can see, the performance of Pulsar B0531+21, B1937+21, B1821−24 are relatively better. So we choose these 3 pulsars as the pulsars used to navigate the spacecraft in this article.

## 4  Simulations

The orbit elements are seen in Table 2.

The simulation time is from March 1, 1997, 00:00:00.00 UT.

The measured right ascension angle and declination angle are in Table 3.

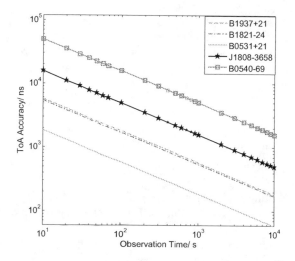

**Fig. 2.** Relationship between TOA and Integration Time

**Table 2.** The orbit elements of the spacecraft

| Orbit Elements | Value |
|---|---|
| Semimajor axis | 12275 km |
| Eccentricity | 0.0038 |
| Inclination | 109.8° |
| Right ascension of ascending node | 0° |
| Argument of perigee | 30° |
| Mean anomaly | 0° |

**Table 3.** The right ascension and declination angle adapted from [9]

| Name | $\varphi$ | $\theta$ |
|---|---|---|
| B0531+21 | 83.63 | 22.01 |
| B1821−24 | 276.13 | −24.87 |
| B1937+21 | 294.92 | 21.58 |

The initial covariance:

$$P_1(0) = \begin{bmatrix} e_r^2 \mathbf{I}_{3\times3} & 0 \\ 0 & e_v^2 \mathbf{I}_{3\times3} \end{bmatrix}$$

where $e_r = 5$ km and $e_v = 10$ m/s are the position and velocity error respectively. The process noise covariance is given as:

$$Q_1(0) = \begin{bmatrix} \sigma_r^2 \mathbf{I}_{3\times3} & \\ & \sigma_v^2 \mathbf{I}_{3\times3} \end{bmatrix}$$

where $\sigma_r = 2 \times 10^{-4}$ m and $\sigma_v = 2 \times 10^{-3}$ m/s.

In this article, the probe area A = 3.5 m$^2$ (optional) and TOA accuracy = 500 ns (optional), the integration time of 3 pulsars are 78 s, 675 s, 755 s. To solve the problem easily, the integration time can be adjusted to 100 s, 600 s, 800 s. We use $x_1$, $x_2$ and $x_3$ to represent the state corresponding to when the 3 detectors obtain the measurement respectively. For the asynchronous observation model, $x_1(k) = x(100 \cdot k)$, $x_2(k) = x(600 \cdot k)$, $x_3(k) = x(800 \cdot k)$. And the TOA accuracy of the asynchronous model are 442 ns, 530 ns, 485 ns.

To ensure all the 3 pulsars have an accuracy of about 500 ns, the integration time of synchronous model are 800 s, 800 s and 800 s. For the synchronous observation model, $x_1(k) = x_2(k) = x_3(k) = x(800 \cdot k)$. The TOA accuracy of synchronous model are 156 ns, 459 ns, 485 ns.

The filter algorithm of asynchronous model is seen in Sect. 2. The filter algorithm of synchronous model is extended Kalman Filter. The other initial conditions are the same with the synchronous model.

We compare the root mean square (RMS) errors of the synchronous observation model and the proposed asynchronous observation model based on 100 Monte Carlo runs. The simulation results are seen in Figs. 3, 4 and 5.

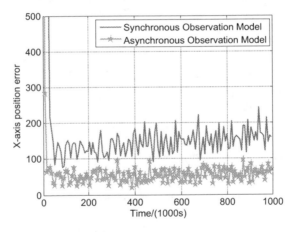

**Fig. 3.** X-axis position errors (m)

As expected, we can see that the proposed model has a better performance than that of the synchronous model. That is because long integration times can only reduce the impact of the measurement noise, but the reduction is too small compared to the system bias caused by the long integration time. From Eq. (26), we can see that long integration time means more iterations to calculate the prediction of the state and more iterations means larger prediction bias. The update rate has been improved heavily compared to that of the synchronous observation model which means much few iterations to calculate the prediction of the state. In the case of the measurement noise are in the same level, that the more accurate prediction makes better performance of asynchronous model is not hard to understand.

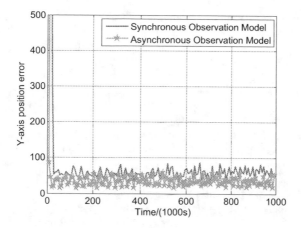

**Fig. 4.** Y-axis position errors (m)

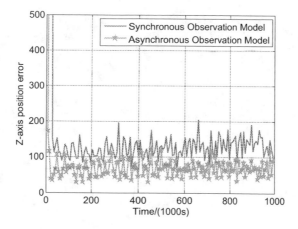

**Fig. 5.** Z-axis position errors (m)

## 5    Conclusion

The main contribution of this paper is that an asynchronous is proposed to improve the update rate of measurement of pulsar navigation. The simulations show that the proposed asynchronous model has better performance than the synchronous model.

## References

1. Matsakis, D.N., Taylor, J., Marshall Eubanks, T.: A statistic for describing pulsar and clock stabilities. Astron. Astrophys. **326**, 924–928 (1997). Berlin
2. Emadzadeh, A.A., Speyer, J.L.: X-Ray pulsar-based relative navigation using epoch folding. IEEE Trans. Aerosp. Electron. Syst. **47**(4), 2317–2328 (2011)

3. Sheikh, S.I., et al.: Spacecraft navigation using X-ray pulsars. J. Guidance Control Dyn. **29** (1), 49–63 (2006)
4. Buist, P.J., et al.: Overview of pulsar navigation: past, present and future trends navigation. J. Inst. Navig. **58**(2), 153–164 (2011)
5. Sheikh, S.I., et al.: The Use of X-ray pulsars for spacecraft navigation. In: Coffey, S.L., et al. (eds.) Spaceflight Mechanics 2004, vol. 119, pp. 105–119 (2005). Pt 1–3
6. Wang, Y., et al.: XNAV/CNS integrated navigation based on improved kinematic and static filter. J. Navig. **66**(06), 899–918 (2013)
7. Wang, Y., et al.: X-ray pulsar-based navigation system with the errors in the planetary ephemerides for earth-orbiting satellite. Adv. Space Res. **51**(12), 2394–2404 (2013)
8. Wei, E., et al.: Autonomous navigation of mars probe using X-ray pulsars: modeling and results. Adv. Space Res. **51**(5), 849–857 (2013)
9. Xiong, K., Wei, C., Liu, L.: Robust Kalman filtering for discrete-time nonlinear systems with parameter uncertainties. Aerosp. Sci. Technol. **18**(1), 15–24 (2012)
10. Liu, J., et al.: Pulsar navigation for interplanetary missions using CV Model and ASUKF. Aerosp. Sci. Technol. **22**(1), 19–23 (2012)
11. Feng, D., et al.: Autonomous orbit determination and its error analysis for deep space using X-ray pulsar. Aerosp. Sci. Technol. **32**(1), 35–41 (2014)
12. Chongzhao, H., Hongyan, Z., Zhansheng, D.: Multi-Source Information Fusion. Tsinghua University Press, Beijing (2010)

# Event-Triggered Adaptive Dynamic Programming for Uncertain Nonlinear Systems

Qichao Zhang[1,2], Dongbin Zhao[1,2(✉)], and Ding Wang[1,2]

[1] The State Key Laboratory of Management and Control for Complex Systems, Institute of Automation, Chinese Academy of Sciences, Beijing 100190, China
zhangqichao2013@163.com, {dongbin.zhao,ding.wang}@ia.ac.cn
[2] University of Chinese Academy of Sciences, Beijing 100049, China

**Abstract.** In this paper, the robust control for a class of continuous-time nonlinear system with unmatched uncertainties is investigated using an event-triggered adaptive dynamic programming method. First, the robust control problem is solved using the optimal control method. Under the event-triggered mechanism, the solution of the optimal control problem can asymptotically stabilize the uncertain system with an designed triggering condition. That is, the designed event-triggered controller is robust to the original uncertain system. Then, a single critic network structure with experience replay technique is constructed to approach the optimal control policies. Finally, a simulation example is provided to demonstrate the effectiveness of the proposed control scheme.

**Keywords:** Adaptive dynamic programming · Event-triggered control · Robust control · Neural network

## 1 Introduction

As many practical control systems become more and more complex, the uncertainties arise in the system models frequently. These uncertainties may severely degrade the system performance, and even lead to system instability, so it is necessary to design the robust controller for uncertain nonlinear systems. Lin *et al.* [1] established a connection between the robust control problem and optimal control problem. They proposed an indirect approach for the robust stabilization by designing a corresponding optimal controller. In [2], the uncertainties was divided into matched and unmatched ones and proved that the optimal controller can stabilize the linear and nonlinear robust control systems in the same way. However, the detailed approach to solve the Hamilton-Jacobi-Bellman (HJB) equation to obtain the optimal control policy was not discussed.

As is known, it is intractable to give an analytic solution to the HJB equation for the nonlinear systems [3]. Recently, adaptive dynamic programming (ADP) which was proposed by Werbos [4] has been widely applied to approximate the solution of the HJB equation. For example, the $H_\infty$ control approach based on ADP was investigated for the uncertain nonlinear systems in [5]. Jiang *et al.* proposed a robust adaptive dynamic programming (RADP) methodology in [6].

© Springer Nature Singapore Pte Ltd. 2017
F. Sun et al. (Eds.): ICCSIP 2016, CCIS 710, pp. 13–26, 2017.
DOI: 10.1007/978-981-10-5230-9_2

Liu *et al.* [7] investigated the optimal robust guaranteed cost control problem using corresponding optimal control method. In [8], the robust control problem of nonlinear systems with matched uncertainties was converted into an optimal control problem of an nominal system. For the nonlinear deterministic systems, Zhao *et al.* developed several ADP methods to solve the corresponding optimal control problems [9,10]. However, the aforementioned approaches are conducted predicated on the traditional time-triggered strategy.

In general, the amount of transmitted data is huge using the traditional time-triggered approach. To mitigate the unnecessary waste of communication resources, event-triggered control (ETC) method has received great interests among the control researchers. Recently, the ETC method has been integrated with the ADP approach to solve the optimal control problems [11]. In [12], Sahoo *et al.* proposed a neural network (NN)-based ETC scheme for nonlinear discrete-time systems using ADP approach. Vamvoudakis proposed an optimal adaptive ETC algorithm based on the actor-critic structure for CT nonlinear systems with guaranteed performance in [13]. In [14], the event-triggered reinforcement learning approach was developed for the nonlinear systems without requiring exact knowledge of system dynamics. However, the system uncertainties are not concerned in the existing work of event-triggered optimal control.

In this paper, we investigate the robust control problem of nonlinear systems with unmatched uncertainties using an optimal control approach.

Section 2 introduces the robust control problem of the nonlinear system with unmatched uncertainties and the traditional optimal control problem. In Sect. 3, the connection between the robust stabilization and the optimal control problem is discussed. In Sect. 4, the event-triggered ADP algorithm is proposed to approximate the optimal control policy. Simulation results and the conclusion are presented in the end.

## 2    Problem Statement

Consider the following CT uncertain nonlinear system

$$\dot{x}(t) = f(x(t)) + g(x(t))u(x) + k(x(t))W(x(t)) \tag{1}$$

where $x = x(t) \subseteq \mathbb{R}^n$ is the state vector, $u = u(x) \in \mathbb{R}^m$ is the control input, $f(\cdot) \in \mathbb{R}^n$, $g(\cdot) \in \mathbb{R}^{n \times m}$ and $k(\cdot) \in \mathbb{R}^{n \times q}$ are differentiable nonlinear dynamics with $f(0) = 0$, and $W(\cdot) \in \mathbb{R}^q$ is the unknown nonlinear perturbation. Assume that $W(0) = 0$, so that $x = 0$ is an equilibrium of system (1).

The uncertainty $W(x)$ is known as an unmatched uncertainty for system (1), if $k(x) \neq g(x)$. In this paper, we aim to find a control policy so that the system (1) is globally asymptotically stable for all unmatched uncertainties $W(x)$ satisfying the following assumption.

*Assumption 1* [2]

1. The uncertainty $W(x)$ is bounded by a known non-negative function $W_M(x)$, i.e., $\|W(x)\| \leq W_M(x)$ with $W_M(0) = 0$.

2. There exists a non-negative function $g_M(x)$ such that

$$\|g^+(x)k(x)W(x)\|^2 \le \frac{g_M^2(x)}{2} \tag{2}$$

where $g^+(x)$ denotes the (Moore-Penrose) pseudoinverse of function $g(x)$.

Motivated by [2], the robust control problem of the uncertain nonlinear system will be converted into an optimal control problem of a corresponding auxiliary system with an appropriate cost function. First, the uncertainty term $k(x)W(x)$ is decomposed into a matched component and an unmatched one in the range space of $g(x)$.

$$k(x)W(x) = g(x)g^+(x)k(x)W(x) + (I - g(x)g^+(x))k(x)W(x) \tag{3}$$

Then, we can transform the robust control problem into an optimal control problem as follows.

*Optimal Control Problem:* For the corresponding auxiliary system

$$\dot{x} = f(x) + g(x)u(x) + \left(I - g(x)g^+(x)\right) k(x)w(x) \tag{4}$$

where $w = w(x) \in \mathbb{R}^q$ is an augmented control to deal with the unmatched uncertainty component, and $[u^{\mathrm{T}}(x), w^{\mathrm{T}}(x)]^{\mathrm{T}}$ is a control policy pair of system (4).

Assume that the auxiliary system (4) is controllable. It is desired to find the optimal control policy pair $[u^{*\mathrm{T}}(x), w^{*\mathrm{T}}(x)]^{\mathrm{T}}$ that minimizes the cost function given by

$$V(x(0)) = \int_0^\infty \|r^{\mathrm{T}}\|^2 g_M^2(x) + \eta^2 \|m^{\mathrm{T}}\|^2 W_M^2(x) + U(x, u, w) \mathrm{d}t \tag{5}$$

where the utility $U(x, u, w) = x^{\mathrm{T}}Qx + u^{\mathrm{T}}(x)Ru(x) + \eta^2 w^{\mathrm{T}}(x)Mw(x)$, and $\eta > 0$ is a designed parameter. Here, $Q$, $R$ and $M$ are positive definite symmetric matrices. According to the principle of Cholesky decomposition, we have $R = rr^{\mathrm{T}}$ and $M = mm^{\mathrm{T}}$, where $r$ and $m$ are two appropriate lower triangular matrices.

**Remark 1.** *For the optimal control problem of the auxiliary system (4), the designed feedback control inputs should be admissible (see [5] for definition). In this paper, we use $\Phi(\Omega)$ to denote the set of admissible policies on a compact set $\Omega$.*

For any admissible policies $u, w \in \Phi(\Omega)$, if the cost function (5) is continuously differentiable, the infinitesimal version of (5) is the so-called nonlinear Lyapunov equation

$$\nabla V^{\mathrm{T}} \left(f(x) + g(x)u(t) + (I - g(x)g^+(x))k(x)w(t)\right)$$
$$+ \|r^{\mathrm{T}}\|^2 g_M^2(x) + \eta^2 \|m^{\mathrm{T}}\|^2 W_M^2(x) + U(x, u, w) = 0, \tag{6}$$

where $\nabla V = \partial V(x)/\partial x$ is the partial derivative of the cost function $V(x)$ with respect to the state $x$, and $V(0) = 0$.

Define the Hamiltonian function of system (4) as

$$
\begin{aligned}
H(x, \nabla V, u, w) =&\|r^{\mathrm{T}}\|^2 g_M^2(x) + \eta^2 \|m^{\mathrm{T}}\|^2 W_M^2(x) + U(x, u, w) \\
&+ (\nabla V)^{\mathrm{T}} \left( f(x) + g(x)u(t) + (I - g(x)g^+(x))k(x)w(t) \right)
\end{aligned}
\tag{7}
$$

Then the optimal cost function of system (4)

$$
\begin{aligned}
V^*(x(0)) = \min_{u, w \in \Phi(\Omega)} \int_0^\infty & \left\{ \|r^{\mathrm{T}}\|^2 g_M^2(x(\tau)) + \eta^2 \|m^{\mathrm{T}}\|^2 \right. \\
&\left. \times W_M^2(x(\tau)) + U(x(\tau), u(\tau), w(\tau)) \right\} \mathrm{d}\tau
\end{aligned}
\tag{8}
$$

satisfies the associated HJB equation

$$
\min_{u, w \in \Phi(\Omega)} H(x, \nabla V^*, u, w) = 0
\tag{9}
$$

where $V^*(x)$ is a solution of the HJB equation.

Assume that the minimum policy pair on the left-hand side of (9) exists and is unique. According to the stationary conditions, the optimal control policies are given by

$$
u^*(x) = -\frac{1}{2} R^{-1} g^{\mathrm{T}}(x) \nabla V^*
\tag{10}
$$

$$
w^*(x) = -\frac{1}{2\eta^2} M^{-1} k^{\mathrm{T}}(x)(I - g(x)g^+(x))^{\mathrm{T}} \nabla V^*
\tag{11}
$$

Denote $d(x) = (I - g(x)g^+(x))k(x)$. Based on (10) and (11), the HJB Eq. (9) can be rewritten as

$$
\begin{aligned}
&H(x, \nabla V^*, u^*, w^*) \\
=& (\nabla V^*)^{\mathrm{T}} f(x) + x^{\mathrm{T}} Q x + \|r^{\mathrm{T}}\|^2 g_M^2(x) + \eta^2 \|m^{\mathrm{T}}\|^2 W_M^2(x) \\
&- \frac{1}{4}(\nabla V^*)^{\mathrm{T}} g(x) R^{-1} g^{\mathrm{T}}(x) \nabla V^* - \frac{1}{4\eta^2}(\nabla V^*)^{\mathrm{T}} d(x) M^{-1} d^{\mathrm{T}}(x) \nabla V^* = 0
\end{aligned}
\tag{12}
$$

So far, the robust control problem is transformed into a corresponding time-triggered optimal control problem. Then the traditional ADP technique can be employed to approximate the solution $V^*(x)$ of the HJB equation. In order to reduce the computational burden and save communication resources, the ETC mechanism is introduced in this paper. And an adaptive triggering condition will be designed to guarantee the stability of the uncertain system with an event-triggered optimal controller.

## 3    Event-Triggered Robust Optimal Controller

To propose the ETC mechanism, we first define a monotonically increasing sequence of triggering instants $\{\tau_j\}_{j=0}^\infty$, where $\tau_j$ is the $j^{\mathrm{th}}$ consecutive sampling instant with $\tau_j < \tau_{j+1}, j \in \mathbb{N}$ with $\mathbb{N} = \{0, 1, 2, \cdots\}$. Then an sampled-data system characterized by the triggering instants is introduced, where the controller is updated based on the sampled state $\hat{x}_j = x(\tau_j)$ for all $t \in [\tau_j, \tau_{j+1})$. Define the event-triggered error as

$$e_j(t) = \hat{x}_j - x(t), \forall t \in [\tau_j, \tau_{j+1}), j \in \mathbb{N} \tag{13}$$

where $x(t)$ and $\hat{x}_j$ denote the current state and the sampled state, respectively.

In the ETC method, the triggering condition is determined by the event-triggered error and a designed state-dependent threshold. When the event-triggered error exceeds the state-dependent threshold, an event is triggered. Then, the system states are sampled that resets the event-triggered error $e_j(t)$ to zero, and be held until the next triggering instant. Accordingly, the designed event-triggered controller $u(\hat{x}_j) \stackrel{\Delta}{=} \mu(\hat{x}_j)$ is updated. Clearly, the control signal $\mu(\hat{x}_j)$ is a function of the event-based state vector, which is executed based on the latest sampled state $\hat{x}_j$ instead of the current value $x(t)$. That is, the event-triggered controller is only updated at the triggering instant sequence $\{\tau_j\}_{j=0}^{\infty}$ and remains unchanged in each time interval $t \in [\tau_j, \tau_{j+1})$. Hence, this control signal $\mu(\hat{x}_j)$ with $j \in \mathbb{N}$ is a piecewise constant function on each segment $[\tau_j, \tau_{j+1})$.

Under the event-triggering mechanism, the transformed optimal control problem in the previous section can be restated as follows.

With the event-triggered control input $\mu(\hat{x}_j)$, the sampled-data version of the auxiliary system (4) can be written as

$$\dot{x}(t) = f(x) + g(x)\mu\left(x(t) + e_j(t)\right) + d(x)w\left(x(t)\right) \tag{14}$$

Considering the event-triggered sampling rule, the optimal control policy (10) becomes

$$\mu^*(\hat{x}_j) = -\frac{1}{2}R^{-1}g^{\mathrm{T}}(\hat{x}_j)\nabla V^*(\hat{x}_j) \tag{15}$$

for all $t \in [\tau_j, \tau_{j+1})$, where $\nabla V^*(\hat{x}_j) = \partial V^*(x)/\partial x|_{x=\hat{x}_j}$.

By using the optimal cost function $V^*(x)$, the event-triggered controller (15) and the augmented controller (11), the Hamiltonian function (7) becomes

$$
\begin{aligned}
&H(x, \nabla V^*, \mu^*(\hat{x}_j), w^*(x)) \\
&= (\nabla V^*)^{\mathrm{T}} f(x) + x^{\mathrm{T}} Q x + \|r^{\mathrm{T}}\|^2 g_M^2(x) + \eta^2 \|m^{\mathrm{T}}\|^2 W_M^2(x) \\
&\quad - \frac{1}{2}(\nabla V^*)^{\mathrm{T}} g(x) R^{-1} g^{\mathrm{T}}(\hat{x}_j)\nabla V^*(\hat{x}_j) \\
&\quad + \frac{1}{4}(\nabla V^*(\hat{x}_j))^{\mathrm{T}} g(\hat{x}_j) R^{-1} g^{\mathrm{T}}(\hat{x}_j)\nabla V^*(\hat{x}_j) \\
&\quad - \frac{1}{4\eta^2}(\nabla V^*)^{\mathrm{T}} d(x) M^{-1} d^{\mathrm{T}}(x)\nabla V^*
\end{aligned}
\tag{16}
$$

For convenience of analysis, results of this paper are based on the following assumptions.

*Assumption 2* [8]: $f + gu + dw$ is Lipschitz continuous on $\Omega \in \mathbb{R}^n$ containing the origin.

*Assumption 3* [13]*:* The controller $u(x)$ is Lipschitz continuous with respect to the event-triggered error,

$$\|u(x(t)) - u(\hat{x}_j)\| = \|u(x(t)) - u(x(t) + e_j(t))\| \leq L\|e_j(t)\| \qquad (17)$$

where $L$ is a positive real constant.

**Remark 2.** *This assumption is satisfied in many applications where the controller are affine with respect to $e_j$. Note that $w(t)$ is not the direct control policy of the robust control system (1), but it plays an important role in finding the event-triggered optimal control policy $\mu^*(\hat{x}_j)$ for the system (14).*

**Remark 3.** *Combined (12) and (16), we have*

$$\begin{aligned}
&H(x, \nabla V^*, \mu^*(\hat{x}_j), w^*(x)) \\
=&(\nabla V^*)^T (f(x) + g(x)\mu^*(\hat{x}_j) + d(x)w^*(x)) + \|r^T\|^2 g_M^2(x) \\
&+ \eta^2\|m^T\|^2 W_M^2(x) + U(x, \mu^*(\hat{x}_j), w^*(x)) \\
=&\left(r^T(u^*(x) - \mu^*(\hat{x}_j))\right)^T \left(r^T(u^*(x) - \mu^*(\hat{x}_j))\right)
\end{aligned} \qquad (18)$$

*It is called the event-triggered HJB equation. Different from the traditional HJB Eq. (12), the event-triggered HJB equation is only equal to zero at every triggering instant. In other words, a transformation error is introduced due to the event-triggered transformation from (10) to (15), which makes the function $H(x, \nabla V^*, \mu^*(\hat{x}_j), w^*(x))$ not equal to zero during each time interval $t \in (\tau_j, \tau_{j+1})$.*

**Theorem 1.** *Suppose that $V^*(x)$ is the solution of the HJB Eq. (12). For all $t \in [\tau_j, \tau_{j+1}), j \in \mathbb{N}$, the control policies are given by (11) and (15), respectively. If the triggering condition is defined as follows*

$$\|e_j(t)\|^2 > \frac{(1 - \beta^2)}{2\|r^T\|^2\|L\|^2}\lambda_{\min}(Q)\|x\|^2 - \frac{\eta^2\|m^T w^*(x)\|^2}{\|r^T\|^2\|L\|^2} \triangleq \|e_T\|^2 \qquad (19)$$

*where $e_T$ denotes the threshold, $\lambda_{\min}(Q)$ is the minimal eigenvalue of $Q$, and $\beta \in (0,1)$ is a designed sample frequency parameter. Then the solution $\mu^*(\hat{x}_j)$ to the optimal control problem is also a solution to the robust control problem. That is, the system (1) can be globally asymptotically stable for all admissible uncertainties $W(x)$ under $\mu^*(\hat{x}_j)$.*

**Remark 4.** *The corresponding proof will be given in a future work. Note that the control input $\mu^*(\hat{x}_j)$ is based on event-triggered mechanism while the augmented control input $w^*(x)$ is based on time-triggered mechanism in this paper.*

## 4    Approximate Optimal Controller Design

In this section, an online event-triggered ADP algorithm with a single NN structure is proposed to approximate the solution of the event-triggered HJB equation.

## 4.1   Event-Triggered ADP Algorithm via Critic Network

In the event-triggered ADP algorithm, only a single critic network with a three-layer network structure is required to approximate the optimal value function. The optimal value function based on NN can be formulated as

$$V^*(x) = W_c^{\mathrm{T}} \phi(x) + \varepsilon \tag{20}$$

where $W_c \in \mathbb{R}^N$ is the critic NN ideal weights, $\phi(x) \in \mathbb{R}^N$ is the activation function vector, $N$ is the number of hidden neurons, and $\varepsilon \in \mathbb{R}$ is the critic NN approximation error. Then, we can obtain

$$\nabla V^*(x) = \nabla \phi^{\mathrm{T}}(x) W_c + \nabla \varepsilon \tag{21}$$

Since the ideal weight matrix is unknown, the actual output of critic NN can be presented as

$$\hat{V}(x) = \hat{W}_c^{\mathrm{T}} \phi(x) \tag{22}$$

where $\hat{W}_c$ represents the estimation of the unknown weight matrix $W_c$.

Accordingly, the augmented control policy (11) and the event-triggered control policy (15) can be approximated by

$$\hat{w}(x) = -\frac{1}{2\eta^2} M^{-1} d^{\mathrm{T}}(x) \nabla \phi^{\mathrm{T}}(x) \hat{W}_c \tag{23}$$

$$\hat{\mu}(\hat{x}_j) = -\frac{1}{2} R^{-1} g^{\mathrm{T}}(\hat{x}_j) \nabla \phi^{\mathrm{T}}(\hat{x}_j) \hat{W}_c \tag{24}$$

Using the neural network expression (20), the event-triggered HJB Eq. (18) becomes

$$\begin{aligned}
& H(x, W_c, \mu(\hat{x}_j), w) \\
= & \|r^{\mathrm{T}}\|^2 g_M^2(x) + \eta^2 \|m^{\mathrm{T}}\|^2 W_M^2(x) + U(x, \mu(\hat{x}_j), w) \\
& + W_c^{\mathrm{T}} \nabla \phi(x) (f(x) + g(x) \mu(\hat{x}_j) + d(x) w) \\
= & \varepsilon_{cH} + (r^{\mathrm{T}}(u(x) - \mu(\hat{x}_j)))^{\mathrm{T}} (r^{\mathrm{T}}(u(x) - \mu(\hat{x}_j)))
\end{aligned} \tag{25}$$

where

$$\varepsilon_{cH} = -(\nabla \varepsilon)^{\mathrm{T}} (f(x) + g(x) \mu(\hat{x}_j) + d(x) w)$$

denotes the residual error. For fixed $N$, the NN approximation errors $\varepsilon$ and $\nabla \varepsilon$ are bounded locally [5]. That is, $\forall \nabla \varepsilon_{\max} > 0, \exists N(\nabla \varepsilon_{\max}) : \sup \|\nabla \varepsilon\| < \nabla \varepsilon_{\max}$. Then, the residual error is bounded locally under the Lipschitz assumption on the system dynamics. That is, there exists $\varepsilon_{cH \max} > 0$ such that $|\varepsilon_{cH}| \le \varepsilon_{cH \max}$.

Using (22) with the estimated weight vector, the approximate event-triggered HJB equation is

$$\begin{aligned}
& H(x, \hat{W}_c, \mu(\hat{x}_j), w) \\
= & \|r^{\mathrm{T}}\|^2 g_M^2(x) + \eta^2 \|m^{\mathrm{T}}\|^2 W_M^2(x) + U(x, \mu(\hat{x}_j), w) \\
& + \hat{W}_c^{\mathrm{T}} \nabla \phi(x) (f(x) + g(x) \mu(\hat{x}_j) + d(x) w) \\
\overset{\Delta}{=} & e_c
\end{aligned} \tag{26}$$

where $e_c$ is a residual equation error.

Define $\varepsilon_u = \left(r^{\mathrm{T}}(u(x) - \mu(\hat{x}_j))\right)^{\mathrm{T}} \left(r^{\mathrm{T}}(u(x) - \mu(\hat{x}_j))\right)$ as the event-triggered transformation error. Letting the weight estimation error of the critic NN be $\tilde{W}_c = W_c - \hat{W}_c$ and by combining (25) with (26), we have

$$e_c = -\tilde{W}_c^{\mathrm{T}} \nabla \phi(x) \left(f(x) + g(x)\mu(\hat{x}_j) + d(x)w\right) + \varepsilon_{cH} + \varepsilon_u \qquad (27)$$

Based on experience replay technique [15], it is desired to choose $\hat{W}_c$ to minimize the corresponding squared residual error

$$E = \frac{1}{2} \left( e_c^{\mathrm{T}} e_c + \sum_{k=1}^{p} e^{\mathrm{T}}(t_k) e(t_k) \right)$$

where $e(t_k) = U\left(x(t_k), \hat{\mu}(\hat{x}_i), \hat{w}(t_k)\right) + \hat{W}_c^{\mathrm{T}}(t)\sigma_k$, $\sigma_k = \nabla \phi(x(t_k))(f(x(t_k)) + g(x(t_k))\hat{\mu}(\hat{x}_i) + k(x(t_k))\hat{w}(t_k))$ are stored data at time $t_k \in [\tau_i, \tau_{i+1})$, $i \in \mathbb{N}$, and $p$ is the number of stored samples.

*PE-Like Condition:* The recorded data matrix $M = [\sigma_1, ..., \sigma_p]$ contains as many as linearly independent elements as the number of the critic NN's hidden neurons, such that $\text{rank}(M) = N$.

The weights of the critic NN are tuned using the standard steepest descent algorithm, which is given by

$$\dot{\hat{W}}_c = -\alpha_c \frac{\partial E}{\partial \hat{W}_c}$$
$$= -\alpha_c \sigma \left( \|r^{\mathrm{T}}\|^2 g_M^2(x) + \eta^2 \|m^{\mathrm{T}}\|^2 W_M^2(x) \right.$$
$$+ \sigma^{\mathrm{T}} \hat{W}_c + U\left(x, \hat{\mu}(\hat{x}_j), \hat{w}(t)\right) \right) \qquad (28)$$
$$- \alpha_c \sum_{k=1}^{p} \sigma_k \left( \|r^{\mathrm{T}}\|^2 g_M^2(x(t_k)) + \eta^2 \|m^{\mathrm{T}}\|^2 W_M^2(x(t_k)) \right.$$
$$+ \sigma_k^{\mathrm{T}} \hat{W}_c + U\left(x(t_k), \hat{\mu}(\hat{x}_i), \hat{w}(t_k)\right) \right)$$

where $\sigma = \nabla \phi(x) \left(f(x) + g(x)\hat{\mu}(\hat{x}_j) + d(x)\hat{w}(t)\right)$, and $\alpha_c$ denotes the learning rate.

Combining (25), (27) and (28), we have

$$\dot{\tilde{W}}_c = -\alpha_c \sigma(\sigma^{\mathrm{T}} \tilde{W}_c - \varepsilon_{cH} - \varepsilon_u)$$
$$- \alpha_c \sum_{k=1}^{p} \sigma_k \left( \sigma_k^{\mathrm{T}} \tilde{W}_c - \varepsilon_{cH}(t_k) - \varepsilon_u(t_k) \right) \qquad (29)$$

where $\varepsilon_{cH}(t_k)$ and $\varepsilon_u(t_k)$ denote the residual error and the event-triggered transformation error at $t = t_k$, respectively.

Note that the closed-loop sampled-data system behaves as an impulsive dynamical system with the flow dynamics and jump dynamics. Define the augmented state $\Psi = [x^{\mathrm{T}}, \hat{x}_j^{\mathrm{T}}, \tilde{W}_c^{\mathrm{T}}]^{\mathrm{T}}$. From (13), (14) and (29), the dynamics of the impulsive system during the flow $t \in [\tau_j, \tau_{j+1}), j \in \mathbb{N}$ can be described by

$$\dot{\Psi} = \left[ \begin{array}{ccc} F(\Psi)^{\mathrm{T}} & 0 & G(\Psi)^{\mathrm{T}} \end{array} \right]^{\mathrm{T}} \tag{30}$$

where the nonlinear functions

$$\begin{aligned} F(\Psi) = {} & f(x) + g(x)\mu^*(\hat{x}_j) + k(x)w^*(x) \\ & + \frac{1}{2}g(x)R^{-1}g^{\mathrm{T}}(\hat{x}_j)\left(\nabla\phi^{\mathrm{T}}(\hat{x}_j)\tilde{W}_c + \nabla\varepsilon\right) \\ & + \frac{1}{2\eta^2}d(x)M^{-1}d^{\mathrm{T}}(x)\left(\nabla\phi^{\mathrm{T}}(x)\tilde{W}_c + \nabla\varepsilon\right), \end{aligned}$$

$$\begin{aligned} G(\Psi) = {} & -\alpha_c\sigma(\sigma^{\mathrm{T}}\tilde{W}_c - \varepsilon_{cH} - \varepsilon_u) \\ & - \alpha_c\sum_{k=1}^{p}\sigma_k\left(\sigma_k^{\mathrm{T}}\tilde{W}_c - \varepsilon_{cH}(t_k) - \varepsilon_u(t_k)\right). \end{aligned}$$

The jump dynamics at the triggering instant $t = \tau_{j+1}$ can be given by

$$\Psi(t) = \Psi\left(t^-\right) + \left[ \begin{array}{ccc} 0 & (x - \hat{x}_j)^{\mathrm{T}} & 0 \end{array} \right]^{\mathrm{T}} \tag{31}$$

where $\Psi\left(t^-\right) = \lim_{\varrho \to 0} \Psi\left(t - \varrho\right)$, and 0 s are null vectors with appropriate dimensions.

## 4.2  Stability Analysis

In this subsection, the main theorem will be presented to guarantee the weight estimation error of the critic NN to be UUB. Meanwhile, the stability of the impulsive dynamical system based on the event-triggered optimal control and the augmented control will be guaranteed with a novel adaptive triggering condition. First, we give the following assumption.

*Assumption 4*

1. $g(x)$ and $d(x)$ are upper bounded by positive constants such that $\|g(x)\| \leq g_{\max}$ and $\|d(x)\| \leq d_{\max}$.
2. The critic NN activation function and its gradient are bounded, i.e., $\| \phi(x) \| \leq \phi_{\max}$ and $\| \nabla\phi(x) \| \leq \nabla\phi_{\max}$, with $\phi_{\max}, \nabla\phi_{\max}$ being positive constants.
3. The critic NN ideal weight matrix is bounded by a positive constant, that is $\|W_c\| \leq W_{\max}$.

**Theorem 2.** *Suppose that Assumptions 1–4 hold. The tuning law for the CT critic neural network is given by (28). Then the closed-loop sampled-data system (14) is asymptotically stable and the critic weight estimation error is guaranteed to be UUB if the adaptive triggering condition*

$$\begin{aligned} \|e_j(t)\|^2 > {} & \frac{1}{L^2\|r^T\|^2}\left((1 - \beta^2)\lambda_{\min}(Q)\|x\|^2 \right. \\ & \left. + \|r^T\hat{\mu}(\hat{x}_j)\|^2 - \eta^2\|m^T\hat{w}(x)\|^2\right) \\ \triangleq {} & \left\|\hat{e}_T\left(x, \hat{x}_j, \hat{W}_c\right)\right\|^2 \end{aligned} \tag{32}$$

*holds and the following inequality*

$$\|\tilde{W}_c\| > \sqrt{\frac{\alpha_c^2 \eta^2 \lambda_{\min}(M) \sum_{k=1}^{p+1} (\varepsilon_{cH\max} + \varepsilon_{u\max})^2 + \Gamma}{4\eta^2(\alpha_c - 1)\lambda_{\min}(H)\underline{\theta}(M)}} \tag{33}$$
$$\overset{\Delta}{=} \Pi_{\max}$$

*is satisfied with* $\alpha_c > 1$, *where* $\Gamma = 2\left(d_{\max}\nabla\phi_{\max}\left(W_{\max} + \nabla\varepsilon_{\max}\right)\right)^2$.

**Remark 5.** *The proof of Theorem 2 will be presented in a future paper. Note that the triggering condition (32) is utilized to approximate the optimal control policy pair* $[\hat{\mu}^{*T}(\hat{x}_j), \hat{w}^{*T}(x)]^T$ *for the auxiliary sampled-date system while the triggering condition (19) in Theorem 1 is utilized to guarantee the robust stabilization of the original uncertain system with the obtained optimal control policy* $\hat{\mu}^*(\hat{x}_j)$.

## 5    Simulation

The example is considered as follows [2]:

$$\begin{bmatrix} \dot{x}_1 \\ \dot{x}_2 \end{bmatrix} = \begin{bmatrix} 0 & 1 \\ 0 & 0 \end{bmatrix} \begin{bmatrix} x_1 \\ x_2 \end{bmatrix} + \begin{bmatrix} 0 \\ 1 \end{bmatrix} u + \begin{bmatrix} 0.2 \\ 0 \end{bmatrix} W(x) \tag{34}$$

where $W(x) = \lambda_1 x_1 \cos\left(\frac{1}{x_2 + \lambda_2}\right) + \lambda_3 x_2 \sin(\lambda_4 x_1 x_2)$, and $\lambda_1, \lambda_2, \lambda_3, \lambda_4$ are the unknown parameters. The last term reflects the unmatched uncertainty in the system. Assume that $\lambda_1 \in [-1, 1]$, $\lambda_2 \in [-100, 100]$, $\lambda_3 \in [-0.2, 1]$, and $\lambda_4 \in [-100, 0]$.

Clearly,

$$g^+(x) = \left(g^T(x)g(x)\right)^{-1} g^T(x) = g^T(x) = [0, 1],$$

$$(I - g(x)g^+(x)) k(x) = \begin{bmatrix} 1 & 0 \\ 0 & 0 \end{bmatrix} \begin{bmatrix} 0.2 \\ 0 \end{bmatrix} = \begin{bmatrix} 0.2 \\ 0 \end{bmatrix},$$

$$\|W(x)\|^2 \le x_1^2 + x_2^2 \overset{\Delta}{=} W_M^2(x),$$

$$2\|g^+(x)k(x)W(x)\|^2 = 0 \overset{\Delta}{=} g_M^2(x).$$

Set $Q, R, r$ and $m$ are the identity matrices with appropriate dimensions. We experimentally choose $\eta = 1$, $p = 10$, $\beta = 0.1$ and $L = 3$.

During the implementation process of the event-triggered ADP method, we choose a three-layer feedforward NN with structure 2-8-1 as the critic network. The critic NN activation function is chosen as $\phi(x) = [x_1^2 \quad x_1 x_2 \quad x_2^2 \quad x_1^4 \quad x_1^3 x_2 \quad x_1^2 x_2^2 \quad x_1 x_2^3 \quad x_2^4]^T$. The initial state is selected as $x_0 = [1, -1]^T$, the learning rate is $\alpha_c = 0.1$, and the sampling time is chosen as $0.05\,\text{s}$. The trajectories of the critic parameters are shown in Fig. 1. At the end of learning process, the parameters converge to $\hat{W}_c = [1.8594\ 0.8845\ 1.1560\ 1.9860\ 0.9272\ 0.5403\ 0.4344\ 0.3737]^{\text{T}}$. From Fig. 2, one can get the event-triggered error $e_j(t)$ and the threshold $e_T$ converge to zero as the states converge to zero. In addition, the event-triggered error is forced to zero when the triggering condition is satisfied, that is the system states are sampled at the triggering instants. The sampling period during the event-triggered learning process for the control policy is provided in Fig. 3. Furthermore, the lower bound on the inter-sample times is found to be $0.15\,\text{s}$. In particular, the event-triggered controller uses 47 samples of the state while the time-triggered controller uses 1000 samples, which means fewer transmissions are needed between the plant and the controller due to event-triggered sampling. That will reduce the number of controller updates during the learning process.

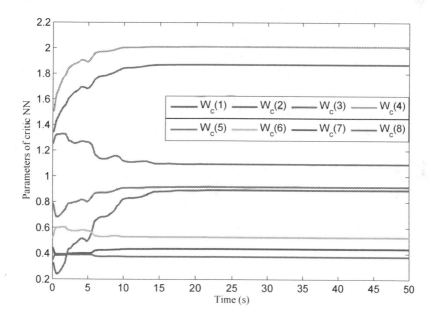

**Fig. 1.** Convergence of the critic parameters

Based on the converged weights $\hat{W}_c$, we can obtain the near-optimal control laws as

$$\begin{bmatrix} \hat{\mu}^*(\hat{x}_j) \\ \hat{w}^*(x) \end{bmatrix} = \begin{bmatrix} -\frac{1}{2}[0\ 1]\nabla\phi^{\text{T}}(\hat{x}_j)\hat{W}_c \\ -\frac{1}{2}[1\ 0]\nabla\phi^{\text{T}}(x)\hat{W}_c \end{bmatrix} \tag{35}$$

From [2], the optimal control laws are given as

$$\begin{bmatrix} u^*(x) \\ w^*(x) \end{bmatrix} = \begin{bmatrix} -1.2906x_1 - 2.1247x_2 \\ -0.5783x_1 - 0.2581x_2 \end{bmatrix} \tag{36}$$

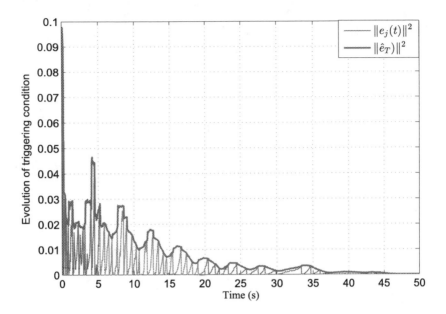

**Fig. 2.** Response of $\|e_j(t)\|^2$ and $\|\hat{e}_T\|^2$

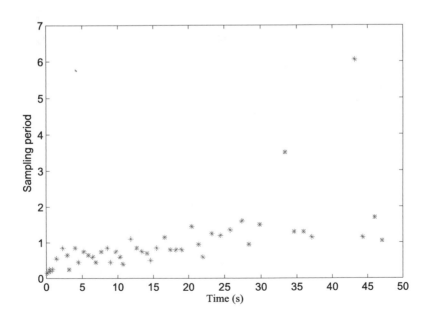

**Fig. 3.** Triggering instants during the learning process of the control input

Now, we apply the near-optimal control laws (35) with the triggering condition (19) and the optimal control laws (36) for the uncertain nonlinear system with $\lambda_1 = -1, \lambda_2 = -100, \lambda_3 = 0, \lambda_4 = -100$. Set the initial state be $x_0 = [1, -1]^T$, and the sampling time be 0.05 s. The simulation results are given in Fig. 4.

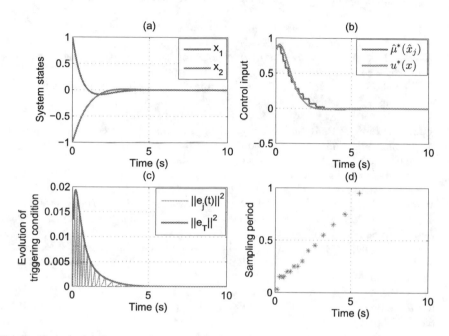

**Fig. 4.** Case 1: (a) State trajectory. (b) Near-optimal and optimal control inputs. (c) Response of $\|e_T\|^2$ and $\|e(t)\|^2$. (d) Sampling period.

We can observe the near-optimal controller is robust for the uncertain nonlinear system and adjusted with events.

## 6   Conclusion

In this paper, we propose an event-triggered ADP algorithm to solve the robust control problem of uncertain nonlinear systems. The robust control problem is described as an optimal control problem with an modified cost function. For implementation purpose, a critic NN is constructed to approximate the optimal value function. Finally, simulation results are given to demonstrate the effective of the event-triggered ADP scheme.

**Acknowledgments.** This research is supported by National Natural Science Foundation of China (NSFC) under Grants No. 61573353, No. 61533017, by the National Key Research and Development Plan under Grants 2016YFB0101000.

# References

1. Lin, F., Brandt, R.D., Sun, J.: Robust control of nonlinear systems: compensating for uncertainty. Int. J. Control **56**(6), 1453–1459 (1992)
2. Lin, F.: An optimal control approach to robust control design. Int. J. Control **73**(3), 177–186 (2000)
3. Lewis, F.L., Liu, D.: Reinforcement Learning and Approximate Dynamic Programming for Feedback Control. Wiley, New Jersey (2013)
4. Werbos, P.J.: Advanced forecasting methods for global crisis warning and models of intelligence. Gen. Syst. Yearb. **22**(12), 25–38 (1977)
5. Abu-Khalaf, M., Lewis, F.L.: Nearly optimal control laws for nonlinear systems with saturating actuators using a neural network HJB approach. Automatica **41**(5), 779–791 (2005)
6. Jiang, Y., Jiang, Z.P.: Robust Adaptive Programming. Reinforcement Learning and Approximate Dynamic Programming for Feedback Control, pp. 281–302 (2012)
7. Liu, D., Wang, D., Wang, F.Y., et al.: Neural-network-based online HJB solution for optimal robust guaranteed cost control of continuous-time uncertain nonlinear systems. IEEE Trans. Cybern. **44**(12), 2834–2847 (2014)
8. Wang, D., Liu, D., Li, H., et al.: Neural-network-based robust optimal control design for a class of uncertain nonlinear systems via adaptive dynamic programming. Inf. Sci. **282**, 167–179 (2014)
9. Zhao, D., Zhu, Y.: MECA near-optimal online reinforcement learning algorithm for continuous deterministic systems. IEEE Trans. Neural Netw. Learn. Syst. **26**(2), 346–356 (2015)
10. Zhao, D., Zhang, Q., Wang, D., et al.: Experience replay for optimal control of nonzero-sum game systems with unknown dynamics. IEEE Trans. Cybern. **46**(3), 854–865 (2016)
11. Zhang, Q., Zhao, D., Zhu, Y.: Event-triggered $H_\infty$ control for continuous-time nonlinear system via concurrent learning. IEEE Trans. Syst. Man Cybern. Syst. doi:10.1109/TSMC.2016.2531680 (2016)
12. Sahoo, A., Xu, H., Jagannathan, S.: Near optimal event-triggered control of nonlinear discrete-time systems using neurodynamic programming. IEEE Trans. Neural Netw. Learn. Syst. **27**(9), 1801–1815 (2016)
13. Vamvoudakis, K.G.: Event-triggered optimal adaptive control algorithm for continuous-time nonlinear systems. IEEE/CAA J. Automatica Sinica **1**(3), 282–293 (2014)
14. Zhong, X., Ni, Z., He, H., et al.: Event-triggered reinforcement learning approach for unknown nonlinear continuous-time system. In: 2014 IEEE International Joint Conference on Neural Networks, pp. 3677–3684. IEEE Press, Beijing (2014)
15. Modares, H., Lewis, F.L., Naghibi-Sistani, M.B.: Adaptive optimal control of unknown constrained-input systems using policy iteration and neural networks. IEEE Trans. Neural Netw. Learn. Syst. **24**(10), 1513–1525 (2013)

# Adaptive Terminal Sliding Mode Control for Formations of Underactuated Vessels

Yuqi Wang[1], Tieshan Li[1(✉)], and C.L. Philip Chen[2]

[1] Navigation College, Dalian Maritime University, Dalian, China
394562998@qq.com, tieshanli@126.com
[2] Department of Computer and Information Science,
University of Macau, Macau, China
philip.chen@ieee.org

**Abstract.** In this brief, the curve line path following problem is considered for formations of underactuated vessels. By using adaptive terminal sliding mode control method and finite time stability theory, the underactuated ships can reach and maintain the desired trajectory in finite time under the influence of unknown disturbance. Simulation results are provided to validate this method.

**Keywords:** Finite time stability · Formation control · Underactuated ships · Sliding mode control

## 1 Introduction

In recent years, the formation control of a group of autonomous marine vessels has received great attention from the control community due to its broad applications in navigation, such as exploration of natural resources, underway ship replenishment, surveillance of territorial waters, rescue missions and so on. Several methods have been proposed to achieve the desired formation, which include behavior-based, virtual structure, leader-follower strategy, and so on. Among these approaches, the leader-follower strategy has been much more preferred because of its simplicity and scalability.

The leader-follower approach plus the Lyapunov and backstepping technique has been used in [1]. A dynamic surface leader-follower formation controller based on neural network has been proposed for such systems in [2]. In [3], a linear sliding mode leader-follower formation control law has been designed. In [4], a Lagrangian formation control method is proposed for underactuated vessels. In [5], the multi-layer neural network and adaptive robust techniques are employed to design the controller for surface vessels with limited torques. However, all the methods mentioned above cannot guarantee the vessels to reach the desired formation in finite time.

This work is supported in part by the National Natural Science Foundation of China (Grant Nos: 61572540, 51179019, 51279106, 61374114), the Macau Science and Technology Development under Grant 008/2010/A1 and UM Multiyear Research Grants, the Fundamental Research Program for Key Laboratory of the Education Department of Liaoning Province (LZ2015006), the Fundamental Research Funds for the Central Universities under Grants 3132016313 and 3132016311.

© Springer Nature Singapore Pte Ltd. 2017
F. Sun et al. (Eds.): ICCSIP 2016, CCIS 710, pp. 27–35, 2017.
DOI: 10.1007/978-981-10-5230-9_3

In contrast, in this brief we develop a decentralized formation controller for underactuated vessels, using terminal sliding mode control (TSMC) approach combined with adaptive law. The TSMC approach proposed in [6] ensures the convergence of the system trajectories to the origin in finite time based on finite time stability theory. Meanwhile, in previous work, environmental disturbances are assumed to be upper bounded which is unrealistic in practical application and may cause acute chattering due to the over gain [12]. In this paper, the effects caused by environmental disturbances are cancelled by on-line upper bounds adaptive identification without any information in advance. Using this approach, a group of underactuated vessels can reach the desired formation in finite time under the influence of unknown disturbance.

## 2 Problem Formulation and Preliminaries

### 2.1 Vessel Communication Network

Graph theory is used to describe the communication (see for instance [7]). The communication network is $G(v, \varepsilon)$, where $v$ is a set of vertices and $\varepsilon$ is a set of edges. The vertices represent the vessels in the formation and the number of vertices is equal to the number of vessels. The edges represent communication channels and are represented by $(v_i, v_j)$. If information transfer from $v_i$ to $v_j$ then $(v_j, v_i) \in \varepsilon$.

The adjacency matrix of the graph $G$ is defined as $A = \{a_{ij}\} \in \mathbb{R}^{n \times n}$, where $a_{ii} = 0$, $a_{ij} = 1$ if $(v_i, v_j) \in \varepsilon$ and $a_{ij} = 0$ otherwise. The in-degree matrix of the graph $G$ is defined as $D_{in} = diag[d_{in}(v_1), \ldots, d_{in}(v_n)]$, where $d_{in}(v_n)$ is equal to the number of edges $(v_j, v_i) \in \varepsilon$. The Laplacian matrix of $G$ is defined as $L = \{l_{ij}\} \in \mathbb{R}^{n \times n}$, where $l_{ii} = \sum_{j \neq i} a_{ij}$ and $l_{ij} = -a_{ij}, i \neq j$. The Laplacian matrix $L = D_{in} - A$, the normalized directed Laplacian matrix is defined as $\ell_{ij} = \frac{l_{ij}}{l_{ii}}$.

In this paper, for the formation control we consider is in the leader-follower framework, where the leader information is known. Moreover, the leader can only transmit information to the follower and does not influence by the follower. Thus the Laplacian matrix can be written as follows

$$\ell = \{\ell_{ij}\}_{(n+1) \times (n+1)} = \begin{bmatrix} 0 & 0_{1 \times n} \\ \ell_1 & \ell_2 \end{bmatrix}$$

Where

$$\ell_{ij} = \begin{cases} 1 & i = j \text{ and } i \neq L \\ \frac{l_{ij}}{l_{ii}} & otherwise \end{cases}$$

$$\ell_1 = \begin{bmatrix} \ell_{1L} \\ \vdots \\ \ell_{nL} \end{bmatrix} \text{ and } \ell_2 = \begin{bmatrix} \ell_{11} & \cdots & \ell_{1n} \\ \vdots & & \vdots \\ \ell_{nL} & \cdots & \ell_{nn} \end{bmatrix}$$

## 2.2 The Vessel Model

Consider a group of N underactuated surface vessels. The kinematics and dynamic models are as follows [8]

$$\dot{\eta}_i = R(\psi_i)v_i, \quad i = 1, 2, \ldots, N, \tag{1}$$

$$M_i\dot{v}_i + C_i(v)v_i + D_i(v)v_i = \tau_i + \omega_i \tag{2}$$

Where $\eta_i = [x_i, y_i, \psi_i]^T \in \mathbb{R}^3$ denotes the position and orientation in the earth-fixed reference frame; $v_i = [v_{xi}, v_{yi}, w_{zi}]^T \in \mathbb{R}^3$ denotes the velocity in the body-fixed reference frame. $M_i \in \mathbb{R}^{3\times3}$ is a symmetric positive-definite inertia matrix; $C_i(v)v_i \in \mathbb{R}^{3\times3}$ is a matrix of coriolis and centripetal matrix, $D_i(v)v_i \in \mathbb{R}^{3\times3}$ is the hydrodynamic damping matrix which is also symmetric and positive-definite; $\tau_i = [F_{xi}, 0, T_{zi}]^T \in \mathbb{R}^3$ denotes the vector of external force and torque; $\omega_i = [\omega_x, \omega_y, \omega_z]^T \in \mathbb{R}^3$ denotes the unknown disturbances from the environment. The rotation matrix $R(\psi)$, and dynamic matrices are defined as follows

$$R(\psi) = \begin{bmatrix} \cos\psi_i & -\sin\psi_i & 0 \\ \sin\psi_i & \cos\psi_i & 0 \\ 0 & 0 & 1 \end{bmatrix}, M_i = \begin{bmatrix} m_{11i} & 0 & 0 \\ 0 & m_{22i} & 0 \\ 0 & 0 & m_{33i} \end{bmatrix}, C_i = \begin{bmatrix} 0 & 0 & c_{13i} \\ 0 & 0 & c_{23i} \\ -c_{13i} & -c_{23i} & 0 \end{bmatrix}$$

Where $c_{13i} = -m_{22i}v_{yi} - \frac{1}{2}(m_{23i} + m_{32i})w_{zi}$ and $c_{23i} = m_{11i}v_{xi}$.

$$D_i = \begin{bmatrix} d_{11i} & 0 & 0 \\ 0 & d_{22i} & 0 \\ 0 & 0 & d_{33i} \end{bmatrix} \tag{3}$$

Then the simplified model can be obtained as follows

$$\begin{aligned} m_{11i}\dot{v}_{xi} - m_{22i}v_{yi}w_{zi} + d_{11i}v_{xi} &= F_{xi} + \omega_x \\ m_{22i}\dot{v}_{yi} + m_{11i}v_{xi}w_{zi} + d_{22i}v_{yi} &= 0 + \omega_y \\ m_{33i}\dot{w}_{zi} + m_{22i}v_{yi}v_{xi} - m_{11i}v_{xi}v_{yi} + d_{33i}w_{zi} &= T_{zi} + \omega_z \end{aligned} \tag{4}$$

# 3 Formation Controller Design and Stability Analysis

The dynamical model of the vehicle is represented by

$$\begin{aligned} \dot{x}_i &= v_{xi}\cos\psi_i - v_{yi}\sin\psi_i \\ \dot{y}_i &= v_{xi}\sin\psi_i + v_{yi}\cos\psi_i \\ \dot{\psi}_i &= w_{zi} \end{aligned} \tag{5}$$

From (4) we can get

$$
\begin{aligned}
\dot{v}_{xi} &= \frac{m_{22i}}{m_{11i}} v_{yi} w_{zi} - \frac{d_{11i}}{m_{11i}} v_{xi} + \frac{1}{m_{11i}} F_{xi} + \frac{1}{m_{11i}} \omega_x \\
\dot{v}_{yi} &= -\frac{m_{11i}}{m_{22i}} v_{xi} w_{zi} - \frac{d_{22i}}{m_{22i}} v_{yi} + \frac{1}{m_{22i}} \omega_y \\
\dot{w}_{zi} &= \frac{m_{11i} - m_{22i}}{m_{33i}} v_{xi} v_{yi} - \frac{d_{33i}}{m_{33i}} w_{zi} + \frac{1}{m_{33i}} T_{zi} + \frac{1}{m_{33i}} \omega_z
\end{aligned}
\tag{6}
$$

Differentiating (5) we can get

$$
\begin{aligned}
\ddot{x}_i(t) &= u_{1i}(t) + \tilde{\omega}_x(t) \\
\ddot{y}_i(t) &= u_{2i}(t) + \tilde{\omega}_y(t) \\
\ddot{\psi}_i(t) &= u_{3i}(t) + \tilde{\omega}_z(t)
\end{aligned}
\tag{7}
$$

Where

$$
u_{1i}(t) = \left( \frac{m_{22i}}{m_{11i}} v_{yi} w_{zi} - \frac{d_{11i}}{m_{11i}} v_{xi} - v_{xi} w_{zi} + \frac{1}{m_{11i}} F_{xi} \right) \cos \psi_i + \left( \frac{m_{11i}}{m_{22i}} v_{xi} w_{zi} - v_{xi} w_{zi} + \frac{d_{22i}}{m_{22i}} v_{yi} \right) \sin \psi_i
$$

$$
u_{2i}(t) = \left( \frac{m_{22i}}{m_{11i}} v_{yi} w_{zi} - \frac{d_{11i}}{m_{11i}} v_{xi} - v_{yi} w_{zi} + \frac{1}{m_{11i}} F_{xi} \right) \sin \psi_i + \left( -\frac{m_{11}}{m_{22}} v_x w_z + v_x w_z - \frac{d_{22}}{m_{22}} v_y \right) \cos \psi
$$

$$
u_{3i}(t) = \frac{m_{11i} - m_{22i}}{m_{33i}} v_{xi} v_{yi} - \frac{d_{33i}}{m_{33i}} w_{zi} + \frac{1}{m_{33i}} T_{zi}
$$

$$
\tilde{\omega}_x(t) = \frac{1}{m_{11i}} \omega_x \cos \psi_i - \frac{1}{m_{22i}} \omega_y \sin \psi_i
$$

$$
\tilde{\omega}_y(t) = \frac{1}{m_{11i}} \omega_x \sin \psi_i + \frac{1}{m_{22i}} \omega_y \cos \psi_i
$$

$$
\tilde{\omega}_z(t) = \frac{1}{m_{33i}} \omega_z
$$

The formation control objective for under-actuated ships can be stated as follows

$$
\lim_{t \to \infty} e_{ij}(t) = \lim_{t \to \infty} \left( \eta_i(t) - \eta_j(t) - l_{ij}(t) \right) = 0 \; i, \; j = L, 1, \ldots, n
\tag{8}
$$

Where $l_{ij}(t)$ denotes the relative position between the i-th ship and the j-th ship. Furthermore, we introduce a generalized error state for the i-th ship as follows

$$
z_i(t) = \eta_i(t) - \frac{a_{ij}}{\sum_{j \neq i} a_{ij}} \sum \left( \eta_i(t) + l_{ij}(t) \right) \; i, \; j = 1, \ldots, n
\tag{9}
$$

**Lemma 1:** Define $z = [z_1^T, \ldots, z_m^T]^T$, where $z_i$ is given by (9) we can get the conclusions as follows [9]

(i)  If $z = 0$, then $e_{ij} = 0$, $i = 1, \ldots, n$, $j = L, 1, \ldots, n$.
(ii) If $e_{ij} = 0, i = 1, \ldots, n$, $j \in \{a_{ij} \neq 0, \; i, \; j = L, 1, \ldots, n\}$, then $z = 0$.

The generalized error dynamics are obtained by taking the second time derivative of (9) and are given by

$$\ddot{z}_i(t) = \ddot{\eta}_i(t) - \frac{l_{ij}}{l_{ii}} \sum \left( \ddot{\eta}_j(t) + \ddot{l}_{ij}(t) \right) = \tilde{u}_i(t) + \varpi_i(t) + \ell_{iL}\ddot{\eta}_L - \frac{l_{ij}}{l_{ii}} \sum \ddot{l}_{ij}(t) \qquad (10)$$

Where $\tilde{u}_i(t) = u_i(t) - \frac{l_{ij}}{l_{ii}} \sum\limits_{j \neq L} u_j(t)$, $\varpi_i(t) = \tilde{\omega}_i(t) - \frac{l_{ij}}{l_{ii}} \sum\limits_{j \neq L} \tilde{\omega}_i(t)$

Next we define i-th nonlinear sliding mode surface respect to (13) as follows

$$S_i(z_i, \dot{z}_i) = \dot{z}_i(t) + C_i R_i(z_i) |z_i|^{\frac{1}{2}} \qquad (11)$$

Where

$C_i = diag[c_{i1}, c_{i2}, c_{i3}], c_{ij} > 0, R_i(z_i) = diag[sign(z_{i1}), sign(z_{i2}), sign(z_{i3})]$

$|z_i|^{\frac{1}{2}} = \left[ |z_{i1}|^{\frac{1}{2}}, |z_{i2}|^{\frac{1}{2}}, |z_{i3}|^{\frac{1}{2}} \right]^T$

By using the sliding mode control theory and let $\dot{S}_i(z_i, \dot{z}_i) = 0$, we get

$$\tilde{u}_i(t) = -\ell_{iL}\ddot{\eta}_L + \frac{l_{ij}}{l_{ii}} \sum \ddot{l}_{ij}(t) - \frac{1}{2} C_i p_i(z_i, \dot{z}_i) - K_i sign(S_i(z_i, \dot{z}_i)) \qquad (12)$$

Where $(z_i, \dot{z}_i) \in q_i, i = 1, \ldots, n, K_i = diag[k_{i1}, k_{i2}, k_{i3}],$

$$p_i(z_i, \dot{z}_i) = \left[ \dot{z}_{i1} |z_{i1}|^{-\frac{1}{2}}, \dot{z}_{i2} |z_{i2}|^{-\frac{1}{2}}, \dot{z}_{i3} |z_{i3}|^{-\frac{1}{2}} \right]^T, i = 1, \ldots, n,$$

$$sign(S_i(z_i, \dot{z}_i)) = \begin{bmatrix} sign(S_{i1}(z_i, \dot{z}_i)) \\ sign(S_{i2}(z_i, \dot{z}_i)) \\ sign(S_{i3}(z_i, \dot{z}_i)) \end{bmatrix}$$

$q_i = \left\{ (z_i, \dot{z}_i) \in \mathbb{R} \times \mathbb{R} : \|p_i(z_i, \dot{z}_i)\|_\infty \leq \lambda_i \right\}$, Where $\lambda_i = \|C_i\|_\infty + \delta_i, \delta_i > 0.$

**Remark 1:** $q_i$ is the set where $p_i(z_i, \dot{z}_i)$ is bounded, and by setting $p_i(z_i, \dot{z}_i) \in q_i$, we can avoid the singularity problem of the controller.

**Lemma 2:** if the sliding mode controller gain $k_{ij}$ satisfies:

$$k_{ij} = \alpha_{ij} + \sup\|\varpi\|_\infty \qquad (13)$$

Where $\alpha_{ij} > \frac{\lambda^2 - c_{ij}\lambda_i}{2} > 0, i = 1, \ldots, n, j = 1, 2, 3$, then $q_i$ is positively invariant set.

However, the upper bound of environment disturbance $M$ is unknown in practical application. According to this circumstance, we introduce adaption law to the controller design. The estimated value of $M$ is $\hat{M}$, define the error between the two values are as follows:

$$\tilde{M} = \hat{M} - M \tag{14}$$

Therefore, $k_{ij} = \alpha_{ij} + \dot{\hat{M}}_i$, where $\dot{\hat{M}}_i$ satisfies

$$\dot{\hat{M}}_i = \frac{\left|S_{ij}(z_i, \dot{z}_i)\right|}{\gamma_i} \tag{15}$$

Next, for the condition $(z_i, \dot{z}_i) \notin q_i$, we design an auxiliary sliding surface

$$S_{iaux}(z_i, \dot{z}_i) = \dot{z}_i \tag{16}$$

Let $\dot{S}_{iaux}(t) = 0$, we obtain

$$u_{iaux} = -\ell_{iL}\ddot{\eta}_L + \frac{l_{ij}}{l_{ii}}\sum \ddot{l}_{ij}(t) - K_{iaux}sign(S_{iaux}(z_i, \dot{z}_i)) \tag{17}$$

Where $(z_i, \dot{z}_i) \notin q_i$ , $K_{iaux} = diag[k_{i1aux}, k_{i2aux}, k_{i3aux}]$

$$sign(S_{iaux}(z_i, \dot{z}_i)) = \begin{bmatrix} sign(S_{i1aux}(z_i, \dot{z}_i)) \\ sign(S_{i2aux}(z_i, \dot{z}_i)) \\ sign(S_{i3aux}(z_i, \dot{z}_i)) \end{bmatrix}$$

$$k_{ijaux} = \alpha_{ijaux} + \hat{M}_{ijaux}, i = 1, \ldots, n, \ j = 1, 2, 3, \ \dot{\hat{M}}_{iaux} = \frac{\left|S_{ijaux}(z_i, \dot{z}_i)\right|}{\gamma_{iaux}}$$

**Proof:** First, for the condition $(z_i, \dot{z}_i) \notin q_i$, we consider a Lyapunov function as follows

$$V_i(S_{iaux}(z_i, \dot{z}_i)) = \frac{1}{2}S_{iaux}^T S_{iaux} + \frac{1}{2}\gamma_{iaux}\tilde{M}_{iaux}^2 \tag{18}$$

Whose time derivative is given by

$$\begin{aligned}
\dot{V}_i &= S_{iaux}^T(-K_{iaux}sign(S_{iaux}(z_i, \dot{z}_i)) + \varpi) + \gamma_{iaux}\tilde{M}_{iaux}\dot{\hat{M}}_{iaux} \\
&= -a_{ijaux}\left|S_{ijaux}(z_i, \dot{z}_i)\right| - M_{iaux}\left|S_{ijaux}(z_i, \dot{z}_i)\right| + \varpi S_{ijaux}(z_i, \dot{z}_i) \\
&\leq -\sum_{j=1}^{3} a_{ijaux}\left|S_{ijaux}(z_i, \dot{z}_i)\right| \leq -\sum_{j=1}^{3}\min_{j=1,2,3}\{a_{ijaux}\}\left|S_{ijaux}(z_i, \dot{z}_i)\right| = -\min_{j=1,2,3}\{a_{ijaux}\}\|\dot{z}_i\|_1 \\
&\leq -\sqrt{2}\min_{j=1,2,3}\{a_{ijaux}\}V_i^{\frac{1}{2}}(S_{ijaux}(z_i, \dot{z}_i))
\end{aligned} \tag{19}$$

Thus, it follows [10] that the sliding surface is finite-time stable. Therefore, there exists a finite time T. At this time, the sliding mode controller switches from (12) to (17). Let $T = \max_{i=1,\ldots,n}\{T_i\}$, when $t \geq T$, we have $(z_i, \dot{z}_i) \in q_i, i = 1, \ldots, n$.

Next consider the Lyapunov function candidate given by

$$V_i(S_i(z_i, \dot{z}_i)) = \frac{1}{2} S_i^T S_i + \frac{1}{2} \gamma_i \tilde{M}_i^2 \tag{20}$$

Differentiating $V_i$ with respect to time, we have

$$
\begin{aligned}
\dot{V}_i &= S_i^T (-K_i sign(S_i(z_i, \dot{z}_i)) + \varpi) + \gamma_i \tilde{M}_i \dot{\tilde{M}}_i \\
&= -a_{ij} |S_{ij}(z_i, \dot{z}_i)| - M_i |S_{ij}(z_i, \dot{z}_i)| + \varpi S_{ij}(z_i, \dot{z}_i) \\
&\leq -\sum_{j=1}^{3} a_{ij} |S_{ij}(z_i, \dot{z}_i)| \leq -\sum_{j=1}^{3} \min_{j=1,2,3} \{a_{ij}\} |S_{ij}(z_i, \dot{z}_i)| = -\min_{j=1,2,3} \{a_{ij}\} \|\dot{z}_i\|_1 \\
&\leq -\sqrt{2} \min_{j=1,2,3} \{a_{ij}\} V_i^{\frac{1}{2}}(S_{ij}(z_i, \dot{z}_i))
\end{aligned}
\tag{21}
$$

Thus, it follows from [10] that the error states can reach the sliding model surface in finite time. Furthermore, while on the sliding surface the close-loop error dynamics are characterized by

$$\dot{z}_i = -C_i R_i(z_i) |z_i|^{\frac{1}{2}} \tag{22}$$

Consider the Lyapunov function as

$$\bar{V}(z_i) = \|z_1\| \tag{23}$$

Whose time derivative is given by

$$\dot{\bar{V}}(z_i) = \sum_{j=1}^{3} sign(z_{ij}) \dot{z}_{ij} = -\sum_{j=1}^{3} c_{ij} |z_{ij}|^{\frac{1}{2}} \leq -\|C_i^{-1}\|_{\infty}^{-1} (V_i(z_i)) \tag{24}$$

From [10], the error states converge to the origin in finite time.

## 4   Simulation

In this section, we consider a group of three ships with a communication network. The model parameters are given [8],

$$m_{11} = 200\,kg,\ m_{22} = 250\,kg,\ m_{33} = 80\,kg, d_{11} = 70\,kg/s,\ d_{22} = 100\,kg/s,\ d_{33} = 50\,kg/s$$

The time-varying disturbances are given in [11], The path of the leader is parameterized as $x_L = t, y_L = 3\cos(0.1t)$. The initial values are $\eta_1 = [-3 \quad 2 \quad \frac{5}{6}\pi], \eta_2 =$

$[-5 \quad -2 \quad \pi]$. The sliding mode surface parameters and the control gain parameters are $C_1 = C_2 = diag[1.2 \quad 1.2 \quad 1.2]$, $a_1 = a_2 = a_{1aux} = a_{2aux} = diag[2.5 \quad 2.5 \, 2.5]$, $\gamma_1 = \gamma_2 = [1 \quad 1 \quad 1]$, $\gamma_{1aux} = \gamma_{2aux} = [1 \quad 1 \quad 1]$, Simulation result is presented as follows (Fig. 1).

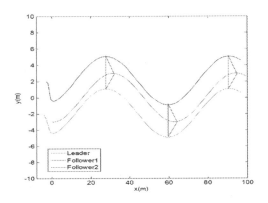

**Fig. 1.** Formation trajectories in 2-D plane.

## 5  Conclusions

In this paper, we investigate the formation control problem of underactuated vessels via adaptive terminal sliding mode control method. To tracking the desired trajectory in finite time, the adaptive sliding mode control method and finite time stability theory are combined to design a decentralized controller for underactuated vessels. Specifically, non-smooth sliding surface are designed to avoid the singularity problem. At last, the simulation results are given to illustrate the performance of the proposed scheme.

## References

1. Ding, L., Guo, G.: Formation control for ship fleet based on backstepping. Control. decis. **27**(2), 299–303 (2012)
2. Peng, Z., Wang, D., Chen, Z., Hu, X., Hu, X., Lan, W.: Adaptive dynamic surface control for formations of autonomous surfaces with uncertain dynamics. IEEE Trans. Control Syst. Technol. **21**(2), 513–520 (2013)
3. Fahimi, F.: Sliding-mode formation control for underactuated surface vessels. IEEE Trans. Robot. **23**(3), 617–622 (2007)
4. Ihle, I.-A.F., Jouffroy, J., Fossen, T.I.: Formation control of marine surface craft: A lagrangian approach. IEEE J. Ocean. Eng. **31**(4), 922–934 (2006)
5. Shojaei, K.: Observer-based neural adaptive formation control of autonomous surface vessels with limited torque. Robot. Auton. Syst. **78**, 83–96 (2016)

6. Venkataraman, S., Gulati, S.: Control of nonlinear systems using terminal sliding modes. J. Dyn. Syst. Meas. Control **115**(3), 554–560 (1993)
7. Godcil, C., Royle, G.: Algebraic Graph Theory. Graduate Texts in Mathematics, vol. 207. Springer, New York (2001)
8. Fossen, T.I.: Handbook of Marine Craft Hydrodynamics and Motion Control. WILEY, Norway (2011)
9. Ghasemi, M., Nersesov, S.G.: Finite-time coordination in multiagent systems using sliding mode control approach. Automatica **50**, 1209–1216 (2014)
10. Nersesov, S.G., Nataraj, C., Avis, J.M.: Design of finite-time stabilizing controllers for nonlinear dynamical systems. Int. J. Robust Nonlinear Control **19**, 900–918 (2009)
11. Peng, Z., Wang, D., Lan, W., et al.: Robust leader-follower formation tracking control of multiple underactuated surface vessels. Chin. Ocean Eng. **26**(3), 521–534 (2012)
12. Zhang, Y.: Adaptive sliding mode control and application for uncertain nonlinear systems. Chongqing University (2011)

# Real-Time Distributed Optimal Control Considering Power Supply Constraint for Deferrable Loads Scheduling

Mengya Kang, Chenglin Wen$^{(\boxtimes)}$, and Chenxi Wu

The School of Automation, Hangzhou Dianzi University,
Hangzhou 310018, Zhejiang, China
wencl@hdu.edu.cn

**Abstract.** In recent years, the ineffective utilization of power resources has attracted much attention. This paper proposes a real-time distributed load scheduling algorithm considering constraints of power supply. Firstly, an objective function is designed based on the constraint, which aims to transform the deferrable loads problem scheduling into a distributed optimal control problem. Then, to optimize the objective function, a real-time scheduling algorithm under power supply constraint is presented. At every time step, the purpose is to minimize the variance of differences between power supply and aggregate load. Finally, simulation examples are provided to illustrate the effectiveness of the proposed algorithm.

**Keywords:** Deferrable loads scheduling · Power supply · Real-time distributed control · Optimal control

## 1 Introduction

In recent years, with the emergence of deferrable loads and the development of renewable generation, power grids have attracted a widespread attention. Renewable generation capacity keeps growing at the rate of 10–60% every year since 2004. By the end of 2014, the consumption of renewable energy accounts for 22.8% of the global energy consumption around the world [1].

As a supplement to the power generation scheduling, deferrable loads scheduling can adjust the load curve, balance the intermittent energy fluctuation and provide auxiliary services. However, deferrable loads scheduling has been confronted with several new challenges, which could certainly add uncertainties of demand side, reduce the lifespan of power distribution circuits and transformers [2], and cause power loss and voltage change [3]. Previous researches manifest that these challenges would be mitigated if we take smart charging strategies. In addition, considering uncertainties in renewable generation and deferrable loads

This work was supported by the National Natural Science Foundation of China under Project Code No. 61273075, No. 61304186.

© Springer Nature Singapore Pte Ltd. 2017
F. Sun et al. (Eds.): ICCSIP 2016, CCIS 710, pp. 36–43, 2017.
DOI: 10.1007/978-981-10-5230-9_4

arrivals, several algorithms for real-time distributed load control have been pro-posed. References [4–6] evaluate algorithms with simulation, and references [6,7] provide analytic performance guarantee. However, these algorithms only can be used when ignoring the constraint of power supply. Given the constraint, this paper develops existing algorithms to propose DLCS-t algorithm.

The rest of this paper is organized as follows: In Sect. 2, we establish mathe-matical models and transform the real-time scheduling problem into an optimal control problem. Section 3 introduce a real-time distributed control algorithm to solve the proposed problem. Simulation results are applied to illustrate the effectiveness of the proposed algorithm in Sect. 4. Finally, we conclude this paper and give some discussions on future works in Sect. 5.

## 2　Problem Description

Consider a discrete-time model over a finite time horizon, we divide the schedul-ing cycle into $T$ slots of equal length labelled $1, 2, \cdots, T$. The aim is to make optimal power consumption schedules for each deferrable load under the con-straint of power supply. Ignoring power losses, it can be achieved by optimizing (minimizing) the objective function $D(s)$, which is defined as the variance of the differences between power supply and aggregate load:

$$D(s) = \frac{1}{T} \sum_{\tau=t}^{T} \left\{ [m(\tau) - s(\tau)] - \frac{1}{T-t+1} \sum_{k=t}^{T} [m(k) - s(k)] \right\}^2, \quad t = 1, 2, \cdots T. \quad (1)$$

where $m = \{m(t)\}_{t=1}^{T}$ denotes the power supply schedule, $s = \{s(\tau)\}_{\tau=t}^{T}$ is aggregate load schedule and it will be described in detail at a later stage.

### 2.1　Model Overview

Non-deferrable load and renewable generation can be denoted by $u = \{u(\tau)\}_{\tau=1}^{T}$ and $g = \{g(\tau)\}_{\tau=1}^{T}$ respectively. Define base load $b = \{b(\tau)\}_{\tau=1}^{T}$ as the difference between them. In this section, $b$ is considered as a stochastic process, and we use a causal filter based model to establish the stochastic model [8].

At time $t$, the prediction of base load $b_t$ can be modeled as a sum of the expectation $\bar{b} = \{\bar{b}(\tau)\}_{\tau=1}^{T}$ and a random deviation $\delta b = \{\delta b(\tau)\}_{\tau=1}^{T}$, where the sequence $\bar{b}$ can be obtained from historical data and weather report. The sequence $\delta b$ can be modeled as an uncorrelated sequence of identically distributed random variables $x = \{x(\tau)\}_{\tau=1}^{T}$ passing through a causal filter. In addition, the mean of $x$ is 0, the variance is $\sigma^2$.

Let $f = \{f(\tau)\}_{\tau=-\infty}^{\infty}$ denote the impulse response of the causal filter, where $f(0) = 1$, $f(\tau) = 0$ $(\tau < 0)$, then:

$$\delta b(\tau) = \sum_{s=1}^{T} x(s) f(\tau - s), \quad \tau = 1, 2, \cdots, T. \quad (2)$$

Define the prediction of $b$ as:

$$b_t(\tau) = \bar{b}(\tau) + \sum_{s=1}^{t} x(s) f(\tau - s), \quad \tau = 1, 2, \cdots, T, \ t = 1, 2, \cdots, T. \quad (3)$$

EVs(Electric Vehicles) represent deferrable loads. The sum of EVs that arrive over the scheduling cycle is $N$, and the total power consumption of each EV before a deadline is certain. But the arrival time is uncertain, independent and random. Define $N(t)$ as the number of deferrable loads that arrive before or at time $t$, which satisfies $N(0) = 0$, $N(T) = N$ ($t = 1, 2, \cdots, T$, and $N$ is a constant number). At time $t$, $v_n(t)$ denotes the power consumption of deferrable load $n$. $\bar{v}_n(t)$ and $\underline{v}_n(t)$ are defined as the upper and lower bounds respectively, i.e.,

$$\underline{v}_n(t) \le v_n(t) \le \bar{v}_n(t), \quad n = 1, \cdots, N, \ t = 1, \cdots, T. \quad (4)$$

Then $v_n = \{v_n(1), \cdots, v_n(T)\}$ is the schedule of deferrable load $n$, i.e., its power consumption profile.

During the scheduling cycle, $V_n$ denotes the total power demand of EV $n$, which implies that

$$\sum_{t=1}^{T} v_n(t) = V_n, \quad n = 1, 2, \cdots, N. \quad (5)$$

Let $c(t)$ denote the total power request of all deferrable loads that arrive at time $t$ ($t = 1, 2, \cdots, T$), then $c(t)$ is defined as the following:

$$c(t) = \sum_{n=N(t-1)+1}^{N(t)} V_n, \quad t = 1, 2, \cdots, T. \quad (6)$$

Assume that $c = \{c(t)\}_{t=1}^{T}$ is an independent and identically distributed random sequence, the mean is $\lambda$ and the variance is $s^2$. Define $C(t)$ as the total power demand after time $t$, then,

$$C(t) = \sum_{\tau=t+1}^{T} c(\tau), \quad t = 1, 2, \cdots, T. \quad (7)$$

It's worth noting that only information about deferrable load 1 to $N(t)$ is available at time $t$, which include $\underline{v}_n(t)$, $\bar{v}_n(t)$, $V_n$. Information about future deferrable load $N(t) + 1, \cdots, N$ is unavailable and thus we use a pseudo deferrable load to represent the future load.

**Definition 1.** $a = \{a(\tau)\}_{\tau=t}^{T}$ is the power consumption of pseudo load, fix $a(t) = 0$. $\bar{a}$ and $\underline{a}$ are defined as the upper and lower bounds respectively. Then it subjects to:

$$\underline{a}(\tau) \le a(\tau) \le \bar{a}(\tau), \quad \tau = t, t+1, \cdots, T. \quad (8)$$

$$\sum_{\tau=t}^{T} a(\tau) = E\{C(t)\}, \quad t = 1, 2, \cdots, T. \tag{9}$$

## 2.2   Real-Time Distributed Optimal Control Problem

**Definition 2.** Aggregate load $s = \{s(\tau)\}_{\tau=t}^{T}$ is defined as:

$$s(\tau) = b_t(\tau) + \sum_{n=1}^{N(t)} v_n(\tau) + a(\tau), \quad \tau = t, t+1, \cdots, T, \ t = 1, 2, \cdots, T. \tag{10}$$

According to the objective function designed in Eq. (1) and the constrained conditions listed above, the load scheduling problem with power supply constraint can be formulated as the following optimal control problem:

$$\min_{a,s,v_n} \frac{1}{T} \sum_{\tau=t}^{T} \left\{ [m(\tau) - s(\tau)] - \frac{1}{T-t+1} \sum_{k=t}^{T} [m(k) - s(k)] \right\}^2, n \le N(t), \ \tau \ge t.$$

$$\text{s.t.} \quad \begin{cases} b(t) = g(t) - u(t), & 1 \le t \le T; \\ s(\tau) = b_t(\tau) + \sum_{n=1}^{N(t)} v_n(\tau) + a(\tau), & t \le \tau \le T; \\ \underline{v}_n(t) \le v_n(t) \le \overline{v}_n(t), & n \le N(t); \\ \sum_{\tau=t}^{T} v_n(\tau) = V_n(t), & n \le N(t); \\ \underline{a}(\tau) \le a(\tau) \le \overline{a}(\tau); \\ \sum_{\tau=t}^{T} a(\tau) = E\{C(t)\}. \end{cases} \tag{11}$$

where $V_n(t) = V_n - \sum_{\tau=1}^{t-1} v_n(\tau)$ is the total power consumption at or after time $t$.

As $m = \{m(t)\}_{t=1}^{T}$ is available, the designed objective function is considered as a function of aggregate load $s$ in fact.

## 3   Algorithm Description

In order to solve the problem in Eq. (11), this section proposes a distributed optimization algorithm: DLCS-t algorithm. At time $t$, the detailed steps of the algorithm are presented as follows:

(1) Set $i = 0$. For load $n = 1, 2, \cdots, N(t)$, the power consumption schedule $v^{(i)}$ is initialized as follows:

$$v_n{}^{(0)}(\tau) = \begin{cases} v_n^{(I)}(\tau), & n \le N(t-1) \\ 0, & N(t-1) < n \le N(t) \end{cases}, \quad \tau = t, t+1 \cdots, T. \tag{12}$$

where $v_n^{(I)}$ is the schedule of load $n$ in the iteration $I$ of the previous time slot $(t-1)$.

(2) For load $N(t)+1, \cdots, N$, the pseudo load schedule $\{a^{(i)}(\tau)\}_{\tau=t}^{T}$ can be obtained by minimizing the differences between power supply and aggregate load as follows:

$$\min_{a(\tau)} \sum_{\tau=t}^{T} \left\{ m(\tau) - \left[ b_t(\tau) + \sum_{n=1}^{N(t)} v_n^{(i)}(\tau) + a(\tau) \right] \right\}^2 \qquad (13)$$

$$\text{s.t.} \quad \begin{cases} \underline{a}(\tau) \le a(\tau) \le \overline{a}(\tau), & \tau \ge t; \\ \sum_{\tau=t}^{T} a(\tau) = \mathrm{E}\{C(t)\}. \end{cases}$$

(3) The mean of the differences between power supply and aggregate load can be chosen as the control signal $c^{(i)}$:

$$c^{(i)}(\tau) = \frac{1}{N(t)} \left\{ m(\tau) - \left[ b_t(\tau) + \sum_{n=1}^{N(t)} v_n^{(i)}(\tau) + a^{(i)}(\tau) \right] \right\} \qquad (14)$$

(4) For load $n = 1, 2, \cdots, N(t)$, $v_n^{(i+1)}$ is updated by solving:

$$\min_{v_n(\tau)} \sum_{\tau=t}^{T} \left\{ c^{(i)}(\tau) \cdot \left[ \frac{m(\tau) - (b_t(\tau) - a(\tau))}{N(t)} - v_n(\tau) \right] + \frac{1}{2} \left[ v_n(\tau) - v_n^{(i)}(\tau) \right]^2 \right\}$$

$$\text{s.t.} \quad \begin{cases} \underline{v}_n(\tau) \le v_n(\tau) \le \overline{v}_n(\tau), & \tau \ge t; \\ \sum_{\tau=t}^{T} v_n(\tau) = V_n(t). \end{cases} \qquad (15)$$

(5) Set $i = i + 1$. If $i < I$, then return to Step (2), else continue Step (6).
(6) Update $V_n(t + 1) = V_n(t) - v_n(t)$. For load $1, 2, \cdots, N(t)$, the algorithm outputs their final schedules as $v_n(t) = v_n^{(I)}(t)$.

Reference [8] has proposed a valley-filling algorithm, and the convergence of its outputs has been proven in the paper. Similarly, it can be proved that, with power supply constraint, the schedules of the deferrable loads obtained by DLCS-t algorithm converge to optimal solutions of the optimal control problem.

## 4    Simulation Results

This section illustrates the effectiveness of the DLCS-t algorithm through MATLAB simulation experiments. We choose 100 households to participate in the experiments, and assume that 20 EVs are available for scheduling. The traces of non-deferrable load come from the average residential load in the service area of Southern California Edison in 2012 [9]. The traces of renewable generation come from the 10-minute historical data for total wind power generation of the Alberta Electric System Operator from 2004 to 2009 [10].

Wind generation is used to represent renewable generation. This section uses normal distribution as the distribution model of wind power prediction error. In addition, the arrival process of the deferrable loads begins at 20:00 on the first day and ends at 12:00 on the next day. After the deadline all EVs have already arrived.

Experiments demonstrate that DLCS-t algorithm converges fairly fast, and iterations will stop after 15 rounds. The algorithm proposed in reference [9] is denoted as VF-t algorithm. We compare the load curves of DLCS-t algorithm with VF-t algorithm in the case that $t = 4$ (0:00), $t = 8$ (4:00) and $t = 12$ (8:00) respectively.

Figures 1(a), 2(a) and 3(a) display the scheduling results of DLCS-t algorithm and VF-t algorithm with scheduling time $t$ taking different values. The aggregate load $s$ of VF-t algorithm in three time periods (1:00–8:00 in Fig. 1(a), 4:00–9:00 in Fig. 2(a) and 8:00–8:40 in Fig. 3(a)) have already exceeded the power supply $m$. It would lead to over-demand in power systems. These three figures manifest that aggregate load of DLCS-t algorithm is invariably lower than power supply except for individual time points (18:00–20:00 in Fig. 2(a)), whose curve is more close to the power supply curve, and it has a stronger potential to track the power supply curve.

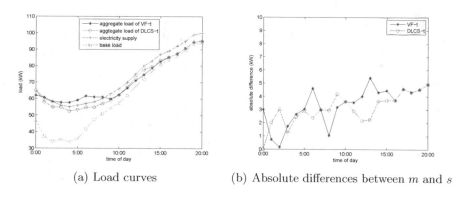

(a) Load curves               (b) Absolute differences between $m$ and $s$

**Fig. 1.** The comparison between DLCS-t algorithm and VF-t algorithm ($t = 4$).

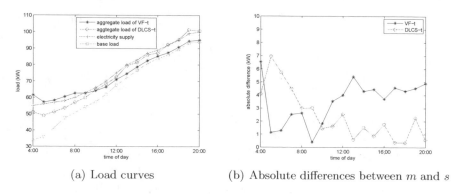

(a) Load curves               (b) Absolute differences between $m$ and $s$

**Fig. 2.** The comparison between DLCS-t algorithm and VF-t algorithm ($t = 8$).

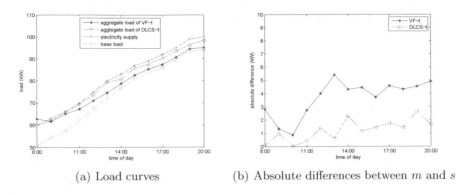

(a) Load curves                    (b) Absolute differences between $m$ and $s$

**Fig. 3.** The comparison between DLCS-t algorithm and VF-t algorithm ($t = 12$).

At different scheduling time slots, Figs. 1(b), 2(b), 3(b) present the absolute differences between power supply $m$ and aggregate load $s$. These figures demonstrate that the differences of DLCS-t algorithm always keep in a lower level and have smaller fluctuations.

The above conclusion can be verified from Table 1 which demonstrates the mean and the variance of absolute differences obtained by the two algorithms at different time slots. From the comparison between the third and fourth columns, it can be found that the mean and the variance of DLCS-t algorithm are invariably smaller than VF-t algorithm.

**Table 1.** Comparison between the two algorithms.

| Scheduling time | Absolute differences between $m$ and $s$ | DLCS-t algorithm | VF-t algoritim |
|---|---|---|---|
| $t = 4$ | Mean | 3.0708 | 3.3571 |
|  | Var | 10.7703 | 13.2016 |
| $t = 8$ | Mean | 2.4179 | 3.5337 |
|  | Var | 9.3558 | 15.0871 |
| $t = 12$ | Mean | 1.2191 | 3.6889 |
|  | Var | 2.0641 | 15.3374 |

## 5    Conclusions and Future Works

To conclude, this paper has studied the real-time distributed control for deferrable loads scheduling problem considering the constraint of power supply. By designing the objective optimization function with power supply constraint, we have transformed the load scheduling problem into an optimal control problem, and propose DLCS-t algorithm to handle this problem.

However, DLCS-t algorithm also has its limitation. For example, it only focus on the optimization effect of the aggregate load curve, and ignores the potential impact that deferrable loads scheduling may incurs on power flow and voltage of power systems. So under the constraint of power supply, the real-time distributed optimal control for deferrable loads scheduling is worth of making a further research.

## 6     The References Section

EVs        Electric Vehicles
DLCS-t     Real-Time Deferrable Loads Control with Power Supply Constraints
VF-t       Real-Time Valley Filling

## References

1. The data and tables of global renewable energy status report. http://news.bjx.com.cn/html/20150625/634314.shtml (2015)
2. Clement, K., Haesen, E., Driesen, J.: Coordinated charging of multiple plug-in hybrid electric vehicles in residential distribution grids. In: IEEE Power Systems Conference and Exposition, pp. 1–7 (2009)
3. Roe, C., Farantatos, E., Meisel, J.: Power system level impacts of PHEVs. In: IEEE 42nd Hawaii International Conference on System Sciences, pp. 1–10 (2009)
4. Caramanis, M., Foster, J.M.: Management of electric vehicle charging to mitigate renewable generation intermittency and distribution network congestion. In: Proceedings of the 48th IEEE Conference, pp. 4717–4722 (2009)
5. Conejo, A.J., Morales, J.M., Baringo, L.: Real-time demand response model. IEEE Trans. Smart Grid **1**(3), 236–242 (2010)
6. Deilami, S., Masoum, A.S., Moses, P.S.: Real-time coordination of plug-in electric vehicle charging in smart grids to minimize power losses and improve voltage profile. IEEE Trans. Smart Grid **2**(3), 456–467 (2011)
7. Chen, S., Tong, L.: iENS for large scale charging of electric vehicles: architecture and optimal online scheduling. In: 3th IEEE International Conference on Smart Grid Communications (SmartGridComm), pp. 629–634 (2012)
8. Gan, L., Wierman, A., Topcu, U., Chen, N., Low, S.H.: Real-time deferrable load control: handling the uncertainties of renewable generation. In: Proceedings of the 4th International Conference on Future Energy Systems, pp. 113–124 (2013)
9. Southern California Edison. 2012 static load profiles. http://www.sce.com/005_regul_info/eca/DOMSM12.DLP
10. Alberta Electric System Operator. Wind power/ail data. http://www.aeso.ca/gridoperations/20544.html

# Robust Adaptive Neural Fault-Tolerant Control of Hypersonic Flight Vehicle

Yuyan Guo, Qiang Wang, and Bin Xu[(⊠)]

School of Automation, Northwestern Polytechnical University, Xi'an, China
binxu@nwpu.edu.cn

**Abstract.** This paper proposes a fault-tolerant back-stepping control method for the hypersonic flight vehicle. An adaptive law is proposed to make sure that the normal actuators could compensate the ineffective actuators while failure exists. Meanwhile, the RBF NN is employed to estimate the unknown nonlinearity of the model. The simulation results verify the effectiveness of the proposed approach.

**Keywords:** Hypersonic flight vehicle · Fault-tolerant control · Neural networks

## 1 Introduction

Hypersonic Flight Vehicle (HFV) could fly with a velocity beyond Mach 5 and fulfill global strike capabilities. HFV has a large flight envelope, meanwhile its model is highly nonlinear and uncertain, therefore its controller design faces multiple challenges. The research [1] has made a review on HFV model and its control approaches. Particularly, due to the hierarchical model of the altitude subsystem of HFV, the back-stepping control has been studied a lot in HFV longitudinal control. Further, to eliminate the "explosion of complexity" caused by derivatives of the virtual control in each step, the dynamic surface control technique is proposed [2].

Due to the lack of the model knowledge as well as the unknown flight environment, the model of the HFV contains uncertain nonlinearity. Some studies have concentrated on the estimation of the uncertainty and multiple approaches have been proposed such as Neural Networks (NN) learning [3,4] and fuzzy logic learning [5,6]. Typically, the study [7] proposed a composite NN learning law, which has been further employed in HFV control [8]. Since HFV actuators have a higher risk of failure due to the severe condition, fault-tolerant control (FTC) has been studied and combined with HFV control. The paper [9] made a brief introduction on current FTC approaches. In addition, actuator compensation

This work was supported by National Natural Science Foundation of China (61622308), Aeronautical Science Foundation of China (2015ZA53003), Natural Science Basic Research Plan in Shaanxi Province (2016KJXX-86), Fundamental Research Funds of Shenzhen Science and Technology Project (JCYJ20160229172341417).

ⓒ Springer Nature Singapore Pte Ltd. 2017
F. Sun et al. (Eds.): ICCSIP 2016, CCIS 710, pp. 44–51, 2017.
DOI: 10.1007/978-981-10-5230-9_5

[10] is often employed when some actuators fail while others remain normal. In the study [11], the actuator adaptive compensation method is employed in the HFV control and reach a good performance.

Based on current studies, this paper proposes an FTC law with NN learning. The paper is organized as follows. Section 2 presents the hypersonic flight vehicle longitudinal model. In Sect. 3, the controller is designed for the altitude and velocity subsystem respectively. The simulation results are shown in Sect. 4. At last the conclusion is drawn in Sect. 5.

## 2 Hypersonic Vehicle Longitudinal Dynamics

In this paper, the Control-Oriented-Model (COM) [12] of hypersonic flight vehicle is used in this study. The model consists of the state variables $X = [V\ h\ \gamma\ \alpha\ q]^T$ and control inputs $U = [\delta_e\ \Phi]^T$, $V$, $h$, $\gamma$, $\alpha$, $q$ represent velocity, altitude, flight path angle, angle of attack and pitching rate respectively. $\delta_e$ is the actuator deflection, $\Phi$ is the fuel equivalence ratio. The equations of states are written as:

$$\dot{V} = \frac{T\cos\alpha - D}{m} - g\sin\gamma \tag{1}$$

$$\dot{h} = V\sin\gamma \tag{2}$$

$$\dot{\gamma} = \frac{L + T\sin\alpha}{mV} - \frac{g\cos\gamma}{V} \tag{3}$$

$$\dot{\alpha} = q - \dot{\gamma} \tag{4}$$

$$\dot{q} = \frac{M_{yy}}{I_{yy}} \tag{5}$$

In the equations, $T$, $D$, $L$, $M_{yy}$ respectively represents thrust, drag force, lift and pitching moment of the HFV with following expressions:

$$T = T_\Phi(\alpha)\Phi + T_0(\alpha)$$
$$\approx \bar{q}S(C_{T\Phi}^{\alpha^3}\alpha^3 + C_{T\Phi}^{\alpha^2}\alpha^2 + C_{T\Phi}^{\alpha}\alpha + C_{T\Phi}^0)\Phi + \bar{q}S(C_T^{\alpha^3}\alpha^3 + C_T^{\alpha^2}\alpha^2 + C_T^{\alpha}\alpha + C_T^0)$$
$$D \approx \bar{q}S(C_D^{\alpha^2}\alpha^2 + C_D^{\alpha}\alpha + C_D^0)$$
$$L = L_0 + L_\alpha\alpha \approx \bar{q}SC_L^0 + \bar{q}SC_L^{\alpha}\alpha$$
$$M_{yy} = M_T + M_0(\alpha) + M_{\delta_e}\delta_e \approx z_T T + \bar{q}S\bar{c}(C_M^{\alpha^2}\alpha^2 + C_M^{\alpha}\alpha + C_M^0) + \bar{q}S\bar{c}C_M^{\delta_e}\delta_e$$

where $\bar{q}$, $\bar{c}$, $S$ and $C_a$, $a = T, M, D, L$ are aircraft and aerodynamic parameters.

## 3 Controller Design

### 3.1 Altitude Subsystem

The control goal of the controller design is to make the altitude $h$ track the reference signal $h_r$, therefore define the altitude tracking error $e_h = h - h_r$, further the flight path angle command could be obtained as:

$$x_{1d} = \arcsin\left[\left(-k_h e_h - k_i \int e_h dt + \dot{h}_r\right)/V\right] \tag{6}$$

where $k_h$, $k_i$ are positive constants.

According to the longitudinal dynamics of the HFV, the altitude subsystem could be written as the following strict-feedback form:

$$\begin{aligned}
\dot{x}_1 &= f_1\left(\bar{x}_1\right) + g_1\left(\bar{x}_1\right) x_2 \\
\dot{x}_2 &= x_3 \\
\dot{x}_3 &= f_3\left(\bar{x}_3\right) + g_3\left(\bar{x}_3\right) u_f
\end{aligned} \tag{7}$$

where $x_1 = \gamma$ is the flight path angle, $x_2 = \theta_p = \gamma + \alpha$ represents the pitching angle, $x_3 = q$ is the pitching rate, $f_1$, $f_3$ are unknown nonlinearity, which could be estimated via radial-basis-function neural networks (RBF NNs):

$$\hat{f}_i = \hat{\omega}_i^T \Theta_i\left(\bar{x}_i\right) \tag{8}$$

where $\hat{\omega}_i$ is the estimation of the optimal NN weights. The components of $\Theta$ are obtained via the basis functions $\theta_i$. In this paper, the Gaussian function is chosen as the basis function with following form:

$$\theta_i(X_{in}) = \frac{1}{\sqrt{2\pi}\sigma_i} \exp(-\frac{\|X_{in} - \xi_i\|^2}{2\sigma_i^2}) \tag{9}$$

where $\xi_i$ is an M-dimensional vector which represents the center of the $i$th basis function, $\sigma$ is the variance of the Gaussian function.

The back-stepping control law for the altitude subsystem is designed as follows:

Step 1: Define the flight path angle tracking error $e_1$ as:

$$e_1 = x_1 - x_{1d} \tag{10}$$

Design the virtual control of the pitching angle $x_2$ as:

$$x_{2c} = \frac{1}{g_1}\left(-\hat{\omega}_1^T \Theta_1(\bar{x}_1) - k_1 e_1 + \dot{x}_{1d}\right) \tag{11}$$

where $\hat{\omega}_1$ is the estimation of the $\omega_1^*$, which is obtained via the learning law:

$$\dot{\hat{\omega}}_1 = \gamma_1 e_1 \Theta_1\left(\bar{x}_1\right) \tag{12}$$

where $\gamma_1$ is a positive designed parameter.

The variable $x_{2d}$ can be obtained via the first-order filter:

$$\alpha_2 \dot{x}_{2d} + x_{2d} = x_{2c} \tag{13}$$

where $\alpha_2$ is the filter parameter.

Step 2: Define the pitching angle tracking error $e_2$ as:

$$e_2 = x_2 - x_{2d} \tag{14}$$

Design the virtual control of the pitching rate $x_3$ as:

$$x_{3c} = -k_2 e_2 + \dot{x}_{2d} \tag{15}$$

Similar to step 1, the variable $x_{3d}$ can be obtained via the first-order filter:

$$\alpha_3 \dot{x}_{3d} + x_{3d} = x_{3c} \tag{16}$$

where $\alpha_3$ is the filter parameter.

Step 3: Define the pitching rate tracking error $e_3$ as:

$$e_3 = x_3 - x_{3d} \tag{17}$$

Design the ideal control input $u^*$ as:

$$u^* = \frac{1}{g_3} \left( -\hat{\omega}_3^T \Theta_3 - k_3 e_3 + \dot{x}_{3d} \right) \tag{18}$$

where $\hat{\omega}_3$ is the estimation of the $\omega_3^*$, which is obtained via the learning law:

$$\dot{\hat{\omega}}_3 = \gamma_3 e_3 \Theta_3 \left( \bar{x}_3 \right) \tag{19}$$

where $\gamma_3$ is a positive designed parameter.

Consider the circumstance that multiple actuators contribute to the control input together, then the actual control input $u_f = \mu u$, where $\mu = [\mu_1 \ \mu_2 \ \cdots \ \mu_m]$ indicates how much ratio each actuator could contribute, $u = [u_1 \ u_2 \ \cdots \ u_m]^T$ is the input vector. Further, consider the following fault model:

$$u_{fault} = \mu \cdot [u + \delta \left( \bar{u} - u \right)] \tag{20}$$

where:

$$\delta = diag\{\delta_1 \ \delta_2 \ \cdots \ \delta_m\} \tag{21}$$

$$\delta_i = \begin{cases} 1 \text{ if the ith actuator fails} \\ 0 \text{ otherwise} \end{cases} \tag{22}$$

$\bar{u} = [\bar{u}_1 \ \bar{u}_2 \ \cdots \ \bar{u}_m]^T$ indicates the failure value of the actuators.

Under such circumstance, there exists ideal controller as:

$$u_i^* = k_{1i} u^* + k_{2i}, i = 1, 2, ..., m \tag{23}$$

where $k_{1i}$ and $k_{2i}$ are parameters which satisfy:

$$\mu \left( I - \delta \right) [k_{11} \ k_{12} \ \cdots \ k_{1m}]^T = 1 \tag{24}$$

$$\mu\left(I-\delta\right)\left[k_{21}\ k_{22}\ \cdots\ k_{2m}\right]^{T}=-\mu\delta\bar{u} \tag{25}$$

Design the adaptive controller as:

$$u_{i}=\hat{k}_{1i}u^{*}+\hat{k}_{2i} \tag{26}$$

The adaptive laws are designed as follows:

$$\begin{aligned}\dot{\hat{k}}_{1i}&=\mathrm{sgn}\left(g_{3}\right)\varGamma_{1i}e_{3}u^{*}\\ \dot{\hat{k}}_{2i}&=\mathrm{sgn}\left(g_{3}\right)\varGamma_{2i}e_{3}\end{aligned} \tag{27}$$

where $\varGamma_{1i}$ and $\varGamma_{2i}$ are designed positive parameters.

## 3.2   Velocity Subsystem

The velocity subsystem could be rewritten with following form:

$$\dot{V}=f_{v}+g_{v}\varPhi \tag{28}$$

where:

$$f_{v}=\frac{T_{0}\cos\alpha-D}{m}-g\sin\gamma,\qquad g_{v}=\frac{T_{\varPhi}\cos\alpha}{m} \tag{29}$$

$\varPhi$ is the fuel equivalence ratio which is the control input of the velocity subsystem.
    Hence for the velocity control, define the velocity tracking error $V=V-V_{r}$, the following dynamic inversion control law is designed:

$$\varPhi=\frac{-k_{v}\tilde{V}-f_{v}+\dot{V}_{r}}{g_{v}} \tag{30}$$

where $k_{v}$ is the control gain parameter.

## 4   Simulation

The initial state variables are set as $h_{0}=86000\,\mathrm{ft}$, $v_{0}=7850\,\mathrm{ft/s}$, $\gamma_{0}=0\,\mathrm{rad}$, $\alpha_{0}=0.064\,\mathrm{rad}$, $q_{0}=0\,\mathrm{rad/s}$. The controller parameters are selected as $k_{1}=2, k_{2}=2, k_{3}=10, k_{v}=2$. The parameters of the command filter are set as $\alpha_{2}=\alpha_{3}=0.05$, while the RBF NN parameters are chosen as $\gamma_{1}=\gamma_{3}=1$. For the fault-tolerant adaptive laws, the parameters are designed as $\varGamma_{11}=\varGamma_{12}=10$, $\varGamma_{21}=\varGamma_{22}=2$.
    The altitude is set to increase 300 ft at the beginning as well as the 40th second, while the velocity reference signal increase by 100 ft/s. The reference signals are obtained via the following filter:

$$\frac{S_{r}}{S_{d}}=\frac{\omega_{1}\omega_{2}^{2}}{\left(s+\omega_{1}\right)\left(s^{2}+2\xi\omega_{2}s+\omega_{2}^{2}\right)}$$

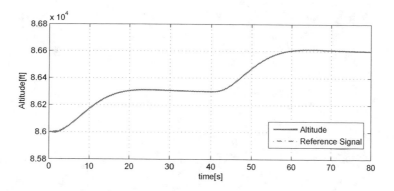

**Fig. 1.** Altitude

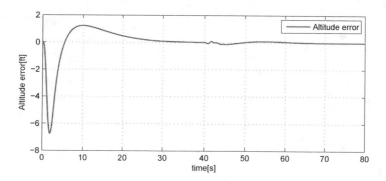

**Fig. 2.** Altitude error

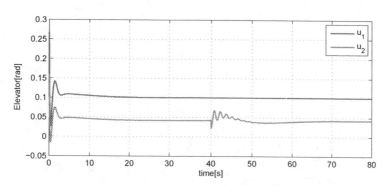

**Fig. 3.** Actuator

where $\omega_1 = 0.5$, $\omega_2 = 0.2$, $\xi = 0.7$.

In this simulation, the actuator 1 is stuck at the 25th second, while the actuator 2 remains normal. The results are as follows:

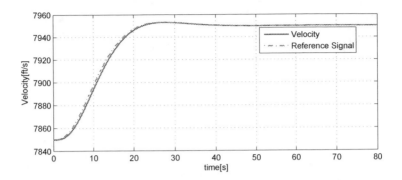

**Fig. 4.** Velocity

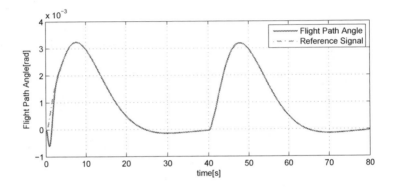

**Fig. 5.** Flight path angle

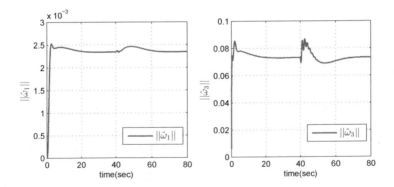

**Fig. 6.** NN weights norm

Figures 1, 2, 3, 4 and 5 show that the designed controller could reach a good tracking performance with actuator faults. Figure 3 clearly presents that the actuator 2 could effectively compensate the control input when the actuator 1 fails. The NN weights norm are shown in the Fig. 6.

# 5   Conclusion

This paper proposes a fault-tolerant control law with NN learning for the longitudinal control of the hypersonic flight vehicle. The proposed adaptive fault-tolerant method could guarantee the system performance under the circumstance that some of the actuators fail. Meanwhile, the RBF NN could estimate the unknown nonlinear function and make the system controllable without precise knowledge of the model. The simulation results verify the effectiveness of the designed method.

# References

1. Bin, X., Shi, Z.K.: An overview on flight dynamics and control approaches for hypersonic vehicles. Sci. Chin. Inf. Sci. **58**, 1–18 (2015)
2. Swaroop, D., Hedrick, J.K., Yip, P.P., Gerdes, J.C.: Dynamic surface control for a class of nonlinear systems. IEEE Trans. Autom. Control **45**(10), 1893–1899 (2000)
3. Bin, X.: Robust adaptive neural control of flexible hypersonic flight vehicle with dead-zone input nonlinearity. Nonlinear Dyn. **80**(3), 1509–1520 (2015)
4. Bin, X., Yang, C., Pan, Y.: Global neural dynamic surface tracking control of strict-feedback systems with application to hypersonic flight vehicle. IEEE Trans. Neural Netw. Learn. Syst. **26**(10), 2563–2575 (2015)
5. Bin, X., Shi, Z., Yang, C.: Composite fuzzy control of a class of uncertain nonlinear systems with disturbance observer. Nonlinear Dyn. **80**(1–2), 341–351 (2015)
6. Bin, X., Sun, F., Pan, Y., Chen, B.: Disturbance observer based composite learning fuzzy control of nonlinear systems with unknown dead zone. IEEE Trans. Syst. Man Cybern. Syst. **PP**(99), 1–9 (2016)
7. Bin, X., Shi, Z., Yang, C., Sun, F.: Composite neural dynamic surface control of a class of uncertain nonlinear systems in strict-feedback form. IEEE Trans. Cybern. **44**(12), 2626–2634 (2014)
8. Zhang, S.M., Li, C.W., Zhu, J.H.: Composite dynamic surface control of hypersonic flight dynamics using neural networks. Sci. Chin. Inf. Sci. **58**(7), 1–9 (2015)
9. Zhang, Y., Jiang, J.: Bibliographical review on reconfigurable fault-tolerant control systems. Annu. Rev. Control **32**(2), 229–252 (2008)
10. Tang, X., Tao, G., Joshi, S.M.: Adaptive actuator failure compensation for nonlinear MIMO systems with an aircraft control application. Automatica **43**(11), 1869–1883 (2007)
11. Bin, X., Guo, Y., Yuan, Y., Fan, Y., Wang, D.: Fault-tolerant control using command-filtered adaptive back-stepping technique: Application to hypersonic longitudinal flight dynamics. Int. J. Adapt. Control Sig. Process. **30**(4), 553–577 (2015)
12. Parker, J.T., Serrani, A., Yurkovich, S., Bolender, M.A., Doman, D.B.: Control-oriented modeling of an air-breathing hypersonic vehicle. J. Guid. Control Dyn. **30**(3), 856–869 (2007)

# Mechanical Design and Tactile Sensing in Dexterous Robot Hands Manipulation

Wenliang Zhang[1], Yiyong Yang[1(✉)], Fuchun Sun[2,3,4], and Bin Fang[2,3,4]

[1] School of Engineering and Technology,
China University of Geosciences, Beijing, China
yangyy@cugb.edu.cn
[2] Department of Computer Science and Technology,
Tsinghua University, Beijing, China
[3] State Key Laboratory of Intelligent Technology and Systems,
Beijing, China
[4] Tsinghua National Laboratory for Information Science and Technology (TNList),
Beijing, China

**Abstract.** Mechanical design and tactile sensing are essential parts for dexterous hands, which decide stability and flexibility of robotics fingers movements. They are used on various application scenarios, IC equipment, medical apparatus and instruments, etc. This paper introduces mechanical structure and tactile sensing in domestic and overseas dexterous hands, such as Robonaut multifingers dexterous hand, Shadow hand, Gifu II hand, etc. The characters of these hands are also introduced in detail. According to various of dexterous hands, mechanical design of them are divided into two series, conventional design and creative design. Tactile sensors layout scheme and application are presented. This paper gives some probable future research directions in the end.

**Keywords:** Dexterous hands · Mechanical design · Tactile sensing

## 1 Introduction

Dexterous robot hands have the same function as human beings which can recognize and grasp objects. Great innovation occurred in robots due to recent advancements in dexterous hands. Dexterous hands are quite complicated in the system of robots. They include multidisciplinary and various fields such as computer graphics, motion path planning, multisensor technology, accurate grasping objects operation, digital processing of signals and robotic emotional interaction, etc. [1]. It is a crucial factor that mastering objects identification and information transmitting for grasping [2]. The most important feature of dexterous hands is precision [3]. Therefore, how to accurately build the kinematics model becoming a challenging problem. Many sensors must be assembled on robots to realize convincing operation capacity and safe automation [4]. Most of tactile sensors are used to get information of target objects shape and hardness, especially for arms and hands [5].

© Springer Nature Singapore Pte Ltd. 2017
F. Sun et al. (Eds.): ICCSIP 2016, CCIS 710, pp. 52–61, 2017.
DOI: 10.1007/978-981-10-5230-9_6

Dexterous hands are also important parts in the new generation of social and service robots. They can replace humans in daily routines and provide assistance to the elderly or disabled. For amputees and paralyzed patients, they should have more functions, such as more human-like appearance, smaller volume, lighter weight, more standardized, commercialized, faster reaction time and preciser feedback strategy. Besides, dexterous hands also apply on some special experiment, for the simulation and control experimental platform of IC equipment, they can take out chip from vacuum cavity. This paper outlines possible research trends in dexterous hands manipulation, the current state-of-the-art mechanical design and tactile sensors in dexterous hands.

## 2   Representative Research

Dexterous hands play an important role in robot. By recent researches on dexterous hands, there are some advancements and drawbacks as Table 1. Because they are mainly applied to disabled as their prosthesis, they must accord with some demands, such as lighter weight, flexible movement, more degrees of freedom (DoFs), more functional and beautiful appearance.

**Table 1.** Advancements and drawbacks of dexterous hands

| Dexterous hands | Robonaut, DLR I, DLR II, Utah/MIT and Stanford/JPL | Shadow, GIFU II, HIT/DLR I, HIT/DLR II, Southampton, Salisbury and Okada |
|---|---|---|
| Advancements | More intelligentized, as space operation background | Structure and function quite simple, weight quite light, can realize simple operation, apply on disabled |
| Drawbacks | System quite complicated, wight quite heavy | Lower robustness and compatibility |

Robonaut multifingers dexterous hand was designed in 1999, which was manufactured by National Aeronautics and Space Administration (NASA) and General Electric Company. This robot hand is mainly applied to aerospace work in global space station and the manufacture of autonomous cars [6]. It has higher reliability and stability, which can bear about 90 N and 550 Nm. NASA dexterous hand was installed on an arm. The arm has a wrist, five fingers and many motors. It had some superfluous joints and 14 DoFs [7]. And its appearance and hand size are similar to human.

DLR I hand was designed in 2000. It has four same modularized fingers. And thumb has adduction-abduction motion. Its drive part adopts direct current brushless motor (DC), harmonic reducer and cog belt. DLR II hands rope decreases to 12 branches. Each fingertip outputs force from 10 N to 30 N [10].

Its main task is grasping bottles, pans and keys. DLR hands have many extrude characters, higher integration, multisensor and modularized design.

Shadow hand was made by Shadow Community in 2004. There are two types of Shadow hand. One has four fingers, the other has five fingers [8]. The latter has 20 DoFs. Its motors and actuated parts are put on forearm. It adopts pneumatic muscles and ropes as drive and transmit parts that endow hand with noticeable grasp functions. And its maximum payload is about 40 N, so its main task is grasping small balls and bulbs. Shadow hand systems have been used for research on grasping, manipulation, neural control, brain computer interface, industrial quality control and hazardous material handing. The hand and forearm weigh about 4.2 kg. The Shadow dexterous hand is an advanced humanoid robot hand system that provides up to 24 joints in total to transmit kinematics and motion. It has been designed to provide comparable force output and movement precision as human hand.

Gifu II hand was researched by Gifu university in 2002. It has five fingers and 16 DoFs. Each finger has three DoFs. The middle and terminal knuckles linked by joints axes are coupled motion. Comparing with palm and others four fingers, thumb has an extra adduction-abduction motion [9]. It is similar to human thumb. It has fingertip six force/torque tactile function and adopts micro motors as actuation.

HIT/DLR I and II dexterous hands were manufactured by Harbin Institute of Technology (HIT) and German Aerospace Center (DLR) [11]. HIT/DLR I hand consists of four modularized fingers. It has 13 DoFs and adopts DC for actuated. So this hand has a lower robustness and compatibility. HIT/DLR II hand consists of 5 fingers, and it has 15 DoFs. Its transducer includes smaller volume, lighter weigh motor, harmonic reducer and cog belt pulley transmission.

By researches on NASA multi-fingered hand, Shadow dexterous hand, GIFI hand, DLR I and DLR II hands, HIT/DLR I and HIT/DLR II hands, the mechanical structure of dexterous hands can be divided into two parts, traditional and creative design.

## 3    Mechanical Structure of Dexterous Hands

The mechanical structure of dexterous hands should accord with many requirements, such as fewer actuators, smaller volume, higher transmit efficiency and lighter weight. In limited operation space, fingers should timely avoid consuming energy and exerting efficient. They should also have stable and flexible movement when catching some objects. In current times, the state of mechanical design in dexterous hands is various. They are mainly divided into two categories, traditional and creative design. For example, tendon-driven, gear-driven, belt-driven and linkages-driven are traditional design, spherical pair joints, hydraulic transmission and Metal Shape Memory Alloy (SMA) are creative design. Their characters as follows.

The theory of tendon-driven is a kind of mechanical transmit device which transmit motion and dynamics based on sheave and ropes friction force. As a kind of flexible drive, ropes play a great role that can change direction and transmit dynamics. Tendon-driven mechanism are usually applied on robotics hands. Many anthropomorphic robotic hands use this actuator, such as Utah/MIT hand, Salisbury hand and Okada hand, etc. Due to the arrangement of tendon and pulleys is various, there are three typical structure forms between them as Fig. 1. The transmit parts mainly are ropes and pulleys. But the wiring way of them is quite complicated [12]. Because it need more pulleys to transmit motion, the whole dexterous hands volume becomes more bigger and lead to interface phenomenon.

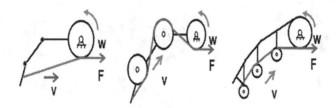

**Fig. 1.** The structure of tendon-driven in dexterous hand

In the tendon-driven design of dexterous hands, tendon-driven can be replaced by gear mechanism. The theory of gears used their gear teeth mesh to transmit dynamics and motion of two shafts. It has many advantages, such as widely transmit power and more accuracy transmit ratio. It is more powerful to grasp objects. But the structure of gear is quite complex so that it increases a lot of weight and inertia. Therefore, it is not fit for micro design. On the other hand, when the length of fingers becomes longer, dexterous hand needs more gear to transmit motion which limit the application of gear mechanism. In order to realize corresponding motion requirement, it is commonly phenomenon that use worm wheel and straight tooth cylinder gear transmission each other in dexterous hands such as Barrett Hand. The compose of it as Fig. 2 [13]. And the intermittent gear mechanism is a kind of intermittent motion mechanism that is evolved by gear mechanism. The static and motion time of driven gear can range widely. On the application of dexterous hands, owing to fingers have a range of degrees when it adopts adduction-abduction motion. Therefore, gears rotate motion changes exist a certain range and part of teeth mesh.

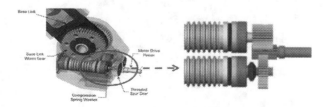

**Fig. 2.** The worm and straight tooth cylinder gear transmission in dexterous hand

Belt pulley transmission system is a kind of flexible connecting mechanism. It uses friction between belt pulley and driving belt to transmit motion and dynamics in dexterous hands manipulation. Belt pulley transmission has many functions such as simple construction, stable transmission and buffer. It can realize fingers flexion motion and accuracy catch some objects. The compose of it as Fig. 3 [14].

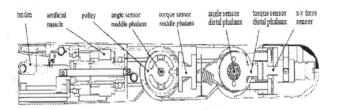

**Fig. 3.** The DLR/HIT hand II

Linkages mechanism can change the direction of motion, expanding stroke, reach reinforcement and remote operation. Owing to linkages mechanism transmit dynamics and motion depend on rigid links, the fingers have stronger grasp force. The links structure is quite compact and its processing of manufacture is quite simple. The touch of two links rely on itself geometry close, so it can get higher accuracy and better simulate human beings to realize naturally grasp. However, its design method is quite complex which results to it is quite difficult to accurately catch object according to specified parameters. Because of its rigid, it has not better adaptability. On dexterous hands operation, designing link mechanism can satisfy dexterous hand motion path planning. Via Fig. 4, by changing the relative length of linkages to make fingers catch objects and complete motion orders. Link mechanism is commonly used in human prosthetic. Truss construction is a kind of construction that connected by linkages and joints [15]. It consists of triangle plane and spatial construction. And it mainly bearing tension or pressure of shaft. Belgrade hand used two plane truss construction. It can put load resolve to a same plane as truss construction. Its computing method adopt finite element.

Spherical pair is three class geometry close and tripod ball sliding joint is four. Both of them are spatial kinematic pair. Manipulate spherical pair and

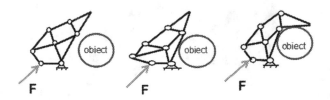

**Fig. 4.** Linkages mechanism in dexterous hand manipulation

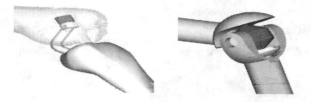

**Fig. 5.** Spherical pair and tripod ball sliding joint in dexterous hand

tripod ball sliding joint can make fingers joints more flexible from Fig. 5 [16]. They are bionic in dexterous hands application.

Hydraulic transmission transmit energy and conduct control by used liquid as working medium. Using hydraulic transmission to drive finger move and produce deformation in dexterous hands. As Fig. 6 [17], it enable make motion stable, work reliable and buffer. But it has some drawbacks, for example, slower reflection and lower transmit ratio.

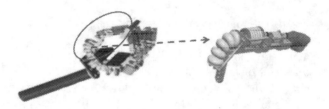

**Fig. 6.** The fluid hand III

SMA uses some alloy to change solid state when crystal structure reach to distortion temperature. When temperature rising to a certain numerical value, the inside structure of crystal could become deformation which lead to the outside appearance change. In dexterous hands application, its curve becomes large and plasticity has great improvement. After above the memory temperature, SMA can recover to the origin shape.

As Fig. 7 [18], the standard of dexterous hand is smaller size, lighter weigh, lower consumption and lighter noise. Besides, it can also realize position operation. Traditional current direct motor own heavy weigh and its drive system exist noisy. When SMA heat to a certain temperature, the motion of SMA will like muscles and can output more power. Usually using Nitinol alloy as their material. Its diameter is about 0.31 mm. Its thermal treatment manner adopt annealing below 450. Mainly research on SMA finger movement angular by use calculation and experience. It has many advancements such as dexterous, easily position control, stable operation, wide spatial application, easy feedback constant position and resolve medical treatment problems. It decreases complicated convert system and reduces heat by ohm resistor. On the other hand, it exists hysteresis, lower replacement and narrow bandwidth phenomenon.

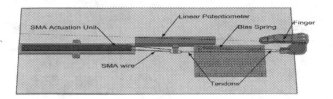

**Fig. 7.** The structure of SMA hand

SMA has own SMA braking unit, braking system and electrical forearm. Its totality mass is lighter, although including brake and electric device. SMA has smaller size and faster cooling time. But its output force is very small. It can only add up to 9 N. In order to generate a series images of temperature and time, doing on a series of static and dynamic experience, researching thermocouple SMA, math function feedback [19]. SMA dexterous hands need to achieve lighter weigh, lower noise and anthropomorphism.

## 4    Tactile Sensing of Dexterous Hands

Multi-fingered hands are known as multi-fingered joints mechanical links. All the fingers are in series of forms and connected together. Multi-fingered hands consist of a palm and fingers whose amount varies from three to five [20]. Each finger has three or four joints, and usually a joint only has one DOF. If fingertips and knuckles are assembled with force sensors or tactile sensors, they can exert appropriate force and grasp fragile objects properly. Some dexterous hands are lack of sensory feedback, so they have poor hand functionality. Tactile sensing can sense the presence of an object in the workspace of dexterous hand and recognize the magnitude of the grasping forces. Recently, the research of multi-fingered dexterous hands intelligence operation and the control of force have become robotics researching hot spot. Neuroscience has long interpretation about the importance of tactile feedback in human manipulation. Shadow hand has position transducers, tactile sensors and pressure sensors, wherein pressure sensors can fit as standard on fingertips. They are high sensitivity region sensors. These sensors can substitute other tactile sensors. And they can detect the full range of sensory information that fingers can detect. NASA multi-fingered dexterous hand used DC motors to reach whole hand moving. It has 43 sensors, not only does hand has tactile sensors, but also it has joint position sensors. Incremental encoders are built in motors. Gifuhand has fingertip six force/torque sensors and tactile sensors. DLR/HIT can measure the size of force, and has many communication interfaces such as CAN, PPSECO. It puts the PCI-DSP control board of DLR/HIT integrated into palm, utilize FPGA chips high capacity and NIOS dual-core processor to realize real-time communication. The three-dimensional effect picture of whole hand and single finger are showed respectively in Fig. 8 [21].

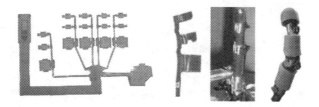

**Fig. 8.** Tactile sensing in whole hand and single finger

Researching the arrangement scheme and background of tactile sensors, robotics programming is the connection point for robotics movement and control. It is the main method for robots. The function of tactile sensors is recognizing objects and tactile feedback. Reflection time depends on two parts. One is the speed of recognition objects surface, the other is catching objects in different environments. Because softer materials increase surface friction, using which will reduce mechanized vibration. Micro switch is the lowest-cost and most ordinary forms in tactile sensors. Its installation should keep objects avoiding collision by accident when working. When fingers are installed with sensitive elements, they can protect object not to bear more applied force.

## 5    Conclusion and Future Research

Through researching relative references and doing some experiments about dexterous hands, the mechanical design and tactile sensors play a crucial role in the whole dexterous hand. First of all, its mechanical design can get some functions like human hand, making the motion of finger more steady and flexible. Secondly, tactile sensors can recognize objects and put appropriate force in order to grasp objects better. Only by dealing with these two key problems, can dexterous hands have stronger self-adaptive ability. Dexterous hands must have manipulative dexterity, grasp robustness and human operability. So that it can accurately and powerfully grasp complicated objects, getting a satisfied result.

There are some perspectives on the future development of dexterous hand from the aspects of mechanical structure, tactile sensors and functionality as follows. Due to current technical constraints on actuators, sensors and control means of dexterous hands cannot completely replace human hands. The future dexterous hand will have more DoFs, perceptional capabilities and superior operation. Undertaking in the future is listed as following: (a) Studying and improving its inside mechanical structure via previous research about dexterous hand. Therefore, devising a better mechanical design is the most important problem. (b) Making sensors more miniature and integrative. Besides, dexterous hands can feedback the information of grasped objects more quickly. Only in this way can fingers transmit stable force and improve dexterous hands grasped capacity.

**Acknowledgments.** This work was financially supported by National Science and Technology Major Project (2011ZX02403-4-3).

# References

1. Kappassov, Z., Corrales, J.-A., Perdereau, V.: Tactile sensing in dexterous robot hands-review. Robot. Auton. Syst. **74**, 195–220 (2015)
2. Liu, H., Nguyen, K.C., Perdereau, V., Bimbo, J., et al.: Finger contact sensing and the application in dexterous hand manipulation. Auton. Robot. **39**, 25–41 (2015)
3. Su, Y., Wu, Y., Soh, H., et al.: Enhanced kinematic model for dexterous manipulation with an underactuated hand. In: International Conference on Intelligent Robots and Systems, pp. 2493–2499. IEEE (2013)
4. Palli, G., Moriello, L., Scarcia, U., et al.: Development of an optoelectronic 6-axis force/torque sensor for robotic applications. Sens. Actuators A Phys. **220**, 333–346 (2014)
5. Feng, G.-H., Chu, G.-Y.: An arc-shaped polyvinylidene fluoride/ionic polymer metal composite dynamic curvature sensor with contact detection and scanning ability. Sens. Actuators A Phys. **208**, 130–140 (2014)
6. Tzvetkova, G.V.: Robonaut2: mission, technologies, perspectives. J. Theor. Appl. Mech. **44**, 97–102 (2014). Sofia
7. Lovchik, C.S., Diftler, M.A.: The Robonaut hand: a dexterous robot hand for space. In: International Conference on Robotics and Automation, pp. 907–912. IEEE (1999)
8. Greenhill, R.M.: Robotic muscular-skeletal jointed structures. United States Patent Application Publication, pp. 901–922 (2012)
9. Mouri, T., Endo, T., Kawasaki, H.: Review of GIFU hand its application. Mech. Based Des. Struct. Mach. **39**, 210–228 (2011)
10. Haidacher, S., Butterfass, J., Fischer, M., et al.: DLR hand 11: hard-and-software architecture for information processing. In: IEEE International Conference on Robotics and Automation, pp. 684–689 (2003)
11. Liu, H., Wu, K., Meusel, P., et al.: Multisensory five-finger dexterous hand: the DLR/HIT hand II. In: International Conference on Intelligent Robots and Systems, IEEE/RSJ, pp. 3692–3697 (2008)
12. Caffaz, A., Cannata, G.: The design and development of the DIST-hand dextrous gripper. In: International Conference on Robotics and Automation, pp. 2075–2080. IEEE (1998)
13. Townsend, W.: The BarretHand grasper programmably flexible part handling and assembly. Ind. Robot Int. J. **27**, 181–188 (2000)
14. Liu, H., Meusel, P., Butterfass, J., et al.: DLRs multisensory articulated hand Part 11: the parallel torque/position control system. In: International Conference on Robotics and Automation, IEEE-RAS, pp. 2087–2093 (1998)
15. Bekey, G.A., Tomovic, R., Zeljkovic, I.: Control architecture for the Belgrade/USC hand. In: Venkataraman, S.T., Iberall, T. (eds.) Dextrous Robot Hands, pp. 136–149. Springer, New York (1990)
16. Weghe, M.V., Rogers, M., Weissert, M., et al.: The ACT hand: design of the skeletal structure. In: International Conference on Robotics and Automation, pp. 3375–3379. IEEE (2004)
17. Gaiser, I., Schulz, S., Kargov, A., et al.: A new anthropomorphic robotic hand. In: International Conference on Humanoid Robot, pp. 418–422 (2008)
18. Andrianesis, K., Tzes, A.: Design of an innovative prosthetic hand with compact shape memory alloy actuators. In: Mediterranean Conference on Control and Automation, pp. 697–702 (2013)

19. Andrianesis, K., Tzes, A.: Design of an anthropomorphic prosthetic hand driven by shape memory alloy actuators. In: International Conference on Biomedical Robotics and Biomechatronics, pp. 517–522. IEEE (2008)
20. Carrozza, M.C., Cappiello, G., Micera, S., et al.: Design of a cybernetic hand for perception and action. Biol. Cybern. **95**, 629–644 (2006)
21. Mouri, T., Kawasaki, H.: A novel anthropomorphic robot hand and its master slave system. In: Humanoid Robots, Human-Like Machines, pp. 29–42 (2007)

# Image and Video

# BAG: A Binary Descriptor for RGB-D Images Combining Appearance and Geometric Cues

Xiuzi Xiao[1], Songhua He[1], Yulan Guo[2,3(✉)], Min Lu[2],
and Jun Zhang[2]

[1] College of Information Science and Engineering,
Hunan University, Changsha 410082, China
`hdxiaoxiuzi@hnu.edu.cn`, `13973132618@139.com`
[2] College of Electronic Science and Engineering,
National University of Defense Technology, Changsha 410073, China
`{yulan.guo,lumin,zhangjun}@nudt.edu.cn`
[3] Institute of Computing Technology, Chinese Academy of Sciences,
Beijing 10080, China

**Abstract.** Feature matching forms the basis for numerous computer vision applications. With the rapid development of 3D sensors, the availability of RGB-D images has been increased stably. Compared to traditional 2D images, the additional depth images in RGB-D images can provide more geometric information. In this paper, we propose a new efficient binary descriptor (namely BAG) for RGB-D image representation by combining appearance and geometric cues. Experimental results show that the proposed BAG descriptor produces better feature matching performance with faster matching speed and less memory than the existing methods.

**Keywords:** Feature matching · Binary descriptor · Local binary pattern · RGB-D image

## 1 Introduction

Feature matching is a fundamental issue for computer vision tasks such as object recognition [1], object detection, 3D reconstruction and image retrieval. The performance of feature matching highly depends on descriptors. Feature descriptors are generally required to be invariant to variations in image scale, rotation and illumination. Therefore, designing descriptors with good performance is very important.

In 2D domain, Lowe et al. [2] proposed the Scale Invariant Feature Transform (SIFT) method using scale space and gradient orientation histograms. Bay et al. [3] proposed the Speeded-Up Robust Features (SURF) method to speed up the keypoint detection step of SIFT. In 3D domain, Tombari et al. [4] proposed a Signature of Histograms of Orientations (SHOT) descriptor using geometric histograms. Later, Tombari et al. [5] proposed a Color-SHOT (CSHOT) descriptor by combining shape and color information. Guo et al. [6] proposed Rotational Projection Statistics (RoPS) based on observations in cognition and multi-view information representation. However, these float descriptors are usually high in dimensionality and matching time and

© Springer Nature Singapore Pte Ltd. 2017
F. Sun et al. (Eds.): ICCSIP 2016, CCIS 710, pp. 65–73, 2017.
DOI: 10.1007/978-981-10-5230-9_7

require a large amount of memory for storage. This issue becomes even challenging when the number of extracted keypoints is large. Consequently, current float feature descriptors are unsuitable for time crucial applications (e.g., mobile computing).

To achieve low memory cost and fast feature generation and matching, binary descriptors have been proposed. In 2D domain, Calonder et al. [7] simply compared the gray values of a specified point pair to generate the Binary Robust Independent Elementary Features (BRIEF) descriptor. In 3D domain, Prakhya et al. [8] used a certain binary mapping rules to propose the Binary SHOT (B-SHOT) descriptor. The aforementioned algorithms generate feature descriptors using RGB information or point cloud information only.

In recent years, with the availability of RGB-D images, few RGB-D image descriptors have been developed. Beksi et al. [9] integrated different features of RGB image and depth image to obtain a covariance descriptor. Feng et al. [10] proposed a Local Ordinal Intensity and Normal Descriptor (LOIND) by constructing a histogram. These descriptors are represented by float vectors, so they require higher memory consumption and more matching time than binary descriptors. Recently, Nascimento et al. [11] proposed a Binary Robust Appearance and Normal Descriptor (BRAND) by detecting variation in the normal or in the intensity on each point pair around a keypoint neighborhood.

In this paper, we propose a new efficient binary descriptor namely BAG for RGB-D images. Experimental results on the datasets **7-Scenes** [12] and **TUM RGB-D** benchmark [13] show that the proposed BAG binary descriptor achieves better performance than other descriptors in terms of recall/1-precision, matching time and memory consumption.

## 2    BAG Binary Descriptor

### 2.1    Local Binary Pattern

Given a keypoint $k$ and a circle patch $p$ with radius $R$ around a keypoint $k$, a specific sampling method is designed to obtain $N$ point pairs from patch $p$, then local binary pattern [14] can be represented as follows:

$$LBP_{R,N}(p) = \sum_{i=0}^{N-1} \tau(p : n_i, m_i)2^i \tag{1}$$

$$\tau(p : n_i, m_i) = \begin{cases} 1, & p(n_i) < p(m_i) \\ 0, & \text{otherwise} \end{cases} \tag{2}$$

where $n_i, m_i$ stands for a point pair from patch $p$, $p(n_i), p(m_i)$ is the gray value at point $n_i$ and $m_i$, respectively.

It can be seen that local binary pattern is robust to illumination variations and fast to compute. Since RGB-D image can provide both color information and depth information, we use 3 bits rather than 1 bit for each point pair to improve the discriminativeness power of feature descriptor.

## 2.2  Scale and Rotation Invariance

To improve the discriminativeness and robustness of a feature descriptor in 2D image, scale invariance should be considered. Generally, it can be achieved by constructing a scale space and then searching for extreme values in the scale space. According to the principle of image formation, the scale of a point in 2D image is approximately inversely proportional to its corresponding depth. So, we can use depth information to estimate the scale $s$ for each keypoint in RGB-D image [11], that is:

$$s = \max\left(0.2, \frac{3.8 - 0.4\max(2, d)}{3}\right) \tag{3}$$

where $d$ is the depth value of the keypoint. Since the depth sensor has a limited working range, part of the depth values measured by depth sensor are inaccurate. Therefore, we filter out the depth value smaller than 2 m.

To achieve rotation invariance, we use the same canonical orientation estimation method as SURF [3].

Then, the patch $p$ with radius $R$ around keypoint $k$ is scaled and rotated:

$$p = \{(T_{\theta,s}(x_i), T_{\theta,s}(y_i)) | (x_i, y_i) \in A\} \tag{4}$$

$$T_{\theta,s} = \begin{pmatrix} \cos\theta & -\sin\theta \\ \sin\theta & \cos\theta \end{pmatrix} \begin{pmatrix} s & 0 \\ 0 & s \end{pmatrix} \tag{5}$$

where $A$ is the $N$ point pairs sampled from patch $p$, $(x_i, y_i)$ is a point pair selected from $A$. After doing this, the proposed descriptor is invariant to scale and rotation. Uniform distribution sampling is used in this paper, an illustration is shown in Fig. 1.

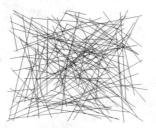

**Fig. 1.** Uniform distribution

## 2.3  Fusion of Color and Depth Information

Once $N$ point pairs have been determined for patch $p$, the BAG descriptor for each point pair is generated using the following three steps.

(1) The average gray value *ave* of patch $p$ in RGB image is first calculate, the gray value of each point in the point pair is then compared with the average gray value to produce a 1-bit representation $\tau_a$. That is:

$$\tau_a(x_i, y_i) = \begin{cases} 1, & \text{if } (p(x_i) > ave \&\& p(y_i) > ave) \| (p(x_i) < ave \&\& p(y_i) < ave) \\ 0, & \text{others} \end{cases}$$
(6)

where $p(.)$ is the gray value.

(2) The gray values of points in the point pair are compared directly, resulting in a 1-bit representation $\tau_b$.

$$\tau_b(x_i, y_i) = \begin{cases} 1, & \text{if } p(x_i) > p(y_i) \\ 0, & \text{others} \end{cases}$$
(7)

(3) The depth image is transformed to a point cloud, geometry information of the point cloud is then extracted and compared within each point pair, resulting in a 1-bit representation. The related geometry information is shown in Fig. 2.

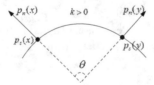

**Fig. 2.** Geometry information

Specifically, the following two features are constructed using surface geometry. The first one is the dot product between surface normals. The second one is the convexity of a surface. The convexity of a surface is defined as follows:

$$k(x_i, y_i) = \; <p_s(x_i) - p_s(y_i), p_n(x_i) - p_n(y_i)>$$
(8)

Where $<,>$ represents the dot product of two vectors, $p_s(x_i), p_s(y_i)$ and $p_n(x_i), p_n(y_i)$ are the 3D positions and the normals of points $x_i$ and $y_i$, respectively.

Finally, the 1-bit representation $\tau_c$ for geometry information [11] can be expressed as:

$$\tau_c(x_i, y_i) = (\;<p_n(x_i), p_n(y_i)> \; < \cos(\rho))^\wedge (k(x_i, y_i) < 0)$$
(9)

where $\rho$ is the normal angle threshold.

Therefore, we have 3 bits for the representation of each point pair. The BAG feature descriptor is then expressed as:

$$b(k) = \sum_{i=0}^{N-1} \left( 2^{3i} \tau_a(x_i, y_i) + 2^{3i+1} \tau_b(x_i, y_i) + 2^{3i+2} \tau_c(x_i, y_i) \right) \qquad (10)$$

### 2.4 Gaussian Filter

To improve the robustness of BAG descriptor with respect to noise, the patch $p$ is smoothed with a Gaussian kernel before the generation of binary features (as described in Sect. 2.3). The Gaussian kernel has a deviation $\sigma$ of 2 and a window of $9 \times 9$ pixels. The 2D Gaussian kernel function with deviation $\sigma$ is defined as:

$$g_\sigma(x, y) = \frac{1}{2\pi\sigma^2} \exp\left(-\frac{x^2 + y^2}{2\sigma^2}\right) \qquad (11)$$

The Gaussian filter value $F(q)$ at point $q$ is defined as:

$$F(q) = \frac{\sum\limits_{(l,k)\in\Omega} g_\sigma(l, k) I_{(l,k)}}{\sum\limits_{(l,k)\in\Omega} g_\sigma(l, k)} \qquad (12)$$

where $(l, k)$ is the relative position to $q$, $I_{(l,k)}$ is the gray value at position $(l, k)$, $\Omega$ is the filter window.

## 3 Experiments

### 3.1 Experimental Setup

In this paper, experiments were conducted on public datasets **7-Scenes** and **TUM RGB-D** benchmark. The integral image method [10, 11] was used to calculate the normals of a depth image. The Nearest Neighbor Distance Ratio (NNDR) criterion was used for descriptor matching and the widely used recall/1-precision curve [15] was used to measure the performance of a feature descriptor. To ensure fair comparison, we used the same keypoint detector method (i.e., STAR) [16] to generate keypoints in all experiments. We then used different keypoint description methods to generate feature matching performance.

To find the optimal parameters for BAG descriptors, we have tested our BAG feature descriptor with different sizes and different thresholds for normal angle. Finally, we set the size for BAG to be 48 bytes and the normal angle to be 45°.

## 3.2    Comparative Experiments

In order to test the performance of the proposed BAG descriptor, we compared BAG with several existing methods, including SIFT [2], SURF [3], SHOT [4] and CSHOT [5] in terms of recall/1-precision, generation time, matching time and memory consumption. Note that, the NNDR matching criterion was used in all experiments. For feature matching, the Euclidean distance was used for all float descriptors, and the Hamming distance was used for our proposed BAG binary descriptor.

The recall/1-precision curves achieved on different sequences of the **7-Scenes** dataset are shown in Fig. 3. The results show that the proposed BAG consistently outperformed SURF. Compared to SIFT, results on the first 3 sequences show that the proposed BAG significantly outperformed SIFT when the recall is low, the proposed BAG is then inferior to SIFT slightly. For the remaining 3 sequences, the proposed BAG achieved almost the same performance when recall is low, the proposed BAG is then slightly inferior to SIFT. That is because, the proposed BAG contains both appearance (RGB) information and geometric (depth) information, its performance is comparable to or better than the SIFT descriptor. Meanwhile, since the proposed BAG is represented by binary strings, its descriptiveness for a local surface is still slightly lower than the float descriptor. Therefore, the number of false positive matches for BAG matching increases when recall is high. Compared to SHOT and CSHOT, it is clear that the proposed BAG outperforms SHOT and CSHOT on all scenes when recall is high. Note that, CSHOT outperforms SHOT all the time.

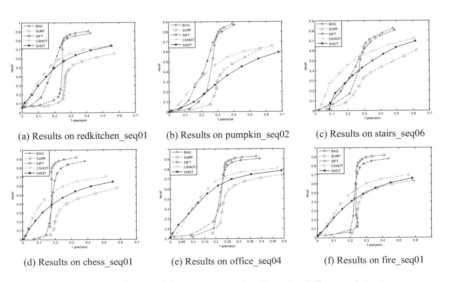

(a) Results on redkitchen_seq01    (b) Results on pumpkin_seq02    (c) Results on stairs_seq06

(d) Results on chess_seq01    (e) Results on office_seq04    (f) Results on fire_seq01

**Fig. 3.** Recall/1-precision curves achieved on the **7-Scenes** dataset

The recall/1-precison curves achieved on the publically available **TUM RGB-D** benchmark are shown in Fig. 4. The results show that the comparative performance of the proposed BAG is consistent with the results achieved on the **7-Scenes** dataset,

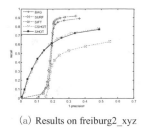

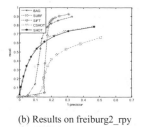

(a) Results on freiburg2_xyz                    (b) Results on freiburg2_rpy

**Fig. 4.** Recall/1-precision curves achieved on the **TUM RGB-D** benchmark

except that CSHOT achieves almost the same performance as SHOT on the **TUM RGB-D** benchmark. The observation indicates that CSHOT does not benefit from the color information of images on the **TUM RGB-D** benchmark.

The feature generation and matching time for different feature descriptors is shown in Table 1. From Table 1, we can see that the descending ranking for descriptors in terms of generation time is CSHOT, SHOT, SIFT, BAG and SURF. Particularly, the generation time of the proposed BAG is smaller than all other algorithms except SURF. That is because, the proposed BAG has to correct the scale and rotation of each point pair to achieve scale invariance and rotation invariance. With the scale and rotation invariance, the proposed BAG consistently outperforms SURF in term of recall/1-precision curves. The descending rank for descriptors in terms of matching time is CSHOT, SHOT, SIFT, SURF and BAG. The reason is that the BAG uses Hamming distance while the other descriptors use Euclidean distance for feature matching. With Euclidean distance, the matching time increases with the feature dimensionality. Note that, the descriptor dimensionalities for CSHOT, SHOT, SIFT and SURF are 1344, 352, 128, 64, respectively.

**Table 1.** Feature generation and matching time for different descriptors

|                      | SIFT  | SURF  | SHOT  | CSHOT | BAG    |
|----------------------|-------|-------|-------|-------|--------|
| Generation time (ms) | 0.691 | **0.047** | 1.912 | 2.467 | 0.215  |
| Matching time (ns)   | 88.3  | 46.64 | 241.9 | 939.4 | **28.64** |

The memory consumption for different descriptors is shown in Table 2. From Table 2, we can see the descending ranking is CSHOT, SHOT, SIFT, SURF and BAG. BAG is significantly smaller in memory cost than others. That is because, the proposed BAG is represented by binary bits while the other descriptors are represented by float values. Since a float vector contains 32 bits, a binary descriptor is more compact than a float descriptor with the same feature dimensionality.

**Table 2.** Memory consumption comparison among different descriptors

|       | SIFT | SURF | SHOT | CSHOT | BAG |
|-------|------|------|------|-------|-----|
| Bytes | 512  | 256  | 1408 | 5376  | **48** |

## 4 Conclusion

The paper has proposed a new efficient binary descriptor for RGB-D images. The proposed descriptor integrates both RGB and depth information and it is highly discriminative. Experiments have been conducted to compare our BAG descriptors with SIFT, SURF, SHOT and CSHOT descriptors. Results show that the proposed BAG produces better keypoint matching performance, it also achieves the fastest matching speed and the smallest memory consumption.

**Acknowledgment.** This work was supported by the National Natural Science Foundation of China (Nos. 61602499 and 61471371), the National Postdoctoral Program for Innovative Talents (No. BX201600172), and China Postdoctoral Science Foundation.

## References

1. Guo, Y., Bennamoun, M., Sohel, F., Lu, M., Wan, J.: 3D object recognition in cluttered scenes with local surface features: a survey. IEEE Trans. Pattern Anal. Mach. Intell. **36**(11), 2270–2287 (2014)
2. Lowe, D.G.: Distinctive image features from scale-invariant keypoints. Int. J. Comput. Vis. **60**(2), 91–110 (2004)
3. Bay, H., Ess, A., Tuytelaars, T., Van Gool, L.: Speeded-up robust features (SURF). Comput. Vis. Image Underst. **110**(3), 346–359 (2008)
4. Tombari, F., Salti, S., Di Stefano, L.: Unique signatures of histograms for local surface description. In: Daniilidis, K., Maragos, P., Paragios, N. (eds.) ECCV 2010. LNCS, vol. 6313, pp. 356–369. Springer, Heidelberg (2010). doi:10.1007/978-3-642-15558-1_26
5. Tombari, F., Salti, S., Di Stefano, L.: A combined texture-shape descriptor for enhanced 3D feature matching. In: 2011 18th IEEE International Conference on Image Processing, pp. 809–812. IEEE, September 2011
6. Guo, Y., Sohel, F., Bennamoun, M., Lu, M., Wan, J.: Rotational projection statistics for 3D local surface description and object recognition. Int. J. Comput. Vis. **105**(1), 63–86 (2013)
7. Calonder, M., Lepetit, V., Strecha, C., Fua, P.: BRIEF: binary robust independent elementary features. In: Daniilidis, K., Maragos, P., Paragios, N. (eds.) ECCV 2010. LNCS, vol. 6314, pp. 778–792. Springer, Heidelberg (2010). doi:10.1007/978-3-642-15561-1_56
8. Prakhya, S.M., Liu, B., Lin, W.: B-SHOT: a binary feature descriptor for fast and efficient keypoint matching on 3D point clouds. In: 2015 IEEE/RSJ International Conference Intelligent Robots and Systems (IROS), pp. 1929–1934. IEEE, September 2015
9. Beksi, W.J., Papanikolopoulos, N.: Object classification using dictionary learning and RGB-D covariance descriptors. In: 2015 IEEE International Conference on Robotics and Automation (ICRA), pp. 1880–1885. IEEE, May 2015
10. Feng, G., Liu, Y., Liao, Y.: Loind: an illumination and scale invariant RGB-D descriptor. In: 2015 IEEE International Conference on Robotics and Automation (ICRA), pp. 1893–1898. IEEE, May 2015
11. do Nascimento, E.R., Oliveira, G.L., Vieira, A.W., Campos, M.F.: On the development of a robust, fast and lightweight keypoint descriptor. Neurocomputing **120**, 141–155 (2013)
12. Glocker, B., Izadi, S., Shotton, J., Criminisi, A.: Real-time RGB-D camera relocalization. In: 2013 IEEE International Symposium Mixed and Augmented Reality (ISMAR), pp. 173–179. IEEE, October 2013

13. Sturm, J., Engelhard, N., Endres, F., Burgard, W., Cremers, D.: A benchmark for the evaluation of RGB-D SLAM systems. In: 2012 IEEE/RSJ International Conference on Intelligent Robots and Systems, pp. 573–580. IEEE, October 2012
14. Ojala, T., Pietikainen, M., Maenpaa, T.: Multiresolution gray-scale and rotation invariant texture classification with local binary patterns. IEEE Trans. Pattern Anal. Mach. Intell. **24** (7), 971–987 (2002)
15. Guo, Y., Bennamoun, M., Sohel, F., Lu, M., Wan, J., Kwok, N.M.: A comprehensive performance evaluation of 3D local feature descriptors. Int. J. Comput. Vis. **116**(1), 66–89 (2016)
16. Agrawal, M., Konolige, K., Blas, M.R.: CenSurE: center surround extremas for realtime feature detection and matching. In: Forsyth, D., Torr, P., Zisserman, A. (eds.) ECCV 2008. LNCS, vol. 5305, pp. 102–115. Springer, Heidelberg (2008). doi:10.1007/978-3-540-88693-8_8

# Self-tuning Motion Model for Visual Tracking

Hangkai Tan[✉], Qingjie Zhao, and Xiongpeng Wang

Beijing Lab of Intelligent Information Technology, School of Computer Science,
Beijing Institute of Technology, Beijing 100081, People's Republic of China
tanhangkai@126.com, zhaoqj@bit.edu.cn,
wangxiongpeng@foxmail.com

**Abstract.** In visual tracking, how to select a suitable motion model is an important problem to deal with, since the movements in real world are always irregular in most cases. We propose a self-tuning motion model for target tracking in this paper, where the current motion model is computed according to the relative distance of the target positions in the last two frames. Our method has achieved excellent performance when experimenting on the sequences where the targets move unstably, abruptly or even when partial occlusion exists, and the method is particularly robust to the unsuitable initial motion model.

**Keywords:** Visual tracking · Self-tuning motion models · Logistic regression

## 1 Introduction

Visual tracking has been playing a critical role in the computer vision field. It can be used in various applications such as video surveillance, human computer interface, motion analysis, intelligent visual surveillance and intelligent transportation [1, 2]. The task of visual tracking is mainly to determine the states of object such as scale, velocity, position and other related information. Large numbers of effective tracking approaches have been proposed in literature [3–7].

A complete target tracking algorithm mainly includes the feature extractor, observation model, motion model, model updater and ensemble post-processor [8]. Some methods focus on global models [9–12]. Some methods focus on local parts or patches, and others combine local model with global model. The observation model is divided into discriminative observation model and generative observation model. Since the top-performing trackers in recent benchmarking studies are exclusively discriminative trackers, in our algorithm we use discriminative observation model.

The significance of an algorithm is that it can be used in real life. Movements in real world tend to be irregular in most cases. Irregular movements mean that the tracking would fail when we use a constant or an unsuitable motion model. Motion has its own complexity, which places a huge challenge to find an excellent motion model [13]. Our paper mainly focuses on studying motion models under the framework of particle filter [14].

---

This work is supported by National Natural Science Foundation (NNSF) of China under Grant 61175096.

F. Sun et al. (Eds.): ICCSIP 2016, CCIS 710, pp. 74–81, 2017.
DOI: 10.1007/978-981-10-5230-9_8

In the tracking algorithms, the motion model represents the change of object state over time and an appropriate motion model can effectively reduce the search space and computational complexity for the optimal target location [15].

The main contribution of this paper is that a self-tuning motion model is proposed to track the target. Our self-tuning motion model mainly solves the problem of initial motion model selection and the change of target motion, which may cause by camera shaking, acceleration and deceleration of target. Self-tuning motion model is not sensitive to the initial setting of motion model.

In the following, we will give overview of the system in Sect. 2. In Sect. 3, the logistic regression discriminative appearance model for tracking is introduced. And our self-tuning motion model for tracking is introduced in Sect. 4. The simulation results show that the proposed algorithm can be used to track target effectively in sequences in Sect. 5. Finally, we give conclusion of this paper in Sect. 6.

## 2   System Overview

We present details of the proposed image representation scheme and tracking algorithm in this section. Our algorithm is formulated within the Bayesian framework in which the maximum a posterior (MAP) estimate of the state given the observations up to time $t$ is computed by

$$p(X_t|Y_{1:t}) = \alpha p(Y_t|X_t) \int p(X_t|X_{t-1}) p(X_{t-1}|Y_{1:t-1}) dX_{t-1}, \tag{1}$$

where $Y_{1:t}$ donates all the observations up to time $t$, $X_t$ is the state at time $t$, and $\alpha$ is a normalization term. In this work, the target state is defined as $X_t = \left(X_t^c, X_t^{sx}, X_t^{sy}\right)$, where $X_t^c$ represents the center location of the target, $X_t^{sx}$ and $X_t^{sy}$ denote its scale in x-axis and y-axis, respectively. As demonstrated by numerous works in the object tracking literature, it is critical to construct an effective observation model $p(Y_t|X_t)$ and an efficient motion model $p(X_t|X_{t-1})$.

In our formulation, a robust discriminative appearance model is constructed which, given an observation, computes the grades of it belonging to the target or the background. Thus, the observation estimate of a certain target candidate $X_t$ is proportional to its confidence:

$$p(Y_t|X_t) \propto \hat{C}(X_t), \tag{2}$$

where $\hat{C}(X_t)$ represents the confidence of an observation at state $X_t$ being the target. The state estimate of the target $\hat{X}_t$ at time $t$ can be obtained by the MAP estimate over the N samples at each time $t$. Let $X_t^{(l)}$ denotes the $l$-th sample of the state $X_t$,

$$\hat{X}_t = \arg\max_{X_t^{(l)}} p(X_t^{(l)}|Y_{1:t}) \, \forall l = 1, \ldots, N \tag{3}$$

## 3  Observation Model and Feature Extractor

In tracking algorithms, feature extractor is very important. So in our algorithm we use the fusion of HOG feature and raw pixel feature. Fusion strategy is:

$$x = [x_h, x_r] = [m_0, m_1, \ldots, m_{h+r}], \tag{4}$$

where $x$ represents the fusion feature, $x_h$ represents the HOG feature and $x_r$ represents the raw pixel feature.

Logistic regression model can be thought of as a linear regression model, through learning the characteristics of the sample to train classifier, and it is defined as:

$$h_\theta(x) = g(\theta^T x) = \frac{1}{1 + e^{-\theta^T x}}, \tag{5}$$

where $x$ is $N$ dimensional vector from formula (4), $g$ is called as Logistic Function or Sigmoid Function. The cost of logistic regression function is:

$$J(\theta) = -\frac{1}{n} \left[ \sum_{i=1}^n y^{(i)} \log \left( h_\theta \left( x^{(i)} \right) \right) + \left( 1 - y^{(i)} \right) \log \left( 1 - h_\theta \left( x^{(i)} \right) \right) \right], \tag{6}$$

where the formula (6) is regression model for maximum likelihood estimation of the likelihood function, $x^{(i)}$ represents the feature of $i$-th sample, $y^{(i)}$ is the label of $x^{(i)}$ and $n$ represents the number of training sample. Because the minimum of the cost function is equal to maximum likelihood estimation, estimation of the parameter $\theta$ can be obtained by minimizing the cost function. And in order to prevent the fitting, $l_2$ regularization is joined to a logistic regression model. So the problem of parameter computation is translated into:

$$argmax(\delta(\theta) - \partial ||\theta||)^2, \tag{7}$$

To join the regular item for the cost function is:

$$J(\theta) = \frac{1}{N} \sum_{i=1}^N \delta \left( y^{(i)}, \theta, x^{(i)} \right) + \frac{\lambda}{2} ||\theta||^2, \tag{8}$$

where $\theta$ represents the parameters of the classifier, $\lambda$ controls the regularization parameter. $x^{(l)}$ represents the feature of $X_t^{(l)}$, which can be calculated using formula (4). Through formula (9) we can calculate all candidate target points, and the maximum score as the tracking results.

$$\hat{C} \left( X_t^{(l)} \right) = 1 / \left( 1 + e^{-\theta^T x^{(l)}} \right) \tag{9}$$

# 4  Self-tuning Motion Model

The traditional motion model is assumed to be Gaussian distributed,

$$p(X_t|X_{t-1}) = N(X_t|X_{t-1}, \varphi) \tag{10}$$

where $\varphi$ is a diagonal covariance matrix whose elements are the standard deviations for location and scale, i.e., $\sigma_c$ and $\sigma_s$ dictate how the proposed algorithm accounts for motion change. And $\sigma_c = [\sigma_x, \sigma_y]$, $\sigma_x$ represents the change of position along the $x$ axis direction, $\sigma_y$ represents the change of position along the $y$ axis direction.

Many tracking algorithms are based on the particle filter framework. And in the process of tracking the $\sigma_x$, $\sigma_y$ are the same, but the target motion model is always changing, which may cause failure. They need to set different motion model according to the specific video sequence. But in practical application, we do not know which motion model we should set. In order to solve the problems above, we put forward an adaptive motion model.

Because the movement of targets is continuous, the displacement distance of object between two consecutive frames video is related. We use the first two frames as a priori information to set the current frame of target motion model. Dynamic $\sigma_x$, $\sigma_y$ settings as follows:

$$\begin{cases} \sigma_x = \gamma \, Sx_{t-1} & \text{if } \sigma_x > \beta \text{ then } \sigma_x = \beta & \text{if } \sigma_x < \mu\sigma_x = \mu \\ \sigma_y = \gamma \, Sy_{t-1} & \text{if } \sigma_y > \beta \text{ then } \sigma_y = \beta & \text{if } \sigma_y < \mu\sigma_y = \mu \end{cases} \tag{11}$$

where $Sx_{t-1}$, $Sy_{t-1}$ respectively denote the relative distance of target in the last two frames in $x$ axis and $y$ axis, $\gamma$ is a coefficient of a constant used to show that the proportion of the relationship between $\sigma_x$ ($\sigma_y$) and $Sx_{t-1}$ ($Sy_{t-1}$), $\beta$ represents the maximum value of $\sigma_x$ and $\sigma_y$, $\mu$ represents the minimum value of $\sigma_x$ and $\sigma_y$. Using the above method to realize the motion model of dynamic adjustment (Table 1).

# 5  Experiment Results

In order to evaluate the robustness and effectiveness of the self-tuning motion model, we test our method on five challenging sequences: Biker, Deer, Human9, Stennis and Woman. All of these are publicly available benchmark video sequences which can be downloaded from the datasets of the website http://www.visual-tracking.net.

In order to illustrate the robustness and effectiveness of the self-tuning motion model, we compare within the algorithms which the other parts are same except for motion model. So it shows that our motion model is effective. Numerous experimental results show that our algorithm can track an object under challenging conditions: camera shake, speed change quickly, partial occlusion, drastic change in velocity, etc. In order to show that our self-tuning motion model is not sensitive to the selection of motion model initial, we choose groups of the initial motion model to illustrate the selection of the initial. In Tables 2 and 3 our self-tuning motion model named "Our", the contrast algorithm named "Original".

**Table 1.** Our self-tuning algorithm

| Algorithm1: self-tuning motion model  tracking |
|---|

Input: state $X_t$, motion model $\sigma_{x_0}$、$\sigma_{y_0}$.

Output: state $X_{t+1}$.

1:    while t< MAX frame do
2:        if t=1  then
3:            calculate observation model of object using Eq.(7)  ;
4:        end if
5:        if t=2  then
6:            Use motion model $\sigma_{x_0}$、$\sigma_{y_0}$ to predict $X_{t+1}$.
7:        End if
8:        if t>2  then
9:            calculate $\sigma_{x_t}$、$\sigma_{y_t}$ through Eq. (10).
10:        Predict $X_{t+1}$ using $\sigma_{x_t}$、$\sigma_{y_t}$.
11:        Calculate the accuracy of particles through Eq. (8).
12:        End if
13:    estimate the confidence of particle to gain state $X_{t+1}$.
14:    update observation model every k frames.
15: end while

**Table 2.**  Average center location error (red bold represent the best performance in average)

| $\sigma_x, \sigma_y$ | Stennis | | Woman | | Human9 | |
|---|---|---|---|---|---|---|
| | Our | Original | Our | Original | Our | Original |
| (3 3) | 1.72 | 30.25 | 7.86 | 7.84 | 2.81 | 47.40 |
| (6 6) | 1.74 | 67.70 | 7.29 | 7.49 | 2.48 | 25.29 |
| (4 13) | 1.71 | 1.83 | 7.90 | 7.01 | 2.61 | 39.45 |
| (13 4) | 1.80 | 27.14 | 8.90 | 7.70 | 2.42 | 4.49 |
| (13 13) | 1.69 | 2.24 | 7.08 | 7.97 | 2.48 | 2.43 |
| Average | 1.73 | 25.83 | 7.8 | 7.6 | 2.56 | 23.81 |

**Table 3.**  Average center location error (red bold represent the best performance in average)

| $\sigma_x, \sigma_y$ | Bike | | Deer | |
|---|---|---|---|---|
| | Our | Original | Our | Original |
| (3 3) | 22.08 | 88.08 | 5.76 | 96.90 |
| (6 6) | 23.64 | 21.08 | 7.66 | 101.46 |
| (4 13) | 21.92 | 59.72 | 6.40 | 91.85 |
| (13 4) | 22.25 | 104.20 | 6.57 | 318.5 |
| (13 13) | 22.46 | 22.41 | 6.26 | 8.39 |
| Average | 22.47 | 59.10 | 6.53 | 123.42 |

Without loss of generality, in our experiments we set $\gamma = 2.15$, $\beta = 16$ and $\mu = 3$.

Besides the qualitative evaluation above, we also evaluate our algorithm quantitatively. The error of center location is the Euclidean distance from the tracking center to the manually labeled ground truth data. The quantitative results are shown in Fig. 1, which indicates that our algorithm is efficient and accurate in dealing with abrupt and camera shake.

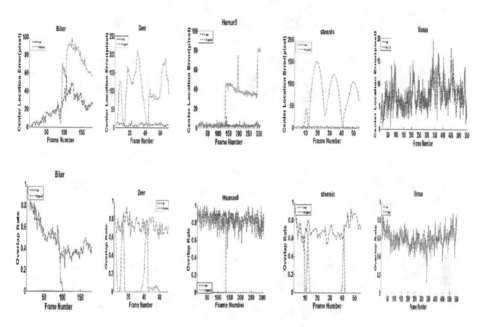

**Fig. 1.** Center location error and overlap rate

The results in Tables 2 and 3 show that for different initial motion models, our algorithm can get better results. As we can see from the experimental results, good results are obtained from the multi group initial motion model. Our algorithm is more robust to the choice of the initial model. The traditional fixed motion model is very sensitive to the choice of the initial model. And the results of different motion models are very different, some of the results are very poor.

Figure 2 shows the screenshots of tracking results on five different datasets and we use the same initial motion model $\left(\sigma_{x_0} = \sigma_{y_0} = 6\right)$. In these challenging video sequences, our method can accurately track the object even in some special circumstances: occlusion (in the sequences woman), abrupt motion (in the sequences biker, Stennis) and camera shake (in the sequences Human9, woman). And from Fig. 2 we can see that in the process of tracking shot shaking suddenly, our tracking algorithm can track successfully such as woman sequence in the frame $562 \sim 577$.

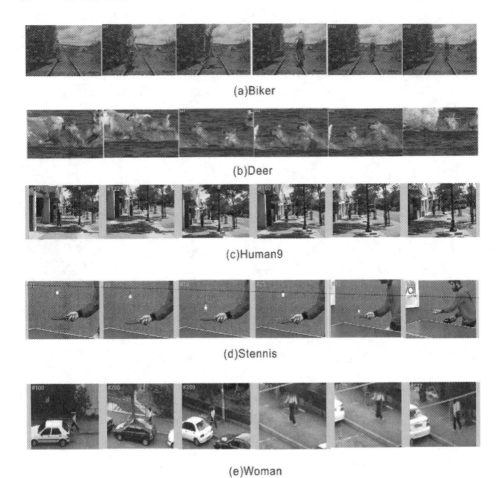

(a)Biker

(b)Deer

(c)Human9

(d)Stennis

(e)Woman

**Fig. 2.** Comparison tracking results of our tracking with Original method on five video sequence: (a) Biker, (b) Deer, (c) Human9, (d) Stennis, (e) Woman. Red box is our algorithm, yellow box is contrast algorithm (Color figure online)

## 6   Conclusion and Future Work

In this paper, we propose a self-tuning motion model algorithm. The application of self-tuning motion model in particle filter can guarantee tracker to capture the target when encountering drastic motion. And it has great significance in practical application. For unknown motion model tracking scenarios our self-tuning motion model can set motion model itself. According to the accuracy of particles in these frame, self-tuning motion model is implemented to make the system stable and robust. Our method effectively addresses the problem of partial occlusion, fast moving, camera shake, sudden acceleration and sudden deceleration. The competitive results demonstrate our algorithm can accommodate scenarios with severe changes. In the future, we will use other relationships to take the place of proportional relationship, which may get better effect. And our self-tuning motion model can be used in other tracking algorithm.

# References

1. Li, M., Chen, W., Huang, K., et al.: Visual tracking via incremental self-tuning particle filtering on the affine group. In: 2010 IEEE Conference on Computer Vision and Pattern Recognition (CVPR), pp. 1315–1322. IEEE (2010)
2. Qie, Z., Li, J., Zhang, Y.: Adaptive particle swarm optimization-based particle filter for tracking maneuvering object. In: 2014 33rd Chinese Control Conference (CCC), pp. 4685–4690. IEEE (2014)
3. Wang, L., Ouyang, W., Wang, X., et al.: Visual tracking with fully convolutional networks. In: International Conference on Computer Vision (2015)
4. Yang, F., Lu, H., Yang, M., et al.: Robust superpixel tracking. IEEE Trans. Image Process. **23**(4), 1639–1651 (2014)
5. Pan, J., Lim, J., Su, Z., et al.: L0-regularized object representation for visual tracking. In: British Machine Vision Conference (2014)
6. Ma, C., Huang, J., Yang, X., et al.: Hierarchical convolutional features for visual tracking. In: International Conference on Computer Vision (2015)
7. Yoon, J.H., Yang, M., Yoon, K., et al.: Interacting multiview tracker. IEEE Trans. Pattern Anal. Mach. Intell. **38**(5), 903–917 (2016)
8. Wang, N., Shi, J., Yeung, D., et al.: Understanding and diagnosing visual tracking systems. In: International Conference on Computer Vision (2015). Kwon, J., Lee, K.M.: Visual tracking decomposition. In: Proceedings of the IEEE Conference on Computer Vision and Pattern Recognition (CVPR), pp. 1269–1276. June (2010)
9. Ross, D.A., Lim, J., Lin, R., et al.: Incremental learning for robust visual tracking. Int. J. Comput. Vis. **77**, 125–141 (2008)
10. Hare, S., Saffari, A., Torr, P.H., et al.: Struck: structured output tracking with kernels. In: International Conference on Computer Vision (2011)
11. Zhuang, B., Lu, H., Xiao, Z., et al.: Visual tracking via discriminative sparse similarity map. IEEE Trans. Image Process. **23**(4), 1872–1881 (2014)
12. Yilmaz, A., Javed, O., Shah, M., et al.: Object tracking: a survey. ACM Comput. Surv. **38**(4) (2006)
13. Kwon, J., Lee, K.M.: Visual tracking decomposition. In: Proceedings of the IEEE Conference on Computer Vision and Pattern Recognition (CVPR), pp. 1269–1276, June 2010
14. Pérez, P., Hue, C., Vermaak, J., Gangnet, M.: Color-based probabilistic tracking. In: Heyden, A., Sparr, G., Nielsen, M., Johansen, P. (eds.) ECCV 2002. LNCS, vol. 2350, pp. 661–675. Springer, Heidelberg (2002). doi:10.1007/3-540-47969-4_44
15. Alper, Y., Omar, J., Mubarak, S.: Object tracking: a survey. ACM Comput. Surv. **38**(4), 13 (2006)

# Bio-Inspired Night Image Enhancement Based on Contrast Enhancement and Denoising

Xinyi Bai[1,2], Steffi Agino Priyanka[2], Hsiao-Jung Tung[2], and Yuankai Wang[2(✉)]

[1] University of Electronic Science and Technology of China, Chengdu, China
babsbxy@outlook.com, wwwbxyl23@163.com
[2] Fu Jen Catholic University, New Taipei City, Taiwan
steffi@islab.tw, ykwang@fju.edu.tw

**Abstract.** Due to the low accuracy of object detection and recognition in many intelligent surveillance systems at nighttime, the quality of night images is crucial. Compared with the corresponding daytime image, nighttime image is characterized as low brightness, low contrast and high noise. In this paper, a bio-inspired image enhancement algorithm is proposed to convert a low illuminance image to a brighter and clear one. Different from existing bio-inspired algorithm, the proposed method doesn't use any training sequences, we depend on a novel chain of contrast enhancement and denoising algorithms without using any forms of recursive functions. Our method can largely improve the brightness and contrast of night images, besides, suppress noise. Then we implement on real experiment, and simulation experiment to test our algorithms. Both results show the advantages of proposed algorithm over contrast pair, Meylan and Retinex.

**Keywords:** Bio-inspired image enhancement algorithm · Nighttime image · Contrast enhancement · Denoising · Intelligent surveillance system

## 1 Introduction

Surveillance system has been widely used to do security work. While the accuracy of these algorithms is largely based on the quality of input videos. Due to the lack of exposure, nighttime images are characterized as low brightness, low contrast, and high noise. This paper proposed a novel bio-inspired chain method to deal with them.

Human eyes can figure out information from different scales and exposure levels quickly and then adapt their pupils to the environmental brightness in order to take corresponding strategies for further detection automatically, because many receptive fields exist in their retinas, which helps to express the overall characteristics from positions under various exposure level. And these complete receptive fields are crucial for attention selection, which makes human eyes only focus on the object and ignore unrelated background and noise. So the first contribution in this paper is to divide nighttime images into three levels as three pseudo receptive fields: low light level (LLL), very low light level (VLLL), and high dynamic range (HDR). According to the three pseudo receptive fields, we simulate three levels of images and enhance the contrast and

F. Sun et al. (Eds.): ICCSIP 2016, CCIS 710, pp. 82–90, 2017.
DOI: 10.1007/978-981-10-5230-9_9

brightness using different parameters. The noise in nighttime images mainly includes Poisson noise and false color noise, so we use bilateral filter as fundamental pseudo attention selection to remove noise in R, G, B channels respectively.

Visual information propagates from the retina issued through the lateral geniculate nucleus finally reaches the primary visual cortex (V1), then signal processing is divided into two pathways, ventral pathway and dorsal pathway. And ventral pathway passes through V2 region to V4 region, finally arrive at inferior temporal cortex to deal with color and shape information, while dorsal pathway passes through V2 region to V3 region and middle temporal cortex, finally reaches posterior parietal cortex to deal with spatial information. So the second contribution in this paper is to divide our contrast enhancement algorithms into two simultaneously pathways, one focuses on the color, the other focuses on the brightness. Besides, human visual system is a hierarchical structure, the latter layer accepts the information processed from the former layer, and performs more advanced operation it, so every pathway of our method is a chain of algorithms. Another contribution in this paper is to count the pros and cons that do contrast enhancement before denoising and denoising before contrast enhancement. Therefore, in this paper, we also analyze and discuss the sequences of contrast enhancement algorithm and denoising algorithm.

In recent years, researches about contrast enhancement mainly include self-enhancement and context-based fusion. For context-based fusion, it aims to fuse multiple images into one image, and it is commonly applied to high dynamic range images such as denight [1], which fuses the night image with corresponding day images under abundant exposure. But this method is applicable to day and night scenes without objects. Because if there are objects in the day image, through denight contrast enhancement, the object will disappear; if there are object in the night image, the enhanced image will have ghosts. Nevertheless, when color light sources exist in the image, the color light sources will lead to color shift [1]. For self-enhancement, the global method such as contrast pair [3] is to obtain the ratio of the target point pixel value and neighboring pixel values, then calculates the mapping function based on these ratios. If the brightness is the same, the change of these pixel values in different region remains a constant, but in local methods such as Retinex and dehaze, the change of the pixel values is related to the neighboring pixel values [4–7]. Moreover, denoising algorithm mainly includes spatial method and spatio-temporal method. Common spatial method contains traditional Gaussian filter, median filter, bilateral filter and non-local mean filter [8, 9]. While spatiotemporal methods in [2, 9, 10] use the filter from the radio based method, which extends the two dimensional filter into three dimensional filter, and takes the combination of the initial video with the enhanced video as the reference of the denoising algorithm.

Main contributions of the bio-inspired image enhancement algorithm are to analogy the ventral and dorsal parallel pathways in visual signaling, and three receptive fields in retina, besides, use chain of contrast enhancement algorithms to analogy a hierarchical structure in human visual system.

## 2  Contrast Enhancement and Denoising

We establish a night image enhancement framework based on contrast enhancement and denoising. Our proposed method aims to convert image $I_N(x, y)$ which has low brightness, low contrast and high noise to a brighter and clearer image $I_{NIE}(x, y)$.

In the chains of contrast enhancement algorithm, we simultaneously implement it with two parallel pathways like the ventral and dorsal pathways. On one pathway, we separate the luminance channel $I_N^L$ from the night image, then improve the global contrast using tone mapping, next we do RBAF on the logarithmic domain to correct the brightness and gain the enhanced luminance channel $I_{CE}^L$, finally with the method of Histogram smoothing, the over strengthened pixels at the peak of Histogram will be solved. On the other pathway, we focus on keeping the consistence of the brightness in color channels, first we obtain a new brightness channel $I_N'$ in the global image, then we separate another two color channels $I_N^{C_1}$ and $I_N^{C_2}$ in the logarithmic domain through PCA conversion, next by multiplying them with a weight $\alpha$, the color saturation is improved. Finally, we convert the enhanced brightness channel $I_{CE}^L$ and two color channel $I_N^{C_1}, I_N^{C_2}$ back to RGB color space. In denoising algorithm, considering the main noise in the night image is false color noise, we use bilateral filter to remove the noise in three channels respectively from image $I_{CE}$. Finally, in the enhanced images, the strength of edges will be maintained, the contrast and brightness can be largely improved, and the noise will be removed. The flow chart of our algorithm is shown in Fig. 1.

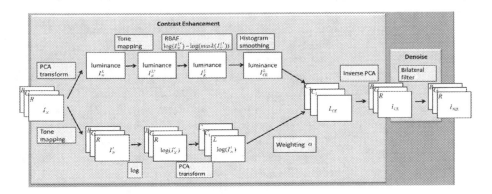

**Fig. 1.** Night image enhancement flow chart.

First we convert night image $I_N$ from RGB to $L, C_1, C_2$. Then we use the average brightness $\overline{I_N^L}$ to adjust the slope in tone mapping, where $\overline{I_N^L}$ ranges in $[0, 1]$. From (1), (2), $\frac{1}{\gamma}$ is the average brightness ranging in $[\varepsilon, 1]$, and the adjusting coefficient $\lambda = \frac{1}{6}$, $\varepsilon = \frac{2}{3}$. Then in (3), p is the value of the pixel, N is the total pixels of the image. After tone mapping, RBAF is adapted for local adjustment. In (4), (5), (6), the coefficient $\beta(x, y)$ is to maintain the consistence of bright areas and dark areas. Where $\beta(x, y)$ is determined by $I_N^{L'}(x, y)$, and $\beta(x, y)$ is close to 0 in the bright area, while in the dark area, $\beta(x, y)$ is close to 1.

$$I_N^{L'} = \left(I_N^L\right)^{1/\gamma} \tag{1}$$

$$\frac{1}{\gamma} = \min(1, \Gamma \overline{I_N^L} + \varepsilon) \tag{2}$$

$$\overline{I_N^L} = \frac{\sum_{p \in I_N^L} \log\left(I_N^L(P)\right)}{N} \tag{3}$$

$$R(x, y) = \log\left(I_N^{L'}(x, y)\right) - \log\left(mask\left(I_N^{L'}(x, y)\right)\right) \tag{4}$$

$$R(x, y) = \log\left(I_N^{L'}(x, y)\right) - \beta(x, y) \cdot \log\left(mask\left(I_N^{L'}(x, y)\right)\right) \tag{5}$$

$$\beta(x, y) = 1 - \frac{1}{1 + e^{-7\left(I_N^{L'}(x,y) - 0.5\right)}} \tag{6}$$

To deal with the halo artifacts in Retinex, in (7), we replace Gaussian filter to adaptive filter, let the contour of the object in accordance with the image itself. And change the $\sigma_{\theta, r}$ in Gaussian filter to kinetic energy as $mask(I_N^{L'}(x, y))$, where $\sigma_{\theta, r}$ is determined by whether the edge of the $mask(I_N^{L'}(x, y))$ has a high contrast. Namely, we scan the edge in eight directions from the mask, when it matches the edge precisely, $\sigma_{\theta, r}^2 = \sigma_1$; when it failed to match the edge and fell to the smooth area, $\sigma_{\theta, r}^2 = \sigma_0$, where $r$ is the distance from the point to the center of the mask, $\theta$ is the angle of Retinex based adaptive filter, when $0 < \sigma_1 \leq \frac{1}{2}\sigma_0$, the halo artifacts can be largely reduced as (8). If the value of the reflection image from (5) is less than 0, histogram stretching is required to do normalization. As is shown in (9), min and max mean the maximum and minimum values selected by $R(x, y)$.

$$mask\left(I_N^{L'}(x, y)\right) = \frac{\sum_{\theta=0}^{360} \sum_{r=0}^{r_{max}} I_N^{L'}(x + r\cos(\theta), y + r\sin(\theta)) \cdot e^{\frac{r^2}{\sigma_{\theta,r}^2}}}{\sum_{\theta=0}^{360} \sum_{r=0}^{r_{max}} e^{\frac{r^2}{\sigma_{\theta,r}^2}}} \tag{7}$$

$$\sigma_{\theta, r}^2 = \left\{ \begin{array}{l} \sigma_0, \ no \ high-contrast \ edge \ was \ crossed \ along \ \theta \\ \sigma_1, \ a \ high-contrast \ edge \ was \ crossed \ along \ \theta \end{array} \right\} \tag{8}$$

$$I_R^L(x, y) = \frac{R(x, y) - min}{max - min} \tag{9}$$

Since the normalization will reduce the contrast of some areas, we use histogram smoothing to improve it. The histogram of the input image $h_i$ is changed into $h$. And we come to its cumulative histogram $H(i)$, then take $H(i)$ as the mapping function, as

(10), (11). Nest, in denoising, as (12), the intensity value at each pixel in an image is replaced by a weighted average of intensity values from nearby pixels. These weights are in Gaussian distribution.

$$I_{CE}^L(x, y) = H(i)I_R^L(x, y) \tag{10}$$

$$h = \left((1 + \lambda)I + \gamma D^T D\right)^{-1}(h_i + \lambda u) \tag{11}$$

$$I_{CE}(x, y) = W^{-1}\left[I_{CE}^L(x, y) + \alpha\left(I_N^{C1'}(x, y) + I_N^{C2'}(x, y)\right)\right] \tag{12}$$

Finally, the noise in the enhanced image $I_{CE}$ is removed. In our output image $I_{NE}(x, y)$, the contrast and brightness are largely improved, besides, the noise is removed, and the sharp edge remains clear.

## 3    Simulation Experiment and Analysis

This paper selects experiment images from TID2008 datasets [11]. We divide night images into three levels like three pseudo receptive fields, low light level (LLL), whose contrast may be well enough in the original image, but the low contrast in night time makes us difficult to recognize; very low light level (VLLL), its dark pixels in the original image do not clear enough, then global image become so dark, it is impossible to recognize; and high dynamic range (HDR), where the existing ambient light source in the image makes partial areas extremely bright or dark. In order to simulate the noise, we bring in colorful Poisson noise. The process of simulating three levels of images is divided into two steps, first decrease the brightness of the global image to $d$ to simulate a certain proportion of distortion t in dark area. Then proportionally reduce the kinetic energy according to the pixel values. In (13), $f(x)$ is the simulation image, $\alpha$ is the reduced weight of the kinetic energy, $d$ is the reduced brightness, which is deduced from (14), calculate the cumulative distribution of the distortion region $t$ in dark areas, where $0 < \alpha < 1$, $0 \leq t \leq 1$.

$$f(x) = \alpha(max(x - d, 0)) \tag{13}$$

$$d = min\{i|cdf(i) \geq t\} \tag{14}$$

The distortion t of the LLL is 0.03, $\alpha$ is 0.7; while the distortion t of VLLL is 0.03, $\alpha$ is 0.3. In the histogram of the simulated images, where the average of brightness in VLLL is 0.077115, the standard deviation is 0.055803. We also simulate the HDR image, from (15), (16), (17), (18), where $t_{low}$ and $t_{high}$ are both 0.05.

$$f(x) = min(\alpha(max(x - d_{low}, 0)), 1) \tag{15}$$

$$d_{low} = min\{i|cdf(i) \geq t_{low}\} \tag{16}$$

$$d_{high} = max\{i|cdf(i) \leq 1 - t_{high}\} \tag{17}$$

$$\alpha = \left(d_{high} - d_{low}\right)^{-1} \tag{18}$$

We use bilateral filter to denoise and compare our contrast enhancement algorithm under VLLL with contrast pair, Retinex, and Melan. In contrast pair, the edge threshold is 10; in Meylan, $\sigma_0 = 16$, $\sigma_1 = 5$, $\alpha = 1.6$; in our method, $\sigma_0 = 16$, $\sigma_1 = 5$, $\alpha = 1.6$, $\lambda = 1$, $\gamma = 1$.

Few researchers test implement orders of the two algorithms, we also analyze the sequences based on LLL-Poisson simulation: denoising after contrast enhancement (Bilateral-CE), and contrast enhancement after denoising (CE-Bilateral). Results are shown in Fig. 2, it is clearer on the edge of the hat and shade region in CE-Bilateral. Moreover, the contrast of the shade from contrast pair is lower than our method; the dark region in Retinex is in bluish hue compared with our method; the contrast is higher in the bright area from our method than Meylan. So our method not only improves the brightness, but also provides good contrast in dark areas. And for sequences, our method performs better under CE-bilateral than under bilateral-CE.

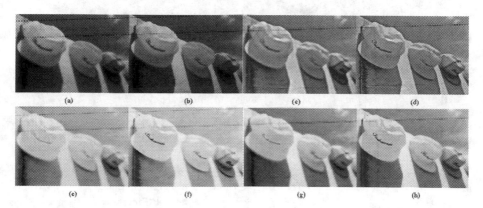

**Fig. 2.** Comparison of CE-Bilateral and Bilateral-CE based on LLL-Poisson, (a)(c)(e)(g) Bilateral-CE, (b)(d)(f)(h) CE-Bilateral, (a)(b) contrast pair, (c)(d) Retinex, (e)(f) Meylan, (g)(h) proposed.

## 4 Real Night Experiments and Analysis

We use SSIM, Luminance and VCM [12] to compare our algorithm with contrast pair, Meylan and Retinex in real night experiments.

As is shown in Figs. 3 and 4, we use digital single lens reflex camera (DSLR) to take VLLL image. Experimental results show that the four methods improve the brightness and contrast. However, contrast pair has the least contrast and brightness among them; Retinex performs better in dark areas but less in bright areas compared with ours, besides, it causes severe noise, the results of our method and Meylan are

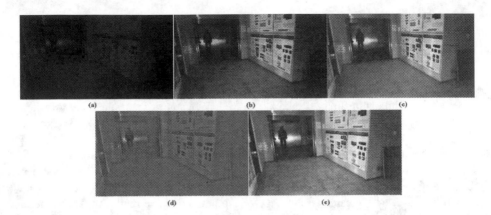

Fig. 3. VLLL night image enhancement I, (a) source, (b) contrast pair, (c) Meylan, (d) Retinex, (e) proposed.

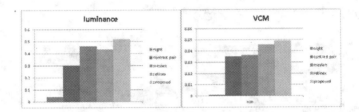

Fig. 4. Quantitative analysis on four algorithms.

both great, but our method improves the contrast of dark areas better than Meylan. Moreover, our method enjoys the highest VCM.

Next, we implement on a second experiment to compare our method with denight and contrast pair, where the edge threshold is 10 in contrast pair; in our method, $\sigma_0 = 10$, $\sigma_1 = 3$, a = 1.6, $\alpha = 1$, $\lambda = 1$, $\gamma = 1$; in bilateral filter, w = 15w, $\sigma_d = 0.5$, $\sigma_r = 3$; in Gaussian filter, $\gamma = 5w = 9$, $\sigma_d = 0.3w$, $\sigma_r = 0.15$. As is shown in Figs. 5 and 6.

Fig. 5. VLLL night image enhancement II, (a) source night image, (b) contrast pair, (c) denight, (d) proposed.

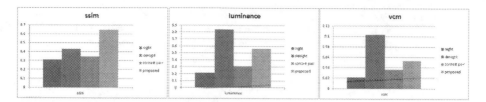

**Fig. 6.** Quantitative analysis on three algorithms.

In the final analysis, the three algorithms all improve the SSIM, brightness and contrast of the image, our method is better than contrast pair in VCM, and performs best in SSIM among them. Denight results in severe ghosts and noise. Our method largely improves the contrast and brightness of night images and nearly has no noise.

## 5 Conclusion

We use chains of image processing algorithms to construct a bio-inspired night image enhancement algorithm including ventral and dorsal parallel pathways and three pseudo receptive fields, which aims to solve the problem of low brightness, low contrast and high noise in night images. First we implement contrast enhancement algorithm dealing with low brightness and low contrast. Then we adopt bilateral filter to remove the noise in the enhanced image. Next we simulate LLL, VLLL, HDR night images and confirm that doing contrast enhancement before denoising is the best. Next, we compare proposed method with various algorithms on real night experiment. Finally, our proposed method provides the best results, which puts out image with higher brightness, higher contrast, less noise, and objects are in no ghosting condition.

## References

1. Yamasaki, A., Takauji, H., Kaneko, S., et al.: Denighting: enhancement of night time images for a surveillance camera. In: Proceedings of the International Conference on Pattern Recognition (2008)
2. Malm, H., Oskarsson, M., Warrant, E., et al.: Adaptive enhancement and noise reduction in very low light-level video. In: Proceedings of the IEEE 11th International Conference on Computer Vision (2007)
3. Rivera, A.R., Byungyong, R., Oksam, C.: Content-aware dark image enhancement through channel division. IEEE Trans. Image Process. **21**(9), 3967–3980 (2012)
4. Xiangdong, Z., Peiyi, S., Lingli, L., et al.: Enhancement and noise reduction of very low light level images. In: Proceedings of the 21st International Conference on Pattern Recognition (2012)
5. Xueyang, F., Delu, Z., Yue, H., et al.: A variational framework for single low light image enhancement using bright channel prior. In: Proceedings of the IEEE Global Conference on Signal and Information Processing (2013)

6. Xuan, D., Guan, W., Yi, P., et al.: Fast efficient algorithm for enhancement of low lighting video. In: Proceedings of the IEEE International Conference on Multimedia and Expo (2011)
7. Dongsheng, W., Xin, N., Yong, D.: A piecewise-based contrast enhancement framework for low lighting video. In: Proceedings of the International Conference on Security, Pattern Analysis, and Cybernetics (2014)
8. Qing, X., Hailin, J., Scopigno, R., et al.: A new approach for very dark video denoising and enhancement. In: Proceedings of the 17th IEEE International Conference on Image Processing (2010)
9. Minjae, K., Dubok, P., Han, D., et al.: A novel approach for denoising and enhancement of extremely low-light video. IEEE Trans. Consum. Electron. **61**(1), 72–80 (2015)
10. Malm, H., Warrant, E.: Motion dependent spatiotemporal smoothing for noise reduction in very dim light image sequences. In: Proceedings of the 18th International Conference on Pattern Recognition (2006)
11. Ponomarenko, N., Lukin, V., Zelensky, A., et al.: TID2008-a database for evaluation of full-reference visual quality assessment metrics. Adv. Modern Radioelectron. **10**(4), 30–45 (2009)
12. In, S.J., Wang, J.K., Lee, T.H., et al.: Local contrast enhancement based on adaptive multiscale retinex using intensity distribution of input image. J. Imaging Sci. Technol. **55**(4), 40502-1–40502-14 (2011)

# A Robust Feature Extraction Method for Image-Based Visual Servoing

Zhoujingzi Qiu[(⊠)], Shiqiang Hu[(⊠)], Lingkun Luo, Fuhui Tang,
Jiyuan Cai, and Hong Zhang

School of Aeronautics and Astronautics,
Shanghai Jiao Tong University, Shanghai, China
qiuzhoujingzi@126.com, sqhu@sjtu.edu.cn

**Abstract.** This paper deals with the visual positioning task in the image-based visual servoing. The controller is based on the discretized model of image Jacobian matrix. The visual servo controller can solve the intractable problems, such as large displacements between the initial and the desired pose of the camera. This controller can achieve a smooth and linear image trajectory in the image space. The developed IBVS controller also enhances the camera trajectory in 3-D space with time-varying depth. The proposed line feature extraction method is robust to the image noises, the dim light condition and the shadows. The simulation test is performed to validate the effectiveness of the proposed image-based visual controller and line feature extraction method.

**Keywords:** Visual positioning · Image-based visual servoing · Smooth trajectory · Time-varying depth · Line feature extraction

## 1 Introduction

Visual servoing has been widely used in the field of robotics to make machines more accurate and more flexible. The aim of the image-based visual servoing system is to eliminate the errors between the current features and the desired features. The controller generates a velocity screw as the input command for the camera system. Then the Jacobian matrix is used to compute a motion command to drive the end-effector towards its target. Visual control systems can be classified into three categories according to the three visual feedback forms: position-based visual servoing (PBVS) [1], image-based visual servoing (IBVS) [2] and hybrid visual servoing [3]. It is complicated to compute the pose of the end-effector with respect to the target in the position-based visual servoing. Compared to the position-based visual servoing, the image-based visual servoing using the 2-D locations of the features is more direct and has lower computational-complexity.[1] And the image-based visual servoing has strong robustness to the image noises, the camera calibration errors and the robot kinematic calibration errors.

[1] This paper is jointly supported by the National Natural Science Foundation of China "61374161", China Aviation Science Foundation "20142057006".

© Springer Nature Singapore Pte Ltd. 2017
F. Sun et al. (Eds.): ICCSIP 2016, CCIS 710, pp. 91–99, 2017.
DOI: 10.1007/978-981-10-5230-9_10

The image-based visual servoing controller is designed by using the image Jacobian matrix to compute a velocity command for the camera system. The visual servoing task is completed when the image errors are eliminated. The image Jacobian can be numerically estimated by using the Broyden method [4], the neural network [5], the fuzzy control, etc. However, the image Jacobian matrix may be coarse estimated, which leads to the visual system unstable. And the features may leave the camera's field of view. In most of the researches, a constant depth value of the feature is considered in the design of the controller, which leads to the visual servo system instability if the desired camera position is far from the initial camera position [6]. In this paper, the visual servo controller based on the discretized model of image Jacobian matrix can deal with the difficult problems, such as the time-varying depth, large displacements between the initial and the desired pose of the camera. The visual servo controller provides the camera velocity command to ensure the smoothness of the feature trajectory and the camera trajectory. And the image features are kept in the field of the image plane. What's more, the classical IBVS often uses points as the image features, however, the points are easily affected by image noises [7]. In this paper, we also propose a robust line feature extraction method to obtain the feature points, which can adapt to the complex environment such as the dim light condition, the shadows and so on.

## 2   The Robust Feature Extraction Method of a "Square" Target

The feature extraction is an important step in the visual servoing. There are various feature extraction methods. Generally, the feature extraction methods include the color feature extraction, the texture feature extraction, the shape feature extraction, the spatial relationship feature extraction and so on. According to the specific image character-istics of the target, the specific feature extraction method should be employed. In this paper, we regard the target as a "square", as shown in Fig. 1(a). Usually, most of the image-based servo control systems use the points as the features, such as the corner points, the hole centers, the contour dominant points and so on. As shown in Fig. 1(a), we choose the four corner points as the image features. There are various corner feature extraction methods which include the Harris corner detection, the Shi-Tomasi corner detection, the fast key point detection, the surf, etc. However, compared with the point features, line features are more robust and stable to the image noises, the large dis-placements, the dim light condition and the shadows. So we adopt the Hough transform theory to detect the lines of the "square". And the lines intersect each other to get the four corner points of the "square". The procedure of extracting the corner points is as follows:

1. The original image of the target is obtained by the camera, as shown in Fig. 1(a);
2. The threshold method is applied to the "square" image and its binary image is obtained. Pixels above a specified level are set to white, the pixels below the specified level are set to black, as shown in Fig. 1(b). This process can separate the target from the background to get the interested area in the image.

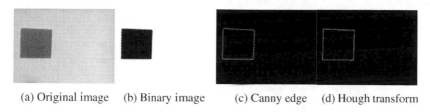

(a) Original image    (b) Binary image        (c) Canny edge    (d) Hough transform

**Fig. 1.** The feature extraction of corner points

3. The canny edge detector is adopted to detect the edge in the binary image, as depicted in Fig. 1(c).
4. Taking advantage of the Hough transform to detect the lines of the edge of the "square" in Fig. 1(c), then the detected lines intersect each other at four corner points as shown in Fig. 1(d).

## 3   The Definition of the Coordinate Systems

The coordinate systems should be defined to describe the position and orientation of the object. Consider a camera coordinate system which is defined as $\sum_C$: $O_C$-$X_C Y_C Z_C$. The image coordinate system is defined as $O_1$-xy. An object coordinate system $\sum_O$: $O$-$X_O Y_O Z_O$ is fixed in the world coordinate system $\sum_W$: $O_W$-$X_W Y_W Z_W$. We use the homogeneous matrix $^W H_C$ to describe the position and orientation of the camera coordinate system $\sum_C$ relative to the world coordinate system $\sum_W$. The homogeneous transformation matrix $^W H_C$ is defined by

$$^W H_C = \begin{bmatrix} ^W R_C & ^W P_C \\ 0 & 1 \end{bmatrix}, \tag{1}$$

where $^W R_C$ is a $3 \times 3$ orientation matrix. And $^W P_C$ is a $3 \times 1$ position vector of the camera coordinate system $\sum_C$ with respect to the world coordinate system $\sum_W$ [9].

The position vector of the object coordinate system $\sum_O$ with respect to the world coordinate system $\sum_W$ is defined by $^W P_O$, the orientation matrix of the $\sum_O$ with respect to the $\sum_W$ is defined by $^W R_O$. Then, the world coordinate system is used to establish the relationship between the camera coordinate system and the object coordinate system. The homogeneous transformation matrix $^C H_O$ can be expressed as

$$^C H_O = \begin{bmatrix} ^C R_O & ^C P_O \\ 0 & 1 \end{bmatrix} = \begin{bmatrix} ^C R_W {}^W R_O & ^C R_W (^W P_O - {}^W P_C) \\ 0 & 1 \end{bmatrix}. \tag{2}$$

As shown in Fig. 2, $O_C$ is the origin of the camera coordinate system and it is the optical center of the camera. $Z_C$ is the optical axis. The origin of the image coordinate system $O_1$ is the intersection of the optical axis $Z_C$ and the image plane. The image axes x and y are parallel to the camera axes $X_C$ and $Y_C$, respectively. The focal length of the

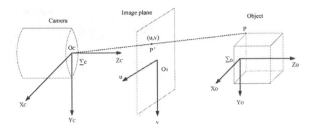

**Fig. 2.** The camera perspective projection model

camera lens is f, and $f = O_CO_1$. And the camera coordinate system moves with the camera.

In the camera perspective projection model, a point P is in 3-D space. Its 3-D position coordinates $^CP_O$ in the camera coordinate system are defined as (X, Y, Z) and its 2-D projection coordinates on the image plane are defined as (x, y). The camera perspective projection model is taken as an ideal pin-hole model. According to the geometric relationship, we obtain

$$x = f\frac{X}{Z}, y = f\frac{Y}{Z}. \tag{3}$$

## 4   The Controller Design

### 4.1   The Solution of the Image Jacobian Matrix

The image Jacobian matrix can be used to describe the relationship between the motion of the camera in 3-D space and the motion of the image feature points in the image plane. The solution of the image Jacobian matrix is important for the design of the image-based visual servo controller. The matrix converts the movement of the camera in 3-D space to the movement of the feature points in the image plane. Differentiating both sides of (3), we yield

$$\dot{x} = \frac{f}{Z^2}(Z\dot{X} - X\dot{Z}), \ \dot{y} = \frac{f}{Z^2}(Z\dot{Y} - Y\dot{Z}). \tag{4}$$

Let the world coordinate system as an intermediate coordinate system to establish the relationship between the camera coordinate system and the object coordinate system. The velocity of the camera in the camera coordinate system includes the linear velocity $^Cv_C$ and the angular velocity $^Cw_C$, let

$$\begin{bmatrix} ^Cv_C & ^Cw_C \end{bmatrix}^T = \begin{bmatrix} v_x & v_y & v_z & w_x & w_y & w_z \end{bmatrix}^T. \tag{5}$$

Then

$$\begin{bmatrix} \dot{X} \\ \dot{Y} \\ \dot{Z} \end{bmatrix} = \frac{d^C P_O}{dt} = {}^C R_W [-{}^W w_C \times ({}^W P_O - {}^W P_C)] + {}^C R_W ({}^W \dot{P}_O - {}^W \dot{P}_C). \qquad (6)$$

Since the target is static in the world coordinate system, then ${}^W \dot{P}_O = 0$. According to the knowledge in robotics, we have:

$$^W \hat{w}_C = {}^W \dot{R}_C {}^W R_C^{-1}, {}^W v_C = \frac{d^W P_C}{dt}, \qquad (7)$$

$$\forall \hat{w} = \begin{bmatrix} w_1 \\ w_2 \\ w_3 \end{bmatrix}, \hat{w}q = w \times q, \hat{w} = \begin{bmatrix} 0 & -w_3 & w_2 \\ w_3 & 0 & -w_1 \\ -w_2 & w_1 & 0 \end{bmatrix}. \qquad (8)$$

Substituting (7) and (8) into (6), we yield

$$\begin{bmatrix} \dot{X} \\ \dot{Y} \\ \dot{Z} \end{bmatrix} = -{}^C w_C \times {}^C P_O - {}^C v_C = -\begin{bmatrix} w_x \\ w_y \\ w_z \end{bmatrix} \times \begin{bmatrix} X \\ Y \\ Z \end{bmatrix} - \begin{bmatrix} v_x \\ v_y \\ v_z \end{bmatrix}$$

$$= \begin{bmatrix} -1 & 0 & 0 & 0 & -Z & Y \\ 0 & -1 & 0 & Z & 0 & -X \\ 0 & 0 & -1 & -Y & X & 0 \end{bmatrix} \begin{bmatrix} {}^C v_C & {}^C w_C \end{bmatrix}^T \qquad (9)$$

And substituting (3) and (4) into (9), we have

$$\begin{bmatrix} \dot{x} \\ \dot{y} \end{bmatrix} = J_{image}(x, y, z) \begin{bmatrix} {}^C v_C & {}^C w_C \end{bmatrix}^T. \qquad (10)$$

Then the image Jacobian matrix is obtained as follows:

$$J_{image}(x, y, z) = \begin{bmatrix} -\frac{f}{Z} & 0 & \frac{x}{Z} & \frac{xy}{f} & -\frac{x^2+f^2}{f} & y \\ 0 & -\frac{f}{Z} & \frac{y}{Z} & \frac{y^2+f^2}{f} & -\frac{xy}{f} & -x \end{bmatrix}. \qquad (11)$$

## 4.2   The Design of the State Feedback Control Laws

Let $u = \begin{bmatrix} v_x & v_y & v_z & w_x & w_y & w_z \end{bmatrix}^T$ denote the control input. For a very short sampling period $\Delta t$, we yield a discrete approximation time system (12) for m image feature points,

$$p(t+1) = p(t) + J_{image}u \cdot \Delta t. \tag{12}$$

Assuming that the expected image feature points are $p_d$, then we obtain an error system

$$e(t+1) = e(t) + M(t)u(t). \tag{13}$$

Define the error function as follows:

$$e(t) = \lambda[p(t) - p_d]. \tag{14}$$

then

$$M(t) = \lambda J_{image} \cdot \Delta t. \tag{15}$$

Where $\lambda$ is a proportional coefficient. The variation range of the proportional coefficient is between 0 and 1. The value of the proportional coefficient $\lambda$ has an effect on the system's convergence, the system's response speed, the system's steady state errors, and the overshoot of the image errors. What's more, the proportional coefficient $\lambda$ has an influence on the smoothness of the camera trajectory in 3-D space. The Moore-Penrose inverse of $J_{image}$ is $J_{image}^{\#} = [J_{image}^{T}J_{image}]^{-1}J_{image}^{T}$, and $C = J_{image}^{\#}$. We obtain the controller by using the state feedback

$$u(t) = -\lambda C[p(t) - p_d]. \tag{16}$$

The block diagram of the image-based servo control is shown in Fig. 3.

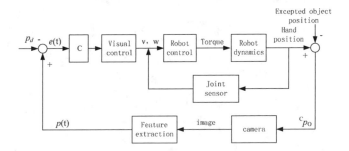

**Fig. 3.** The block diagram of the image-based servo control

## 5   Simulations

Simulations are conducted to indicate the correctness and the validity of the visual servo control algorithm. The feature points should be guaranteed from the initial positions to the desired positions on the image plane by the controller algorithm. There is no limit to the depth information. The depths of the feature points are time-varying.

Also, the proposed feature extraction method can adapt to the case of the image noises, the dim light condition, the shadows and so on. The simulation test is performed to validate the effectiveness of the algorithm. The initial and the desired images are taken during a positioning task. The images are obtained by a CCD camera with the focal length f = 5 mm. The image resolution is 1292 × 964 and the dimension of the CCD is 4.8 × 3.6 mm. The dimension of the "square" is 5 cm and the target is stationary.

In the test, a long distance visual servoing task is performed. The desired locations of feature points are far away from the initial locations of feature points. As shown in Fig. 4(a), the image of the target is obtained by the camera in an initial camera position. As shown in Fig. 4(b), the image of the target is obtained by the camera in the desired camera position. The initial image of the target is shown in Fig. 4(c). The desired image of the target is shown in Fig. 4(d).

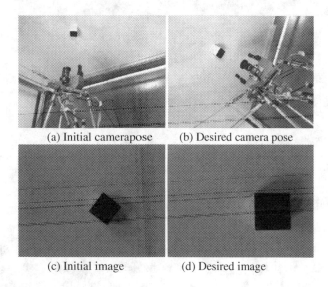

(a) Initial camerapose       (b) Desired camera pose

(c) Initial image       (d) Desired image

**Fig. 4.** Obtain the "square" image in the initial camera pose and desired camera pose

The corner points can be extracted directly by the proposed line feature extraction method under the situation of the image noises, the dim light condition and the shadows which are both the difficult problems in the image processing. The results of the visual servo test are shown in Fig. 5. The feature trajectory in the image space is shown in Fig. 5(a). The trajectory is kept in the camera's field of view. And the trajectory is smooth, linear without any unnecessary motion. Also, each feature point converges to the desired location. Figure 5(b) shows the image errors which asymptotically converge close to zero. Figure 5(c) shows the camera's linear velocity and angular velocity in 3-D space, the velocity converge to zero smoothly with a little overshoot. Figure 5(d) illustrates the camera trajectory in 3-D space with a circular motion. The camera does not move along a straight line, because there exists large displacement and rotation between the initial pose and the desired pose of the camera

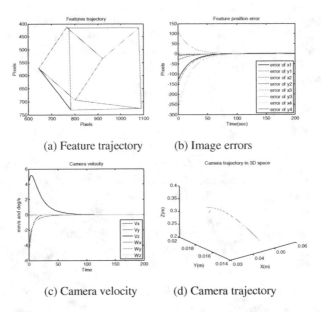

(a) Feature trajectory    (b) Image errors

(c) Camera velocity    (d) Camera trajectory

**Fig. 5.** The behavior of the control system by using four corner points

with respect to the target. The depth varies in a long vertical translation. The test is performed successfully under the proposed image-based visual servo control.

## 6    Conclusion

Unlike most of the IBVS controllers use a constant depth value, the designed controller can deal with the time-varying depth of the feature point. And the controller manages the large displacement task while keeping the features within the camera's field of view. The trajectory of the features on the image space and the trajectory of the camera in 3-D space are smooth. What's more, the proposed line feature extraction method is robust to the image noises, the shadows and the large displacement of the camera. Future work will address the problem of the local minima and the singularity of the Jacobian matrix.

## References

1. Chaumette, F.: Potential problems of stability and convergence in image-based and position-based visual servoing. In: The Confluence of Vision and Control, pp. 66–78. Springer, London (1998)
2. Gans, N.R., Hu, G., Shen, J., Zhang, Y., Dixon, W.E.: Adaptive visual servo control to simultaneously stabilize image and pose error. Mechatronics **22**(4), 410–422 (2012)
3. Chaumette, F., Hutchinson, S.: Visual servo control. II. Advanced approaches [Tutorial]. IEEE Robot. Autom. Mag. **14**(1), 109–118 (2007)

4. Mansard, N., Lopes, M., Santos-Victor, J., Chaumette, F.: Jacobian learning methods for tasks sequencing in visual servoing. In: International Conference on Intelligent Robots and Systems, pp. 4284–4290. IEEE Press, Beijing (2006)
5. Zhao, Y.M., Xie, W.F., Liu, S., Wang, T.: Neural network-based image moments for robotic visual servoing. J. Intell. Rob. Syst. **78**(2), 239–256 (2016)
6. Chaumette, F., Hutchinson, S.: Visual servo control. I. Basic approaches. IEEE Robot. Autom. Mag. **13**(4), 82–90 (2006)
7. Wang, H., Liu, Y.H., Zhou, D.: Adaptive visual servoing using point and line features with an uncalibrated eye-in-hand camera. IEEE Trans. Rob. **24**(4), 843–857 (2008)

# Visual-Cognition-Driven SAR Multiple Targets Robust Feature Extraction, Recognition and Tracking

Hongqiao Wang[✉], Yanning Cai, Guangyuan Fu, and Ming Wu

Xi'an Research Institute of Hi-Tech, 710025 Xi'an, China
ep.hqwang@gmail.com

**Abstract.** Aiming at the multiple targets recognition and tracking in SAR images, a robust feature extraction method and a combined recognition and tracking method for multi-class slow-moving targets based on visual cognition is presented in this paper. To obtain robust feature and high classification precision, a local multi-resolution analysis and feature extraction method based on the visual attention mechanism and a multiple kernel classifier is studied, which realizes the quick classification with high accuracy for multi-class image targets. According to the recognition result and the corresponding relationship of targets in the adjacent frames, the targets' motion parameters are estimated utilizing the unscented Kalman filter (UKF) based on the "what" and "where" pathways information processing mechanism. As a result, the high performance tracking of multi-class slow-moving targets in complicated background is realized. The simulation results show that the feature extraction and recognition method has good robustness and high classification correct ratio, the combining recognition and tracking method also has high location precision.

**Keywords:** SAR · Visual cognition · Feature extraction · Target recognition · Target tracking

## 1  Introduction

Moving target detected and tracked by airborne radars, such as the synthetic aperture radar (SAR), especially the slow-moving target called in many literatures can be defined from two aspects. Firstly, in speed, the slow-moving target is called relatively to the rapid movement of the radar aircraft (100–300 m/s), so the common ground wheeled and tracked vehicles are all belong to the domain of slow-moving targets, but some other targets such as the hedgehopped cruise missiles are not in the domain. Secondly, in frequency spectrum, the slow-moving target is named relatively to the static targets. The ordinary airborne imaging radar system only considers the focus of the ground static targets. For the slow-moving targets, their echo signals fall into the main lobe clutter, and as their moving parameters are different from the static targets, the slow-moving targets are transformed into the defocusing and shifting information in radar images.

The echoes from slow-moving targets are confused with the main lobe clutter, so it is difficult to detect and locate these targets. But the above mentioned targets are the

© Springer Nature Singapore Pte Ltd. 2017
F. Sun et al. (Eds.): ICCSIP 2016, CCIS 710, pp. 100–112, 2017.
DOI: 10.1007/978-981-10-5230-9_11

military ones such as tanks, fighting vehicles, which should be paid significant attention. In the ground moving target tracking field based on SAR, the early research is
focused on ice-motion tracking in the sea. For example, Kwok [1] analysized the
motion of iceberg in the sea area of Alaska based on SAR image series using a simple
feature and region based tracking algorithm. Daida [2] presented an object-oriented
feature tracking technique. Strozzi [3] proposed a density tracking technology for the
glacier. Yang [4] studied the adaptive subspace filtering method and its application in
moving target tracking. Kirubarajan [5] proposed a interactive multi-model filtering
based tracking method, which overcomes the shortcoming of the traditional Kalman
filtering method, for example, the Kalman filter is hard to be used for complex
movement tracking.

In the field of ground target tracking using SAR image series, Xia [6] proposed a
moving ground target detection method based on SAR multi-look image sequence
tracking, in which an improved dynamic programming approach with directional
constraints is used to track the moving target. Henke [7] presented a novel method for
moving-target tracking using single-channel SAR with a large antenna beamwidth, the
main technologies include subaperture SAR processing, image statistics, and multi-
target unscented Kalman filtering. Gao [8] studied a detection and tracking algorithm
for moving target using SAR Images with the particle filter based on an idea of
Track-Before-Detect. These methods can improve the detection performance of the
weak target, but it ignores the inherent information of target in high resolution SAR
image, and doesn't make full use of the size, the structure, the direction and the deeper
features of the targets.

With the gradually improvement of SAR in imaging resolution and system integrated level, it becomes an important research direction on how to realize the
multi-class slow-moving targets recognition and tracking based on the SAR imaging
and the high resolution image series, especially based on the feature information of
target. On the basis of large-scale scene high resolution airborne SAR image series, an
efficient ground multi-class slow-moving targets classification and tracking method is
realized in this paper using a combination recognition method of local multi-resolution
analysis and multiple kernel classifier, also includes the tracking filter of UKF.

In the remainder of this paper, we go along through different sections organized as
follows: in Sect. 2, we present a robust feature extraction and multiple target recognition method based on visual attention mechanism. Then a combining recognition and
tracking method based on "what" and "where" pathways information processing
mechanism is introduced in Sect. 3. In Sect. 4, several simulation experiments are
carried out to testify the effectiveness of the method. Finally, we conclude in Sect. 5.

## 2  Robust Feature Extraction and Multiple Target Recognition Based on Visual Attention Mechanism

For SAR target recognition, two aspects must be concerned, firstly, there must have a
robust and low-dimensional feature extraction method according to the image's characters, especially for the SAR images with much speckle and complicated background.

Secondly, a high efficient classifier should be used to realize the high precision classification for targets.

## 2.1    Robust Feature Extraction Based on Visual Attention Mechanism

For the ground slow-moving target classification and tracking in high resolution SAR images, without loss of generality, the Moving and Stationary Target Acquisition and Recognition (MSTAR) dataset is taken as the investigation object. The targets in the MSTAR chips have the following characters: the dataset are composed by chips with equal image size; there is only one target in a chip; the target lies in the center of the chip; the targets in the dataset have the same resolution, and are distributed around the centers of the chips with a certain angle. The image examples of the three classes of targets in the MSTAR dataset are shown in Fig. 1. In view of this, according to the method in reference [9], an image-based multilevel difference of Gaussian (DOG) like scale space is constructed based on the mechanism of receptive field model and the scale invariant feature transform (SIFT) method. Then, a 8-neighborhood orthogonal basis is designed, using which an image can be processed with a multi-level sampling filter, in addition, the features in eight directions and one low frequency filtering feature of the image can be achieved. The structure of the 8-neighborhood orthogonal basis is shown in Fig. 2.

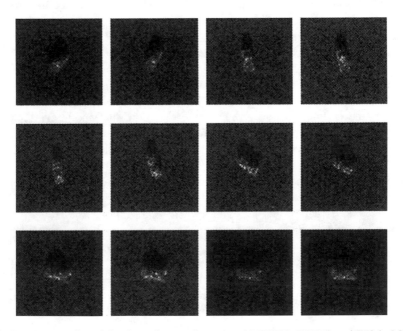

**Fig. 1.** Image examples of the three classes of targets with BMP2, BTR70 and T72 in MSTAR dataset

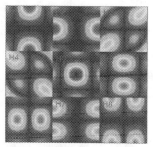

| H0 | H1 | H2 |
|---|---|---|
| 1 1 1 / 1 1 1 / 1 1 1 | -0.5 -0.5 -0.5 / 1 1 1 / -0.5 -0.5 -0.5 | -0.5 1 -0.5 / -0.5 1 -0.5 / -0.5 1 -0.5 |

| H3 | H4 | H5 |
|---|---|---|
| 1 -0.5 -0.5 / -0.5 1 -0.5 / -0.5 -0.5 1 | -0.5 -0.5 1 / -0.5 1 -0.5 / 1 -0.5 -0.5 | 1 1 1 / 0 0 0 / -1 -1 -1 |

| H6 | H7 | H8 |
|---|---|---|
| 1 0 -1 / 1 0 -1 / 1 0 -1 | -0.5 1 -0.5 / 0 0 0 / 0.5 -1 0.5 | -0.5 0 0.5 / 1 0 -1 / -0.5 0 0.5 |

(a) 8-neighborhood orthogonal basis   （b） Frequency spectrum of the 8-neighborhood orthogonal basis

**Fig. 2.** 8-neighborhood orthogonal basis and its frequency spectrum

Using the sampling filter idea of the traditional wavelet, a local extension sampling method based on visual attention mechanism is presented, which extends from a local point to surroundings, and can guarantee the generated basis are right toward the local region. In this way, the same local characteristics have the similar projection coefficients onto the basis, which is beneficial to the feature description and target recognition. About the implementation of this method, an image can be processed with a multistage filtering beginning from a local point (for example, the point of interest) of the image by adopting a fast filter, namely the multi-resolution decomposition to an image. As a result, the DOG like space image of the original image can be obtained. Then, by directly sampling from the key pixels in each stage image, the local multi-resolution features of the original image can be rapidly acquired.

Aiming at the images in MSTAR dataset, the targets first can be detected using the constant false alarm rate (CFAR) method. In consideration of the targets only occupy the central location of the chips, for convenience, the central area with the size of $81 \times 81$ in each $128 \times 128$ chip is taken as the research target. Then, the obtained image is processed by a 4-level local multi-resolution decomposition. As for the feature extraction, we can directly choose the pixels in each level of the image as follows: in the highest level, the image size is $3 \times 3$, all the 9 pixels are choose as the 9-dimension feature; in the second level, the 8 image blocks with the size of $3 \times 3$ corresponding to the 8 peripheral pixels in the highest level are choose as the feature, so the feature dimension is 72; the feature extraction method in the third level is similar to the second level, the eight $3 \times 3$ image blocks corresponding to the block centers in the second level are selected, the feature dimension is also 72; in the fourth level, the peripheral 8 central pixels are directly selected, so the feature dimension is 8. So, for a given image, the total feature dimension is $9 + 72 + 72 + 8 = 161$.

## 2.2   Multiple Kernel Classifier Designing

The fusion of kernels with multiple scales is a special condition of multiple kernel learning [10–13]. This kernel method has better flexibility, and can bring more completed scale choice than other method, such as the composite kernel method.

In addition, with the wavelet theory and the multi-scale analysis theory continue to mature, the multiple kernel method gains good theory background by introducing the scale space.

The foundation of multi-scale kernel method is seeking for a set of kernel functions owning the multi-scale representation capability. Among the kernel functions being widely used, the Gaussian radial basis function (RBF) (1) is the most popular one, because of its general approximation ability, simultaneously, it is also a typical kernel can be multi-scaled.

$$k(x,z) = \exp(-\frac{\|x-z\|^2}{2\sigma^2}) \tag{1}$$

Take the RBF kernel as the example, it can be multi-scaled as (2) (Suppose the generated kernels have the translation invariant).

$$k(\frac{\|x-z\|^2}{2\sigma_1^2}), \ldots, k(\frac{\|x-z\|^2}{2\sigma_m^2}) \tag{2}$$

where $\sigma_1 < \ldots < \sigma_m$. From (2), we can see when $\sigma$ is small, the support vector classifier (SVC) using the RBF kernel can fit the samples which have drastic variability. And when $\sigma$ is larger, the same classifier can well classify the samples with mild variability. So the multi-scale kernels can obtain better generalization. When it is implemented, the values of $\sigma$ can be determined as (3) by borrowing the scale-variant rule of wavelet transformation.

$$\sigma_i = 2^i\sigma, \ i = 0, 1, 2, \ldots \tag{3}$$

Utilizing the multi-scale kernel matrix fused from multiple scaled kernels, the discrimination of features and the classification accuracy can both be promoted than the simple kernel matrix in common support vector machine (SVM). For a 2-class classification problem, the decision function of the simple SVC is

$$f(x) = \text{sgn}\left(\sum_{i=1}^{n} \alpha_i y_i \langle \phi(x), \phi(x_i) \rangle + b\right). \tag{4}$$

After substituting the kernel function, the function can be transformed as (5)

$$f(x) = \text{sgn}\left(\sum_{i=1}^{n} \alpha_i y_i K(x, x_i) + b\right). \tag{5}$$

For a typical multiple kernel learning method with the convex combination of multiple kernels, the decision function of the SVC is

$$f(\boldsymbol{x}) = \operatorname{sgn}\left(\sum_{j=1}^{m} \beta_j \sum_{i=1}^{n} \alpha_i y_i \langle \phi_j(\boldsymbol{x}), \phi_j(\boldsymbol{x}_i)\rangle + b\right), \tag{6}$$

namely,

$$f(\boldsymbol{x}) = \operatorname{sgn}\left(\sum_{j=1}^{m} \beta_j \sum_{i=1}^{n} \alpha_i y_i K_j(\boldsymbol{x}, \boldsymbol{x}_i) + b\right). \tag{7}$$

On the other hand, it is also an effective approach for the improvement of target recognition accuracy if we synthesize the features having multi-resolution character and the multi-scale kernel functions. In this paper, the 4-level local multi-resolution decomposition and the 4-scale Gaussian kernels are synthesized, the scales of corresponding kernel functions are increased with 2 times. At the same time, the weights of kernels are determined by equal coefficients, namely $\beta_1 = \beta_2 = \beta_3 = \beta_4 = 1/4$, the schematic diagram is shown in Fig. 3.

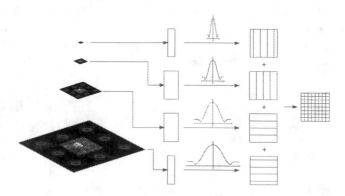

**Fig. 3.** Synthesis schematic diagram of 4-level local multi-resolution feature and 4-scale Gaussian kernel

The target recognition procedure includes two stages which are the offline training and the online recognition. The offline training is mainly based on the MSTAR dataset. Firstly, the CFAR detection is carried out respectively for all the training target chips and we can get the target segmentation results. Then from the centers of the chips (namely the centers of targets), the 4-level local multi-resolution decompositions of the targets are executed, and then the feature vectors of every targets can be extracted. Using these multi-level feature vectors, the multiple kernel classifier can be trained.

The online recognition is based on the large-scale scene series image samples being acquired in real time. Firstly, the CFAR detection is done for every frame of large-scale scene image and targets are segmented. On this basis, the centers of gravity of the targets can be calculated, then from the centers of gravity, execute the 4-level local multi-resolution decomposition for the original image, and extract the feature vectors of targets. Finally, the feature vectors are fed into the multiple kernel classifier, and then the recognition result can be obtained.

## 3   Combining Recognition and Tracking Method Based on "What" and "Where" Pathways Information Processing Mechanism

Recent studies on human brain visual processing mechanism find that there are two main pathways in the vision system, the "what" pathway and the "where" pathway, which can form the feeling to target and the location in space respectively.

Based on the findings, to track the multiple targets in SAR images, the multi-class targets should first be classified, and then the trend of motion of different target can be continuously predicted. According to this idea, a combing recognition and tracking method is proposed using the "what" and "where" pathways information processing mechanism. Based on the recognition result and the corresponding relationship of targets in the adjacent frames, the targets' motion parameters are estimated utilizing the UKF based on the "what" and "where" pathways information processing mechanism. As a result, the high performance tracking of multi-class slow-moving targets in complicated background is realized.

For the target tracking based on SAR images, the hypotheses are all difficult to be satisfied. So, the unscented Kalman filtering (UKF) algorithms [14] are introduced in this paper. These algorithms can effectively overcome the influences of the nonlinear dynamics and the non-Gaussian noise [15]. The algorithms also have lower computational complexity than the other methods, such as particle filtering, and the error of the algorithms only appears in the moments beyond the third rank, which can be easily accepted in practical applications. On the other hand, for multi-target tracking and location, the UKF shows great superiority than the other tracking methods.

Utilizing the above mentioned feature extraction method, multi-scale kernel classifier and target recognition system, we further study and design a target tracking system based on detection and recognition results aiming at the target image series. The flow diagram is shown in Fig. 4. The main ideas are as follows: firstly, get the image segmentation results (namely the regions of interest (ROI)) of the large scale scene image series in real time. Secondly, calculate and obtain the center of gravity of each ROI by the image binary conversion. On the one hand, the center of gravity is an important target parameter of KF and UKF tracking, through which the predicted coordinates of target can be gained after passing the filter, and it can be used for the next step prediction via a parameter correction. On the other hand, the center of gravity is also the reference point of image's local multi-resolution decomposition and getting the feature vector. Thirdly, send the feature vectors into the multi-scale kernel classifier, and we can obtain the classification result, which can also be used to discriminate the false-alarm. As a result, the target type and coordinates are obtained, which is the basis of the target tracking.

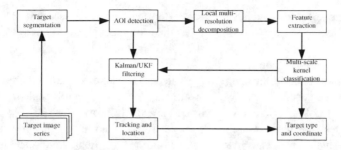

**Fig. 4.** Flow diagram of target recognition and tracking

After the target recognition and location in each frame of image, the motion parameters of the target can be estimated by the tracking filter based on the corresponding relationship of the targets between the adjacent frames, and the parameters are continuously renewed using the practical measured values. Ultimately, we can gain the type and coordinate information of targets in real time, and realize the target indication in the frames.

# 4    Simulation Experiment and Result Analysis

## 4.1    Target Recognition Experiment

After the features of the testing set being extracted, the feature vectors are sent to the classifier and the recognition precision is outputted. To analyze the adaptability against noise, the speckle with mean 0 and variance 0.04 is added to the MSTAR testing set, the final recognition results are shown in Table 1.

**Table 1.** Single target ATR result under different speckle adding degree

| Speckle adding degree (SAD) | Number of testing set | Correct recognition number | Recognition precision |
| --- | --- | --- | --- |
| SAD = 0 (No adding speckle) | 1365 | 1348 | 98.75% |
| SAD = 1 | 1365 | 1275 | 93.41% |
| SAD = 2 | 1365 | 1196 | 87.62% |
| SAD = 3 | 1365 | 1044 | 76.48% |

From the experimental result, we can see that the fusion method with the multi-scale feature and the multi-scale kernel classifier gives a very high classification precision of 98.75% when there is not adding speckle. In addition, the algorithm realizes the fast access and storage to nearly 3000 SAR images in a short time, which indicates good real-time performance. Comparing with the traditional method, the presented algorithm has far more advanced in fast detection of target and the dimension of feature vectors.

When the speckle is added into the testing samples, the recognition precision is 93.41% while SAD = 1. With the enhancement of speckle, the recognition precisions are reduced to 87.62% and 76.48% when SAD = 2 and SAD = 3 respectively, which are still the preferably correct ratios. That is because there is only one target in each sample, and we already know the targets lie in the center of sample chips. So, even though the target structure changes, we still can do the local multi-scale decomposition from the center of sample and can extract the exactly proper features.

Further tests with the rotation and scale transformations of the targets are introduced based the large-scene SAR images. In the tests, 3 degrees of speckle are added into Image I and Image II. Then utilizing the same target segmentation, mathematical morphological processing with modulation of parameters, center of gravity calculation, we can achieve the target detection and marking result. Figure 5 shows the image target segmentation, detection and marking result under the SAD = 1. Then, begin from the center of gravity, execute the multi-scale decomposition, feature extraction, and gain the feature vectors. Finally, send the feature vectors into the multi-scale classifier, and output the recognition results.

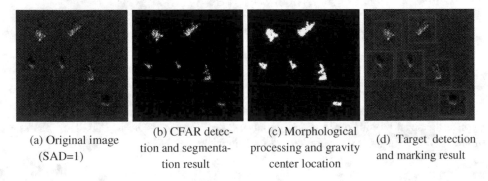

(a) Original image (SAD=1)  (b) CFAR detection and segmentation result  (c) Morphological processing and gravity center location  (d) Target detection and marking result

**Fig. 5.** Multiple targets detection and marking result of the large-scene sample Image I with rotation and scale transformation

## 4.2   Target Tracking Experiment

The tracking experiments based on series images are carried out as the following steps. Firstly, segment the image frame and find the regions that might contain the targets. Secondly, after the target detection, local multi-resolution decomposition, and recognition in real time, eliminate the false targets and get the real targets. Thirdly, add the coordinate information of the targets into the tracking filter, measure and estimate the motion of all the targets. Fourthly, continuously record the target positions in each frame; ultimately realize the target UKF tracking and location with the center of gravity. The comparison experiments using the common Kalman filter and the UKF method are carried out. By drawing the tracking curves of targets, we can analysis the tracking performance of the algorithm.

Figure 6 shows the multi-class and multiple vehicle targets tracking results using UKF based on image series. From the recognition and tracking of every frame, we can see that the targets are almost been correct recognized except the beginning several frames, and the error-labeled targets and missing targets didn't appear in the tracking process. At the same time, the estimated value of the target position could rapidly converge to the measured value (namely the true value) using the UKF. Figure 7 is the horizontal and vertical coordinates tracking curves with KF and UKF for target marked "2". From the curves we can find that UKF method can more rapidly converge to the actual position of target than Kalman filter, the tracking result once again verifies the perfect convergence speed and tracking performance of UKF.

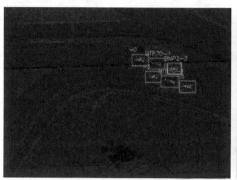 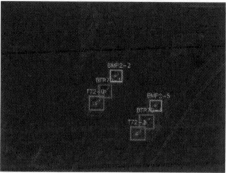

(a) Result of the 108th frame          (b) Result of the 360th frame

**Fig. 6.** Target UKF tracking result of image series II

### 4.3   Target Tracking Accuracy Analysis

Still utilizing the UKF tracking method, the location data and errors in 4 random frames of the two image series are recorded in Table 2. There are respectively 6 targets in the experiments. According to the statistics of the estimated values and true values on the coordinates of the target center of gravity, we can calculate the distances (namely the estimation error) of the two coordinate points. In the case of the image resolution has already been known, the absolute errors of target tracking and location can be figured out (the marks "-" in the tables mean the targets have not appeared or have not been detected in this frame).

From the data in the tables, we can see that the method has high location accuracy in the tracking and location process. Suppose the SAR image has a resolution of 0.5 m, the maximum value of location error is 1.58 m and the minimum value is 0.5 m in the image series I; in the image series II, the corresponding maximum value is 2.55 m, and the minimum value is 0, which shows the accuracy of tracking and location once again.

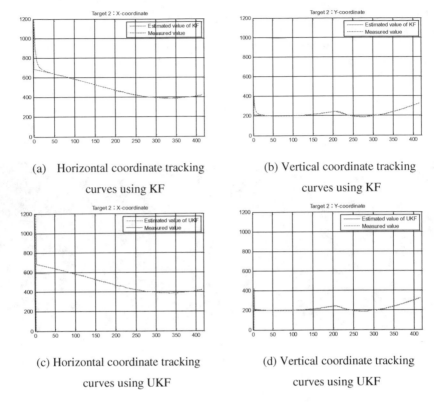

(a)  Horizontal coordinate tracking
curves using KF

(b) Vertical coordinate tracking
curves using KF

(c) Horizontal coordinate tracking
curves using UKF

(d) Vertical coordinate tracking
curves using UKF

**Fig. 7.** Horizontal and vertical coordinates tracking curves with KF and UKF for target marked "2"

**Table 2.** Target tracking error of image series (Random 4 frames)

| Absolute error (m) | Target number | | | | | |
|---|---|---|---|---|---|---|
| Frame number | 0 | 1 | 2 | 3 | 4 | 5 |
| 114 | - | 0 | 0 | - | 0.5 | - |
| 165 | 1.00 | 1.12 | 0.50 | 0.71 | 1.12 | 0.50 |
| 229 | 0.71 | 0.50 | 0.50 | 0.71 | 1.12 | 0.50 |
| 307 | 0.71 | 1.12 | 2.00 | 1.12 | 2.55 | 1.00 |

## 5    Conclusions

Aiming at the large-scale multi-target recognition and tracking demands, a multiple targets recognition and tracking method is systematically studied in this paper. Firstly, a robust feature extraction method based on a local multi-resolution decomposition is proposed. Then with the introduction of multiple kernel classifier, the multi-scale features and the multi-scale kernel method can be organically combined. Moreover, according to the recognition result and the corresponding relationship of targets in the adjacent frames, the targets' motion parameters are estimated utilizing the unscented Kalman filter (UKF) based on the "what" and "where" pathways information processing mechanism. As a result, the high performance tracking of ground multi-class slow-moving targets in complicated background is realized. Simulation results with large-scale scene SAR image series show that the effectiveness of the given method. Besides the vehicle targets in SAR image series, the presented feature extraction, pattern classification and tracking filtering methods can also be used for some other moving target with the fixed structure, which possesses important significance and practical values in target detection, target positioning, real-time situation monitoring and damage effect evaluation.

**Acknowledgments.** This work was jointly supported by the National Natural Science Foundation for Young Scientists of China (Grant No: 61202332, 61403397, 61503389), China Postdoctoral Science Foundation (Grant No: 2012M521905) and Natural Science Basic Research Plan in Shaanxi Province of China (Grant No: 2015JM6313).

# References

1. Kwok, R., Curlander, J.C., McConnell, R., Pang, S.S.: An ice-motion tracking system at the Alaska SAR facility. IEEE J. Oceanic Eng. **15**(1), 44–54 (1990)
2. Daida, J., Vesecky, J.: Object-oriented techniques for feature-tracking algorithms of marginal ice zone SAR images. In: Proceedings of Annual International Symposium on Geoscience and Remote Sensing, pp. 1885–1886 (1990)
3. Strozzi, T., Luckman, A., Murray, T., Wegmuller, U., Werner, C.L.: Glacier motion estimation using SAR offset-tracking procedures. IEEE Trans. Geosci. Remote Sens. **40**(11), 2384–2391 (2002)
4. Yang, Z., Soumekh, M.: Adaptive along-track multi-channel SAR interferometry for moving target detection and tracking. In: Proceedings of IEEE International Radar Conference, pp. 337–342 (2005)
5. Kirubarajan, T., Bar-Shalom, Y., Pattipati, K.R., Kadar, I.: Ground target tracking with variable structure IMM estimator. IEEE Trans. Aerospace Electron. Syst. **36**(1), 26–46 (2000)
6. Xia, B., Xu, J., Tang, J., Peng, Y.-N.: Moving ground target detection based on SAR multi-look image sequence tracking. J. Tsinghua Univ. (Sci. Technol.) **51**(7), 977–982 (2011)
7. Henke, D., Magnard, C., Frioud, M., Small, D., Meier, E., Schaepman, M.E.: Moving-target tracking in single-channel wide-beam SAR. IEEE Trans. Geosci. Remote Sens. doi:10.1109/TGRS.2012.2191561
8. Gao, H., Li, J.: Detection and tracking of a moving target using SAR images with the particle filter-based Track-Before-Detect algorithm. Sens. (Basel) **14**(6), 10829–10845 (2014)
9. Wang, H.-Q., Sun, F.-C., Cai, Y.-N., Chen, N., Pei, D.-L.: SAR image automatic target recognition based on local multi-resolution features. J. Tsinghua Univ. (Sci. Technol.) **51**(8), 1049–1054 (2011)
10. Bach, F.R., Lanckriet, G.R.G., Jordan, M.I.: Multiple kernel learning, conic duality, and the SMO algorithm. In: Proceedings of the 21st International Conference on Machine Learning (2004)

11. Sonnenburg, S., Rätsch, G., Schäfer, C., Schölkopf, B.: Large scale multiple kernel learning. J. Mach. Learn. Res. **7**, 1531–1565 (2006)
12. Hong-qiao, W., Fu-chun, S., Yan-ning, C., Ning, C., Lin-ge, D.: On multiple kernel learning methods. Acta Automatica Sin. **36**(8), 1037–1050 (2010)
13. Gönen, M., Alpaydin, E.: Regularizing multiple kernel learning using response surface methodology. Pattern Recogn. **44**, 159–171 (2011)
14. Julier, S., Uhlmann, J., Durrant-Whyte, H.F.: A new method for the nonlinear transformation of means and covariances in filters and estimators. IEEE Trans. Autom. Control **45**(3), 477–482 (2000)
15. Madhan Kumar, K., Kanthavel, R.: An efficient road tracking from aerial images by means of filter methods. J. Theoret. Appl. Inf. Technol. **62**(2), 424–437 (2014)

# Stixel World Based Long-Term Object Tracking for Intelligent Driving

Liuyuan Deng[1], Ming Yang[1(✉)], Chunxiang Wang[2], and Bing Wang[1]

[1] Key Laboratory of System Control and Information Processing,
Department of Automation, Ministry of Education of China,
Shanghai Jiao Tong University, Shanghai 200240, China
MingYANG@sjtu.edu.cn
[2] Research Institute of Robotics,
Shanghai Jiao Tong University, Shanghai 200240, China

**Abstract.** Long-term object tracking is key for a higher level of semantic interpretation of driving environment. One of the state-of-the-art approaches for long-term tracking is Tracking-Learning-Detection (TLD), which, however, suffers from variability of on-road objects and moving cluttered background. This paper presents a long-term object tracking method for intelligent driving based on Stixel World to address the drifting problem. First, this method adopts TLD framework, and integrates intensity and depth cues into the detector and learning component. Next, this method introduces Stixel World for compact medium-level representation of the 3D world, and Attention Guiding Filter (AGF) is proposed to focus on relevant areas in the image. Experiments in real traffic scene show the outstanding long-term tracking performance for intelligent driving.

**Keywords:** Object tracking · Stixel World · Stereo vision · TLD

## 1 Introduction

Long-term object tracking constitutes an essential component of intelligent driving, and is being used in Advanced Driver Assistance Systems (ADAS) applications, e.g. high level of semantic interpretation or specifically on-road behavior analysis. In the complex driving environment, object varies in size, shape and color due to different viewpoints and changing illumination, and extensive scene clutter is inevitable due to the movement of platform. These lead to ambiguous visual features and accumulated error with each update (the drifting problem [1]) for long-term object tracking.

Online learning based tracking methods are used to handle appearance variations of object. TLD [2] as an online learning framework decomposes the tasks into three components: tracking, learning, and detection. In this framework, tracking errors are estimated online to update the tracking model. To make TLD more suitable for pedestrian and bicycle tracking, gradient feature is used instead of gray feature in our previous paper [3]. Whereas, when the visual features get ambiguous, drifting problem still emerges. Depth cues can be introduced to make the features more discriminative. Stereo information provides cues on another dimension, making a difference especially encountering low-textured regions.

© Springer Nature Singapore Pte Ltd. 2017
F. Sun et al. (Eds.): ICCSIP 2016, CCIS 710, pp. 113–118, 2017.
DOI: 10.1007/978-981-10-5230-9_12

To analyze numerous values in dense disparity image which is reconstructed by stereo image pair using dense stereo matching algorithm like "Semi-Global Matching" (SGM) [4], Stixel World [5] is proposed to bridge the gap between the pixel and the object level, which is a compact but flexible medium level representation of the three-dimensional traffic situation. The idea is to approximate all objects within the three dimensional environment using sets of thin, vertically oriented rectangles, the so-called Stixels. Stixel World has been widely used in traffic situations [6, 10].

This paper presents a long-term object tracking method based on Stixel World for intelligent driving to address drifting problem. This method adopts TLD framework and intensity and depth cues are integrated in the detector and learning component. Attention guiding filter (AGF) is proposed to guide the attention to object regions such as vehicles, pedestrians, cyclists, etc., benefiting from Stixel World.

The block diagram of the proposed method is shown in Fig. 1. Grayscale and dense disparity images acquired from an embedded stereoscopic system are taken as inputs. Each frame the dense disparity image is compactly represented by Stixel World. AGF in the detector acts directly on Stixel World to reject patches which don't satisfy certain constraints. In addition, gradient features extracted on both grayscale and dense disparity images are integrated into a discriminative feature termed as composite feature. We use the composite feature to replace the gray feature of the original TLD. In the following of this paper, Sect. 2 introduces the composite feature and AGF is detailed in Sect. 3.

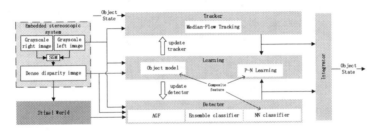

**Fig. 1.** Detailed block diagram of the proposed method.

## 2   Composite Feature

In driving environment, the grayscale feature is susceptible to variability in the size, shape and color of the objects and variations in illumination, background and scene complexity. Depth cues from the stereo images and intensity cues from grayscale image are integrated into composite feature, which provide an enhanced 3D scene understanding in conjunction with appearance information.

The complementary property of the two modalities is illustrated by Fig. 2(a). In grayscale image, it is easy to capture gradients within the object, while in disparity image, no significant gradients appear in areas corresponding to the object but the depth discontinuity around the object is highlighted, which is a distinctive feature. HOG features extracted from grayscale image and HOG features extracted from disparity image are concatenated into a single joint feature space as illustrated in Fig. 4(b). Composite feature benefits from the various salient regions in grayscale and disparity image.

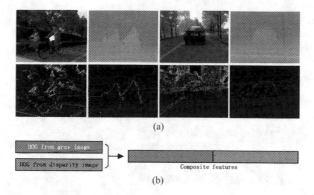

(a)

(b)

**Fig. 2.** (a) Raw grayscale images and disparity images are in the first row. In the second row are the corresponding gradient feature. (b) The formation of composite feature.

Online object model is a collection of composite features of learned positive and negative patches, instead of gray features in the original TLD. Each frame detector uses the online model and classifies patches using NN classifier with composite feature and the learning component updates the online object model using P-expert and N-expert.

## 3   Attention Guiding Filter Based on Stixel World

The detector scans the input image by a scanning window and for each patch decides about the presence or absence of the object. Tens of thousands of bounding boxes are produced, leading to a huge search space. We introduce an attention mechanism to reject non-object patches. Stixel World is used to guide TLD's attention to object areas.

Two aspects are considered using the Stixel World to guide the attention. One aspect is the area of overlap $a_o$ between the patch bounding box $B_p$ and stixel area $S$ by the formula: $a_o = \dfrac{area(B_p \cap S)}{area(B_p)}$, where $B_p \cap S$ denotes the intersection of $B_p$ and $S$. If $a_o$ is zero, this patch may be sky or ground in-stead of object which is represented by Stixels. The other aspect is the ratio of disparity $d$ and observed height $h$ in image plane. In the pinhole camera model, it can be easily derived that the ratio is inversely proportional to the 3D object height $H$ ($\frac{d}{h} \propto \frac{1}{H}$). For objects of fixed size that ratio keeps constant. We define the scaling ratio $R_s$ by the formula: $R_s = \frac{R_p}{R_o}$, where $R_o = \frac{d_o}{h_o}$ is the ratio for tracking object which is set when model initialization, $R_p = \frac{d_p}{h_p}$ is the ratio for patch. The disparity $d_o$ of tracking object and $d_p$ of the patch can be obtained from the Stixels and the height $h_o$ of tracking object and $h_p$ of the patch are the heights of corresponding bounding boxes. When object is exactly tracked, scaling ratio is ideally equal to 1. If that value is too small or too large, the patch can't be the tracking object.

AGF will reject the patch if $a_o$ is too small or the constraint of $R_s$ isn't satisfied. The scaling ratio $R_s$ is allowed to change in certain ranges for the transformation of the object in the image plane. As a consequence, the patches of background and those with incorrect scaling ratio are ignored. Therefore, the object regions is focused on.

## 4  Experiments

In this section, we evaluate the system in real traffic scene. The grayscale image and dense disparity image are acquired on a moving platform from 3DV-E [7] with a resolution of $640 \times 480$ pixels and a baseline of 12 cm, which is a standalone stereoscopic embedded system with improved SGM algorithm [8]. The 3DV-E is mounted in front of the vehicle above the bumper. An Intel Core i5-4200M CPU at 2.5 GHz is used to execute the system at 13 frames per second.

### 4.1  Attention Guiding with Stixel World

First, Stixel World is built from dense disparity image following [5]. We estimate the road plane by V disparity [9] for low computational complexity. As described in [10], solving the dynamic programming problem has a complexity $O(Q \cdot B^2)$ where $Q$ is the number of Stixels in the image, and $B$ is the number of rows considered. To speed up the algorithm, large width of a Stixel is set to reduce the number of Stixels. Besides, only the region less than 2 m above the ground is considered to reduce the number of rows. Although it makes the representation coarse, but the computational cost is decreased greatly. The result of Stixel World is shown in Fig. 3(b).

Each frame detector scans the image plane to find the tracking object. AGF is used to constrain the attention towards the likeliest areas. The patch is rejected if its area of overlap $a_o$ is less than 80% or scaling ratio $R_s$ is less than 0.8 or great than 1.2. Figure 3(c) illustrates the result by AGF. The white bounding boxes are the remaining patches which satisfy the constraints of AGF. We note that the patches of background such as sky, road and trees are ignored and all patches satisfy scaling ratio constraint as it is supposed. In contrast, the result by variance filter in original TLD is scattered when objects have no significant variance as illustrated in Fig. 3(d). In our experiments detector with AGF instead of variance filter can decrease false alarms and more than 80% patches are rejected which is much more efficient.

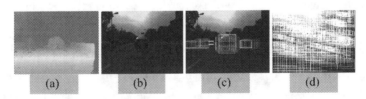

**Fig. 3.** (a) Dense disparity image. (b) Corresponding simplified visualization of Stixel World. The green sticks are Stixels and the distance between two adjacent sticks is the width of a Stixel. Here the width is 10 pixels. (c) The remaining patches by AGF. (d) The remaining patches by variance filter. The white bounding box denotes the remaining patches. (Color figure online)

## 4.2    Long-Term Object Tracking in Driving Environment

The method is tested in several sequences of traffic scene to compare with the original TLD. Figure 4 shows the tracking results of the two methods in a sequence. In this sequence, the tracking object, a vehicle in front, is the same in both methods, which is manually selected in the first frame. In Fig. 4(a), it shows that the tracking bounding box drifted out gradually in original TLD, especially when ahead vehicle made a turn, and erroneously tracked the background. However, as illustrated in Fig. 4(b), method of this paper is stable in this situation, owing to two aspects: one is the composite feature which integrates gray and depth cues and maintains discriminative even when the appearance of the tracking object isn't textual enough but depth cues still work; the other is the AGF which guides the attention to the objects above the ground and exists no chance to track the background with these constraints. In addition, false positives are reduced in our method, indicated in the 2nd, 3rd, and 4th images in Fig. 4(a) and corresponding images in Fig. 4(b).

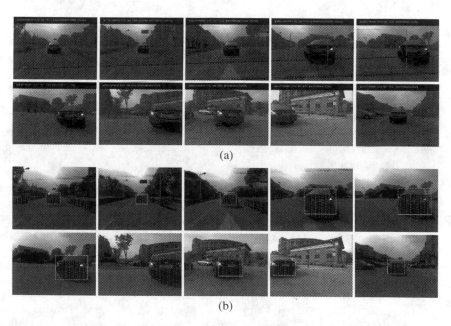

(a)

(b)

**Fig. 4.** The tracking results in a sequence of driving environment. Sequential images in (a) are sampled from results of original TLD, denoted with blue bounding box. Sequential images in (b) are corresponding tracking results using method of this paper, denoted with yellow bounding box and the green sticks are visualization of Stixel World. (Color figure online)

To conclude, with the discriminative composite feature and the constraints of AGF, false alarms of background are reduced and drifting problem is well prevented, which makes longer and more robust tracking possible in driving environment.

## 5   Conclusion

This paper presents a long-term traffic object tracking method based on Stixel World specifically for intelligent driving. Depth cues are integrated and Stixel World is used as an attention mechanism for TLD. Experiments demonstrate the effectiveness of on-road long-term tracking by preventing the drifting problem and reducing the false alarms in the background. Future work will focus on the combination of monocular tracking at near-range and binocular tracking at long-range, for the poor accuracy of stereo matching in the long distance.

**Acknowledgements.** This work was supported by the National Natural Science Foundation of China (91420101), National Magnetic Confinement Fusion Science Program (2012GB102002).

## References

1. Matthews, L., Ishikawa, T., Baker, S.: The template update problem. IEEE Trans. Pattern Anal. Mach. Intell. **26**, 810 (2004)
2. Kalal, Z., Mikolajczyk, K., Matas, J.: Tracking-learning-detection. IEEE Trans. Pattern Anal. Mach. Intell. **34**, 1409 (2012)
3. Xue, L., Yang, M., Dong, Y., Wang, C., Wang, B.: TLD based real-time weak traffic participants tracking for intelligent vehicles. In: 5th Workshop on Planning, Perception and Navigation for Intelligent Vehicles (PPNIV 2013) (2013)
4. Hirschmuller, H.: Accurate and efficient stereo processing by semi-global matching and mutual information. In: IEEE Computer Society Conference on Computer Vision and Pattern Recognition, CVPR 2005, vol. 2, p. 807 (2005)
5. Badino, H., Franke, U., Pfeiffer, D.: The Stixel World - a compact medium level representation of the 3D-world. In: Denzler, J., Notni, G., Süße, H. (eds.) DAGM 2009. LNCS, vol. 5748, pp. 51–60. Springer, Heidelberg (2009). doi:10.1007/978-3-642-03798-6_6
6. Franke, U., Pfeiffer, D., Rabe, C., Knoeppel, C., Enzweiler, M., Stein, F., Herrtwich, R.G.: Making bertha see. In: 2013 IEEE International Conference on Computer Vision Workshops (ICCVW), Sydney, NSW, vol. 214 (2013)
7. 3DV-E system. http://vislab.it/products/3dv-e-system/
8. Camellini, G., Felisa, M., Medici, P., Zani, P., Gregoretti, F., Passerone, C., Passerone, R.: 3DV — An embedded, dense stereovision-based depth mapping system (2014) 1435 p.
9. Labayrade, R., Aubert, D., Tarel, J.P.: Real time obstacle detection in stereovision on non flat road geometry through "v-disparity" representation. In: Intelligent Vehicle Symposium, vol. 2, p. 646. IEEE (2002)
10. Benenson, R., Mathias, M., Timofte, R., Gool, L.: Fast stixel computation for fast pedestrian detection. In: Fusiello, A., Murino, V., Cucchiara, R. (eds.) ECCV 2012. LNCS, vol. 7585, pp. 11–20. Springer, Heidelberg (2012). doi:10.1007/978-3-642-33885-4_2

# Hand Gestures Recognition
# from Multi-channel Forearm EMG Signals

Zehua Chen, Nannan Zhang, Zhihua Wang, Zongtan Zhou[✉],
and Dewen Hu

College of Mechatronic Engineering and Automation,
National University of Defense Technology,
Changsha 410073, Hunan, People's Republic of China
zehuachenchn@gmail.com

**Abstract.** The control system based on the surface Electromyography (sEMG) signal provides a wireless, convenient and natural choice to Human Computer Interaction (HCI). The identification of human hand gestures can offer enough kinds of controlling commands to intelligent devices in real time. In order to improve the classification accuracy in recognizing hand gestures, this paper explored the signal acquisition, signal processing and feature extraction methods of 6-channel forearm EMG signals. By utilizing Chebyshev II filter (25–450 Hz), 9 time domain features in sliding windows, PCA algorithm and SVM classifier, 17 hand gestures (HG), which include 6 wrist actions (WR) and 11 finger gestures (FG), are recognized with the accuracy of more than 95%.

**Keywords:** Hand gestures recognition · Wrist actions · Finger gestures · Multi-channel EMG signals · Time domain features · SVM

## 1 Introduction

In recent years, in order to improve the quality of life of the disabled people and break through the limitation of the conventional ways of Human Computer Interaction (HCI) such as keyboard, mouse, joystick, etc., many researchers have been committed to develop innovative and user-friendly interfaces. The highlighted problems mainly include the selection and acquisition of input signal, the preprocessing techniques, the feature extraction and classification methods. All these points significantly contribute to the performance of the HCI system because they have a considerable influence on the information transfer rate (ITR).

As to the choice of signals, image and video have been widely explored and used by many scientists and researchers. Various kinds of advanced image processing methods and theories have been developed to strengthen the applicability of the system. Danica and kulic [1] proposed several methods to recognize the action primitives and their sequencing in human motion from images and videos. However, the light, texture and surroundings inevitably restrict the performance of the system in outdoor and mobile environment. In addition to image, the data glove has also been employed to measure human hand and finger movements with bending sensors, pressure sensors and accelerometers. The data glove-based techniques achieved high performance in sign

© Springer Nature Singapore Pte Ltd. 2017
F. Sun et al. (Eds.): ICCSIP 2016, CCIS 710, pp. 119–125, 2017.
DOI: 10.1007/978-981-10-5230-9_13

language recognition and human motion demonstration, but the wearable device impedes the convenience and naturalness in HCI [2]. Besides the above options, bio-signals are good choices for HCI as well, which mainly include Electro-encephalogram (EEG), Electro-oculogram (EOG), and Electromyogram (EMG). Many attempts have been made to establish HCI system using such signals, especially for the physically disabled people. Compared to others, EMG signal can be acquired with portable surface electrodes and higher information transfer rate. This bioelectric signal can directly reflects the muscle activities in human motion and it has been explored and used in clinical analysis, gait analysis and HCI in recent years. In order to explore and realize a real neural-linked and natural HCI system, this paper employed the forearm surface EMG signal as the only input to identify human wrist actions and hand gestures.

The recognition accuracy of the EMG system is the primary demand to researchers, which mainly depends on EMG electrode position, signal processing techniques, feature extraction and classification methodology. The electrode position not only influence the quality of signal, but also affect the applicability and feasibility of the experimental design. The issue of electrode location had been summarized by L. Mesin, R. Merletti [3]. The most detailed work was accomplished by the European Project on "Surface EMG for Non Invasive Assessment of Muscles" (SENIAM) [www. seniam.org], where careful analysis and explanation were presented. The results of this project contributed a lot to other EMG researchers. When reviewing previous work in EMG-based gesture identification, we found that most systems mounted two to eight EMG sensors on the forearm of subject [4–6]. After lots of attempts, on the purpose of acquiring high quality EMG signal and developing a convenient and feasible experimental design for all subjects, we placed six EMG sensors on forearm. The method has been illustrated in Fig. 1. The six sensors were divided into two groups. The first group were mounted near the elbow and the other one were placed near the wrist.

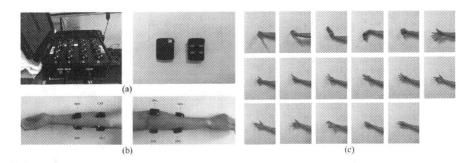

**Fig. 1.** (a) Delsys Trigno, a portable and wireless 16-channel EMG device; (b) The design of EMG sensors position. They are divided into two groups. The first three sensors are placed near elbow and the second group are mounted near wrist; (c) The 17 hand gestures include 6 wrist actions and 11 finger gestures.

After having been collected from the forearm muscles, the EMG signals are required to be amplified and filtered. Then in order to improve classification results, the features of the EMG need to be carefully selected. Generally, the features of EMG can be divided into three categories, including time domain, frequency domain and time-frequency domain [7, 8]. Because features in time domain provide high recognition accuracy and low computational cost, they are very suitable to EMG system. Hudgins et al. [9, 10] developed time domain features and achieved good performance. Alkan et al. [11] employed mean absolute value (MAV) to classify four arm movements, where the window length is the single parameter. Lin et al. [6] used MAV and the first 3 parameters of 4 order AR model as features. Phinyomark et al. [12] used 26 time domain features and few frequency domain features as the inputs of classifier. In this paper, we employed 9 time domain features as the input of classifier. As to the classification algorithm, the Artificial Neural Network (ANN), Linear Discriminant Analysis (LDA), k-Nearest Neighbor (KNN) and Support Vector Machines (SVM) have been employed. In our work, the SVM classifier achieves the highest accuracy. Hence the lib-SVM 3.21 classifier is finally employed in this paper.

The contribution of this paper is the exploration of the methods which can improve EMG signal classification accuracy. We utilized six-channel EMG signals to classify 17 hand gestures, including 6 wrist actions and 11 finger gestures. By exploring the method of data acquisition and optimizing the time length of signal, we realized a natural HCI system with the recognition accuracy more than 95%.

## 2    Data Acquisiton

### 2.1    Experimental Equipment

One portable and wireless 16-channel EMG device (DELSYS TRIGNO) was used to collect EMG data, which has been shown in Fig. 1. The sample rate was set to 1000 Hz and the acquired data was transferred to PC by wireless module. Then the collected data was processed and analyzed by EMGworks Analysis and MATLAB programs.

### 2.2    Experimental Design

There are totally 5 subjects (4 males and 1 female) took part in the experiments. All of them are right handed. Before the experiment, they were instructed to practice all of the gestures. The forearm skin of the electrodes location was cleaned by alcohol and six wireless electrodes were mounted on the right forearm as Fig. 1. The 6 wrist actions and 11 finger gestures were listed in Fig. 1. After they were familiar with the gestures and well prepared, the MATLAB experiment program begun. In detail, each trial contained two parts: the preparing time and action time, both of which were set as 5 s. In order to make the subjects well-prepared in the action time, we displayed the gesture in the preparing time. Hence the subjects were able to see the following gesture in advance. In the action time, the subjects were demanded to maintain the gesture which was displayed on the screen. Each gesture were displayed 30 times. Hence there were 510 trials for each subject. This experimental design has been shown in Fig. 2.

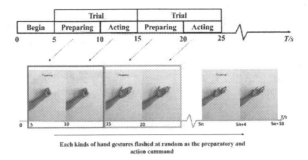

**Fig. 2.** The design of the data acquisition experiment. The subjects are instructed by the preparatory and action commands to perform the corresponding gesture. In the preparing time, subjects can relax their hands to avoid excessive muscle fatigue.

# 3   Methods

After six-channel surface EMG signals had been collected from all subjects, the materials for further processing steps were prepared. The methods of data segmentation, data filtering, feature extraction and classification are introduced below.

## 3.1   Preprocessing

For each subject, we acquired 30 samples of each gesture. The time length of the data samples is 5 s. In order to discuss the influence of signal time length on classification results, we set the signal time length as 5 s, 3 s, 1 s and 0.5 s respectively. Then the signal amplitude was amplified. Because the main noise of EMG is low frequency component, the amplified signal was filtered by Chebyshev II filter (25–450 Hz).

## 3.2   Feature Extraction

This study totally employed 9 time domain features. They were extracted by sliding windows and reduced by PCA algorithm. The selected features includes Integrated EMG, Mean Absolute Value, Mean Square Root, Variance, Waveform Length, Simple Square Intergral, Slope Sign Changes, Zero Crossings, Willison Amplitude. Features such as the correlation coefficient between any two channels of EMG signal were also attempted, but they contributed little to the final classification results.

As it can be seen in Fig. 3, when we extracted these features of the six channel EMG signals, the features between the first and forth channel are partly similar. They are similar between the other two pairs of channels as well, because the two groups of EMG sensors reflect the activity of some same muscles. In order to reduce redundant information, we attempted to reduce sensor number and employed PCA algorithm.

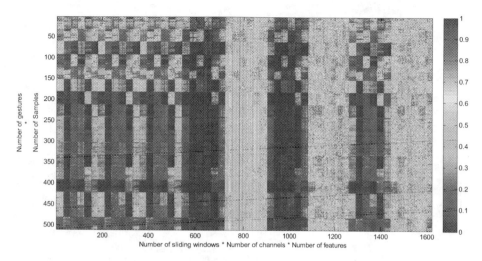

**Fig. 3.** The feature matrix of six-channel EMG signals

### 3.3    Classification

This paper employed lib-SVM as the classification tool for pattern recognition. In addition, 10-fold Cross Validation was used to test the sensitivity.

## 4    Results

We obtained 30 samples for each gestures for five subjects (4 males and 1 female). The method of data filtering, feature extraction, feature selection and classification has been introduced above. In this section, we will exhibit the classification results and discuss the effect of EMG sensor number and time length of EMG Signal. When we use two groups of the EMG sensors and the time length is set as 5 s, the recognition results have been listed in Table 1.

We divided the EMG sensors into two groups. The effect of each group was tested. The time length is set as 3 s. Average identification results are listed in Table 2.

The time length of EMG signal not only has an influence on classification accuracy, but also affect the practicability of the EMG-based HCI system. Hence we explored the effect of time length. The test results are listed in Table 3.

According to Table 1, for each subject, the recognition accuracy of the 6 wrist actions is usually higher than 98.5%. As to the 11 finger gestures and 17 hand gestures, the recognition accuracy are generally higher than 90%, which shows lower separability than the wrist actions. All the average recognition accuracy of wrist actions, finger gestures and hand gestures is above 95%, which proves the effectiveness of the system.

According to Table 2, when the complexity of gestures increases, we need more EMG sensors. Generally, the performance of the first group of sensors is better than the second group. In fact, the signals from either group is enough to wrist actions

**Table 1.** The recognition accuracy(%) of WA, FG and HG

| Subjects | CZH | ZNN | XHZ | ZLF | LYR | Average rate |
|----------|------|------|------|------|------|--------------|
| WA(6) | 100 | 98.92 | 100 | 99.18 | 99.65 | 99.55 |
| FG(11) | 96.65 | 96.16 | 97.28 | 93.45 | 94.27 | 95.56 |
| HG(17) | 96.06 | 95.68 | 97.02 | 92.75 | 93.88 | 95.08 |

**Table 2.** The average recognition accuracy(%) for five subjects with different sensor number

| Sensor Number | WA | | FG | | HG | |
|---------------|------|------|------|------|------|------|
| | Mean | Std | Mean | Std | Mean | Std |
| Sensor 1–3 | 96.99 | 1.97 | 89.16 | 3.92 | 80.06 | 5.63 |
| Sensor 4–6 | 95.97 | 2.02 | 77.85 | 5.94 | 77.74 | 6.61 |
| Sensor 1–6 | 97.83 | 1.36 | 95.12 | 2.79 | 91.81 | 3.85 |

**Table 3.** The average recognition accuracy(%) for five subjects with different time length

| Time length (s) | WA | | FG | | HG | |
|-----------------|------|------|------|------|------|------|
| | Mean | Std | Mean | Std | Mean | Std |
| 0.5 s | 95.52 | 3.52 | 73.18 | 6.65 | 58.16 | 9.21 |
| 1 s | 96.11 | 1.93 | 88.82 | 4.73 | 73.00 | 6.38 |
| 3 s | 97.83 | 1.36 | 95.12 | 2.79 | 91.81 | 3.85 |
| 5 s | 99.55 | 0.49 | 95.56 | 1.63 | 95.08 | 1.73 |

identification (above 95%). However, in order to recognize finger gestures and hand gestures, six-channel EMG signals are required. The redundant information can be removed by PCA algorithm.

According to Table 3, the time length of EMG signal is of importance for classification. When we use the information in 0.5 s, the average classification accuracy of 17 hand gestures is 58.16%, which cannot meet the requirement in reality at all. In summary, the more controlling commands is expected, the longer time length is required.

## 5    Conclusion and Discussion

To realize a natural HCI using surface EMG signal, stable and accurate controlling commands are required at first. In this paper, 17 kinds of hand gestures exhibit high separability which including 6 wrist actions and 11 fingers actions. In the experiments, all the five subjects achieved high performance, proving the hand gestures can be efficiently transformed into effective controlling commands to peripheral devices or computer software.

In addition to the realization of EMG controlling system, the paper explored the functions of the number of EMG sensors and the time length of EMG signals. All in all, more EMG sensors and longer time length provide more information about muscle activities, which is of importance for complex gestures recognition.

In further work, two problems is worthy to be concerned. The first one is the method of reducing training data. If we can ensure the recognition accuracy above 90% with less than 5 or 10 samples, the applicability of the system will be improved. The second problem is the method of feature extraction. The effective and efficient features will decrease the required time length. If the time length of each sample could be reduced to 1 s, the user experience of this system will be improved.

**Acknowledgement.** This work is partly supported by National Natural Science Foundation of China (Project 61375117 and Project 91320202).>

# References

1. Kulić, D., Kragic, D., Krüger, V.: Learning action primitives. In: Moeslund, T.B., Hilton, A., Krüger, V., Sigal, L. (eds.) Visual Analysis of Humans, pp. 333–353. Springer, London (2011). doi:10.1007/978-0-85729-997-0_17
2. Fang, G., Gao, W., Zhao, D.: Large vocabulary sign language recognition based on fuzzy decision trees. IEEE Trans. Syst. Man Cybern. Part A: Syst. Hum. **34**(3), 305–314 (2004)
3. Mesin, L., Merletti, R., Rainoldi, A.: Surface EMG: the issue of electrode location. J. Electromyogr. Kinesiol. **19**(5), 719–726 (2009)
4. Zhang, X., et al.: A framework for hand gesture recognition based on accelerometer and EMG sensors. IEEE Trans. Syst. Man Cybern. Part A: Syst. Hum. **41**(6), 1064–1076 (2011)
5. Chen, X., et al.: Hand gesture recognition research based on surface EMG sensors and 2D-accelerometers. In: 2007 11th IEEE International Symposium on Wearable Computers. IEEE (2007)
6. Lin, K., et al.: A robust gesture recognition algorithm based on surface EMG. In: 2015 Seventh International Conference on Advanced Computational Intelligence (ICACI). IEEE (2015)
7. Chowdhury, R.H., et al.: Surface electromyography signal processing and classification techniques. Sensors **13**(9), 12431–12466 (2013)
8. Ahsan, M., Ibrahimy, M.I., Khalifa, O.O.: EMG signal classification for human computer interaction: a review. Eur. J. Sci. Res. **33**(3), 480–501 (2009)
9. Hudgins, B., Parker, P., Scott, R.N.: A new strategy for multifunction myoelectric control. IEEE Trans. Biomed. Eng. **40**(1), 82–94 (1993)
10. Englehart, K., Hudgins, B.: A robust, real-time control scheme for multifunction myoelectric control. IEEE Trans. Biomed. Eng. **50**(7), 848–854 (2003)
11. Alkan, A., Günay, M.: Identification of EMG signals using discriminant analysis and SVM classifier. Expert Syst. Appl. **39**(1), 44–47 (2012)
12. Phinyomark, A., Phukpattaranont, P., Limsakul, C.: Feature reduction and selection for EMG signal classification. Expert Syst. Appl. **39**(8), 7420–7431 (2012)

# An Optimized Naive Bayesian Method
# for Face Recognition

Rui Yan[1(✉)], Jie Wen[1], Jian Cao[1], Yong Xu[1], and Jian Yang[2]

[1] Shenzhen Graduate School, Bio-Computing Research Center,
Harbin Institute of Technology, Shenzhen 518055, Guangdong, China
reeyree@163.com
[2] School of Computer Science and Technology,
Nanjing University of Science and Technology,
Nanjing 210094, Jiangsu, China

**Abstract.** Naive Bayesian is a simple and powerful classification algorithm. In this paper, we propose an optimized naive Bayesian algorithm with the application to face recognition. Firstly, the algorithm estimates the probability distribution of each pixel at each gray level. Secondly, it performs Laplace smoothing to resolve the zero probability problem. Thirdly, the maximum filtering is used to optimize the probability distribution matrix for classification. Experiments on three face databases show that the proposed algorithm is effective and performs better than some state-of-the-art algorithms.

**Keywords:** Face recognition · Naive bayesian · Laplace smoothing · Maximum filtering

## 1 Introduction

The naive Bayesian classifier is a probabilistic approach to classification [1]. It assumes that the effect of an attribute value is independent of other attributes on a given class [3]. This assumption is called class conditional independence. It is made to simplify the computation cost.

As a popular classification algorithm, the naive Bayesian algorithm shows its excellence for the text classification [4]. However, the naive Bayesian classifier does not perform well in image classification, because the way to get priori probability in text classification is not very suitable for image classification. A possible reason is that there is a significant relationship between associated neighborhood pixels, thus it is unreasonable to assume them to be independent.

Face recognition has a long history dating back to 1960s with the work of Bledsoe [5]. It is still one of the most challenging problem and an active research field in compute vision and biometric identification.

Various algorithms based on Bayesian theory are widely used in pattern recognition. Bayesian face recognition [6] is a representative and effective algorithm. It proposes the probabilistic similarity measures based on the Bayesian theorem. In Bayesian face recognition, $\Delta = x_1 - x_2$ stands for the difference of two face images $x_1$ and $x_2$. Bayesian face recognition classifies $\Delta$ as intra-personal variation $\Omega_I$ (i.e., the variations

© Springer Nature Singapore Pte Ltd. 2017
F. Sun et al. (Eds.): ICCSIP 2016, CCIS 710, pp. 126–135, 2017.
DOI: 10.1007/978-981-10-5230-9_14

are from the same individual) or extra-personal variation $\Omega_E$ (i.e., the variations are from different individuals). The similarity measure between $x_1$ and $x_2$ can be expressed by the logarithm likelihood ratio of $p(\Delta \mid \Omega_I)$ to $p(\Delta \mid \Omega_E)$, where both $p(\Delta \mid \Omega_I)$ and $p(\Delta \mid \Omega_E)$ are assumed to follow one multivariate Gaussian distribution [6].

However, one limitation has restricted the performance of Bayesian face recognition. Existing Bayesian face methods just exploit the difference of a given face pair, not taking into serious account the discriminative information and separability of different faces [7]. Recently, Chen et al. [8] proposed a joint formulation for Bayesian face recognition, which has solved this problem successfully. Chen et al. directly modeled the joint distribution of $\{x_1, x_2\}$ for the face verification problem in the same Bayesian framework and introduced an appropriate prior for face representation, where each face is the summation of two independent Gaussian latent variables [9], i.e., intrinsic variable and intra-personal variable [8]. Based on this prior, it can effectively learn the parametric models of two latent variables by an EM-like algorithm [8] and can derive a closed-form expression of the log likelihood ratio.

Our main contributions can be summarized as follows:

a. Different from the traditional naive Bayesian method, our method takes the pixel position information into account and proposes a new approach to estimate priori probability.
b. In the proposed algorithm, the relationship of associated neighborhood is utilized to obtain the optimal priori probability, which makes the proposed algorithm has the potential to obtain better performance than other methods.
c. We provide a very large number of experiments and the experimental results show that the proposed method is very effective.

The remainder of this paper is organized as follows. In Sect. 2, we describe the naive Bayesian method for face recognition. Section 3 gives the detail step of the proposed methods. Section 4 presents the experimental results. Finally, Sect. 5 offers our conclusion and provides an analysis of the proposed method.

## 2   Related Works

### 2.1   Symbol Description

We assume that there are $L$ classes and $m$ training samples of each class, $x^{(i,j)}(1 \leq i \leq L, 1 \leq j \leq m)$ represents the $jth$ training sample of the $ith$ class and it is defined as:

$$x^{(i,i)} = \begin{bmatrix} x_{1,1}^{(i,j)} & x_{1,2}^{(i,j)} & \cdots & x_{1,c}^{(i,j)} \\ x_{2,1}^{(i,j)} & x_{2,2}^{(i,j)} & \cdots & x_{2,c}^{(i,j)} \\ \vdots & \vdots & \vdots & \vdots \\ x_{r,1}^{(i,j)} & x_{r,2}^{(i,j)} & \cdots & x_{r,c}^{(i,j)} \end{bmatrix}.$$

If a training sample is from the *ith* class, we take $y_i$ as the class label of this training sample, Let the test sample be $x = \begin{bmatrix} x_{1,1} & x_{1,2} & \cdots & x_{1,c} \\ x_{2,1} & x_{2,2} & \cdots & x_{2,c} \\ \vdots & \vdots & \vdots & \vdots \\ x_{r,1} & x_{r,2} & \cdots & x_{r,c} \end{bmatrix}$, $r$ and $c$ represent the height and width of the input image.

## 2.2    Naive Bayesian Classification Algorithm

Naive Bayesian classifier is a term dealing with probabilistic classifier based on Bayesian theorem with strong independence assumptions [13]. In naive Bayesian classification algorithm, test sample $x$ is classified to

$$\arg \max_{y_i} \{p(y_i \,|\, x)\}, i = 1, 2, \cdots, L \tag{1}$$

According to the Bayesian' theorem, the posterior probability $p(y_i \,|\, x)$ can be represented as $p(y_i \,|\, x) = \frac{p(x \,|\, y_i) p(y_i)}{p(x)}$. For face recognition; $\frac{1}{p(x)}$ is a constant, (1) is equivalent to the following formula $\arg \max_{y_i} \{p(x \,|\, y_i) p(y_i)\}, i = 1, 2, \cdots, L$.

$$p(x \,|\, y_i) = p(x_{1,1}, \cdots\cdots, x_{r,c} \,|\, y_i) = p(x_{1,1} \,|\, y_i) p(x_{1,1}, x_{1,2} \,|\, y_i, x_{1,1}) \\ \cdots\cdots p(x_{1,1}, \cdots\cdots, x_{r,c} \,|\, y_i, x_{1,1}, \cdots\cdots, x_{r,c-1}) \tag{2}$$

The naive Bayesian classification algorithm assumes that each attribute of image $x$ is independent. So metric $p(x \,|\, y_i)$ can be expressed as follows.

$$p(x \,|\, y_i) p(y_i) = p(y_i) \prod_{u=1}^{r} \prod_{v=1}^{c} p(x_{a,b} \,|\, y_i) \tag{3}$$

To improve the computation efficiency, we transform it (3) into the following formula

$$\ln(p(x \,|\, y_i) p(y_i)) = \ln p(y_i) + \sum_{u=1}^{r} \sum_{v=1}^{c} \ln(p(x_{u,v} \,|\, y_i)). \tag{4}$$

Finally we use the following equation to classify the test sample

$$\arg \max_{y_i} \{\ln p(y_i) + \sum_{u=1}^{r} \sum_{v=1}^{c} \ln(p(x_{u,v} \,|\, y_i))\}, i = 1, 2, \cdots, L \tag{5}$$

According to the Maximum a Posterior rule, we can get the priori probability

$$\phi_{x_\theta = k \,|\, y_i} = p(x_\theta = k \,|\, y_i) = \frac{\sum\limits_{j=1}^{n} \sum\limits_{u=1}^{r} \sum\limits_{v=1}^{c} g(x_{u,v}^{(i,j)}, k)}{n.r.c} \quad (0 \le k \le 255) \tag{6}$$

$$g(x, k) = \begin{cases} 1 & , x = k \\ 0 & , x \ne k \end{cases}$$

$$\phi_{y_i} = p(y_i) = \frac{1}{L} \tag{7}$$

where $\phi_{x_\theta = k \,|\, y_i} = p(x_\theta = k \,|\, y_i)$ denotes the probability of event $x_\theta = k$ $(x_\theta \in x)$ of *ith* class and $p(y_i)$ represents the probability of samples from *ith* class. Since the gray level of an image is [0, 255], thus $k \in [0, 255]$ in the proposed algorithm.

## 3   The Proposed Method

The accuracy of naive Bayesian classification algorithm is determined by the priori probability. As presented in Sect. 2, tradition naive Bayesian classification algorithm only uses statistics to calculate the priori probability, and supposes information of neighborhood pixels are independently. It is not reasonable to directly apply naive Bayesian for image classification.

In fact, three limitations have restricted the performance of naive Bayesian classification for face recognition. First, the naive Bayesian face method is based on the priori probability of all image, it ignores the position information of each gray level. Second, the value of priori probability $p(x_\theta = k \,|\, y_i)$ can be zero without smoothing operation. Third, pixels in a local neighborhood of digital image are not independent while having large correlation. In other words, the priori probability of some pixels is influenced by its neighborhood, but the traditional naive Bayesian classification algorithm does not take into account it.

Based on above analysis, in this paper, we propose a new approach to estimate the priori probability so as to improve the performance for image classification. The frame of our method is shown in Fig. 1, and then we describe each step in detail. We call the proposed method naive Bayesian with position information and maximum filtering (NBPIMF).

### 3.1   The Probability Distribution Matrix of Gray Level

Compared with traditional naive Bayesian classification method, we take into account the position information of pixels to estimate the priori probability.

Suppose that $X^{(i,k)}$ represents the probability distribution matrix of the training sample from *ith* class at gray level $k$. According to the Maximum a Posterior rule, the probability distribution matrix is calculated by scanning training sample $x^{(i,j)}$ $(1 \le j \le m)$ and computing the probability at each gray level $x_{u,v}^{(i,j)} = k$.

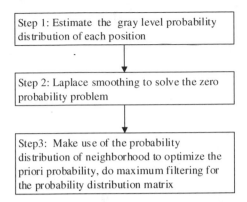

**Fig. 1.** The proposed method to optimize the priori probability.

Probability distribution matrix $X^{(i,k)}$ is calculated as

$$X^{(i,k)}_{u,v} = \phi_{x_{u,v}=k \mid y_i} = p(x_{u,v} = k \mid y_i)$$

$$= \frac{\sum\limits_{j=1}^{n} g(x^{(i,j)}_{u,v}, k)}{n} \quad (1 \le u \le r, 1 \le v \le c, 0 \le k \le 255)$$

$$g(x, k) = \begin{cases} 1 & , x = k \\ 0 & , x \ne k \end{cases}$$

### 3.2  Laplace Smoothing

The zero probability occurs when a feature value does not appear in the training data. Naive Bayesian classification algorithm uses a smoothing filter to solve this problem. In this paper, we perform the Laplace smoothing (add-one smoothing) [10] on the matrix $X^{(i,k)}$

$$X^{(i,k)}_{u,v} = \phi_{x_{u,v}=k \mid y_i} = p(x_{u,v} = k \mid y_i)$$

$$= \frac{1 + \sum\limits_{j=1}^{n} g(x^{(i,j)}_{u,v}, k)}{n + \tau} \quad (1 \le u \le r, 1 \le v \le c, 0 \le k \le 255)$$

$$g(x, k) = \begin{cases} 1 & , x = k \\ 0 & , x \ne k \end{cases}$$

where $\tau$ is the total number of possible values of $k$.

### 3.3    Maximum Filtering for the Probability Distribution Matrix

After the previous operation, we can get probability distribution matrix $X^{(i,k)}$, where $i$ means the label of training sample and $k$ means the value of gray level. The probability distribution matrix is shown in Fig. 2.

| $X_{1,1}^{(i,k)}$ | $X_{1,2}^{(i,k)}$ | $X_{1,3}^{(i,k)}$ | $\cdots$ | $X_{1,c}^{(i,k)}$ |
|---|---|---|---|---|
| $X_{2,1}^{(i,k)}$ | $X_{2,2}^{(i,k)}$ | $X_{2,3}^{(i,k)}$ | $\cdots$ | $X_{2,c}^{(i,k)}$ |
| $X_{3,1}^{(i,k)}$ | $X_{3,2}^{(i,k)}$ | $X_{3,3}^{(i,k)}$ | $\cdots$ | $X_{3,c}^{(i,k)}$ |
| $\vdots$ | $\vdots$ | $\vdots$ | $\vdots$ | $\vdots$ |
| $X_{r,1}^{(i,k)}$ | $X_{r,2}^{(i,k)}$ | $X_{r,3}^{(i,k)}$ | $\cdots$ | $X_{r,c}^{(i,k)}$ |

**Fig. 2.**  Probability distribution matrix $X^{(i,k)}$.

Pixels in a local neighborhood of an image have great correlation. In general, the nearer the two pixels, the greater the correlation will be. This indicates that the priori probability of pixel is influenced by its neighborhood. Thus, taking into account this information has the potential to improve the performance of Bayesian based classification methods for image classification. Inspired by that the naive Bayesian algorithm uses the Maximum a Posterior rule to estimate the priori probability, we use the maximum filter to optimize the priori probability in this paper.

The maximum filter is a typical morphological filter that works by considering a neighborhood around each pixel. For a pixel, it chooses the largest pixel value in a local neighborhood around the pixel as the output value. Suppose in a local area with a square size of $s \times s$, where $s$ is an odd number and the smallest box size is $3 \times 3$, the maximum filtering operation can be expressed as:

$$X_{u,v}^{(i,k)} = \max\{X_{u+a,v+b}^{(i,k)}\} \quad \left(-\frac{s-1}{2} \leq a \leq \frac{s-1}{2}, \ -\frac{s-1}{2} \leq b \leq \frac{s-1}{2}\right).$$

For $X_{u+a,v+b}^{(i,k)}$, where $u+a \notin [1,r]$, $v+b \notin [1,c]$, we set the value of it to be zero, then test sample $x$ can be classified by

$$\arg\max_{y_i}\{\ln p(y_i) + \sum_{u=1}^{r}\sum_{v=1}^{c}\ln(X_{(u,v)}^{(i,x_{u,v})})\}, i = 1, 2, \cdots, L.$$

## 4    Experiments

To evaluate the proposed algorithm, several state-of-the-art classification methods such as sparse representation classification (SRC) algorithm [11], linear regression classification (LRC) [12], collaborative representation classification (CRC) [13], principal component analysis (PCA) [14], and linear discriminant analysis (LDA) [15] are compared. The above algorithms are tested on two face datasets, including ORL [16], the Georgia Tech (GT) [17] face databases and AR [18] face databases. In the experiment, we also adopt Laplace smoothing on the naive Bayesian classifier algorithm to obtain a fairly comparison result. In the experiment, the square size of the maximum filtering is selected as $3 \times 3$ and $5 \times 5$ for the proposed algorithm, and we use short NBPIMF ($3 \times 3$) and NBPIMF ($5 \times 5$) to denote the two options.

**Fig. 3.** Some face images of the ORL database.

### 4.1    Experiments on the ORL Face Database

The ORL database includes 400 face images taken from 40 subjects, and each subject provides 10 face images. The size of face image in the ORL database is 46 by 56. The images were taken at different times, with varying lighting, facial expressions (open/closed eyes, smiling/not smiling), and facial details (glasses/no glasses).

In the experiment, the first 2, 3, 4, 5, and 6 samples of each class are selected as the training samples, and the remaining samples are treated as test sample. Figure 3 shows some typical face images of the ORL face databases. The experiment results of above classification algorithms on the ORL face database are shown in Table 1.

**Table 1.** Classification accuracies of different algorithms on the ORL face database (%)

| Training sample per class | 2 | 3 | 4 | 5 | 6 |
|---|---|---|---|---|---|
| Naive Bayesian | 67.50 | 64.64 | 72.50 | 76.50 | 80.63 |
| CRC | 83.44 | 83.33 | 89.17 | 88.50 | 91.50 |
| LRC | 79.06 | 81.79 | 85.00 | 87.80 | 90.06 |
| LDA(39) | 79.06 | 81.79 | 90.16 | 95.20 | 96.30 |
| SRC | 84.32 | 86.42 | 87.50 | 89.50 | 95.80 |
| PCA(50) | 79.06 | 80.42 | 86.25 | 92.80 | 94.80 |
| NBPIMF ($3 \times 3$) | 82.19 | 85.36 | 90.42 | 95.50 | 99.38 |
| NBPIMF ($5 \times 5$) | **84.69** | **85.86** | **91.67** | **96.00** | **99.38** |

The experiment results on the ORL face database shows that the proposed algorithm performs much better than the compared algorithms. For example, the

**Fig. 4.** Some face images of the GT database.

**Table 2.** Classification accuracies of different algorithms on the GT face database (%)

| Training sample per class | 3 | 4 | 5 | 6 | 7 |
|---|---|---|---|---|---|
| Naive Bayesian | 57.67 | 54.55 | 53.80 | 55.11 | 58.50 |
| CRC | 45.33 | 47.09 | 48.08 | 55.60 | 58.50 |
| LRC | 51.00 | 55.27 | 59.40 | 68.00 | 72.00 |
| LDA(49) | 53.00 | 57.82 | 60.00 | 68.89 | 70.89 |
| SRC | 49.50 | 50.73 | 52.60 | 57.00 | 59.75 |
| PCA(50) | 46.67 | 48.72 | 51.20 | 60.67 | 68.20 |
| NBPIMF (3 × 3) | 65.00 | 64.91 | 63.40 | 67.78 | 75.50 |
| NBPIMF (5 × 5) | **66.83** | **65.64** | **65.60** | **70.44** | **76.75** |

classification accuracy of the proposed algorithm is approximate 20% higher than naive Bayesian classification algorithm. The accuracy of the well-known SRC is 6.50% lower than that of the proposed method in which the first five samples of each class is selected as training samples.

## 4.2 Experiments on the GT Face Database

The GT database includes 50 individuals taken from two or three sessions. Each individual contains 15 color JPEG images with cluttered background. The image size is 640 × 480. The database contains frontal or tilted faces with different facial expressions, lighting conditions and scale. Each image was manually labeled to determine the position of the face. The face images used in the experiment are with the background removed. And then the downsampling algorithm is performed to resize the image into a 40 by 30 matrix in advance. Figure 4 shows some face images of the GT face database.

In the experiment, the first 3, 4, 5, 6, and 7 samples of each class are selected as the training samples, and the remaining samples are treated as test sample. Table 2 shows the experiment result of different algorithms on the GT face database.

Experiment results shows that the proposed method performs much better than other methods when testing on GT face database.

## 4.3 Experiments on the AR Face Database

For the AR face database, we select 2600 color images from 100 subjects to test the above algorithms. Each subject provides 26 images, and the size of each image is 120 × 100. Each image is transformed into the gray image in advance. Figure 5 shows some face images of the AR face databases.

**Fig. 5.** Some face images of the AR database.

Table 3 shows the experiment results on the AR face database, in which the first 6, 7, 8, 9, and 10 samples of each class are selected as training set, and the remaining samples are regard as test set.

The experiment results on the AR face database shows that our method achieves the best performance. For example, the accuracy of the proposed algorithm are 50% higher than the naive Bayesian classification.

All the experiment results on the ORL, GT and AR face database show that the performance of the proposed algorithm with the maximum filtering size of $5 \times 5$ is much better than that of size $3 \times 3$.

**Table 3.** Classification accuracies of different algorithms on the AR face database (%)

| Training sample per class | 6 | 7 | 8 | 9 | 10 |
|---|---|---|---|---|---|
| Naive Bayesian | 9.10 | 8.53 | 9.06 | 9.00 | 8.50 |
| CRC | 64.84 | 63.37 | 62.96 | 62.07 | 60.63 |
| LRC | 62.37 | 61.23 | 59.63 | 57.16 | 55.16 |
| LDA(49) | 64.70 | 64.10 | 63.70 | 60.95 | 60.19 |
| SRC | 63.90 | 65.10 | 63.30 | 60.09 | 59.23 |
| PCA(50) | 56.70 | 55.73 | 54.30 | 52.23 | 51.93 |
| NBPIMF ($3 \times 3$) | 65.34 | 64.50 | 63.11 | 61.65 | 60.17 |
| NBPIMF ($5 \times 5$) | **66.36** | **64.74** | **63.50** | **61.94** | **60.39** |

## 5  Conclusion

The paper analyzes the drawbacks of the naive Bayesian classification algorithm and proposes an improved algorithm with the application to face recognition. Considering the fact that pixels in a local area of image have great correlation whereas the naive Bayesian classification ignores it, we propose a new approach to estimate the priori probability. By using the maximum filtering, the position information of pixels is properly utilized to obtain the optimal prior probability for classification. In addition, Laplace smoothing is implemented on the priori probability to resolve the zero probability problem which makes the algorithm more stable. Various experiments show that the proposed algorithm is effective and outperforms some state-of-the-art algorithms for face recognition.

**Acknowledgment.** This work was supported by the National Natural Science Foundation of China under Grant 61300208.

# References

1. Leung, K.M.: Naive bayesian classifier. Polytechnic University Department of Comptuter Science Finance and Risk Engineering (2007)
2. Maxwell, J.C.: A Treatise on Electricity and Magnetism, 3rd edn., vol. 2, pp. 68–73. Oxford, Clarendon (1892)
3. Yager, R.R.: An extension of the naive Bayes classifier. J. Inf. Sci. **176**(5), 577–588 (2006)
4. Zhang, L., Zhu, J., Yao, T.: An evaluation of statistical spam filtering techniques. J. ACM Trans. Asian Lang. Inf. Process. **3**(4), 243–269 (2004)
5. Bledsoe, W.W.: The model method in facial recognition. Panoramic Research, Inc., Palo Alto (1966)
6. Moghaddam, B., Jebara, T., Pentland, A.: Bayesian face recognition. J. Pattern Recogn. **33**(11), 1771–1782 (2000)
7. Wang, X., Tang, X.: Bayesian face recognition using Gabor features. In: Proceedings of ACM SIGMM Workshop on Biometric Methods and Applications, pp. 70–73 (2003)
8. Chen, D., Cao, X., Wang, L., Wen, F., Sun, J.: Bayesian face revisited: a joint formulation. In: Fitzgibbon, A., Lazebnik, S., Perona, P., Sato, Y., Schmid, C. (eds.) ECCV 2012. LNCS, vol. 7574, pp. 566–579. Springer, Heidelberg (2012). doi:10.1007/978-3-642-33712-3_41
9. Lyu, S.: Bayesian supervised learning with non-Gaussian latent variables. In: ChinaSIP, pp. 659–663 (2013)
10. Hafilizara, M.: Metode Smoothing dalam Naïve Bayes untuk Klasifikasi Email Spam. UT - Computer Science (2014)
11. Wright, J., Ma, Y., Mairal, J.: Sparse representation for computer vision and pattern recognition. J. Proc. IEEE **98**(6), 1031–1044 (2010)
12. Shi, Q., Eriksson, A., Hengel, A.: Is face recognition really a compressive sensing problem? In: CVPR, pp. 553–560 (2011)
13. Zhang, L., Yang, M., Feng, X.: Sparse representation or collaborative representation: which helps face recognition?. In: ICCV, pp. 471–478 (2011)
14. Debruyne, M., Verdonck, T.: Robust kernel principal component analysis and classification. J. Adv. Data Anal. Classif. **4**(2–3), 151–167 (2010)
15. Xu, Y., Zhang, D.: Represent and fuse bimodal biometric images at the feature level: complex-matrix-based fusion scheme. Opt. Eng. **49**, 037002 (2010)
16. The Database of Faces. http://www.cl.cam.ac.uk/research/dtg/attarchive/facedatabase.html
17. The Georgia Tech (GT) face databases: http://www.anefian.com/research/face_reco.htm
18. http://cobweb.ecn.purdue.edu/ ∼ aleix/aleix−face−DB.html

# Development of Operation Estimation Method Based on Tracking Records Captured by Kinect

Bin Wang[1,2], Fuchun Sun[1,2], Huaping Liu[1,2(✉)], Xuan Guo[1,2],
Sota Yoshii[3], Naoyuki Fujiwara[3], Weihang Wu[3], and Guangyu Zhao[4]

[1] Department of Computer Science and Technology,
Tsinghua University, Beijing, China
hpliu@tsinghua.edu.cn
[2] State Key Laboratory of Intelligent Technology and Systems,
Tsinghua University, Beijing, China
[3] Yokohama R&D Center, Mitsubishi Heavy Industries, Tokyo, Japan
[4] Little Wheel Robot Co., Beijing, China

**Abstract.** In order to evaluate workers' progress in the factory, we developed a model of operation estimation method based on tracking records captured by Kinect. In this paper, we use Kinect sensors to capture the human motion process (such as broadcast gymnastics), extract the skeleton frame sequence from training data as a template, then improve the DTW algorithm to match the skeleton frame in the test data and in the training data, to estimate the percentage of the action's completion. The improved DTW algorithm achieves state-of-the-art performances on our dataset, higher than 90%.

**Keywords:** Working progress completion estimation · DTW · Kinect

## 1 Introduction

In order to enhance competitiveness and improve work efficiency, the factory's manager need to get the worker's progress in real-time. In the traditional method, the wearable device (such as a microphone, PDA and other devices) were used, they were cumbersome and ineffective compared to Kinect, which can capture the human skeleton, the skeleton data is more easily identified for body gesture recognition than RGB data, and is not prone to be interfered by the back ground (Fig. 1).

In this paper, we used Kinect to record some person's whole working progress as xef file, extracted body skeleton as feature from it, labeled one of them as training template, and used other person's data as testing data (Fig. 2).

In the Sect. 2, the improved Dynamic Time Warping algorithm (DTW) was explained, In the Sect. 3, we will show how DTW could be employed to identify similar to query subsequences in the long data streams. In the Sect. 3, the evaluation result was shown. In the Sect. 4, we summarized.

© Springer Nature Singapore Pte Ltd. 2017
F. Sun et al. (Eds.): ICCSIP 2016, CCIS 710, pp. 136–143, 2017.
DOI: 10.1007/978-981-10-5230-9_15

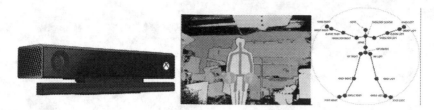

**Fig. 1.** Kinect v2 and skeleton frame

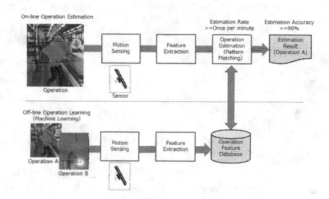

**Fig. 2.** System architecture

## 2 Development of Operation Estimation Method

### 2.1 Introduce of Dynamic Time Warping Algorithm (DTW)

The Dynamic Time Warping algorithm (DTW) is a well-known algorithm in many areas: handwriting and online signature matching [1, 2], sign language recognition [3] and gestures recognition [3, 4], data mining and time series clustering (time series databases search) [5–10], computer vision and computer animation [11], surveillance [12], protein sequence alignment and chemical engineering [13], music and signal processing [11, 14, 15].

DTW algorithm has earned its popularity by being extremely efficient as the time-series similarity measure which minimizes the effects of shifting and distortion in time by allowing "elastic" transformation of time series in order to detect similar shapes with different phases. Given two time series $X = (x_1, x_2, \ldots x_N), N \in N$ and $Y = (y_1, y_2, \ldots y_M), M \in N$ represented by the sequences of values (or curves represented by the sequences of vertices) DTW yields optimal solution in the O (MN) time which could be improved further through different techniques such as multi-scaling [14, 15]. The only restriction placed on the data sequences is that they should be sampled at equidistant points in time (this problem can be resolved by re-sampling). If sequences are taking values from some feature space $\Phi$ than in order to compare two different

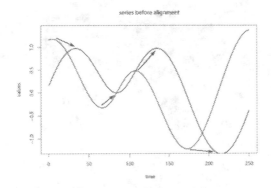

**Fig. 3.** Raw time series, arrows show the desirable points of alignment

sequences $X, Y \in \Phi$ one needs to use the local distance measure which is defined to be a function:

$$d : \Phi \times \Phi \rightarrow R \geq 0 \tag{1}$$

Intuitively d has a small value when sequences are similar and large value if they are different. Since the Dynamic Programming algorithm lies in the core of DTW it is common to call this distance function the "cost function" and the task of optimal alignment of the sequences becoming the task of arranging all sequence points by minimizing the cost function (or distance). Algorithm starts by building the distance matrix $C \in R^{N \times M}$ representing all pairwise distances between X and Y (Fig. 4). This distance matrix called the

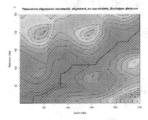

**Fig. 4.** Time series alignment, cost matrix heat map.

local cost matrix for the alignment of two sequences X and Y:

$$C_1 \in R^{N \times M} : c_{i,j} = kx_i - y_ik, \ i \in [1 : N], j \in [1 : M]$$

Once the local cost matrix built, the algorithm finds the alignment path which runs through the low-cost areas - "valleys" on the cost matrix, Fig. 5. This alignment path (or warping path, or warping function) defines the correspondence of an element $x_i \in X$ to $y_i \in Y$ following the boundary condition which assigned first and last elements of X

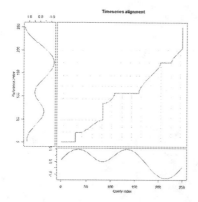

**Fig. 5.** The optimal warping path aligning time series from the Fig. 3.

and Y to each other, Fig. 6. Formally speaking, the alignment path built by DTW is a sequence of points $p = (p_1, p_2, \ldots, p_k)$ with $pl = (pi, pj) \in [1 : N] \times [1 : M]$ for $I \in [1 : k]$.

## 2.2    The Improved DTW

We optimized the DTW algorithm according to the order of the human motion. In the whole action routines, every section is in a certain sequence, will not be disorder. For example, the Sect. 3 can only happen before the Sect. 4, and not happen before the Sect. 2. Therefore, according to the sequence of section, we can fix the error results, the evaluation accuracy were improved more than 10%.

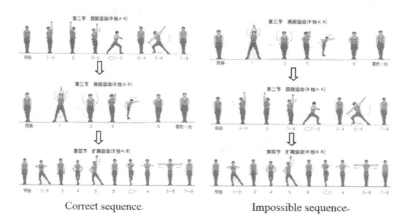

Correct sequence.                          Impossible sequence.

**Fig. 6.** Correct sequence and impossible sequence

## 3    Experiment Conclusion

### 3.1    Data and Evaluation Formula

6 persons (Fig. 7) did Chinese gymnastic (Fig. 8) as data set. Each section has n activities, which are labeled as 1, 2 …, n.

**Fig. 7.** Collecting data

**Fig. 8.** Chinese gymnastic

The evaluation formula:

$$D(m) = |R(m) - C(m)|$$

$$A = 1 - \frac{\sum_{m=1}^{M} D(m)}{M}$$

(a)  m: Number of frames
(b)  C(m): the estimated completion of work
(c)  R(m): the practical completion of work
(d)  A: Accuracy

## 3.2    Results

The average accuracy of DTW is 86% (Fig. 9). The blue line is ground truth and the red line is test result. X axis: Length of the test job, Y axis: Activities and the complete degree.

**Fig. 9.**  The DTW results (Color figure online)

The average accuracy of improved DTW is 97.63% (Fig. 10).

**Fig. 10.**  The improved DTW results

## 4    Conclusion and Future Work

In this paper, we improved DTW algorithm to estimate the whole working progress completion, to use gymnastics data of 6 person's to cross test, the average accuracy is more than 90%. The result show when to use one person's data as template, himself data as test data, the result is almost 99%. If to use other person data as test data, or when the skeleton was lost by Kinect, the result is not good enough. In the future research we will resolve above problems.

**Acknowledgment.** This project was completed with the Mitsubishi Heavy Industries cooperation, and was funded by the Mitsubishi Heavy Industries research project No.14-36.

# References

1. Efrat, A., Fan, Q., Venkatasubramanian, S.: Curve matching, time warping, and light fields: new algorithms for computing similarity between curves. J. Math. Imaging Vis. **27**(3), 203–216 (2007). http://dx.doi.org/10.1007/s10851-006-0647-0
2. Tappert, C.C., Suen, C.Y., Wakahara, T.: The state of the art in online handwriting recognition. IEEE Trans. Pattern Anal. Mach. Intell. **12**(8), 787–808 (1990). http://dx.doi.org/10.1109/34.57669
3. Kuzmanic, A., Zanchi, V.: Hand shape classification using DTW and LCSS as similarity measures for vision-based gesture recognition system. In: EUROCON, 2007. The International Conference on Computer as a Tool 2007, pp. 264–269. http://dx.doi.org/10.1109/EURCON.2007.4400350
4. Corradini, A.: Dynamic time warping for off-line recognition of a small gesture vocabulary. In: RATFG-RTS 2001: Proceedings of the IEEE ICCV Workshop on Recognition, Analysis, and Tracking of Faces and Gestures in Real-Time Systems (RATFG-RTS'01). IEEE Computer Society, Washington, D.C. (2001). http://portal.acm.org/citation.cfm?id=882476.883586
5. Niennattrakul, V., Ratanamahatana, C.A.: On clustering multimedia time series data using k-means and dynamic time warping. In: International Conference on Multimedia and Ubiquitous Engineering, MUE 2007, pp. 733–738 (2007). http://dx.doi.org/10.1109/MUE.2007.165
6. Gu, J., Jin, X.: A simple approximation for dynamic time warping search in large time series database, pp. 841–848 (2006). http://dx.doi.org/10.1007/11875581101
7. Bahlmann, C., Burkhardt, H.: The writer independent online handwriting recognition system frog on hand and cluster generative statistical dynamic time warping. IEEE Trans. Pattern Anal. Mach. Intell. **26**(3), 299–310 (2004). http://dx.doi.org/10.1109/TPAMI.2004.1262308
8. Kahveci, T., Singh, A.: Variable length queries for time series data. In: 17th International Conference on Data Engineering, 2001. Proceedings, pp. 273–282 (2001). http://dx.doi.org/10.1109/ICDE.2001.914838
9. Kahveci, T., Singh, A., Gurel, A.: Similarity searching for multiattribute sequences. In: 14th International Conference on Scientific and Statistical Database Management, 2002. Proceedings, pp. 175–184 (2002). http://dx.doi.org/10.1109/SSDM.2002.1029718
10. Euachongprasit, W., Ratanamahatana, C.: Efficient multimedia time series data retrieval under uniform scaling and normalisation, pp. 506–513 (2008). http://dx.doi.org/10.1007/978-3-540-78646-749

11. Dtw-based motion comparison and retrieval, pp. 211–226 (2007). http://dx.doi.org/10.1007/978-3-540-74048-310

12. Zhang, Z., Huang, K., Tan, T.: Comparison of similarity measures for trajectory clustering in outdoor surveillance scenes. In: ICPR 2006: Proceedings of the 18th International Conference on Pattern Recognition (ICPR 2006), pp. 1135–1138. IEEE Computer Society, Washington, D.C. (2006). http://dx.doi.org/10.1109/ICPR.2006.392

13. Vial, J., Nocairi, H., Sassiat, P., Mallipatu, S., Cognon, G., Thiebaut, D., Teillet, B., Rutledge, D.: Combination of dynamic time warping and multivariate analysis for the comparison of comprehensive two-dimensional gas chromatograms application to plant extracts. J. Chromatogr. A (2008). http://dx.doi.org/10.1016/j.chroma.2008.09.027

14. Muller, M., Mattes, H., Kurth, F.: An efficient multiscale approach to audio synchronization, pp. 192–197 (2006)

15. Dynamic time warping, pp. 69–84 (2007). http://dx.doi.org/10.1007/978-3-540-74048-34

# Sex Difference of Saccade Patterns in Emotional Facial Expression Recognition

Yaohui Han, Badong Chen[✉], and Xuetao Zhang

Institute of Artificial Intelligence and Robotics,
Xi'an Jiaotong University, Xi'an, China
chenbd@mail.xjtu.edu.cn

**Abstract.** In this work, we conduct two experiments: the first aims at emotional (sadness, happiness, disgust, fear, anger, shame) and neutral facial expressions recognition and the second investigates how the emotional audio (cry, laugh) affects the recognition for emotional (sadness, happy) and neutral facial expressions. The eye movements data in both experiments are recorded by an SMI eye tracker with 120 Hz sampling frequency. The hidden Markov model (HMM) is then applied to extract the fixation patterns in data. For each emotional block, two HMMs are learned, which are related, respectively, to the emotional and neutral faces. The HMM models are trained using 70% saccade data and tested using the remaining 30% data. The first experiment indicates that the saccade patterns not only relate to the task, but also relate to the emotional stimulations and contexts. In particular, the males and females show significant difference in that the females are more easily affected by sadness facial expressions (negative emotion). The second experiment maintains that the emotional audio has greater impact on the females than on the males while the subjects recognizing the neutral facial expressions. This implies that men and women also display significant difference in audio modulated facial expressions cognition. The findings in this study may be still inconclusive, possibly the results of methodological differences.

**Keywords:** Saccade · HMM · Facial expression recognition · Multi-modality

## 1 Introduction

Cognitive difference between male and female has been an interesting research topic for a long time. So far many efforts have been devoted to this topic, and lots of gender differences in cognition have been found. The females are generally reported to perform better on emotional cognition (Broverman et al. 1972) and in particular, females are well known to evaluate negative emotional stimuli as more arousing than males (Spalek et al. 2015), and masculine characteristics are positively valued more often than feminine characteristics (Broverman et al. 1972). In consideration of the sex difference, a common idea is that male and female show significant distinction in emotional processing. In the past few years, the difference between male and female in emotional facial expression recognition was studied with fMRI, PET, EEG or ERP records (van Hooff et al. 2011; Spalek et al. 2015). However, to date little study has

© Springer Nature Singapore Pte Ltd. 2017
F. Sun et al. (Eds.): ICCSIP 2016, CCIS 710, pp. 144–154, 2017.
DOI: 10.1007/978-981-10-5230-9_16

been conducted with eye movement records, which are quite easy to acquire (few restrictions are placed on the subjects).

Facial expression recognition has been an active research area for several decades. The facial expression recognition was not associated with the eye movements before the first eye tracker was published. Because the eye movement is random and rapid, it is very hard to interpret reasonably. Some early studies showed that the eye movement can be described as the 'saccade and fixation' and the majority of information should be contained in fixation rather than saccade. In many approaches to address the eye movement data, using a Gaussian Mixture Model (GMM) to fit the fixation map is one of the most commonly used methods. Then, the saccade pattern is modeled by the GMM and in particular, the distances among the saccade patterns can be described by the Kullback-Leibler divergences among GMMs. However, the GMM contains simply the spatial information and ignores the temporal information. The eye movement should contain both spatial and time information. So, the eye movement data regarded as dynamic time-series should be more reasonable. However, modeling the eye movement time-series is quite hard because the length of time-series is irregular. The Dynamic Time Warping (DTW) (Petitjean et al. 2014) and Hidden Markov Model (HMM) are two typical dynamic models for eye movement modeling. DTW needs less training data, but its accuracy is worse than that of HMM. In general, the HMM is a better choice (Oates et al. 1999). In recent years, eye movement has been successfully introduced into the facial expression recognition studies. Schurgin pointed out that a unique fixation pattern may emerge for each emotion (Schurgin et al. 2014). Moreover, Schurgin demonstrated that the emotion could be inferred from the fixation data. However, previous studies only considered the vision modality. In fact, the stimulus signals that affect the cognitive response should be multi-modal. Human beings are born to receive different modalities simultaneously during a cognitive process. Some researchers suggest that classification of the emotional facial expressions may be altered by information from the context in which they are embedded, such as body postures (Van den Stock et al. 2007; Aviezer et al. 2008) and speech prosody (Paulmann and Pell 2010). In a word, the emotional cognition could be affected by mixed signals from different modalities. The saccade patterns are related to emotional cognition, and multi-modalities (vision, audio, etc.) should work together on the saccade patterns.

In the present work, we apply the HMM with Gaussian emission densities to model the eye movement. We learn the HMMs directly from the experiment data. Each hidden state in HMM corresponds to a region of interest (ROI). The emission densities of the hidden states are modeled by GMMs. First of all, the eye movement data are divided into testing set and training set. The training set is used to train an HMM that is devoted to interpret an emotional saccade pattern. Then, the testing set is used to evaluate the prediction accuracy with the trained model. In particular, we study the eye movements related to the emotional facial expression recognition from three aspects. First, whether different stimuli will result in distinct saccade patterns under the same task. Second, how about the sex difference related to the emotional facial expression recognition. Third, how will the emotional audio affect the saccade patterns of male and female?

# 2  Experiments

## 2.1  Materials

Twelve subjects that are all college students complete the Experiment 1 and Experiment 2 and the total subjects reap the rewards (7 males, 5 female). During addressing the fixation data, additional 4 subjects were not analyzed due to unreliable eye recordings, typically due to interference from phone, eyeglasses, or bad mood. Picture stimulus consist of 228 gray scale photos got from the Montreal Set of Facial Displays of Emotion (Beaupré and Hess 2005). All pictures are standardized for size (800 * 600 pixels) and background color (gray). The photo set contains 12 different facials. For each of identities, we creak four levels between each emotion and neutral face (Fig. 1): 0% emotional (the neutral face without contribution from the emotional face), 20%, 40%, and 60% emotional intensity. Each identity contains an equal number of three cultures: African, Asian, Caucasian. The SMI eye tracker with 120 Hz sample frequency is essential. The screen was 19-in and with a resolution of 1600 * 900 pixels.

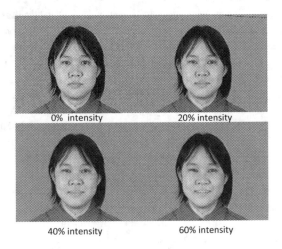

Fig. 1.  Stimulus materials of four levels of emotional intensity.

## 2.2  Experiment 1

The Experiment 1 consists of six emotional blocks (Fig. 2) and each block contains a kind of emotion with different emotional intensity and different cultures. In each block, the emotional intensity (except the neutral face) and cultures are homogeneous and each block contains half of neutral face. The Experiment 1 contains 144 trials and each trial consists of an emotional facial stimulus that is presented on the screen until the subjects make decision (press the space bar) and a question page. The task is to recognize the intensity of emotional face according to their own experiences. In all trails, the task is all the same and the difference is simply the stimulus. In order to improve the accuracy, at the beginning of each block, the calibration (nine-point

**Fig. 2.** Trials sequence in emotional block. Each block contains half of neutral faces and half of emotional faces (20%, 40%, 60%) and the emotional faces are homogeneous in each emotional block.

calibration) is needed. During the calibration, subjects are asked to stare the red dot that moves around the screen fleetly. The calibration is finished until the error is lower than 0.5. At the beginning of the experiment, subjects need to familiarize the operation at the next step.

### 2.3    Experiment 2

The Experiment 2 consists of two emotional blocks (sadness, happy) and each block plays the emotional audio related to the emotional block (crying, laughter). Each block consists of a kind of emotion with different emotional intensity and three cultures (African, Asian, Caucasian). In each block the emotional intensity (except 0% intensity) and cultural backgrounds are homogeneous and each block contains half of neutral faces. The Experiment 2 contains 48 trails and each trial consists of an emotional face stimulus with emotional audio which is presented on the screen until the subjects make decision (press the space bar) and a question page. In all trials, the tasks are all the same and the only difference is the emotional stimulation with corresponding audio. Calibration is also needed as in Experiment 1.

## 3    Methods

### 3.1    Hidden Markov Model

Hidden Markov Model ($\mathcal{M}$) is a generative model involving a double stochastic process, which can be used to model a time-series generated from a Markov process (whose next state is determined only by its current state). The hidden states of an HMM cannot be observed. The transition probability matrix describes the probability with which the current state will transfer to the next state. The emission probability of a hidden state is used to generate the observation data. The prior probability determines the probability of the initial hidden state in HMM. Transition probability matrix, emission probability and prior probability are three key elements of the HMM. In the past decades, HMM was widely used in speech recognition. In recent years, the HMM was applied to model the eye movement (Chuk et al. 2013; 2014). In this work, the hidden states associate with the ROIs and the emission probability of a hidden state is modeled as a two-dimensional GMM in Cartesian space. The HMM can be described by the following mathematical notations:

$$M = \{\pi, A, \{\{C_{\beta m}, \mu_{\beta m}, \Sigma_{\beta m}\}_{m=1}^{M}\}_{\beta}^{S}\}$$

$\beta$ : hidden state

$\pi$ :  prior probability

A: transition probability matrix                                                                  (1)

$C_{\beta m}$ : weight of gauss in GMM of hidden state $\beta$

$\mu_{\beta m}$ : mean value

$\Sigma_{\beta m}$ : variance

The parameters of an HMM can be estimated by the popular *forward-backward* algorithm (Bilmes 1998). The probability value of a time-series could be computed by the *forward* algorithm.

# 4    Results

## 4.1    Insight of Saccade Patterns in Emotional Expression

The fixation locations of participants will result in different saccade patterns such as the eyes for sadness and the lips for happiness. Different fixation areas on the human faces imply different emotional cognition results. Fixation regions contain only spatial information. However, the fixation orders of relevant regions related to a certain emotion are also extremely significant. If one wants to interpret the saccade patterns precisely, the model of saccade patterns should contain both spatial and time information. According to the previous studies, the HMM is a good choice for the time series of eye movement (Chuk 2015). In Fig. 3, we show the saccade regions relating to six emotions that come from the Experiment 1.

## 4.2    Infer the Emotion from Fixation Data

We model the fixation data recorded in Experiment 1 using HMM with Gaussian emission densities for each emotional block. In each emotional block, the fixation data related to emotional face (60% emotional intensity) and neutral face (0% emotional intensity) both are modeled by HMM. In order to calculate the prediction accuracy, we adopt the leave-one-out method. We run leave-one-out method 100 times. Then, we calculate the prediction accuracy of emotional and neutral face respectively. Yarbus illustrated the different tasks will result in distinct saccade patterns (Greene et al. 2012). The inverse Yarbus that is the task could be inferred from the fixation data related to the

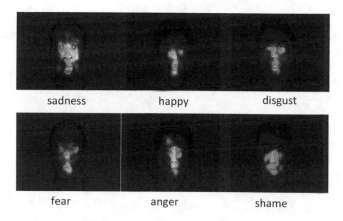

**Fig. 3.** Total fixations of all subjects in each emotional face.

**Table 1.** Results of 100 runs with leave-one-out in 60% emotional intensity. The average prediction accuracy is 28.67% (larger than 1/6).

| 60% Emotional | | | | | | |
|---|---|---|---|---|---|---|
| | Sadness | Happy | Disgust | Fear | Anger | Shame |
| Sadness | 35 | 12 | 9 | 24 | 20 | 0 |
| Happy | 28 | 33 | 5 | 14 | 18 | 2 |
| Disgust | 13 | 7 | 37 | 11 | 20 | 12 |
| Fear | 25 | 4 | 21 | 21 | 15 | 14 |
| Anger | 24 | 12 | 17 | 27 | 12 | 8 |
| Shame | 6 | 12 | 7 | 30 | 11 | 34 |

**Table 2.** Results of 100 runs with leave-one-out in neutral faces (0% emotional intensity). The average prediction accuracy is 27.67% (larger than 1/6). The cause resulting in distances between saccade patterns could not attribute to both stimulation and task (stimulation and task are all the same in six emotional blocks). Actually, in Experiment 1, the difference of neutral faces among six blocks is simply the stimulating context corresponding to different emotional block. In a word, the saccade patterns (paths of eye movement) are not only associated with the task, but also associated with stimulation and corresponding context.

| Neutral face | | | | | | |
|---|---|---|---|---|---|---|
| | Sadness | Happy | Disgust | Fear | Anger | Shame |
| Sadness | 34 | 25 | 16 | 10 | 10 | 5 |
| Happy | 31 | 26 | 11 | 13 | 13 | 6 |
| Disgust | 21 | 15 | 24 | 9 | 11 | 20 |
| Fear | 15 | 13 | 15 | 20 | 17 | 20 |
| Anger | 17 | 23 | 8 | 21 | 18 | 13 |
| Shame | 9 | 7 | 11 | 12 | 17 | 44 |

task has been verified in 2014 (Haji-Abolhassani and Clark 2014). In the Experiment 1, the task is all the same but the stimulus intensity and identity are different. In Table 1, however, we verify the theory that the different emotional stimulus will result in the significant difference of saccade patterns (60% emotional face). In Table 2, we verify stimulating context also extremely associates with saccade patterns (neutral face).

### 4.3  Sex Difference in Emotion Cognition

Gender difference is a hot topic in the past several decades. In recent years, some new research methods (fMRI, PET, ERP, etc.) have been successfully introduced into the research of sex difference (Robin et al. 2003; van Hooff et al. 2011; Spalek et al. 2015). Eye movement has become a pivotal tool in cognitive field since the first eye tracker was invented. However, there is little research about gender difference. According to modern medicine some diseases show significant otherness between male and female. By this taken, the sex difference is very important in medical science. Here, we study the sex difference based on the eye movement that is much easier to use than the previous tools (fMRI, PET, ERP, etc.) in emotional cognition. In particular, we only consider the most classical emotion in Experiment 1: happy (positive), sadness (negative).

First, we divide the eye movement data into two parts according to the gender of subjects and we address fixation data of the male and female respectively. Then, we model each block's fixation data with 60% emotional intensity using HMM with Gaussian emission densities. We adopt the leave-one-out method as in Sect. 4.2.

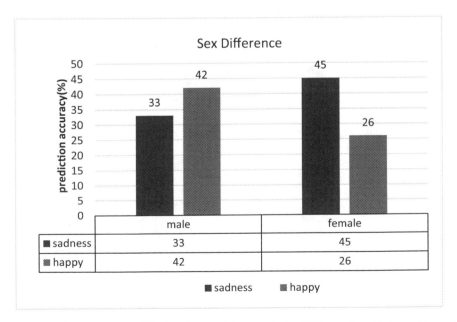

**Fig. 4.** Prediction accuracy of both sadness and happy blocks (60% emotional intensity) in male and female.

Generally, it is well-known that the females are more easily affected by the negative emotions (Spalek et al. 2015). On the other hand, the males are more rational than females. Broverman reported that characteristics ascribed to men are positively valued more often than characteristics ascribed to women (Broverman et al. 1972). The results of this work support the viewpoints mentioned above. The differences are obvious in statistics as shown in Fig. 4.

Results in Fig. 4 show that the saccade patterns of female are more characteristic in sadness faces (negative emotion) than male and the saccade patterns of male are more characteristic in happy faces (positive emotion) than female. In a sense, the results are consistent with the previous study by Spalek and Broverman (Broverman et al. 1972; Spalek et al. 2015). However, the findings are still inconclusive, possibly the results of methodological differences.

### 4.4   Audio Influence on the Saccade Patterns

In emotional cognition science, the facial expression is usually considered to be independent of other modal information. In fact, human can receive different modal information at one moment and combine the signals from different modalities, such as audio, facial, body and so on. In 1985, Noller studied how the signals from different modalities are combined to form the cognitive perception (Noller 1985). Audio plays an important role in human cognition, and in particular, emotional audio can affect

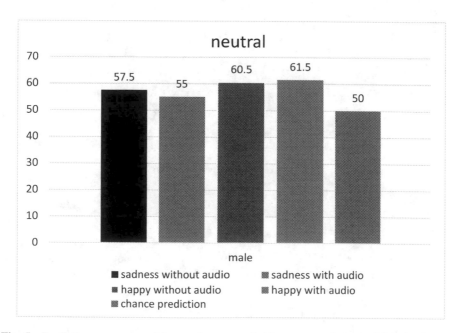

**Fig. 5.** Prediction accuracies with saccade patterns (with respect to the neutral faces) of male in Experiment 1 (without audio) and Experiment 2 (with audio). The figure indicates that the emotional audio has little influence on the saccade patterns of male.

other cognitive modalities such as visual modal. Several studies have applied the audio method in modality recognition (Zeng et al. 2009; Lavan et al. 2014). Recently, Nadine Lavan studied the Multi-modal Information Fusion in emotional cognitive field and demonstrated that the same type of emotional audio can affect the human emotion (laughter on the happy scale and crying on the sad scale) (Lavan et al. 2014).

Here, we model the fixation data related to the neutral faces in sadness and happy blocks of Experiment 1and 2 with HMM. Then, we apply the leave-one-out method as in Sect. 4.2 to evaluate the accuracy. Different from the Experiment 1, the Experiment 2 has the emotional audio. In Experiment 2, when the stimuli are shown on the center of screen, the sadness block plays various cry sounds and the happy block plays various laugher sounds. According to our study, the saccade patterns of the females in Experiment 2 is more obvious than those in Experiment 1. But the saccade patterns of the males in Experiment 2 don't show significant difference when compared with those in Experiment 1. In a word, the females are more sensitive to the emotional audio than the males (Fig. 5).

In this work, we find that the saccade patterns of female are more easily influenced by the emotional audio than the male. In a sense, if not considering the sex, the results are consistent with a previous conclusion that ratings will become higher for laughter on the happy scale and crying on the sad scale (Lavan et al. 2014). The results also support the general viewpoint that the male is more rational than female and the female is more susceptible than male (Fig. 6).

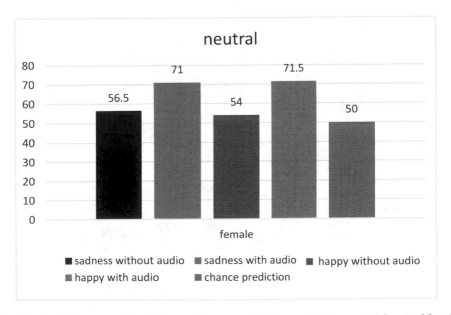

**Fig. 6.** Prediction accuracies with saccade patterns (with respect to the neutral faces) of female in Experiment 1 (without audio) and Experiment 2 (with audio). The figure indicates that the emotional audio has larger influence on the saccade patterns of female.

# 5   Concluding Remarks

In this paper, we use the eye movement data to study the sex difference in emotional facial expression recognition. Two similar experiments are conducted: first experiment based on emotional (sadness, happy, disgust, fear, anger, shame) and neutral facial expressions recognition task and second experiment based on emotional (sadness, happy) and neutral facial expressions with emotional audio (cry, laugh) recognition task. The hidden Markov model (HMM) with Gaussian emission densities is used to model the fixation data recorded using SMI eye tracker with 120 Hz sample frequency. In view of sex difference, we obtain the following results. First, we study the factors (stimulation, context) that impact on the saccade patterns. We find that the context and stimulation are both critical factors associated with saccade patterns. Second, we study the sex difference in saccade patterns based on facial expression recognition tasks. The males and females show significant difference in that the females are more easily affected by sadness facial expressions (negative emotion) than happy facial expressions (positive emotion). Third, we study how the multi-modalities involving vision and audio impact on the saccade patterns of emotional expression recognition. We find that the saccade patterns of the females are more easily influenced by the emotional audio than the males. Maybe the findings in this work are inconclusive, possibly the result of methodological differences.

**Acknowledgements.** This work was supported by the 973 Program (2015CB351703) and the National Natural Science Foundation of China (No. 61372152).

# References

Aviezer, H., et al.: Angry, disgusted, or afraid? Studies on the malleability of emotion perception. Psychol. Sci. **19**(7), 724–732 (2008)

Beaupré, M.G., Hess, U.: Cross-cultural emotion recognition among Canadian ethnic groups. J. Cross Cult. Psychol. **36**(3), 355–370 (2005)

Bilmes, J.A.: A gentle tutorial of the EM algorithm and its application to parameter estimation for Gaussian mixture and hidden Markov models. Int. Comput. Sci. Inst. **4**(510), 126 (1998)

Broverman, I.K., et al.: Sex-role stereotypes: a current appraisal1. J. Soc. Issues **28**(2), 59–78 (1972)

Chuk, T., Chan, A.B., Hsiao, J.: Hidden Markov model analysis reveals better eye movement strategies in face recognition. In: Proceedings of the 37th Annual Conference of the Cognitive Science Society (2015)

Chuk, T., et al.: Understanding eye movements in face recognition using hidden Markov models. J. Vis. **14**(11), 8 (2014)

Chuk, T., et al.: Understanding eye movements in face recognition with hidden Markov model. In: Proceedings of the 35th Annual Conference of the Cognitive Science Society (2013)

Greene, M.R., et al.: Reconsidering Yarbus: a failure to predict observers' task from eye movement patterns. Vis. Res. **62**, 1–8 (2012)

Haji-Abolhassani, A., Clark, J.J.: An inverse Yarbus process: predicting observers' task from eye movement patterns. Vis. Res. **103**, 127–142 (2014)

Lavan, N., Lima, C.F., Harvey, H., et al.: I thought that I heard you laughing: contextual facial expressions modulate the perception of authentic laughter and crying. Cog. Emot. **29**(5), 935–944 (2015)

Noller, P.: Video primacy—A further look. J. Nonverbal Behav. **9**(1), 28–47 (1985)

Oates, T., et al.: Clustering time series with hidden markov models and dynamic time warping. In: Proceedings of the IJCAI-99 workshop on neural, symbolic and reinforcement learning methods for sequence learning. Citeseer (1999)

Paulmann, S., Pell, M.D.: Contextual influences of emotional speech prosody on face processing: how much is enough? Cogn. Affect. Behav. Neurosci. **10**(2), 230–242 (2010)

Petitjean, F., et al.: Dynamic Time Warping averaging of time series allows faster and more accurate classification. In: 2014 IEEE International Conference on Data Mining (ICDM). IEEE (2014)

Robin, O., et al.: Gender influence on emotional responses to primary tastes. Physiol. Behav. **78**(3), 385–393 (2003)

Schurgin, M., et al.: Eye movements during emotion recognition in faces. J. Vis. **14**(13), 14 (2014)

Spalek, K., et al.: Sex-dependent dissociation between emotional appraisal and memory: a large-scale behavioral and fMRI study. J. Neurosci. **35**(3), 920–935 (2015)

Van den Stock, J., et al.: Body expressions influence recognition of emotions in the face and voice. Emotion **7**(3), 487 (2007)

van Hooff, J.C., et al.: The wandering mind of men: ERP evidence for gender differences in attention bias towards attractive opposite sex faces. Soc. Cogn. Affect. Neurosci. **6**(4), 477–485 (2011)

Zeng, Z., et al.: A survey of affect recognition methods: audio, visual, and spontaneous expressions. IEEE Trans. Pattern Anal. Mach. Intell. **31**(1), 39–58 (2009)

# Machine Learning

# Efficient CNN-CRF Network for Retinal Image Segmentation

Yuansheng Luo, Lu Yang, Ling Wang, and Hong Cheng(✉)

Center for Robotics, University of Electronic Science and Technology of China,
Chengdu 611731, Sichuan, China
hcheng@uestc.edu.cn

**Abstract.** The research of retinal vessel segmentation prevails since retinal vessels well indicate the diseases, such as diabetic retinopathy, glaucoma and hypertension. This paper proposes an efficient CNN-CRF framework to segment the vessels from digital retinal images. Our approach combines the prediction ability of CNN and the segmentation ability of CRF, and trains an end-to-end deep learning segmentation model for retinal images. Unlike pixel-wise segmentation, our network is able to segment one image during once network forward computation. When applying our CNN-CRF to the DRIVE database, the average accuracy achieves 0.9536 with the average recall rate of 0.7508, outperforming the state-of-art approaches. And our approach requires only 0.53 s per image, the fastest among deep learning approaches.

**Keywords:** CNN-CRF · Deep learning · Retinal image · Segmentation

## 1 Introduction

The retinal images have an intimate relationship with some ocular diseases, such as diabetic retinopathy, glaucoma and hypertension [4,19] which are the most of crimes making patients blind. It's a fundamental procedure to segment retinal vessels for digitalization analysis of the retinal images [3]. Manual segmentation of retinal images is very arduous and time-consuming, so automatic segmentation by computers becomes mainstream.

Approaches which have been proposed to deal with the retinal image segmentation problem can be categorized into two groups: Rule-based approaches and learning-based approaches.

Rule-based approaches utilize the well-tuned parameters which compose the rules of segmentation to process the images. Chaudhuri *et al.* [5] proposed a Gaussian shape curve to approximate the gray-level profile, and 12 different matched filter were used to detect vessels. Al-Rawi *et al.* [1] used 12 templates with matched filter parameters $\{L, \sigma, T\}$ in different directions to filtering the retinal images, and then choose the best response. Azzopardi *et al.* [3] novelly introduced a B-COSFIRE filter for orientation selectivity to detect vessels. The matched filtering approaches have advantages in detecting bar-shape objects due

© Springer Nature Singapore Pte Ltd. 2017
F. Sun et al. (Eds.): ICCSIP 2016, CCIS 710, pp. 157–165, 2017.
DOI: 10.1007/978-981-10-5230-9_17

to a series of templates which are used to obtain the maximum response, but it also complicate the computation. And the matched filters enhance some bar-shape noises, too. And Martinez-Perez *et al.* [13] proposed an approach utilizing the local maximum over scales of magnitude of the gradient and the maximum principal curvature of the Hessian tensor in a multiple pass region growing procedure. The region growing approaches have to solve a problem that the initial growing seeds must be well assigned. Zana *et al.* [25] proposed an approach based on mathematical morphology and curvature evaluation to detect the vessel-like patterns. Bankhead *et al.* [4] proposed an Isotropic Undecimated Wavelet Transform (IUWT) to process the green-channel retinal image.

Traditional learning-based approaches focus on selecting proper features. Niemeijer *et al.* [16] used kNN classifier, linear classifier and quadratic classifier whose feature vector of each pixel is constructed. And its maximum average accuracy was 0.9416. Soares *et al.* [21] put forward a Bayesian classifier with class-conditional probability dense function with feature vector which included pixel intensity, two-dimensional Gabor wavelet transform responses. Xu *et al.* [24] used adaptive local threshold to produce a binary image then extract large connected components as large vessels, and trained a Support Vector Machine (SVM) to classify pixels of residual binary fragments. Based on the evaluation of the average grey level along lines of fixed length, Ricci *et al.* [18] considered line detector and SVM to classify the retinal image pixels.

Deep learning approaches focus on designing frameworks. [14] proposed a 10-layer deep Convolutional Neural Network (CNN) to do pixel-wise classification. [7] also used it to predict each pixels of electron microscopy images. [10,12] proposed deep learning frameworks to segment retinal images (Figs. 1, 2 and Table 1).

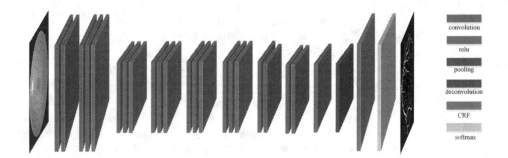

convolution
relu
pooling
deconvolution
CRF
softmax

**Fig. 1.** The structure of our CNN-CRF network

In this paper, our contribution can be summarized as follow:

– The approach this paper proposed is the first that segmentation of one image only requires once forward computation among deep learning approaches. Due to this computation advantage, our network is so efficient that it costs only 0.53 seconds per image.

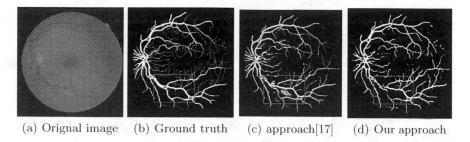

(a) Orignal image    (b) Ground truth    (c) approach[17]    (d) Our approach

**Fig. 2.** The segmentation result. [17] easily misclaissify exudate, important features for diagnosis, but our approach can overcome this problem.

- In this paper, we delicately design a CNN to extract features of vessels. And to better consider spatial information, we concatenate the CRF [26] at the end of CNN to form a deep CNN-CRF network. Our approach achieves average accuracy of 0.9536 with the recall rate of 0.7508.

The rest of this paper is organized as follow. The framework of CNN-CRF is described in Sect. 2. Experiments and analysis are given in Sect. 3. And in Sect. 4, conclusions are drawn.

## 2   CNN-CRF Framework

Our approach can be divided as two parts: CNN is for calculating the energy field, and CRF is for the segmentation.

### 2.1   CNN Energy Supporter

Our CNN part mainly comprises of four different operations–convolution, Rectified Linear Units (ReLU), max-pooling and deconvolution–which can be summarized as the Eq. 1.

$$y_{ij}^l = f_{ks}^l(\{x_{si+\delta i}^l, x_{sj+\delta j}^l\}, 0 < \delta i, \delta j < k) \tag{1}$$

where l is the l-th layer, k the kernel size, s the stride, and $f_{ks}$ the function which is determined by the layer type that a matrix convolution for convolutional layer, a spatial max function for max-pooling layer, and an nonlinear function $max\{0, x\}$ for Relu, an activation layer. And a two connected layers' operation can be presented as Eq. 2.

$$y_{ij}^{l+1} = f_{ks}^{l+1}(\{y_{si+\delta i}^l, y_{sj+\delta j}^l\}, 0 < \delta i, \delta j < k). \tag{2}$$

Convolution performs as a 2D linear filter filtering the whole image. But different from the Gaussian filter whose parameters are fixed during processing, their parameters are learned from training data. So it performs much better. As

**Table 1.** The 25-layer architecture

| Layer | Type | Input shape | Output shape | Filter size | Filter number | Stride |
|---|---|---|---|---|---|---|
| 1 | Convolution | $3 \times 584 \times 564$ | $16 \times 584 \times 564$ | $3 \times 3$ | 16 | 1 |
| 2 | Relu | $16 \times 584 \times 564$ | $16 \times 584 \times 564$ | − | - | - |
| 3 | Convolution | $10 \times 584 \times 564$ | $16 \times 584 \times 564$ | $3 \times 3$ | 16 | 1 |
| 4 | Relu | $16 \times 584 \times 564$ | $16 \times 584 \times 564$ | − | - | - |
| 5 | Max-pooling | $16 \times 584 \times 564$ | $16 \times 293 \times 283$ | $3 \times 3$ | - | 2 |
| 6 | Convolution | $24 \times 293 \times 283$ | $24 \times 293 \times 283$ | $3 \times 3$ | 24 | 1 |
| 7 | Relu | $24 \times 293 \times 283$ | $24 \times 293 \times 283$ | − | - | - |
| 8 | max-Pooling | $24 \times 293 \times 283$ | $24 \times 293 \times 283$ | $3 \times 3$ | - | 1 |
| 9 | Convolution | $24 \times 293 \times 283$ | $24 \times 293 \times 283$ | $3 \times 3$ | 24 | 1 |
| 10 | Relu | $24 \times 293 \times 283$ | $24 \times 293 \times 283$ | − | - | - |
| 11 | Max-pooling | $24 \times 293 \times 283$ | $24 \times 293 \times 283$ | $3 \times 3$ | - | 1 |
| 12 | Convolution | $32 \times 293 \times 283$ | $32 \times 293 \times 283$ | $3 \times 3$ | 32 | 1 |
| 13 | Relu | $32 \times 293 \times 283$ | $32 \times 293 \times 283$ | − | - | - |
| 14 | Max-pooling | $32 \times 293 \times 283$ | $32 \times 293 \times 283$ | $3 \times 3$ | - | 1 |
| 15 | Convolution | $32 \times 293 \times 283$ | $48 \times 293 \times 283$ | $3 \times 3$ | 32 | 1 |
| 16 | Relu | $48 \times 293 \times 283$ | $48 \times 293 \times 283$ | − | - | - |
| 17 | Max-pooling | $48 \times 293 \times 283$ | $48 \times 293 \times 283$ | $3 \times 3$ | - | 1 |
| 18 | Convolution | $48 \times 293 \times 283$ | $48 \times 292 \times 282$ | $3 \times 3$ | 48 | 1 |
| 19 | Relu | $48 \times 292 \times 282$ | $48 \times 292 \times 282$ | − | - | - |
| 20 | Convolution | $48 \times 292 \times 282$ | $48 \times 292 \times 282$ | $3 \times 3$ | 48 | 1 |
| 21 | Relu | $48 \times 292 \times 282$ | $48 \times 292 \times 282$ | − | - | - |
| 22 | Convolution | $48 \times 292 \times 282$ | $2 \times 292 \times 282$ | $3 \times 3$ | 2 | 1 |
| 23 | Deconvolution | $2 \times 292 \times 282$ | $2 \times 584 \times 564$ | $4 \times 4$ | 2 | 2 |
| 24 | CRF | $2 \times 584 \times 564$ | $2 \times 584 \times 564$ | − | - | - |
| 25 | Softmax | $2 \times 584 \times 564$ | $2 \times 584 \times 564$ | - | - | - |

for the ReLU, it sparses receiving data by applying function $max\{0, x\}$, which makes the output of ReLU contains lots of zero whose corresponding position value is negative. In order to keep the size of output of the network as the input label, which is indispensable to compute the loss, a deconvolutional layer is used to upsample data of the last convolutional layer.

## 2.2 CRF Segmentation

CRF is frequently used in pixel-wise label prediction which can be regarded as random variables when conditional upon a global observation [26]. The energy of a fully connected pairwise CRF model can be presented as Eq. 3:

$$E(X) = \sum_i \psi_u(x_i) + \sum_{i<j} \psi_p(x_i, x_j), \qquad (3)$$

where $X$ is a vector of pixels, $x_i$ the i-th pixel's label, $\psi_u(x_i)$ the cost that the i-the pixel is predicted as $x_i$, and $\psi_p(x_i, x_j)$ the cost that the i-th pixel and j-th pixel are simultaneously predicted as $x_i, x_j$ respectively. The $X$ which minimizes the energy $E(X)$ is the exact solution we try to find. But it's intractable for its complexity. We utilize the mean-field CRF inference proposed by [26].

### 2.3  The CNN-CRF Network

The CNN-CRF network is delicately designed to segment vessels from retinal digital images. Different like [6,11,26] finely tuned from VGG [20] designed for recognition, our CNN-CRF network comprises of only one downsample, since results shown in these papers did not deal well with the edges of objects. However, in our task, retinal vessels spread to the image like branches of a tree, and their edges cover 55.99% of the all vessels' pixels. More importantly, the VGG comprising considerable number of parameters in the network, our data are far from enough to train a VGG network.

The CNN part of our CNN-CRF network primarily utilizes convolutional layers to extract the vessels' features, and a deconvolutional layer to upsample the data to the same size as input. And the unary term $\psi_u(x_i)$ and the pairwise energy term $\psi_p(x_i, x_j)$ in Eq. 3 of the CRF are provided by the output of CNN.

One of the most important contribution of this paper is that we introduce the CNN, which is originally designed by ourselves according to the vessel segmentation task, to the full image segmentation. And combined with CRF that obtains its variables which already are very abstract features from the result of CNN, our network performs better on retinal image segmentation.

## 3  Experimental Results

All our experiments are conducted on a computer with one GTX 770 GPU with 2 GB GPU memory. And the deep learning framework we use is caffe [9]. The data set we conduct our experiments on is the DRIVE [22,23] which contains 40 images. But 20 training images are far from enough to optimize the parameters of CNN-CRF network. So we take 10 images (No.1 to No.10) as testing set, and 30 images (No.11 to No.40) as training set. Since the DRIVE images is randomly picked by its author [22], this action is still solid. More importantly, we expand the 30 images to 15750 images by rotating, and flipping each image.

### 3.1  Loss

We have mentioned that our network is trained by two steps. 300,000 iterations are done to train of CNN part. As is shown in Fig. 3(a), the loss of CNN declines dramatically at the first 500 iterations. After 4,000 iterations, the loss decreases again. Finally, at 300,000 iteration, the loss decreases to about 35,000. We concatenate the CRF with CNN, and initiate it with pre-trained parameters. Figure 3(b) illustrates that loss of the full network decreases from about 35,000 to about 30,000 after CNN has been well optimized.

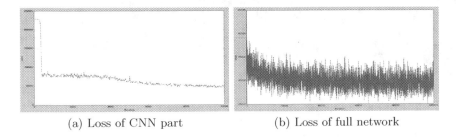

(a) Loss of CNN part          (b) Loss of full network

**Fig. 3.** The loss our experiments.

**Table 2.** Vessel segmentation algorithm times. A comparison of vessel segmentation time for different algorithms applied to DRIVE database. CNN is implemented by ourselves with caffe, and the data is tested on our machine too. And the rest of data is from [4]. It's easy to find that our approach is efficient among learning based approaches, and the accuracy is highest.

| Approach | Processor | RAM | Implementation | Training | Accuracy | Time |
|---|---|---|---|---|---|---|
| **Our approach** | 3.6 GHz | 8 GB | Caffe | Yes | **0.9536** | **0.53 s** |
| CNN [14] | 3.6 GHz | 8 GB | Caffe | Yes | 0.9466 | 452.21 s |
| IUWT [4] | 2.13 GHz | 2 GB | Matlab | No | 0.9371 | 0.093 s |
| Al-Rawl [1] | 1.7 GHz | - | Matlab | Yes | 0.9420 | 2.156 s |
| Anzalone [2] | 2.4 GHz | 192 MB | Matlab | Yes | 0.9419 | < 6 s |
| Espona [8] | 1.83 GHz | 2 GB | C++ | No | 0.9352 | 38.4s |
| Mendonca [15] | 3.2 GHz | 960 MB | Matlab | No | 0.9463 | < 150 s |
| Soares [21] | 2.1 GHz | 1 GB | Matlab | Yes | 0.9466 | 180 s |

## 3.2  Accuracy and Efficiency

The output of the CNN-CRF network is the result of the softmax layer. Therefore, each output pixel is the probability of the corresponding input pixel predicting to be vessel. As is presented in Table 2, the average accuracy of our approach achieves 0.9536. The maximum accuracy is 0.9572 with the recall rate of 0.7428, and the minimum accuracy is 0.9445 with the recall rate of 0.7957. Since the very imbalanced classes of background and vessels, a little improvement of accuracy means a great improvement of segmentation result. It can be proved by recall rate. So the improvement of our approach shown in Table 2 is impressing.

To prove that CRF indeed makes a difference for segmentation, we test the pre-trained CNN too. The segmentation results present that the average accuracy is 0.9486 with the average recall rate of 0.7405. Thus, compared with CNN, the average accuracy of CNN-CRF improves 0.5%.

Our approach, which cost only average 0.53 s per image, is very efficient among the learning-based approaches. The efficiency is due to the framework of our network that takes the full image as the input, and exports the prediction of the full image. Compared with the pixel-wise classification [14] that took a window of pixels to predict the center pixel and predict all pixels of an image one by one in this way and that cost 452.21 s per image, our approach segments one image merely requires once forward of the network.

## 4 Conclusion

In this paper, we propose an efficient CNN-CRF network to segment retinal images. We originally design the network to maintain information of small vessel to improve segmentation. And our network is the first among deep learning approaches that can process one image only requiring once forward computation, leading to the high efficiency of the segmentation, 0.53 s per image. Due to CRF, which widely takes the spatial structure information into consideration, the experiment demonstrates there is an improvement of average accuracy compared with the pure CNN, shown in Sect. 3.2.

Our future work will focus on the refinement of the CNN-CRF network by assigning different proper weights of different labels so that the imbalanced labels make equivalent contribution the loss function.

**Acknowledgment.** The authors would like to thank all the reviewers for their insightful comments. This work was supported by the National Natural Science Foundation of China (Grant No. 61305033, 61273256 and 6157021026), Fundamental Research Funds for the Central Universities (ZYGX2014Z009).

## References

1. Al-Rawi, M., Karajeh, H.: Genetic algorithm matched filter optimization for automated detection of blood vessels from digital retinal images. Comput. Methods Programs Biomed. **87**(3), 248–253 (2007)
2. Anzalone, A., Bizzarri, F., Parodi, M., Storace, M.: A modular supervised algorithm for vessel segmentation in red-free retinal images. Comput. Biol. Med. **38**(8), 913–922 (2008)
3. Azzopardi, G., Strisciuglio, N., Vento, M., Petkov, N.: Trainable cosfire filters for vessel delineation with application to retinal images. Med. Image Anal. **19**(1), 46–57 (2015)
4. Bankhead, P., Scholfield, C.N., McGeown, J.G., Curtis, T.M.: Fast retinal vessel detection and measurement using wavelets and edge location refinement. PloS one **7**(3), e32435 (2012)
5. Chaudhuri, S., Chatterjee, S., Katz, N., Nelson, M., Goldbaum, M.: Detection of blood vessels in retinal images using two-dimensional matched filters. IEEE Trans. Med. Imaging **8**(3), 263–269 (1989)
6. Chen, L.C., Papandreou, G., Kokkinos, I., Murphy, K., Yuille, A.L.: Semantic image segmentation with deep convolutional nets and fully connected CRFs. arXiv preprint arXiv:1412.7062 (2014)
7. Ciresan, D., Giusti, A., Gambardella, L.M., Schmidhuber, J.: Deep neural networks segment neuronal membranes in electron microscopy images. In: Advances in Neural Information Processing Systems, pp. 2843–2851 (2012)

8. Espona, L., Carreira, M.J., Penedo, M., Ortega, M.: Retinal vessel tree segmentation using a deformable contour model. In: 19th International Conference on Pattern Recognition 2008, ICPR 2008, pp. 1–4. IEEE (2008)
9. Jia, Y., Shelhamer, E., Donahue, J., Karayev, S., Long, J., Girshick, R., Guadarrama, S., Darrell, T.: Caffe: Convolutional architecture for fast feature embedding. arXiv preprint arXiv:1408.5093 (2014)
10. Li, Q., Xie, L., Zhang, Q., Qi, S., Liang, P., Zhang, H., Wang, T.: A supervised method using convolutional neural networks for retinal vessel delineation. In: 2015 8th International Congress on Image and Signal Processing (CISP), pp. 418–422. IEEE (2015)
11. Long, J., Shelhamer, E., Darrell, T.: Fully convolutional networks for semantic segmentation. In: Proceedings of the IEEE Conference on Computer Vision and Pattern Recognition, pp. 3431–3440 (2015)
12. Maji, D., Santara, A., Mitra, P., Sheet, D.: Ensemble of deep convolutional neural networks for learning to detect retinal vessels in fundus images. arXiv preprint arXiv:1603.04833 (2016)
13. Martinez-Perez, M.E., Hughes, A.D., Thom, S.A., Bharath, A.A., Parker, K.H.: Segmentation of blood vessels from red-free and fluorescein retinal images. Med. Image Anal. 11(1), 47–61 (2007)
14. Melinščak, M., Prentašić, P., Lončarić, S.: Retinal vessel segmentation using deep neural networks. In: VISAPP 2015 (10th International Conference on Computer Vision Theory and Applications) (2015)
15. Mendonca, A.M., Campilho, A.: Segmentation of retinal blood vessels by combining the detection of centerlines and morphological reconstruction. IEEE Trans. Med. Imaging 25(9), 1200–1213 (2006)
16. Niemeijer, M., Staal, J., van Ginneken, B., Loog, M., Abramoff, M.D.: Comparative study of retinal vessel segmentation methods on a new publicly available database. In: Medical Imaging 2004, pp. 648–656. International Society for Optics and Photonics (2004)
17. Orlando, J.I., Blaschko, M.: Learning fully-connected CRFs for blood vessel segmentation in retinal images. In: Golland, P., Hata, N., Barillot, C., Hornegger, J., Howe, R. (eds.) MICCAI 2014. LNCS, vol. 8673, pp. 634–641. Springer, Cham (2014). doi:10.1007/978-3-319-10404-1_79
18. Ricci, E., Perfetti, R.: Retinal blood vessel segmentation using line operators and support vector classification. IEEE Trans. Med. Imaging 26(10), 1357–1365 (2007)
19. Sangeetha, K., Karthiga, R., Jeyanthi, K.: Advanced analysis of anatomical structures using hull based neuro-retinal optic cup ellipse optimization in glaucoma diagnosis. In: 2012 International Conference on Computer Communication and Informatics (ICCCI), pp. 1–12. IEEE (2012)
20. Simonyan, K., Zisserman, A.: Very deep convolutional networks for large-scale image recognition. arXiv preprint arXiv:1409.1556 (2014)
21. Soares, J.V., Leandro, J.J., Cesar Jr., R.M., Jelinek, H.F., Cree, M.J.: Retinal vessel segmentation using the 2-D gabor wavelet and supervised classification. IEEE Trans. Med. Imaging 25(9), 1214–1222 (2006)
22. Staal, J., Abràmoff, M.D., Niemeijer, M., Viergever, M.A., Van Ginneken, B.: Drive database. http://www.isi.uu.nl/Research/Databases/DRIVE/
23. Staal, J., Abràmoff, M.D., Niemeijer, M., Viergever, M.A., Van Ginneken, B.: Ridge-based vessel segmentation in color images of the retina. IEEE Trans. Med. Imaging 23(4), 501–509 (2004)
24. Xu, L., Luo, S.: A novel method for blood vessel detection from retinal images. Biomed. Eng. Online 9(1), 14 (2010)

25. Zana, F., Klein, J.C.: Segmentation of vessel-like patterns using mathematical morphology and curvature evaluation. IEEE Trans. Image Process. Publ. IEEE Sig. Process. Soc. **10**(7), 1010–1019 (2001)
26. Zheng, S., Jayasumana, S., Romera-Paredes, B., Vineet, V., Su, Z., Du, D., Huang, C., Torr, P.H.: Conditional random fields as recurrent neural networks. In: Proceedings of the IEEE International Conference on Computer Vision, pp. 1529–1537 (2015)

# A Novel Prediction Scheme for Hot Rolled Strip Thickness Based on Extreme Learning Machine

Yonghong Xie[1,2], Jingyu Liu[1,2], Dezheng Zhang[1,2(✉)], and Xiong Luo[1,2(✉)]

[1] School of Computer and Communication Engineering,
University of Science and Technology Beijing, Beijing 100083, China
zdzchina@126.com, xluo@ustb.edu.cn
[2] Beijing Key Laboratory of Knowledge Engineering for Materials Science,
Beijing, China

**Abstract.** In order to predict the hot-rolled strip thickness, two extreme learning machine (ELM)-based thickness modeling algorithms based on clustering and differential evolution algorithm are proposed in this paper. These two kinds of modeling methods are used to predict the thickness, and the experimental results are compared with the standard ELM. The final results show that the two models proposed in this paper are better than the standard ELM model, and these two kinds of modeling methods can be selected according to different production conditions.

**Keywords:** Extreme learning machine (ELM) · Differential evolution · Thickness prediction

## 1 Introduction

To improve the control accuracy of hot-rolled strip thickness, the accuracy of the prediction model of strip thickness can be improved. Since the rolling process of hot-rolled strip has the characteristics of nonlinear, strong coupling and many influence factors, so the prediction accuracy of the traditional setting calculation methods (such as regression empirical formula) has been unable to meet the needs of modern rolling. And because of the high real-time requirements of rolling process, the use of iterative modeling method for modeling in the hot-rolled field is very weak [1].

Artificial neural networks have two characteristics: nonlinearity and adaptive capacity. The network contains a large number of neurons. By adjusting the network connection weights and thresholds, artificial neural networks can approximate nonlinear function with arbitrary accuracy. Therefore, application of artificial neural network modeling in the hot-rolled field is very suitable. Now with the rise of the extreme learning machine theory [2], more and more researchers have applied it to the industrial field.

F. Sun et al. (Eds.): ICCSIP 2016, CCIS 710, pp. 166–172, 2017.
DOI: 10.1007/978-981-10-5230-9_18

## 2 Principle of Extreme Learning Machine

ELM algorithm was first proposed by Guang-Bin Huang in 2004. It is a simple and effective single hidden layer feedforward neural networks (SLFNs). The learning efficiency of ELM is high, and the generalization ability is higher than that of the traditional feedforward neural network [2].

The typical single hidden layer feedforward neural network structure is composed of input layer, hidden layer and output layer. The input vector for the sample set is $[x_1, x_2, \ldots, x_n]^T$, the output vector of the network is $[y_1, y_2, \ldots, y_m]^T$. The connection between two adjacent layers is determined by the connecting factors $\omega$ and $\beta$ [3]. These connecting factors make up the connection weight matrixes.

The mathematical expression of the standard SLFNs, which contains L hidden layer nodes and the activation function $g(x)$, is as follows:

$$\sum_{i=1}^{L} \beta_i g(W_i \cdot X_j + b_i) = o_j, \ j = 1, 2, \cdots, N \tag{1}$$

$\beta_i$   - the ith hidden layer node to the output layer weight matrix, $\beta_i = [\beta_{i1}, \beta_{i2}, \ldots, \beta_{im}]^T$;

$W_i$   - the ith hidden layer node to the input layer weight matrix, $W_i = [\omega_{i1}, \omega_{i2}, \ldots \omega_{in}]^T$;

$b_i$   - the ith hidden layer node threshold.

The single hidden layer neural network learning goal is to make the output of the minimum error. That can be expressed as

$$\sum_{j=1}^{N} \|o_j - t_j\| = 0 \tag{2}$$

That is, there are $\beta_i, W_i$ and $b_i$ making

$$\sum_{i=1}^{L} \beta_i g(W_i \cdot X_j + b_i) = t_j, \ j = 1, 2, \cdots, N \tag{3}$$

That can be expressed as a matrix

$$H\beta = T \tag{4}$$

Among them, $H$ is the output of the hidden layer node, $\beta$ is the output weight, and $T$ is the expected output. That can be expressed

$$H(W_1, \cdots, W_L, b_1, \cdots, b_L, X_1, \cdots, X_L)$$

$$= \begin{bmatrix} g(W_1 \cdot X_1 + b_1) & \cdots & g(W_L \cdot X_L + b_L) \\ \vdots & \cdots & \vdots \\ g(W_1 \cdot X_N + b_1) & \cdots & g(W_L \cdot X_N + b_N) \end{bmatrix}_{N*L} \tag{5}$$

$$\beta = \begin{bmatrix} \beta_1^T \\ \vdots \\ \beta_L^T \end{bmatrix}_{L*m} \qquad T = \begin{bmatrix} T_1^T \\ \vdots \\ T_N^T \end{bmatrix}_{N*m} \tag{6}$$

In most cases, the number of hidden layer nodes is much smaller than the number of samples. In order to be able to train a single hidden layer neural network, we hope to obtain $\beta'$, making

$$\|H\beta' - T\| = min\|H\beta - T\| \tag{7}$$

At the beginning of the learning algorithm, arbitrarily given $\omega$ and $b$ values and then calculate $H$ and make it unchanged, then we need to determine the parameter of only $\beta$. The training of a single hidden layer neural network can be transformed into solving a linear system $H\beta = T$. And the output weight matrix $\beta$ can be determined as

$$\beta' = H^+ T \tag{8}$$

Among them, the matrix $H^+$ is the generalized inverse of matrix $H$. And it can be proved that the norm of the solution $\beta'$ is the smallest and the only one [4].

## 3   ELM Thickness Modeling Based on Clustering

Due to the complicated process and many technical parameters in the strip thickness control, qualitatively classifying by experience or professional knowledge is not able to be exact classification. We use the method of clustering [5]. The samples with greater similarity are classified as a class, then each kind of sample set is modeled. When the production requires a certain thickness of steel, we find the steel with this kind of thickness and use its training model to predict in order to guide production.

Through the establishment of the thickness prediction model, we combine with production data of Beihai Steel Factory and randomly select 522 data items from it to carry on thickness prediction experiment. The 522 data items using the k-mean algorithm is divided into three categories [6].

After determining the centroid position, the three categories of data are obtained. The first category contains 193 data items, the second category contains 193 data items, and the third category contains 136 data items. The three categories of data according to the training sets and test sets respectively use ELM model to train and predict in the group. The predicted results are shown in Fig. 1.

It can be seen that the predicted results of the exit thickness using ELM are very close to the actual results. The predicted results are used to calculate the RMSE, MAE, and MAPE values of the clusters. The values obtained are shown in Table 1.

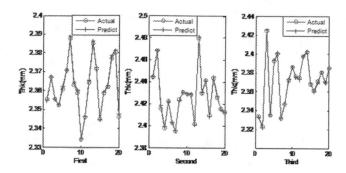

**Fig. 1.** Three kinds of clustering results

**Table 1.** The results of the clustering experiment

|  | The first cluster | | The second cluster | | The third cluster | |
|---|---|---|---|---|---|---|
|  | Train | Test | Train | Test | Train | Test |
| Time(s) | 0.005100 | 0.001000 | 0.005203 | 0.001164 | 0.004433 | 0.001977 |
| RMSE | 0.000369 | 0.000894 | 0.000453 | 0.001010 | 0.000302 | 0.000891 |
| MAE | 0.000311 | 0.000819 | 0.00 | 0.000813 | 0.000241 | 0.000779 |
| MAPE | 1.2 | 3.1 | 1.6 | 3.6 | 1.0 | 3.3 |

It can be seen that the average absolute percent error of the training results and test results of the three categories is all less than 10, and the average absolute error is in the range between 0.0002 and 0.0009. The accuracy of prediction is high, and the thickness prediction is feasible by clustering.

## 4 ELM Thickness Modeling Based on Differential Evolution

As the input weights and thresholds of ELM algorithm are randomly generated, it's hard to avoid appearing the situation of the local optimal solution. Differential evolution algorithm can effectively solve the problem of parameter optimization [7]. Which is realized through four steps.

- Initializing population. Generate random initial population, i = 1, 2,..., NP, where NP is the size of the population.
- Differential mutation. After initialization, the individual in the population is scaled by the differential vector, and the other vector in the population is disturbed to generate a new mutation vector. The equation is

$$v_{i,G+1} = x_{r1,G} + F \cdot \left( x_{r2,G} - x_{r3,G} \right) \tag{9}$$

In formula, F - variation factor, acts on the scaling factor of the differential vector, which interval is in the [0, 2]. $v_{i,G+1}$-mutation vector.

- Cross recombination. When all the mutation vectors are generated, generating test vectors by crossing. The equation of crossover operation is

$$u_{j,i,G+1} = \begin{cases} v_{j,i,G+1} \ if \ rand_{j,i} \leq CR \, or \, j = I_{rand} \\ x_{j,i,G} \ if \ rand_{j,i} > CR \, and \, j \neq I_{rand} \end{cases} \tag{10}$$

In formula, $rand_{j,i} \sim U[0,1]$, and $I_{rand}$ is a random integer in the $(1,2,3,\cdots D)$, where D is the sample dimension. CR - the crossover rate is in the range (0, 1).

- Choice. By comparing the target vector with the test vector, the vector that satisfies the minimum fitness function is selected as the target vector of the next generation. The equation of selecting operation is

$$x_{i,G+1} = \begin{cases} u_{i,G+1} & if f(u_{i,G+1}) \leq f(x_{i,G}) \\ x_{i,G} & others \end{cases} \quad i = 1,2,\ldots,N \tag{11}$$

- Repeat the operation until the required standard is reached.

Using differential evolution algorithm to optimize the parameter values of ELM to predict the thickness of hot rolled strip. The different population variation rate CR and the scaling factor F will affect the differential evolution algorithm and the prediction accuracy [8], so we choose four different F and CR values for comparison. The initial selection coefficients are divided as follows, C1: F = 0.5, CR = 0.8; C2: F = 0.5, CR = 0.3; C3: F = 1, CR = 0.8; C4: F = 1, CR = 0.3.

The population number is set as 200, and the number of iterations is set as 10. The corresponding training sets error is shown in Fig. 2.

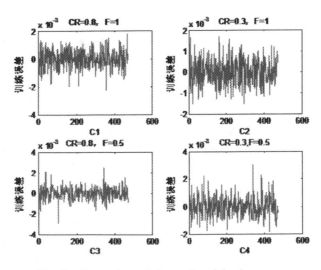

**Fig. 2.** Comparison of the results of the four cases

It can be observed that when the variation rate is different and the scaling factor is same, the training error range of C1 and C2 is between [−0.0002, 0.0002]. In the same case, the C3 and C4 training error are kept in the [−0.004, 0.004]. So it is concluded that the variation rate has no effect on the prediction of the steel rolling thickness. The C1 and C3, C2 and C4 are compared, when the variation rate is same and the scaling factor is different, the scaling factor has influence on the training error. Therefore, we can draw the scaling factor selected for the steel exit thickness prediction has a direct impact.

From the above experiments, when the scaling factor F is 1, the training result of the model is more ideal. Therefore, set it as the setting parameters of the hot rolling strip thickness model, and set the variation rate as 0.8. The comparison chart of the forecast exit thickness and the actual exit thickness is obtained by using the model to learn, which is shown in Fig. 3.

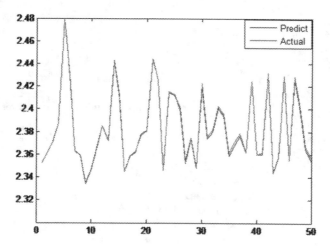

**Fig. 3.** Comparison of actual thickness and forecast thickness

**Table 2.** The results of different methods

| Modeling method | Training set(RMSE) | Test set(RMSE) | Training time(s) |
|---|---|---|---|
| ELM | 0.000463 | 0.001126 | 0.0150 |
| ELM based on clustering | 0.000375 | 0.000936 | 0.0013 |
| DE_ELM | 0.000634 | 0.000823 | 84.4277 |

## 5    Conclusion

The above two modeling methods and the standard ELM in the thickness prediction are compared, as shown in Table 2.

As can be seen from the table, the two modeling methods proposed in this paper are superior to the standard ELM in the training accuracy. ELM based on clustering in thickness prediction application is compared with the standard ELM, the accuracy is improved by about 20% on the original basis and the training time is reduced by 10 times. It can be drawn that the forecasting model of ELM based on clustering is superior to the standard ELM. DE_ELM algorithm compensates the deficiency of the standard ELM, which has local optimal solution due to the input weights and the bias randomly generated. The training accuracy is improved compared with the clustering algorithm. But the overall training time of the network is longest because of the parameters selection. Therefore, in the selection of DE_ELM algorithm to establish a prediction model, we need to be based on the actual production situation.

## References

1. Sun, Y.K.: Model of Control Hot Strip Mill, pp. 124–163. Metallurgical Industry Press, Beijing (2002)
2. Huang, G.B., Zhu, Q.Y., Siew, C.K.: Extreme learning machine: theory and applications. Neurocomputing **70**, 489–501 (2006)
3. Huang, G.B., Zhu, Q.Y., Siew, C.K.: Extreme learning machine: a new learning scheme of feedforward neural networks. In: Proceedings International Joint Conference Neural Networks (IJCNN 2004), pp. 985–990 (2004)
4. Huang, G.B., Chen, L.: Convex incremental extreme learning machine. Neurocomputing **70**, 3056–3062 (2007)
5. Xie, J., Jiang, S., Xie, W., et al.: An efficient global K-means clustering algorithm. J. Comput. **6**(2), 271–279 (2011)
6. Al-Zoubi, M.B., Hudaib, A., Huneiti, A., et al.: New efficient strategy to accelerate k-means clustering algorithm. Am. J. Appl. Sci. **5**(9), 1247–1250 (2008)
7. Lonen, J., Kamarainen, J.-K., Lampinen, J.: Differential evolution training algorithm for feed-forward neural networks. Neural Process. Lett. **7**(1), 93–105 (2003)
8. Gaemperle, R., Mueller, S.D., Koumoutsakos, P.: A parameter study for differential evolution. In: Grmela, A., Mastorakis, N.E. (eds.) Advances in Intelligent Systems, Fuzzy Systems, Evolutionary Computation, pp. 293–298. WSEAS Press, Spain (2002)

# Extreme Learning Machine Based Modified Deep Auto-Encoder Network Classifier Algorithm

Ruimin Cao, Fengli Wang, and Lina Hao[✉]

School of Mechanical Engineering and Automation,
Northeastern University, Shenyang, China
xiaojiacaoruimin@126.com, sdwangfl@163.com,
haolina@me.neu.edu.cn

**Abstract.** Aiming to solving the problem of slow training speed and learning efficiency existed in the deep auto-encoder network, this paper puts forward a new kind of modified deep auto-encoder network model based on extreme learning machine (ELM-MDAE). Through training the deep auto-encoder networks with the training method of extreme learning machine, the classification accuracy and training time of ELM-MDAE are compared with traditional deep auto-encoder network utilizing the rolling bearing fault vibration dataset released by Case Western Reserve University in United States. Experiments turn out to be that the average diagnostic accuracy rate could reach to 98.42%, and the average training time is 3.70 s with the method established in this paper. Therefore, ELM-MDAE possesses a better classification ability and fewer training time.

**Keywords:** ELM-MDAE · Extreme learning machine · Auto-encoder network · Rapid training speed

## 1 Introduction

Due to the development of parallel computing technology, the accumulation of big data and continuous improvement of deep learning algorithms, artificial intelligence has been developed by leaps and bound in a decade, some original applications such as autonomous vehicles, body control recognition, machine translation, natural language recognition and cognitive computing have been reached the practical level [1]. Among them, a great number of deep learning algorithms could realize a deeper abstract level in order to make the distributed feature representation come true [2]. Hin-ton et al. [3] put forward the greedy unsupervised training algorithm based on the Deep Belief Networks (DBN), which brought the hope for solving optimization problems of the deep neural networks. However, due to the explosive growth of data volume and the increasing complexity of the problem, the training time of the traditional deep neural network algorithm increases exponentially, which could not fully meet the requirement of rapid learning and recognition in the era of big data currently.

Professor Guang-bin Huang [4] firstly put forward the Extreme Learning Machine (ELM) theory based on the generalized neural network theory, control theory, matrix

© Springer Nature Singapore Pte Ltd. 2017
F. Sun et al. (Eds.): ICCSIP 2016, CCIS 710, pp. 173–180, 2017.
DOI: 10.1007/978-981-10-5230-9_19

theory and systems theory in 2004. ELM is a kind of Single Hidden Layer Feed-forward Network (SLFN) essentially. During the learning process, it needn't to adjust the weights and biases of the whole network over and over again, thus could greatly improve the learning speed. ELM theory has been successfully applied in signal processing, face recognition, fault diagnosis, market analysis, and aerospace, etc. [5].

Nevertheless, since SLFN has limited capability in the feature abstracting and extracting of big data, some researchers began to explore the combination of ELM theory and traditional deep learning algorithms, i.e. improved the training speed with the training method of extreme learning machine and extracted features utilizing deep learning algorithms. Shi-fei Ding et al. [6] proposed convolution extreme learning machine model through adding the sampling kernels of the convolution layers into the hidden layers of the original ELM for feature extraction and classification. Aiming to solving the problem of high dimension and multi-class in text messages, Hang-xia Zhou et al. [7] put forward the regularized extreme learning machine based on the fast auto-encoder(FA-RELM). Fu-xian Huang et al. [8] put forward the dynamic cost-sensitive extreme learning machine based on the deep imputation network for the classification of the incomplete data.

This paper puts forward a new kind of modified deep auto-encoder network model based on extreme learning machine. Through training the deep auto-encoder networks utilizing the training methods of extreme learning machine, the classification accuracy and training time of ELM-MDAE are compared with traditional deep auto-encoder network utilizing the rolling bearing fault vibration dataset released by Case Western Reserve University in United States.

## 2    ELM-MDAE Algorithm

### 2.1    Deep Auto-Encoder Network

Auto-encoder network is a kind of unsupervised learning network which is put forward by Hinton et al. [9] in 2006. It is a triple-layer network structure. Supposing that there are totally N unlabeled samples $\{x_i | x_i \in R^n\}_{i=1}^N$, it essentially trains the identity function which is shown as formula (1)

$$h_{w,b}(x) = x \tag{1}$$

The training process of auto-encoder network is divided into two parts: encoding and decoding. Figure 1 shows the training process of auto-encoder network. Encoder is the mapping process between input data $x$ and hidden layer $h$; meanwhile, decoder is the mapping between the hidden layer $h$ and the reconstructed data $\hat{x}$ in the output layer, which is shows as formulas (2) and (3)

$$h = f(W \cdot x + b) \tag{2}$$

$$\hat{x} = g(W' \cdot h + b') \tag{3}$$

Where $f$ and $g$ represent the firing function respectively, $f$ could be some nonlinear function typically, such as Sigmoid function, Gaussian function and so on. $g$ could be some linear function or Sigmoid function; $W$ and $W'$ assign the weights of input-hidden layer and hidden-output layer respectively, $b$ and $b'$ assign the biases of hidden layer and output layer.

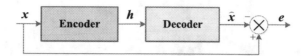

**Fig. 1.** The training process of auto-encoder network

Auto-encoder network could obtain hidden layer $h$ through the encoding process. Decoder reconstructs the hidden layer to be $\hat{x}$ during the decoding process, thus the target of the training process of auto-encoder is to minimize the reconstruction error, as shown in formula (4)

$$e = |x - \hat{x}| \tag{4}$$

Generally, the optimization target could be described as the formula (5)

$$J(w, b) = \frac{1}{2}\|\hat{x} - x\|^2 = 0 \tag{5}$$

Deep auto-encoder network is a kind of deep neutral network, whose training process is consist of two parts, i.e. unsupervised pre-training process and supervised trimming process. Through extracting the complex representation of high-dimensional data, finally we could obtain the distributed feature of original data. Figure 2 shows the training process of auto-encoder network, which includes the following steps:

(1) Unsupervised pre-training
  (1) The input data could generate the encoded data $h_1$ with encoder $E_1$, and reconstructs the input data utilizing the decoder $D_1$. When the reconstruction error is minimized in proposed limit, we could get a well-trained encoder $E_1^*$ and encoded data $h_1^*$;
  (2) Taking the encoded data $h_1^*$ as the input data, we could generate the encoded data $h_2$ with encoder $E_2$, and reconstructs the encoded data $h_2$ utilizing the decoder $D_2$. When the reconstruction error is minimized in proposed limit, we could get a well-trained encoder $E_2^*$ and encoded data $h_2^*$;
  (3) Repeating the training process of the steps (1) and (2),taking the former encoded data $h_{i-1}^*$ as the input of the next encoder $E_i^*$, until all the training process of the hidden layers are completed.

(2)  Supervised trimming

   In order to obtain the classification capability in the deep auto-encoder network, we add a classifier after the encoders. The function of supervised trimming is to further adjust the weights and biases to the well-trained network with labelled samples. After iterated for several times, the weights and biases could be further optimized.

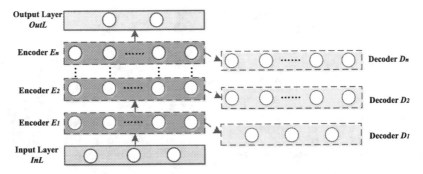

**Fig. 2.** The training process of deep auto-encoder network

## 2.2  Extreme Learning Machine

Extreme learning machine is essentially a generalized single hidden layer feed-forward networks (SLFN) [10], as is shown in Fig. 3.

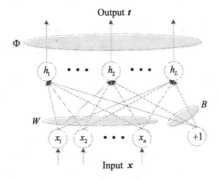

**Fig. 3.** The model of extreme learning machine

For a given N training samples $\{x_i, t_i | x_i \in R^n, t_i \in R^m\}_{i=1}^N$, its model is expressed as formula (6)

$$\sum_{i=1}^N g(w_j \cdot x_i + b_j)\phi_j = o_i, j = 1, 2, \cdots, L \qquad (6)$$

Where $w_j$ and $b_j$ are the weights and biases associated with the neurons of $j^{th}$ hidden layers respectively, both of them are given randomly. $\phi_j \in R^m$ represents the output weights of $j^{th}$ hidden layers. $g$ and $L$ represent the firing function and number of neurons of hidden layers respectively, $o$ represents the desired output. The learning goal of the extreme learning machine is shown as formula (7)

$$\sum_{i=1}^{N} \|o_i - t_i\| = 0 \tag{7}$$

Where $t$ assigns the actual output. Then the solution to extreme learning machine could be translated as the following optimal problem

$$\min_{W,B,\Phi} \sum_{j=1}^{L} \left\| \sum_{i=1}^{N} g(w_j \cdot x_i + b_j)\phi_j - t_i \right\|^2 \tag{8}$$

Since $W$ and $B$ satisfied some continuous probability distribution are given randomly, we could say, when $W$ and $B$ are regulated, and $H = H(W,B) = (h_{ij})_{N \times L}$, $h_{ij} = g(w_j \cdot x_i + b_j)$, $T = [t_1, t_2, \cdots, t_N]$, $\Phi = [\phi_1, \phi_2, \cdots, \phi_L]$, then the formulas (6) and (7) could be translated as formula (9)

$$H\Phi = T \tag{9}$$

Formula (8) is equivalent to solving the generalized Moore-Penrose inverse of formula (9) through least norm least square to get the output weights $\Phi$:

$$\Phi = H^{\dagger}T = (H^T H)^{-1} H^T T \tag{10}$$

Where $H^{\dagger}$ assigns the generalized Moore-Penrose inverse.

## 2.3    ELM-MDAE Algorithm

In the traditional constructing process of deep auto-encoder network, some auto-encoder networks should be established at first, and then adjust parameters of each encoder utilizing BP algorithm, which drop the training speed and make generalization ability worse. Extreme learning machine directly calculates the generalized Moore-Penrose inverse to get the output matrix $\Phi$ based on the least square theory, which greatly improves the training speed and efficiency.

In addition, we make some improvements based on the formula (10) by adding a regularization item to become the following formula [11]:

$$\Phi = \begin{cases} H^T \left(\frac{I}{C} + H^T H\right)^{-1} T & \text{if } N \leq L \\ \left(\frac{I}{C} + H^T H\right)^{-1} H^T T & \text{if } N > L \end{cases} \tag{11}$$

Among them, $C$ assigns the regularization coefficient, $I$ assigns the unit matrix, $N$ and $L$ assign the number of samples and hidden layer neurons respectively. This difference could improve the generalization and robustness of the network.

Thus, we train the auto-encoder network with the training method of extreme learning machine instead of the repeated training process to improve the training efficiency of deep auto-encoder network. Figure 4 shows the flowchart of modified deep auto-encoder network algorithm.

## 3  Simulation

We test the performance of ELM-MDAE utilizing the rolling bearing fault vibration dataset released by Case Western Reserve University in United States. A total of 3600 samples of the bearing health status are divided into 4 categories, namely, normal, fault at outer rings, fault at inner rings and fault at rolling elements.

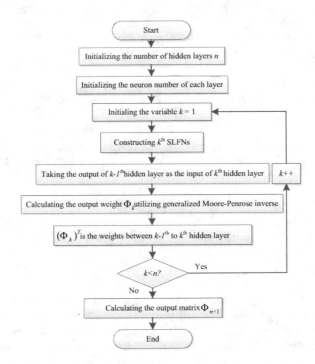

**Fig. 4.** The flowchart of modified deep auto-encoder network algorithm

Then construct an ELM-MDAE network with 6 layers whose structure is 1600-1500-100-400-100-4. Correspondingly, a DAE network with 6 layers is also established, and its structure is 1600-400-200-100-50-4. In order to reduce the influence of random factors to the test results, the experiment is repeated for 10 times. The simulation environment is MATLAB2014a on 64-bit Windows7.0, RAM is 8 GB.

Figure 5 shows the 10 times' diagnostic results of both networks respectively and statistics results are shown in Table 1. As we could see, the average and maximal diagnostic accuracy of DAE reached to 97.73% and 98.44% respectively; on the other

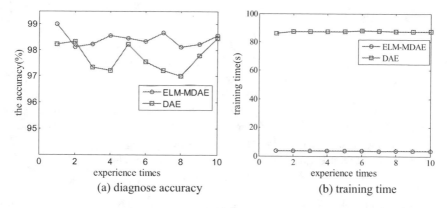

Fig. 5. Diagnose performance with 10 simulation times

hand, the average and maximal diagnostic accuracy of ELM-MDAE reached 98.42% and 99.00% respectively. In addition, the standard deviation of diagnostic results utilizing the ELM-MDAE network is only 0.28%, which is extremely better than 0.54% of the DAE network. These results show that the proposed method can not only achieve a better classification performance, but also be more stable than the DAE, which also indicates that the deep auto-coder network with the extreme learning machine methods could find the optimal solution, while the traditional training methods tends to find the suboptimal solutions.

Traditional training methods require adjusting the weights and biases of each layer reiteratively and therefore consume a lot of learning time; while in the method proposed in this paper, the weights and biases of each layer is training by directly calculating the generalized Moore-Penrose inverse, thus it can greatly improve the training speed. As it can be seen from Table 1, the average training time of the traditional methods is 87.34 s, while the average training time of the proposed method is only 3.70 s, the train speed increases by 23 times.

Literature [7] trained the two-layer auto-encoder utilizing extreme learning machine, and had good classification efficiency. However, literature [7] didn't put forward a deeper network structure. ELM-MDAE proposed in this paper could construct a deep layer network structure, thus greatly improve the training speed.

Table 1. Statistics values with 10 simulation times

| Methods | Classification accuracy | | | Training time | |
|---|---|---|---|---|---|
| | Maximal (%) | Average (%) | Std (%) | Average (s) | Std (%) |
| ELM-MDAE | 99.00 | 98.42 | 0.28 | 3.70 | 7.843 |
| DAE | 98.44 | 97.73 | 0.54 | 87.34 | 55.33 |

## 4  Conclusion

With respect to the problem of slow training speed and learning efficiency existing in Deep auto encoder network, we put forward the ELM-MDAE network, which means training the DAE network utilizing the training methods of ELM. Taking the fault vibration dataset of rolling bearing released by Case Western Reserve University in United States as samples, we compare the classification accuracy and training time of both networks. Experiments turn out to be that the average diagnostic accuracy and the average training time of the ELM-MDAE network could reach 98.42% and 3.70 s respectively. Therefore, ELM-MDAE possesses a better classification ability and lower training time.

**Acknowledgements.** This work was particularly supported by the National High Technology Research, Development Program of China (863 program) under Grant No. 2015AA042302, NSFC under grant 61573093. The authors would also like to sincerely thank the reviewers and editors for their very pertinent remarks that helped this article become clearer and more precise.

## References

1. Kelly, K.: The three breakthroughs that have finally unleashed AI on the world. Wired Online Edition (2014)
2. Schmidhuber, J.: Deep learning in neural networks: an overview. Neural Netw. **61**, 85–117 (2015)
3. Hinton, G.E., Osindero, S., Teh, Y.W.: A fast learning algorithm for deep belief nets. Neural Comput. **18**(7), 1527–1554 (2006)
4. Huang, G.B., Zhu, Q.Y., Siew, C.K.: Extreme learning machine: a new learning scheme of feedforward neural networks. In: 2004 IEEE International Joint Conference on Neural Networks, Proceedings, vol. 2, pp. 985–990. IEEE (2004)
5. Ding, S., Zhao, H., Zhang, Y., et al.: Extreme learning machine: algorithm, theory and applications. Artif. Intell. Rev. **44**(1), 103–115 (2015)
6. Ding, S., Guo, L., Hou, Y.: Extreme learning machine with kernel model based on deep learning. Neural Comput. Appl. 1–10 (2016)
7. Zhou, H., Ye, J., Ren, H.: Text classification based on fast Auto-encoder RELM. Comput. Eng. Sci. **5**, 871–876 (2016). (in Chinese)
8. Huang, F., Liu, C., Huang, Y., et al.: Dynamic cost-sensitive extreme learning machine for classification of incomplete data based on the deep imputation network. Int. J. Database Theor. Appl. **9**(6), 285–298 (2016)
9. Hinton, G.E., Salakhutdinov, R.R.: Reducing the dimensionality of data with neural networks. Science **313**(5786), 504–507 (2006)
10. Huang, G.B., Zhu, Q.Y., Siew, C.K.: Extreme learning machine: theory and applications. Neurocomputing **70**(1), 489–501 (2006)
11. Huang, G.B., Bai, Z., Kasun, L.L.C., et al.: Local receptive fields based extreme learning machine. IEEE Comput. Intell. Mag. **10**(2), 18–29 (2015)

# An Approach of Ship Routing Plan Based on Support Vector Machine

Chuang Zhang[1(✉)] and Chen Guo[2]

[1] Navigation College, Dalian Maritime University, Dalian 116026, China
zhchuangdmu@163.com
[2] School of Information Science and Technology,
Dalian Maritime University, Dalian 116026, China
dmuguoc@126.com

**Abstract.** This paper focuses on a new approach of applying a pattern classification technique to ship routing plan. A safe path between a start point and a destination provides information about the space region partition. In the case of 2D routing plan, the route classifies the space into two districts. This means a dual problem of first classifying the entire space into two districts and then picking out the border as a route. We propose a novel approach to solve this dual problem based on support vector machine (SVM). SVM produces a non-linear separating surface on the basis of the margin maximization principle. This feature is applied to the objective of common routing plan problems, that is, generating a non-collision and smooth route. The effectiveness of the proposed approach is demonstrated by using several routing plan results in 2D spaces.

**Keywords:** Routing plan · Support vector machine · Margin maximization

## 1 Introduction

From its inception, the research of ship routing plan has generated wonderful hopes. To this day the subject persists wide open and is incessantly evolving. Routing plan is normally reckoned as finding a consecutive safe route, given a start point and a destination, and obstacles in the space.

Early in works, Graph-based routing plan essays to shrink the world of robot to a chart and then apply search algorithms of chart to find a solution. Voronoi diagram is another common idea [1] and requests surrounded obstacles within 2D polygon. Grid-based routing plan separates the surroundings into cells, shrinking the problem to a C-space search. It is convenient for used in practical problems in virtue of the fact that no former knowledge of the environment is indispensable. An additional benefit is that they can work with observations of the environment.

At present, the randomized methods [2–4] come out in lots of actual applications that request high-dimensional routing plan. Searching algorithms run through all these works. Formers works about routing plan majorly take an empirical approach that a route is set up from a set of pervious route elements. This paper focuses on routing plan from a different perspective. Let us consider a ship moving among planar obstructions. A safe route, connecting a start point and a destination, classifies the entire space into.

© Springer Nature Singapore Pte Ltd. 2017
F. Sun et al. (Eds.): ICCSIP 2016, CCIS 710, pp. 181–188, 2017.
DOI: 10.1007/978-981-10-5230-9_20

two districts: one on the left and the other on the right of the routing plan. This means a dual problem of first classifying the entire space into two districts and then picking out the border as a route. Classify the entire space into two districts can be regarded as a two-class classification problem. In the pattern recognition domain, various classification methods have been deduced.

We make use of support vector machine among them [5]. SVM is a powerful machine learning methods for classification and regression problems of small samples and high dimensions, and has been applied to many fields such as fault diagnosis, face recognition, and pattern matching-based tracking.

SVM has the many advantages can be highlighted in routing plan:

- The first one uses SVM to generate non-linear separating surfaces, which apply to improving or smoothing routes.
- The second one uses idea of margin maximization of SVM to apply to the strategy of finding safety in routing plan.
- SVM can compute optimal separating surfaces with a lower cost, compared to integrated methods.

This paper narrates routing plan based on support vector machine.

## 2  Support Vector Machine Scheme

### 2.1  Margin Maximization

SVM is a binary classification system that seeks the optimal separating hyper plane on the basis of the method of margin maximization [6].

Supposing there is a sample dataset $\{(x_1, t_1), \cdots, (x_N, t_N)\}, x_i \in R^m, t_i \in \{-1, +1\}$, let dataset as the training data as divided by a hyper plane $w^T x - h = 0$. The training data are linearly separable, then $w$ and $h$ are given by:

$$t_i(w^T x_i - h) \geq 1, (i = 1, 2, \cdots, N) \tag{1}$$

According to these parameters, the two classes are divided into two hyper planes, $H_1 : w^T x - h = 1$ and $H_2 : w^T x - h = -1$, and without data exist between the hype planes. Owing to the range between the hyper planes is $2/\|w\|$, the optimum parameters are decided by minimizing the target function, meanwhile Eq. (1) bound Eq. (2).

$$L(w) = \|w\|^2/2 \tag{2}$$

To solve this problem, a scheme is proposed by dealing with the following dual problem that is to maximize:

$$L_D(\alpha) = \sum_{i=1}^{N} \alpha_i - \frac{1}{2} \sum_{i,j=1}^{N} \alpha_i \alpha_j t_i t_j x_i^T x_j \tag{3}$$

under the constraints:

$$\sum_{i=1}^{N} \alpha_i t_i = 0, \alpha_i \geq 0 (i = 1, 2, \cdots, N) \tag{4}$$

The training sample $x_i$ with non-zero $\alpha_i$ are belong to the hyper planes $w^T x - h = 1$ or $w^T x - h = -1$. These data are defined as support vectors on account of they are the sole data that decide the parameters. A discrimination function is obtained by considering these data:

$$y = \text{sign}(w^T x - h) = \text{sign}(\sum_{i \in S} \alpha_i t_i x_i^T x - h) \tag{5}$$

where $S$ demonstrates the set of index for support vectors.

## 2.2   Soft Margin

In the case of linearly separable, all data are beyond the district constructed by two hyper planes, $H_1$ and $H_2$. We move some samples of any hyper plane into the opposite region condition that data are not linearly separable. Replace Eq. (2), we use this formula:

$$L(w) = \frac{1}{2} \|w\|^2 + \gamma \sum_{i=1}^{N} \xi_i \tag{6}$$

where $\xi_i \geq 0$ is slack variable and $\gamma$ is a weight that measures the error decrease and the margin maximization. $\alpha_i$ will not only satisfies the support vectors in the hyper planes, $\alpha_i = \gamma$, but also satisfies the support vectors on one of hyper planes, $H_1$ and $H_2$, includes the in equation $0 < \alpha_i < \gamma$.

## 2.3   Not Linearly SVM

SVM are suitable for ensure the not linearly separable surfaces using kernel function [7].

In this study, proper kernel function is adopted because its good properties and universal usage, we can alter the puzzles of seeking a not linearly separable surface in the primitive space into that of seeking a separable hyper plane in the high dimensional space, therefore decreasing computational cost and making it possible to achieve an optimum not linearly separable surface in the primitive space.

Supposed $\pi$ is the mapping from the primitive to the high-dimensional space, the mapping can be described by kernel function $K$:

$$\pi(x_1)^T \pi(x_2) = K(x_1, x_2) \tag{7}$$

Considering the discrimination of the high-dimensional space, the primitive target function, such as Eq. (3), is amended by

$$L_D(\alpha) = \sum_{i=1}^{N} \alpha_i - \frac{1}{2} \sum_{i,j=1}^{N} \alpha_i \alpha_j t_i t_j K(x_i, x_j) \qquad (8)$$

Meanwhile the discriminant function, such as Eq. (5), is amended by

$$y = \text{sign}(\sum_{i \in S} \alpha_i t_i K(x_i, x) - h) \qquad (9)$$

As the whole essential calculations inside the high-dimensional space is provided by kernel function from the primitive space, not linearly separating surfaces can be given. Not linearly classification is shown in Fig. 1. Where small box symbols mean positive data and cross symbols mean negative data. Blue, wathet and white districts mean positive, intermediate, and negative districts, respectively. Samples with larger boxes are support vectors.

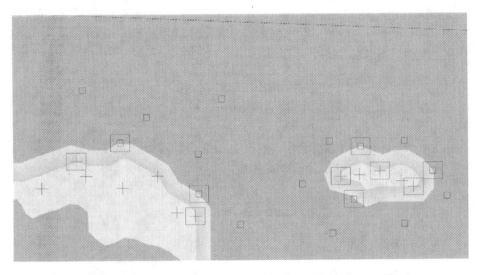

**Fig. 1.** Gaining not linearly separating surfaces (Color figure online)

## 3  Routing Plan Based on SVM

### 3.1  Pre-processing and Post-processing for Using SVM to Route Plan

Supposed $V$ is the outcome of Eq. (10):

$$V = \sum_{i \in S} \alpha_i t_i K(x_i, x) - h \qquad (10)$$

The total space is separated into the three districts according to the size of $V$. in Fig. 1: $V \geq 1$ and $V \leq -1$ are positive and negative district, respectively, however $-1 < V < 1$ means intermediate district.

On condition that we construct the three districts in order to whole obstacles are within positive or negative regions, a safe route can be generated inside intermediate regions. In order to do this, obstacles are indicated by two classes, and positive sample data which support vector learning have constructed by one class, whereas another class generate negative samples. Meanwhile we also lay fictitious obstacles near a start point and a destination in order to make them inside intermediate districts.

Sometimes both a start point and a destination lie inside intermediate districts, it is not possible that the two points are within the identical intermediate district, because different portions are included inside intermediate districts in Fig. 1. This state occurs primarily because uneven distribution of sample data. Hence we increase a number of data on the name of lead samples to deal with this.

## 3.2    2D Routing Plan Scheme

(1) The summary of the scheme is following:
   (a) Lay fictitious obstacles near a start point and a destination.
   (b) Initialize and define positive and negative samples for the obstacle.
   (c) Set lead samples in order to involve the wide district.
   (d) Create samples and gain a credible route by researching the learned model using SVM.
   (e) Repeat the step (b) until a termination condition has been reached.
(2) Lay fictitious obstacles near a start point and a destination:
   We lay fictitious obstacles near a start point and a destination in order to comprises the points in the intermediate district as shown in Fig. 2(b). More specifically, we compute the line linking the points and define as nominal line, and define $N_v$ as positive on the right side of nominal line and $N_v$ negative on the opposite side at a fixed interval $d_v$ and make sure parallel with the nominal line.
(3) Initialize and generate sample:
   Supposed the nominal line lies in left side of the centroid of an obstacle, the obstacle is marked as positive, and vice versa. In terms of every obstacle, we create samples which contain all the vertices of edges as shown in Fig. 2(c).
(4) Assigning lead samples:
   Lead samples are connected by solid lines in Fig. 2(d) and (f) are set to the nominal line parallel and fixed distance is $d_g$ away the line, meanwhile distance $d_p$ is also certain between samples. In the event of an obstacle proceeds to the opposite side, the lead samples on the same side are transformed base on how far the obstacle have shifted as shown in Fig. 2(f).
(5) Utilizing SVM and dissecting the learning outcome:
   We utilize an SVM learning scheme for the samples. Then we gain a group of support vectors and its weights by learning scheme, they form a decision function to distinguish to which district every point belong.

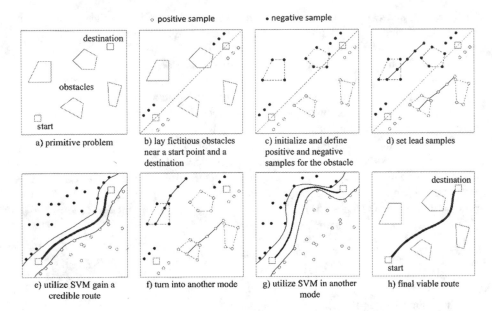

Fig. 2. Steps for routing plan based on SVM

In this paper, a safe route is determined by the separating surface. But the surface is not sole line and is definitely indicated by the support vectors and weights. We must ensure the separating line by seeking the adjacent point where $V = 0$ in Eq. (10). Search algorithm is seen in [8].

In Fig. 2(e), we hope to gain a route from a start point to a destination by this search. Sometimes the two points are part of different intermediate districts for a spot of obstacle. Hence termination condition is either steps exceeds a threshold or adjacent point is safe.

We choose an obstacle at random and overturn it so that turn into another mode. If the mode is new, we create samples and use the above scheme to create another route. The process is continue unless satisfy the termination condition and a viable route is found as shown in Fig. 2(h).

### 3.3    Experimental Results

There are some obstacles in a four square work area and its dimension is identical. If some obstacles overlay one another, it is deem to a single obstacle. In this paper, the kernel function used is a Gaussian kernel.

Figure 3 shows a set of planned paths for a routing plan problem. The size of the square work area is $2.0^2$, the start point and the destination are in (0.1, 0.1) and (1.9, 1.9), the size of obstacle is $0.2^2$ and obstacles are seventeen yet combine into seven, because the superposition of obstacles.

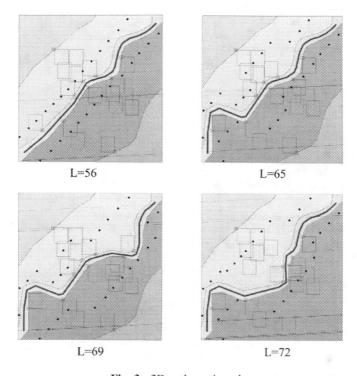

L=56  L=65

L=69  L=72

**Fig. 3.** 2D path routing plan

The chart indicates the routing plan for seven obstacles. Despite diverse patterns create diverse routes, a smooth route is created in all any cases. The shortest route is the first one.

In this test, parameters are listed below. Gaussian kernel is 10 and soft margin weight is 1000, $N_v = 3$, $d_v = 0.05$.

We inspect the computation time for 17 obstacles. The mean time of using SVM for one obstacle is about 105.5 ms, and its standard deviation $\sigma = 79.5$ ms, however, route generation using this pattern is 78.3 ms, and its standard deviation $\sigma = 28.8$ ms. Discrimination is more easily than using SVM and spends less time and less non determinacy. The whole route creation time is about 54 ms, and its standard deviation $\sigma = 9.5$ ms.

## 4 Conclusions

This paper has proposed a novel approach of using SVM to routing plan. SVM has a fine attribute which it can create a consecutive not linear separating surface. We have narrated Pre-processing and post-processing for applying SVM to route plan in 2D. Integrated SVM methodology with other routing plan schemes are future works.

**Acknowledgements.** This work was supported by the National Nature Science Foundation of China (Nos. 51579024, 61374114) and the Fundamental Research Funds for the Central Universities (DMU nos. 3132016311, 3132016005).

# References

1. Avidan, S.: Support vector tracking. IEEE Trans. Pattern Anal. Mach. Intell. **26**(8), 1064–1072 (2004). IEEE Press, New York
2. Caprin, S., Pillonetto, G.: Robot motion planning using adaptive random walks. In: Proceedings of 2003 IEEE International Conference on Robotics and Automation, pp. 3809–3814 (2003)
3. Lu, D.V., Hershberger, D., Smart, W.D.: Layered cost maps for context-sensitive navigation. In: 2014 IEEE/RSJ International Conference on Intelligent Robots and Systems (IROS 2014), pp. 709–715. IEEE Press, New York (2014)
4. Su, K.H., Lian, F.L., Yang, C.Y.: Navigation design with SVM path planning and fuzzy-based path tracking for wheeled agent. In: 2012 International Conference on Fuzzy Theory and it's Applications, pp. 273–278 (2012)
5. Davoodi, M., Panahi, F., Mohades, A., Hashemi, S.N.: Clear and smooth path planning. Appl. Soft Comput. **32**, 568–579 (2015)
6. Cossell, S., Guivant, J.: Concurrent dynamic programming for grid-based problems and its application for real-time path planning. Robot. Auton. Syst. **62**, 737–751 (2014)
7. Do, Q.H., Mita, S., Nejad, H.T.N., Han, L.: Dynamic and safe path planning based on support vector machine among multi moving obstacles for autonomous vehicles. IEICE Trans. Inf. Syst. **E96D**, 314–328 (2013)
8. Miura, J.: Support vector path planning. In: 2006 IEEE/RSJ International Conference on Intelligent Robots and Systems, pp. 2894–2899. IEEE (2006)

# Mobile Data Traffic Prediction Based on Empirical Mode Decomposition and Kernel Extreme Learning Machine

Wenxu Xie, Wendong Xiao[✉], and Chunhong Wu

School of Automation and Electronical Engineering,
University of Science and Technology Beijing, Beijing, China
xiaoxu7810@163.com

**Abstract.** In view of the nonlinear and non-stationary characteristics of mobile data traffic, this paper proposes a mobile data traffic prediction model based on empirical mode decomposition (EMD) and kernel extreme learning machine (KELM). It uses EMD algorithm to decompose the mobile data traffic to obtain a series of Intrinsic Mode Function (IMF) with distinct frequency component. KELM is proposed for modeling and prediction for each IMF, based on which the mobile data traffic can be predicted by aggregating the predicted results of all KELM. Real mobile data traffic is used to verify the feasibility and effectiveness of the proposed method in this paper.

**Keywords:** Mobile data traffic prediction · Empirical mode decomposition · Kernel extreme learning machine

## 1 Introduction

In recent years, with the increasing of mobile devices and improvement of cellular network speed, mobile data traffic expands rapidly [1]. In order to ensure the reliable transmission of mobile data and reasonable allocation of resources, high quality mobile data traffic prediction has important theoretical significance and practical value for network planning, management and design.

Network data traffic sequence is a kind of time series, which can be predicted by the time series prediction modeling method. Traditional traffic prediction based on time series analysis method, such as Markov model and ARIMA model based on MA and AR algorithm [2, 3]. But they can only perform linear modeling of the network traffic with poor adaptability and large prediction error. In recent years, with the discovery of the chaos of the network traffic, the prediction models based on support vector machine and neural network have been introduced [4, 5]. They can fit the nonlinear variation trend of network traffic, and improve the prediction effect.

Although these methods have improved the predictive effect to a certain extent, the following problems still exist. Compared with the traditional Internet traffic, mobile data traffic is more random and volatile which make it difficult to predict. At the same time, the single prediction model has the limitations on the computation speed and prediction accuracy.

© Springer Nature Singapore Pte Ltd. 2017
F. Sun et al. (Eds.): ICCSIP 2016, CCIS 710, pp. 189–196, 2017.
DOI: 10.1007/978-981-10-5230-9_21

Empirical mode decomposition (EMD) is an effective sifting method [6], it can adaptively decompose any signal into a series of Intrinsic Mode Function (IMF). It provides a good manner to smooth mobile data traffic. KELM, which proposed by Huang [7], overcomes the shortcomings of the slow calculation speed of each IMF in building the prediction model. KELM replaces the hidden layer mapping of ELM with kernel function in SVM and it avoids the optimal structure determination problem and retains the advantage of fast training speed of ELM. At the same time, it improves the accuracy and the generalization ability of the model.

Based on the advantages of EMD and KELM, this paper proposed a mobile data traffic prediction model based on empirical mode decomposition (EMD) and kernel extreme learning machine (KELM) in order to achieve high quality prediction.

## 2    EMD-KELM Model

This paper proposed a mobile data traffic prediction model by combining of EMD and KELM. First, it uses EMD to smooth the mobile data traffic sample with nonlinear and non-stationary into a series of IMF and a residual. Each component is input into KELM for modeling and prediction, respectively. At last we can get the final forecast by aggregating the predicted results of all KELM models. The structure of the prediction model is shown in Fig. 1.

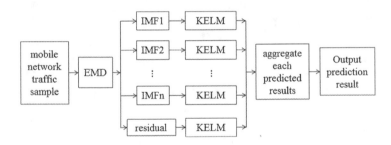

**Fig. 1.** The structure of EMD-KELM model for mobile data traffic

## 3    Empirical Mode Decomposition

Empirical mode decomposition (EMD) is the essence of Hibert-Huang Transform. With EMD, any signal can be adaptively decomposed into a series of Intrinsic Mode Function (IMF), each IMF with distinct frequency component.

IMF satisfies the following two conditions: (1) in the whole data set, the number of extrema and the number of zero crossings must either equal or differ at most by one; (2) at any point, the mean value of the envelope defined by the local maxima and minima is zero.

Usually EMD algorithm implemented as follows:

Step1: Find all local extrema of the original signal s(t), by using cubic spline curve interpolation to connect, we can get maximum envelope $s_{max}(t)$ and minimum envelope $s_{min}(t)$ of s(t) separately. The mean $m_1(t)$ is estimated as the average of two envelopes.

$$m_1(t) = \frac{s_{max}(t) - s_{min}(t)}{2} \tag{1}$$

Step2: $h_1(t)$ is the difference between s(t) and $m_1(t)$, which usually may not be the final IMF component. The sifting process has to be repeated a number of times (assume for k times), until $h_k(t)$ meet the second condition of IMF. Then it is designated as $c_1(t)$, the first IMF component from the data. $c_1(t)$ contain the minimal scale or the shortest period component of the signal.

$$h_k(t) = h_{k-1}(t) - m_{k-1}(t) = c_1(t) \tag{2}$$

Step3: We can get $r_1(t)$ by separating $c_1(t)$ from the signal s(t).

$$r_1(t) = s(t) - c_1(t) \tag{3}$$

Then $r_1(t)$ is referred as a new group of signal to repeat the above EMD procedure, and we can obtain $r_2(t) = r_1(t) - c_2(t)$ by EMD repeatedly. When $r_n(t)$ become a monotone or DC signal, EMD procedure will be finished.

Thus, the signal s(t) is decomposed into n IMFs and a residual.

$$s(t) = \sum_{i=1}^{n} c_i(t) + r_n(t) \tag{4}$$

# 4    Kernel Extreme Learning Machine

## 4.1    Basic Extreme Learning Machine

ELM is a flexible computing architecture, which is widely used in nonlinear problems. It is a simple and effective SLFN learning algorithm.

Suppose there are N arbitrary samples $(x_i, t_i)$, $x_i = [x_{i1}, x_{i2}, \ldots, x_{in}]^T \in R$, $t_i = [t_{i1}, t_{i2}, \ldots, t_{im}]^T \in R$. Then standard SLFNs with L hidden nodes can be mathematically expressed as following:

$$\sum_{i=1}^{L} \beta_i g(a_i \cdot x_j + b_i) = y_j, \quad j = 1, \cdots, N \tag{5}$$

$a_i = [a_{i1}, a_{i2}, \ldots, a_{in}]^T$ is the weight vector connecting the hidden node and the input nodes, $b_i$ is the threshold of the hidden node. $\beta_i = [\beta_{i1}, \beta_{i2}, \ldots, \beta_{in}]^T$ is the weight vector connecting hidden node and the output nodes.

If the SLFN with activation function can approximate these $N$ training samples with zero error, the following liner system is set up.

$$\sum_{i=1}^{L} \|y_j - t_j = 0\|$$ (6)

Regression models can be expressed as follow:

$$\sum_{i=1}^{L} \beta_i g(a_i \cdot x_j + b_i) = t_j, \quad j = 1, \cdots, N$$ (7)

the above equation can also be simplified as $H\beta = T$, where

$$H = \begin{bmatrix} g(a_1 \cdot x_1 + b_1) & \cdots & g(a_L \cdot x_1 + b_L) \\ \vdots & \ddots & \vdots \\ g(a_1 \cdot x_N + b_1) & \cdots & g(a_L \cdot x_N + b_L) \end{bmatrix}_{N \times L}$$ (8)

The weight $\beta$ can be obtained by solving the following equations by least-square method.

The solution is $\hat{\beta} = H^* T$, where $H^*$ is the Moore-Penrose generalized inverse of matrix $H$.

### 4.2    Kernel Extreme Learning Machine

When using ELM to solve practical matter, actual data sample may cause $HH^T$ non-singular, to improve the stability of ELM, we can have:

$$\hat{\beta} = H^T \left(\frac{I}{C} + HH^T\right)^{-1} T$$ (9)

Where C is a penalty parameter, I is the identity matrix. Then the corresponding output function of ELM is:

$$f(x) = g(x)\beta = g(x)H^T \left(\frac{I}{C} + HH^T\right)^{-1} T$$ (10)

If the hidden layer feature mapping g(x) is unknown to users, an ELM kernel function can be constructed to replace $HH^T$.

$$HH^T = \Omega_{ELM} = \begin{bmatrix} K(x_1, x_1) & \cdots & K(x_1, x_j) \\ \vdots & \ddots & \vdots \\ K(x_i, x_1) & \cdots & K(x_i, x_j) \end{bmatrix} = K(x_i, x_j)$$ (11)

$$g(x)H^T = \begin{bmatrix} K(x, x_1) \\ \vdots \\ K(x, x_N) \end{bmatrix}^T$$ (12)

Thus we can get the output of KELM model as follow:

$$f(x) = \begin{bmatrix} K(x,x_1) \\ \vdots \\ K(x,x_N) \end{bmatrix}^T \left(\frac{I}{C} + \Omega_{ELM}\right)^{-1} T \qquad (13)$$

In selecting kernel function, as long as meeting Mercer theory, it can be used as the kernel function. The radial based function (RBF) kernel function is chosen for KELM prediction model in our paper, whose expression is:

$$K(x,x_i) = exp\left(-\|x - x_i\|^2/\sigma^2\right) \qquad (14)$$

## 5   Method Evaluation

### 5.1   Data Sources

The testing sample in this paper was obtained from a mobile advertisement company, which is collected from October 14 to October 27, 2015. The paper chooses 14 days' real mobile data traffic samples. It samples the data every 15 min and 1344 data elements totally. The original mobile data traffic time series is shown in Fig. 2.

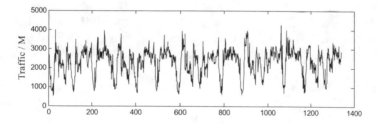

**Fig. 2.**   The mobile data traffic time series

### 5.2   Data Preprocessing

Firstly, the time series are normalized, and then decomposed by the EMD in order to sift IMFs and the residual. The mobile data traffic time series is decomposed into 8 IMF components and a residual $R$, as shown in Fig. 3. After the decomposition each IMF highlights the local characteristics of the original sequence. From the figure, we can clearly see the stochastic term, periodic term and trend of original mobile data traffic sample.

The delay time $\tau = 1$ and embedding dimension m = 8 is obtained by adopting experimental method. After the phase space reconstruction, we can get 1336 sets of data. The first 1200 are used as training sets and the rest are used as testing sets to validate the prediction model.

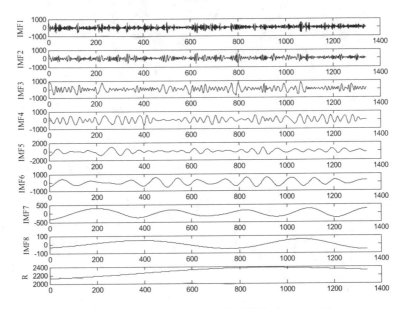

**Fig. 3.** IMFs and residual after the EMD decomposition

## 5.3    Experiment Results

Due to there are a series of IMFs, IMF3 to IMF8 and residual are aggregated to a new sequence (IMFm) in order to reduce the simulation time. We can get 3 sequences (IMFm, IMF1 and IMF2) with another two high frequency IMFs. We select RMSE as the performance index and use cross validation to optimize the KELM penalty factor and kernel parameter. The optimum parameters with the minimum RMSE are selected to establish KELM model.

Figure 4 shows the comparison between predicted value and actual value of IMF1, IMF2, IMFm. From the figure, the predicted result of IMF1 with higher oscillation frequency has deviation; with the reducing of frequency, the predicted result of IMF2 shows better effect; the predicted curve of IMFm is in a good coincidence with the actual value.

Figure 5 shows the comparison between the predicted value and the actual value of mobile data traffic time series, and the absolute errors. From the figure, it is clear to us that EMD-KELM model has a good fitting effect for the sample with less predicting error.

We select root mean square error (RMSE) defined in (15) as the performance index to evaluate the mobile data traffic prediction model. RMSE has no positive and negative offset to errors, the evaluation of the overall performance of the system is very important.

$$RMSE = \sqrt{\frac{1}{N} \sum_{i=1}^{N} (y_i - \hat{y}_i)^2} \tag{15}$$

where $y_i$ is the actual value of the mobile data traffic, and $\hat{y}_i$ is the predicted value.

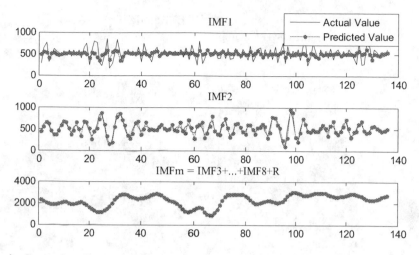

**Fig. 4.** Comparison between the predicted value and the actual value of IMF1, IMF2, IMFm

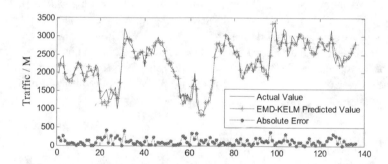

**Fig. 5.** Comparison between the predicted value and the actual value of mobile data traffic

**Table 1.** The RMSE value of each IMF by three prediction models

|      | ELM    | SVM    | KELM   |
|------|--------|--------|--------|
| IMF1 | 132.23 | 137.86 | 119.98 |
| IMF2 | 65.56  | 61.29  | 59.17  |
| IMFm | 37.36  | 32.86  | 18.35  |

Table 1 is the RMSE value of three different prediction models to predict the IMF component. In the prediction of the IMF component, the RMSE values of the KELM model are lower than those of ELM and SVM model.

In order to further verify the prediction accuracy of the model proposed in this paper, compare EMD-KELM predicted value with EMD-ELM model, ELM model and SVM model, experiments were carried out and the results are shown in Table 2.

As can be seen from Table 2, the EMD-KELM model proposed in this paper has the best results. Without the EMD decomposition, the prediction result has a large error with only ELM or SVM model to predict the mobile network time series.

**Table 2.** The RMSE value of four prediction models

| Times | ELM | SVM | EMD-ELM | EMD - KELM |
|---|---|---|---|---|
| 1 | 315.55 | 306.81 | 158.68 | 135.61 |
| 2 | 306.00 | 312.27 | 149.42 | 137.52 |
| 3 | 307.87 | 305.70 | 153.43 | 136.89 |
| 4 | 310.53 | 304.44 | 156.53 | 136.26 |
| 5 | 312.34 | 306.09 | 149.00 | 135.30 |

# 6  Conclusions

In this paper, we propose a mobile data traffic prediction model based on empirical mode decomposition (EMD) and kernel extreme learning machine (KELM). The high frequency time series is decomposed by EMD algorithm, and then each IMF component is input to KELM for modeling and prediction.

The results show that, compared to the prediction model without EMD, the prediction performance of EMD-KELM has greatly improved. It has better fitting capability and higher prediction accuracy for the nonlinear mobile data traffic.

# References

1. Cisco: Visual networking index: global mobile data traffic forecast update. White paper (2014–2019)
2. Yao, Q.F., Li, C.F., Ma, H.L.: Novel network traffic forecasting algorithm based on grey model and Markov chain. J. Zhejiang Univ. **34**(4), 396–400 (2007)
3. Yu, G., Zhang, C.: Switching ARIMA model based forecasting for traffic flow. In: IEEE International Conference on Acoustics, Montreal. IEEE (2004)
4. Chen, X.T., Zhang, S.Y., Tian, T.: Internet traffic forecasting based on BP neural network. J. Nanjing Univ. Posts Telecommun. **30**(2), 16–21 (2010)
5. Luo, A.Q., Xia, J.B., Wang, H.B.: Application of Chaos-support vector machine regression in traffic prediction. Comput. Sci. **36**(7), 244–246 (2009)
6. Huang, N.E., Shen, Z., Long, S.R.: The empirical mode decomposition and the Hilbert spectrum for nonlinear and non-stationary time series analysis. Proc. Math. Phys. Eng. Sci. **454**(1971), 903–995 (1998)
7. Huang, G.B., Zhu, Q.Y., Siew, C.K.: Extreme learning machine: a new learning scheme of feedforward neural networks. Neural Netw. **2**(2), 985–990 (2004)

# Abnormal Events Detection Using Deep Networks for Video Surveillance

Binghao Meng[1], Lu Zhang[1], Fan Jin[1], Lu Yang[1], Hong Cheng[1(✉)], and Qian Wang[2]

[1] School of Automation Engineering, Center for Robotics, University of Electronic Science and Technology of China, Chengdu, China
hcheng@uestc.edu.cn
[2] Ricoh Software Research Center of Beijing, Beijing, China

**Abstract.** In this paper, a novel method is proposed to detect abnormal events. This method is based on spatio-temporal deep networks which can represent sequential video frames. Abnormal events are rare in real world and involve small samples along with large amount of normal video data. It is difficult to apply with deep networks directly which usually require amounts of labeled samples. Our method solves this problem by pre-training the networks on videos which are irrelevant to abnormal events and refining the networks with fine tuning. Furthermore, we employ the patch strategy to improve the performance of our method in complex scenes. The proposed method is tested on real surveillance videos which only contain limited abnormal samples. Experimental results show that the proposed approach can outperform the conventional abnormal event detection algorithm which utilized hand-crafted features.

**Keywords:** Spatio-temporal networks · Deep learning · Abnormal events detection · Small sample events

## 1 Introduction

In the past decades, with the development of the technology in computer vision and pattern recognition, smart surveillance systems are increasingly being used to detect potential dangerous situations. But the recognition of complex events in videos continues to be a challenging problem [2,3,9]. For detection of complex events in videos, recent researches in this aspect emphasized on concept based methods as they provided high-level complex event recognition and proposed an approach to discover data-driven concepts to represent high level semantics of video [13,22], so as to improve complex event recognition, [1] developed a model that captured the temporal dynamics of windowed mid-level concept detectors. Based bottom up approach was presented to recognize events [1]. To detect abnormal event in scenes, various approaches were categorized into two classes, one was based on trajectory pedestrians or object-tracking, nevertheless, these methods were not the best choice because tracking was extremely

© Springer Nature Singapore Pte Ltd. 2017
F. Sun et al. (Eds.): ICCSIP 2016, CCIS 710, pp. 197–204, 2017.
DOI: 10.1007/978-981-10-5230-9_22

difficult in complex scene [18,24]. Another was based on motion representation which avoided tracking, the method of mainstream was optical flow such as [3,7], Markov Random Field (MRF) model such as [14,19]. [12] developed a 3DCNN models, and achieved superior performance in the recognition of human actions.

Deep learning has won amounts of contests in pattern recognition and machine learning, and it allows models to learn representations of data with multiple levels of abstraction. Deep convolution nets have brought about break-throughs in image and video processing. Recently, deep models were led into video event analysis, as the great performance of Convolution Neural Networks (CNN) in image classification, it was expanded to time domain to temporal clues of videos [12]. Video level pooling or encoding to frame features extracted by CNN were implemented to obtain the video level representation [6]. Another way to extract the video level representation was to combine CNN/3DCNN with Recurrent Neural Networks (RNN) with Long Short-Term Memory (LSTM) [4,20], which has been proved to be efficient in sequential data processing [8]. [5,15] proposed a fully automated deep model which learned to recognize human actions directly from video.

In this paper, we aim to detect abnormal events of crowding and escape behaviors in videos. We are more inclined to post-processing in our emergency plan systems, which lack of beforehand prevention. Mass incident in public place tends to have greater security risks. It is necessary to develop a system which can implement real-time monitoring of the mass incident, judging whether any mass incident, predicting the state of abnormal behavior in a short time, and making corresponding warning or alarm. For abnormal behavior detection, approaches based on Social Force Model (SFM) such as [17,23] has already proved effective. In this work we propose an automated deep learning model that address this problem. The contributions include: (1) solve the problem of small sample abnormal event by pre-training on irrelative videos and fine-tuning on abnormal videos. (2) efficiently detect events which occur in local area of surveillance view-point. The rest of this paper is organized as follows: we describe the overview of the approach in Sect. 2. The details of the proposed method described in Sect. 3. The experimental results on the dataset are analyzed in Sect. 4. We conclude in Sect. 5.

## 2     Overview of the Proposed Framework

We propose a novel abnormal event detection approach using spatio-temporal deep networks. Figure 1 summarizes the main steps of the method. We first extract five low-level features as inputs of different pathway of the deep net-works: gray, gradient-x, gradient-y, optflow-x and optflow-y. The gray contains the original information of image for that color information has little impact on event detection. Gradient can represent the edge information efficiently, so the gradient-x and gradient-y are obtained by computing gradients along the hori-zontal and vertical directions respectively. The optflow-x and optflow-y contain the optical flow fields along the horizontal and vertical directions, respectively, computed from adjacent input frames which contain the motion information.

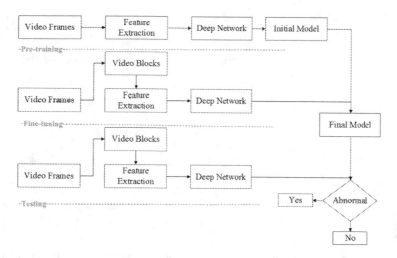

**Fig. 1.** Framework of the proposed method. (a) Pre-training: videos are irrelevant with abnormal behavior. (b) Fine-tuning: videos contain few abnormal samples and are decomposed into blocks. (c) Testing: videos are decomposed into blocks.

The selection of initial weights has great influence on the networks, furthermore, the detection of abnormal event is more depending on better weights. We pre-train our model on vast irrelative videos which are easy to obtain. Abnormal behavior often occurs in a small area while the entire scene covers large area in surveillance videos, we propose a patch strategy by decomposing video into blocks which avoids that local abnormal behavior weakened by global information. Video blocks taken as new inputs of networks to refine the weights. When performing abnormal event detection, the test videos will also be processed as before. Finally, the experiential rule is used to classify the video frames into an abnormal event or normal one.

## 3    The Proposed Method

### 3.1    Spatio-Temporal Deep Networks

The convolutional architecture was introduced in [16], since the early 2000s, CNN has been applied with great success to the detection, segmentation and recognition of objects in images. There are four key ideas behind CNN that take advantage of the properties of natural signals: local connections, shared weights, pooling and the use of many layers. CNN is a deep model which possesses strong ability of self learning.

The traditional CNN performs 2D convolution which only computes spatial information. In the application of video, time domain information is necessary. We use 3DCNN to obtain the time domain information, this kind of hierarchical learned high-level features are much stronger than the low-level temporal feature such as optical flow.

3DCNN applies 3D convolution instead of 2D convolution in CNN. 3D convolution extends the 2D convolution by which computes the convolution in temporal dimension. In 3DCNN, we apply it based on Eq. (1) and the details refer to [12],

$$v_{st}^{xyz} = f(b_{st} + \sum_m \sum_{p=0}^{P_s-1} \sum_{q=0}^{Q_s-1} \sum_{r=0}^{R_s-1} w_{stm}^{pqr} v_{(s-1)m}^{(x+p)(y+q)(z+r)}), \quad (1)$$

where, the value of an unit at position $(x, y, z)$ in the $t$-th feature map in the $s$-th layer, denoted as $v_{st}^{xyz}$, $b_{st}$ is the bias for this feature map, $w_{stm}^{pqr}$ is the value at the position $(p, q, r)$ of the kernel connected to the $m$th feature map.

Our spatio-temporal deep networks have five pathways and different low-level features are the input of each pathway. In addition, the five pathways have the same structure based on [12]. After then, the uniform feature representation is obtained by fully connected layer from five pathways. Ultimately, softmax is applied to classify the outputs. Figure 2 shows the framework of the networks. The structure of mixture multi-channels obtains variant different properties from original videos. Therefore, the extracted features contain more hidden information with better representation of video content.

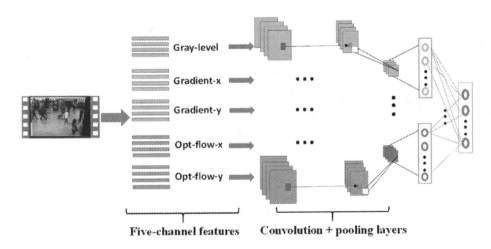

Fig. 2. The framework of networks.

Although CNN was designed for processing a huge number of training samples, we find that if the related class and unrelated class have some common properties, CNN can transfer the model pre-trained on the plenty of samples of unrelated class to the target class by fine-tuning on few related samples. In the detection of events, whether abnormal event or normal event, both of the motion representations are similar in videos. Therefore, we pre-train our deep networks with normal event videos and fine-tune on few abnormal events which demonstrated to be effective.

## 3.2    Patch Strategy

Considering abnormal behavior only locates in a certain area which accounts for a small proportion in surveillance video image, local event is likely to be weakened by global information if process the whole image directly. So as to solve this problem well, we develop a patch strategy. We use a sequence of $N$ fixed-length clips without overlapping frames to characterize video, each clip contains $m$ frames, the $k$-th frame in the $C$-th clip is divided into $d_1 \times d_2$ patches, where $i = 1, 2, \ldots, d_1$, $j = 1, 2, \ldots, d_2$, $k = 1, 2, \ldots, m$, $C = 1, 2, \ldots, N$. Then combining multiple patches together at same location in temporal dimension, the patch clip denoted as $P^n(i, j)$ and labeled simultaneously. The Dividing process as shown Fig. 3.

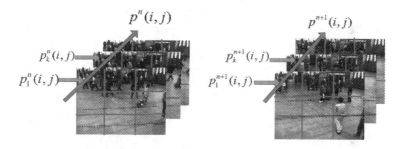

**Fig. 3.** Dividing process from continuous frames.

The testing videos are decomposed into blocks according to above method, then we apply the learned model for detecting abnormal events in videos. To prevent the false detection, we introduce an experiential rule works as follows, if $k$ continuous clips belong to the category of abnormality simultaneously, it is regarded as abnormal event follows Eq. (2).

$$Result = \begin{cases} abnormal, p^n \bigwedge p^{n+1} \bigwedge \cdots \bigwedge P^{n+k-1} = 1 \\ normal, others \end{cases} \tag{2}$$

Where $P^n$ denotes the result of detection at the same location, we denote $P^n = 1$ with respect to abnormal event. The value of $k$ is set to 2 empirically.

## 4    Experimental Results

This section details our experimental protocols and describes the three videos datasets. We focus on the RICOH data to evaluate the developed method for abnormal detection. Meanwhile, we also compare with previous method which was evaluated in the same dataset [11]. Our method is implemented over CAFFE (Convolutional Architecture for Fast Feature Embedding) with respect to an open-source and high-efficiency deep learning framework.

### 4.1   Dataset

The Fudan-Columbia video Dataset (FCVID) consists of 91,223 Web videos annotated manually according to 239 categories. We choose six kinds of events in FCVID dataset to pre-training. RICOH dataset consists of two view points from different cameras (TYZX camera and Point-Gray camera) and includes amount of crowd events. The publicly available dataset from University of Minnesota (UMN) is used to detect escape event.

### 4.2   Experiments

In this experiment, ten frames of size $64 \times 64$ as inputs ($64 \times 64 \times 10$) to this model. The parameters of the nets are set as $C1(11 \times 11 \times 4) - S2(2 \times 2) - C3(7 \times 7 \times 3) - S4(3 \times 3) - C5(7 \times 7 \times 1) - FC6(256) - FC7(2)$. $C(H \times W \times T)$ represents convolutional layer, in this layer, $H, W, T$ represent the height, width and size of temporal dimension in kernel respectively. After each convolutional processing, a *tanh* function is stacked as activation function. $S(H \times W)$ as the layer of subsampling, $H$ and $W$ represent the height and width of pooling. After the multiple layers of convolution and subsampling, we apply fully connected layers $FC(N)$ which consist of $N$ feature maps. Obviously, the outputs, in the last layer, include two cases of abnormal and normal. The layers from $C1$ to $C5$ are common structures and $FC6$, $FC7$ are fusion layers. Finally, softmax shows promising capability in classification. All the parameters are initialized randomly and trained by back-propagation algorithm based on [10].

Figure 4 shows the results of crowd detection on RICOH dataset. In order to embody the effect of proposed method, we obtain the statistical result by decomposing the Point-Gray data into clips and each clip consists of 20 frames. The experiment shows that the accuracy of our method is 0.9658 and the F-measure is 0.9658. Both accuracy and F-measure are slightly better than method of [11], which are 0.9607 and 0.9578. It is worth noting that the model is trained and tested in different positions by two different cameras, which implies our method is robust for variation of viewpoints. However, the method in [7, 21] is specially designed for specific scenes.

**Fig. 4.** The localization of crowd behaviors in the frames.

We also test the model over UMN dataset, Fig. 5 shows the result of escape event detection. The escape event can be detected accurately, but along with

**Fig. 5.** The localization of escape behaviors in the frames.

delay. On the one hand, the experiential rule will lead to delay. On the other hand, the velocity is fast when human escape suddenly.

## 5   Conclusion

In this paper, we have developed a method for abnormal event detection based on deep learning. The proposed method pre-trains deep spatio-temporal networks over unrelated dataset and shows promising capability in abnormal event detection of small sample problem. We also introduce an experiential rule by which improving the effect of classification. Extensive experimental results illustrate that our method is robust of variant scenes. As part of future work, we plan to add statistic model which represents priori knowledge into deep networks, further improve its ability of small sample events detection.

## References

1. Bhattacharya, S.: Recognition of complex events in open-source web-scale videos: a bottom up approach. In: Proceedings of the 21st ACM International Conference on Multimedia, pp. 1035–1038. ACM (2013)
2. Cho, S.H., Kang, H.B.: Abnormal behavior detection using hybrid agents in crowded scenes. Pattern Recogn. Lett. **44**, 64–70 (2014)
3. Cong, Y., Yuan, J., Liu, J.: Abnormal event detection in crowded scenes using sparse representation. Pattern Recogn. **46**(7), 1851–1864 (2013)
4. Donahue, J., Anne Hendricks, L., Guadarrama, S., Rohrbach, M., Venugopalan, S., Saenko, K., Darrell, T.: Long-term recurrent convolutional networks for visual recognition and description. In: Proceedings of the IEEE Conference on Computer Vision and Pattern Recognition, pp. 2625–2634 (2015)
5. Foggia, P., Saggese, A., Strisciuglio, N., Vento, M.: Exploiting the deep learning paradigm for recognizing human actions. In: 2014 11th IEEE International Conference on Advanced Video and Signal Based Surveillance (AVSS), pp. 93–98. IEEE (2014)
6. Gan, C., Wang, N., Yang, Y., Yeung, D.Y., Hauptmann, A.G.: Devnet: a deep event network for multimedia event detection and evidence recounting. In: Proceedings of the IEEE Conference on Computer Vision and Pattern Recognition, pp. 2568–2577 (2015)
7. Gnanavel, V.K., Srinivasan, A.: Abnormal event detection in crowded video scenes. In: Satapathy, S.C., Biswal, B.N., Udgata, S.K., Mandal, J.K. (eds.) Proceedings of the 3rd International Conference on Frontiers of Intelligent Computing: Theory and Applications (FICTA) 2014. AISC, vol. 328, pp. 441–448. Springer, Cham (2015). doi:10.1007/978-3-319-12012-6_48

8. Graves, A.: Generating sequences with recurrent neural networks. arXiv preprint arXiv:1308.0850 (2013)
9. Gu, X., Cui, J., Zhu, Q.: Abnormal crowd behavior detection by using the particle entropy. Optik-Int. J. Light Electron Opt. **125**(14), 3428–3433 (2014)
10. Hansen, L.K., Salamon, P.: Neural network ensembles. IEEE Trans. Pattern Anal. Mach. Intell. **10**, 993–1001 (1990)
11. Hu, D., Meng, B., Fan, S., Cheng, H., Yang, L., Ji, Y.: Real-time understanding of abnormal crowd behavior on social robots. In: Ho, Y.-S., Sang, J., Ro, Y.M., Kim, J., Wu, F. (eds.) PCM 2015. LNCS, vol. 9315, pp. 554–563. Springer, Cham (2015). doi:10.1007/978-3-319-24078-7_56
12. Ji, S., Xu, W., Yang, M., Yu, K.: 3d convolutional neural networks for human action recognition. IEEE Trans. Pattern Anal. Mach. Intell. **35**(1), 221–231 (2013)
13. Jiang, Y.G., Bhattacharya, S., Chang, S.F., Shah, M.: High-level event recognition in unconstrained videos. Int. J. Multimedia Inf. Retriev. **2**(2), 73–101 (2013)
14. Kim, J., Grauman, K.: Observe locally, infer globally: a space-time MRF for detecting abnormal activities with incremental updates. In: IEEE Conference on Computer Vision and Pattern Recognition, CVPR 2009, pp. 2921–2928. IEEE (2009)
15. Le, Q.V., Zou, W.Y., Yeung, S.Y., Ng, A.Y.: Learning hierarchical invariant spatio-temporal features for action recognition with independent subspace analysis. In: 2011 IEEE Conference on Computer Vision and Pattern Recognition (CVPR), pp. 3361–3368. IEEE (2011)
16. LeCun, Y., Kavukcuoglu, K., Farabet, C., et al.: Convolutional networks and applications in vision. In: ISCAS, pp. 253–256 (2010)
17. Mehran, R., Oyama, A., Shah, M.: Abnormal crowd behavior detection using social force model. In: IEEE Conference on Computer Vision and Pattern Recognition, CVPR 2009, pp. 935–942. IEEE (2009)
18. Popoola, O.P., Wang, K.: Video-based abnormal human behavior recognition - a review. IEEE Trans. Syst. Man Cybern. Part C: Appl. Rev. **42**(6), 865–878 (2012)
19. Qin, L., Ye, Y., Su, L., Huang, Q.: Abnormal event detection based on multi-scale markov random field. In: Zha, H., Chen, X., Wang, L., Miao, Q. (eds.) CCCV 2015. CCIS, vol. 546, pp. 376–386. Springer, Heidelberg (2015). doi:10.1007/978-3-662-48558-3_38
20. Sun, L., Jia, K., Yeung, D.Y., Shi, B.E.: Human action recognition using factorized spatio-temporal convolutional networks. In: Proceedings of the IEEE International Conference on Computer Vision, pp. 4597–4605 (2015)
21. Wang, T., Snoussi, H.: Detection of abnormal events via optical flow feature analysis. Sensors **15**(4), 7156–7171 (2015)
22. Yang, Y., Shah, M.: Complex events detection using data-driven concepts. In: Fitzgibbon, A., Lazebnik, S., Perona, P., Sato, Y., Schmid, C. (eds.) ECCV 2012. LNCS, vol. 7574, pp. 722–735. Springer, Heidelberg (2012). doi:10.1007/978-3-642-33712-3_52
23. Zhang, Y., Qin, L., Yao, H., Huang, Q.: Abnormal crowd behavior detection based on social attribute-aware force model. In: 2012 19th IEEE International Conference on Image Processing (ICIP), pp. 2689–2692. IEEE (2012)
24. Zhou, S., Zhang, Z., Zeng, D., Shen, W.: Abnormal events detection in crowded scenes by trajectory cluster. In: International Symposium on Precision Engineering Measurement and Instrumentation, p. 944614. International Society for Optics and Photonics (2015)

# Sparse Extreme Learning Machine Using Privileged Information for Classification

Michele Mukeshimana, Xiaojuan Ban$^{(\boxtimes)}$, and Nelson Karani

School of Computer and Communication Engineering,
University of Science and Technology Beijing,
Beijing 100083, People's Republic of China
michele.mukeshimana@ub.edu.bi, banxj@ustb.edu.cn,
nyachiro.rirubi@rediffmail.com

**Abstract.** In human learning process, teachers play an important role of transferring knowledge and providing some additional information for better understanding. In machine learning, the role of the teacher has been mostly ignored. Introduction of a new learning paradigm named Learning Using Privileged Information (LUPI) includes the elements of human teaching in machine learning. This paper proposes a learning method using privileged information based on a Sparse Extreme Learning Machine (ELM). Our method aims to improve the classification performance by reducing the testing error. Experimental results show improvements in training accuracy and testing error reduction over the classical methods in classification.

**Keywords:** Extreme Learning Machine (ELM) · Sparse ELM · Learning Using Privileged Information (LUPI) · Support Vector Machine (SVM) · Machine learning

## 1 Introduction

In machine learning, classification is the best treated problem; many algorithms and methods have been proposed. Most of them don't consider the role played by the teachers. The new learning paradigm proposed by Vapnik et al. [1, 2] has brought into account the importance of the additional information on the training samples [16]. Such additional information is called privileged information because it is only available during the training stage.

Learning using privileged information has been largely applied with Support Vector Machine (SVM). It has been applied in cluster analysis [3], in multitask multiclass problems [4] in the improvement of v-Support Vector for Classification and Regression [5] and in many other applications [6, 17]. In all the experiments, the most used algorithm is the SVM+ algorithm [15, 22]. Because of the complexity related to SVM parameters the training time is considerably increased. As an alternative solution, the exploitation of privileged information has been extended to the Extreme Learning Machine (ELM) method which is faster and has less parameterization [17].

ELM is a recent machine learning method which studies the generalized Single Layer Feed-forward Networks (SLFNs) whose hidden layers need not to be tuned.

© Springer Nature Singapore Pte Ltd. 2017
F. Sun et al. (Eds.): ICCSIP 2016, CCIS 710, pp. 205–213, 2017.
DOI: 10.1007/978-981-10-5230-9_23

It was introduced by Huang et al. [18–20] and it has outperformed the SVM in learning speed because the hidden layer of the generalized SLFNs in ELM does not need to be tuned. Learning Using Privileged Information based on ELM was introduced as ELM+ in Zhang et al. [17] to improve the learning accuracy. Their work showed that the use of privileged information improves performance over classical ELM and SVM+. However, the ELM+ inherits the compactness of the unified ELM because of the use of equality constraints. Therefore, it needs a lot of memory storage and is slow in testing. In the work of Bai et al. [13], a sparse ELM was proposed to solve the problem of the storage space and testing time improvements.

The Sparse ELM scope is to be applied in the growing-scale problems. In many real-life situations, large scale problems [24] such as health related problems, human social studies problems like emotion recognition needs a lot of memory in processing. By the use of inequality constraints there is a cutback of storage memory and reduction of computations.

Our work proposes the use of privileged information with sparse ELM to take advantage of privileged information to improve the training accuracy and the testing accuracy. At the same time the sparsity of ELM permits the memory storage economical usage and testing time reduction. In this view, along with the emerging research in multimodal information fusion, our method aims to solve the problem of using two different modalities in training only to improve the testing accuracy when only one modality is available at the testing stage.

The remaining part of the paper is organized in four sections in which we firstly give a brief introduction to basic ELM and Sparse ELM, secondly, we show our proposed method, and thirdly, the experimental results and the analysis are presented before the closing conclusion.

## 2  Background: Basic ELM and Sparse ELM

Extreme Learning Machine (ELM) [18, 20] was originally proposed for the single layer forward neural networks and was extended to the generalized single-hidden layer where the hidden layer needn't be neuron like [7–9, 19].

Given a set of N training samples $(x_i, t_i), i = 1, \ldots, N$ with $x_i \in X^d$ as the input vector for the i[th] sample and $t_i \in T$ its target value. The output of ELM with L hidden nodes can be represented by:

$$f(x) = \sum_{i=1}^{l} \beta_i G(a_i, b_i, x) = \beta.h(x) \tag{1}$$

Where $a_i$ and $b_i$ are respectively the input weight and bias between inputs and hidden nodes, $\beta_i$ is the output weight connecting the i[th] hidden node to the output node.

$G(a_i, b_i, x)$ is the output of the i[th] hidden node with respect to the input $x$, it is a nonlinear piece-wise continuous function satisfying ELM universal approximation capability [14, 19, 21]. $h(x)$ is the output matrix of the hidden layer with respect to the input $x$. The ELM Eq. (1) can be written as:

$$H\beta = T \tag{2}$$

Where

$$H = \begin{bmatrix} h(x_1) \\ \vdots \\ h(x_N) \end{bmatrix} = \begin{bmatrix} G(a_1, b_1, x_1) & \cdots & G(a_L, b_L, x_1) \\ \vdots & \ddots & \vdots \\ G(a_1, b_1, x_N) & \cdots & G(a_L, b_L, x_N) \end{bmatrix}_{N*L}, \beta = \begin{bmatrix} \beta_1^T \\ \vdots \\ \beta_L^T \end{bmatrix}_{L*C}, T = \begin{bmatrix} t_1^T \\ \vdots \\ t_N^T \end{bmatrix}_{N*C} \tag{3}$$

L is the number of the hidden nodes and C is the number of classes. If $H$ is a non-square matrix, the smallest norm least-square solution of the above linear system is:

$$\hat{\beta} = H^\dagger T \tag{4}$$

Where $H^\dagger$ is the Moore-Penrose generalized inverse matrix $H$. Different methods can be used to calculate the Moore-Penrose generalized inverse of matrix.

A sparse ELM network is obtained when the inequality constraints are used in an optimization method based ELM [8, 13].

In general, ELM tends to reach the smallest training error both with the smallest norm output weight [12]. The optimization aims to solve:

$$\text{Minimize: } L_p = \frac{1}{2}\|\beta\|^2 + C\sum_{i=1}^{N}\xi_i \tag{5}$$

$$\text{Subject to: } t_i\beta.h(x_i) \geq 1 - \xi_i, i = 1, \ldots, N, \xi_i \geq 0, i = 1, \ldots, N \tag{6}$$

The Lagrange function is:

$$L_{ELM}(\beta, \xi, \lambda, v) = \frac{1}{2}\|\beta\|^2 + C\sum_{i=1}^{N}\xi_i - \sum_{i=1}^{N}\lambda_i.(t_i\beta.h(x_i) - (1 - \xi_i)) - \sum_{i=1}^{N}v_i\xi_i \tag{7}$$

Where $\lambda_i$ and $v_i$ are the Lagrange multipliers and are non-negative values. The dual form of sparse ELM becomes:

$$\text{Minimize: } L_{D_{ELM}} = \frac{1}{2}\sum_{i=1}^{N}\sum_{j=1}^{N}t_it_j\lambda_i\lambda_j\Omega_{ELM}(x_i, x_j) - \sum_{i=1}^{N}\lambda_i \tag{8}$$

Where $\Omega_{ELM}(x_i, x_j) = h(x_i).h(x_j)^T = K(x_i, x_j)$. So, the output of sparse ELM is:

$$f(x) = h(x)\beta = h(x)\left(\sum_{i=1}^{N}\lambda_it_ih(x_i)^T\right) = h(x)\left(\sum_{s=1}^{N_s}\lambda_st_sh(x_s)^T\right) = \sum_{s=1}^{N_s}\lambda_st_s\Omega_{ELM}(x, x_s) \tag{9}$$

Where $x_s$ is a support vector (SV) and $N_s$ is the number of SVs. For more details, we refer the reader to [13] and the references therein.

# 3  Our Proposed Method: Sparse ELM Learning Using Privileged Information

As mentioned in the above sections, privileged information is the additional information available to the input data vector [10, 11].

When using the privileged information, the training set becomes a set of triplets $(x_i, x_i^*, t_i)$ containing non-privileged variables $x_i$, privileged variables $x_i^*$ and their classification label $t_i$. We map the vector $X$ of the non-privileged information to the hidden-layer feature space by $h(x)$ and the vector $X^*$ of the privileged information to the hidden-layer correcting function by $h^*(x^*)$, the two kernel functions can be different or the same. The optimization problem becomes:

$$\min_{\beta, \beta^*} L_p = \frac{1}{2}[\|\beta\|^2 + \gamma\|\beta^*\|^2] + C\sum_{i=1}^{l} h^*(x_i^*).\beta^* \tag{10}$$

$$\text{subject to}: t_i(\beta.h(x_i)) \geq 1 - (h^*(x_i^*).\beta^*), h^*(x_i^*).\beta^* \geq 0$$

Where $\beta_i^*$ is the correcting weight connecting the $i^{th}$ hidden node to the output nodes in the correcting space and $\gamma$ is introduced. To minimize the above functional (10), we construct The Lagrangian function as:

$$L_D = \frac{1}{2}[\|\beta\|^2 + \gamma\|\beta^*\|^2] + C\sum_{i=1}^{l} h^*(x_i^*).\beta^* - \sum_{i=1}^{l} \alpha[(t_i(\beta.h(x_i))) - (1 - (h^*(x_i^*).\beta^*))]$$

$$- \sum_{i=1}^{l} \mu_i(h^*(x_i^*).\beta^*) \tag{11}$$

Where $\alpha_i$ and $\mu_i$ are the Lagrangian multipliers and are non-negative values. The dual function:

$$\max_{\alpha, \mu} L_D = \sum_{1=1}^{l} \alpha_i - \frac{1}{2}\sum_{i,j=1}^{l} \alpha_i\alpha_j t_i t_j K(x_i, x_j)$$

$$- \frac{1}{2\gamma}\sum_{i,j=1}^{l} (\alpha_i + \mu_i - C)(\alpha_j + \mu_j - C)K*(x_i^*, x_j^*) \tag{12}$$

$$\text{Such that}: \sum_{i=1}^{l} (\alpha_i + \mu_i - C) = 0, \alpha_i \geq 0, \mu_i \geq 0 \tag{13}$$

There are two kernels defining similarity between two objects in different spaces (decision and correcting spaces). The decision function depends on the kernel defined in the decision space. Still, the coefficient $\alpha$ depends on the similarity measure in both spaces.

The new algorithm for the training step is summarized as following:
Given the training set $X$, and the privileged information $X^*$

- Random generation of the respective input weights $W, W^*$.
- Calculate the hidden node output matrices $H, H^*$ and solve the optimization (12)
- Compute $\beta = \sum_{i=1}^{l} \alpha_i t_i h(x_i)$ and the decision function: $f(x) = \sum_{i=1}^{l} \alpha_i t_i h(x_i, x)$.

# 4  Experiment Results and Analysis

In this section, we present the experiments' setup and the evaluation of the performance of the Sparse ELM using privileged information, and its comparisons with Sparse ELM and ELM+ on publically available datasets from UCI machine learning repository [23] and on the ELM official web site.

## 4.1  Experiments Description

We have worked on three different datasets from the UCI machine learning repository namely, Bank Marketing dataset [25] (referred to as Bank names), Breast Cancer Wisconsin dataset [26] (referred to as BreastCancer), Heart Disease dataset [27] (referred to as Heart Disease) and one dataset from the ELM website (referred to as Diabetes). The Table 1 shows the original information of the datasets.

We utilized five-fold cross validation to evaluate the algorithms. All the simulations and evaluations are done with MATLAB R2014b running on an Intel® Core™ i5-4590 CPU @ 3.30 GHz with 4.00 GB RAM. Parts of the codes are taken from the codes available on the Extreme Learning Machine (ELM) official web site[1].

**Table 1.**  Description of the used datasets

| Dataset | Diabetes | Bank names | Breastcancer | Heartdisease |
|---|---|---|---|---|
| Dataset characteristics | Multivariate | Multivariate | Multivariate | Multivariate |
| Number of instances/attributes/Date | 756/ 8/N/A | 45211/ 17/2012 | 198/ 34/1995 | 303/ 75/1988 |
| Random permutation | No | Yes | Yes | Yes |

## 4.2  Experimental Results and Analysis

The performance comparison with classic methods is represented in the Table 2:

According to the results in Table 2, our proposed method has improved the testing time in most of the cases. Training and testing accuracies are also higher in our method because of the use of the quadratic programming algorithm which reaches the global minimum.

---

[1] www.ntu.edu.sg/home/egbhuang.

**Table 2.** Performance comparison of the proposed methods with other methods.

| Datasets | ELM PLUS | | | | S-ELM | | | | Our method | | | |
|---|---|---|---|---|---|---|---|---|---|---|---|---|
| | Train time | Test-time | Train Accu | Test Accu | Train time | Test-time | Train Accu | Test Accu | Train time | Test-time | Train Accu | Test Accu |
| Diabetes | 0.3594 | 0.0156 | 66.17 | 71.43 | 0.0078 | 0.0000 | 66.17 | 71.43 | **0.0117** | **0.000** | **66.17** | **71.43** |
| Bank names | 2.4297 | 0.3203 | 93.26 | 96.67 | 1.9688 | **0.0469** | 93.26 | 96.67 | **1.0938** | 0.1406 | **93.26** | **96.67** |
| Banks Proce | 2.3984 | 0.1719 | **88.19** | 88.89 | 2.7188 | 0.0625 | 87.78 | 88.57 | **1.5156** | **0.0313** | 88.16 | **88.89** |
| Heart Disea. | 0.0254 | **0.0020** | **98.56** | **76.59** | 0.0279 | 0.0042 | 56.67 | 61.90 | **0.0164** | 0.0023 | 56.67 | 61.90 |
| Breast Canc. | 0.0201 | 0.0015 | **100.0** | **87.50** | 0.0145 | 0.0040 | ~ | ~ | 0.0134 | 0.0014 | 74.67 | 83.33 |

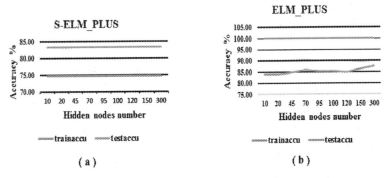

**Fig. 1.** Training and testing accuracy comparison on the Breast Cancer dataset (a) and (b) respectively.

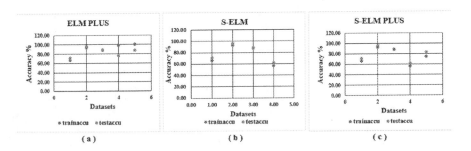

**Fig. 2.** Accuracies comparison

Though in some cases, the ELM plus outperforms our method (S-ELM_PLUS), our method is more stable than the ELM plus as shown on Fig. 1. The use of the quadratic optimization algorithm helps to quickly generalize and stabilize, while the ELM plus is sensitive to the number of the hidden nodes.

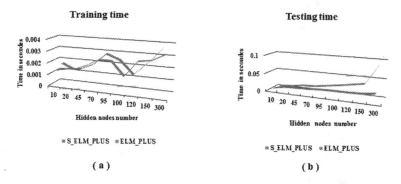

**Fig. 3.** Heart disease dataset

In most of the cases, the testing accuracy is improved in our method. As displayed on Fig. 2 our method performs better than the ELM plus and the Sparse ELM in testing accuracy. For rational comparison the sparse ELM algorithm, used the optimization algorithm. When the hidden nodes number increases the ELM plus tends to overfitting while our method attains the global optimum and stabilizes, it is not affected by the number of the hidden nodes.

The sparsity of our method compared to the unified ELM is proven by the execution time which is smaller for our method than ELM plus. By using equality constraints most of the values are not null in ELM-PLUS while for our proposed method we only compute for the support vectors. Figure 3 shows the execution time comparison for the heart disease dataset.

## 5    Conclusion

The sparse ELM using privileged information offers solutions to three challenges in machine learning research namely, memory storage saving, implementation on large scale datasets and testing time reduction. In addition, privileged information improves the training accuracy and reduces classification error. Its use in many social cases like in emotion recognition should solve the challenge of combining modalities from different sources to reinforce the prediction of the strongest signal by relating privileged information from the weak one.

The reduction of the testing time combined with the testing accuracy improvements, make the Sparse ELM using privileged information candidate to a real-time application. For future work, we will extend our method to the use of real life data.

**Acknowledge.** This work is supported by the National Key Research and Development Program of China under Grant No. 2016YFB0700502, 2016YFB1001404.

# References

1. Vapnik, V., Vashist, A.: A new learning paradigm: Learning using privileged information. Neural Netw. **22**(5–6), 544–557 (2009)
2. Vapnik, V., Vashist, A., Pavlovich, N.: Learning using hidden information: master class learning. In: Proceedings of NATO Workshop on Mining Massive Data Sets for Security, pp. 3–14 (2008)
3. Feyereisl, J., Aickelin, U.: Privileged information for data clustering. Inf. Sci. **194**, 4–23 (2012)
4. Ji, Y., Sun, S.-L., Lu, Y.: Multitask multiclass privileged information Support Vector Machines. In: 21st International Conference on Pattern Recognition (ICPR 2012), pp. 2323–2326. IEEE Press, Tsukuba (2012)
5. Liu, J., Zhu, W.-X., Zhong, P.: A New Multi-class Support Vector Algorithm Based on Privileged Information. J. Information & Computational Science **10**(2), 443–450 (2013)
6. Wang, S.-F., Zhu, Y.-C., Yue, L.-H., Ji, Q.: Emotion recognition with the help of privileged information. IEEE Trans. Auton. Ment. Dev. **7**(3), 189–200 (2015)
7. Huang, G.-B., Zhou, H.-M., Ding, X.-J., Zhang, R.: Extreme learning machine for regression and multiclass classification. IEEE Trans. Syst. Man. Cybern. **42**(2), 513–529 (2012)
8. Huang, G.-B., Ding, X.-J., Zhou, H.-M.: Optimization method based extreme learning machine for classification. Neurocomputing **74**, 155–163 (2010)
9. Yu, W.-C., Zhuang, F.-Z., He, Q., Shi, Z.-Z.: Learning deep representations via extreme learning machines. Neurocomputing **149**, 308–315 (2015)
10. Vapnik, V., Izmailov, R.: Learning Using Privileged Information: Similarity Control and knowledge Transfer. J. Mach. Learn. Res. **16**, 2023–2049 (2015)
11. Vapnik, V.: Empirical Inference Science (2007)
12. Deng, C.-W., Huang, G.-B., Xu, J., Tang, J.-X.: Extreme learning machines: new trends and applications. Sci. Chin. Inf. Sci. **58**, 1–16 (2015)
13. Bai, Z., Huang, G.-B., Wang, D.-W., Wang, H., Westover, M.B.: Sparse extreme learning machine for classification. IEEE Trans. Cybern. **44**(10), 1858–1870 (2015)
14. Huang, G.-B.: An insight into extreme learning machines: random neurons. Random Features and Kernels. Cogn. Comput. **6**, 376–390 (2014)
15. Cai, F., Cherkassky, V.: SVM+ regression and multi-task Learning. In: International Joint Conference on Neural Networks, IJCNN 2009, pp. 418–424. IEEE, Press, Georgia (2009)
16. Vapnik, V.: Empirical Inference Science Afterword of 2006. Springer, New York (2006)
17. Zhang, W.-B., Ji, H.-B., Liao, G.-S., Zhang, Y.-Q.: A Novel Extreme Learning Machine using privileged information. Neurocomputing **168**, 823–828 (2015)
18. Huang, G.-B., Zhu, Q.-Y., Siew, C.-K.: Extreme learning machine: Anew learning scheme of feedforward neural networks. In: Proceeding of International Joint Conference on Neural Networks IJCNN, vol. 2, pp. 985–990 (2004)
19. Huang, G.-B., Chen, L., Siew, C.-K.: Universal approximation using incremental constructive feedforward networks with random hidden nodes. IEEE Trans. Neural Netw. **17**(4), 879–892 (2006)
20. Huang, G.-B., Zhu, Q.-Y., Siew, C.-K.: Extreme learning machine: Theory and applications. Neurocomputing **70**, 489–501 (2006)
21. Huang, G.-B., Chen, L.: Convex incremental extreme learning machine. Neurocomputing. **70**, 3056–3062 (2007)
22. Vapnik, V.: Estimation of Dependencies Based on Empirical Data, 2nd edn. Springer, New York (2006)

23. Blake, C., Keogh, E., Merz, C.: UCI Repository of Machine Learning Database. University of California, Irvine (1998)
24. Cherkassky, V., Dai, W.: Empirical study of the universum svm learning for high-dimensional data. In: Alippi, C., Polycarpou, M., Panayiotou, C., Ellinas, G. (eds.) ICANN 2009. LNCS, vol. 5768, pp. 932–941. Springer, Heidelberg (2009). doi:10.1007/978-3-642-04274-4_96
25. Moro, S., Cortez, P., Rita, P.: A data-driven approach to predict the success of bank telemarketing. Decis. Support Syst. **62**, 22–31 (2014). Elsevier
26. http://archive.ics.uci.edu/ml/machine-learning-databases/breast-cancer-wisconsin/
27. http://archive.ics.uci.edu/ml/datasets/heart+Disease

# Traffic Sign Detection with Convolutional Neural Networks

Evan Peng[1(✉)], Feng Chen[2], and Xinkai Song[2]

[1] Taipei American School, Taipei, Taiwan
evanp17112141@tas.tw
[2] Department of Automation, Tsinghua University, Beijing, China
chenfeng@mail.tsinghua.edu.cn, sxk018@163.com

**Abstract.** This research focuses on improving traffic sign detection in cars using Convoluted Neural Networks (CNN), with images from the German Traffic Sign database. In order to generate more accurate detection results of traffic signs, different algorithms were used to generate the detection and classification tasks. The Faster Region Based Convolutional Neural Network (Faster R-CNN) and You Only Look Once networks were compared beforehand to determine which CNN to use. The Faster R-CNN was decided upon based off of previous results, then used to generate the classification and detection tasks. Pre-training weights were made using Caffe based off of the German Traffic Sign Recognition Benchmark database. Different methods of generation of training data were then used and compared. The Faster R-CNN network was used to create a classification task based off the images from the self-generated training images, which was tested against the German Traffic Sign Detection Benchmark database.

**Keywords:** Traffic sign detection · Traffic sign classification · Automation · R-CNN · Convolutional · Neural networks · Faster R-CNN · Fast R-CNN

## 1 Introduction

The automation of cars is becoming a more and more prominent subject in the current progression of artificial intelligence today. Companies such as Google, Uber, and Tesla have all announced plans of developing autonomous cars, with Tesla already having fully function autonomation capabilities on all 3 of their current models [1], available for consumers today. Laws are also being shifted in order to accommodate autonomous cars. In order to ensure that autonomous vehicles do not endanger the lives of humans on the road, the accurate detection and classification of traffic signs is vital.

For this research paper, in pertinence to the dataset used, traffic sign detection will be defined as the detection and classification of traffic signs, while traffic sign classification will be defined as solely the classification of traffic signs. Ensuring that the divide between the two is defined is necessary for this paper so results for detection do not get confused with the results of classification. Traffic sign detection is done by determining and detecting the area in which the traffic sign could potentially be located. Afterwards, the area is then classified to determine what the traffic sign represents. In

F. Sun et al. (Eds.): ICCSIP 2016, CCIS 710, pp. 214–224, 2017.
DOI: 10.1007/978-981-10-5230-9_24

this paper, 43 various traffic signs were used from the German Traffic Sign Recognition Benchmark (GTSRB) [2] for the classification of the traffic signs (Fig. 1).

**Fig. 1.** All 43 GTSRB signs

These signs present difficulty in the detection and classification of such images as many of them are quite similar to each other. Difficulty is further increased as the signs are detected from further distances, which would result in a higher chance of confusing the signs with other signs during the detection and classification task. Lighting and weather conditions can also affect the detection and classification of such images, which again may result in either mis-classification or non-detection such signs. Speed is also an issue that must be acknowledged in the detection such traffic signs. When an autonomous car is operating under real time circumstances the car must be able to accurately detect and classify the traffic sign as soon as possible to minimize the risk of danger (Fig. 2).

**Fig. 2.** An example of difficult detection circumstances (the sign is designated by the red box) (Color figure online)

In order to account for the above issues, the neural network model that is used must be able to efficiently detect images while also having high classification accuracy and detection/classification speed rates. Convolutional Neural Networks (CNN) are the most widely-used model of neural networks in image-based detection. Over 50,000 various traffic sign images from the GTSRB of various noise levels were used to generate training data for the German Traffic Sign Detection Benchmark (GTSDB) [2] test. After examination and light testing of various versions of different CNN implementations, the Faster Region Based Convolutional Neural Network (Faster R-CNN) was decided upon and used to generate the classification and detection tasks. After having viewed the testing results from Tim Dettmers of various Graphics Processing Units (GPU) [3] and his analysis of hardware requirements for deep learning [4], a NVIDIA GTX 1070 8 GB GPU, Intel Core i5 6500 Skylake Processor, and 16 GB of RAM were used to perform the training, detection, and classification tasks.

## 2   Related Works

There are not many modern papers regarding the usage of neural networks besides for CNNs for the application of image based detection. This is due to the high performance that CNNs present when image based detection tasks are needed. The CNN is modeled after a study by D. H. Hubel and T.N Wiesel in their paper on the monkey striate cortex [5], in which Hubel and Wiesel found that the visual cortex of a monkey contains receptive fields that detect light in overlapping sub-regions. The usage of CNNs grew especially prominent in image based detection with the LeNet-5, a 7 level convolutional network by Yann LeCun et al. [6], with focus around the detection of handwritten digits. On the Mixed National Institute of Standards and Technology (MNIST) database, a CNN based model resulted from Dan Ciregan et al. [7] achieved the highest accuracy to date, with a 99.77% accuracy rate.

**Object Detection with Neural Networks.** A CNN, GoogLeNet from Christian Szegedy et al. of Google [8], the University of North Carolina, and the University of Michigan scored a 43.9% detection rate with a classification error of 6.66% on the ImageNet Large Scale Visual Recognition Challenge database, which won the competition in 2014. The ImageNet Challenge database consisted of several millions of images of various objects and scenes. The GoogLeNet consisted of around 100 layers, going 22 layers deep with parameters, and 27 layers deep when counting pooling. The team behind GoogLeNet proposed a CNN called Inception which focused on the stacking of modules upon each other, similar to the Faster R-CNN method, which will be discussed later. The difference between the 2 being the Inception region classifier compared to the R-CNN classifier.

**Traffic Sign Recognition with GTSRB.** For the GTSRB database, work had been done by Dan Cireşan et al. [9] in which a 9 layer single CNN was proposed, with 7 hidden layers. It consisted of the input layer, 3 convolutional layers with another 3 max pooling layers, followed by 2 fully connected layers. For training data, they had just cropped down the images of testing data to be the same size, then plain-fed the images through the CNN. With just the usage of a CNN, they achieved a 98.73% recognition rate.

Using a Multi-Layer Perceptron (MLP) and a CNN they achieved a 99.15% recognition rate. However due to the usage of the MLP, the error rate increased by 4%.

**Convolutional Neural Networks (CNN).** CNNs operate similarly to a standard Neural Network (NN); however, they take in images better than a standard NN would be able to. A CNN takes in images and moves the images through the input layer, creating a 3D volume of neurons with dimensions of width, height, and color channels/depth, which is then output to the next 3D neuron layer. The input layer will have a 3rd dimension of value 3 (representing the 3 color channels of R, G, B). However further outputs from the hidden layers will have a different 3rd dimension value depending on the amount of filters used in the convolution layer (Fig. 3).

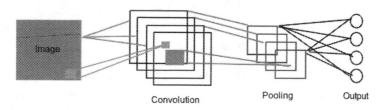

Convolution          Pooling          Output

**Fig. 3.** Example CNN

An issue that is displayed with larger images is the issue of Fully Connected Networks, in which learning features which span the entire image would computationally take a very long time to process if every neuron was connected to every neuron. In order to solve this, for larger images Locally Connected Networks are used instead, and Fully Connected layers are placed at the end in order to compute the final class scores. This consists of only small subsets of the input to be sent to each neuron, and ensures that computation moves along speedily. This is more similar to how the visual cortex is used in which receptive fields only respond to certain areas rather than the entire area.

In order to process the image after the Convolutional layer, as per standard NN, an activation layer is needed. It is standard practice to use the Rectifier Linear Unit (ReLU) activation layer in NN and CNN due to not changing gradient when passing back through Back-Propagation (BPP) during training, which otherwise would result in the vanishing gradient problem. The vanishing gradient problem occurs when the activation layer has a changing gradient, such as with a sigmoid activation layer.

The Sigmoid function presents a changing gradient while, as shown in Fig. 4, the ReLU function does not. With the backpropagation algorithm, when the gradients are multiplied together, if the gradient is changing, the resulting product will begin to exponentially decrease, resulting in a 0 output, which will then result in a loss of accuracy/stagnation in cost. Thus, the ReLU function is the best choice for the CNN and most NN in general. There might follow many convolutional layers and ReLU layers followed by each other.

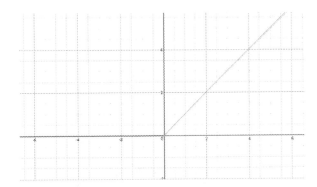

**Fig. 4.** ReLU function

After going through the variable amount of convolutional and ReLU layers, a Pooling layer will then follow to perform downsampling to create a volume with the same depth, but different height and width. After obtaining the features from the convolutional and ReLU layers, the features are pooled over a smaller region. In this case, the maximum value of each feature is taken to develop a single, smaller feature region. These pooling layers may also be inserted periodically between the convolutional and ReLU layers in larger CNN. Finally, a fully connected layer, which has full connections to all the activations from the previous layer, computes the final class scores and determines the resulting classification.

**Faster Region Based CNN (Faster R-CNN).** The Faster R-CNN differs from a standard CNN with its usage of Region Proposal Networks (RPN). RPNs are neural networks which focus on splitting the input image into around 2,000 different region proposals using Selective Search [10], which computes regions which have the highest probability of containing an object. The RPN in Faster R-CNN however does not use Selective Search to divide the regions, and is only present in R-CNN and Fast R-CNN. The region proposals are then warped into a single region, which is then fed through the CNN, resulting in a CNN known as Region Based Convolutional Neural Networks (R-CNN).

As shown in Fig. 5, the image first goes through the RPN and then through the CNN. While this resulted in more accurate results compared to a standard CNN, computation and detection time was very slow due to the multiple stages generated by the R-CNN with the multiple region proposals. Fast R-CNN was then created by Ross Girschick [11] in order to solve this issue by splitting the computation of the convolution layers between proposals and having the CNN run first and then generate the region proposals rather than have the Regions of Interest (RoI) feed into the CNN. Each object proposal from the CNN has a feature vector extracted by a RoI max pooling layer which then connects to the fully connected layers which outputs the classification outputs of a probability (softmax layer) and 4 values of the object class (bbox regressor) (Fig. 6).

Faster R-CNN was further created by Ross Girschick et al. [12] in order to account for the complex training and detection pipeline of Fast R-CNN. Faster R-CNN focused

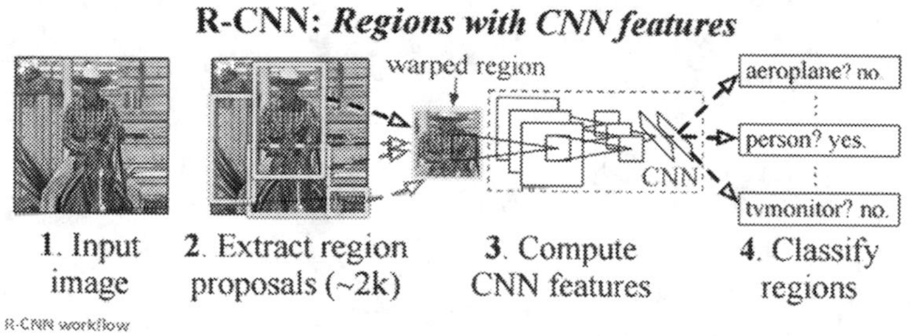

## R-CNN: *Regions with CNN features*

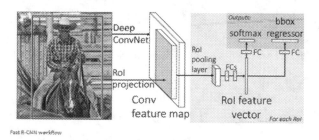

1. Input image
2. Extract region proposals (~2k)
3. Compute CNN features
4. Classify regions

**Fig. 5.** Region based convolutional neural network [11]

**Fig. 6.** Fast-RCNN [12]

on the usage of a CNN followed by a 4-step alternating training of the RPN and Fast-RCNN algorithms. The 4-step alternating training path consisted of first training an RPN off just the feature maps from the initial CNN, which already proves to be faster than training the RPN off the entire image. Using these proposals, a Fast R-CNN detection network is then trained, with pre-trained weights used to ensure learning occurs. In the third step, the RPN training is initialized based off the Fast R-CNN detections with any convolutional layers shared between the 2 fixed and only the unique RPN layers are adjusted. In the final step, the Fast R-CNN uses the proposals from the previous step RPN to initialize itself, in which the convolutional layers shared between the two are fixed once again, and unique layers are adjusted. Once again, with these two networks sharing the same convolutional layers to form a unified network, two outputs are generated with the classification of the object from a probability layer and the region of the object detected with the bbox regressor (Fig. 7).

**You Only Look Once (YOLO).** You Only Look Once is a CNN created by Joseph Redmon et al. [13] that works by resizing the image then running a convolutional network to increase training speed and detection speed, being a reported 100 times faster in training than Fast R-CNN as per the paper from Joseph Redmon. However, when tested against the Fast R-CNN, the Fast R-CNN managed to beat it heavily in terms of accuracy by 10.5% in terms of mean average precision regarding the detection and classification of objects on the VOC 2012 database. While the YOLO network is a lot faster than the Fast R-CNN, the speed of both is still quite fast, and the accuracy trade-off of YOLO does not seem worth it in the event of traffic signs detection, since a

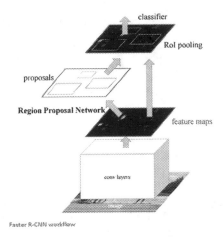

**Fig. 7.** Faster-RCNN [12]

car would still have some time to process the sign before it would need to act upon it, in which the Fast R-CNN time is still a fraction of the time needed.

## 3 Experiments

The Faster R-CNN was used to train the network. The network was trained, as previously mentioned, with a NVIDIA GTX 1070 8 GB GPU, Intel Core i5 6500 Skylake Processor, and 16 GB of RAM. The network was tested against the GTSDB database.

**Training Process.** First, the Faster R-CNN was trained in its original state with the pre-trained weights of the ImageNet weights, with only the GTSRB images as training. This resulted in low results, and a low mean average precision (mAP) of 24.19%.

This was probably a result of there being little background for the Faster R-CNN to detect, as the GTSRB images ranged from $34 \times 34$ to $127 \times 127$, and the GTSDB test images area $1360 \times 800$. A method was then used which just used the GTSDB training images. However, there were only 600 images, and a similar result was made when compared to the 300 testing images with a final mAP of 24.9%. This was probably due to the low amount of training images and lack of noise with the signs in the images that the GTSRB images have. In order to compensate for the both of this, a script was written which pasted GTSRB images over images from the Road/Lane Detection Evaluation 2013 (RLDE) by Jannick Fritsch and Tobias Kuehnl [13]. Annotation files were also generated. Figure 8 which displays an example training image generated is on the next page for easier viewing. Around 19,000 images were generated in total. This ensured that appropriate background was generated while also ensuring that noise is present for the traffic signs.

The Fast R-CNN and RPN networks for the 4 step alternating training process had 7 convolutional layers each to ensure higher accuracy. Pre trained weights were made using Caffe off the GTSRB images to train off of instead of using the ImageNet weights for the Faster-RCNN algorithm.

**Fig. 8.** Example training image generated

**Results and Efficiency.** Across the 300 GTSDB testing images, a mAP of 77.21% was achieved. The 0 indexes present were not counted towards the mAP, as those classes were just not present in the GTSDB testing images. When testing with all 800 GTSDB images from the training and testing database, a mAP of 72.15% is achieved (Figs. 9 and 10).

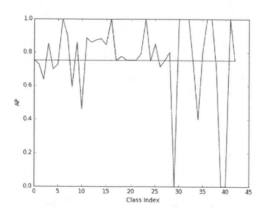

**Fig. 9.** 300 GTSDB images

Detection images on the GTSDB set will be shown on the last page for easier viewing (Fig. 11). In Fig. 12 the previous issue of distance and bad weather/lighting affecting the results of the detection is shown to have been resolved with this issue through the training data generation, as the 2 signs are placed quite a distance away from the car. While still being quite close together, the model was able to differentiate between these signs with a high accuracy of 99.7% and 94.5% accuracy for each sign respectively. While most of the detection results were quite high, there were some issues. Especially when considering the signs bluer in appearance, there tended to be an issue of accuracy. Figure 13 shows a blue sign with a lower accuracy present of 60.6%,

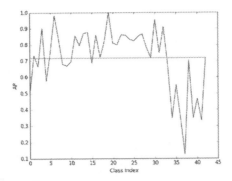

**Fig. 10.** 800 GTSDB images

showing how ineffective the model could be when detecting more "blue" signs. Occasionally the model also detected an area that was not a sign due to similar coloring (Fig. 14). This is an issue as this would result in a vehicle performing actions it should not be performing. This was potentially generated due to some of the signs in the RLDE dataset not being annotated as they were not generated from the GTSRB, and thus the model considered those background, resulting in awry detections. This was more prominent with images that displayed the color blue more.

The detection speed when the demo was run was a mere 0.2818 s per image on average, even with multiple signs. This demonstrates the high speed of the neural network, which is a goal that was set forward with the research of the application of Faster R-CNN on traffic signs. Earlier a potential issue that must be analyzed is the issue of speed, and YOLO was considered as a response to this issue. However, we see with the results from Faster R-CNN that speed is not an issue, and YOLO would only have resulted in potentially lower results.

**Fig. 11.** Red sign with 99.8% accuracy (Color figure online)

**Fig. 12.** Image of 2 signs with 99.7% and 94.5% accuracy respectively

**Fig. 13.** Image with blue sign detected with a lower 60.6% accuracy. (Color figure online)

**Fig. 14.** Failed detection with supposed accuracy of 89.6%

## 4   Conclusions

In this paper, we presented the usage of Faster R-CNN on the generation of detection and classification tasks. The detector proved to be very fast and had quite high results of around 90% accuracy for multiple images, but there were images where accuracy was quite low or detection was completely off due to potential issues regarding the background of the RLDE dataset. In the future, road images should be used that do not include direct signs in the background that are not annotated. However, including images or colors that are similar to the color on signs in the background would ensure that the images which are similar to signs in the future are ignored.

Higher resolution pictures of Figs. 11, 12, 13 and 14 and additional detection images are available at http://imgur.com/a/MHlPY.

**Acknowledgments and Institution.** 我单位的置名格式: Department of Automation and CBICR Center, Tsinghua University; Beijing KLSBDPA Key Laboratory.

论文的资助项目: This work is supported in part by the National Natural Science Foundation of China under Grants 61671266, 61327902, and in part by the Research Project of Tsinghua University under Grant 20161080084, and in part by National High-tech Research and Development Plan under Grant 2015AA042306.

Acknowledgment must be given to the Tsinghua University Department of Automation, for supporting me and allowing me to work with them for this research, and Yan Qi for helping solve issues regarding implementation.

# References

1. https://www.tesla.com/presskit/autopilot
2. Houben, S., Stalkamp, J., Salmen, J., Schilpsing, M., Igel, C.: Detection of traffic signs in real-world images: the German traffic sign detection benchmark. In: International Joint Conference on Neural Networks
3. Dettmers, T.: Which GPU for deep learning http://timdettmers.com/2014/08/14/which-gpu-for-deep-learning/
4. Dettmers, T.: A full hardware guide to deep learning http://timdettmers.com/2015/03/09/deep-learning-hardware-guide/
5. Hubel, D.H., Wiesel, T.N.: Receptive fields and functional architecture of monkey striate cortex. J. Physiol. **195**, 215–243 (1968)
6. Lecun, Y., Bottou, L., Bengio, Y., Haffner, P.: Gradient-based learning applied to document recognition. In: Proceeding of Institute of Electrical and Electronical Engineers (1998)
7. Ling, S., Wu, D., Li, X.: Learning deep and wide: a spectral method for learning deep networks. IEEE Trans. Neural Netw. Learn. Syst. **25**, 2303–2308 (2014)
8. Szegedy, C., Liu, W., Jia, Y., Sermanet, P., Reed, S., Anguelov, D., Erhan, D., Vincent, V., Andrew, R.:Going deeper with convolutions, computer vision foundation CVPR (2015)
9. Ciresan, D., Meier, U., Masci, J., Schmidhuber, J.: A committee of neural networks for traffic sign classification. In: Dalle Molle Institute for Artificial Intelligence (2011)
10. Uijlings, J.R.R., van de Sande, K.E.A.; Gevers, T., Smeulders, A.W.M.: Selective search for object recognition. In: IJCV Technical report (2012)
11. Girshick, R.: Fast R-CNN in arXiv:1504.08083
12. Girschik, R., Ren, S., He, K., Sun, J.: Faster R-CNN: Towards real-time object detection with region proposal networks arXiv:1506.01497
13. Redmon, J., Divvala, S., Girschik, R., Farhadi, A.: You only look once: unified, real-time object detection arXiv:1506.02640
14. Fritsch, J., Tobias, K.: Road/lane detection evaluation. In: Honda Research Institute Europe, Karisruhe Institute of Technology (2013)

# License Plate Recognition Using Deep FCN

Yue Wu[1(✉)] and Jianmin Li[2]

[1] Shenzhen College of International Education, Shenzhen, China
wuyueholmes@qq.com
[2] State Key Laboratory of Intelligent Technology and Systems,
Tsinghua National Laboratory for Information Science and Technology,
Department of Computer Science and Technology,
Tsinghua University, Beijing, China
lijianmin@mail.tsinghua.edu.cn

**Abstract.** In our work, we concentrate on the problem of car license plate recognition after the plate has been extracted from an image. Traditional methods approach this problem as three separate steps: preprocessing, segmentation, and recognition. In this paper, we propose a unified approach that integrates these steps using a fully convolutional network. We train a 36-class FCN on a dataset of single characters and apply it to height-normalized license plates. The architecture of this model successfully reduces the loss in detail during end-to-end convolution. Finally, we extract the results from the output sequences of probabilities using a variant of the NMS algorithm. The experiments on public license plate datasets show that our approach outperforms the state-of-the-art methods.

**Keywords:** Computer vision · Fully Convolutional Network · License plate recognition · End-to-end recognition · Residual learning

## 1 Introduction

In recent years, the rapid growth of automobiles has created the need for reliable automatic car License Plate Detection and Recognition (LPDR) systems. The increase in traffic produces an increasing amount of data, which makes manual processing impossible [1, 2]. Hence, the field of LPDR has attracted considerable interest among researchers.

Recognizing sequences of characters in an open environment is much more difficult than recognizing a single character since the algorithm needs to first separate the text. Existing systems and algorithms work well under controlled conditions. LPDR in an open environment remains a challenging topic: changes in the direction of the camera, the size of the plate, the font and color of the numbers, and even the illumination and background of the picture directly affect the results of license plate recognition [3].

---

This research is conducted during the Research Science Initiative — Tsinghua 2016.

F. Sun et al. (Eds.): ICCSIP 2016, CCIS 710, pp. 225–234, 2017.
DOI: 10.1007/978-981-10-5230-9_25

Previous work on license plate recognition mainly relies on delicate preprocessing [4] and transformations [5], using brightness, color [5], or size as features to help segment the characters [6]. Characters on the plate are then segmented and provided to a classifier to produce the final results.

Attempts toward a unified solution have been made using probabilistic models transferred from sequential natural language processing [7], but they too incorporate lots of prior knowledge which does not generalize well to complicated real-world situations.

We optimize the sliding window solution in [8] by extending the idea in [9] to a fully convolutional network (FCN). We feed a whole height-normalized car plate into the FCN and produce a matrix of probabilities. One axis represents the possible characters, and the other the index of the character in the license plate. Each element in the matrix represents the probability that indexed location on the plate is a certain character. At last, the output is refined by a customized NMS [10] algorithm to produce the final output.

The rest of the paper is organized as follows. Section 2 gives a brief discussion on related work. Section 3 describes the method and algorithms on license plate recognition. Experimental results are shown in Sect. 4, and conclusions drawn in Sect. 5.

## 2  Related Works

This section introduces previous work on license plate recognition and suggests their contribution to our proposal.

### 2.1  License Plate Recognition

Traditional approaches to license plate segmentation can be mainly classified into three groups: connectivity based, projection based and knowledge based [3].

The first group classifies each pixel in an image based on connectivity. Classes with similar size and aspect ratio are candidates for license plate characters [11]. However, this method depends on the color and brightness of the image, which are widely affected by external factors such as dust, illumination, and background.

The second method is popular because of the high contrast between characters and the background of the license plate. Horizontal and vertical projection of the license plate is used to determine the position of each character [12]. With 99.2% accuracy and a 10 – 20 ms per picture processing speed, this method is the simplest and most common method to separate characters in license plates [3]. Nevertheless, noise and tilts may still make the projection values difficult to interpret.

The third method segments the characters with designed templates. The program can use the template to locate the position of every character [13]. If the picture is skewed, however, the system will fail.

License plate character recognition is a subset of scene character recognition. The existing algorithms mainly follow two approaches: template matching and learning based methods.

Template matching methods [3] recognize characters by comparing them to pre-stored templates. Although simple and straightforward, they only work with brightness and size normalized pictures.

Learning-based methods include hidden Markov models (HMM) [4] and neural networks [13]. They are more robust than template matching, but their performance is still limited by the quality of segmented characters.

A novel, unified approach is provided by [12] using a recurrent neural network (RNN) with long short term memory (LSTM). The RNN network makes predictions based on the feature extracted by a pre-trained CNN. Although this model is currently state-of-the-art in LPDR, the use of RNN complicates the solution and does not improve the results effectively since there is no correlation between the characters on the car plate.

## 2.2 Convolutional Neural Network and Space Displacement Neural Network

In recent years, CNN and its variants have taken over the field of computer vision.

The Oxford VGG team [14] proposes an excellent end-to-end solution. Its model improves the performance of [8, 9] by incorporating various techniques including maxout and dropout. Weight sharing between the detection model and classification model reduces overall computations and uses training data more efficiently. VGG also makes use of the space displacement architecture [9] which reduces redundant computations during convolution.

Our approach to license plate recognition improves upon these architectures with a deep FCN, which performs as both a character detector and a classifier. In other words, we treat spaces as a character in our FCN. Since we only concern about the characters in a finite area – the license plate, this design saves time and computations. Experiments show that this scheme can produce promising results.

## 2.3 Deep Residual Learning

Even though very deep networks can converge due to the efforts of [14–16], they often cannot outperform shallower designs due to the degradation problem. In [17], a very deep residual neural network is proposed to solve this problem. Shortcut connections are established, and residual functions are learned with reference to the layer of inputs. This architecture enables us to train a 30-layer residual network for character recognition in license plates.

## 2.4 Fully Convolutional Network

Space displacement neural network iterates the fully connected layers through a feature matrix produced by convolving the entire input image with the convolutional layers of the network. Inspired by this idea, we propose a deep FCN with residual design to perform the task of end-to-end license plate recognition.

FCNs have not been widely used in accurate end-to-end recognition. Most current FCNs performs object-wise tasks [18] which require less accuracy than character recognition. To structure a fully convolutional network for accurate end-to-end license plate character recognition or scene text recognition is not an easy task. As is widely known, most convolutional layers learn features or approximation to the inputs, which can be considered as learning effective ways to compress the inputs. Therefore, there are is always lost detail during compression, especially in designs that have small kernel size and relatively large stride.

# 3   License Plate Recognition

In the traditional sequence of LPDR, as we introduced above, preprocessing and character segmentation play a significant role in the success of the system. Bad pre-processing and segmentation may cause the digits to be unreadable by the classifier. Former approaches apply many post-processing techniques to handle the miss-segmented blocks [19], making the results more reliant on prior knowledge of the shape of the characters and the length of the text. Therefore, we propose an FCN to handle this task.

## 3.1   Network Architecture

Inspired by the methods used in [8, 9], we train a 30-layer CNN model with 36-classes on 32 × 20 gray-scale images of single characters. The network consists of 29 convolutional layers and one fully connected layers. A softmax layer outputs the predicted probability for each class. Since letter "I" never appears in license plates, it is replaced with a class for non-characters. By doing this, we merge a character detector and a classifier into a single model.

## 3.2   Deep Residual Learning

As mentioned earlier, very deep neural networks are often difficult to train, and lots of them perform poorly compared to the shallower networks. In our model, residual design [17] is adopted to tackle this problem.

**Deep Residual Network.** To prove the superiority of residual architecture on deep convolutional neural networks, we propose a "plain" version of our residual net and test it on our test set. With the same initialization techniques as [17], the networks consist of 29 convolutional layers and one fully connected layer. Details of the model are shown in Fig. 1.

We apply batch normalization to the outputs of each convolutional layer. Outputs of each layer are then weighted. The weights are implemented as Scale layer in Caffe and learned through back propagation.

We carefully choose stride, kernel size and padding for each layer to keep as much detail as possible. The kernel size is always bigger than or equal to the stride value in

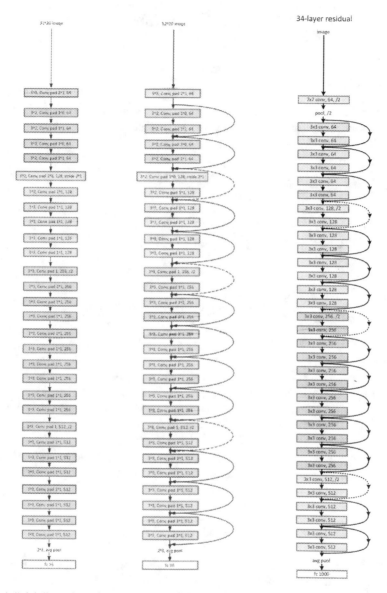

**Fig. 1.** A "plain" version of our proposed 30-layer deep residual network, the proposed model, and the 34-layer deep residual model from [17].

our design to reduce the loss in information. This architecture helps to achieve better results on license plates.

**Fully Convolutional Network.** Our ultimate design is a fully convolutional network. The network is produced by replacing the final fully connected layer of the deep residual network in the previous section with a convolutional layer with kernel size

$2 \times 2$ and 36 output filters. We can, therefore, feed the whole image with height 32 of a license plate to the network to get a vector of predicted classes and their probabilities.

### 3.3    Post-processing

As mentioned before and shown in Fig. 2, our models output a matrix of probabilities. We need to refine the outputs to get the desired sequence.

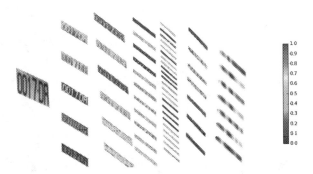

**Fig. 2.** An example license plate processed by 6 layers chosen from the layers that resize the input in the 30-layer neural network.

**NMS Using Length Information.** We propose an NMS [10] post-processing algorithm in which we incorporate prior knowledge about the length of the characters. In this algorithm, we let our NMS algorithm produce a sequence of possible words with their likelihoods.

Because we scan the output features with a fixed step-size, we can infer the overlap in the area of each bounding box based on their position in the sequence. Therefore, instead of suppressing bounding according to overlapping area, we suppress bounding boxes that have

$$\theta d < \varphi \tag{1}$$

where $\theta$ stands for the probability of predicted class, d represents the distance between two characters and $\varphi$ is a hyperparameter set to be 1.55. The likelihood of each refined character P(c) is calculated during NMS by the formula

$$P(c) = \sum p \tag{2}$$

to sum over the probabilities of the outputs merged into one.

Since we expect a character list of fixed length, we could output words that have top k probabilities, where k is the expected length of the characters in the license plate. If there are less than k elements, we continue splitting the element with the highest probability until the requirement is met.

# 4    Experiments and Results

In this section, experiments are performed to verify the successfulness of the proposed architectures. We conduct experiments on NVIDIA Titan X GPU with 12 GB memory.

We train the model using the AdaDelta solver with Delta value set to $1 \times 10^{-8}$ in Caffe with Python 2.7 interface. The initial learning rate (a hyperparameter to Ada-Delta) is set to 1 and is divided by 5 once the error plateaus. AdaDelta solver saves us from having to decide learning rate for different models and reduces the number of times we decrease the learning rate.

## 4.1    Dataset

To create a training set of appropriate size, we combine data from multiple sources. In particular, our dataset includes the English subset of Chars74 k dataset [20], KAIST [21] and SVT-CHAR [22, 23]. A 32 × 20 dataset is generated by ourselves using the datasets mentioned above. We carefully create the none-text class using both computer-generated data and images cropped and concatenated from the datasets above to model the blank between adjacent characters. About 500 pictures of characters cropped from Chinese car plates were added to improve the performance of our classifier on license plates. We carry out four types of data augmentation including adding noise, rotation, translation and stretching. Computer generated images for spaces and individual characters, with distractions on either side, are added to the train set. We test our single character classifier on a combination of the test set of ICDAR 2003 dataset, and some computer generated data similar to the characters on the license plates to give us a solid reflection of the effectiveness our model.

For license plate recognition, we test our model on standard license plate datasets, including the AOLP dataset [19] and the Caltech cars dataset [24]. All the license plates are manually located in the Caltech dataset. We normalize the height of plates to 32 and stretch the width of each image by a factor of 1.2 to produce more outputs after convolution.

## 4.2    Evaluation Criterion

It is hard [3] to compare the performance of different LPDR systems since the systems are not defined or trained on the same datasets, even though they may be tested on the same dataset. To quantify the recognition results, we calculate the recognition accuracy, which is defined as the number of true positives (correctly recognized license plates) over the total number of ground truth images tested. A correctly recognized license plate is one where all the characters on the plate are identified correctly under the correct sequence and with the right number of occurrences. Since most of the previous works present license plate segmentation accuracy and character recognition instead of overall accuracy, we calculate an expectation E of their overall accuracy by a formula

$$E = sc^n \tag{3}$$

where s is the segmentation accuracy, c is the character recognition accuracy, and n stands for the number of characters in the license plate (Tables 1 and 2).

**Table 1.** The accuracy of the deep neural networks on our proposed $30 \times 20$ dataset. The input images are resized for the 9-layer models.

|  | Test accuracy (%) |
|---|---|
| 9-layer CNN [12] | 93.4 |
| Plain 30-layer FCN | 94.7 |
| **Proposed 30-layer FCN** | **97.2** |

**Table 2.** The accuracy of other methods compared with the proposed method on different datasets. The accuracies of the first three approaches are calculated by Eq. (3). The first three are the three segments of AOLP [19].

|  | AC (%) | LE (%) | RP (%) | Caltech (%) |
|---|---|---|---|---|
| Hsu et al. [19] | 78.2 | 69.0 | 73.5 |  |
| V. Ganesh et al. [25] |  |  |  | 49.5 |
| 1st approach from [12] | 84.21 | 84.20 | 71.11 | 47.18 |
| 2nd approach from [12] | 94.85 | 94.19 | 88.38 |  |
| **Proposed FCN** | **97.9** | **97.6** | **98.2** | **92.1** |

### 4.3    License Plate Recognition

**Performance on Customized Character Datasets.**

**Performance on Public License Plate Datasets.** We test our 30-layer FCN on several standard license plate datasets and compare the results with the other proposals. We correct the mislabeled data and eliminate the license plates which has character length not equal to 7 in the Caltech dataset [24]. The accuracy we report on RP segment of AOLP dataset is the accuracy of our model on first 344 images, because we do not have segmented plate images for the rest of the images. The second approach of [12] does not report results on the Caltech dataset because it requires training data that is similar to the test data.

## 5    Conclusion

In this paper, we have presented a unified approach to license plate recognition. We have reduced loss in details during convolution with a 30-layer fully convolutional network. Our network exhibits impressive performance across a wide range of dataset.

Compared to the RNN with **LSTM** [12], our FCN shows better generalization ability and runs in much less time. Our model takes an average of 14.4 ms to process one image on NVIDIA Titan X and 573.4 ms on i7-6700HQ. The results illustrate that our license plate recognition algorithm has an enormous potential of being deployed in the real world.

Further improvements can include training the model directly on car license plates by back propagating from the NMS, or from better post-processing algorithms such as CTCs [12].

In addition, it would be interesting to apply FCNs to end-to-end scene text recognition in the fashion of a Faster RCNN [26]. Since 98% of the training set characters in this framework are not from license plates, its applications are not only limited to license plate recognition.

**Acknowledgements.** I want to give special thanks to Ruoqi Zhang and Fanfu Shentu, who helped me during data collection and network visualization. Also, I would like to thank my writing coach, Aradhana Sinha, and tutor, Ms. Qianhui Wu, who helped me revise my paper.

Last but not the least, I would like to show my gratitude to Tsinghua University and Center for Excellence in Education for the computational resources and for providing me with such a wonderful research opportunity this summer.

# References

1. Liu, G., Ma, Z., Du, Z., Wen, C.: The calculation method of road travel time based on license plate recognition technology. In: Tan, H., Zhou, M. (eds.) Advances in Information Technology and Education. Communications in Computer and Information Science, vol. 201, pp. 385–389. Springer, Heidelberg (2011)

2. Chiou, Y.C., Lan, L.W., Tseng, C.M., Fan, C.C.: Optimal locations of license plate recognition to enhance the origin-destination matrix estimation. In: Proceedings of the Eastern Asia Society for Transportation Studies, vol. 2011, p. 297. Eastern Asia Society for Transportation Studies (2011)

3. Du, S., Ibrahim, M., Shehata, M., Badawy, W.: Automatic license plate recognition (ALPR): a state-of-the-art review. IEEE Trans. Circ. Syst. Video Technol. **23**(2), 311–325 (2013)

4. Llorens, D., Marzal, A., Palazón, V., Vilar, J.M.: Car license plates extraction and recognition based on connected components analysis and HMM decoding. In: Marques, J.S., Pérez de la Blanca, N., Pina, P. (eds.) IbPRIA 2005. LNCS, vol. 3522, pp. 571–578. Springer, Heidelberg (2005). doi:10.1007/11492429_69

5. Lee, E.R., Kim, P.K., Kim, H.J.: Automatic recognition of a car license plate using color image processing. In: IEEE International Conference on Image Processing, 1994 Proceedings, ICIP-1994, vol. 2, pp. 301–305. IEEE, November 1994

6. Busch, C., Domer, R., Freytag, C., Ziegler, H.: Feature based recognition of traffic video streams for online route tracing. In: 48th IEEE Vehicular Technology Conference, 1998, VTC 1998, vol. 3, pp. 1790–1794. IEEE, May 1998

7. Fan, X., Fan, G.: Graphical models for joint segmentation and recognition of license plate characters. IEEE Sig. Process. Lett. **16**(1), 10–13 (2009)

8. Wang, T., Wu, D.J., Coates, A., Ng, A.Y.: End-to-end text recognition with convolutional neural networks. In: 2012 21st International Conference on Pattern Recognition (ICPR), pp. 3304–3308. IEEE, November 2012

9. Matan, O., Burges, C.J., LeCun, Y., Denker, J.S.: Multi-digit recognition using a space displacement neural network. In: NIPS, pp. 488–495 (1991)

10. Neubeck, A., Van Gool, L.: Efficient non-maximum suppression. In: 18th International Conference on Pattern Recognition (ICPR 2006), vol. 3, pp. 850–855. IEEE, August 2006

11. Wen, Y., Lu, Y., Yan, J., Zhou, Z., von Deneen, K.M., Shi, P.: An algorithm for license plate recognition applied to intelligent transportation system. IEEE Trans. Intell. Transp. Syst. **12** (3), 830–845 (2011)

12. Li, H., Shen, C.: Reading Car License Plates Using Deep Convolutional Neural Networks and LSTMs. arXiv preprint arXiv:1601.05610 (2016)

13. Paliy, I., Turchenko, V., Koval, V., Sachenko, A., Markowsky, G.: Approach to recognition of license plate numbers using neural networks. In: Proceedings of IEEE International Joint Conference on Neural Networks, vol. 4, pp. 2965–2970, July 2004

14. Jaderberg, M., Vedaldi, A., Zisserman, A.: Deep features for text spotting. In: Fleet, D., Pajdla, T., Schiele, B., Tuytelaars, T. (eds.) ECCV 2014. LNCS, vol. 8692, pp. 512–528. Springer, Cham (2014). doi:10.1007/978-3-319-10593-2_34

15. Ioffe, S., Szegedy, C.: Batch normalization: Accelerating deep network training by reducing internal covariate shift. arXiv preprint arXiv:1502.03167 (2015)

16. He, K., Zhang, X., Ren, S., Sun, J.: Delving deep into rectifiers: surpassing human-level performance on imagenet classification. In: Proceedings of the IEEE International Conference on Computer Vision, pp. 1026–1034 (2015)

17. He, K., Zhang, X., Ren, S., Sun, J.: Deep residual learning for image recognition. arXiv preprint arXiv:1512.03385 (2015)

18. Long, J., Shelhamer, E., Darrell, T.: Fully convolutional networks for semantic segmentation. In: Proceedings of the IEEE Conference on Computer Vision and Pattern Recognition, pp. 3431–3440 (2015)

19. Hsu, G.S., Chen, J.C., Chung, Y.Z.: Application-oriented license plate recognition. IEEE Trans. Veh. Technol. **62**(2), 552–561 (2013)

20. de Campos, T.E., Babu, B.R., Varma, M.: Character recognition in natural images. In: VISAPP, no. 2, pp. 273–280, February 2009

21. Lee, S., Cho, M.S., Jung, K., Kim, J.H.: Scene text extraction with edge constraint and text collinearity. In: 2010 20th International Conference on Pattern Recognition (ICPR), pp. 3983–3986. IEEE, August 2010

22. Mishra, A., Alahari, K., Jawahar, C.V.: Top-down and bottom-up cues for scene text recognition. In: 2012 IEEE Conference on Computer Vision and Pattern Recognition (CVPR), pp. 2687–2694. IEEE, June 2012

23. Wang, K., Babenko, B., Belongie, S.: End-to-end scene text recognition. In: 2011 International Conference on Computer Vision, pp. 1457–1464. IEEE, November 2011

24. Caltech plate dataset (2003). http://www.vision.caltech.edu/html-files/archive.htm

25. Ganesh, V.: Parking lot monitoring system using an autonomous quadrotor UAV (2015)

26. Ren, S., He, K., Girshick, R., Sun, J.: Faster R-CNN: towards real-time object detection with region proposal networks. In: Advances in Neural Information Processing Systems, pp. 91–99 (2015)

# A Novel Time-Frequency Analysis in Nonstationary Signals Based Multiscale Radial Basis Functions and Forward Orthogonal Regression

Xudong Wang[1], Lina Wang[2], and Yang Li[1($\boxtimes$)]

[1] Department of Automation Sciences and Electrical Engineering,
Beihang University, Beijing 100191, China
liyang@buaa.edu.cn

[2] National Laboratory of Aerospace Intelligent Control Technology, Beijing
Aerospace Automatic Control Institute, Beijing 100854, China

**Abstract.** For time-frequency analysis of nonstationary signals, an adaptive and efficient time-varying autoregressive (TVAR) modeling method based on the multiscale radial basis function (MRBF) network and forward orthogonal regression (FOR) algorithm is investigated in this paper. Specifically, time-varying coefficients in the TVAR model is firstly approximated by the MRBF which has a better performance of tracking the time-varying parameters in nonstationary signals. Thus, the time-varying modeling problem is simplified to the selection of optimal centers and scales of MRBF, which a modified particle swarm optimization (MPSO) method aided by a FOR algorithm are resolved. Secondly, recursive least squares (RLS), Legendre polynomials expansion method and single scale radial basis function approach (SSRBF) are used to compare with the proposed method to evaluate the performance. Finally, the experimental results indicate that the proposed approach outperforms competing techniques in terms of mean absolute error and root mean squared error, and show the effectiveness of the proposed method for extracting the nonstationary signals. *abstract* environment.

**Keywords:** Forward orthogonal regression (FOR) · Multiscale radial basis functions (MRBF) · Modified particle swarm optimization (MPSO) · Time-frequency analysis · Time-varying autoregressive (TVAR)

## 1 Introduction

For nonstationary signals, traditional spectral analysis methods like Fourier transform generally cannot accurately extract the features of nonstationary signals, where the Fourier transform is assumed that the signals are stationary [1]. It is most appropriate to employ time-frequency domain such as short-time

Fourier transform (STFT), wavelet transform (WT), and parametric methods [2] for analysing these nonstationary signals [3–5].

Among these time-frequency analysis methods, STFT algorithm has the limitation of time-frequency resolution because it employs a fixed window for processing and extracting the nonstationarity of EEG signals [6]. Although WT can adjust the window size and achieve better time-frequency estimates for nonstationary signals, the application of WT method mainly depends on the selection of wavelet basis and discretization of scales. To overcome these limitations, parametric modelling method can be used to improve the time-frequency resolution, which are mainly based on time-varying models including the classical time-varying autoregressive (TVAR) model [7].

Generally, there are mainly two approaches in time-varying parameter modeling problems, one is adopted the traditional adaptive estimation algorithms like the classical recursive least squares (RLS) or Kalman filter algorithm [8], where the estimation algorithms tracks lag present in the estimated parameters when time-varying parameters change quickly or abrupt [9]. The other is that Li et al. [2, 7, 10] introduced a new basis function expansion approach for processing nonstationary signals. They employed the multi-wavelet or multiscale radial basis function (MRBF) methods to determine the instantaneous frequencies from the nonstationary time series. These approaches can produce a high-resolution spectral estimation results, even for data corrupted by a low signal-to-noise ratio, compared to the traditional adaptive parametric spectral estimation or nonparametric spectral estimation like FFT or STFT algorithms. Li et al. [7] also combined the MRBF methodology with a modified particle swarm optimization (MPSO) algorithm to detect the transient time-dependent spectrum information of EEG recordings. However, the MRBF expansion method generally involves many redundant terms or regressors, which normally results in the overfitting model. Furthermore, the low time-frequency resolution is produced. Therefore, in this paper an improvement of particle swarm optimization aided by forward orthogonal regression algorithm is proposed to achieve a better time-frequency resolution performance of processing nonstationary signals.

The rest of the paper is organized as follows. Section 2 introduces the time-varying autoregressive model briefly. In the next Section, the proposed multiscale radial basis function method is derived. The performance evaluation and the experimental results are discussed in Sect. 4. Finally, the effectiveness and remarks of the proposed method is summarized in Sect. 5.

## 2    TVAR Model Based on Multiscale Radial Basis Functions

The time-varying autoregressive (TVAR) model is a special AR model with associated model parameters are time-varying. The TVAR model of order p is given by [11,12]

$$y(t) = \sum_{i=1}^{p} a_i(t) y(t-i) + e(t) \tag{1}$$

where $t(t = 1, 2, \cdots, N, N$ is the length of samples) is the sampling index or time instant of the output signal $y(t)$, $a_i(i = 1, 2, ..., p)$ is the time-varying coefficients of the TVAR model, $\{y(t-i)\}_{i=1}^{p}$ are delayed samples of $y(t)$ and the term $e(t)$ is a sequence of independent and normal distributed random variables with zero mean and a variance $\sigma_e^2$.

To estimate the time-varying coefficients, an efficient solution is expand the time-varying coefficients $a_i(t)$ in Eq. (1) onto a set of basis functions $\varphi_m(t)$ for $m = 1, 2, \cdots, M$, as the following expression holds:

$$a_i(t) = \sum_{m=1}^{M} \chi_{i,m} \varphi_m(t) \tag{2}$$

where the $\chi_{i,m}$ represent the time-invariant expansion parameters of the basis functions $\varphi_m(t)$, $M$ is the dimension of the basis functions. Substituting Eqs. (2) to (1), the TVAR model can also be described as

$$y(t) = \sum_{i=1}^{p} \sum_{m=1}^{M} \chi_{i,m} \varphi_m(t) y(t-i) + e(t) \tag{3}$$

Once proper basis functions $\varphi_m(t)$ have been determined, Eq. (3) could be rewritten as following

$$y(t) = \sum_{i=1}^{p} \sum_{m=1}^{M} \chi_{i,m} \psi_m(t-i) + e(t) \tag{4}$$

where $\psi_m(t-i) = \varphi_m(t)y(t-i), m = 1, 2, \cdots, M, i = 1, 2, \cdots, p$

Since the TVAR model could be converted into a time invariant model with a set of basis functions and the form of the converted model is a standard linear regression model, thus the coefficients $c_{i,m}$ could be accurately estimated using the classical least squares algorithm [7].

## 3    Multiscale Radial Basis Functions

Radial basis function (RBF) is a common basis function with a three-layer neural network, which depends on the distance between input vector $\mathbf{x} = \{y(t-1), y(t-2), \cdots, y(t-p)\}$ and the center of RBF $c$ and the scale $\sigma$ decide the width of RBF [13,14]. Given the sample data set $D_N = \{\mathbf{x}_n, y_n\}_{n=1}^{N}$, the TVAR model described in Eq. (4) could be identified by using RBF network model as following

$$\hat{y}_n^{(M)} = \hat{f}_{RBF}^{(M)}(\mathbf{x}_k) = \sum_{i=1}^{M} \chi_i \psi_i(\mathbf{x}_k) = \psi_M^T(n) \chi_M \tag{5}$$

where $\hat{f}_{RBF}^{(M)}(\cdot)$ is the mapping of the M-dimension RBF model, $\chi_M$ is the RBF weight vector and $\psi_M$ is the response vector of the M-dimension RBF $\{\varphi_m\}_{m=1}^{M}$ multiply the input $\mathbf{x}_n$.

Define the model error at the $n$th sample data point $(\mathbf{x}_n, y_n)$ as

$$\varepsilon_n^{(M)} = y_n - \hat{y}_n^{(M)} \tag{6}$$

Thus the regression model (5) could be rewritten as in the matrix form

$$\mathbf{y} = \psi_M^T(n)\chi_M + \varepsilon^{(M)} \tag{7}$$

where $\mathbf{y} = [y_1, y_2, \cdots y_N]^T$ is the desired output vector, $\varepsilon^{(M)} = \left[\varepsilon_1^{(M)}, \varepsilon_2^{(M)}, \cdots, \varepsilon_N^{(M)}\right]$ is model error vector of the $M$-dimension model.

Let an orthogonal decomposition of the matrix $\psi_M$ be $\psi_M = \mathbf{W}_M \mathbf{A}_M$, where $\mathbf{A}_M$ is a upper triangular matrix, which defined as following

$$\mathbf{A}_M = \begin{bmatrix} 1 & \alpha_{1,2} & \cdots & \alpha_{1,M} \\ 0 & 1 & \ddots & \vdots \\ \vdots & \ddots & 1 & \alpha_{M-1,M} \\ 0 & \cdots & 0 & 1 \end{bmatrix} \tag{8}$$

and $\mathbf{W}_M = [w_1, w_2, \cdots, w_M]$ is an orthogonal matrix with columns satisfy $w_i^T w_l = 0$ for $l \neq i$. The regression model (7) could be alternated as

$$\mathbf{y} = \mathbf{W}_M \mathbf{g}_M + \varepsilon^{(M)} \tag{9}$$

where the orthogonal weight vector $\mathbf{g}_M = [g_1, g_2, \cdots, g_M]^T$ satisfies $\mathbf{A}_M \chi_M = \mathbf{g}_M$. The space spanned by the original model bases $\psi_m(\cdot), 1 \leq m \leq M$ is identical to the space spanned by the orthogonal model bases $w_m(\cdot), 1 \leq m \leq M$, and the model is equivalently expressed by

$$\hat{y}_n^{(M)} = \mathbf{w}_{(M)}^T(n)\mathbf{g}_{(M)} \tag{10}$$

where $\mathbf{w}_{(M)}^T(n) = [w_1(n), w_2(n), \cdots, w_M(n)]$ is the $n$th row of $\mathbf{W}_{(M)}$.

There are many radial basis functions which have the property of non-singularity, where the Gaussian kernel is wildly used because of its localized function and positive definiteness. The RBF with Gaussian kernel could be presented as follow [15]:

$$\varphi_m(n) = \exp\left[-\frac{\|n - c_m\|^2}{2\sigma_m^2}\right] \tag{11}$$

where $c_m$ is the center of $m$th Gaussian radial basis function, $\sigma_m$ is the scale of the $m$th basis function and $\|\cdot\|$ denotes the Euclidean norm.

To assure the RBF distribute throughout the wholly time-varying parameters range and guarantee the time-varying parameters is estimated accurately, the centers of RBF are chosen as uniformly distributed [16]. The $m$th center of the RBF are defined by [17]

$$c_m = \frac{m \times N}{M} \tag{12}$$

where $m$ is the center of the $m$th RBF and $M$ is the dimension of RBF.

To obtain a proper scales, a modified particle swarm optimization (MPSO) aided forward orthogonal regression (FOR) is used to determine and verify the optimal scales of RBF. Let denote $C_{best}^{(h)}$ the best previous position at the $i$th particle, $g_{best}^{(h)}$ denotes the global best position and h denotes the iteration counter. The current velocity $v_i^{(h)}$ and position $u_i^{(h)}$ of the $i$th dimension of the $i$th particle at time $h$ is as following functions [18,19]

$$v_i^{(h+1)} = \omega \times v_i^{(h)} + \theta \times c_1 \times (C_{best}^{(h)} - u_i^{(h)}) + \theta \times c_2 \times (g_{best}^{(h)} - u_i^{(h)}) \tag{13}$$

$$u_i^{(h+1)} = u_i^{(h)} + v_i^{(h+1)} \tag{14}$$

where $\omega$ is the inertia weight which controls exploration degree of the search, $c_1, c_2$ is uniform random number between 0 and 1, $\theta$ is the acceleration coefficients that influence the divergence of each particle for each iteration.

The inertia weight $\omega$ is usually a constant in traditional PSO algorithm, which maybe inflexible in searching the optimal particles and even leads to inaccurate results [7]. Therefore, to obtain a faster convergence performance and higher accuracy in the process of searching optimization, the modified inertia weight is defined as below [20]

$$R_i^{(h)} = \frac{H-h}{h}$$
$$\omega^{(h+1)} = \exp\left(-\exp\left(-R_i^{(h)}\right)\right) \tag{15}$$

where $H$ is the maximum of iteration, $h$ is the current iteration, $g_{best}^{(h)}$ is the global best position and $C_{gbest}^{(h)}$ is the best previous position at the $i$th particle.

The parameters $c_1$ and $c_2$ also play an important role in searching optimal results [21] and the parameter $c_1$ could be chosen from 2.5 to 0.5 and $c_2$ is between 0.5 to 2.5, where $c_1$ and $c_2$ can be calculated as $c_1 = 2.5 - \frac{2 \times h}{H}$ and $c_2 = 0.5 + \frac{2 \times h}{H}$ [19].

To obtain a satisfying RBF scales, the candidate scales of RBF can be given as follows [13,22]

$$\sigma_k^2 = \frac{N^2 \times 2^{-S_k}}{M} \tag{16}$$

where $N$ is the length of the sampled data, $M$ is the dimension of the RBF, $s_k$ is an arbitrary integer tuned, where the maximum value of it is usually under 10 [13]. Thus, the particle position $u_i$ can be represented as a $M$-dimension vector $u_i = [s_1, s_2, \cdots, s_M]$.

The LOO MSE $J_M$ is evaluated as a fitness function in the modified PSO algorithm, which is defined as [17]

$$J_M = E\left[\left(\varepsilon_n^{(M,-n)}\right)^2\right] \approx \frac{1}{N}\sum_{n=1}^{N}\left(\varepsilon_n^{(M,-n)}\right) \tag{17}$$

where $\varepsilon_n^{(M,-n)}$ is the LOO modelling error, defined by Eq. (18) and could be calculated recursively by Eqs. (19) and (20) [23].

$$\varepsilon_n^{(M,-n)} = \frac{\varepsilon_n^{(M)}}{\eta_n^{(M)}} \tag{18}$$

$$\varepsilon_n^{(M)} = y_n - \sum_{i=1}^{M} g_i w_i(n) = \varepsilon_n^{(M-1)} - g_M w_M(n) \tag{19}$$

$$\eta_n^{(M)} = 1 - \sum_{i=1}^{M} \frac{w_i^2(n)}{w_i^T w_i + \lambda} = \eta_n^{(M-1)} - \frac{w_M^2(n)}{w_M^T w_M + \lambda} \tag{20}$$

where $g$ and $w$ are described in model (9), $\lambda \geq 0$ is a small regularization parameter, which could be set to zero (no regularisation) or a very small value $10^{-6}$ [23].

Once the TVAR parameters are calculated in model (1), the time-varying power spectrum could be estimated by the parameters. Define $\hat{a}_i(t)$ as the estimate of time-varying parameter $a_i(t)$ and $\hat{\sigma}_e^2$ as the estimate of the variance of the error $\sigma_e^2$. The time-dependent spectral function relative to the TVAR model is then given by [24,25]

$$S(t, f) = \frac{\sigma_e^2}{\left| 1 - \sum_{i=1}^{p} \hat{a}_i(t) e^{-j2\pi if/f_s} \right|^2} \tag{21}$$

where $j = \sqrt{-1}$ and $f_s$ is the sampling frequency. It should be careful that the power spectral function in Eq. (21) is a continuous function of the frequency $f$ and then could be employed to estimate the power spectral at any desired frequency from 0 to the Nyquist frequency $f_s/2$ [26].

## 4    Simulation Example

The reliability and availability of the proposed approach is tested in an artificial EEG time-varying signal, which is nonstationary signal. The simulations consist of five distinct components with four frequencies and durations. The signal was defined as below:

$$y(t) = \begin{cases} 2|t|^\zeta \sin(2\pi f_\theta t) + 2|t|^\zeta \sin(2\pi f_\beta t) & t \in (0, 2) \\ 2|t|^\zeta \sin(2\pi f_\theta t) + |t|^\zeta \sin(2\pi f_\beta t) + |t|^\zeta \sin(2\pi f_\alpha t) & t \in [2, 4) \\ |t|^\zeta \sin(2\pi f_\beta t) + 2|t|^\kappa \sin(2\pi f_\alpha t) & t \in [4, 5) \\ |t|^\zeta \sin(2\pi f_\alpha t) + |t|^\zeta \sin(2\pi f_\gamma t) & t \in [5, 6) \\ 2|t|^\kappa \sin(2\pi f_\gamma t) & t \in [6, 8] \end{cases} \tag{22}$$

where $\zeta = 0.5$ and $\kappa = 0.25$, the frequency components $f_\theta = 6$, $f_\alpha = 12$, $f_\beta = 25$ and $f_\gamma = 40\,\mathrm{Hz}$ correspond to typical EEG frequency components and are meant to emulate the *theta, alpha, beta* and *gamma* bands of EEG recording data, respectively. The signal $f(t)$ was sampled with a sampling interval of 0.01, thus a total of 800 observations were obtained. A Gaussian white noise sequence, with mean zero and variance of 0.16, was added to the 800 data points to achieve a more realistic simulation.

Different methods of time-varying frequency analysis, including recursive least squares (RLS), Legendre polynomials approach (LP), traditional single scale radial basis function (SSRBF) and the proposed method multiscale radial basis function (MRBF) with modified particle swarm optimization (PSO) aided forward orthogonal regression (FOR) method based on time-dependent spectral estimation, are compared using the artificial EEG signals in Eq. (22).

Figure 1 shows a comparison of time-frequency spectra among four methods based on time-dependent spectral estimation. It could be find that the MRBF method presents the best performance of the time-dependent spectral estimation. One advantage of MRBF method, compared to RLS, LP and SSRBF, is that it could track fast and slow signals, especially rapidly changing signal like EEG signal, by including both small and large scales of radial basis functions.

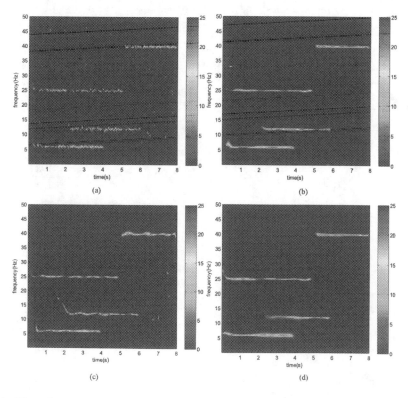

**Fig. 1.** Time-frequency spectral characteristics of the simulated nonstandard signals. (a) RLS, (b) Legendre polynomials, (c) SSRBF, (d) MRBF with PSO and FOR algorithm.

The quantitation of the time-frequency resolution is evaluated by comparing the mean absolute error (MAE) and root mean squared error (RMSE) for the four sinusoidal components at $f = 6, 12, 25$ and $40\,\mathrm{Hz}$. The MAE and RMSE are defined as

$$MAE\left(\hat{f}_I\right) = \frac{1}{N} \sum_{t=1}^{N} \left| S\left(t, f\right) - \hat{S}\left(t, \hat{f}_I\right) \right|, \qquad I = \{\theta, \alpha, \beta, \gamma\} \qquad (23)$$

$$RMSE\left(\hat{f}_I\right) = \frac{1}{N} \sqrt{\sum_{t=1}^{N} \frac{\left\| S\left(t, f\right) - \hat{S}\left(t, \hat{f}_I\right) \right\|^2}{\left\| S\left(t, f\right) \right\|^2}}, \qquad I = \{\theta, \alpha, \beta, \gamma\} \qquad (24)$$

where $N$ is the length of the data, $S\left(t, \hat{f}_I\right)$ is the estimated power spectrum of the real power spectrum $S\left(t, f\right)$ from the simulation signal.

Table 1 shows the MAE and RMSE of the time-frequency estimation of the four frequency components, where both MAE and RMSE values of proposed method in this paper are smaller than the other methods, which illustrates the performance of the proposed method is better than the others.

**Table 1.** Performance comparison of MAE and RMSE using four approaches

| Approach | Estimated frequency components | MAE | RMSE |
|---|---|---|---|
| RLS | $\hat{f}_\theta$ | 25.3278 | 31.1238 |
| | $\hat{f}_\alpha$ | 22.8162 | 61.7663 |
| | $\hat{f}_\beta$ | 21.7277 | 189.2301 |
| | $\hat{f}_\gamma$ | 26.3409 | 36.3478 |
| Legendre polynomials | $\hat{f}_\theta$ | 24.8439 | 30.2699 |
| | $\hat{f}_\alpha$ | 22.7906 | 61.7064 |
| | $\hat{f}_\beta$ | 21.3683 | 187.8091 |
| | $\hat{f}_\gamma$ | 26.2781 | 36.1535 |
| SSRBF | $\hat{f}_\theta$ | 25.0041 | 30.4518 |
| | $\hat{f}_\alpha$ | 22.8131 | 61.7644 |
| | $\hat{f}_\beta$ | 21.4862 | 187.8355 |
| | $\hat{f}_\gamma$ | 26.3028 | 36.2102 |
| MRBF with MPSO and FOR | $\hat{f}_\theta$ | 24.6587 | 30.077 |
| | $\hat{f}_\alpha$ | 22.6872 | 61.3419 |
| | $\hat{f}_\beta$ | 21.1962 | 187.3705 |
| | $\hat{f}_\gamma$ | 26.2180 | 36.0559 |

# 5  Conclusions

In this paper, a novel time-frequency analysis method that expands the time-varying parameters onto the multiscale radial basis function has been proposed for analysing nonstationary signals. A significant step of constructing MRBF is employed to determine the optimal scales from multiple kernel widths, where a modified PSO algorithm aided by a FOR algorithm is utilized. Compared with the traditional RLS approach, Legendre polynomials expansion and single scale radial basis function, the proposed approach is more powerful on extracting the time-frequency resolution for the nonstationary signals. In the simulation example, compared to the state-of-art methods, the proposed method indeed achieves the best performance on the four frequency bands, and shows the effectiveness of the proposed method.

# References

1. Fu, K., et al.: Classification of seizure based on the time-frequency image of EEG signals using HHT and SVM. Biomed. Sig. Process. Control **13**, 15–22 (2014)
2. Li, Y., Luo, M.L., Li, K.: A multiwavelet-based time-varying model identification approach for time-frequency analysis of EEG signals. Neurocomputing **193**, 106–114 (2016)
3. Boashash, B., Mesbah, M., Golditz, P.: Time-Frequency Detection of EEG Abnormalities, pp. 663–669. Elsevier, Amsterdam (2013). Chap. 15
4. Boashash, B., Boubchir, L., Azem, G.: A methodology for time-frequency image processing applied to the classification of non-stationary multichannel signals using instantaneous frequency descriptors with application to newborn EEG signals. Eurasip J. Adv. Sig. Process. **1**, 1–12 (2012)
5. Tzallas, A.T., Tsipouras, M.G., Fotiadis, D.I.: Epileptic seizure detection in EEGs using time-frequency analysis. IEEE Trans. Inf. Technol. Biomed. **13**, 703–710 (2009)
6. Cohen, L.: Time-frequency analysis: theory and applications. J. Acoust. Soc. Am. **134**, 4002–4002 (2013)
7. Li, Y., et al.: High-resolution time-frequency analysis of EEG signals using multiscale radial basis function. Neurocomputing **195**, 96–103 (2016)
8. Li, Y., et al.: Time-varying linear and nonlinear parametric model for Granger causality analysis. Phys. Rev. E **85**, 041906 (2012)
9. Chon, K.H., et al.: Multiple time-varying dynamic analysis using multiple sets of basis functions. IEEE Trans. Biomed. Eng. **52**, 956–960 (2005)
10. Guo, L., et al.: Automatic feature extraction using genetic programming: an application to epileptic EEG classification. Expert Syst. Appl. **38**, 10425–10436 (2011)
11. Lee, J., Chon, K.H.: Time-varying autoregressive model-based multiple modes particle filtering algorithm for respiratory rate extraction from pulse oximeter. IEEE Trans. Biomed. Eng. **58**, 790–794 (2011)
12. Wang, G.F., et al.: Fault identification and classification of rolling element bearing based on time-varying autoregressive spectrum. Mech. Syst. Sig. Process. **22**, 934–947 (2008)
13. Billings, S.A., Wei, H.L., Balikhin, M.A.: Generalized multiscale radial basis function networks. Neural Netw. **20**, 1081–1094 (2007)

14. Chang, L.C., Chang, F.J., Wang, Y.P.: Auto-configuring radial basis function networks for chaotic time series and flood forecasting. Hydrol. Process. **23**, 2450–2459 (2009)
15. Xie, J.C., Wang, T.P.: A method of flood forecasting of chaotic radial basis function neural network. In: International Workshop on Intelligent Systems and Application, pp. 1–5 (2010)
16. Wei, H.L., Billings, S.A.: Forecasting the geomagnetic activity of the Dst index using multiscale radial basis function networks. Adv. Space Res. **40**, 1863–1870 (2007)
17. Chen, S., et al.: Non-linear system identification using particle swarm optimisation tuned radial basis function models. Int. J. Bio Inspired Comput. **1**, 246–258 (2009)
18. Bao, Y., Hu, Z., Xiong, T.: A PSO and pattern search based memetic algorithm for SVMs parameters optimization. Neurocomputing **117**, 98–106 (2014)
19. Ratnaweera, A., Halgamuge, S., Watson, H.: Self-organizing hierarchical particle swarm optimizer with time-varying acceleration coefficients. IEEE Trans. Evol. Comput. **8**, 240–255 (2004)
20. Chauhan, P., Deep, K., Pant, M.: Novel inertia weight strategies for particles swarm optimization. Memetic Comput. **5**, 229–251 (2013)
21. Farid, M., Yakoub, B.: Classification of electrocardiogram signals with support vector machines and particle swarm optimization. IEEE Trans. Inf. Technol. Biomed. **12**, 667–677 (2008)
22. Billings, S.A.: Nolinear System Identification: NARMAX Methods in the Time, Frequency, and Spatio-temporal Domains, 1st edn. John Wiley and Sons, Chichester (2013)
23. Chen, S.H., Harris, C.J., Sharkey, P.M.: Sparse modelling using orthogonal forward regression with PRESS statistic and regularization. IEEE Trans. Syst. Man Cybern. B **34**, 898–911 (2004)
24. Wei, H.L., Billings, S.A.: Time-varying parametric modelling and time-dependent spectral characterisation with applications to EEG signals using multiwavelets. Int. J. Model. Ident. Control **9**, 215–224 (2010)
25. Zhang, Z.G., Hung, Y., Chan, S.C.: Local polynomial modeling of time-varying autoregressive models with application to time-frequency analysis of event-related EEG. IEEE Trans. Biomed. Eng. **58**, 557–566 (2011)
26. Wei, H.L., Billings, S.A., Liu, J.: Time-varying parametric modelling and time-dependent spectral characterisation with applications to EEG signals using multiwavelets. Int. J. Model. **9**, 215–224 (2010)

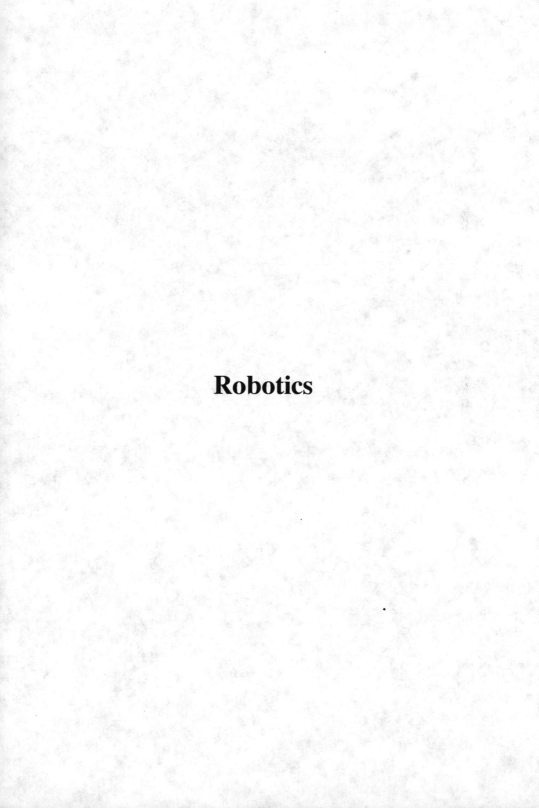

# Robotics

# Experiment on Impedance Adaptation for an Under-Actuated Gripper Grasping an Unknown Object with Tactile Sensing

Shaobo Yan[1($\boxtimes$)], Zhongyi Chu[1], and Fuchun Sun[2]

[1] School of Instrument Science and Opto-Electronics Engineering,
Beihang University, Beijing 100191, China
yan7shark@126.com
[2] Department of Computer Science and Technology,
Tsinghua University, Beijing, China

**Abstract.** This paper presents an experiment on impedance adaptation for an under-actuated gripper grasping an unknown object. Under-actuated gripper has broad applications in the field of industrial robotics and on-orbit services because of its better self-adaption. However, subject to uncertain characteristics of the object, it is difficult for an under-actuated gripper to achieve stable grasp. To address this problem, this paper develops impedance adaptation for an under-actuated gripper manipulation with the tactile sensing. A cost function that measures the contact force, velocity and positioning errors of the contact point is defined and the critical impedance parameters are determined that minimize it; this adaptation is feasible for an under-actuated gripper to guarantee a stable grasp without requiring information on the object dynamics. Finally, an experimental setup is established to verify the validity of the proposed method. The experimental results demonstrate that the under-actuated gripper can stably grasp an unknown object.

**Keywords:** Stable grasp · Impedance adaptation · Under-actuated gripper · Tactile sensing · Unknown object

## 1 Introduction

In the fields of industrial robotics and on-orbit services, end effectors play an important role. As a type of end effector, an under-actuated gripper [1] has a broad range of applications because of its better self-adaption abilities, which permit the grasp of objects of various shapes. Due to the under-actuated characteristics, many different types of passive elements, such as springs, are considered to resolve the non-uniqueness question involved with null space grasping and ensuring the shape-adaptation of the finger to the object grasped [2]. It is worth mentioning that the balance between the contact force, the input torque and the spring passive torque contribute to various grasping types and has a significant effect on stable grasping. A proper contact force is necessary for stable grasp. Commonly, the contact force applied is either too weak or too strong, resulting in slipping or mechanical deformation of the grasped object [3]. Generally, the necessary contact force is different for the

© Springer Nature Singapore Pte Ltd. 2017
F. Sun et al. (Eds.): ICCSIP 2016, CCIS 710, pp. 247–260, 2017.
DOI: 10.1007/978-981-10-5230-9_27

objects with different parameters. However, the contact force is a passive parameter one cannot directly control. Considering the balance between the contact force, the spring torque and the input torque, the contact force can be adjusted by controlling the input torque. Hence, it is essential to control the input torque depending on the properties of the object.

In this field, impedance control [4] can be employed to achieve a stable grasp [5]. Under impedance control, an under-actuated gripper's compliance is determined by contact force exerted by the object. Moreover, impedance control regulates the contact force implicitly by specifying the desired impedance [6]. In early research works on impedance control, the uncertainties in robotic dynamics are considered in order to obtain the desired impedance model [7]. However, in many situations, the environmental dynamics should be taken into account. A good control strategy is to choose the proper impedance parameters based on the object. As a result, impedance adaptation has been widely investigated. In [8], an impact controller based on the switching of the impedance parameters depending on dissipated and generated forms of energy is discussed. In [9], the position data and contact force are used to obtain the desired impedance parameters based on adaptive optimal control. In many studies on impedance control, the environmental parameters are estimated to design the impedance controller. For example, the stiffness of a human operator's arm is estimated in real-time based on which controller is designed to adjust the impedance coefficients of the robot [10].

For impedance adaptation, optimization is necessary because that the control objective of impedance control includes both force regulation and trajectory tracking. In [11], a cost function measuring trajectory errors and contact force is defined. The desired impedance parameters are obtained to minimize the cost function. However, the system dynamics are assumed to be known. To achieve optimal control in the case of unknown system dynamics, adaptive dynamic programming (ADP) has been widely studied [12]. In many studies of ADP, a learning process is still required to obtain the desired impedance parameters, which causes the robot to repeat operations to learn the desired impedance parameters [13]. In [9], this problem is avoided by modifying the ADP for systems with unknown dynamics. Although impedance adaptation has been broadly developed it is challenging to employ it to solve the stable grasp problem because the parameters of the object are unknown. This is especially for an under-actuated gripper. It is difficult to develop impedance adaptation because it is impossible to control the position of each phalanx independently.

In our previous works, an under-actuated gripper was designed and manufactured. The under-actuated gripper consists of two under-actuated fingers with a rotational spring which is placed in a different location from that of the SARAH hand to resolve the indeterminacy so that the distal phalanges can move relative to one another in a parallel manner with less energy consumption [14]. Moreover, an impedance joint torque controller has been designed to control the grasping system dynamics [15]. However, the parameters of the controller are treated as a constant, and a controller with fixed parameters does not suffice in many applications. For example, the parameters of the grasped object are usually unknown. To achieve stable grasp with an unknown object, this paper develops an impedance adaptation on a two-finger under-actuated gripper using tactile sensing. First, a terrestrial experimental setup is established using the two-finger under-actuated gripper, an unknown grasped object and hardware control architecture. Second, the object dynamics are taken into consideration to develop the impedance adaptation, and the unknown grasped object is described as a mass-damping-stiffness system with unknown dynamics. Then, the desired impedance model is obtained based on the unknown dynamics, and the critical impedance parameters are determined that minimize the cost function which is defined to describe the grasp performance. Furthermore, an impedance model is imposed on the under-actuated gripper to guarantee a stable grasp. Finally, the experimental results are used to validate the stability and adaptability of the design at grasping an unknown object.

The remainder of this paper is organized as follows. In Sect. 2, the mechanism and experimental setup are described. In Sect. 3, the impedance adaptation is developed based on an estimation of the parameters of the unknown object and optimal control so that the stable grasping is achieved based on the unknown object. In Sect. 4, the validity of the proposed method is verified through experimentation. Section 5 concludes the paper.

## 2 Mechanism and Experimental Setup

As shown in Fig. 1, the experimental system consists of two parts: a supervisor computer and an implementation controller. Based on the SCI (Serial Communication Interface) software, the supervisor computer displays the measurements. The implementation controller consists of a 2-finger under-actuated gripper, the unknown grasped object and the hardware control architecture, which comprise a closed-loop control system.

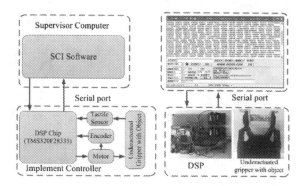

**Fig. 1.** The experimental system.

### 2.1 Mechanism

The model of the under-actuated gripper and unknown grasped object is shown in Fig. 2. The under-actuated gripper consists of four parts: the driving and transmission portion, the gripper portion, the tactile sensor and the support portion, as shown in

Fig. 3. The driving and transmission portion consists of one driving motor, two gear wheels, two worm gears and two worm screws. The gripper portion consists of two under-actuated fingers with rotational springs, i.e., passive actuators. Each under-actuated finger is a closed-loop system with five linkages, the driving linkage, the driven linkage, the middle linkage, the contact linkage and the linkage embedded in the base. The spring is located between the driving and middle linkages. Most importantly, a PPS (Pressure Profile System) tactile sensor SN5570 is fixed on the contact linkage used to measure the contact force. The support portion is the base that supports the entire system. The parameters of the under-actuated gripper are listed in Table 1.

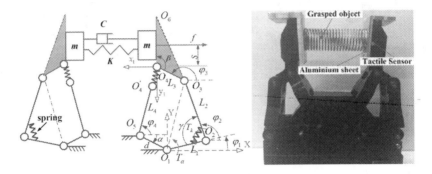

**Fig. 2.** The under-actuated gripper with an unknown grasped object.

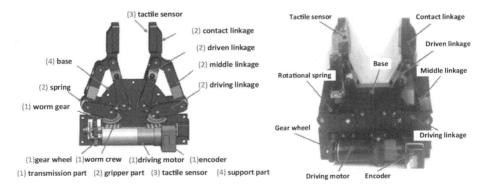

**Fig. 3.** The structure of the under-actuated gripper.

**Table 1.** The parameters of the gripper.

| Symbol | Value | Symbol | Value |
|--------|-------|--------|-------|
| $L_1$ | $3.18 \times 10^{-2}$ m | $d$ | $1.90 \times 10^{-2}$ m |
| $L_2$ | $4.80 \times 10^{-2}$ m | $\alpha$ | 0.46 rad |
| $L_3$ | $1.90 \times 10^{-2}$ m | $\beta$ | 2.09 rad |
| $L_4$ | $5.71 \times 10^{-2}$ m | | |

In this paper, the grasped objects are chosen to be three sets of springs with different stiffnesses, as shown in Fig. 4. An aluminium sheet (shown in Fig. 2) is placed between the grasped spring and the PPS tactile sensor to ensure that the spring contact with the PPS sensor is over a large area.

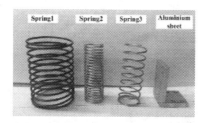

**Fig. 4.** Springs and aluminium sheet

## 2.2 Hardware Control Architecture

As illustrated in Fig. 1, the proposed hardware control architecture consists of a multisensory system, a controller and communication system. The multisensory system consists of motor and sensors. The under-actuated gripper is driven by a Maxon motor and a worm gear (gear ratio 1:35). A photoelectric encoder (HEDS 5X40) with a 500 pulse/rev capability is embedded in the motor to provide rotor position/speed. An integrated circuit converts the two-phase input pulses into a four-phase-count, which improves the precision of measurement. From on this data, the positional data of contact point is obtained based on the kinematic of the under-actuated gripper. Additionally, the PPS sensor on the contact linkage provides the contact force data, which consists of $4 \times 4$ sensing cells and signal processing circuitry. This array of sensors ensures the accuracy of the measurement, and the signal processing circuitry is used to transmit of the measured data.

For the under-actuated gripper and unknown grasped object, the controller is integrated onto a DSP chip (TMS320F28335), which is used to perform sensor signal processing and motor control, as well as communicating between the under-actuated gripper and the PC. The position and contact force data are sent to the DSP to ensure closed-loop control. Combined with the control algorithm, several PWM pulses with the proper duty ratio are output from the DSP depending on the particular motor being driven by the driving circuit (L298N) to grasp an unknown grasped object.

## 3 Impedance Adaptive Control

This section is dedicated to develop impedance adaptive control. The proposed impedance adaptive control scheme of the system is shown in Fig. 5. A desired impedance model is imposed on the under-actuated gripper to ensure stable grasping, and the impedance parameters determined from an unknown grasped object are based on the estimation of the object's parameters. In particular, the desired impedance model is given by

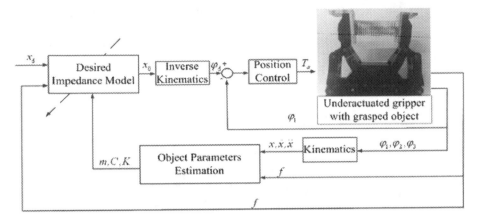

**Fig. 5.** Schematic of the impedance adaptive control.

$$f = Z(x_0, x_d),  \tag{1}$$

where $x_d$ is the desired trajectory of the contact point, $x_0$ is the virtual desired trajectory and $Z(\cdot)$ is a target impedance function that needs to be determined. For an ideal position controller, it is obvious that $x_0(t) = x(t)$. Then, the desired impedance model can be rewritten as

$$f = Z(x, x_d).  \tag{2}$$

The method to determine $Z(\cdot)$ is presented in the following subsections. It is worth mentioning that the desired impedance model is based on the unknown grasped object. Therefore, the unknown grasped object is analysed to develop the impedance adaptive control, and the description of the unknown grasped object is presented in Sect. 3.1.

### 3.1  Description of the Unknown Grasped Object

As shown in Fig. 3, and without the loss of generality, the unknown grasped object is described as mass-damping-stiffness system. The dynamic equation for the unknown grasped object is given by:

$$f = -m\ddot{x} - 2C\dot{x} - 2Kx,  \tag{3}$$

where $m$, $C$ and $K$ are the unknown contact mass, damping and stiffness of the grasped object model, respectively. The variable $f$ denotes the force exerted by the contact linkage. The variables $\ddot{x}$, $\dot{x}$ and $x$ are the acceleration, velocity and position of the contact point, respectively, which change along the $x_1$ axis. For a mass-damping-stiffness system, the state function is defined as:

$$\xi = A\xi + Bu, \tag{4}$$

where $\xi$ is the system state, $u$ is the system input, and $A$ and $B$ are unknown constant matrices related to the parameters of grasped object ($m$, $C$ and $K$). In this paper, the system input is $u = [f]$, and the system state is $\xi = [\dot{x} \quad x \quad z]^T$, in which $z \in R^m$ is the state of the following system [11]:

$$\begin{cases} \dot{z} = Uz, \\ x_d = Vz, \end{cases} \tag{5}$$

Where $U \in R^{m \times m}$ and $V \in R^{n \times m}$ are two known matrices. Substituting Eq. (3) into Eq. (4), the state function can be rewritten as:

$$\begin{bmatrix} \ddot{x} \\ \dot{x} \\ \dot{z} \end{bmatrix} = \begin{bmatrix} -2Cm^{-1} & -2Km^{-1} & 0 \\ I & 0 & 0 \\ 0 & 0 & U \end{bmatrix} \begin{bmatrix} \dot{x} \\ x \\ z \end{bmatrix} + \begin{bmatrix} -m^{-1} \\ 0 \\ 0 \end{bmatrix} f. \tag{6}$$

We denote

$$A = \begin{bmatrix} -2Cm^{-1} & -2Km^{-1} & 0 \\ I & 0 & 0 \\ 0 & 0 & U \end{bmatrix}, B = \begin{bmatrix} -m^{-1} \\ 0 \\ 0 \end{bmatrix}. \tag{7}$$

Note that $A$ and $B$ include the grasped object dynamics and that they are unknown.

## 3.2 Impedance Adaptation

By addressing the grasped object dynamics, we develop an impedance adaptation to minimize the following cost function:

$$\begin{aligned} \Gamma &= \int_0^\infty (\dot{x}^T Q_1 \dot{x} + (x - x_d)^T Q_2 (x - x_d) + f^T rf) dt \\ &= \int_0^\infty (\dot{x}^T Q_1 \dot{x} + [x^T \quad z^T] \begin{bmatrix} Q_2' & -Q_2' V \\ -V^T Q_2' & V^T Q_2' V \end{bmatrix} \begin{bmatrix} x \\ z \end{bmatrix} + f^T rf) dt \\ &= \int_0^\infty [\xi^T Q\xi + f^T Rf] dt. \end{aligned} \tag{8}$$

The cost function presented in Eq. (8) represents the compromise/combination of the force regulation and trajectory tracking and determines the grasping performance. In Eq. (8), $Q$ and $R$ are the weighting matrices which satisfy:

$$Q = Q^T = \begin{bmatrix} Q_1 & 0 & 0 \\ 0 & Q_2' & -Q_2' V \\ 0 & -V^T Q_2' & V^T Q_2' V \end{bmatrix}, R = [r]. \tag{9}$$

The factors $Q_1$ and $Q_2'$ satisfy: $Q_1 > 0$, $Q_2' > 0$, and $r > 0$. If we assume the contact force $f$ in Eq. (6) to be the 'system input' to the grasped object dynamics, we are able to obtain a minimized version of the cost function (Eq. 8). The optimal control state is then can be employed to determine the contact force $f$, which is obtained as follow

$$f = -\mathbf{K}_k \xi = -\mathbf{R}^{-1}\mathbf{B}^{\mathrm{T}}\mathbf{P}\xi, \tag{10}$$

where $\mathbf{K}_k$ is the optimal feedback gain matrix and $\mathbf{P} = \mathbf{P}^{\mathrm{T}}$ is the solution of the following Riccati equation

$$\mathbf{P}\mathbf{A} + \mathbf{A}^{\mathrm{T}}\mathbf{P} - \mathbf{P}\mathbf{B}\mathbf{R}^{-1}\mathbf{B}^{\mathrm{T}}\mathbf{P} + \mathbf{Q} = \mathbf{0}. \tag{11}$$

We denote that

$$\mathbf{P} = \begin{bmatrix} \mathbf{P}_1 & \mathbf{P}_2 & \mathbf{P}_3 \\ * & * & * \\ * & * & * \end{bmatrix}, \tag{12}$$

where $\mathbf{P}_1 \in \mathbf{R}^{n \times n}$, $\mathbf{P}_2 \in \mathbf{R}^{n \times n}$ and $\mathbf{P}_3 \in \mathbf{R}^{n \times n}$, and '*' represents the elements that do not concern this problem. Substituting Eq. (12) into Eq. (10) leads to

$$\begin{aligned} f &= m^{-1}\mathbf{R}^{-1}\mathbf{P}_1\dot{x} + m^{-1}\mathbf{R}^{-1}\mathbf{P}_2 x - m^{-1}\mathbf{R}^{-1}\mathbf{P}_3 z \\ &= m^{-1}\mathbf{R}^{-1}[\mathbf{P}_1\dot{x} + \mathbf{P}_2 x - \mathbf{P}_3\mathbf{V}^{\mathrm{T}}(\mathbf{V}\mathbf{V}^{\mathrm{T}})^{-1}x_{\mathrm{d}}] \\ &= -k_0\dot{x} - k_1 x - k_2 x_{\mathrm{d}}. \end{aligned} \tag{13}$$

For certain values of $\mathbf{A}$, $\mathbf{B}$, $\mathbf{Q}$ and $\mathbf{R}$, the values of $k_0$, $k_1$ and $k_2$ may be obtained by solving the Riccati equation:

$$k_0 = -\sqrt{Q_1^2/r - 2mk_1 + 4C^2} + 2C, \tag{14}$$

$$k_1 = -\sqrt{Q_2'/r + 4K^2} + 2K, \tag{15}$$

$$k_2 = Q_2'\mathbf{V}r^{-1}(k_0\mathbf{U} - 2C\mathbf{U} + m\mathbf{U}^2 + 2K\mathbf{I} - k_1\mathbf{I})^{-1}\mathbf{V}^{\mathrm{T}}(\mathbf{V}\mathbf{V}^{\mathrm{T}})^{-1}. \tag{16}$$

For the unknown parameters (m, $C$ and $K$) of the grasped object, an estimation method is developed based on the Recursive Least Squares (RLS) algorithm. For the detailed implementation, we recall from the Eq. (3) that each $k \in \mathbf{Z}^+$, where $k$ stands for step $k$ and $\mathbf{Z}^+$ is positive integer. The discretization of Eq. (3) is defined as:

$$f(k) = -m\ddot{x}(k) - 2C\dot{x}(k) - 2Kx(k). \tag{17}$$

Equation (17) can be rewritten as matrix form as:

$$\mathbf{f}(k) = -\mathbf{r}^{\mathrm{T}}(k)\mathbf{w}, \tag{18}$$

where

$$\mathbf{r}(k) = [\ddot{x}(k) \quad 2\dot{x}(k) \quad 2x(k)]^{\mathrm{T}}, \tag{19}$$

$$\mathbf{w} = [m \quad C \quad K]^{\mathrm{T}}. \tag{20}$$

The RLS estimation of $\mathbf{w}$ from [15] is defined as:

$$\hat{\mathbf{w}}(t) = \hat{\mathbf{w}}(t-1) + \mathbf{L}(t)[\mathbf{f}(t) - \mathbf{r}^{\mathrm{T}}(t)\hat{\mathbf{w}}(t-1)], \tag{21}$$

where

$$\mathbf{L}(t) = \mathbf{P}(t-1)\mathbf{r}(t)[1 + \mathbf{r}^{\mathrm{T}}(t)\mathbf{P}(t-1)\mathbf{r}(t)]^{-1}, \tag{22}$$

$$\mathbf{P}(t) = [\mathbf{I}_3 - \mathbf{L}(t)\mathbf{r}^{\mathrm{T}}(t)]\mathbf{P}(t-1). \tag{23}$$

The variable $\mathbf{P}(t)$ is the covariance matrix for a matrix size of $3 \times 3$, and $\mathbf{P}(0) = p_0\mathbf{I}_3$, where $p_0$ is a large positive number, e.g., $p_0 = 10^6$. We defining the estimation error as $\delta = \hat{w}(t) - w$, which approaches zero when the input signal is persistently excited, and when the noise has a zero mean and finite variance [16]. Thus, the parameters of grasped object are obtained using the RLS algorithm.

Comparing Eq. (13) with the desired impedance model (Eq. (2)), the exact impedance parameters are obtained. As shown in Fig. 6, the object parameter estimation is for developing the preliminary impedance adaptation, which requires the contact force and the position data of the contact point. The contact force $f$ is measured by tactile sensing with the PPS sensor, and the position data $x$ is calculated according to the geometric relationship between the joint space and work space (as shown in Fig. 6),

$$x = \|\mathbf{D}\|_2 \cdot \cos(\varphi_3 - \varphi_{30}), \tag{24}$$

where

$$\mathbf{D} = \begin{bmatrix} d_x \\ d_y \end{bmatrix} - \begin{bmatrix} d_{x0} \\ d_{y0} \end{bmatrix} = \begin{bmatrix} \cos\varphi_1 & \cos\varphi_2 & \cos\varphi_3 & \cos(\beta+\varphi_3-\pi) \\ \sin\varphi_1 & \sin\varphi_2 & \sin\varphi_3 & \sin(\beta+\varphi_3-\pi) \end{bmatrix} \begin{bmatrix} L_1 \\ L_2 \\ L_3 \\ S \end{bmatrix}$$
$$- \begin{bmatrix} \cos\varphi_{10} & \cos\varphi_{20} & \cos\varphi_{30} & \cos(\beta+\varphi_{30}-\pi) \\ \sin\varphi_{10} & \sin\varphi_{20} & \sin\varphi_{30} & \sin(\beta+\varphi_{30}-\pi) \end{bmatrix} \begin{bmatrix} L_1 \\ L_2 \\ L_3 \\ S_0 \end{bmatrix}, \tag{25}$$

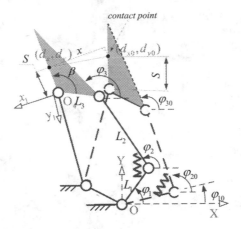

**Fig. 6.** Geometric relationship between the joint space and the work space.

where $[d_{x0}, d_{y0}]^T$ is the initial position of the contact point, and $[d_x, d_y]^T$ is the current position. The variable $S$ is the distance from the contact point to the joint $O_4$, and $S_0$ is the initial value of $S$. The variable $\varphi_{i0}$ (i = 1, 2, 3) is the initial value of the joint angle $\varphi_i$ (i = 1, 2, 3), the joint angle $\varphi_1$ is obtained from the photoelectric encoder and the joint angles $\varphi_2$ and $\varphi_3$ are obtained by solving the following dynamics function for the under-actuated gripper [19].

$$\mathbf{T} = \mathbf{M}(\varphi)\ddot{\varphi} + \mathbf{C}(\dot{\varphi}, \varphi) + \mathbf{H}(\varphi) + \mathbf{T}_{ext}, \tag{26}$$

where $\varphi = [\varphi_1 \ \varphi_2 \ \varphi_3 \ \varphi_4]^T$ is the vector matrix of the joint angle, $\mathbf{M}(\varphi)$ is the inertia matrix of the gripper, $\mathbf{C}(\dot{\varphi}, \varphi)$ denotes the Coriolis and Centrifugal forces, respectively, $\mathbf{H}(\varphi)$ is the elastic forces, $\mathbf{T}$ is the vector of the driving motor torque and $\mathbf{T}_{ext}$ is the reaction torque imposed by an external force.

In brief, based on the object parameter estimation, the parameters presented in Eq. (13) can be determined according to Eqs. (14)–(16). Thus, the virtual desired trajectory $x_0$ is obtained according to Eq. (13) using the measured $f$ and the given $x_d$, and the inner-position controller is used to ensure the trajectory tracking. In this way, impedance adaptive control is achieved and Eq. (13) provides the resulting critical impedance function in the presence of an unknown grasped object.

## 4   Experiment Results

### 4.1   Experimental Conditions

The proposed method is verified based on the hardware platform presented in Sect. 2. In the control scheme (as shown in Fig. 6), the position control is used to ensure trajectory tracking in joint space, which is achieved by the PID controller. The parameters of the PID controller are chosen as P = 1, I = 0.1 and D = 0. The weighting matrices are chosen as: $Q_1 = 1$, $Q_2' = 800 \times 800$ and $r = 1$. The matrices $\mathbf{U}$ and $\mathbf{V}$ are chosen as: $\mathbf{U} = \begin{bmatrix} 0 & -1 \\ 0 & 0.5 \end{bmatrix}$ and $\mathbf{V} = [1 \quad 0.01]$, and the desired trajectory is designed

to be $x_d = 0.01 - 0.01e^{-0.5t}$. We employing $f = -\mathbf{K}_0 \xi + v$ as the impedance model over the time interval [0 s, 3 s], where $\mathbf{K}_0$ is the initial value of the impedance parameters and $v$ is the exploration noise to satisfy the persistent excitation (PE) condition [9]. In the experiment, $\mathbf{K}_0$ is chosen as $\mathbf{K}_0 = [-1{-}1000 \; 1000]$ and the exploration noise is chosen to be $v = \sum_{w=1}^{10} \frac{3}{w} \sin(wt)$. The impedance model for this time period is $f = \dot{x} + 1000x - 1000x_d + v$. The parameters for the grasped object are estimated during the entire process at the same time that the impedance parameters are calculated according to Eqs. (14)–(16). The impedance parameters are used to update the impedance model over the time interval (3 s, 120 s).

## 4.2   Experimental Results

The experimental results for the position and contact force are shown in Figs. 7(a) and (b). For the three sets of springs with aluminium sheets, the position and contact force converge to constants, and for different springs, the stable position and contact force are different. To observe the effect of the exploration noise, the results over the time interval (0 s, 30 s) are presented in Figs. 7(c) and (d). During the first 3 s, the under-actuated gripper has a high-frequency movement, which ensures an accurate estimation of the parameters of the grasped object. After 3 s, the desired impedance model is obtained and imposed upon the under-actuated gripper, and the action of the

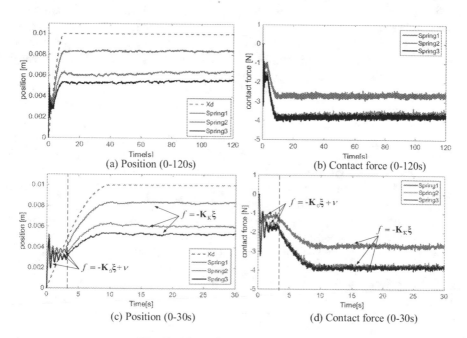

**Fig. 7.** The position and contact force.

under-actuated gripper during this time absolutely relies on the impedance parameters. The convergence performance of the impedance parameters are shown in Fig. 8. For a certain spring with an aluminium sheet, the impedance parameters have a good convergent effect.

For the impedance adaptive control method proposed in Sect. 3, the impedance parameters rely on the estimated values of the dynamics parameters of the springs with an aluminium sheet. The estimated values of the dynamics parameters are presented in Fig. 9, which exhibit good convergent performance.

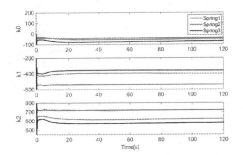

**Fig. 8.** Impedance parameters.    **Fig. 9.** The estimated values.

The mean values of the estimated results at a stable stage are listed in Table 2, which are compared with the nominal value. The nominal value of the stiffness is measured according to the Hooke's law, and the nominal value of contact mass is given as the mass of the aluminium sheet. However, it is difficult to measure the nominal damping of the spring with an aluminum sheet. From Table 2, we see that the estimation of the stiffness is very near to the nominal value, which has a much larger magnitude than the estimation of the contact mass and damping. Therefore, the stiffness plays a primary role in the grasping process, and an accurate estimation of stiffness is crucial to ensure stable grasping. Although good convergent performance is achieved, there is a significant gap between the nominal mass of the aluminium sheet and the estimation of the contact mass. Additionally, the estimation of the damping is negative and which should be positive in practice. The reason for this result may be that the contact mass and damping of the system composed of the spring and aluminium sheet are much smaller than the stiffness. Thus the estimation of the damping and contact mass is significantly affected by many factors, e.g., measurement error and noise. Despite the fact that a large number of common characteristics are attributed to such a system in which the stiffness is much larger than the contact mass and damping, this work provides a good reference for the stable grasp of an unknown object. Future work should be dedicated to exploring the reason behind the inaccurate estimation of the contact mass and the damping terms. For this work, the selection of a proper grasped object is optional, as well as a viable approach to measuring the damping and contact mass of a grasped object.

**Table 2.** Estimated results and the nominal value.

| | Stiffness (N/m) | | Damping (Ns/m) | | Contact mass (kg) | |
|---|---|---|---|---|---|---|
| | Nominal value | Estimation | Nominal value | Estimation | Nominal value | Estimation |
| Spring1 | 168.9 | 161.6 | DTD | −7.3 | 0.028 | 0.37 |
| Spring2 | 306.3 | 299.4 | DTD | −11.5 | 0.028 | 0.22 |
| Spring3 | 362.9 | 357.1 | DTD | −16.2 | 0.028 | 0.49 |

Note: difficult to determine (DTD).

## 5    Conclusions

This paper presents an experiment on impedance adaptation for an under-actuated gripper grasping an unknown grasped object with tactile sensing. The experimental setup uses hardware control architecture and a two-finger under-actuated gripper with an unknown grasped object. The unknown grasped objects are chosen as three sets of springs with different stiffness. Based on the hardware platform, an impedance adaptive control is developed to obtain the desired impedance parameters when manipulating an unknown grasped object. The unknown grasped object is described using mass-damping-stiffness system. From this, the desired impedance model is obtained and the critical impedance parameters are determined to minimize a cost function including the velocity, trajectory errors and contact force. The desired impedance model is imposed on the under-actuated gripper to ensure gripper actions during the grasping process. The experimental results show that the under-actuated gripper can stably grasp an unknown grasped object using the proposed method.

**Acknowledgements.** This work is supported by the Natural Science Foundation of China (Grant Nos. 51375034 and 61327809).

## References

1. Kragten, A., van der Helm, F.C.T., Herder, J.L.: A planar geometric design approach for a large grasp range in underactuated hands. Mech. Sci. **46**, 1121–1136 (2011)
2. Birglen, L., Gosselin, C.M.: On the force capability of underactuated fingers. In: Proceedings of IEEE International Conference on Robotics and Automation (2003)
3. Tiwana, M.I., Shashank, A., Redmond, S.J., Lovell, N.H.: Characterization of a capacitive tactile shear sensor for application in robotic and upper limb prostheses. Sens. Actuators A, Phys. **165**(29), 164–172 (2011)
4. Hogan, N.: Impedance control: an approach tomanipulation-part i: theory; part ii: implementation; part iii: applications. Trans. ASME J. Dyn. Syst. Measur. Control **107**, 17–24 (1985)
5. Xu, Q.S.: Robust impedance control of a compliant microgripper for high-speed position/force regulation. IEEE Trans. Ind. Electron. **62**(2), 1201–1209 (2015)
6. Li, M., Hang, K.Y., Kragic, D., Billard, A.: Dexterous grasping under shape uncertainty. Rob. Auton. Syst. **75**(Part B), 352–364 (2016)

7. Colbaugh, R., Seraji, H., Glass, K.: Direct adaptive impedance control of manipulators. J. Rob. Syst. **10**(2), 217–248 (1991)
8. Stanisic, R.Z., Fernandez, A.V.: Adjusting the parameters of the mechanical impedance for velocity, impact and force control. Robotica **30**(4), 583–597 (2012)
9. Ge, S.S., Li, Y.N., Wang, C.: Impedance adaptation for optimal robot–environment interaction. Int. J. Control **87**(2), 249–263 (2013)
10. Tsumugiwa, T., Yokogawa, R., Hara, K.: Variable impedance control based on estimation of human arm stiffness for human-robot cooperative calligraphic task. In: Proceedings of the IEEE International Conference on Robotics and Automation, pp. 644–650 (2002)
11. Johansson, R., Spong, M.W.: Quadratic optimization of impedance control. In: Proceedings of IEEE International Conference of Robotics and Automation, pp. 616–621 (1994)
12. Jiang, Y., Jiang, Z.P.: Computational adaptive optimal control for continuous-time linear systems with completely unknown dynamics. Automatica **48**, 2699–2704 (2012)
13. Kim, B., Park, J., Park, S., Kang, S.: Impedance learning for robotic contact tasks using natural actor-critic algorithm. IEEE Trans. Syst. Man Cybern.-Part B: Cybern. **40**, 433–443 (2010)
14. Chu, Z.Y., Hu, J., Lei, Y.A.: An adaptive gripper of space robot for space on-orbit services, CN 201310326633.7, China patent (2013)
15. Zhou, M., Chu, Z.Y.: Impedance joint torque control of an active-passive composited driving self-adaptive end effector for space manipulator. In: Proceedings of the 11th World Congress on Intelligent Control and Automation, Shenyang, China (2014)
16. Liu, Y.J., Ding, F.: Convergence properties of the least squares estimation algorithm for multivariable systems. Appl. Math. Modell. **37**, 476–483 (2013)

# Experiment on Self-adaptive Impedance Control of Two-Finger Gripper with Tactile Sensing

Zhongyi Chu[1], Ye Ma[1(✉)], Miao Zhou[1], and Fuchun Sun[2]

[1] School of Instrument Science and Opto-Electronics Engineering,
Beihang University, Beijing, China
15210806985@163.com
[2] Department of Computer Science and Technology,
Tsinghua University, Beijing, China

**Abstract.** The end effector is crucial for handling and manipulating objects with a space manipulator during on-orbit service. In this paper, a new self-adaptive impedance controller for an underactuated two-finger gripper is proposed based on tactile sensing. The impedance controller makes the finger appear as mechanical impedance when it touches an unknown object. In particular, the impedance stiffness parameter can be adjusted using the stiffness recognition of tactile sensing in real time. Thus, there is no switching mode between motion in free space and the capture process, and the gripper can self-adapt the capture force to different stiffness of objects. Finally, a terrestrial experimental setup is established to validate the efficiency of the proposed controller for the gripper.

**Keywords:** Gripper · Self-adaptive · Impedance control · Stiffness recognition · Tactile sensing

## 1 Introduction

On-orbit services, such as repairing, refuelling and re-orbiting, are essential for space missions, and they increasingly rely on the end effector, which is the most critical device in space manipulators. To perform diverse on-orbit tasks, many types of end effectors have been examined. Recently, studies on human hands have inspired new research in this field, particularly regarding underactuated systems [1]. Underactuated end effectors can grasp various objects, because the fingers adapt themselves to the shape of the object by their mechanical behaviour [2]. However, to design an appropriate autonomous control scheme to achieve the stability of grasp and the flexibility to the environment is difficult for the underactuated end effector [3].

The common control objective of end effectors is to drive away from any arbitrary initial position and balance at the equilibrium position to obtain fine object grasping; accordingly, researchers have presented many control schemes. However, the most frequently used method is a hybrid position/force controller T. Reisinger proposed hybrid position/force-control to implement skill primitives [4]. The hybrid control

© Springer Nature Singapore Pte Ltd. 2017
F. Sun et al. (Eds.): ICCSIP 2016, CCIS 710, pp. 261–275, 2017.
DOI: 10.1007/978-981-10-5230-9_28

method only attempts to control forces and motions in orthogonal directions, and it cannot actively control the complete system dynamics of capturing objects, particularly regarding the system damping property; hence, it cannot comply with the environment. To address this disadvantage, Hogan introduced the impedance control scheme [5], which is currently considered a classical control approach in robotics [6]. Based on the general concept of impedance control, the impedance position controller was presented in [7]. However, it should be noted that the impedance position controller has position feedback, which is modified by a second-order impedance model, but no force/torque control, which leads to stability problems [8]. To overcome this problem, H. Liu proposed an impedance joint torque control scheme [9], where the impedance parameters determined the dynamic behaviour of the capture so that each finger could comply with the force control. However, the impedance parameters of these controllers cannot vary with different objects, which results in poor flexibility to the seized object. Therefore, self-adapting the dynamic property of the capture to different objects is a great challenge for the control of the end effector.

To realise flexible and adaptive manipulation in an unknown environment, various sensors are mounted in the gripper to mimic the human hand, such as the sensor-based space robotics ROTEX [10]. In general, the sensors can be classified into noncontact sensors and contact sensors [11]. Noncontact sensors, such as laser scanners and cameras, are essential for the gripper to recognise an object and plan the location to grasp it [12]. Recognition and planning instruct the grasping action, such as providing information about the material, shape and position trajectory of the object, to adaptively handle an unknown object and remain robust to inevitable uncertainties [13], any a priori information must be complemented with real-time contact sensors, such as force/torque sensors and tactile sensors [14]. Tactile sensors, which are similar to human skin structure, are extremely sensitive and capable to measure dynamic contact forces and their distribution. Therefore, tactile sensors are better than other sensors at perceiving interactive events, which inspired the development of its application in robotic grasp control. Based on tactile sensing, Fernandez and Yussof studied the slipping detection and object hardness classification [15], and Chitta analysed the internal state recognition for mobile manipulation [16]. Although significant efforts were made to recognise the object and contact state by tactile sensing, researchers had to pursue an appropriate computation scheme to apply the detection information to the controller.

This paper presents a new self-adaptive impedance controller for a two-finger gripper with tactile sensing. First, the kinematics and dynamics of the gripper are briefly reviewed. Second, a new self-adaptive impedance control scheme is proposed for the gripper, the stiffness parameter of which can be adjusted using the stiffness recognition of tactile sensing in real time. Based on the proposed scheme, there is no switching mode during the transition from the free space to the constraint space, and the finger can autonomously adapt appropriate forces to different objects, which acts as a programmable mechanical spring with variable impedance parameters to the environment. Finally, the experimental results validate the efficiency of the proposed controller to adapt the capture force to different stiffness of the objects.

The paper is organised as follows. Section 2 briefly reviews the kinematics and dynamics of the two-finger gripper. The self-adaptive impedance controller with tactile sensing is proposed in Sect. 3. The experimental results are presented in Sect. 4. Finally, the conclusions are provided in Sect. 5.

## 2 Model

### 2.1 Brief View of the Gripper

The structure of the two-finger gripper is shown in Fig. 1. It consists of four parts: (1) motor and gearing, (2) two fingers, (3) tactile sensors and (4) the base. The motor and gearing parts are used to transmit energy and forces to guide the gripper in grasping. The two-finger part consists of 2 underactuated fingers with passive springs. Each finger is a closed-loop system with four moving linkages and a fixed linkage embedded in the base. As a 5-bar link with only one input torque is indeterminate, a spring which is in a different location from that of the gripper [17] is used to resolve the indeterminacy so that distal phalanges can move relative to one another in the parallel manner with less energy consumption. In addition, the tactile sensors in the contact linkages are used to measure the contact force and its distribution. The base supports the entire system.

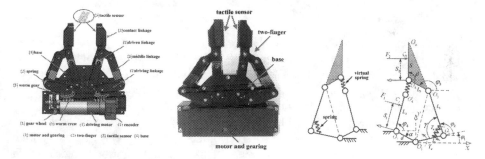

**Fig. 1.** Structure of the two-finger grip

**Fig. 2.** Model of the two-finger gripper

### 2.2 Kinematics

The model of the active-passive composited driving end effector is shown in Fig. 2, which is a symmetrical design with two fingers. Each finger consists of five linkages $L_1$, $L_2$, $L_3$, $L_4$, $d$ and five joints $O_1, O_2, O_3, O_4(O_4'), O_5$, where linkages $O_4O_6$ and $L_3$ are coupled with the invariant angle $\beta$, and $d$ is rooted in the base. The frame $\{O_1\text{-}xy\}$ is located with the finger base coordinate system. The state parameters of the system $\varphi = [\varphi_1 \ \varphi_2 \ \varphi_3 \ \varphi_4]^T$ are the angles between the linkages $(L_1, L_2, L_3, L_4)$ and the $x$ axis of the base coordinate system and $\alpha$ is the angle between linkage $d$ and the opposite direction of the $x$ axis as the base coordinate system.

According to the closed-loop system of the finger, one can obtain the restricted functions as follows [18]:

$$
\begin{cases}
f_1 = d\,\cos\alpha + L_1\cos\varphi_1 + L_2\cos\varphi_2 + L_3\cos\varphi_3 - L_4\cos\varphi_4 = 0 \\
f_2 = d\,\sin\alpha + L_1\sin\varphi_1 + L_2\sin\varphi_2 + L_3\sin\varphi_3 - L_4\sin\varphi_4 = 0 \\
f_3 = d^2 + L_1^2 + L_2^2 + L_3^2 - L_4^2 + 2dL_1\cos(\alpha-\varphi_1) + 2dL_2\cos(\alpha-\varphi_2) + 2dL_3\cos(\alpha-\varphi_3) \\
\quad\ + 2L_1L_2\cos(\varphi_1-\varphi_2) + 2L_1L_3\cos(\varphi_1-\varphi_3) + 2L_2L_3\cos(\varphi_2-\varphi_3) = 0 \\
f_4 = d^2 + L_1^2 + L_2^2 + L_4^2 - L_3^2 + 2dL_1\cos(\alpha-\varphi_1) + 2dL_2\cos(\alpha-\varphi_2) - 2dL_4\cos(\alpha-\varphi_4) \\
\quad\ + 2L_1L_2\cos(\varphi_1-\varphi_2) - 2L_1L_4\cos(\varphi_1-\varphi_4) - 2L_2L_4\cos(\varphi_2-\varphi_4) = 0
\end{cases}
\tag{1}
$$

After differentiating Eq. (1) with respect to the state parameters $\varphi_1$, $\varphi_2$, $\varphi_3$, $\varphi_4$, one obtains Jacobian matrix as follows:

$$
A = \left[\frac{\partial f_1}{\partial\varphi_1}\frac{\partial f_1}{\partial\varphi_2}\frac{\partial f_1}{\partial\varphi_3}\frac{\partial f_1}{\partial\varphi_4};\frac{\partial f_2}{\partial\varphi_1}\frac{\partial f_2}{\partial\varphi_2}\frac{\partial f_2}{\partial\varphi_3}\frac{\partial f_2}{\partial\varphi_4};\frac{\partial f_3}{\partial\varphi_1}\frac{\partial f_3}{\partial\varphi_2}\frac{\partial f_3}{\partial\varphi_3}\frac{\partial f_3}{\partial\varphi_4};\frac{\partial f_4}{\partial\varphi_1}\frac{\partial f_4}{\partial\varphi_2}\frac{\partial f_4}{\partial\varphi_3}\frac{\partial f_4}{\partial\varphi_4}\right]
\tag{2}
$$

### 2.3    Dynamics and Modelling

The two-finger gripper is an underactuated system, which is usually formulated using differential-algebraic dynamic equations and results in a complex computational burden. To address this problem, the Virtual Spring Approach (VSA) [19] is adopted to derive the dynamic equation. Then, one can use a Lagrangian formulation to derive the dynamic equations of the equivalent mechanism [20].

In Fig. 2, ignoring the undesirable effects of the transmission part, there is an active torque $T_a$ of the driving motor and a passive torque $T_k$ of the spring; $F_1$ and $F_2$ are external forces caused by the contact between the finger and the grasped object, which is measured using the tactile sensors, and $S_1$ and $S_2$ are the arms of external forces that act on the corresponding joints. The dynamic equation for the gripper is rewritten in matrix form:

$$
\mathbf{M}(\varphi)\ddot{\varphi} + \mathbf{C}(\dot{\varphi},\varphi) + \mathbf{H}(\varphi) = \tau
\tag{3}
$$

i.e.

$$
\begin{bmatrix}
M_{11} & M_{12} & M_{13} & 0 \\
M_{12} & M_{22} & M_{23} & 0 \\
M_{13} & M_{23} & M_{33} & 0 \\
0 & 0 & 0 & M_{44}
\end{bmatrix}
\begin{bmatrix}
\ddot{\varphi}_1 \\ \ddot{\varphi}_2 \\ \ddot{\varphi}_3 \\ \ddot{\varphi}_4
\end{bmatrix}
+
\begin{bmatrix}
C_1 \\ C_2 \\ C_3 \\ C_4
\end{bmatrix}
+
\begin{bmatrix}
H_1 \\ H_2 \\ H_3 \\ H_4
\end{bmatrix}
=
\begin{bmatrix}
\tau_1 \\ \tau_2 \\ \tau_3 \\ \tau_4
\end{bmatrix}
\tag{4}
$$

where $\mathbf{M}(\varphi)$ is the $4\times 4$ inertia matrix of the finger, $\mathbf{C}(\dot{\varphi},\varphi)$ is the $4\times 1$ vector that contains the centrifugal and Coriolis terms, $\mathbf{H}(\varphi)$ is the $4\times 1$ vector of the elastic forces, and $\tau$ is the $4\times 1$ vector of the generalised forces.

$$M_{11} = J_1 + m_1 L_{c_1}^2 + m_2 L_1^2 + m_3 L_1^2, \ M_{12} = (m_2 L_{c_2} + m_3 L_2) L_1 \cos(\varphi_1 - \varphi_2), M_{13} = m_3 L_1 L_{c_3} \cos(\varphi_1 - \varphi_3)$$

$$M_{22} = J_2 + m_2 L_{c_2}^2 + m_3 L_2^2, M_{23} = m_3 L_2 L_{c_3} \cos(\varphi_2 - \varphi_3), M_{33} = J_3 + m_3 L_{c_3}^2, M_{44} = J_4 + m_4 L_{c_4}^2$$

$$C_1 = \dot{\varphi}_2^2 L_1 (m_2 L_{c_2} + m_3 L_2) \sin(\varphi_1 - \varphi_2) + \dot{\varphi}_3^2 m_3 L_1 L_{c_3} \sin(\varphi_1 - \varphi_3)$$

$$C_2 = -\dot{\varphi}_1^2 L_1 (m_2 L_{c_2} + m_3 L_2) \sin(\varphi_1 - \varphi_2) + \dot{\varphi}_3^2 m_3 L_2 L_{c_3} \sin(\varphi_2 - \varphi_3)$$

$$C_3 = -\dot{\varphi}_2^2 m_3 L_2 L_{c_3} \sin(\varphi_2 - \varphi_3) - \dot{\varphi}_1^2 m_3 L_1 L_{c_3} \sin(\varphi_1 - \varphi_3)$$

$$H_1 = -L_1 k_1 \Delta_x \sin \varphi_1 + L_1 k_1 \Delta_y \cos \varphi_1 + T_k, H_2 = -L_2 k_1 \Delta_x \sin \varphi_2 + L_2 k_1 \Delta_y \cos \varphi_2 - T_k$$

$$H_3 = -L_3 k_1 \Delta_x \sin \varphi_3 + L_3 k_1 \Delta_y \cos \varphi_3, H_4 = L_4 k_1 \Delta_x \sin \varphi_4 - L_4 k_1 \Delta_y \cos \varphi_4$$

$$\tau_1 = T_a - F_{2x} L_1 \sin \varphi_1 + F_{2y} L_1 \cos \varphi_1, \tau_2 = -F_{2x} L_2 \sin \varphi_2 + F_{2y} L_2 \cos \varphi_2$$

$$\tau_3 = -F_{2x} [L_3 \sin \varphi_3 + S_2 \sin(\varphi_3 - \pi/3)] + F_{2y} [L_3 \cos \varphi_3 + S_2 \cos(\varphi_3 - \pi/3)]$$

$$\tau_4 = -F_{1x} S_1 \sin \varphi_4 + F_{1y} S_1 \cos \varphi_4$$

$$(5)$$

where $F_{1x}$, $F_{1y}$, $F_{2x}$ and $F_{2x}$ are the projections of $F_1$ and $F_2$ onto the $x$ and $y$ axes, respectively, and $\Delta_x$ and $\Delta_y$ are the projections of $\Delta$ onto the $x$ and $y$ axes, respectively, which can be described as: $\Delta_x = L_1 \cos \varphi_1 + L_2 \cos \varphi_2 + L_3 \cos \varphi_3 - L_4 \cos \varphi_4 - d \cos(\pi + \alpha)$ and $\Delta_y = L_1 \sin \varphi_1 + L_2 \sin \varphi_2 + L_3 \sin \varphi_3 - L_4 \sin \varphi_4 - d \sin(\pi + \alpha)$, accordingly.

It can be observed from Eqs. (4) and (5) that every joint torque contains an inertia force, the centrifugal and Coriolis forces of the linkages and external forces. Evidently, the VSA increases the degrees of freedom in modelling the mechanism.

As discussed in Sect. 2.1, the gripper is an underactuated mechanism that consists of an active motor and a passive spring. We can obtain the desired motor torque $T_a$ based on the commanded trajectories of the linkages using inverse dynamics. When applied to the inverse dynamics computation, some parameters for the gripper must already be known from the forward dynamics, where the torque $T_k$ of the passive spring is a function of angles $\varphi_1$ and $\varphi_2$, and $F_1$, $F_2$, $S_1$ and $S_2$ can be measured using the tactile sensor. Then, Eq. (4) can be transformed into a system of four equations by eliminating the internal action forces $k_1 \Delta_x$ and $k_1 \Delta_y$.

According to the forward dynamics in Eqs. (3), (4) and (5), one can obtain

$$\mathbf{M}(\varphi)\ddot{\varphi} + \mathbf{C}(\dot{\varphi}, \varphi) = \mathbf{Y} \begin{bmatrix} T_a \\ k_1 \Delta_x \\ k_1 \Delta_y \\ 1 \end{bmatrix} = \begin{bmatrix} 1 & L_1 \sin \varphi_1 & -L_1 \cos \varphi_1 & -T_k + \tau_1' \\ 0 & L_2 \sin \varphi_2 & -L_2 \cos \varphi_2 & T_k + \tau_2 \\ 0 & L_3 \sin \varphi_3 & -L_3 \cos \varphi_3 & \tau_3 \\ 0 & -L_4 \sin \varphi_4 & L_4 \cos \varphi_4 & \tau_4 \end{bmatrix} \begin{bmatrix} T_a \\ k_1 \Delta_x \\ k_1 \Delta_y \\ 1 \end{bmatrix}$$

$$(6)$$

$$\begin{bmatrix} T_a \\ k_1 \Delta_x \\ k_1 \Delta_y \\ 1 \end{bmatrix} = \mathbf{Y}^{-1} [\mathbf{M}(\varphi)\ddot{\varphi} + \mathbf{C}(\dot{\varphi}, \varphi)]$$

$$(7)$$

where $\tau_1' = -F_{2x}L_1 \sin \varphi_1 + F_{2y}L_1 \cos \varphi_1$. From Eq. (7), we can find the values of $k_1\Delta_x$ and $k_1\Delta_y$.

According to Eq. (5), Eq. (4) can be transformed into

$$\mathbf{M}(\varphi)\ddot{\varphi} + \mathbf{C}(\dot{\varphi}, \varphi) + \mathbf{H}(\varphi) = \mathbf{T} - \mathbf{T}_{ext} \tag{8}$$

where $\mathbf{T} - \mathbf{T}_{ext} = \tau$, $\mathbf{T}$ is the $4 \times 1$ vector of the active motor torque of the joint, i.e., $\mathbf{T} = [T_a\ 0\ 0\ 0]^T$, and $\mathbf{T}_{ext}$ is the $4 \times 1$ vector of the joint torques of the external forces $\mathbf{T}_{ext} = \left[-\tau_1' - \tau_2 - \tau_3 - \tau_4\right]^T$.

Accordingly, the inverse dynamics can be written as

$$\mathbf{T} = \mathbf{M}(\varphi)\ddot{\varphi} + \mathbf{C}(\dot{\varphi}, \varphi) + \mathbf{H}(\varphi) + \mathbf{T}_{ext} \tag{9}$$

# 3    Controller Design

This section presents the self-adaptive impedance controller for the two-finger gripper, which consists of two parts: impedance control and stiffness recognition. The objectives are to cause the finger to follow the desired trajectory and autonomously control the dynamic grasping behaviour. The control scheme of the system is shown in Fig. 3.

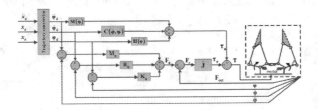

**Fig. 3.** Block diagram of the impedance controller

## 3.1    Impedance Control

Using the proposed control scheme, we can control the desired impedance property of the finger:

$$\mathbf{F}_{ext} = \mathbf{M_d}\delta\ddot{x} + \mathbf{B_d}\delta\dot{x} + \mathbf{K_d}\delta x \tag{10}$$

where $\mathbf{F}_{ext} = [F_{1x}\ F_{1y}\ F_{2x}\ F_{2y}]^T$ are the external forces acting on the finger; $\mathbf{M_d}$, $\mathbf{B_d}$ and $\mathbf{K_d}$ are the $4 \times 4$ diagonal desired target impedance parameters of the finger; $\delta x = x_d - x$ is the $4 \times 1$ vector of the position errors; and $x_d$ and $x$ are $4 \times 1$ vectors of the desired positions and the actual positions of the finger, respectively.

According to the closed-loop system of the finger, as shown in Fig. 3, the positions of the contact points between the external forces and the finger can be written as

$$\begin{cases} S\_F_1 = O_1 O_5 + O_5 C_1 \\ S\_F_2 = O_1 O_2 + O_2 O_3 + O_3 O_4 + O_4 C_2 \end{cases} \tag{11}$$

Based on the projections of the positions onto the $x$ and $y$ axes, Eq. (11) can be transformed into

$$\mathbf{x} = \begin{bmatrix} x\_F_1 \\ y\_F_1 \\ x\_F_2 \\ y\_F_2 \end{bmatrix} = \begin{bmatrix} -d\cos\alpha + S_1\cos(\varphi_4) \\ -d\sin\alpha + S_1\sin(\varphi_4) \\ L_1\cos(\varphi_1) + L_2\cos(\varphi_2) + L_3\cos(\varphi_3) + S_2\cos(\varphi_3 - \frac{\pi}{3}) \\ L_1\sin(\varphi_1) + L_2\sin(\varphi_2) + L_3\sin(\varphi_3) + S_2\sin(\varphi_3 - \frac{\pi}{3}) \end{bmatrix} \tag{12}$$

By differentiating Eq. (12) with respect to the state parameters $\varphi_1$, $\varphi_2$, $\varphi_3$ and $\varphi_4$, one obtains the following relationship between $\delta\mathbf{x}$ and $\delta\varphi$:

$$\delta\mathbf{x} = \mathbf{J} \cdot \delta\varphi = \begin{bmatrix} 0 & 0 & 0 & -S_1\sin(\varphi_4) \\ 0 & 0 & 0 & S_1\cos(\varphi_4) \\ -L_1\sin(\varphi_1) & -L_2\sin(\varphi_2) & -L_3\sin(\varphi_3) - S_2\sin(\varphi_3 - \frac{\pi}{3}) & 0 \\ L_1\cos(\varphi_1) & L_2\cos(\varphi_2) & L_3\cos(\varphi_3) + S_2\cos(\varphi_3 - \frac{\pi}{3}) & 0 \end{bmatrix} \cdot \begin{bmatrix} \delta\varphi_1 \\ \delta\varphi_2 \\ \delta\varphi_3 \\ \delta\varphi_4 \end{bmatrix}$$

$$\tag{13}$$

By combining Eqs. (10) and (13), $\mathbf{F}_{ext}$ can be written as:

$$\begin{aligned} \mathbf{F}_{ext} &= \mathbf{M_d}\delta\ddot{\mathbf{x}} + \mathbf{B_d}\delta\dot{\mathbf{x}} + \mathbf{K_d}\delta\mathbf{x} \\ &= \mathbf{M_d}\left(\dot{\mathbf{J}}\delta\dot{\varphi} + \mathbf{J}\delta\ddot{\varphi}\right) + \mathbf{B_d}\mathbf{J}\delta\dot{\varphi} + \mathbf{K_d}\mathbf{J}\delta\varphi \\ &= \mathbf{M_\varphi}\delta\ddot{\varphi} + \mathbf{B_\varphi}\delta\dot{\varphi} + \mathbf{K_\varphi}\delta\varphi \end{aligned} \tag{14}$$

where $\mathbf{M_\varphi} = \mathbf{M_d}\mathbf{J}$, $\mathbf{B_\varphi} = \mathbf{M_d}\dot{\mathbf{J}} + \mathbf{B_d}\mathbf{J}$, $\mathbf{K_\varphi} = \mathbf{K_d}\mathbf{J}$, and $\mathbf{M_\varphi}$, $\mathbf{B_\varphi}$ and $\mathbf{K_\varphi}$ are the $4 \times 4$ matrices that represent the joint inertia, damping and stiffness, respectively.

As discussed in Sect. 2.3, by substituting Eqs. (3), (4) and (5) into Eq. (8), the relationship between the joint torques and the external forces can be written in matrix form:

$$\mathbf{T}_{ext} = \begin{bmatrix} \tau'_1 \\ \tau_2 \\ \tau_3 \\ \tau_4 \end{bmatrix} = \tilde{\mathbf{J}}\mathbf{F}_{ext} \tag{15}$$

Where,

$$\tilde{\mathbf{J}} = \begin{bmatrix} 0 & 0 & L_1 \sin\varphi_1 & -L_1 \cos\varphi_1 \\ 0 & 0 & L_2 \sin\varphi_2 & -L_2 \cos\varphi_2 \\ 0 & 0 & L_3 \sin\varphi_3 + S_2 \sin(\varphi_3 - \frac{\pi}{3}) & -L_3 \cos\varphi_3 - S_2 \cos(\varphi_3 - \frac{\pi}{3}) \\ S_1 \sin\varphi_4 & -S_1 \cos\varphi_4 & 0 & 0 \end{bmatrix}$$

To maintain the target impedance, we can deduce the following active motor torque by substituting Eqs. (14) and (15) into the inverse dynamics in Eq. (9).

$$\mathbf{T} = \mathbf{M}(\varphi)\left\{\ddot{\varphi}_d - \mathbf{M}_\varphi^{-1}\left(\mathbf{F}_{ext} - \mathbf{B}_\varphi \delta\dot{\varphi} - \mathbf{K}_\varphi \delta\varphi\right)\right\} + \mathbf{C}(\dot{\varphi},\varphi) + \mathbf{H}(\varphi) + \tilde{\mathbf{J}}\mathbf{F}_{ext} \quad (16)$$

The above equation shows that one can perfectly calculate active motor torque based on the feedback linearization with precise knowledge of the gripper dynamics and accurate sensors, and the finger will present the desired impedance parameters $\mathbf{M_d}$, $\mathbf{B_d}$ and $\mathbf{K_d}$ to the environment. However, in reality, the gripper dynamics are not precisely known, the gearing part introduces some hysteresis, and the accuracy of the position and force sensors are always affected by some noises, so it is difficult to realise a perfect linearisation. Hence, the desired impedance parameters cannot be achieved. Alternatively, to maintain Eq. (16) as equal as possible, we can introduce an explicit force control scheme [9].

$$\mathbf{F_d} = \mathbf{M}_\varphi \delta\ddot{\varphi} + \mathbf{B}_\varphi \delta\dot{\varphi} + \mathbf{K}_\varphi \delta\varphi \quad (17)$$

We define the error function

$$\mathbf{F_e} = \mathbf{F_d} - \mathbf{F_{ext}} \quad (18)$$

where $\mathbf{F_{ext}}$ is the external forces that are measured using the tactile sensor.

Then, the torque $\tau_e$ caused by the error function can be obtained:

$$\tau_e = \tilde{\mathbf{J}}\mathbf{F_e} \quad (19)$$

Combining Eqs. (9), (16) and (19), the impedance control moment of the driving motor is defined as:

$$\tau = \tau_a + \tau_e \quad (20)$$

Where,

$$\tau_a = \mathbf{M}(\varphi)\ddot{\varphi} + \mathbf{C}(\dot{\varphi},\varphi) + \mathbf{H}(\varphi).$$

Ultimately, we can build an impedance controller, as is shown in Fig. 3. If $\mathbf{F_e}$ approaches zero, the desired target impedance parameters $\mathbf{M_d}$, $\mathbf{B_d}$ and $\mathbf{K_d}$ will converge to the actual values. In the steady state, the measured and desired velocities and accelerations are zero, so the capture force is proportional to the deformation $\delta\varphi$, which implies that the steady force is the stiffness $\mathbf{K}_\varphi$ multiplied by the deformation $\delta\varphi$, where the joint stiffness $K_\varphi$ depends on the desired target stiffness $K_d$. However, the desired target stiffness $K_d$ is constant and cannot vary with the environment, which results in the poor flexibility of the capture force to the different seized objects. To address this problem, in the following subsection, the tactile sensing is applied to recognise the stiffness of object in real time, so that the desired target stiffness parameter $K_d$ can vary with the environment.

## 3.2 Stiffness Recognition

This section presents the stiffness recognition algorithm with the tactile signals of tactile sensors, which consists of two parts: contact event detection and stiffness recognition. Here, we describe the two tactile sensory signals, including the force and force disturbance, which are required to analyse the contact state.

Each fingertip of the gripper is equipped with a tactile sensor that consists of $4 \times 4$ individual cells. The total fingertip force can be calculated by summing the readings from all 16 elements in the tip of one finger:

$$F_L = \sum_{i=1}^{4} \sum_{j=1}^{4} f_{L(i,j)} \tag{21}$$

where $f_{L(i,j)}$ is the force that acts on the left fingertip at location $(i,j)$. The same method is used to calculate $F_R$ on the right finger using $f_{R(i,j)}$. The mean grip force is obtained by averaging the force of two fingers:

$$F = \frac{1}{2}(F_L + F_R) \tag{22}$$

To obtain the force disturbance, we take the sum of the high-pass-filtered forces using the 16 fingertip cells:

$$\tilde{F}_L(z) = \sum_{i=1}^{4} \sum_{j=1}^{4} H_F(z) f_{L(i,j)}(z) \tag{23}$$

where $H_F(z)$ is a discrete-time first-order Butterworth high-pass filter with a cutoff frequency of 5 Hz, which is designed for the 50 Hz sampling rate of the pressure signals. Then the resulting filtered signals are summed to obtain an estimation of the >5 Hz force disturbances $\tilde{F}_L(z)$ that acts on the left finger. The procedure is identical for the right finger to obtain $\tilde{F}_R(z)$.

Based on the above tactile signals, to recognise the stiffness of grasped object, the contact event during the transition from the free space to the constraint space is detected first:

$$\begin{cases} \text{LeftContact} = (F_L > \text{FLIMIT}) \ || \ (\tilde{F}_L > \text{DLIMIT}) \\ \text{RightContact} = (F_R > \text{FLIMIT}) \ || \ (\tilde{F}_R > \text{DLIMIT}) \end{cases} \tag{24}$$

where FLIMIT and DLIMIT are the thresholds of the force signal and force-disturbance signal of each fingertip for the contact event, respectively. We define LeftContact and RightContact as the contact event.

After contact is detected, the finger pauses for a short settling time ($\Delta t$) with a moderate closing speed ($v$). The force response during this contact settling time is a notably useful indicator of the object firmness [21]. Thus, the gripper records the maximum average force detected by the fingers during the settling time and calculates the target stiffness of the object as:

$$K = \max_{\Delta t}(F)\frac{\text{KHARDNESS}}{v} \tag{25}$$

where KHARDNESS is a constant coefficient. The values of KHARDNESS and $v$ strongly contribute to estimate the stiffness of the grasped objects. Therefore, KHARDNESS and $v$ should be obtained from experiments that are implemented for a generic set of objects.

In the capture process, the desired position trajectory depends on the movement of the fingertip along the $x$ axis, i.e., $x\_F_{2d}$. In addition, there is zero value in $F_{1x}$, $F_{1y}$, and $F_{2y}$, and the desired target stiffness parameter $\mathbf{K_d}$ is related to only the stiffness of the perpendicular compressive force $F_{2x}$ of the fingertip, i.e.

$$K_d = [0\,0\,0\,0;\ 0\,0\,0\,0;\ 0\,0\,K\,0;\ 0\,0\,0\,0]$$

Consequently, from Eq. (25), $\mathbf{K_d}$ varies according to the stiffness $K$ towards different objects. Therefore, when the finger contacts the grasped object, it appears as active mechanical impedance with variable impedance stiffness $\mathbf{K_\varphi}$, which makes the capture process smoother to avoid capture failure or damage to the object. Furthermore, in the steady state, the gripper can self-adapt the capture force to different stiffness of the objects. Accordingly, the impedance controller with stiffness recognition using tactile sensing makes the gripper behave similarly to a programmable spring with variable impedance parameters, which can adapt to the environment.

## 4    Experiment Study

### 4.1    Experimental Setup

As shown in Fig. 4, the experimental system consists of two parts: a supervisor computer and an implement controller. Based on the GUI software, the supervisor computer shows the sensor measurements and gives the desired trajectory of the gripper. The implement controller consists of the gripper and hardware control architecture, which comprise a closed-loop control system.

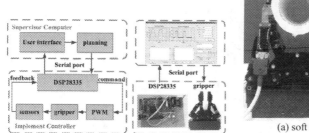

Fig. 4. Experimental system of the gripper

(a) soft object    (b) hard object

**Fig. 5.** Two experimental situations

## 4.2    Experimental Results

In this section, two situations are experimented to validate the adaptability of the proposed controller: capturing a soft object (Fig. 5(a)) and capturing a hard object (Fig. 5(b)). The parameters of the two-finger gripper are listed in Table 1.

**Table 1.** Parameters of the gripper.

| Symbol | $L_1$ | $L_2$ | $L_3$ | $L_4$ | $m_1$ | $m_2$ | $m_3$ | $m_4$ | $\alpha$ | $\beta$ | $d$ |
|--------|-------|-------|-------|-------|-------|-------|-------|-------|----------|---------|-----|
| Value | $3.18\times10^{-2}$m | $4.80\times10^{-2}$m | $1.90\times10^{-2}$m | $5.71\times10^{-2}$m | 0.0195kg | 0.03kg | 0.0409kg | 0.0335kg | $-26.57°$ | $120°$ | $1.9\times10^{-2}$m |

| Symbol | $s$ | $k_1$ | $L_{c1}$ | $L_{c2}$ | $L_{c3}$ | $L_{c4}$ | $\varphi_{10}$ | $\varphi_{20}$ | $\varphi_{30}$ | $\varphi_{40}$ | $k_2$ |
|--------|-----|-------|----------|----------|----------|----------|----------------|----------------|----------------|----------------|-------|
| Value | $4.8\times10^{-2}$m | $10^6$ N/m | $1.59\times10^{-2}$m | $2.4\times10^{-2}$m | $0.95\times10^{-2}$m | $2.85\times10^{-2}$m | $-4.482°$ | $86.547°$ | $153.43°$ | $52.71°$ | 1.25 N/m |

| Symbol | $I_1$ | $I_2$ | $I_3$ | $I_4$ |
|--------|-------|-------|-------|-------|
| Value | $1.643\times10^{-4}$m$^2$kg | $5.76\times10^{-6}$m$^2$kg | $1.23\times10^{-6}$m$^2$kg | $9.102\times10^{-4}$m$^2$kg |

Simultaneously, to demonstrate the improved performance of the new self-adaptive impedance controller with stiffness recognition, the presented method is compared with the traditional impedance controller without stiffness recognition, and the optimal parameters of these two controllers are listed in Table 2. The desired position trajectory of the gripper is shown in Fig. 6; three components of the desired position trajectory represent the closing, grasping and opening stages.

**Table 2.** Optimal parameters of two controllers.

| Symbol | Self-adaptive impedance controller | | | | | | | Traditional impedance control | | |
|--------|------------------------------------|---|---|---|---|---|---|-------------------------------|---|---|
| | $M_d$ | $B_d$ | FLIMIT | DLIMIT | $v$ | $\Delta t$ | KHRADNESS | $M_d$ | $B_d$ | $K_d$ |
| Value | 0.001 Ns$^2$/m | 6.5 Ns/m | 0.475 N | 0.158 N | 1.15 mm/s | 0.05 s | 0.082 s$^{-1}$ | 0.001 Ns$^2$/m | 6.5 Ns/m | 1750 N/m |

The experimental results of the position trajectories and capture forces are shown in Figs. 7 and 8. Figures 7(a) and (b), 8(a) and (b) show that the position trajectories of the soft and hard objects are almost identical in both controllers. For the capture force,

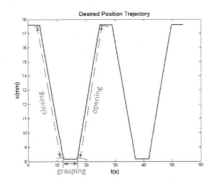

**Fig. 6.** Desired position trajectory

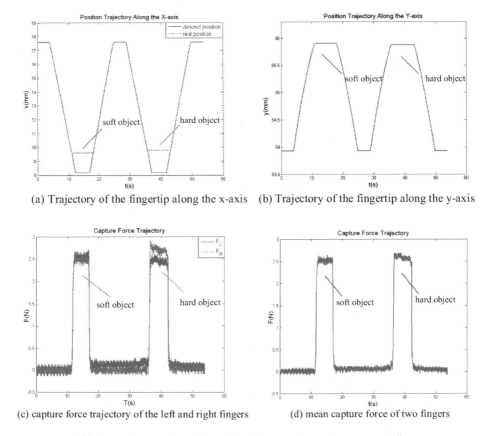

(a) Trajectory of the fingertip along the x-axis     (b) Trajectory of the fingertip along the y-axis

(c) capture force trajectory of the left and right fingers     (d) mean capture force of two fingers

**Fig. 7.** The experimental results of traditional impedance controller

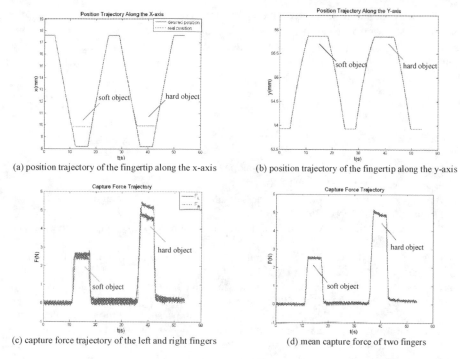

(a) position trajectory of the fingertip along the x-axis

(b) position trajectory of the fingertip along the y-axis

(c) capture force trajectory of the left and right fingers

(d) mean capture force of two fingers

**Fig. 8.** The experimental results of self-adaptive impedance controller

the traditional impedance controller maintains the same force for the soft and hard objects (Figs. 7(c) and (d)). However, in the self-adaptive impedance controller, the capture force of hard object is larger than that of soft object (Figs. 8(c) and (d)), because the impedance stiffness of the self-adaptive impedance controller can vary with different objects by stiffness recognition of tactile sensing, whereas the impedance stiffness of the traditional impedance controller remains constant, which poorly adapts to the environment. Simultaneously, because of the noises of the tactile sensors and asymmetrical surfaces of the grasped object, the forces of the left and right fingers have some asymmetry, as is shown in Figs. 7(c) and 8(c). In general, the self-adaptive impedance controller adapts the grasp control of the gripper better than the traditional impedance controller.

## 5   Conclusion

The self-adaptive impedance controller was proposed for a two-finger gripper, the impedance stiffness of which is adjusted by the stiffness recognition of tactile sensing in real time. Accordingly, the finger acts as a programmable spring with variable impedance parameters and self-adapts the capture force to different stiffness of objects to adapt to the environment. Finally, terrestrial experiments were implemented to validate the adaptability of the proposed control scheme for the gripper.

The experimental results show that the proposed controller can be used for adaptive robotic grasp control. And in future work, based on tactile sensing and slipping detection, we hope to recognise other dynamic impedance parameters besides stiffness, including damping and inertia, to model the dynamics of the grasping process to adapt the dynamic properties for the capture process.

# References

1. Shigeo, H., Umetani, Y.: The development of soft gripper for the versatile robot hand. Mech. Mach. Theor. **13**(3), 351–359 (1978)
2. Belzile, B., Birglen, L.: A compliant self-adaptive gripper with proprioceptive haptic feedback. Auton. Robots **36**, 79–91 (2014)
3. Ciocarlie, M., Allen, P.: A constrained optimization framework for compliant underactuated grasping. Mech. Sci. **2**, 17–26 (2011)
4. Reisinger, T.: Hybrid position/force-control for implementing skill primitives. In: ACSE 05 Conference, CICC, Cairo, Egypt, pp. 191–196 (2005)
5. Hogan, N.: Impedance control: an approach to manipulation: Part III-applications. J. Dyn. Syst. Meas. Contr. **107**, 17–24 (1985)
6. Xiong, R., Sun, Y.C., Zhu, Q.G., Wu, J., Chu, J.: Impedance control and its effects on a humanoid robot playing table tennis. Int. J. Adv. Rob. Syst. **9**, 1–11 (2012)
7. Hun, L., Setiawan, S.A., Takanishi, A.: Position-based impedance control of a biped humanoid robot. Adv. Rob. **18**, 415–435 (2004)
8. Ott, C.: Cartesian impedance control of redundant and flexible-joint robots. Adv. Rob. **49**, 4–37 (2008)
9. Liu, H., Liu, Y.C., Jin, M., Sun, K., Huang, J.B.: An experimental study on cartesian impedance control for a joint torque-based manipulator. Adv. Rob. **22**, 1155–1180 (2007)
10. Hirzinger, G., Brunner, B., Dietrich, J.: Sensor-based space robotics-ROTEX and its telerobotics features. IEEE Trans. Rob. Autom. **9**, 649–662 (1993)
11. Abielmona, R., Petriu, E.M., Harb, M., Wesolkowski, S.: Mission-driven robotic intelligent sensor agents for territorial security. IEEE Comput. Intell. Mag. **6**, 55–67 (2011)
12. Chen, G.C., Juang, C.F.: Object detection using color entropies and a fuzzy classifier. IEEE Comput. Intell. Mag. **8**, 33–45 (2013)
13. Guo, D., Sun, F.C., Liu, C.F.: A system of robotic grasping with experience acquisition. Sci. China Inf. Sci. **57**, 120202 (2014)
14. Kim, M.J., Choi, M., Kim, Y.B., Liu, F., Moon, H., Koo, J.C., Choi, H.R.: Exploration of unknown object by active touch of robot hand. Int. J. Control Autom. Syst. **12**(2), 406–414 (2014)
15. Fernandez, R., Payo, I., Vazquez, A.S., Becedas, J.: Micro-vibration-based slip detection in tactile force sensora. Sensors **14**, 709–730 (2014)
16. Chitta, S., Piccoli, M., Sturm, J.: Tactile object class and internal state recognition for mobile manipulation. In: IEEE International Conference on Robotics and Automation, Anchorage, Alaska, USA, pp. 2342–2348 (2010)
17. http://robotiq.com/en/products/industrial-robot-gripper/
18. Chu, Z.Y., Zhou, M., Hu, J., Lu, S.: Gripper mode analysis of an active-passive composited driving self-adaptive mechanism. Acta Aeronautics et Astronuatica Sinica. **35**(12), 3451–3458 (2014)

19. Wang, J.G., Gosselin, C.M., Cheng, L.: Modeling and simulation of robotic systems with closed kinematic chains using the virtual spring approach. Multibody Syst. Dyn. **7**, 145–170 (2002)
20. Khan, W.A., Tang, C.P., Krovi, V.N.: Modular and distributed forward dynamics simulation of constrained mechanical systems-a comparative study. Mech. Mach. Theor. **42**, 558–579 (2007)
21. Romano, J.M., Hsiao, K., Niemeyer, G., Chitta, S., Kuchenbecker, K.J.: Human-inspired robotic grasp control with tactile sensing. IEEE Trans. Rob. **27**, 1067–1079 (2011)

# An Evaluation of 2D SLAM Techniques Based on Kinect and Laser Scanner

Qingyang Lang[1,3], Fuchun Sun[2,3], Huaping Liu[2,3(✉)], Bin Wang[2,3],
Meng Gao[1,3], Jiakui Li[4], and Qing Zhang[4]

[1] Department of Electrical and Electronic Engineering,
Shijiazhuang Tiedao University, Shijiazhuang, China
[2] Department of Computer Science and Technology,
Tsinghua University, Beijing, China
hpliu@tsinghua.edu.cn
[3] State Key Laboratory of Intelligent Technology and Systems,
Tsinghua University, TNLIST, Beijing, China
[4] Samsung Research Institute, Beijing, China

**Abstract.** Both Laser scanner and Kinect has been widely used in robotic application for 2D Simultaneous Localization and Mapping (SLAM). The feasibility of sensors to build acquired maps are often due to the limited field of view of the sensors. In this work, we applied four methods of sensor patterns for SLAM: a single Kinect, two Kinects, a Laser scanner, a Kinect combine with a Laser scanner. For the two-sensor patterns, we proposed an efficient approach to merge the data from the both two sensors. Several SLAM algorithms (i.e. Gmapping, Hector and Crsm SLAM) were tested using the four methods to build accurate 2D maps. All the methods have been evaluated and compared in real world experiments with slight and complex features, then the performance of the three SLAM algorithms were compared particularly in the map accuracy by using the assessment algorithm of Local Grid Map Recursion Matching.

**Keywords:** SLAM · Kinect · Laser scanner · Robotics

## 1 Introduction

The SLAM problem has been widely researched theoretically and has been successfully implemented on mobile robots in 2D and 3D environments. The main idea of this technique is to leave the robot at an unknown location and let it move and build a consistent map of its surroundings [1]. The solution to the SLAM problem allows deployment of robots in many applications such as search and rescue operations. A custom mobile robot was built which provides hardware and software for development of robot algorithms. The Robot Operating System (ROS) is the most popular robotics framework nowadays. It provides a set of tools, libraries and drivers in order to help researchers develop robot applications with hardware abstraction and easily perform real world experiments [2]. The robot needs to localize itself and map the environment which makes it a challenging problem to solve because of the mutual dependency of the map and robot's pose. The purpose of mapping is used for

© Springer Nature Singapore Pte Ltd. 2017
F. Sun et al. (Eds.): ICCSIP 2016, CCIS 710, pp. 276–289, 2017.
DOI: 10.1007/978-981-10-5230-9_29

navigation [3, 4]. Navigation has been a subject of interest in mobile robotics over the past two decades. Navigation relates to a precise map, accurately location, path planning and obstacle-avoiding while the robot move itself to the target point. The methods of SLAM are often device-specific due to the different sensing modalities and capabilities of each sensor. Now mobile robots carry precise sensors such as wheel encoders, gyroscopes, accelerometers, Kinect, ultrasonic sensors and Laser scanners to perform the 2D mapping and navigation. Optical sensors are much cheaper, but have a limited resolution and require complex algorithms to determine depth values from the camera images. Sensor application is also subject to environmental impact in indoor and outdoor or complex and featureless environments. With a single sensor to complete mapping is usually can not receive good results. In order to solve this problem, we consider using sensor fusion [13]. With a single Kinect or Laser scanner, in an environment of single structure (such as gallery, corridor) typically lead to mapping errors because of incorrect scan matching. Fused sensor data from various sensors offers several advantages when compared to data from a single sensor [5]. Most SLAM algorithm can only utilize one laser scan data as input. We take the depth data from Kinect and convert the data to laser scan type [6], then we use two Kinects or a Laser scanner with a Kinect to combine the data into a single laser scan to perform SLAM with Gmapping [7], Hector SLAM [8], and Crsm SLAM [9]. Meanwhile, we also use a single Kinect and a single Laser scanner to perform the three SLAM for comparison. All the tested SLAM use occupancy grids as the final output. With the occupancy grid map, we can analyze the performance of the three algorithms using a metric for map similarities.

## 2   2D SLAM Algorithms

Presently, nearly all of the recognized algorithms used to solve the problem of mapping rely in probabilities. Most of the probabilistic models rely on Bayes estimation [1]. There are numerous algorithms developed by past researchers such as Kalman Filter [1], Extended Kalman Filter [10], UKF [11], RPBF [7], TreeMap [5] and Occupancy Grid Map [12]. Most of the algorithms used odometry and proximity sensors to implement localization and mapping. Some SLAM algorithms do not require wheel odometry information, the 2D robot pose is estimated based on the scan matching process alone.

We present a brief description of Gmapping, Hector SLAM and Crsm SLAM to provide an overview of the strengths and weaknesses of all the three algorithms.

### 2.1   Gmapping

Gmapping is a laser-based SLAM and it is the most widely used algorithm in 2D mapping program. Gmapping was developed based on the Rao-Blackwellized Particle Filter (RBPF), the RBPF was proposed to solve grid-based SLAM problems and it requires odometry information and the sensor's observations (i.e., scans). It usually requires a high number of particles to obtain good results, which increases its computational complexity. The particle - depletion problem related to the re-sampling process decreases the algorithm accuracy. This phenomenon occurs because the importance weights of particles may become insignificant. An adaptive re-sampling technique has been used which minimizes the particle depletion problem, since this process is only performed when is needed. By working with the scan matching process, the number of particles required is decreased since the uncertainty is lower, the robot pose will be accurate.

## 2.2    Hector SLAM

Hector SLAM combines a 2D SLAM system based on robust scan matching and 3D navigation technique using an inertial sensing system [8]. In comparison to the majority of grid-map SLAM techniques, Hector SLAM does not require wheel odometry information. Thus, the 2D robot pose is estimated based on the scan matching process alone. Hector SLAM does not provide an explicit loop closure approach. The algorithm focuses on using a high update rate and low distance measurement noise to estimation the robot movement in real-time. For these conditions, it might have problems when the scan rate is low. The 2D pose estimation is based on optimization of the observation and the map stored so far. The scan matching program is solved using a Gaussian-Newton equation, which calculates the best fit transformation through the laser beams to the map that stored. The endpoints are projected in the actual map and the grid occupancy probabilities are estimated in the same time. In addition, a multi resolution map representation is used, to avoid getting stuck in local minima.

## 2.3    Crsm SLAM

Crsm SLAM stands for Critical Rays Scan Match SLAM. For the aiming of noise accumulation reduction, it uses scan-to-map matching instead of the usual scan-to-scan matching. The scan matching program is performed via a Random Restart Hill Climbing algorithm (RRHC) which is a local search optimization procedure. Only the critical rays take part in the algorithm as critical are denoted the rays which contain more spatial information than the others. The algorithm makes absolutely no use of odometry or robot kinematics, in order to compute the robot's pose. The map update intensity is depending on the current environmental structure. The main idea is to reduce complexity and time needed for matching by preprocessing the scan and selecting rays. In order to minimize the accumulated errors the scan matching is performed between the current scan and the global robot map. Crsm SLAM also uses an occupancy grid map in order to depict the environment. Crsm SLAM does not have a close loop behaviour, but it gives very good results in featured spaces.

# 3 Our Approach to Merge Two Sensors into One Laser Scanner

A good field of view sensor is important in mobile robots, because the wider the field of view, the more features from the environment robot catch. With more features used for scan matching, the robot localization will be more accurate. Simultaneously, the map will be more precise. A mobile robot with poor field of view must constantly maneuver to fill up the missing map. When the robot moving to a corner, rotated 90° for example, entering a new scene, features that before does not exist in this new scene and the scan matching does not work, the robot will occur a localization error because of the odometry deviation in rotate degrees.

During this research, We use Turtlebot, Kinect and Hokuyo UST-10LX Laser Range Finder to perform the three SLAM with four methods as mentioned in the preceding article. The 3D vision of the Kinect can be converted into a 2D laserscan type and compressed 3D obstacle onto a 2D plane with the ROS package depthimage to laserscan as methods shown in [6]. To use this package, we can detect small obstacles below the 2D scan plane through Kinect. The narrow field of view and the close range are limitations of the Kinect. The depth scan range on the Kinect has a field of view (FOV) of 57° while the Laser scanner has a field of view of 270° as Fig. 1 shows.

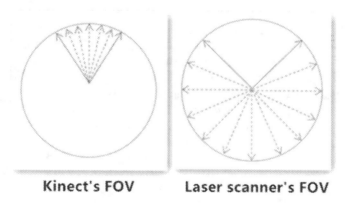

**Kinect's FOV          Laser scanner's FOV**

**Fig. 1.** Kinect's FOV and Laser scanner's FOV.

The maximum range of the Kinect is about 8 m but there will be more error data when we use the maximum range as the input scan range. The UST-10LX has a maximum detection range of 30 m. To know more comparisons between the two sensors consult [14]. The specifications of the two sensors are shown in Fig. 2. To increase the field of view of sensor used for SLAM and to increase more features used for localization, We suggested that it is possible to use two or more sensors for performing SLAM.

| | UST-10LX | Kinect |
|---|---|---|
| Light Source | Laser semiconductor | Infrared |
| Detection Range | 0.06m to 10m (white Kent sheet) 0.06m to 4m (diffuse reflectance 10%) Max. detection distance : 30m | 0.35m to 6m |
| Field of View | Horizontal 270 deg Vertical 0 deg | Horizontal 57 deg Vertical 43 deg |
| No. of Points | 1080 | 640x480=307,200 |
| Scan Time | 25ms | 33ms |
| Angular Resolution | 0.25 deg | 0.098 deg |
| Interface | Ethernet 100BASE-TX | USB |
| Dimensions (W×D×H) | 50×50×70mm (sensor only) | 307x62x51mm |

**Fig. 2.** The specifications of UST-10LX and Kinect

### 3.1  Two Kinects

Most SLAM algorithm can only utilize one laser scan data as input. We use two Kinects to compare with a single one. One Kinect mounted in front of the robot and the other one mounted on the same horizontal plane rotating 180° facing behind, like Fig. 3 shows. Therefore the data from the two Kinects need to be merged into a single scan. A single Kinect has a angular resolution of 0.098° in 57° with 640 points. The merged scan has a angular resolution of 0.196° (twice of the single one) in almost 114° with 640 points. The scans which fall in the blind spot area are represented by fake laser scans with high value (i.e. 20 m) and then be abandoned by the SLAM algorithms.

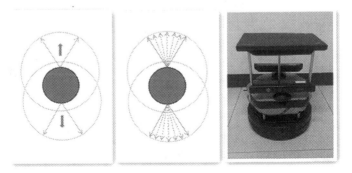

**Fig. 3.** The position of the two Kinects and the merged scan; The gray circle is the robot.

### 3.2    A Kinect and a Laser Scanner

The Kinect with horizontal FOV of 57° was mounted to face forward while the Laser scanner with FOV of 270° faced backwards. The Laser scanner has a angular resolution of 0.25° in 270°, if we took the merged angular resolution smaller than the angular resolution of Laser scanner, there would be some ineffectiveness reasons for using the laser scan data. So in case of getting more points and leave the laser scan data more entirely, we take up the merged scan with a angular resolution of 0.25° the same with laser scan. We extracted the Kinect scan data and do some process to make the data useful for SLAM. Figure 4 shows the mounting position of the two sensors for this method.

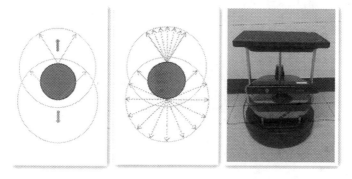

**Fig. 4.** The position of the Kinect and the Laser scanner.

With a angular resolution of 0.098°, our purpose is to take the Kinect scan into the angular resolution of 0.25°. The nearest angle approximation which both Kinect and Laser scanner get close to is 0.50° (0.25 × 2 = 0.50, 0.098 × 5 = 0.49), We set 228 points to become the merged scan points with each step size of 0.25°. To due with the 228 points, we set each point as a center, around the center (0.50° range) we take 4–5 nearest Kinect scan points to calculate average and assign it to the point value. Then the merged scan giving a useful FOV of almost 327° (We assume the robot is a point) with 1308 points and a angular resolution of 0.25°.

## 4    Experiments

We set the Kinect detection range to 0.35 m to 5 m and the Hokuyo UST-10LX detection range to 0.35 m to 10 m in all the real world environment experiments. We performed each SLAM algorithm with default parameter values and moved the robot in real-time. For example, the number of particle for the Gmapping algorithm was 30, the map update interval is 5.

### 4.1    Corridor with Less Feature

We made the experiments in a corridor with less feature. In every test we took 3 min, using the same robot's starting pose, speed and the same path along with the wall, to ensure that all the twelve experiments were carried out under the same exact conditions. Figure 5 shows the drawing of the environment being tested. The purpose select a featureless space to perform SLAM is to inspect how FOV of sensors effect the map precision. Gmapping employ the odometry data in computing the robot's pose except the scan matching program making a contrast with Hector SLAM and Crsm SLAM. Figure 6 shows the comparison of the maps obtained using Gmapping, Hector SLAM and Crsm SLAM with different sensor methods. For the reason of gray background, we did some process with the maps obtained from Crsm SLAM to make free grids as Gmapping and Hector SLAM.

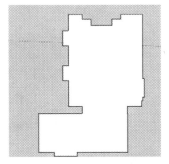

**Fig. 5.** The actual map of featureless corridor being test.

The maps obtained using both single Kinect and two Kinects for Gmapping, Hector SLAM and Crsm SLAM are seen to deviate precision from the actual map dimension. For the single Kinect method, Gmapping algorithm performed better than the other two because of the usage of the odometry data in robot localization, but there was a ghost map for the reason of localization take a greater confidence in scan matching than odometry. Hector SLAM couldn't build a map because of the FOV of Kinect restriction lead to scan matching lost as well as Crsm SLAM, but Crsm SLAM performed a better result than Hector SLAM. For the two Kinects method, getting benefit from the increase of FOV and detection distance, all the SLAM operated better than the single one especially Hector SLAM. Both the single Laser scanner method and Laser combine with Kinect method created relatively accurate maps compare with the first two methods. The method proposed to merge laser scan data and Kinect scan data is able to provide available input for SLAM techniques. We can use the method to produce a comparable map accuracy with respect to the single Laser scanner method. Comparing the four kinds of methods we know that the map accuracy can be influenced by the FOV, the max detection distance, the noise and the measurement accuracy of sensors.

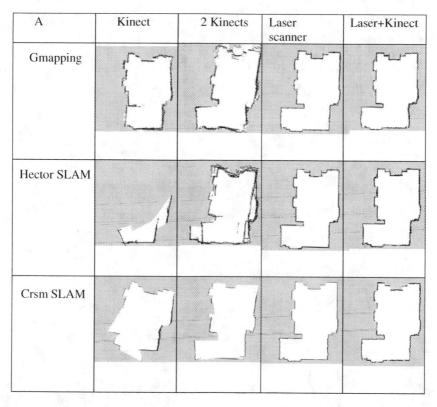

| A | Kinect | 2 Kinects | Laser scanner | Laser+Kinect |
|---|--------|-----------|---------------|--------------|
| Gmapping | | | | |
| Hector SLAM | | | | |
| Crsm SLAM | | | | |

**Fig. 6.** Comparison of maps obtained using different SLAM techniques and scan types in corridor with less feature present.

## 4.2 Corridor with Known Features

We made the experiments in the same place added five boxes with different sizes, placed in five location. All the configurations and conditions are same with the featureless one. The purpose to layout like that is to analyze the robot localization accuracy for using scan matching program with more features. Two boxes in the height were below the sensor horizontal plane, thus we set the scan_height value to 100 (pixel) in depthimage_to_laserscan package. Figure 7 shows the drawing of the environment being tested.

With known features, the maps obtained using both single Kinect and two Kinects for Gmapping, Hector SLAM and Crsm SLAM are better than the featureless ones. Figure 8 shows the Hector SLAM was still could not build a map using a single Kinect, but Crsm SLAM performed better than the featureless one. A single Kinect method and two Kinects method could mark small obstacles but the Laser scanner couldn't. In the aspect of marking obstacles, Hector SLAM obtained a better result than the other two SLAM that it marked all the obstacles in the FOV of sensor. Crsm SLAM did better in dealing with the details or small objects. For Laser combine with Kinect method, some of the obstacles went missing from the final map because of the small boxes were not in the horizontal plane of the Laser scanner. Kinect marked small boxes as obstacles but the Laser scanner couldn't detect them and when the laser scanning these areas, the value of grids would be updated to zero then the map would be instead of free space. Overall, in these experiments, Hector SLAM performed better especially in the Laser combine with Kinect method.

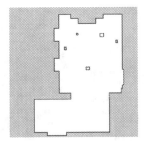

**Fig. 7.** The actual map with known features being test.

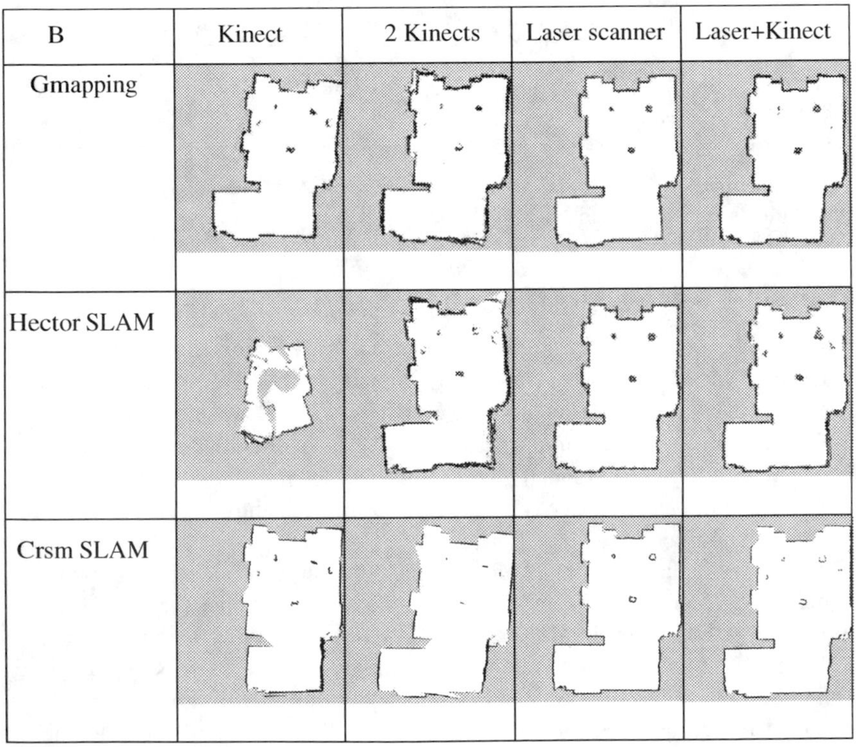

| B | Kinect | 2 Kinects | Laser scanner | Laser+Kinect |
|---|---|---|---|---|
| Gmapping | | | | |
| Hector SLAM | | | | |
| Crsm SLAM | | | | |

three SLAM.

**Fig. 8.** The comparison of the maps obtained using four methods for performing the three SLAM.

## 4.3    Long Corridor with Known Features

We selected the experiment environment where various objects are present. Figure 9 shows the drawing of the corridor being tested. All the conditions are the same with featureless one expect the running time set to 5 min.

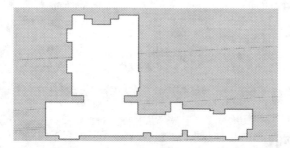

**Fig. 9.** The actual map of the long corridor with various features being test

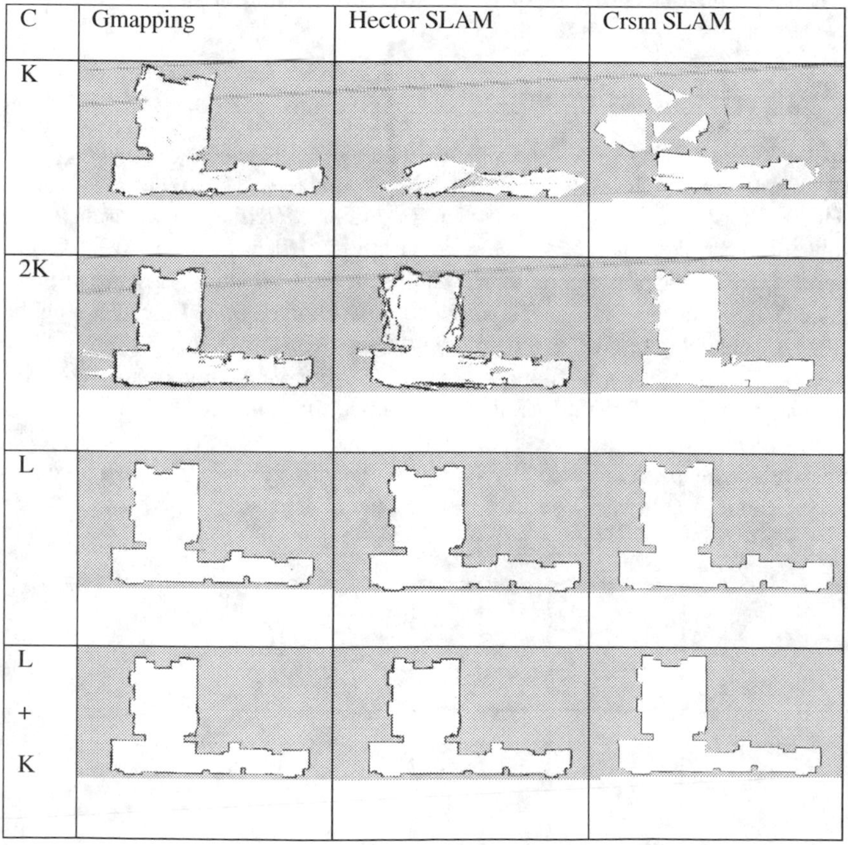

| C | Gmapping | Hector SLAM | Crsm SLAM |
|---|---|---|---|
| K | | | |
| 2K | | | |
| L | | | |
| L + K | | | |

**Fig. 10.** The comparison of the maps obtained using four methods for performing the three SLAM in long corridor.

In this large scene, the length and the width are both beyond the four methods sensor detection range. The robot was controlled remotely to move around the corridor for covering as many areas as possible. The maps obtained using single Kinect for Gmapping, Hector SLAM and Crsm SLAM were ever so disappointing. With a single Kinect to build map or with a small FOV of sensor to build map, the scan matching program can not perform better even though there are various features. Once the robot lost itself, it is hard to retrieve the pose and the position in the map. Hector SLAM and Crsm SLAM rely on largely in scan matching with successive measurements. Hector SLAM and Crsm SLAM are inapplicable with a small FOV of sensor, especially in large scale environments. The capability of relocation for Hector SLAM is better than the Crsm SLAM.

The maps based on single Laser scanner method and combined method are seen to be more accurate than the map based on the first two methods Fig. 8. The Laser combine with Kinect method seen to indicate relatively more features than the single laser method through the thick wall and some features were not described in the map. Figure 10 shows the comparison of the maps obtained using four methods for performing the three SLAMWe used a Local Gird Map Recursion Matching algorithm to evaluate the map accuracy to analyze the three SLAM.

# 5    Result and Conclusion

To evaluate the quality of the maps obtained, an analysis by calculating the map accuracy between the generated maps and the ground actual map was conducted. We advance a algorithm called Local Gird Map Recursion Matching. A performance metric reckon from the grid map covariance descriptor [15] was used. We extract the covariance descriptor of each grid map take part in the computing, then we use the dtw distance [16] calculated from each covariance descriptor with the k-nearest neighbor to get the map matching degree as the accuracy. Our algorithm is different from [17], we do not use a set of Matlab functions in the Image Processing Toolbox to align with the respective ground actual map. We clip the obtained maps in $480 \times 480$ or $960 \times 480$ resolutions and then divide the maps into N (for example N = 9) pieces of local occupancy grid maps in fixed pixels. With each local occupancy grid map, we make a down subdivide in N pieces continuously as Fig. 11 shows.

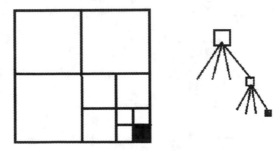

**Fig. 11.**  The local grid map split graphic.

Firstly, we set the weight $\frac{1}{N}$ for the using of N. For the second time to subdivide the local grid map in N pieces, the weight is $\frac{1}{N^2}$, then the third time $\frac{1}{N^3}$...

Secondly, We use knn to compute the whole map matching degree. The complete algorithm executive program follow the steps like this:

The first level local grid maps matching value is $a$,

the mismatching total is $N - a$.

The map matching degree is $acc_1$,

$$acc_1 = \frac{1}{N} \bullet a, \tag{1}$$

The second level local grid maps matching values are

$$b_1, b_2, \ldots, b_{N-a},$$

each mismatching values are

$$N - b_1, N - b_2, \ldots, N - b_{N-a};$$

The map matching degree is $acc_2$,

$$acc_2 = \frac{1}{N^2} \bullet \sum_{n=1}^{N-a} b_n. \tag{2}$$

The third level local grid maps matching values are

$$c_{11}, c_{12}, \ldots, c_{1N-b_1}, c_{21}, c_{22}, \ldots, c_{2N-b_2} \ldots;$$

The map matching degree is $acc_3$,

$$acc_3 = \frac{1}{N^3} \bullet \left( \sum_{n=1}^{N-b_1} c_{1n} + \sum_{n=1}^{N-b_2} c_{2n} + \ldots + \sum_{n=1}^{N-b_{N-a}} c_{N-an} \right). \tag{3}$$

The whole map matching degree is $acc$,

$$acc = acc_1 + acc_2 + acc_3 + \ldots. \tag{4}$$

We selected the single Laser scanner method and the Laser combine with Kinect method in the three groups of experiments to be applied on the assessment algorithm. The results are presented in the Tables 1, 2 and 3.

In general, the Gmapping, Hector SLAM and Crsm SLAM have been able to produce accurate results in the experiments using the single Laser scanner method and the Laser combine with Kinect method. When using the single Kinect method and the two Kinects method the results were not well. This suggests that a wide and comprehensive FOV of the sensor are the important factors to ensure reliable SLAM

**Table 1.** The map accuracy in corridor with less feature.

| A | Gmapping | Hector SLAM | Crsm SLAM |
|---|---|---|---|
| Laser scanner | 0.8932 | 0.9006 | 0.8610 |
| Laser + Kinect | 0.9069 | 0.9072 | 0.8644 |

**Table 2.** The map accuracy in corridor with known features.

| B | Gmapping | Hector SLAM | Crsm SLAM |
|---|---|---|---|
| Laser scanner | 0.8912 | 0.8948 | 0.8542 |
| Laser + Kinect | 0.9125 | 0.9203 | 0.8505 |

**Table 3.** The map accuracy in long corridor with various features.

| C | Gmapping | Hector SLAM | Crsm SLAM |
|---|---|---|---|
| Laser scanner | 0.9072 | 0.9084 | 0.8612 |
| Laser + Kinect | 0.9205 | 0.9240 | 0.8695 |

operation. If we require to build a map with small FOV of sensors, it would be nice to use some other sensors as appurtenance. Kinect has the ability of marking small obstacles but the Laser scanner hasn't. When using the Laser combine with Kinect method, Gmapping executed the marking and cleaning behaviors due to the different scan data from Kinect and Laser scanner lead to the small obstacles disappeared.

While the three SLAM algorithms have both advantages and disadvantages. Gmapping is able to close the loop since it is based on particle filter. Hector SLAM and Crsm SLAM with no odometry information and only relies on scan registration to estimate the robot pose also made good results in these experiments especially in the last two methods. The more obstacles or features in the environment the more accuracy in robot localization. Crsm SLAM with only the critical rays take part in building maps but not the entire scan data make it a lack of coverage rate relative to Gmapping and Hector SLAM for running the same duration. Crsm SLAM itself performed a better result in small scene with multiplicate features than in large scale with less feature. The merged scan methods both use two Kinects and Laser combine with Kinect were feasible, but the position of sensors should be calibrated precisely. In large scale scene with less feature, the most effective way to build a accurate map is to use a wide FOV of sensor.

# References

1. Thrun, S., Burgard, W., Fox, D.: Probabilistic Robotics. MIT press, Cambridge (2005)
2. Quigley, M., et al.: ROS: an open-source robot operating system. In: IEEE International Conference on Robotics and Automation (ICRA), Workshop on Open Source Software (2009)

3. Leonard, J.J., Durrant-Whyte, H.F.: Directed Sonar Sensing for Mobile Robot Navigation, vol. 175. Springer, New York (1990)
4. Bruce, J., Veloso, M.M.: Real-time randomized path planning for robot navigation. In: Kaminka, G.A., Lima, P.U., Rojas, R. (eds.) RoboCup 2002. LNCS, vol. 2752, pp. 288–295. Springer, Heidelberg (2003). doi:10.1007/978-3-540-45135-8_23
5. Chávez, A., Karstoft, H.: Improvement of KinectTM sensor capabilities by fusion with laser sensing data using octree. Sensors 12(4), 3868–3878 (2012)
6. Kamarudin, K., Mamduh, S.M., Shakaff, A.Y.M., Saad, S.M., Zakaria, A., Abdullah, A.H., et al.: Method to convert kinect's 3D depth data to a 2D map for indoor SLAM. In: 9th IEEE Colloquium on Signal Processing and its Applications (CSPA 2013), Kuala Lumpur (2013)
7. Grisetti, G., Stachniss, C., Burgard, W.: Improved techniques for grid mapping with Rao-Blackwellized particle filters. Trans. Rob. 23(1), 34–46 (2007)
8. Kohlbrecher, S., Meyer, J., Von Stryk, O., Klingauf, U.: A Flexible and Scalable SLAM System with Full 3D Motion Estimation. In: The International Symposium on Safety, Security and Rescue Robotics (SSRR), November (2011)
9. Tsardoulias, E., Petrou, L.: Critical rays scan match SLAM. J. Intell. Rob. Syst. 72(3), 441–462 (2013)
10. Huang, S., Dissanayake, G.: Convergence and consistency analysis for extended Kalman filter based SLAM. IEEE Trans. Rob. 2(5), 1036–1049 (2007)
11. Wan, E.A., Merwe, R.V.D.: The unscented Kalman filter for nonlinear estimation. In: Adaptive Systems for Signal Processing, Communications, and Control Symposium, pp. 153–158. IEEE (2000)
12. Moravec, H.P., Elfes, A.: High resolution maps from angle sonar. In: ICRA 1985, pp. 116–121 (1985)
13. Srinivasan, K., Gu, J.: Multiple sensor fusion in mobile robot localization. In: Canadian Conference on Electrical & Computer Engineering, pp. 1207–1210 IEEE (2007)
14. Zug, S., Penzlin, F., Dietrich, A., et al.: Are laser scanners replaceable by Kinect sensors in robotic applications? In: IEEE International Symposium on Robotic and Sensors Environments, pp. 144–149. IEEE (2012)
15. Tuzel, O., Porikli, F., Meer, P.: Region covariance: a fast descriptor for detection and classification. In: Leonardis, A., Bischof, H., Pinz, A. (eds.) ECCV 2006. LNCS, vol. 3952, pp. 589–600. Springer, Heidelberg (2006). doi:10.1007/11744047_45
16. Salvador, S., Chan, P.: Toward accurate dynamic time warping in linear time and space. Intell. Data Anal. 11(5), 561–580 (2007)
17. Santos, J.M., Portugal, D., Rocha, R.P.: An evaluation of 2D SLAM techniques available in Robot Operating System. In: IEEE International Symposium on Safety, Security, and Rescue Robotics, pp. 1–6 (2013)

# An Intraoperative Localization Method of Femoral Tunnel Entry Point for ACL Reconstruction

Long Lei[1], Yang Liu[2], Yu Sun[1], Kailin Ma[3], Ji Chen[2(✉)],
Ying Hu[4(✉)], and Jianwei Zhang[5]

[1] Harbin Institute of Technology Shenzhen Graduate School,
Shenzhen Institutes of Advanced Technology,
Chinese Academy of Sciences, Shenzhen, China
{long.lei,yu.sun}@siat.ac.cn
[2] Shenzhen People's Hospital, Shenzhen, China
{sumsly,chenji710727}@163.com
[3] Xi'an Jiaotong University, Xi'an, China
kl.ma@siat.ac.cn
[4] Guangdong Provincial Key Laboratory of Robotics and Intelligent System,
Shenzhen Institutes of Advanced Technology,
Chinese Academy of Sciences, Shenzhen, China
ying.hu@siat.ac.cn
[5] University of Hamburg, Hamburg, Germany
zhang@infomatik.uni-hamburg.de

**Abstract.** The Anterior Cruciate Ligament (ACL) is one of the four main ligaments of the knee and crucial to stabilizing the knee. In the surgery of arthroscopic ACL reconstruction after ruptures, the precise intraoperative localization of the entry point of the femoral tunnel is one of the key factors affecting the function of knee. In this paper, a new method is proposed to rapidly achieve the localization of the entry point. A special probe should be registered firstly so that its tip position is measured in real time. Then the point cloud of probe tip's trajectories is obtained when outlining the cartilage posterior edge of lateral condyle. In order to simplify the way to confirm if the entry point of the femoral tunnel is in the preoperative planning position, a projection transformation is applied finally to reduce the dimensions. Besides, the experimental results show that the method can meet the demands of the surgery for ACL reconstruction.

**Keywords:** ACL reconstruction · Probe registration · Precise localization · Projection transformation · Femoral tunnel

## 1 Introduction

The Anterior Cruciate Ligament (ACL, Fig. 1) is one of a pair of cruciate ligaments, which attaches in front of the intercondyloid eminence of the tibia and the distal femur. It provides the major restraining force to anterior translation and medial rotation of the

© Springer Nature Singapore Pte Ltd. 2017
F. Sun et al. (Eds.): ICCSIP 2016, CCIS 710, pp. 290–302, 2017.
DOI: 10.1007/978-981-10-5230-9_30

tibia [1]. ACL reconstruction is one of the most common surgeries for stabilizing the knee with torn ligament [2], and the precise intraoperative localization of the entry point of the ACL footprint is crucial to creating the femoral tunnel [3]. ACL tearing without reconstruction in time can result in progressive wearing away of the cartilage and meniscus and even osteoarthritis [4]. Therefore, the diagnosis and treatment for ACL rupture are very important.

The surgery of ACL reconstruction under the arthroscope is the most common operation for ACL rupture [5, 6]. In this process, the precise localization of entry point of the femoral tunnel is one of the key factors affecting the success of operation [7, 8]. Generally, doctors determine the entry point of the femoral tunnel upon personal experience. However, there are a lot of uncertainties increasing the risk of surgery for the subjective judgments [9]. Navigation technology also has an application in ACL reconstruction surgery [10, 11], while the limb positioning requires the repeated X-ray, which increases the operation time and the risk of infection [12]. Therefore, a precise and convenient method is needed to locate the entry point of the femoral tunnel during the ACL reconstruction.

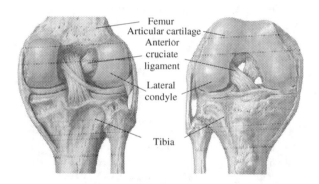

**Fig. 1.** Schematic diagram of knee joint

In order to realize the entry point localization for the femoral tunnel, a simple and precise method is proposed for operating during the surgery. The information about the entry point and posterior edge of lateral condyle can be obtained in medical image planning. According to the position relations, a special probe is used to outline the contour of the posterior edge and observe the tip's coordinates in tracking system. The main steps are described as follows: firstly, the position of the probe tip in the probe tool frame is obtained by pivoting the probe, and further we measure the tip position in the base coordinate system in real time, which is called tool registration; secondly, a series of points are collected when the probe tip walks along the posterior edge of the cartilage; finally, the available sampling points are projected onto an appropriate plane by genetic algorithm (GA). According to the distribution of these points and the image information, doctors can make reasonable judgment if the entry point of the femoral tunnel is in the preoperative planning position.

The rest of the paper is organized as follows: the probe registration algorithm is described in Sect. 2; the projection plane acquired by GA is optimized in Sect. 3; the experiment and analysis are conducted in Sect. 4; and we concluded in Sect. 5.

## 2 The Probe Registration Algorithm

A tracking system, polaris vicra (NDI, Canada), is used to obtain the point cloud coordinate using binocular infrared vision technology. Before tracking the position of probe tip to outline the contour of cartilage and find the entry point of the femur tunnel, the probe should be registered to transform the coordinates from the passive infrared markers to the tip. The probe tip registration directly affects the sampling accuracy of the trajectories; therefore, it is crucial to find an effective method to register the probe tip.

The tracking system records the probe's position and attitude in 10 Hz sampling frequency while the probe is rotated around its tip. The origin of the tool frame of the probe is in the center of a sphere, and the position of the tip in the base coordinate system is determined by solving the corresponding equations with the least squares algorithm [13, 14]. After the tool registration, the probe tip is being tracked by tracking system in real time.

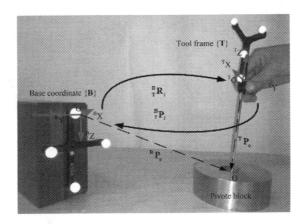

**Fig. 2.** The probe registration process

The coordinate systems in probe registration are shown in Fig. 2. The $_T^B\mathbf{R}_i$ and $_T^B\mathbf{P}_i$ are respectively the probe's attitude matrix and position vector in base coordinate system $\{\mathbf{B}\}$. The $^T\mathbf{P}_o$ and $^B\mathbf{P}_o$ are the probe tip's position vectors respectively in tool frame $\{\mathbf{T}\}$ and $\{\mathbf{B}\}$.

### 2.1  Method of Calculating $^B\mathbf{P}_o$

A set $\left\{_T^B\mathbf{P}_i | i = 1, 2, \ldots, n\right\}$ is obtained by pivoting the probe, with $_T^B\mathbf{P}_i = \left(^b x_i, ^b y_i, ^b z_i\right)$. The iteration variables should be determined firstly. The appropriate selection of the iteration variables can improve the convergence of the iteration and avoid falling into a local optimum. $^{B}\mathbf{P}_o$ is with elements $(^{b}x_o^i, ^{b}y_o^i, ^{b}z_o^i)$ for the $i$th iteration and initialized by the average value of the $_T^{B}\mathbf{P}_i$ vectors, as shown in Formula (1).

$$\begin{bmatrix} ^{b}x_o^0 \\ ^{b}y_o^0 \\ ^{b}z_o^0 \end{bmatrix} = \frac{1}{n} \cdot \sum_{i=1}^{n} \begin{bmatrix} ^{b}x_i \\ ^{b}y_i \\ ^{b}z_i \end{bmatrix} \tag{1}$$

where $^{b}x_o^0$, $^{b}y_o^0$ and $^{b}z_o^0$ are the initial values for iteration.

Then, the iteration formula (2) and (3) are obtained by using the least squares method, and $^{b}y_o$ and $^{b}z_o$ have the same expression. The iteration can be stopped after the difference less than $\delta$ set as 0.05 mm.

$$^{b}x_o^{k+1} = ^{b}x_o^0 + \frac{1}{n^2} \sum_{i=1}^{n} d_{oi} \cdot \sum_{i=1}^{n} \frac{^{b}x_o^k - ^{b}x_i}{d_{oi}} \tag{2}$$

$$d_{oi} = \sqrt{\left(^{b}x_o^k - ^{b}x_i\right)^2 + \left(^{b}y_o^k - ^{b}y_i\right)^2 + \left(^{b}z_o^k - ^{b}z_i\right)^2} \tag{3}$$

## 2.2 Method of Calculating $^{T}\mathbf{P}_o$

Another set $\{_T^{B}\mathbf{R}_i | i = 1, 2, \ldots, n\}$ is also obtained by pivoting the probe. $^{T}\mathbf{P}_o$ is calculated by several times with elements $(^{t}x_o, ^{t}y_o, ^{t}z_o)$ obtained according to formula (4).

$$\begin{bmatrix} ^{t}x_o \\ ^{t}y_o \\ ^{t}z_o \end{bmatrix} = \frac{1}{n} \cdot \sum_{i=1}^{n} {_T^{B}}\mathbf{R}_i^{-1} \begin{bmatrix} ^{b}x_o - ^{b}x_i \\ ^{b}y_o - ^{b}y_i \\ ^{b}z_o - ^{b}z_i \end{bmatrix} \tag{4}$$

The suspected bad data can be automatically filtered out according to the formula (5) with the threshold c, then the $^{T}\mathbf{P}_o$ is recalculated by using the remaining data. The process is repeated until no data can be removed.

$$[-c]_{3\times1} < {_T^{B}}\mathbf{R}_i^{-1} \begin{bmatrix} ^{b}x_o - ^{b}x_i \\ ^{b}y_o - ^{b}y_i \\ ^{b}z_o - ^{b}z_i \end{bmatrix} - \begin{bmatrix} ^{t}x_o \\ ^{t}y_o \\ ^{t}z_o \end{bmatrix} < [c]_{3\times1} \tag{5}$$

The real-time position of the tip is obtained according to the formula (6).

$$^{B}\mathbf{P} = {_T^{B}}\mathbf{P}_r + {_T^{B}}\mathbf{R}_r \cdot {^{T}}\mathbf{P}_o \tag{6}$$

where $^{B}\mathbf{P}$ is the probe tip's position in base coordinate $\{B\}$, and r means the tracking matrix and vector are in real time.

## 3 Display of Posterior Edge in Special Plain

### 3.1 Special Plane Optimization

A special plane is optimized by the GA method, and it is necessary to determine the appropriate decision variables and the fitness function before optimizing [15–17].

The plane equation can be written as Eq. (7).

The points, $(x_i, y_i, z_i)$, are the position coordinates of tip collected by the tracking system, and they are treated as the variables reducing the searching range of GA for speeding up the convergence and shortening the searching time.

$$\begin{vmatrix} x & y & z & 1 \\ x_1 & y_1 & z_1 & 1 \\ x_2 & y_2 & z_2 & 1 \\ x_3 & y_3 & z_3 & 1 \end{vmatrix} = 0 \tag{7}$$

The objective special plane should contain the sampled points as much as possible, while the posterior edge has both convex and concave and the measuring error of the tracking system also exists, which affects the expression of posterior edge. For filtering the redundant points, the distance between an arbitrary point and the special plane is treated as the filter condition to determine if the point was located on the plane. The threshold $d_0$ is the measuring error of tracking system, as shown in formula (8).

$$d_i = \frac{|Ax_i + By_i + Cz_i + D|}{\sqrt{A^2 + B^2 + C^2}} \le d_0 \tag{8}$$

The GA is always searching the minimum of the fitness function; therefore, the number of the points which not meet the formula (8) are treated as the individual fitness values.

### 3.2 Points Projection Transformation

The point with the distance less than $d_0$ is defined as the available point. The available points filtered by formula (8) are projected onto the special plane, while the rest of points are eliminated. The relation between a point $(x_{ap}, y_{ap}, z_{ap})$ and its projection point $(x_{pp}, y_{pp}, z_{pp})$ on the special plane can be expressed as formula (9) which also used to solve the position of projection point in real time.

$$\begin{bmatrix} 1 & 0 & -A \\ 0 & 1 & -B \\ -A & -B & -C^2 \end{bmatrix} \begin{bmatrix} x_{pp} \\ y_{pp} \\ m \end{bmatrix} = \begin{bmatrix} x_{ap} \\ y_{ap} \\ z_{ap}C + D \end{bmatrix} \tag{9}$$

where $m$ is an interim parameter to calculate the $z_{pp}$.

Assume O, P, Q are three non-collinear points on the special plane, and they can be displayed following the steps below (Fig. 3).

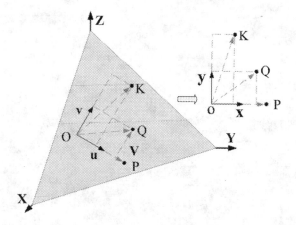

**Fig. 3.** The diagram of dimension reduction

$$u = \frac{OP}{|OP|} \tag{10}$$

The unit vector **u** is calculated by formula (10), which is set as the **x** axis of the special plane.

$$V = OQ - (OQ \cdot u) \cdot u \tag{11}$$

$$v = \frac{V}{|V|} \tag{12}$$

The vector **v** is calculated by formula (11) and formula (12), which is set as the **y** axis of the special plane. The coordinate for an arbitrary point can be retreated by the orthogonal vectors **u** and **v**.

## 4  The Experiments and Analysis

An experiment was conducted to verify the practicality and reliability of the proposed method, and the results were analyzed. The experiment is divided into two parts: the first part is for the probe registration, and the second part is about the display of the posterior edge on the special plane.

### 4.1  Probe Registration Analysis

Before registering the probe, a good pivot block is made according to the size of the tip and the way of pivoting, which can reduce the registration error.

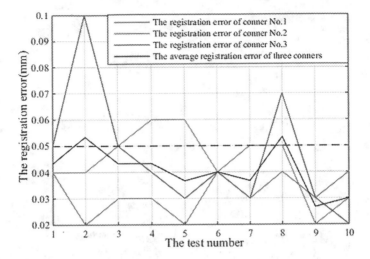

**Fig. 4.** The operation error of three conners

There are three untrained conners did the registration for ten times respectively, and each test last 10 s. The error of their operations is calculated by formula (13) and (14) and shown in Fig. 4 which also including the average error.

$$\varepsilon = \frac{1}{n} \cdot \sum_{i=1}^{n} \left| \left\| {}_{\mathbf{T}}^{\mathbf{B}}\mathbf{P}_i - {}^{\mathbf{B}}\mathbf{P}_o \right\| - \varepsilon_0 \right| \tag{13}$$

$$\varepsilon_0 = \frac{1}{n} \cdot \sum_{i=1}^{n} \left\| {}_{\mathbf{T}}^{\mathbf{B}}\mathbf{P}_i - {}^{\mathbf{B}}\mathbf{P}_o \right\| \tag{14}$$

As shown in Fig. 4, there are obvious differences among these conners, and the performances in the different tests are not identical for each conner. Although there are fluctuations in the operation error, all the stabilities can meet the surgical demands. Otherwise, the operation error decreases with the increasing times of the test as a whole, which indicates the registration results are related to the proficiency. Thus, some training is needed for doctors to obtain a better accuracy in the clinical application. The average operation error is basically within 0.05 mm, which satisfies the actual requirement.

In addition, the real-time display of the operation error provides a basic reference for the doctor, and the registration will be executed again if the operation error is not accepted.

## 4.2  Projection Transformation Optimization

In this experiment, the model of femur is used instead of the real one. The point cloud is sampled by the registered probe, shown in Fig. 5, with 10 Hz frequency. There are some precautions that need to be taken: the femur model and the base coordinate should be fixed during the experiment; the probe tip should run across the posterior edge smoothly; and the direction of the probe markers should face the tracking system while outlining the contour. The process and analysis of the tracking points are described below.

**The Special Plane Optimization by GA.** The Matlab (MathWorks, the USA) is used to realize the optimization with its GA Toolbox. The real number coding is adopted for genetic manipulation, that is, the float gene value of each individual is within a certain range and the individual length is equal to the number of decision variables. The real coding method, without the mapping errors for discretization of continuous function, can improve the efficiency of GA and satisfies the demands of the application. With the GA method, the coefficients of the special plane can be obtained.

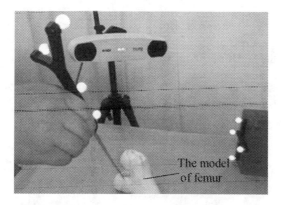

**Fig. 5.** The sampling process of the posterior edge

The following operators are chosen due to the repeated tests to obtain the best results. The initial population with a uniform distribution is generated with the uniform function. The operator named Rank is chosen to transform the fitness scaling. The function named Stochastic Uniform is set as the selecting operator and the Constraint Dependent is set as the mutation operator.

The Arithmetic Crossover (AC) function is chosen as the cross operator. The AC is applied to the two individuals $X_A^h$ and $X_B^h$, and then, new individuals are obtained according to formulas (15), where the scale parameter $\alpha$ is determined by the evolution generations [18].

$$\begin{cases} X_A^{h+1} = \alpha X_B^h + (1 - \alpha)X_A^h \\ X_B^{h+1} = \alpha X_A^h + (1 - \alpha)X_B^h \end{cases} \tag{15}$$

The tracking system has 0.25 mm inherent error, and the probe registration is within 0.05 mm, and the error resulting related to the diameter of the probe tip is 0.2 mm. Therefore, the threshold in formula (8) is set to 0.5 mm.

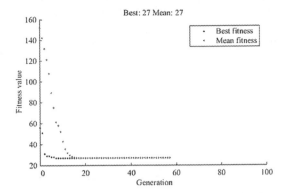

**Fig. 6.** The special plane optimization process

Based on the above analysis, the optimization process is shown in Fig. 6, which convergence of the process tends to a certain value within 20 generations of evolution.

For verifying the stability of the optimization algorithm, five tests are carried on, and the results are shown in Table 1. Figure 7 shows the 5 special planes intuitively. Based on Table 1 and Fig. 7, the algorithm is stable enough due to the biases between different results are small.

**Table 1.** The planes of optimization tests

| Test no. | Best fitness | Mean fitness | Special plane parameters | | | |
|---|---|---|---|---|---|---|
| | | | A | B | C | D |
| 1 | 27 | 27 | −1.0 | 0.67 | 14.82 | 1255.62 |
| 2 | 27 | 27 | −1.0 | 0.74 | 15.70 | 1329.86 |
| 3 | 27 | 27 | −1.0 | 0.69 | 14.05 | 1202.62 |
| 4 | 27 | 27.02 | −1.0 | 0.65 | 14.55 | 1231.68 |
| 5 | 27 | 27.02 | −1.0 | 0.71 | 15.52 | 1311.21 |

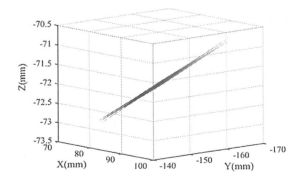

**Fig. 7.** The planes of optimization tests

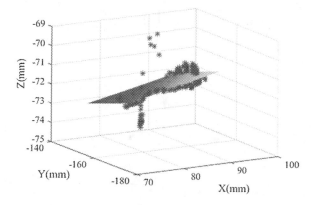

**Fig. 8.** The optimal plane and the point cloud

The sampled points and the special plane optimized by GA are shown in Fig. 8 which illustrates the optimization can effectively avoid the disturbance of singular points to optimize an appropriate special plane, which can reflect the posterior edge information as much as possible.

As shown in Fig. 8, the GA adopted in this paper not only has good convergence and stability, but also can optimize an appropriate plane to reflect the distribution characteristics of the posterior edge and the entry point.

**Final Result Expression with Dimension Reduction.** The available points are projected on the optimal plane while the singular points are eliminated after the optimization. The coordinates of the projection points are transformed from the special plane according to the formulas (10) and (12). The actual posterior edge and the entry point assumed to be sought are displayed correspondingly in Fig. 9.

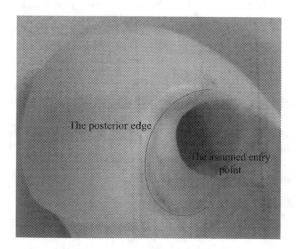

**Fig. 9.** The actual posterior edge and the entry point

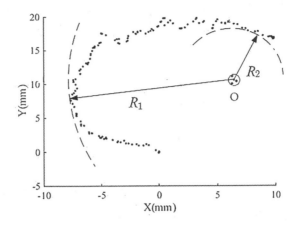

**Fig. 10.** The relation between posterior edge and entry point

After projection transformation, the position information between the posterior edge and the assumed entry point is shown in Fig. 10, where O is the center of the smallest circle including the points on behalf of the entry point, and we consider O as the real entry point during the application. The $R_1$ and $R_2$ represent respectively the closest distance and the farthest distance between posterior edge and entry point. The error is small for both $R_1$ and $R_2$ comparing with the actual distances, and doctors can make judgments if the entry point of the femoral tunnel was in the preoperative planning position according to the results.

## 5 Conclusion

In this study, we proposed a new method for the surgery of ACL reconstruction, and it can achieve the localization of the femoral tunnel entry point accurately and measurably. For this method, the operation is simple enough for the clinical application and there is no damage to the patients. The probe tip is registered before obtaining the coordinates information by the tracking system, while GA method is used to optimize the special plane to acquire the projection transformation and be displayed after reducing the dimensions. This process can simplify the way to confirm if the femoral tunnel entry point was in the position planned perioperatively. There are several experiments conducted to test the efficiency of the projection transformation for the algorithm validation and result analysis, which shows the method can meet the demands of the surgery for ACL reconstruction.

This method has a simple operation to measure the entry point related to the posterior edge in the ACL reconstruction, which can be treated as a quantitative reference in the clinical operation. However, there is room to improve the accuracy of the method. The future works will focus on how to improve the sampling conditions.

**Acknowledgments.** This research is supported by the National High-tech R&D Program of China (No. 2015AA043201), Key Fundamental Research Program of Shenzhen (No. JCYJ20140 417113430650), Guangdong Science and Technology Scheme (No. 2014A020215027 and 2014A020215030) and Research and Development Project of Guangdong Key Laboratory of Robotics and Intelligent Systems (No. ZDSYS20140509174140672).

# References

1. Swischuk, L.E., Jadhav, S.P.: Knee and Leg. Springer, New York (2014)
2. Maffulli, N., Osti, L.: ACL stability, function, and arthritis: what have we been missing. Orthopedics **36**(36), 90–92 (2013)
3. Stergiou, N., Ristanis, S., Moraiti, C.: Tibial rotation in anterior cruciate ligament (ACL)-deficient and ACL-reconstructed knees. Dept. Comput. Sci. **38**(8), 2638–2641 (1998)
4. Zabala, M.E., Favre, J., Andriacchi, T.P.: Relationship between knee mechanics and time since injury in ACL-deficient knees without signs of osteoarthritis. Am. J. Sports Med. **5**, 1189–1196 (2015)
5. Lubowitz, J.H.: Editorial commentary: ACL reconstruction: single-bundle versus double-bundle. Arthrosc. J. Arthrosc. Relat. Surg. **6**, 1197–1198 (2015)
6. Kostov, H., Stojmenski, S., Kostova, E.: Reliability assessment of arthroscopic findings versus MRI in ACL injuries of the knee. Acta Inform. Med. **2**, 111–114 (2014)
7. Kawakami, Y., Hiranaka, T., Matsumoto, T., et al.: The accuracy of bone tunnel position using fluoroscopic-based navigation system in anterior cruciate ligament reconstruction. Knee Surg. Sports Traumatol. Arthrosc. **20**(20), 1503–1510 (2012)
8. Fernandes, T.L., Fregni, F., Weaver, K., et al.: The influence of femoral tunnel position in single-bundle ACL reconstruction on functional outcomes and return to sports. Knee Surg. Sports Traumatol. Arthrosc. **1**, 97–103 (2014)
9. Domnick, C., Herbort, M., Raschke, M.J., et al.: Conventional over-the-top-aiming devices with short offset fail to hit the center of the human femoral ACL footprint in medial portal technique, whereas medial-portal-aiming devices with larger offset hit the center reliably. Arch. Orthop. Traumatol. Surg. **136**, 499–504 (2015). Fischer, H., Vogel, B., Pfleging, W., Besser, H.: Flexible distal tip made of nitinol (NiTi) for a steerable endoscopic camera system, Materials Science and Engineering, P273–275, 780–783 (1999)
10. Plaweski, S., Rossi, J., Merloz, P., et al.: Analysis of anatomic positioning in computer-assisted and conventional anterior cruciate ligament reconstruction. Orthop. Traumatol. Surg. Res. **97**(6), S80–S85 (2011)
11. Luites, J.W.H., Wymenga, A.B., Blankevoort, L., et al.: Accuracy of a computer-assisted planning and placement system for anatomical femoral tunnel positioning in anterior cruciate ligament reconstruction. Int. J. Med. Rob. Comput. Assist. Surg. **10**(4), 438–446 (2014)
12. Ortmaier, T., Weiss, H., Döbele, S., et al.: Experiments on robot-assisted navigated drilling and milling of bones for pedicle screw placement. Int. J. Med. Rob. **2**, 350–363 (2006)
13. Axelsson, O., Neytcheva, M.: The algebraic multilevel iteration methods – theory and applications (1994)
14. Blanchet, G., Charbit, M., Blanchet, G., et al.: The Least Squares Method. Digital Signal and Image Processing Using Matlab®, 2nd edn., pp. 349–395. Wiley, Hoboken (2014)
15. Hu, R., Yue, C., Xie, J.: Joint optimization of age replacement and spare ordering policy based on genetic algorithm. In: International Conference on Computational Intelligence & Security, pp. 156–161 (2008)

16. Dastani, M., Ardebili, M.: Optimal design and analysis simulation of an outer rotor hybrid excited generator for wind energy conversion systems. In: Proceedings of Electrical Engineering. IEEE (2015)
17. Su, C.H., Hou, T.H.: Using multi-population intelligent genetic algorithm to find the pareto-optimal parameters for a nano-particle milling process. Expert Syst. Appl. **34**(4), 2502–2510 (2008)
18. Ling, S.H., Lam, H.K., Leung, F.H.F., et al:. A novel GA-based neural network for short-term load forecasting. In: Proceedings of the 2002 International Joint Conference on Neural Networks, IJCNN 2002, pp. 2761–2766. IEEE (2002)

# A Flexible Capacitive Tactile Sensor for Manipulator

Jintao Zhang[1], Jing Cui[1], Yuanshen Lu[1], Xu Zhang[2(✉)],
and Xiaohui Hu[2]

[1] Beijing University of Technology, Beijing, China
[2] Institute of Semiconductors, Academy of Sciences, Beijing, China
zhangxu@semi.ac.cn

**Abstract.** A flexible capacitive tactile sensor with micro needle structure is designed in this paper for the palm and fingers of the manipulator. The sensor has better sensitivity, stability and repeatability and the spatial layout of the manipulator tactile sensor is designed in this paper. The main raw material PDMS is prepared to meet the requirements of a flexible tactile sensor. The silicon-based MEMS technology is used to achieve a tiny micro needle structure. Experimental results show that the sensor is proved to work well and able to guarantee a better sensitivity at 30 N pressure.

**Keywords:** Flexible tactile sensor · Micro needle · Silicon-based MEMS technology

## 1 Introduction

During the developing process of the tactile sensor, researchers from all over the world have been doing a lot of research and exploration [1, 2]. The flexible capacitive tactile sensor with plate capacitor has simple structure [3], small temperature coefficient, high sensitivity, better output stability and dynamic response characteristic. Also, because of the small amount of heat emission and low power dissipation, it has a very good application prospect.

To a great extent, the character of dielectric layer decides the performance of the capacitor when using the capacitive structure as the sensing unit. There are two different dielectrics of the traditional flexible capacitor, air and PDMS. Usually, the sensor using air as the dielectric has a better sensitivity than those using PDMS. However, the elastic ability will be weaken when using air medium so that it cannot recover to the previous position after repeatedly press for a long time [4]. The sensor using PDMS as the dielectric has a better ability of deformation resistance and has great advantages in repeatability and stability [5]. The other new type dielectric structure is micro needle [6, 7]. Such structure can be compressed and altered the distance of polar plates when there is an outer pressure. Because of the elasticity of micro needle, the gap of capacitor will return to origin position after the outer force is cancelled. The capacitor with micro needle structure has advantages like high sensitivity, high repeatability, high stability and prolonging lifetime of sensor, which makes it an ideal capacitive sensor structure.

From the analysis above, to satisfy the tactile sensor to have a better flexibility, sensitivity and repeatability, this paper decides to use PDMS as material and capacitive

© Springer Nature Singapore Pte Ltd. 2017
F. Sun et al. (Eds.): ICCSIP 2016, CCIS 710, pp. 303–309, 2017.
DOI: 10.1007/978-981-10-5230-9_31

structure with dielectric layer of micro needles as the unit of tactile sensor to manufacture flexible tactile sensor.

## 2 Design

As shown in Fig. 1, the size of flexible tactile sensor unit structure is 3 mm × 3 mm, which including bump layer, deposition layer, top electrode layer, dielectric layer, bottom electrode layer and substrate layer. The structure of bump layer is designed to concentrate the contact force of outside to the capacitive sensors.

Figure 2 is the manipulator. The installed position of the manipulator will be placed on the part of the palm and five fingers (as shown in Fig. 2 of the red areas).

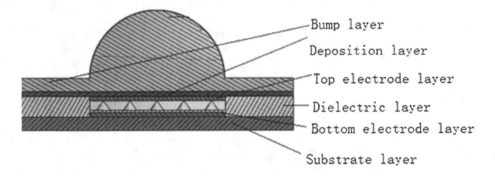

**Fig. 1.** The diagram of capacitor structure

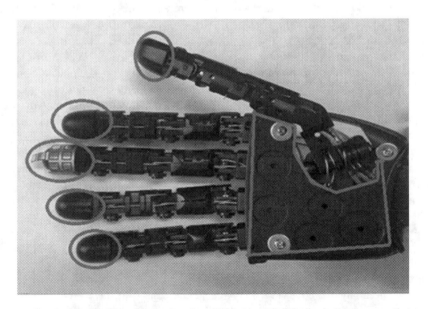

**Fig. 2.** The schematic of manipulator (Color figure online)

Figure 3 is the 3D models of the flexible tactile sensor placed on palm and fingertips which is designed by three dimensional software.

**Fig. 3.** Three dimensional schematic of the palm and fingertips tactile sensor

## 3   Fabrication

In this paper, the main raw material PDMS is prepared to meet the requirements of the flexible tactile sensor. The proportion of polymer of PDMS and curing agent is 20:1. The material with this proportion have a better flexible ability.

### 3.1   Upper Dielectric Layer

Upper dielectric layer includes bump layer, deposition layer and top electrode layer. The bump layer is made by an aluminum mold turning model in the system. PDMS material and metal material thermal expansion coefficients are greatly different. In order to prevent metal plates which attach directly onto the PDMS plate damaging or rupturing [8], we deposited a thin film of parylene to enhance the metal adhesion and relieve the destruction by vacuum vapor deposition and sputtering the deposited gold film on the deposited layer.

### 3.2   Dielectric Layer with Micro Needle

As shown in Fig. 4, it is the whole process of fabricating micro needle: silicon mold preparation, rolling over the mold of PDMS. Silicon mold preparation process ((a) to (d) of Fig. 4) mainly uses silicon-based MEMS technology. Then the silicon mold is rolled over by the PDMS and the mold of PDMS can be got. At last, PDMS dielectric layer can be manufactured by rolling over the mold of PDMS. ((e) to (h) of Fig. 4)

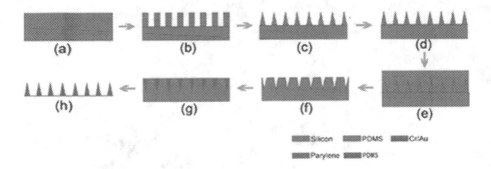

**Fig. 4.** The fabrication of micro needle dielectric layer

## 3.3    Bottom Dielectric Layer

Bottom dielectric layer includes bottom electronic layer and substrate layer. Palm uses a normal PCB board and fingertips part uses the flexible PCB. The palm and fingers of the PCB layout are shown in Fig. 5.

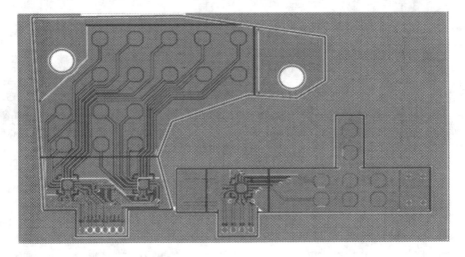

**Fig. 5.** Palm with fingers PCB Board

## 3.4    The Sensor Integration

The surface of the PDMS membrane without treatment has a thin layer of oligomer which is hydrophobic and has a poor surface adhesion. So we have to treat the PDMS surface and improve the surface activity to enhance its adhesion by using oxygen plasma treatment technology. Figure 6 is the final tactile sensors.

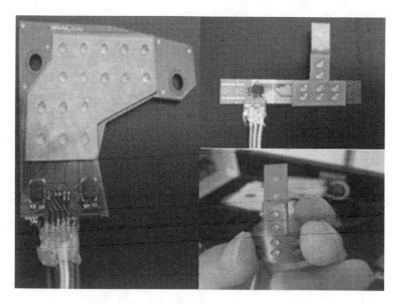

**Fig. 6.** The flexible tactile sensors of the palm and fingertip

## 4 Measurement and Discussion

The palm and fingertips tactile sensors are placed on static pressure machine for the integral pressure test. At the same time, a sampling circuit is used to collect the change of the voltage value. Increasing the press loads gradually from 0 N to 30 N at a speed of 0.15 mm/min and collecting capacitance variation of each test point at the same time.

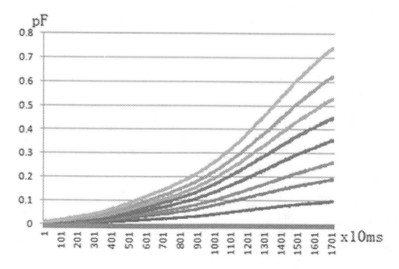

**Fig. 7.** Time - the capacitance value curve of each test point of the fingertip

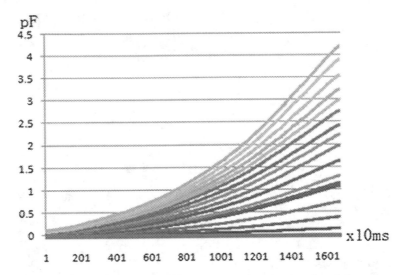

**Fig. 8.** Time - the capacitance value curve of each test point of the palm

**The results of analysis:** From Figs. 7 and 8, we can know that the capacitance-displacement relationship corresponds with the variation tendency in the ideal status because the displacement is proportional to the change of time and the relationship between capacitance and time is linear. The sensor has a large measuring range and a good sensitivity. An upward trend of each collection point capacitance is basically the same. This suggests that flexible tactile sensors of the palm and fingers have a good integrity.

**Problem analysis:** Under the circumstance of compressing the whole sensor, the variation value of each test point is relatively different. The reason is that it cannot guarantee the force condition of each test point is exactly the same in the real stress test.

## 5   Conclusion

This paper improves the sensitivity, stability and repeatability of the sensor by using micro needles structure as the dielectric layer of the capacitance in a tactile sensor unit. To satisfy the request of flexibility of the tactile sensor, this paper uses PDMS as the main raw material and utilizes MEMS technology to achieve processing tiny structure. After experimental test, the results show that this tactile sensor has a large measuring range and a high sensitivity.

**Acknowledgements.** The authors would like to thank National High Technology Research and Development Program of China (863) (Grant Nos. 2012AA030308, 2013AA032204, 2014AA 032901) National Basic Research Program of China (Grant No. 2011CB933203) National Natural Science Foundation of China (Grant Nos. 81300803, 61327809, 61474107, 61372060,

61335010, 61275200, 61178051) Grant for Capital Clinical Application Research with Characteristics (Grant No. Z141107002514061) Chinese Academy of Sciences Focus Fund (Grant No. KJZD-EW-L11-01). Also, we want to thank CHU ZHONG YI of Beijing University of Aeronautics & Astronautics.

# References

1. Markham, H.C., Brewer, B.R.: Development of a skin for intuitive interaction with an assistive robot, Minneapolis, MN, United states, pp. 5969–5972 (2009)
2. Kerpa, O., Weiss, K., Worn, H.: Development of a Flexible Tactile Sensor System for a Humanoid Robot, Las Vegas, NV, United states, vol. 1, pp. 1–06 (2003)
3. Lee, H.-K., Chang, S.-l., Yoon, E.: A flexible polymer tactile sensor: fabrication and modular expandability for large area deployment. J. Microelectromech. Syst. **15**(6), 1681–1686 (2006)
4. Lei, K.F., Lee, K., Lee, M.: Development of a flexible PDMS capacitive pressure sensor for plantar pressure measurement. Microelectron. Eng. **99**, 1–5 (2012)
5. Pritchard, E., Mahfouz, M., Evans Iii, B., et al.: Flexible capacitive sensors for high resolution pressure measurement. In: Proceedings of Sensors, Lecce, pp. 1484–1487 (2008)
6. Hu, X., Zhang, X., Liu, M., Chen, Y., Li, P., Pei, W., Zhang, C., Chen, H.: A flexible capacitive tactile sensor array with micro structure for robotic application. Sci. China Inf. Sci. **57**(12), 120204 (2014)
7. Hu, X., Zhang, X., Liu, M., Chen, Y., Li, P., Liu, J., Yao, Z., Pei, W., Zhang, C., Chen, H.: High precision intelligent flexible grasping front-end with CMOS interface for robots application. Sci. China Inf. Sci. **59**(3), 032203 (2016)
8. Hotta, Y., Zhang, Y., Miki, N.: Flexible distributed capacitive sensor with encapsulated ferroelectric liquid. In: Proceedings of Micro Electro Mechanical Systems, Cancun, pp. 573–576 (2011)

# Robot Path Planning for Human Search in  Indoor Environments

Ye Tang[1], Meiqin Liu[1(✉)], Weihua Sheng[2], and Senlin Zhang[1]

[1] College of Electrical Engineering, Zhejiang University, Hangzhou 310027, China
{21410133,liumeiqin,slzhang}@zju.edu.cn
[2] School of Electrical and Computer Engineering, Oklahoma State University,
Stillwater, OK 74078, USA
weihua.sheng@okstate.edu

**Abstract.** Aiming at the problem of a mobile robot searching human in home environments, a gird model is built and a path planning method based on a modified genetic algorithm and an improved A\* algorithm is proposed. First, the grid map is divided into several unit regions using Boustrophedon cellular decomposition. Then, a unit region planning method based on a genetic algorithm is applied to generate a region transition sequence, and an effective strategy to search every region is adjusted according to the robot's sensors. Meanwhile, the optimal path between two points is generated by an improved A\* algorithm, so that the path is much shorter and the number of turns is greatly reduced. Finally, the simulation results verify that this method can provide an optimized path in known home environments effectively, based on that the robot can find human in the shortest possible time.

**Keywords:** Indoor mobile robot · Grid method · Path planning · Genetic algorithm · A\* algorithm

## 1 Introduction

Nowadays indoor intelligent robots are being developed by researchers due to their wide variety of applications in everyday life, especially as Smart Home attracts more and more attention. Since mobility is the most basic capability of a indoor robot, path planning [1] and area coverage [2] are the two of the main problems in mobile robots. Path planning aims to find a least-cost path from a starting point to the target point while avoiding obstacle, and it is usually applied to autonomous navigation, such as the Google Driverless Car. Area coverage means the robot can traverse the entire workspace under a certain motion control

This work was supported by the National Natural Science Foundation of China under Grant 61328302, and it is also supported by the National Science Foundation (NSF) Grant CISE/IIS 1231671 and CISE/IIS 1427345, the Open Research Project of the State Key Laboratory of Industrial Control Technology, Zhejiang University, China (No. ICT1600217).

© Springer Nature Singapore Pte Ltd. 2017
F. Sun et al. (Eds.): ICCSIP 2016, CCIS 710, pp. 310–323, 2017.
DOI: 10.1007/978-981-10-5230-9_32

strategy, which requires both avoiding obstacle and avoiding repeated coverage. Area coverage has been widely used in many fields, such as robotic demining [3], oil spill cleaning [4], etc.

Taking the actual scene into account, indoor intelligent robots not only can play an important role with respect to the health and psychological well-being of the elderly [5], but also can be used by doctors and nurses to remotely check on patients, even in their own homes [6]. Obviously, most jobs of the robot involves interacting with human, so that our robots are always equipped with natural human interfaces and sensing sensors like RGB cameras or Kinects [7]. But when the human is not within the detection range of the robot, an important issue to be solved is to find the location of that person. Some of our previous research has developed indoor human localization algorithm that estimates human pose by using environmental PIR sensors [8], then the search space for the robot may be reduced. While without the Passive Infrared (PIR) sensors' priori information, our robot have to plan a global path to explore the whole home. Besides, path should satisfy a number of optimization parameters, such as the shortest distance, minimum time and minimum energy consumption and so on.

This paper aims at planning a time optimal search path, based on that the indoor mobile robot can explore the home environments effectively to find human. Since the vision sensor has a limited detection range, after properly dividing the known static map into several unit regions [9], robot's detection in each region is an area coverage problem, while robot's transition among regions is an unsymmetrical Traveling Salesman Problem. Therefore, in Sect. 2, we firstly consider the cell decomposition problem and solve it with Boustrophedon cellular decomposition method. Then in Sect. 3, we propose a modified genetic algorithm to accomplish the task of region transition sequence planning, and discuss how to improve A* algorithm for optimization of path planning between two points. Finally, in Sect. 4, simulation results are presented to verify the effectiveness of our method. Conclusion of this paper is provided in Sect. 5.

## 2    Establishment of Environmental Model

This section formulates the environmental model by a grid method. Then, according to the detection range of robot's vision sensor, we divide the grid map into several regions using Boustrophedon cellular decomposition.

### 2.1    Raster Modelling

For the purpose of path planning, a suitable map model based on real home environments is very important. As we know, obstacles in home environments do not move very often, and on the other hand, when the furniture do move, the robot can update its map information through Simultaneous Localization and Mapping (SLAM) [10], so that the global map can be considered as a static map. Since using a two-dimensional grid method is very simple and effective to represent the static information environments, and it can greatly reduce the complexity of modeling, to facilitate computer storage and processing, and to prevent the loss of part of a feasible path, we choose this method to model the environments.

As shown in Fig. 1(a), the home environments is modelled as a $26 \times 31$ grid model with obstacle distribution. The black grids represent the obstacle space, while white grids abstract free space for robot to move back and forth, and size of each grid is $35\,\mathrm{cm} \times 35\,\mathrm{cm}$, which is slightly larger than the size of our robot.

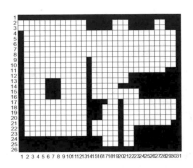

(a) Home model by the grid method

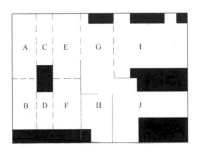

(b) Sketch map of regional division

**Fig. 1.** Establishment of environmental model

## 2.2   Division of the Grid Map

Choset. H and Pignon. P proposed Boustrophedon cellular decomposition by improving Trapezoidal cellular decomposition [9]. In this method, there is given a tangential direction, and it will sweep the work area from left to right (top to bottom), then new unit will generate when connectivity of swept area changes. When connectivity increases, related old unit will be terminated and several new units will be generated, while in contrast, we terminate multiple old units and generate new unit. After cellular decomposition, the environments can be viewed as a collection of several unit regions, in where there are no obstacles.

In our raster model, as the size of each grid equals the real robot's diameter, robot's movement is considered transferring among the center of each grid. Besides, our robot is equipped with vision sensors to identify human behavior, then when dividing the map, the max size of each unit region must be limited by the maximum detection range of vision sensors. Therefore, as shown in Fig. 1(b), the global map is divided into region $A \sim J$. In each region, our robot uses the same strategy to detect, then it can determine whether there is anyone in it, regardless of the specific size of each region for the reason of vision sensor's detection range.

As previously mentioned, robot's detection in each region differs from traditional area coverage for the same reason of vision sensor. In other words, instead of travelling everywhere by round-trip coverage strategy like a sweeping robot, our robots can detect its complete surroundings while rotating in the center of a region. So, the detect problems in each region can be simplified to determine the center coordinates of the region, and then do a rotation detection.

An other issuer is the time and energy consumption when robot rotating, and it is the significant optimization parameter of the optimal path, which is an essential variable in the fitness function of the genetic algorithm in Sect. 3.1.

# 3 Global Path Planning Methods

With a priori information of human's position from the PIR sensors network or not, the global path for robot to find human can be quite different, for the reason that we can reduce the numbers of regions based on the probability. This section presents details of the algorithm, including how to get the optimal region transition sequence by the genetic algorithm and how to generate obstacles avoiding path by A* algorithm which fit the actual situation.

## 3.1 Region Transition Sequence by Modified GA

The sequence planning problem is an unsymmetrical TSP problem, as the worst case needs robot to travel all the regions and each region exactly once. The access order of each region will lead to different time-consuming, then our target is to find the minimum consumption sequence. Genetic algorithms are relatively optimization technique and can be applied to various problems, including those that are NP-hard [11]. Therefore, we applied a genetic algorithm in this sequence planning problem and achieved good results.

The genetic algorithm is based on the natural process of evolution. This idea is applied to a problem by first guessing solutions and then combining the fittest solutions to create a new generation of solutions which should be better than the previous generation. We improved the traditional genetic algorithm in the following several aspects to solve the practical problem.

**A. Encoding.** The first task is to convert every region transition sequence into the structure of genotype string, which can be recognized by genetic algorithms. Swap coding is used to solve sort problems such as the traveling salesman problem and scheduling problems. After numbering region $A \sim J$ to gene $0 \sim 9$, a gene string indicates the order of region traversal. For example, gene string [3, 2, 5, 7, 8, 0, 6, 1, 9, 4] means the region transition sequence $D \to C \to F \to H \to I \to A \to G \to B \to J \to E$.

**B. Fitness Function.** Many researchers used fitness functions like follows, which although concerned about the turns in the path, they treats different turn angle with the same attitude [12]:

$$f = \sum_{i=1}^{N-1} (D(k_i, k_{i-1}) + T(k_i, k_{i-1})) \tag{1}$$

where $T(k_i, k_{i-1})$ is the number of turns, meaning that the time spent on each exact corner is considered constant.

Since in practical applications, the robot is looking for the optimal path rather than the shortest path, in order to fit the actual situation, we introduce distance time-consuming, turn time-consuming and probability of next region as evaluation parameters to construct a comprehensive fitness function.

$$f = \sum_{i=1}^{N-1} \frac{D(k_i, k_{i-1})/v + T(k_i, k_{i-1})/\omega}{P_i \times P_i} \tag{2}$$

where $N$ is the number of regions. $D(k_i, k_{i-1})$ is the path length between the two adjacent nodes, $T(k_i, k_{i-1})$ is the total turn angle, and the path between $k_i$ and $k_{i-1}$ is constructed by improved A* Algorithm in Sect. 3.2. $v$ and $\omega$ represent the robot's linear and angular velocity, which are regarded as constant. Finally, $P_i$ means the possibility of human in this region. Note that each region's possibility may depend upon a priori information, we initialize the regions' possibilities a vector of the same value and adaptively update it. Then, when a region's probability is obviously higher than other, it may have a high chance to be the first area for robot to search.

As we can see, this fitness function describes the time our robot may spend to search human in the whole process, because our primary focus is to get the robot to reach the people as soon as possible to complete a variety of tasks.

**C. Crossover.** Since Goldberg and Grefenstette used genetic algorithms for the traveling salesman problem the first time, several crossover methods have been developed to improve the convergence speed and seek better results, such as Partial Match Crossover(PMX) and Ordered Crossover(OX) [13]. But, when facing our unsymmetrical TSP problem, as each region must be covered for only once before and after crossover, many of the traditional methods don't work well, except the new one named as 3-exchange crossover heuristic algorithms [14].

As we know, the main purpose of crossover operator is to promise the progeny generation can inherit more advantages of the parents, and the truth is the farther parents' relationship is, the better excellent progeny will be. The 3-exchange crossover heuristic algorithms choose three chromosomes as the parents, then generate one progeny by calculating the cost and select one minimal cost region sequentially. This process is illustrated as follows. Let the three parents be:

$$\begin{bmatrix} A \\ B \\ C \end{bmatrix} = \begin{bmatrix} 3\ 2\ 1\ 4\ 8\ 7\ 6\ 5\ 0\ 9 \\ 2\ 4\ 9\ 6\ 8\ 0\ 1\ 3\ 5\ 7 \\ 8\ 6\ 0\ 5\ 3\ 4\ 9\ 2\ 7\ 1 \end{bmatrix} \tag{3}$$

where the fitness function value is $f_A = 42$, $f_B = 40$, $f_C = 46$.

Firstly, we choose a region as an initial area randomly, for instance region $D$, and do right rotation on the three parents to make region $D$ the first region.

$$\begin{bmatrix} A \\ B \\ C \end{bmatrix} = \begin{bmatrix} 3\ 2\ 1\ 4\ 8\ 7\ 6\ 5\ 0\ 9 \\ 3\ 5\ 7\ 2\ 4\ 9\ 6\ 8\ 0\ 1 \\ 3\ 4\ 9\ 2\ 7\ 1\ 8\ 6\ 0\ 5 \end{bmatrix} \tag{4}$$

Then, we calculate the cost between the first two regions of each parent, and select the minimum one to generate the child chromosome. In this case, if $f_{ffitness}(3,2) > f_{ffitness}(3,5) > f_{ffitness}(3,4)$, then the region $F$ will be the second gene of the child, and the parents may update to:

$$\begin{bmatrix} A \\ B \\ C \end{bmatrix} = \begin{bmatrix} \times\,5\,0\,9\,2\,1\,4\,8\,7\,6 \\ \times\,5\,7\,2\,4\,9\,6\,8\,0\,1 \\ \times\,5\,4\,9\,2\,7\,1\,8\,6\,0 \end{bmatrix} \tag{5}$$

So forth, we may finally obtain the progeny:

$$O = \begin{bmatrix} 3\,5\,7\,6\,0\,4\,8\,9\,2\,1 \end{bmatrix} \tag{6}$$

The child's fitness cost is superior to its parents in general. By this crossover method, we can totally control the first eight regions' transition costs, yet although we have nothing to do with the last transition to promise it won't be shortcoming, a high probability of optimization has completely achieved our goal.

**D. Operating Parameters.** With other aspects as same as the conventional method, including selection operator and mutation operator, the last thing to consider is setting appropriate parameters. In order to get better results, after several tests, we finally set the parameters as shown in Table 1.

**Table 1.** The parameters of the genetic algorithm

| Parameters | Values |
|---|---|
| Population size | 50 |
| Maximum generation | 25 |
| Crossover probability | 0.9 |
| Mutation probability | 0.1 |
| Selection proportion | 0.6 |

As the initial cost map and segmentation results shown in Fig. 1, if ignoring the initial position of the robot, the finally region transition sequence by the modified genetic algorithm will be $J \rightarrow I \rightarrow H \rightarrow G \rightarrow E \rightarrow C \rightarrow A \rightarrow B \rightarrow D \rightarrow F$. When setting robot's initial position in region $A$, the finally will be $A \rightarrow C \rightarrow B \rightarrow D \rightarrow F \rightarrow E \rightarrow G \rightarrow H \rightarrow I \rightarrow J$, and so on.

## 3.2   Path Planning Based on the Improved A* Algorithm

Besides obtaining the sequence of regions, the path planning between two points while avoiding obstacles is the other key task. Today there are many useful path planning algorithms based on grid method, such as Dijkstra, A*, D*, D*

Lite [15]. A* algorithm is more effective in a known static environment, as it guarantees to find the optimal path as good as what Dijkstras algorithm found and uses a heuristic algorithm to guide the pathfinding process like Greedy Best-First-Search algorithm.

In the standard terminology used when talking about A*, the core part is the design of the evaluation function (7):

$$f(x) = g(x) + h(x) \tag{7}$$

where $g(x)$ represents the exact cost of the path from the initial point to any point $x$, and $g(x)$ represents the heuristic estimated cost from point $x$ to the goal. A* balances the two as it moves from the starting point to the goal. In the actual environments, we usually select Euclidean distance (straight line distance) between two nodes as the estimated cost:

$$h(x) = \sqrt{(x_G - x_X)^2 + (y_G - y_X)^2} \tag{8}$$

where $(x_X, y_X)$ represents the robot's current position $X$, and $(x_G, y_G)$ is the position of target node $G$.

The A* algorithm maintains two sets, OPEN and CLOSED. The OPEN set contains those nodes that are candidates for examining. Initially, the OPEN set contains only one element: the starting position. The CLOSED set contains those nodes that have already been examined. Initially, the CLOSED set is empty. Each node also keeps a pointer to its parent node so that we can determine how it was found. Its pseudo-code is shown in Algorithm 1.

However, since A* algorithm regards the center of each grid as a node, the neighbor nodes' number on each node is limited to eight, so that the final path may contain too many unnecessary corners comparing to the real optimal path, which is a straight line directly, as shown in Fig. 2. Then we take some measures to address this problem.

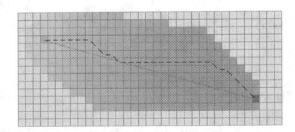

**Fig. 2.** The A* algorithm path and the real shortest path

Extending the number of searchable neighbourhood to infinite is a good solution, as in this way, the robot's search direction will be arbitrary and then unnecessary corners are avoided [16]. But this method may be a little complicated, for the reason that it has to discuss all the possibilities of the grid's different

**Algorithm 1.** Basic A* Algorithm

```
OPEN = priority queue containing START;
CLOSED = empty set;
while lowest rank in OPEN is not the GOAL do
    current = lowest rank item in OPEN;
    remove current from OPEN and add current to CLOSED;
    for each neighbor of current do
        cost = g(current) + movecost(current, neighbor);
        if neighbor in OPEN & cost < g(neighbor) then
            remove neighbor from OPEN;
        end if
        if neighbor in CLOSED & cost < g(neighbor) then
            remove neighbor from CLOSED;
        end if
        if neighbor not in OPEN & not in CLOSED then
            set g(neighbor) to cost;
            add neighbor to OPEN;
            set priority queue rank to g(neighbor) + h(neighbor);
            set neighbor's parent to current;
        end if
    end for
end while
return path(X_start, X_goal) by reverse the nodes' paternity list.
```

positions and applies different valuation function. However, without complex derivation, there is a smooth optimization method dealing with the generated path by A* algorithm, which consists of two steps: combining the collinear nodes and getting rid of excess inflection nodes as possible.

**A. Combine the Collinear Nodes.** Determining whether three nodes collinear or not is the first task, and it can be obtained by comparing the slope of any two lines. For example, given three points $A$, $B$, $C$, if the slope of line $AB$ equals the slope of line $BC$, these three points are exactly collinear. Secondly, we remove the middle node successively when adjacent three points are collinear. After this step, all nodes in the path are turns, regardless of necessary, then we come the next procedure.

**B. Remove Excess Inflection Nodes.** As we known, the shortest distance between two points is a straight line. Therefore, when there are no obstacles between the straight line of two nodes, all other nodes among the two points' sequence can be completely removed. Then determining whether there is an obstacle on the straight line of the two points is our focus, and the method of grids traversal on this line is applied.

As shown in Fig. 3, the upper and lower graphs display the nodes(the black grids) of A* path after the two operation. The final path which only consists

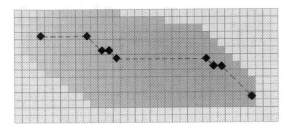

(a) The path after combining the collinear nodes

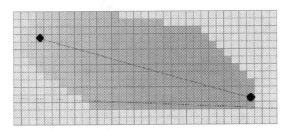

(b) The path after removing excess inflection nodes

**Fig. 3.** Smooth optimization on the A* path

of two nodes is as same as the shortest one in Fig. 2, so it clearly proves the effectiveness of our smooth optimization A* algorithm.

## 4    Simulations

In this section, simulations are carried out to validate the proposed path planning algorithm for searching humans in a known static environment on a simulation test-bed. In order to comparatively evaluate the performance of the proposed algorithm, a benchmark algorithm is also tested in the same scenario. In the benchmark algorithm, the robot implements back and forth motion and avoids obstacles as needed, and direction of motion inside each region is consistent with the tangential direction when decomposing.

### 4.1    Experimental Parameters and Performance Metrics

We use the actual robot' parameters in the simulator, which is equipped with a 360° Laser Radar and a RGB-D vision sensor. The robot radius is 17 cm, and robot's velocity $v = 0.25$ m/s, $\omega = 1.0$ rad/s are used in function (2). The vision sensor's detection radius is $0.8 \sim 3.5$ m and detection angle is $\alpha = 1$ rad in the horizontal direction, then when the target human is in the robot's detected area, we say the human searching task has been completed.

Although we use this exact robot for validation, the human searching path planning algorithm presented in the paper is meant to be generic and not platform dependent. The home environments are modelled as shown in Fig. 1. The selection of the robot's starting point can be random in the environments, and in this simulation exercise, the starting point is the upper left corner for the reason of facilitating the operation of benchmark algorithm.

The probability $P_i$ that human in region $i$ depends on the circumstances of a priori (9):

$$P_i = \begin{cases} 1/N & \text{if without a priori} \\ C_i / \sum_{j=0}^{N-1} (C_j) & \text{if with PIR priori} \end{cases} \quad (9)$$

where $N$ is the number of regions; $C_i$ is the number of particles in region $i$, under the premise of each particle represents a possible position of the person, for the reason that we may use Particle filters to deal with the PIR sensor information.

Four different performance metrics are used to compare the effectiveness of the proposed algorithm with that of the benchmark algorithm in searching human:

- $T_{cover}$: total time to search the entire map
- $T_{search}$: total time to find the target human
- $Distance$: total distance of the path
- $Angle$: total steering angle of the path

The algorithm that has smaller $Distance$ and $Angle$ is considered to be more effective, and these two metrics affect $T_{search}$ together in the case that the robot's velocity $v$ and $\omega$ are considered constant. Finally, the algorithm with smaller $T_{search}$ is preferred because the major task in this application is to find the target human in the shortest time. $T_{cover}$ may be the final time spent in the worst case that the human position is in the last region in the region transition sequence, then we can have a more comprehensive understanding of the two methods.

## 4.2   Simulation Results

When there is no priori information, the simulation results of robot searching the human in the known indoor environments is shown in Fig. 4, in which Fig. 4(a) shows the result of proposed path planning algorithm in this paper and Fig. 4(b) shows that of the benchmark method.

The red circles represent the initial position of our robot, which is the upper left corner in the map. The blue circles represent the human's position, which may be any passable place, and we generate it randomly. The red tracks are the robot's moving paths to search human by the two path planning methods adapted to human's exact location and blue tracks shows the motion paths under actual conditions. As we seen, the two paths scanning the entire environments differ from each other significantly as they are generated by different methods.

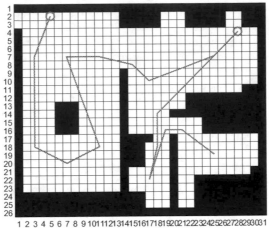

(a) Path planning result by the proposed method

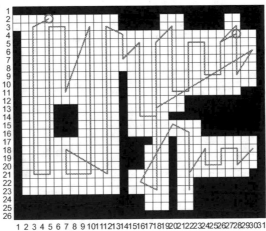

(b) Path planning result by the benchmark method

**Fig. 4.** Result of searching human by the two algorithms (Color figure online)

After visual representation, the comparison of performance are as follows to quantitatively analyze which method is better. The proposed method and the benchmark method are comparatively evaluated using those four performance metrics, and the results are shown in Table 2. As indicated by $T_{cover}$ and $T_{search}$ of two algorithms, the proposed one's improvement is quite significant, which takes less than 50% time to complete the task of finding humans. When it comes to the travelled motion consumption, the proposed method takes 63.8%

less distance, although it takes 16.5% more turn angles to finish scanning the search area, for the reason that robot has to rotate almost 360° in the center of each region. Besides, in numerous simulation experiments in different situations, the performance of the two algorithms are all compared, and regardless of the distance between human's position and robot's initial position, the proposed method is much more efficient in human searching than the benchmark method.

**Table 2.** Comparative evaluation of the two methods

| Metrics | Benchmark | Proposed | Improvement |
|---|---|---|---|
| $T_{cover}$ /s | 410.23 | 183.42 | 55.3% |
| $T_{search}$ /s | 279.83 | 127.55 | 54.4% |
| $Distance$ /m | 58.71 | 21.27 | 63.8% |
| $Angle$ /rad | 44.99 | 52.42 | −16.5% |

Meanwhile, when there is a priori information, our algorithm also works well and the result is shown in Fig. 5. This situation is entirely different from the previous, as we have a fundamental grasp that some places do not deserve to be detected. Then, each chromosome will only contain the possible areas, which means the region transition sequence will be greatly shortened. According to formula (9), the greater the number of particles contained in a region, the higher searching priority it will be. This time, we can easily determine the benchmark algorithm and other methods based on area coverage are not appropriate, because they can not effectively use this prior information.

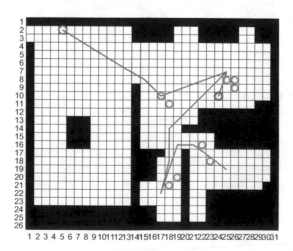

**Fig. 5.** Optimal paths by the proposed algorithm

In summary, our proposed path planning algorithm is proved to be an effective method in the scenes that robot is asked to find humans in the home environments as soon as possible.

## 5    Conclusion

This paper presents a path planning algorithm for indoor mobile robot to find humans in a static environment, which gives full consideration to environmental information and sensor information available to the robot. It mainly consists of three core steps: Boustrophedon cellular decomposition on the grid map, the genetic algorithm to generate a region transition sequence and an improved A* algorithm to obtain two point's optimal path.

The proposed algorithm has been validated in human-search examples with and without a priori information. Along the generated path by this algorithm, robot can roam throughout the home environments to find the human's position in the possible shortest time. Compared to the benchmark algorithm that uses back and forth motion and obstacle avoidance algorithm, the proposed algorithm is more efficient in reducing the time spent on finding humans. Further research will focus on applying this algorithm to real environments and considering dynamic maps.

## References

1. Souligma, M.: Feasible and optimal path planning in strong current field. IEEE Trans. Robot. **27**, 89–98 (2011)
2. Acar, E.U., Choset, H., Lee, J.Y.: Sensor-based coverage with extended range detectors. IEEE Trans. Robot. **22**, 189–198 (2006)
3. Acar, E.U., Choset, H., Zhang, Y.G., et al.: Path planning for robotic demining: robust sensor-based coverage of unstructured environments and probabilistic methods. Int. J. Robot. Res. **22**, 441–466 (2003)
4. Jin, X., Ray, A.: Navigation of autonomous vehicles for oil spill cleaning in dynamic and uncertain environments. Int. J. Control **87**, 787–801 (2014)
5. Tapus, A., Mataric, M.J., Scassellati, B.: The grand challenges in socially assistive robotics. IEEE Robot. Autom. Mag. Spec. Issue Grand Challenges Robot. **14**, 1–7 (2007)
6. Dillow, C.: Children's Hospital Boston Sends Telepresence Robots Home With Post-Op Patients (2013). http://www.popsci.com/technology/article/2011-12/childrens-hospital-boston-sends-telepresence-robots-post-op-patient-care
7. Desai, M., Tsui, K.M., Yanco, H.A., Uhlik, C.: Essential features of telepresence robots. In: 2011 IEEE Conference on Technologies for Practical Robot Applications, pp. 15–20 (2011)
8. Li, Y., Liu, M., Sheng, W.: Indoor human tracking and state estimation by fusing environmental sensors and wearable sensors. In: 2015 IEEE International Conference on Cyber Technology in Automation, Control, and Intelligent Systems (CYBER), pp. 1468–1473 (2015)

9. Choset, H., Pignon, P.: Coverage path planning: the boustrophedon cellular decomposition. In: Zelinsky, A. (ed.) Field and Service Robotics, pp. 203–209. Springer, London (1998)
10. Arumugam, R., et al.: DAvinCi: a cloud computing framework for service robots. In: 2010 IEEE International Conference on Robotics and Automation, pp. 3084–3089 (2010)
11. Homaifar, A., Guan, S., Liepins, G.E.: Schema analysis of the traveling salesman problem using genetic algorithms. Complex Syst. **6**, 183–217 (1992)
12. Zhu, L., Fan, J., Zhao, J., et al.: Global path planning and local obstacle avoidance of searching robot in mine disasters based on grid method. J. Cent. South Univ. (Sci. Technol.) **42**, 3421–3428 (2011)
13. Grefenstette, J.J., Gopal, R., Rosmaita, B., et al.: Genetic algorithm for TSP. In: Proceedings of the First International Conference on Genetic Algorithms and their Applications, pp. 160–168 (1985)
14. Lixin, T.: Improved Genetic Algorithms for TSP. J. Northeast. Univ. (Nat. Sci.) **20** (1999)
15. Yap, P.: Grid-based path-finding. In: Cohen, R., Spencer, B. (eds.) AI 2002. LNCS, vol. 2338, pp. 44–55. Springer, Heidelberg (2002). doi:10.1007/3-540-47922-8_4
16. Xin, Y., Liang, H.W., Du, M.B., et al.: An improved A* algorithm for searching infinite neighbourhoods. Robot **36**, 627–633 (2014)

# Multimodal Electronic Skin Integrated with 3-D Force Detection and High Precision Position Estimation

Xiaohui Hu[1], Xu Zhang[1(✉)], Ming Liu[1], Weihua Pei[1], Zhongyi Chu[2], Chun Zhang[3], Fuchun Sun[3], and Hongda Chen[1]

[1] Institute of Semiconductor, Academy of Science, Beijing, China
zhangxu@semi.ac.cn
[2] Beihang University, Beijing, China
[3] Tsinghua University, Beijing, China

**Abstract.** This paper proposed a novel electronic skin, which can detect 3-D force, and estimate accurate touch position at the same time. The proposed multimodal electronic skin is designed to capacitive sensing mechanism. Through the densely covered driving electrode, the detection area is divided into a number of staggered subareas. When the contact point is transferred from one subarea to another, outputs of the adjacent subareas change regularly. Then contact position can be estimated. Pressure sensitive layer is designed to needle shaped structure to increase the range and sensitivity of tactile sensor. After measurement, pressure change and slip of touch point can be detected simultaneously.

**Keywords:** 3-d force · Touch position · Capacitive sensor

## 1   Introduction

Tactile sense is an important channel for robots to perceive the world, as well as an indispensable man-machine interface for portable devices. As robots and wearable devices are becoming more functional and versatile, how to improve the ability of tactile perception becomes very important. In this case, tactile sensor is proposed to perceive the information of the contact object [1]. Recently, tactile sensors have evolved to be flexible or even stretchable so that they can be compatible with flexible applications.

Studies of tactile sensor has never ceased, and various structures have been proposed in the literature during the past years. Silicon-based MEMS technology

The authors would like to thank NSFC (No. 81300803, 61327809, 61474107, 61372060, 61335010, 61275200, 61178051), National Basic Research Program of China (No. 2011CB933203,), National 863 plans projects (No. 2012AA030308, 2013AA032204, 2014AA032901, 2016YFC0105604), Chinese Academy of Sciences Focus Fund (No. KJZD-EW-L11-01) and Capital Clinical Application Research (Z141107002514061) for financial support.

© Springer Nature Singapore Pte Ltd. 2017
F. Sun et al. (Eds.): ICCSIP 2016, CCIS 710, pp. 324–330, 2017.
DOI: 10.1007/978-981-10-5230-9_33

is commonly used before, but with the rapid development of flexible printing and flexible electronics, flexible tactile sensor got rapid progress. Many flexible material is applied to tactile sensors, and shows excellent properties of their respective peculiarity. For example, piezoresistive properties of conductive rubber has been used to detect pressure by Y.J. Yang et al. [2]. They found that doping PDMS with conductive particles, such as carbon nanotubes, graphene, silver powder and so on, can change the conductive properties of PDMS. When doping proportion reaches a certain level, the conductivity of PDMS will positively related to the increase of pressure. PDMS is a commonly kind of material usually used in flexible substrate as well, owing to its softness and ductility. In [3], Mohd Haris et al. used silicon on insulator as structural material and PDMS as flexible substrate to fit more irregular surfaces. In [4], Eun-Soo Hwang et al. embedded four strain gauges in four directions of the center of polymer substrate. In [5], M.-Y. Cheng et al. proposed a sandwiched capacitive structure, embedding an air groove made by PDMS between two electrodes. Excellent tactile sensing measurement results have been achieved by all of them. In the past, the flexible tactile sensor is mainly used to provide tactile sense. Since the launch of iPhone 6s, tactile sensor sparked a revolution in wearable devices market. According to their different sensing mechanisms, tactile sensor cannot be combined with the existing capacitive screen. Two sensors are overlaid to obtain the ideal output in wearable devices nowadays, which is undoubtedly the waste of hardware and software resources.

In this paper, a novel multimodal electronic skin integrated with 3-D force detection and high precision position estimation is proposed. Through the densely covered driving electrode, the detection area is divided into a number of staggered subareas. When the contact point is transferred from one subarea to another, outputs of the adjacent subareas are varied regularly. Then contact position can be estimated.

## 2 Design

The proposed multimodal electronic skin is designed to capacitive sensing mechanism. There are three layers: the top layer (sensing layer) for sensing the touch position, the middle layer (pressure sensitive layer) for pressure transmission, and

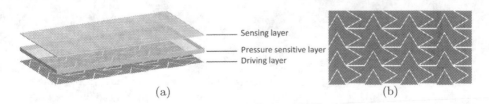

(a)                                              (b)

**Fig. 1.** (a) Schematic of the multimodal electronic skin, (b) Schematic of the driving layer.

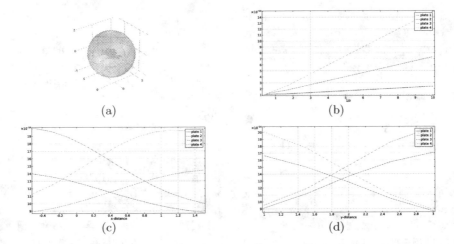

**Fig. 2.** Relationship between output of four parts and (a) Inverse ratio of distance (1/Z), (b) Moving distance x, and (c) Moving distance y.

the bottom layer (driving layer) for detection and analysis. Figure 1(a) shows the schematic diagram, and Fig. 1(b) shows the design of the driving layer.

## 2.1   Design of Driving Layer

Driving layer is the core of touch position estimation, which is designed to figure cross structure. As shown in Fig. 1(b), these intercross electrodes divide the sensing surface into 16 parts. Each part forms a detection subarea with adjacent eight parts. When the touching point moves from one subarea to another, outputs of the 16 parts are varied regularly. Then contact position can be estimated. In Fig. 2, four adjacent parts are extracted to form a basic detection network, and the simulation is carried out by COMSOL Multiphysics. As shown in Fig. 2(a), four adjacent parts are set to terminal, while the upper block which is simulated as finger contact point is set to ground. Simulation environment is set to vacuum. Figure 2(b)–(d) is the simulation results. Figure 2(b) exhibits the relationship between output of four parts and inverse ratio of distance (1/Z), when the touch point moves gradually from the distance to the sensing surface. According to the equation,

$$C = \varepsilon S/d. \tag{1}$$

output should have a linear relationship to 1/Z, which is consistent with simulation results. The difference of the output slope mainly depends on the relative area between the touch point and the sensing surface. Figure 2(c) and (d) exhibit the relationship between output of four parts and moving distance (x, y), when the touch point moves gradually from one side to another along X/Y axis respectively. In the process of moving, change trend of the four parts is obviously different. When touch point moves along X axis, plate 3 and plate 1 decrease

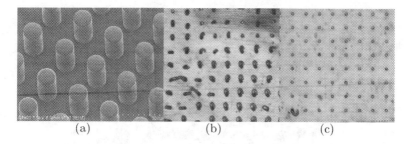

**Fig. 3.** (a) SEM of the needle shaped structure, and microscopic diagram of micro needles under (b) state of stress, (c) pressure release moment.

gradually, and plate 2 and plate 4 increase gradually. When touch point moves along Y axis, plate 3 and plate 4 decrease gradually, and plate 2 and plate 1 increase gradually. Above all, when touch points locates in different region, proportion of the four parts is different. When touch point moves, change trend of the four parts is obviously different. Therefore, position information of the contact point can be calculated by analyzing the change value of the adjacent parts.

### 2.2  Design of Pressure Sensitive Layer

Pressure sensitive layer is designed to needle shaped structure to increase the range and sensitivity of tactile sensor. All the pressure sensitive layers is fabricated by PDMS to guarantee the flexibility. Figure 3(a) shows the scanning electron microscope (SEM) of the needle shaped structure. The micro needles are arranged in order to transfer the pressure well. Figure 3(b) is the microscopic diagram of micro needles under state of stress, while Fig. 3(c) is the microscopic diagram of micro needles at the pressure release moment. When pressed, micro needles are bent to resist the pressure, and micro needles are instantly restored to the initial state when the release is released.

## 3  Fabrication

The proposed multimodal electronic skin is fabricated by flexible MEMS processing technology. The driving layer is made by FPCB processing technology. FPCB processing technology guarantees the softness of the electronic skin, as well as ensures the excellent electrical properties. The sensing layer is made by conductive fabric, which has a nice electrical conductivity. The pressure sensitive layer is made by flexible formwork technology. These three layers are bonded by Oxygen plasma bonding technique. Figure 4(a) is the proposed multimodal electronic skin. It is flexible enough to fit the curved surface, as shown in Fig. 4(b).

(a)                                  (b)

**Fig. 4.** (a) proposed multimodal electronic skin, (b) softness exhibition of the electronic skin.

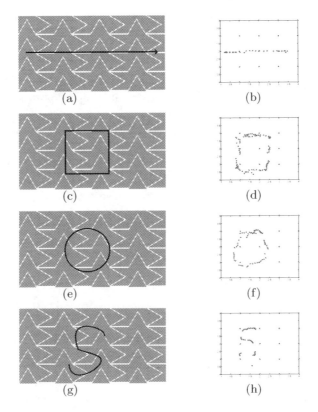

(a)                                  (b)

(c)                                  (d)

(e)                                  (f)

(g)                                  (h)

**Fig. 5.** (a) (c) (e) (g) Path of touch point,(b) (d) (f) (h) Position calculation result.

# 4   Measurement

Measurement has been done on the proposed multimodal electronic skin. Since the proportion and change trend of each driving layer mainly depends on the location of the touch point. Meanwhile, scale of the driving layer output represents the size of the pressure. According to this characteristic, an algorithm has been designed to get the location of the touch points. First, these 16 points is divided into a 4 × 4 matrix. Then, maximal value in the matrix is found as a reference point for the analysis of the whole matrix. Taking the reference point as the center, the horizontal and vertical axis as the limit, the matrix will be divided into four regions. Through proportion between the center point and the sum of horizontal and vertical axis, a rough location can be determined. Finally, through the modeling and analysis of the value of the four regions, the location of the calculation is refined. Figure 5 is the result of position calculation. Figure 5(a), (c), (e), (g) is the path of touch point across the sensor surface, and Fig. 5(b), (d), (f), (h) is the position calculation result. The proposed multimodal electronic skin can detect the position of the touch point accurately, and also can calculate the moving speed according to changing of relative distance.

# 5   Conclusion

A novel multimodal electronic skin is designed in this paper. Three layers is need to form a capacitive sensing mechanism: sensing layer for sensing the touch position, pressure sensitive layer for pressure transmission, and driving layer for detection and analysis. To get the touch point information, driving layer is designed to figure cross structure. Each part forms a detection subarea with adjacent eight parts. When the touching point moves from one subarea to another, outputs of the 16 parts are varied regularly. All the pressure sensitive layer is fabricated by PDMS needle like structure to guarantee flexibility. Micro needles are arranged in order to transfer the pressure well. Proportion and change trend of each driving layer mainly depends on the location of the touch point, while scale of the driving layer output represents the size of the pressure. Position information of the contact point can be calculated by analyzing the value and change of the adjacent parts.

**Acknowledgments.** The authors would like to thank NSFC (No. 81300803, 61327809, 61474107, 61372060, 61335010, 61275200, 61178051), National Basic Research Program of China (No.2011CB933203,), National 863 plans projects (No. 2012AA030308, 2013AA032204, 2014AA032901, 2016YFC0105604), Chinese Academy of Sciences Focus Fund (No. KJZD-EW-L11-01) and Capital Clinical Application Research (Z141107002514061) for financial support.

# References

1. Wei, Y., Torah, R., Yang, K., et al.: Screen printing of a capacitive cantilever-based motion sensor on fabric using a novel sacrificial layer process for smart fabric applications. Meas. Sci. Technol. **24**, 75104 (2013)
2. Hwang, E., Seo, J., Kim, Y.: A polymer-based flexible tactile sensor for normal and shear load detection. In: Proceedings of Micro Electro Mechanical Systems, Istanbul, Turkey, pp. 714–717 (2006)
3. Khasnobish, A., Singh, G., Jati, A., et al.: Object-shape recognition and 3D reconstruction from tactile sensor images. Med. Biol. Eng. Comput. **52**, 353–362 (2014)
4. Haris, M., Qu, H.: A CMOS-MEMS nano-newton force sensor for biomedical applications. In: Proceedings of Nano/Micro Engineered and Molecular Systems, Xiamen, China, pp. 177–181 (2010)
5. Yang, Y.J., Cheng, M.Y., Chang, W.Y., et al.: An integrated flexible temperature and tactile sensing array using PI-copper films. Sens. Actuators, A **143**, 143–153 (2008)

# A Stable and Efficient Vision-Based Tactile Sensor with Tactile Detection Using Neural Network

Chao Yang, Fuchun Sun$^{(\boxtimes)}$, Bin Fang, and Luxuan Li

Department of Computer Science and Technology,
State Key Laboratory of Intelligent Technology and Systems,
Tsinghua National Laboratory for Information Science and Technology (TNList),
Tsinghua University, Beijing, China
yang-c15@mails.tsinghua.edu.cn, fcsun@tsinghua.edu.cn

**Abstract.** In this paper, we design a vision-based tactile sensor which can capture the two-dimensional deformation images when stressed. The sensor mainly consists of a transparent elastomer, a $4 \times 4$ or $8 \times 8$ array of single layer markers on the surface of the elastomer and a camera which is used to capture the markers. According to Hooke's law, we propose a scheme using the nonlinear fitting and activation function of neural network with three layers to fit stiffness coefficient of elastomer, then we can calculate the three-dimensional tactile information. Compared to the tactile sensor with two layers having markers of different colors, our method has the advantage of simpler manufacturing process. Besides, it does not need expensive camera and precise focusing process, which is necessary for DFD(Depth from defocus) algorithm to calculate depth displacement information of markers. Further more, our method adapts neural network to fit the stiffness coefficient of elastomer, making the parameters have physical significance, which accords with the physical properties of elastomer. The sensor can reconstruct three-dimensional tactile information in real time with a speed of about 30fps.

**Keywords:** Tactile sensor · Neural network · Fitting · Stiffness coefficient

## 1 Introduction

Applications of robots draw attention to more and more researchers today. Although great success has been made today when operating the robotic manipulation devices in some structured or even complex environments, it's still a developing task to make humanoid robots perform simple manipulation tasks like humans, which can help humans and are increasingly required in current society. Just like humans, tactile information is very important for robots to recognize environment they live in. Thus a robot can do more dexterous manipulation like grasping an unknown object without slipping or shape deformation.

© Springer Nature Singapore Pte Ltd. 2017
F. Sun et al. (Eds.): ICCSIP 2016, CCIS 710, pp. 331–340, 2017.
DOI: 10.1007/978-981-10-5230-9_34

Therefore, today there are various tactile sensors using different sensing materials such as piezoelectric, resistive, capacitive, optical and so on.

A novel flexible tactile sensor consists of piezoelectric and resistive transducers has been proposed [1] for detecting slippage. Also, the sensor can detect small contact force. However, the noise, and temperature change can affect the sensor's capacity. A robust and scalable capacitive sensor [2] designed with capacitive array has solved the issue through the use of shielding and local sensor processing, but easily caused the circuit and cable broken in multiple manipulation tasks. Later, a flexible capacitive tactile sensor array with micro needle structure [3] has been proposed for robotic application. It shows better precision, sensitivity and restorative in analysis for the calibration. However, it still has the weakness that the sensor elements may be invalid within short using time. Early research on fingertip-shaped optical tactile sensor for robotic application was introduced in [4]. This sensor can detect the pressure distribution and determine the touch position well by frustration of total internal reflection when light is injected into the contact locations on edge of waveguide. Nevertheless, just detecting the normal(vertical) force cannot satisfy today's requirement for dexterous manipulation.

In order to obtain sensor with flexible surfaces, compact structure and capacity of obtaining various types of tactile information, researchers pay attention to the vision-based sensors, whose basic components are the following two parts. One is an elastomer which can deform on the contact surface when contacting an object. The other is a camera which can observe the deformation. Ito Yuji, Goro Obinata et al. contributed a lot in the research for vision-based tactile sensor [5–8]. They devote to propose a vision-based tactile sensor and relative methods which can obtain multiple types of tactile information simultaneously including the slippage, the contact region, shape of object, 3D-axis contact force and so on. This sensor, consists of an elastic/fluid-type touch pad, CCD camera and LED lights, is relatively low-cost.

GelForce is a vision-based sensor which can be used to measure the surface traction field [9]. We can get the movement of two layer markers in the elastic sensor body when exerting force on it, and calculate this force by solving the linear equation between captured displacement filed and contact force filed. Gelsight sensor is another kind of vision-based sensor [10]. It uses three lights with different source in the environment and adds thermoplastic elastomers with a metal flake skin which is sensitive to small changes of contact surface. Both of these two sensors obtain the three-dimensional tactile information just through shear displacement of markers printed on elastomer, ignoring the normal displacement. Besides, the two-layer structure of markers in elastomer will increase the coupling between normal force and shear force and the complexity of configuration and processing.

In order to avoid the weakness of GelForce and Gelsight, a new vision-based sensor is proposed [11], which can measure the three-dimensional tactile information by using a DFD (Depth from defocus) algorithm for measuring the normal displacement. The study shows that this sensor can sense shear load, normal load and torque effectively.

In this paper, we make calibration for the vision-based tactile sensor proposed in [11]. Differently, we use the two-dimensional displacement of the elastomer which has been proved to be more stable and effective. First, we need to obtain the relationship between the force and two-dimensional displacement. We design a special experimental calibration platform for the tactile sensor and write two programs for platform and sensor respectively to adjust the value of force collect the data of three-dimensional displacement of markers in elastomer. Then,we propose a novel regression algorithm based on nerual network to find the relationship between the force and two-dimensional displacement. Finally, we design some experiments to evaluate the outcome of calibration.

## 2 Overview of Experiment Device

### 2.1 Vision-Based Tactile Sensor

The prototype and the configuration of our sensor is shown in Fig. 1. The top layer is a 1 mm-thick black silicon rubber. Its softness can protect the marker layer and its color can insulate external light. We choose PDMS as the material of the second layer due to the following three points. First, there is a good adhesion ability between this material and silicon so that the tactile information can be transmitted between the first two layers preferably. Second, the Young's modulus of this material is low, which makes it easier to detect and transduce tiny force. Third, its optical transparence helps the camera sample a clear image of the markers. By changing the mix ratio of elastomer base and curing agent and adjusting the curing temperature, the elastomer gains the similar elasticity as human finger successfully. Between the first two layers, we placed a 4 × 4 array of white and circular marker. The color contrast makes the image much clearer. The third layer consists of 12 LEDs around the elastomer which provide stable and uniform illumination for the camera at the bottom. The top 3 layers are supported by the acrylic plate to keep the camera safe, which is used to capture the markers. After getting the image data, we can calculate the three-dimensional displacement of makers in real time.

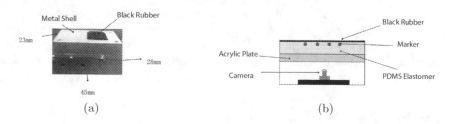

**Fig. 1.** Model of tactile sensor (a) Prototype (b) Principle structure

**Fig. 2.** The Experimental Platform: (a) Calibration device (b) Entirety (c) Force sensor

## 2.2    Calibration Platform

The experimental calibration platform we design performs as Fig. 2. The top of the platform is a three-dimensional force sensor back seated. We convert the three-dimensional force to three set of analog voltage by differential amplification circuit. Then we can calculate the magnitude of the three-dimensional force by linear conversion. The surface of the probe is plat, which is used to simulate the contact surface of vision-based three-dimensional tactile sensor and outside. We use the motion platform to drive the three-dimensional force sensor move, so that we can apply different direction and magnitude force to vision-based three-dimensional tactile sensor. On the premise of ignoring the quality of probe, we can know that the magnitude of force created by three-dimensional sensor is equal to that of vision-based three-dimensional tactile sensor applied to outside according to Newton's third law. Thus, the three-dimensional force sensor can reproduce the force produced by fingers of dexterous hand preferably.

## 2.3    Expermentation Process

In the experiment, we fix the vision-based three-dimensional tactile sensor in a certain position. Then we apply a force we can adjust in any direction to the sensor by rotating the three-axis $(X, Y, Z)$ micrometer of the motion platform. The magnitude of the force can be measured by the three-dimensional force sensor. And the strain pattern of the vision-based sensor can be sampled by the camera in Fig. 1 in the bottom of the sensor. The strain pattern and the three-dimensional force are input and output of neural network introduced later. The aim of neural network is to recover the three-dimensional force of vision-based tactile by image sampled in real time, which can provide environment information for dexterous hand.

## 3    Principles of Visual Preception

### 3.1    Measuring Displacement of Marker

As the process of core point detection you can see in the Fig. 3, we need to sample the original image from CCD camera as preprocessing in order to measure

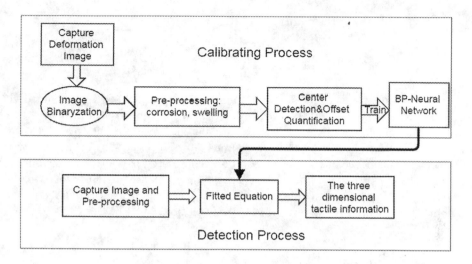

**Fig. 3.** The workflow of 3-dimensional force detection system.

the coordinate of marker when stressed. Next, we need to remove the noise included in the original image due to design technics. We apply the approach of dilate-erode in graphics to remove the noise around markers. Then we detect the center of the circle focus on the marker by the approach of Hough transform circle detection and set it as the center of the marker. Finally, we can calculate the displacement in the two-dimensional coordinate department by difference between the latter image and the original image.

### 3.2 Mapping Relation

As the paper in [12] says, we can infer the force applied on the elastomer by displacement of markers in the two-dimensional coordinate department according to theory of elasticity [13]. Following Eqs. 1 and 2, we express the movement vector $u = (u_x, u_y)$ of the interior point $r = (x, y, z)$ within a plane parallel to the $xy$-plane when a force vector $f = (f_x, f_y, f_z)$ is applied to the surface of the elastomer. Here, $\sigma$ is a Possion ratio, which is set to 0.5 assuming that the elasomer is ideally incompressible. $E$ is Young's modulus and must be appropriately defined according to the actual elastomer used. However, from this equation it is apparent that $E$ is in effect only when multiplying the whole equation by a constant, so it is set to 1 in the sequel.

$$u_x = \frac{1+\sigma}{2\pi E}\{[\frac{xz}{r^3} - \frac{(1-2\sigma)x}{r(r+z)}]f_z + \frac{2(1-\sigma)r+z}{r(r+z)}f_x + \frac{[2r(\sigma r+z)+z^2]x}{r^3(r+z)^2}(xf_x+yf_y)\}$$

(1)

$$u_y = \cdot \frac{1+\sigma}{2\pi E} \{ [\frac{yz}{r^3} - \frac{(1-2\sigma)y}{r(r+z)}]f_z + \frac{2(1-\sigma)r+z}{r(r+z)}f_y$$
$$+ \frac{[2r(\sigma r+z)+z^2]y}{r^3(r+z)^2}(xf_x + yf_y)\} \tag{2}$$

From these equations, when an unit force $\boldsymbol{f} = (f_x, f_y, f_z)$ is applied in each direction $x, y, z$, i.e. $(1,0,0),(0,1,0),(0,0,1)$, the displacement vector of the point in the plane at certain depth $z = z_1$ is calculated. We represent this vector by $\boldsymbol{u}_{f_x} = (h_{xx1}, h_{yx1})$, $\boldsymbol{u}_{f_y} = (h_{xy1}, h_{yy1})$, $\boldsymbol{u}_{f_z} = (h_{xz1}, h_{yz1})$. When the force applied to the surface of the elastic body is reconsidered as a vector distribution experssed as $\boldsymbol{f}(x,y) = (f_x(x,y),(f_y(x,y),(f_z(x,y))$, the displacement vector $\boldsymbol{m}_1(x,y) = (m_{x1}(x,y), m_{y1}(x,y), m_{z1}(x,y))$ for each point $(x,y)$ in the plane at a depth $z_1$ is calculated in the form of a convolution, by (Eq. 3).

$$m_{x1}(x,y) = h_{xx1} * f_x + h_{xy1} * f_y + h_{xz1} * f_z$$
$$m_{y1}(x,y) = h_{yx1} * f_x + h_{yy1} * f_y + h_{yz1} * f_z \tag{3}$$

A discrete form of this calculation can be experssed as a matrix representation. By doing so, Eq. 3 is rewritten in matrix form Eq. 4.

$$\begin{bmatrix} M_{x1} \\ M_{y1} \end{bmatrix} = \begin{bmatrix} H_{xx1} & H_{xy1} & H_{xz1} \\ H_{yx1} & H_{yy1} & H_{yz1} \end{bmatrix} \begin{bmatrix} F_x \\ F_y \\ F_z \end{bmatrix} \tag{4}$$

$M = HF$ is short for Eq. 4. Since this equation calculates displacement of an interior point when a force vector distribution is applied to the surface of the elastic body, we can calculate the force vector distribution by $F = H^{-1}M$. In the following chapter, we use neural network to gain the fitting matrix of $H$.

## 4    Neural Network Regression

The paper is aimed at predicting the three-dimensional tactile information by using the two-dimensional displacement image of the $4 \times 4$ array of markers. By Hooke's law, the amount of deformation is directly proportional to the applied stress. Considering the displacement of marker in our device is two-dimensional and the applied stress is three-dimensional, we can use the nonlinear characteristic of neural network to establish the mapping relation between them.

### 4.1    Construction

The input-output relation of neuron shows the nonlinear mapping relation preferably. Considering the intercoupling of displacement of markers, the input-output relation built by MLP(Multilayer Perceptron) has a great preponderance. In the three-layer BP neural network in this paper, there is a connecting weight between

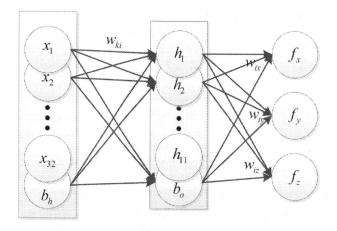

**Fig. 4.** Neural network structure.

neurons of adjacent layers shown in Fig. 4. The mapping relation of input layer and hidden layer in three-layer neural network is

$$hI_i = \sum_{k=1}^{32}(x_k w_{ki}^1) - b_{hi} \quad (i = 1, 2, ..., n) \tag{5}$$

$$hO_i = f(hI_i) = \frac{1}{1 + e^{-\alpha * hI_i}} \quad (i = 1, 2, ..., n) \tag{6}$$

There into, $(x_1, x_2, ..., x_32)$ is feature vector of marker displacement. $w_{ki}^1$ is connecting weight of $k$-th neuron in the input layer and $i$-th neuron in the hidden layer. $b_{hi}$ is input bias of $i$-th neuron in the hidden layer. $f(hI_i)$ is Sigmoid function. The value of $\alpha$ is calculated by random samples of the training set of samples above. $f(hI_i)$ and $f(hO_i)$ are input and output of hidden layer in three-layer neural network.

The mapping relation of hidden layer and output layer in three-layer neural network is

$$\hat{f}_x = f(\sum_{i=1}^{n}(hO_i w_{ix}^2) - b_x) \tag{7}$$

$$\hat{f}_y = f(\sum_{i=1}^{n}(hO_i w_{iy}^2) - b_y) \tag{8}$$

$$\hat{f}_z = f(\sum_{i=1}^{n}(hO_i w_{iz}^2) - b_z) \tag{9}$$

There into, $\hat{f}_x, \hat{f}_y, \hat{f}_z$ are predicted value of three-axis components of external force. $w_{ix}^1$ is connecting weight of $i$-th neuron in the hidden layer and $x$-th neuron in the output layer. $b_x$ is input bias of neuron $x$ in the hidden layer. Other variables use the same rule.

## 4.2  Training

Any optimizing process of neural network is a process of solving parameters by pre-existing samples. In the process, we will set an optimizing target function, also called cost function. The setting of target function will influence the network training converging or not and the velocity of converging. Meanwhile, to avoid overfitting, especially in the experimental scene of dexterous hand grasping, the motion posture of dexterous hand is restricted in a certain set of motion posture. The data sampled by sensor at the end of the dexterous hand has a strong sparsity, thus there is a great probability that the phenomenon of overfitting occur on the neural network trained by samples.In order to avoiding overfitting,we add the term of the network's parameters' two norm to target function as following:

$$e = \frac{1}{2}(\hat{f}_x - f_x)^2 + (\hat{f}_y - f_y)^2 + (\hat{f}_z - f_z)^2 + \beta \parallel w \parallel^2 \qquad (10)$$

$\hat{f}_x, \hat{f}_y, \hat{f}_z$ are predictive values of three-axis component. $f_x, f_y, f_z$ are real values of three-axis component. In the training process, we initiate the connecting weight $w$ and input bias $b$ randomly. And we minimize the target function through BP algorithm [14]. If target function e $< \epsilon$($\epsilon$ is pre-set error limit, which is 0.00001) or the training times exceeds the pre-set maximum training times $M$, we record the connecting weight and input bias of the three-layer neural network we get and end the training. Otherwise, we continue the iteration according to Eqs. 5–9.

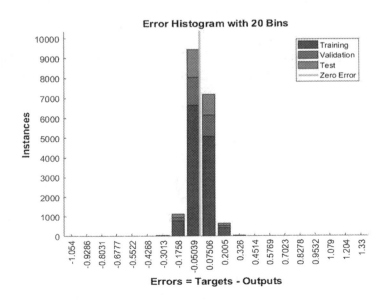

**Fig. 5.** The error distribution of all the samples.

# 5  Result

In this paper, we sample experimental specimens by calibration platform. The specimens include images sampled by camera in real time and three-dimensional force sampled by force sensor. We generates sample set through Calibrating processing in Fig. 3 and divide it into three parts, including Training Set, Validation Set and Test Set. According to the training process in [14], we generate the mapping function in Eqs. 5–9 by iteration. The coefficient in Eqs. 5–9, the connecting weight $w$ and input bias $b$, is already gotten in the training process. So Eqs. 5–9 become fitted Equation at the moment. We can see from Fig. 5 that the measuring errors of most samples using the neural network regression algorithm in this paper are at the limit of $0.05N$, which can meet the demand of dexterous hand operating.

# 6  Conclusion

The approach of vision-based tactile three-dimensional neural network detection in this paper has the following advantages. First, compared to traditional approaches of tactile detection, it can provide three-dimensional force information such as tactile sense sliding sense and pressure sense for dexterous hand since it gets deformation information of elastomer in the contact area through image information. Second, it is in real time and has the advantage of stabilized detection. Third, it fit the stiffness coefficient of elastomer according to Hooke's law, making the fitting parameters have corresponding physical magnificence. Forth, the three-layer neural network build in this paper use pre-existing samples to gradually approach the stiffness coefficient, therefore getting the advantage of high detection accuracy.

However, the contact surface in the paper is plat while the surface of human hands is a little curving. And it can be a difficulty for camera to get image when using the fingertip since there is a great chance that the marker of elastomer is out of focal distance of the camera. One facet of later work is to solve the problem of contact surface of tactile sensor elastomer. Meanwhile, though the cost function of neural network has solved part of overfitting, it will still occur when amount of samples keeps increasing. The problem of cost function should be discussed further.

**Acknowledgment.** The work was supported by the National Natural Science Foundation of China (Grant Nos. 91420302, 91520201).

# References

1. Chuang, CH., et al.: Flexible tactile sensor for the grasping control of robot fingers. In: 2013 International Conference on Advanced Robotics and Intelligent Systems (ARIS). IEEE (2013)
2. Ulmen, J., Cutkosky, M.: A robust, low-cost and low-noise artificial skin for human-friendly robots. In: InternationaL Conference on Robotics and Automation (ICRA) (2010)
3. Hu, X., et al.: A flexible capacitive tactile sensor array with micro structure for robotic application. Sci. Chin. Inf. Sci. **57**(12), 1–6 (2014)
4. Begej, S.: Fingertip-shaped optical tactile sensor for robotic applications. In: Proceedings of IEEE 1988 International Conference on Robotics and Automation, pp. 1752–1757. IEEE (1988)
5. Ito, Y., Kim, Y., Obinata, G.: Contact region estimation based on a vision-based tactile sensor using a deformable touchpad. Sens. **14**(4), 5805–5822 (2014)
6. Ito, Y., Kim, Y., Obinata, G.: Slippage degree estimation for dexterous handling of vision-based tactile sensor. In: IEEE Sensors 2009, IEEE (2009)
7. Ito, Y., et al.: Contact state estimation by vision-based tactile sensors for dexterous manipulation with robot hands based on shape-sensing. Int. J. Adv. Robot. Syst **8**(4), 225–234 (2011)
8. Ito, Y., et al.: Vision-based tactile sensing and shape estimation using a fluid-type touchpad. IEEE Trans. Autom. Sci. Eng. **9**(4), 734–744 (2012)
9. Sato, K., et al.: Finger-shaped gelforce: sensor for measuring surface traction fields for robotic hand. IEEE Trans. Haptics **3**(1), 37–47 (2010)
10. Johnson, M.K., Adelson, E.H.: Retrographic sensing for the measurement of surface texture and shape. In: 2009 IEEE Conference on Computer Vision and Pattern Recognition, CVPR 2009. IEEE (2009)
11. Guo, F., Zhang, F., et al.: Measurement of Three-Dimensional Deformation and Load Using Vision-based Tactile Sensor
12. Kamiyama, K., Kajimoto, H., Kawakami, N., et al.: Evaluation of a vision-based tactile sensor. In: Proceedings of 2004 IEEE International Conference on Robotics and Automation 2004, (ICRA 2004), vol. 2, pp. 1542–1547. IEEE (2004)
13. Sokolnikoff, I.S., Specht, R.D.: Mathematical Theory of Elasticity. McGraw-Hill, New York (1956)
14. Li, J., Cheng, J., Shi, J., Huang, F.: Brief introduction of Back Propagation (BP) neural network algorithm and Its improvement. In: Jin, D., Lin, S. (eds.) Advances in Computer Science and Information Engineering. AISC, vol. 169, pp. 553–558. Springer, Heidelberg (2012)

# Picking from Clutter: An Object Segmentation Method for Robot Grasping

Ying Chen, Yue Wang, Jin Hu, and Rong Xiong[✉]

State Key Laboratory of Industrial Control and Technology, Zhejiang University,
Hangzhou, People's Republic of China
rxiong@zju.edu.cn

**Abstract.** Picking in a unstructured environment is an important task for the further autonomy of the robot manipulation in real applications. A primary challenge for the task is to identify the object from the cluttered sensor readings. In this paper, a real time segmentation algorithm is proposed to partition the scene into objects using only depth and geometry information. We employ a graph to model the scene, in which the surfaces are regarded as nodes while the geometric relations between surfaces as edges. The relations are represented by the convexity and connectivity of the two neighbor surfaces. Upon the segmentation result, a measure was developed for robot grasping proposal suggestion. Our method has advantages over the RGB and learning based methods as it is robust against the illumination variation and does not require the collection of samples, thus achieving more convenient deployment. The method was evaluated on public datasets to validate its feasibility and effectiveness, demonstrating better performance compared to other depth information based image segmentation method. Besides, a real-world robot grasping experiment is conducted to investigate the possibility of on-site production. *abstract* environment.

**Keywords:** Image segmentation · Depth image

## 1 Introduction

Grasping unknown objects from a cluttered environment is an important task to further improve the autonomy of the robot manipulation, so that the grasping application can be extended from restricted working platform to more open and unstructured human shareable space. One of the primary challenges to achieve this goal is to identify the object from the cluttered sensor readings.

Conventionally, the RGB image from the camera is utilized, in which the visual features, like SIFT [17] and SURF [4], are detected and matched to a prior object model for pose estimation [6]. This class of methods gives impressive performance on highly textured objects, even under half occlusion. But for the low textured objects, or non-textured objects, which are common in industrial environment, the performance degenerates significantly. Another class of segmentation on RGB image giving the very good performance is based on

© Springer Nature Singapore Pte Ltd. 2017
F. Sun et al. (Eds.): ICCSIP 2016, CCIS 710, pp. 341–354, 2017.
DOI: 10.1007/978-981-10-5230-9_35

learning algorithm [2], especially the deep learning which achieves big success in artificial intelligence [7,23]. However, both kinds of methods are not adaptive to segment the objects which is unknown in prior. For the learning based methods, tons of training examples is required to capture the large variations for training the models. More importantly, using pure RGB information, only bearing of the object can be estimated, is insufficient for robot grasping. Thanks to the consumer level RGBD camera like Xtion and Kinect, applying the methods above using RGBD images can identify objects with high accuracy and give the target position at the same time [9]. But this advantage still cannot remove the constraints that objects should be known in prior in our scenario.

Methods dealing with grasping utilized only geometric information [19], indicating that the grasp planning can be satisfied by leveraging only depth information, regardless of the object class recognition. Motivated by these works, the grasp learning was studies in recent years, which is seemly promising [13,14]. Even big company like Google, is developing its large scale grasp learning system [15]. These methods works on single object for grasping pose generation, hence do not solve the segmentation problem.

Inspired by hypothesis from the grasp learning that the class of the object can be ignored, we set to develop a geometry based segmentation method from a pile of unknown objects in this paper, which does NOT require expensive training data so that the class set of identified object is open, the deployment of the robot in real application can be much easier, and the variations in RGB image, like illumination and low texture, can be ignored. The contribution of the paper is two-folded:

– A method of object partition and assessment is proposed based on graph model which achieves the robust to the boundary noise in RGBD camera and overcomes the problem of singularity mentioned in [22].
– A benchmark on dataset with other methods based on depth information is conducted, and a completed robot object grasping system is implemented for investigation of the possibility in on-site production.

The remainder of the paper is organized as follow: Sect. 2 presents a review of related works. The object segmentation framework is introduced in Sect. 3, and the experimental results are shown in Sect. 4. The study is concluded and the future works are explored in Sect. 5, which completes the paper.

## 2    Related Works

There are many existing methods for image segmentation which is one of the fundamental problems in computer vision and has been studied extensively. In general, the approaches of objects segmentation consists of three main categories: RGB segmentation, learning based segmentation and geometry based segmentation.

RGB segmentation methods employs hand crafted features like image texture, color and contour for image pixels parsing. Felzenszwalb et al. used a highly efficient graph based approach to model the image with standards-based or global features [9], representing the problem into a graph cut problem. Achantaet al. proposed a algorithm called simple linear iterative clustering (SLIC), which is a superpixel extraction method based on the similarity between the color of the pixel and proximity, calling for higher level merging methods [1]. Quickshift is a mode seeking algorithm which forms a tree of links to the nearest neighbor which increases the density [25]. The RGB segmentation is a main trend in the early studies, but it is hard to design features that is robust to the illumination variance and perspective, which is unavoidable for RGB sensors.

Learning based segmentation analyzes RGBD or RGB images using a large amount of data samples collected from the specific application. Henry et al. utilized deep convolutional neural networks to train classifier, which is successful at learning a good representation of the visual inputs [12]. Shelhamer et al. proposed a fully convolutional networks for image segmentation [21]. Chen et al. employed deep convolution neural networks and probabilistic graphical models to address the task of pixel-level classification [5]. Gupta et al. introduced a new geocentric embedding for depth images and used a decision forest approach to label each pixel [11]. In [16], a bi-modal neural network architecture was proposed to strengthen the object segmentation by mixing the place classification, pushing up the state-of-art performance. With the success of deep learning, this kind of approaches became the research focus in the recent decade. The main obstacle is the massive volume of the supervised data. Especially in the field of segmentation, the supervised data is very expensive.

Geometry based segmentation focuses on the depth data or point cloud by using the geometry structure, which is naturally invariant under the different illumination and perspective. This stability may enable the generalization across the applications without the large scale data annotation and training. In [26], the property of stability against the perspectives was utilized to segment the objects changing across sessions. Ecins et al. supposed that the three dimensional shape of common objects is bilaterally symmetric so that they only need to detect symmetry for segmentation [8]. Uckermann et al. extracted the boundary of depth to build a probabilistic graph to segment image which lacks the theoretic explanation of mechanism [24]. Moosmann et al. also utilized a graph-based approach to segment ground and objects from 3D laser scans [18]. Stein et al. utilized geometry features of surface normal and curvature to over-segment the point cloud into supervoxels and estimates all adjacency surfaces relationship of convexity base on their algorithm [22]. Their work was most similar to ours. But their LCCP algorithm processed the supervoxels whose parameters is very sensitive, causing unstable result. Comparatively, our approach depended on surfaces which are more useful than supervoxels as the size is in the level of objects.

## 3   Methods

Our goal is to classify the image pixels into different categories without learning. Our segmentation proceeds in three stages: (1) surface segmentation,

(2) adjacency graph build, (3) object partitioning. In the first stage, our algorithm produces partitioning of the current scene in a series of surfaces. In the second stage, the algorithm judge the connection of the 3D convex hull vertex and the 3D-relationship of convex-concave between adjacency surfaces. Finally, the adjacent nodes are partitioned into clusters as proposal of objects for possibly successive robot grasping.

## 3.1   Segmentation Scene into Surfaces

In [22], supervoxels are utilized to over-segment cloud point data in real-time. But it is not across different combination of parameters about $R_{voxel}$, $R_{seed}$ and $\beta_{Thresh}$. Segmenting into too small voxels would increase the computational burden of convexity judgment and boundary searching and reduce the stability of the geometric property. However large voxels would merge different object points into the same cluster, resulting in undesired under-segmentation. To avoid the massive parameter tuning, we use region growing algorithm with stationary parameter to over segment scene into surfaces. Each surface had smooth curvature with similar normals. Although, the region growing also need parameters tuning, it is much more stable across the scene. Specifically, we utilize the local feature of normal, distance as well as global features of view angle to describe the closeness of the query point to the region where the seed lies in.

For each point $p_i$ in the point cloud, their corresponding normals are computed using the principal component in their neighborhood respectively, denoted as $n_i$. The neighborhood in radius $\sigma$ is defined as $\Omega^i = \{p_i^1, p_i^2, \ldots, p_i^{N_i}\}$ where $N_i$ is the number of points in the neighborhood. Upon the normals, a description of the local smoothness can be described by the mean angle as

$$Fl_{i,j} = \|\frac{\sum_{k \in \Omega^i} \arccos(n_i^T n_k)}{N_i} - \frac{\sum_{m \in \Omega^j} \arccos(n_j^T n_m)}{N_j}\| \tag{1}$$

If the local properties of the neighborhoods around two points $p_i$ and $p_j$ are similar that means the neighborhood of the two points are both smooth or non-smooth, the $Fl_{i,j}$ should be small. Obviously only this measure is not enough to constrain the region growing, we introduce the global feature $Fg$, describing the relationship at the viewpoint as

$$Fg_{i,j} = \|arccos(n_i^T v_i^c) - arccos(n_j^T v_j^c)\| \tag{2}$$

where $v_i^c$ is the direction vector from viewpoint to point $p_i$ with unit length. the Euclidean distance between points is also employed to describe the degree of similarity between the points as

$$d_{i,j} = \|p_i - p_j\|^2 \tag{3}$$

If both of $Fl_{i,j}$ and $d_{i,j}$ are less than a threshold value then the point is added to the current region, otherwise the point will be regarded as a new seed and the process is circulated until finished.

After the first round of region growing, some clusters can be with very small number of points caused by the noise, especially in the boundary whose normal are unstable and thus adversely impact the initial segmentation of surface. We set a threshold for the segmentation size of surfaces $\Omega_{s_i}$, if the size of surface is less than $\Omega_s$, these clusters are separated into points again. At this point, we have a series of clustered surfaces set as $S = \{S_1, S_2, \ldots, S_M\}$ where $M$ is number of surfaces, and a set of un-clustered points $\tilde{P} = \{\tilde{p}_1, \tilde{p}_2, \ldots, \tilde{p}_{\tilde{N}}\}$ where $\tilde{N}$ is number of un-clustered points. In the second step, $\tilde{P}$ should be clustered into to any of $S$ if there is more than 10% points are in $\tilde{P}$. To facilitate the efficiency of second round of clustering, we build a kd-tree for all points belonging to $S$. Then we query each point in $\tilde{P}$ for neighborhood search within a specified radius of $\sigma$ as

$$\|\tilde{p}_i - p\| \leq \sigma, \quad p \in S \tag{4}$$

all the searched neighbors vote for their corresponding surfaces. The query point $\tilde{p}_i$ is finally clustered into the surface with the highest votes. After this step, small surfaces encoded by sensor noise will be merged to large region, achieving better robust. The processing is shown in Fig. 1.

**Fig. 1.** Example of segmentation when the boundary points normal are unstable. The un-clustered points are in red, of which 90% are small patches of noise. Filtering these small patches and merge them to large surfaces lead to better initial segmentation of current scene. (Color figure online)

## 3.2 Building the Surface-Patch Adjacency Graph

To build an adjacency graph for all segmented surfaces, our clustering algorithm identify a special connection judgment based on a criterion complied by the connectivity and convex-concave separation. In the algorithm, the connectivity is tested by through the adjacency of vertices of neighbor surfaces' convex hulls. The convex hull vertices set of $S_i$ is $C_i = \{c_1^i, c_2^i, \ldots, c_{m_i}^i\}$ where $m_i$ is the number of vertices. For any two surfaces of $S_i$ and $S_j$, a set of vertex distance is computed as $D_{i,j} = \{d_{i,j}^1, d_{i,j}^2, \ldots, d_{i,j}^{m_i,m_j}\}$ in ascending order, i.e. $d_{i,j}^1 < d_{i,j}^2 < \ldots < d_{i,j}^{m_i,m_j}$. To determine the connectivity of the two surfaces, the vertex distance satisfies following criteria,

$$L_{i,j} = \begin{cases} true & \sum_{k=1}^{\delta_n} d_{i,j}^k < \delta_d \\ false & o.w. \end{cases} \tag{5}$$

where $\delta_d$ is a threshold of distance, in this paper we set $\delta_d$ to $0.001\,\mathrm{m}$. The parameter of $\delta_d$ is the threshold of vertex number. Considering the connection of two surfaces of a cuboid, the minimal connected convex hull vertex number is 2, so we set $\delta_n = 3$ for robust. Although two surfaces are connected but majority of them can belong to the different objects, so we need to strengthen constrains by introducing convexity constraints.

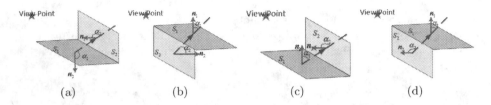

    (a)              (b)              (c)              (d)

**Fig. 2.** If the surface centroid normal are not orienting to the view point such as the (a) and (b), it is difficult to judge whether the connection of the two surfaces is convex or not. In (c) the relationship of surface satisfies the concavity and (d) the relationship of surface satisfies the convexity.

We define $p_{s_i}^c$ to the centroid of surface $S_i$ and $\boldsymbol{n}_{s_i}$ is the normal at the centroid of surface $p_{s_i}^c$. In order to determine the convexity between two surfaces, we need unify all the surface centroid normal vector orienting toward the viewpoint, which is to keep

$$\boldsymbol{n}_{s_i}^T (V_p - p_{s_i}^c) > 0 \tag{6}$$

where $V_p$ is the viewpoint of current scene. As show in Fig. 2, if the normal direction is not unified, it is difficult to judge the connection of two surfaces. Some geometry features could be calculated from current normal and position to judge the whether two surfaces are connected in convexity or concavity. According to the definition in Fig. 2, the inequality $\alpha_1 < \alpha_2$ could be transformed to

$$\alpha_1 < \alpha_2 \Leftrightarrow (\boldsymbol{n}_{s_i}^T - \boldsymbol{n}_{s_j}^T) v_{i,j} > 0 \tag{7}$$

The angle of the two normals, denoted as $\beta$, can be derived as

$$\beta = \arccos(\boldsymbol{n}_{s_i}^T \boldsymbol{n}_{s_j}) = |\alpha_1 - \alpha_2| \tag{8}$$

leading to the judgement of the convexity or concavity as

$$C_{i,j} = \begin{cases} convex & (\boldsymbol{n}_{s_i}^T - \boldsymbol{n}_{s_j}^T) v_{i,j} > 0 \vee \beta < \beta_{thresh} \\ concave & o.w. \end{cases} \tag{9}$$

By calculating this criteria, we can label the property of the connectivity across each pair of surfaces.

### 3.3    Object Partitioning and Grasp

In the previous two subsections, we get the over-segmented surfaces and the relationship across each pair of surfaces with property of the convexity and connectivity, which forms an undirected graph with nodes being the surfaces and edges being the property of the relations, representing the current scene in a compactly. In our algorithm we encode the graph into an adjacency matrix $L$ and an relation matrix $C$, with entries being $L_{i,j}$ and $C_{i,j}$ indicating for the pairwise relations. Then the two matrices are combined into a 0–1 matrix $O$ as follows

$$O = \begin{pmatrix} L_{11} \cap C_{11} & L_{12} \cap C_{12} & \dots & L_{1N} \cap C_{1N} \\ L_{21} \cap C_{21} & L_{22} \cap C_{22} & \dots & L_{2N} \cap C_{2N} \\ \vdots & \vdots & & \vdots \\ L_{N1} \cap C_{N1} & L_{N2} \cap C_{N2} & \dots & L_{NN} \cap C_{NN} \end{pmatrix} \tag{10}$$

which is an element-wise operation between $L$ and $C$. Given a pair of surfaces, the matrix $O$ can tell the whether the relation between the two surfaces is convex and connected simultaneously. As we need merge all connected nodes in the matrix $O$, a common method is disjoint-set [10], but this method needs to know the superiors node. In this paper, we only care about the relations in the same level instead of the hierarchy, so we define an appropriate matrix arithmetic based on this kind of relation to complete the merger as

$$C_{n \times n} = A_{n \times n} \times B_{n \times n} \tag{11}$$

where the operation of $\times$ is defined as

$$c_{ij} = \cup_{k=1}^{n} a_{ik} \cap b_{kj} \tag{12}$$

with $a \cap b = \min(a, b)$ and $a \cup b = \max(a, b)$. To extract the partition from $O$, we compute the matrix $C = O^{\lambda}$ with elements $c_{ij} = 1$ indicating that there is a path from node $i$ to node $j$ with length of $\lambda$. By aggregating the $C$ with different steps on $O$, we have

$$H = O + O^2 + \dots + O^{\lambda} \tag{13}$$

After that we can extracted the all connected components from $H$, each of which indicated for a single object, i.e. the result of the object segmentation. An example is shown in Fig. 3.

### 3.4    Pose Estimation and Grasping Selection

Our main grasping application is picking objects in logistics industry. Most of objects in this scenario are packaged by textureless boxes that means we need to partition boxes from the scenes of shelves, estimate the pose of the boxes and determine which box to grasp first. By applying the segmentation algorithm, we could get the surfaces set $S_i = \{S_i^1, S_i^2, \dots, S_i^{M_i}\}$ of an object $obj_i$ and the surfaces centroid normals set $\boldsymbol{N}_i = \{\boldsymbol{n}_i^1, \boldsymbol{n}_i^2, \dots, \boldsymbol{n}_i^{M_i}\}$ of the object $obj_i$.

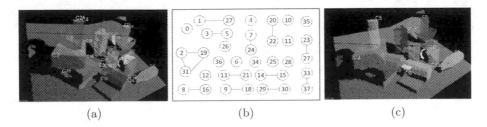

|     |     |     |
| (a) | (b) | (c) |

**Fig. 3.** (a) is over segmented result of a scene and right is the undirected graph of (b) and all edges are satisfied the Euclidean distance requirement and convex shape relationship. (c) is the result of merging all connected nodes in undirected graph of left.

The surfaces are sorted by the number of points contained. At the initial step, we need to select the surface with largest number of points, $S_i^{max}$ and the second largest surface, $S_i^{mid}$ as the major surfaces. Then rotate the largest surface normal in parallel to the z-axis and move the centroid of box to the origin of the coordinate system. Finally the object is rotated so that the normal of the second largest surface can coincide with y-axis. The processing of this bounding box computation is shown in Fig. 4.

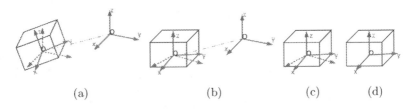

|     |     |     |     |
| (a) | (b) | (c) | (d) |

**Fig. 4.** (a) is the original pose which need to be rotated and transformed to center coordinate. (b) is the result of rotating the largest surface normal parallel to z-axis. (c) is the result of moving the box centroid to the origin and (d) is the result of rotating the second largest surface normal coincides with y-axis.

The hypothesis we make is that the more points contained in a bounding box, the easier object can be grasped. It is equivalent to that the more information we use to estimate the object bounding box, the less uncertainty the estimated pose is, and hence can be grasped accurately. As we see in Fig. 5, some boxes cannot bound the corresponding object well because some of them are only estimated by very limited surfaces, leading to the low confident estimation. This measure relates the uncertainty of the pose estimation to the grasping planning. For the second hypothesis, we consider that if the object is at the bottom, it is obviously harder to grasp rather than the other objects above. This measure is more direct, an object at the bottom generally occluded by the top objects, which can also confuse the segmentation algorithm which we mentioned before as failure case.

Therefore, with this measure, the occlusion can be better controlled. When the top objects are removed, the segmentation and pose estimation of object originally occluded can be increased undoubtedly. We combine both hypothesis that the most covered and the top object should be grasped first. Specifically, we define the size of $obj_i$ as $Size_i = \{w_i, h_i, l_i\}$ which is easy to obtain after the processing shown in Fig. 4. The coverage ratio $cov_i = Ps_i/Es_i$ of object $obj_i$ is calculated on the binary masks $Es_i$ which is a overlapping operation between the re-projected box and the re-projected point cloud of object $obj_i$ in the current view. The object $obj_i$ centroid center in z-axis is $z_i$ and the maximum in z-axis of all objects is $z_{max}$. So the ratio of position in z-axis is $zcov_i = z_i/z_{max}$. The two factors are combined by the importance that the position is more important than the coverage ratio, deriving the confidence of grasping about $obj_i$:

$$confidence_i = 0.3cov_i + 0.7zcov_i \tag{14}$$

$confidence_i$ is employed to order the objects for grasping proposal suggestions.

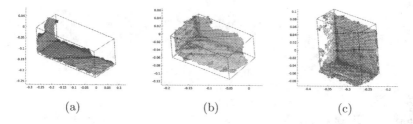

(a)                          (b)                          (c)

**Fig. 5.** Some objects pose estimation results.

## 4    Experiments and Results

In this section we evaluate our algorithm both qualitatively and quantitatively. The employed dataset used in the experiment are all public open datasets, called Object Segmentation Database (OSD) [20] and Cluttered Table Database (CTD) [8]. The proposed algorithm is compared with other segmentation algorithm from [22,24]. In addition, the proposed framework was connected to a robot arm for real-world grasping experiment to investigate the possibility of deployment in practical applications.

### 4.1    Object Segmentation Database

The database of OSD contains training set and testing set. The objects in the dataset are mainly isolated boxes or stacked boxes and cylindric objects. There is occlusion between the objects. The proposed algorithm does not require the training set, so we evaluated our algorithm on both training set and testing set. Some qualitative results are shown in Fig. 6. As we can see that even in very cluttered environment, the objects can be segmented clearly. Besides, the quantitative result is also conducted. The version of the OSD is V0.2. In the experiment, the indicator to performance evaluation includes false negative $f_n$, false positive $f_p$ and true positive $t_p$. The pipeline of the result evaluation is shown in Fig. 7. Both segmented result and ground truth are converted into a series of binary masks, of which each mask indicate for one object. Then the overlap of the two masks are used to derive the indicators $f_n$, $f_p$ and $t_p$. Given the $i$th resultant segmentation mask, the positive pixels are denoted as $S_i$, each segmentation mask in the ground truth denoted as $R_j$ is overlapped to $S_i$, deriving $\tilde{t}_{pij}$. Then the $t_p$ for the $i$th mask is assigned as $t_{pi} = \max \tilde{t}_{pij}$. The final average indicator is

$$t_p = \frac{1}{N} \sum_i \tilde{t}_{pi}, \ f_p = \frac{1}{N} \sum_i \tilde{f}_{pi}, \ f_n = \frac{1}{N} \sum_i \tilde{f}_{ni} \qquad (15)$$

where $N$ is the number of objects. Correspondingly, $\tilde{f}_{pi} = S_i - S_i \cap R_{\hat{j}}$ and $\tilde{f}_{ni} = R_{\hat{j}} - S_i \cap R_{\hat{j}}$, where $\hat{j}$ is the index of associated ground truth mask derived from $t_{pi}$.

The quantitative results of the segmentation algorithm with respect to each object in the OSD is shown in Fig. 8. Most of them $t_p$ is high but some of them are low due to irregular shape of the objects or occlusions by other objects. The benchmark on OSD of the quantitative results is shown in Table 1, demonstrating that our approach is able to compete with the state-of-the-art methods in the task of segmenting objects using only depth information. Compared with the method in [22], our method achieves better performance. Besides, our method does not need to change different parameters comparing while careful tuning of parameters $R_{voxel}$, $R_{seed}$ and $\beta_{thresh}$ is required in [22]. As the reference, the method proposed in [24] is slightly better, but not significantly. However, the boost is brought by the RGB information, which however, can be unstable to illumination invariance, possibly calling for feature design tuning in real world deployment. The failure cases are shown in Fig. 9, indicating the two typical reasons: occlusion and non-convex object. We consider that these two cases cannot be handled without other RGB information or higher level of semantics clues.

## 4.2   Grasping Experiment

From both the qualitative and quantitative results conducted above, we can draw the conclusion that the main failure causes are the objects with irregular

Table 1. The performance of the methods on OSD dataset

| Method | Sensor model | $t_p$ | $f_n$ | $f_p$ | Times (s) |
|---|---|---|---|---|---|
| Our method | Depth | $91.3 \pm 6.2$ | $8.7 \pm 6.2$ | $6.3 \pm 8.2$ | 0.8 |
| Stein [22] | Depth | $90.7 \pm 8.7$ | $9.3 \pm 8.7$ | $4.3 \pm 2.5$ | 0.55 |
| Uckermann [24] | RGBD | $96.3 \pm 4.1$ | $3.7 \pm 4.1$ | $2.5 \pm 4.5$ | 0.04 |

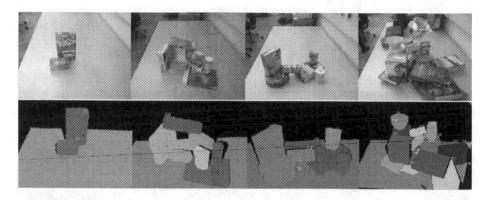

**Fig. 6.** Example results of scenes from OSD dataset and points beyond a distance of 2 m were cropped for visualization.

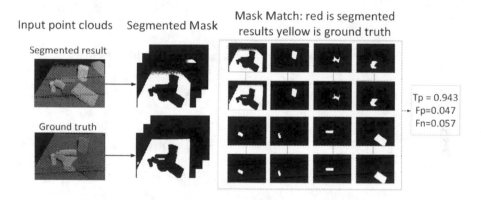

**Fig. 7.** Input the segmented result and ground truth to convert both of them to a series of binary masks. Calculate the overlap of each mask to match the maximum overlap mask and compute the parameters of $f_p$, $f_n$ and $t_p$. (Color figure online)

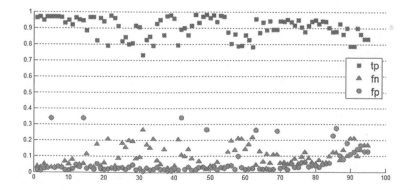

**Fig. 8.** Evaluation results of OSD dataset.

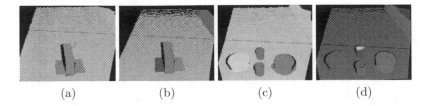

(a)                    (b)                    (c)                    (d)

**Fig. 9.** Images (a), (c) are ground truth of over segmented scenes. And (b) is over segmented result as the deep purple object divided another object into two parts that is difficult to merge just using geometry information. (d) is over segmented as the cup see in the single view but the two part are not tight connection. (Color figure online)

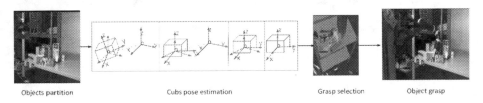

Objects partition            Cubs pose estimation            Grasp selection        Object grasp

**Fig. 10.** Segment current working environment into different objects and estimate each objects pose to plane grasp. (Color figure online)

shapes or the object is occluded by others. For the latter, its is actually not a problem in the scenario of grasping, since it is impossible for the planner to guide the robot to grasp the occluded objects without picking away the objects occluding that. For the former, the scenario is more complex. However, we can control the application to avoid these kind of objects. Therefore the advantage of the proposed algorithm which is robust to the illumination invariance and free of large scale supervised data can be guaranteed. To investigate the possibility of real world deployment for production, we equip the segmentation approach to the Kinova JACO Robotics arm to for completed objects segmentation and grasping. The depth information is provided by ASUS Xtion sensor. The shelf was removed in prior to reduce the computational burden and disturbance. A pipeline of the system is shown in Fig. 10. In our segmentation algorithm we could get the surfaces of object to estimate the pose of objects to decide which object need to grasp or recognize object in the segmented mask that could accelerate the calculation of recognition without sliding window. The video is uploaded in https://youtu.be/RW6pa5SWN-Q. In the video, the object bounded by a red box, is suggested by our system based on the confidence for next-best proposal, which is also highlighted in Fig. 10.

## 5    Conclusion and Further Work

In this work we presented a framework for object segmentation from the cluttered environment using the depth information only, thus robust against the illumination variance and perspective change. Besides, the method does not depends on the model learning, getting rid of collecting massive amount of supervised data. The method is evaluated both qualitatively and quantitatively on OSD and CTD dataset, outperforming the algorithm using the depth information too. The main drawback is that the occlusion and the objects with irregular shape cannot be perfectly handled. However, these drawbacks can be overcame in robot grasping applications with advantages guaranteed at the same time. The success of the deployment of the algorithm in real world experiment indicate that it is possible for real application. In the future, we will focus on solution of the segmentation of objects with non-convex/irregular shapes, so that the application scenario can be further extended.

**Acknowledgment.** This work is supported by the National Nature Science Foundation of China (Grant No. NSFC: U1609210, 61473258 and U1509210).

# References

1. Achanta, R., Shaji, A., Smith, K., Lucchi, A., Fua, P., Süsstrunk, S.: SLIC superpixels compared to state-of-the-art superpixel methods. IEEE Trans. Pattern Anal. Mach. Intell. **34**(11), 2274–2282 (2012)
2. Anguelov, D., Taskar, B., Chatalbashev, V., Koller, D., Gupta, D., Heitz, G., Ng, A.: Discriminative learning of Markov random fields for segmentation of 3D scan data. In: IEEE Computer Society Conference on Computer Vision Pattern Recognition, vol. 2, pp. 169–176 (2005)
3. Barber, B.C., Dobkin, D., Huhdanpaa, H.: The quickhull algorithm for convex hull (2015)
4. Bay, H., Tuytelaars, T., Gool, L.V.: Surf: speeded up robust features. Comput. Vis. Image Underst. **110**(3), 404–417 (2006)
5. Chen, L.C., Papandreou, G., Kokkinos, I., Murphy, K., Yuille, A.L.: Semantic image segmentation with deep convolutional nets and fully connected CRFs. Comput. Sci. **4**, 357–361 (2014)
6. Collet, A., Martinez, M., Srinivasa, S.S.: The moped framework: object recognition and pose estimation for manipulation. Int. J. Robot. Res. **30**(10), 1284–1306 (2011)
7. Couprie, C., Farabet, C., Najman, L., Lecun, Y.: Indoor semantic segmentation using depth information. Eprint arXiv (2013)
8. Ecins, A., Fermuller, C., Aloimonos, Y.: Cluttered scene segmentation using the symmetry constraint. In: IEEE International Conference on Robotics and Automation (2016)
9. Felzenszwalb, P., Huttenlocher, D.: Efficient graph-based segmentation algorithm. IJCV **59**, 167–181 (2014)
10. Gabow, H.N., Tarjan, R.E.: A linear-time algorithm for a special case of disjoint set union. J. Comput. Syst. Sci. **30**(2), 209–221 (1985)
11. Gupta, S., Girshick, R., Arbeláez, P., Malik, J.: Learning rich features from RGB-D images for object detection and segmentation. In: Fleet, D., Pajdla, T., Schiele, B., Tuytelaars, T. (eds.) ECCV 2014. LNCS, vol. 8695, pp. 345–360. Springer, Cham (2014). doi:10.1007/978-3-319-10584-0_23
12. Henry, P., Krainin, M., Herbst, E., Ren, X., Fox, D.: RGB-D mapping: using kinect-style depth cameras for dense 3D modeling of indoor environments. Int. J. Robot. Res. **31**(5), 647–663 (2012)

13. Kappler, D., Bohg, J., Schaal, S.: Leveraging big data for grasp planning. In: IEEE International Conference on Robotics and Automation, pp. 4304–4311 (2015)

14. Lenz, I., Lee, H., Saxena, A.: Deep learning for detecting robotic grasps. Int. J. Robot. Res. **34**(4–5), 705–724 (2013)

15. Levine, S., Pastor, P., Krizhevsky, A., Quillen, D.: Learning hand-eye coordination for robotic grasping with deep learning and large-scale data collection. In: Kulić, D., Nakamura, Y., Khatib, O., Venture, G. (eds.) ISER 2016. Springer, Cham (2016)

16. Liao, Y., Kodagoda, S., Wang, Y., Shi, L., Liu, Y.: Understand scene categories by objects: a semantic regularized scene classifier using convolutional neural networks. In: 2016 IEEE International Conference on Robotics and Automation (ICRA), pp. 2318–2325. IEEE (2016)

17. Lowe, D.G.: Distinctive image features from scale-invariant keypoints. Int. J. Comput. Vis. **60**(60), 91–110 (2004)

18. Moosmann, F., Pink, O., Stiller, C.: Segmentation of 3D lidar data in non-flat urban environments using a local convexity criterion. In: 2009 IEEE in Intelligent Vehicles Symposium, pp. 215–220 (2009)

19. Rao, D., Le, Q.V., Phoka, T., Quigley, M., Sudsang, A., Ng, A.Y.: Grasping novel objects with depth segmentation. In: IEEE/RSJ International Conference on Intelligent Robots and Systems, pp. 2578–2585 (2010)

20. Richtsfeld, A., Mörwald, T., Prankl, J., Zillich, M., Vincze, M.: Segmentation of unknown objects in indoor environments. In: 2012 IEEE/RSJ International Conference on Intelligent Robots and Systems, pp. 4791–4796. IEEE (2012)

21. Long, J., Shelhamer, E., Darrell, T.: Fully convolutional networks for semantic segmentation. In: Proceedings of the IEEE Conference on Computer Vision and Pattern Recognition, pp. 3431–3440 (2015)

22. Stein, S.C., Schoeler, M., Papon, J., Worgotter, F.: Object partitioning using local convexity. In: IEEE Conference on Computer Vision and Pattern Recognition, pp. 304–311 (2014)

23. Sung, J., Jin, S.H., Saxena, A.: Robobarista: object part based transfer of manipulation trajectories from crowd-sourcing in 3D pointclouds. arXiv preprint arXiv:1504.03071 (2015)

24. Uckermann, A., Haschke, R., Ritter, H.: Real-time 3D segmentation of cluttered scenes for robot grasping, pp. 198–203 (2012)

25. Vedaldi, A., Soatto, S.: Quick shift and kernel methods for mode seeking. In: Forsyth, D., Torr, P., Zisserman, A. (eds.) ECCV 2008. LNCS, vol. 5305, pp. 705–718. Springer, Heidelberg (2008). doi:10.1007/978-3-540-88693-8_52

26. Wang, Y., Huang, S., Xiong, R., Wu, J.: A framework for multi-session RGBD slam in low dynamic workspace environment. CAAI Trans. Intell. Technol. **1**, 90–103 (2016)

# 3D Motions Planning of Humanoid Arm Using Learned Patterns

Shaofeng Chen[1], Yi Cui[1], Yu Kang[1,2,3(✉)], Yang Cao[1], and Weiguo Song[1]

[1] Department of Automation, University of Science and Technology of China,
Hefei, China
China.kangduyu@ustc.edu.cn
[2] State Key Laboratory of Fire Science, Department of Automation,
Institute of Advanced Technology, University of Science and Technology of China,
Hefei, China
[3] Key Laboratory of Technology in GeoSpatial Information Processing and
Application System, Chinese Academy of Sciences, Beijing, China

**Abstract.** Humanoid arm has a wide range of applications such as automatic assembly and welding. Due to its complex and nonlinear properties, it is difficult to achieve high robustness and fast response synchronously for the motion planning of humanoid arm. Very recently, it has been proved that imitating human movement system can improve the performance of robot control [11]. This paper proposes a new 3D motion planning method of humanoid arm based on habitual planning theory. The method we proposed is a pre-training algorithm to map the target inputs into a series of patterns of the 3D motion space. Therefore, our proposed method can realize 3D motion planning of humanoid arm. The simulation experimental results demonstrate that our proposed method can use a finite number of patterns (143 patterns used in our experiment) to cover most areas (more than 99%) of the 3D motion space of humanoid arm.

## 1 Introduction

Humanoid arm has been widely used in many applications such as automatic assembly and welding after a long period of progress [13]. To complete those intricate tasks, many complicated manipulations are required to be accomplished with high precision and fast response [17]. However, it is difficult to achieve all requirements in practice. Especially when encountering with different application scenarios, high robustness and learning ability of robot are also required [18].

To meet the requirements, not only have some complicated traditional methods achieved great development [3,8,15], but some intelligent control methods is

This work was supported in part by the National Natural Science Foundation of China (61422307 and 61673361) and the Scientific Research Staring Foundation for the Returned Overseas Chinese Scholars. Authors also gratefully acknowledge supports from the Youth Innovation Promotion Association, Chinese Academy of Sciences, the Youth Top-notch Talent Support Program and the Youth Yangtze River Scholar.

F. Sun et al. (Eds.): ICCSIP 2016, CCIS 710, pp. 355–365, 2017.
DOI: 10.1007/978-981-10-5230-9_36

also applied, such as intelligent control [5], neural networks [9] and deep learning [6]. Very recently, H. Qiao et al. [11] proposes to leverage information propagation mechanism of human movement system into motion control of robotics control, firstly apply the habitual planning theory [2] of the motion model of upper limb. This model shows its self-learning ability and robustness to accomplish the motion task. However, it has an important guiding significance, the proposed model in [11] is still a preliminary work. There are still many problems to be solved before applying to the practical scenarios.

In this paper, we extend the initial human-inspired motion model in [11] from the 2D to 3D case, which means that our method can achieve 3D motion planning of humanoid arm. Then we use 3D delaunay triangulation to achieve the decomposing of 3D motion space, thus corresponding patterns of positions in the space are computed by the dynamic and kinematic models [4]. A pre-training algorithm is proposed to design the target positions under an optimization criterion on all the training samples. Our proposed motion planning method is constructed as follows:

⬦ The dynamic model of upper limb is provided by Opensim [10, 12], whose input and output are the neural excitations and the final positions of the upper limb under the restriction of shoulder joint fixed. In order to achieve 3D motion, we relax the limitation on the shoulder joint by using kinematic equation in Sect. 2.1. Training patterns are defined as the final positions of the upper limb in the 3D motion space.

⬦ In the training process, the 3D motion space is first decomposed into k target positions by using 3D delaunay triangulation. A learning algorithm is applied to select m best candidates of target positions (training patterns) on training samples.

⬦ In the testing process, for a new target position, it's generated by a linear combination of its convex hull of the trained patterns. Simulation experiments conducted on the upper limb demonstrate the effectiveness of our proposed method, which used a finite number of patterns (143 patterns used in our experiment) to cover most areas (more than 99%) of the 3D motion space of humanoid arm.

## 2   The Models of the Humanoid Arm

Human upper limb can be seen as a biomechanical system, it can be seen as a four-link system, from top to bottom are the humerus, ulna, radius and hand [10]. In this section, we present the kinematic and dynamic models of humanoid arm. In this section, we will give two different types of humanoid arm model, these two models can be associated with final position.

### 2.1   The Kinematic Model of the Humanoid Arm

Shoulder can be seen as a ball joint having three degrees of freedom. The elbow joint is the hinge connection, with two degrees of freedom. Wrist joint

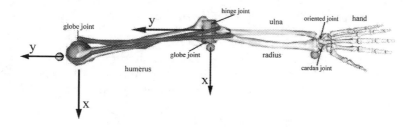

**Fig. 1.** The upper limb

has two degrees of freedom. In our paper, the model is composed of shoulder and elbow joint.

The coordinate system of shoulder and elbow is shown in Fig. 1. The basic coordinate transformation between joint coordinates is as follows:

$$R\left(X, \theta_i\right) = \begin{bmatrix} 1 & 0 & 0 & 0 \\ 0 & \cos\theta_i & -\sin\theta_i & 0 \\ 0 & \sin\theta_i & \cos\theta_i & 0 \\ 0 & 0 & 0 & 1 \end{bmatrix} \quad R\left(Y, \theta_i\right) = \begin{bmatrix} \cos\theta_i & 0 & \sin\theta_i & 0 \\ 0 & 1 & 0 & 0 \\ -\sin\theta_i & 0 & \cos\theta_i & 0 \\ 0 & 0 & 0 & 1 \end{bmatrix}$$

$$R\left(Z, \theta_i\right) = \begin{bmatrix} \cos\theta_i & -\sin\theta_i & 0 & 0 \\ \sin\theta_i & \cos\theta_i & 0 & 0 \\ 0 & 0 & 1 & 0 \\ 0 & 0 & 0 & 1 \end{bmatrix} \quad T\left(a, b, c\right) = \begin{bmatrix} 1 & 0 & 0 & a \\ 0 & 1 & 0 & b \\ 0 & 0 & 1 & c \\ 0 & 0 & 0 & 1 \end{bmatrix} \quad (1)$$

Here, $R\left(X, \theta_i\right)$, $R\left(Y, \theta_i\right)$, $R\left(Z, \theta_i\right)$ are the rotation matrices about $X, Y, Z$ axis. $T\left(a, b, c\right)$ is the translation matrix. The coordinate transformation matrix from the actuator hand to the shoulder is as follows:

$$_{shoulder}\mathrm{W}^{hand} = R\left(X, \theta_1\right) \cdot R\left(Y, \theta_2\right) \cdot R\left(Z, \theta_3\right) \cdot T\left(l_{1x}, l_{1y}, l_{1z}\right) \cdot R\left(Z, \theta_4\right) \cdot T\left(l_{2x}, l_{2y}, l_{2z}\right) \quad (2)$$

Here, $\theta_1$, $\theta_2$ and $\theta_3$ represent the shoulder joint around the $X$ axis, $Y$ axis and $Z$ axis angle, respectively. $\theta_4$ represents the elbow around its own $Z$-axis angle. $l_1$ and $l_2$ are the lengths of the boom and the arm, respectively. Table 1 shows the rotation range of each joint:

**Table 1.** The limit of the joint angle

| Joint angle | Maximumvalue (°) | Minimum value (°) |
|---|---|---|
| $\theta_1$ | −80 | 45 |
| $\theta_2$ | −100 | 25 |
| $\theta_3$ | −90 | 135 |
| $\theta_4$ | 0 | 130 |

## 2.2   The Dynamic Models of the Humanoid Arm

Pennestri et al. [10] and Reinbolt et al. [12] proposed a simplified model of the upper limb by Opensim, which fixes the shoulder joint in the state of nature and has two joints and six muscles. The motion of the upper arm in response to the neural excitation [1] can be described by the following equations:

$$
\begin{cases}
\dot{a}\,(t) = \begin{cases} (u\,(t) - a\,(t)) \left[ \frac{u(t)}{\tau_{act}} + \frac{1-u(t)}{\tau_{deact}} \right] & u\,(t) \geq a\,(t) \\ \frac{u(t)-a(t)}{\tau_{deact}} & u\,(t) < a\,(t) \end{cases} \\
F_m = F_0 \left( f_1 f_2 a\,(t) + f_3 \right) \\
\ddot{q} = A^{-1(q)} \left\{ R\,(q)\, F_m + G\,(q) \right\}
\end{cases}
\tag{3}
$$

Where $a\,(t)$ is the muscle activation, $u\,(t)$ is the muscle excitation and $\tau_{act}$ and $\tau_{deact}$ are the time constants for activation and deactivation, respectively. Equation (3) shows that, the muscle forces $F_m$ depends on the fiber $l_m$, contraction velocity $v_m$ and the state of the muscle activation $a_t$ [16,19]. The specific forms of $f_1$, $f_2$ and $f_3$ are shown as below:

$$
\begin{cases}
f_1 = e^{\left[ -40(x-0.45)^4 + (x-0.95)^2 \right]} \\
f_2 = 1.6 - 1.6 e^{\left[ \frac{-1.1}{(-v+1)^4} + \frac{0.1}{(-v+1)^2} \right]} \\
f_3 = 1.3 \arctan \left[ 0.1 \left( (x - 0.22)^{10} \right) \right] \\
x = \frac{l_m}{l_0} \text{ and } v = \frac{v_m}{2.5}
\end{cases}
\tag{4}
$$

In the Eq. (3), $q$ is the generalized coordinates of the model and $\ddot{q}$ is the accelerations. $A^{-1}$ is the inverse of system mass matrix, $G$ is other environment forces, $R$ is a matrix of muscle moment arms.

To estimate the motion in the space, we don't fix the shoulder joint, we combine the equations in this section to get a series of the joint angles.

$$
\begin{cases}
x = l_1 \sin \alpha \cos \gamma + l_2 \sin (\alpha + \beta) \cos \gamma \\
y = -l_1 \cos \alpha - l_2 \cos (\alpha + \beta) \\
z = l_1 \sin \alpha \sin \gamma + l_2 \sin (\alpha + \beta) \sin \gamma
\end{cases}
\tag{5}
$$

where $\alpha$, $\beta$ and $\gamma$ are the angles of the upperlower joint and shoulder rotate, respectively.

## 3   Motion Control Method Based on Patterns

Habitual planning theory [2] proposed that people tend to use the learned patterns to accomplish a new motion task. Our control task is the position which we expect the humanoid arm to reach. In this section, we explain how to construct patterns and use them to generate target positions, realize the motion control of the humanoid arm, prove the convergence of the method.

## 3.1   Constructing Patterns in the Motion Space

Through the relationship of the two models in Sect. 2, when given a final position, we can get the shoulder joint and muscle excitations when shoulder joint fixed on this angle. So we can only give muscle excitations corresponding a series of different shoulder angles. The pattern is composed of these two parts. The specific processes are shown in below:

Step 1: According to the motion space, design a series of positions which can describe the motion space sufficiently. Here we use $P = \{p_1, p_2, p_3, \cdots, p_k\}$ to represent them.

Step 2: According to the inverse dynamic process and the kinematic model of the humanoid arm, we get the shoulder joint and muscle excitations of these designed positions of the shoulder joint $\gamma$. Here, we use $U = \{u_1, u_2, u_3, \cdots, u_k\}$ to represent them, and $u_i \in \mathbb{R}^{6 \times m}$, where six represents neural excitation of the six muscles, and n is the dimension of each neural excitation.

Step 3: Using the forward dynamic and kinematic model, we can get the actual positions the upper limb reaches, here we use $P' = \{p_1', p_2', p_3', \cdots, p_k'\}$ to represent them.

Step 4: We select appropriate $m$ positions $P'$, corresponding neural excitations $U$, shoulder joint angles $\gamma$ as patterns. And we should design appropriate patterns, according to the size of the motion space and the requirement of control accuracy. The 47 patterns constructing process schematic is shown in Fig. 3.

## 3.2   3-D Delaunay Triangulation Based on Patterns

Here, we use $P = \{p_1, p_2, p_3, \cdots, p_k\}$ to represent the positions corresponding to the patterns. These positions constitute the sample set in the three-dimensional space. In this paper, we use the synthetic algorithm [7] to divide the space. The motion space is divided into a series of tetrahedrons. Every vertice of the tetrahedron represents a pattern. Here we restrict the motion space to a cube (Fig. 2).

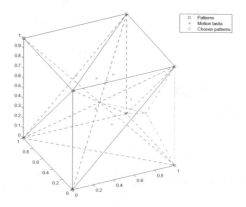

**Fig. 2.** Nine patterns division diagram

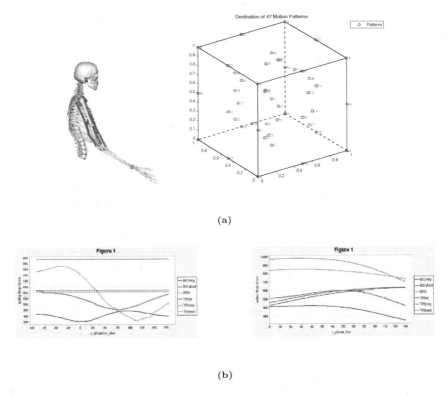

(a)

(b)

**Fig. 3.** The constructed patterns. **Note:** (a) is the positions of the 47 patterns generated by the inverse dynamic process; (b) is the neural excitations of the third pattern in (a)

When given a target position $p_t = \{x_t, y_t, z_t\}$, we need to find the tetrahedron including the position firstly. Then, we use the four vertices to generate the target position. The specific algorithm is as follows:

$$p_t = \sum_i \omega_i p_i \ , \ i = 1, 2, 3, 4 \tag{6}$$

$$\omega_i = \frac{\frac{1}{\|\Delta p_i\|}}{\sum_j \frac{1}{\|\Delta p_j\|}} \ , \ j = 1, 2, 3, 4 \tag{7}$$

$$\|\Delta p_i\| = \sqrt{(x_i - x_t)^2 + (y_i - y_t)^2 + (z_i - z_t)^2} \tag{8}$$

Here $\omega_i$ represents the weight that each pattern contributes to the target position $p_t$.

### 3.3    The Convergence of the Control Algorithm

As shown in Sect. 3.1, we let the input signal $u \in \mathbb{R}$, which represents 6 dimensional signals from the beginning to the end. The output $p \in \mathbb{R}^3$ represents the final position. We have got a series of patterns which we need in the motion space, we use $Q = \{q_1, q_2, \cdots, q_n\}$ to represent them, here $q_i = \{p_i{'}, u_i, v_i, a_i\}, i = 1, 2, 3, \cdots, n$.

We define function $G : \mathbb{R}^{6 \times T} \to \mathbb{R}^3$, $G$ represents the series of transformations from input signal $u$ to the output signal $p$. As shown in above, we have got $(u_i, p_i), i = 1, 2, \cdots, n$, subject to $p_i = F(u_i)$. The domain of definition is the combination of all convex domain that include $u_i$, represented by A. Similarly, we can get the local domain that contains all covex domain combination of $p_i$.

According to the judgement of convex function in the three dimensional [14], we assume that G is invertible and has second order continuous partial derivative on A. Then $G', G^{-1}$ is all bounded on $A : \exists C_1, C_2 \geq 0, \|G'\| \leq 0, \left\|\left(G^{-1}\right)'\right\| \leq C_2$ on A. When given a target position $p_t = \{x_t, y_t, z_t\}$, the error shrinks as the $p_i$ getting closer to each other:

$$
\begin{aligned}
\Delta e &= \|\tilde{p} - p(t)\| \\
&= \|G(\tilde{u}) - G(u_t)\| \\
&= \left\| G\left(\sum_i \omega_i(u_i - u_t) + \omega_i u_t\right) - G(u_t) \right\| \\
&\approx \left\| G(u_t) + G'(u_t) \sum_i \omega_i(u_i - u_t) - G(u_t) \right\| \\
&\leq \left\| C_0 \sum_i \omega_i(u_i - u_t) \right\| \\
&\approx C_0 \left\| \sum_i \omega_i F^{-1}(p_t) \Delta p_i \right\| \\
&\leq C_0 C_1 \left\| \sum_i \omega_i \Delta p_i \right\| \\
&\leq C \cdot n \cdot max\left(\|p_i - p_j\|\right)
\end{aligned}
\tag{9}
$$

Here $p(t)$ is the target position, $\tilde{p}$ is the position which we use our algorithm to generate.

The above proof illustrates that as more patterns are generated, the control accuracy is convergent, and it won't cause the loss of response rapidity.

## 4    Simulation Experiment

The simulation experiment are implemented by Matlab2015a, OpenSim3.3 and VisualStudio2013. The neuromusculoskeletal system of upper limb is constructed by OpenSim3.3 fixed shoulder joint, the platform gives the neural excitation of the six muscles in designed positions. We use VisualStudio2013 to realize three-dimensional Delaunay triangulation algorithm.

### 4.1    Experimental Process and Results

An illustration of the presented motion control method is provided in Fig. 4. It displays the motion of the humanoid arm under the control of the calculated excitation. Because we don't have shoulder muscle model, it is replaced with the rotation angle. As shown in Fig. 4, the actual position and the target position are very close, as the presented control method can attain a small control error. To confirm the effectiveness and precision of the presented motion control method, we devise a series of experiments. The experiment steps are as follows:

Step 1: Construct nine patterns via the method of Sect. 3.1 in given motion space $\Omega$ for target positions.

Step 2: Randomly select 24 target positions $P$ within the space $\Omega$. The actual positions $P'$ are generated with the presented method described in Sect. 3.2.

Step 3: Append new patterns within the space $\Omega$. Then repeat step 1–2 to validate the motion control method has a growing number of patterns.

Step 4: Repeat steps 1–3 for three times.

For each of the target positions, we examine the control errors of the presented method. The control error is computed by the absolute error, as follows:

$$e = \frac{\sqrt{(x - x')^2 + (y - y')^2 + (z - z')^2}}{\sqrt{x^2 + y^2 + z^2}} \tag{10}$$

Here $(x, y, z)$, $(x', y', z')$ mean the target position and actual position, correspondingly. The result is displayed in Table 2.

A series of experimental results are shown in Fig. 4. The patterns are denoted as red circles in the figure. The target positions are represented by blue stars. The actual positions are denoted as pink plus sign. The neural excitations corresponding to the actual positions are generated by a combination of the nearest tetrahedron as shown in Sect. 3.2.

The error of the control method is computed by the following method:

$$E = \sum_i \frac{\|p_i - p_i'\|^2}{n} \tag{11}$$

Here $n$ is the number of the target positions, $p_i$ is the position of the target $i$ and $p_i'$ is the actual position gained by the presented control method. The results are shown in Fig. 4(f).

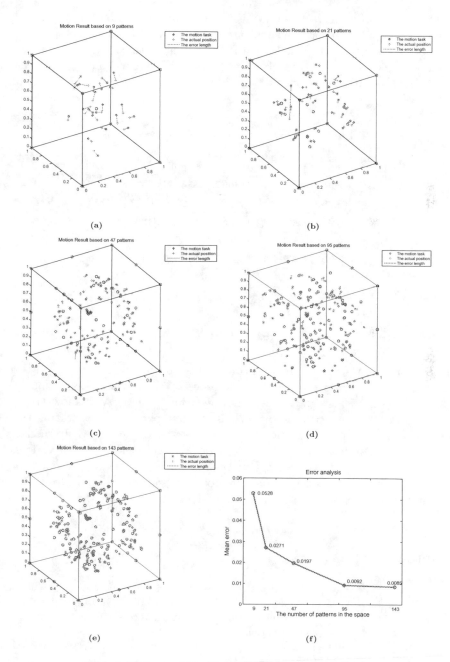

**Fig. 4.** The experiment results (Color figure online)

Over the experiments above, we can obtain the conclusions below:

1. The actual positions recline very near to the target positions in all the experiments. The experiments demonstrate the efficiency of the presented method.
2. The control errors get smaller with denser patterns. When there are more patterns in space, the control accuracy becomes higher. The average error reduces promptly in the opening and progressively converges to a small value.

**Table 2.** The control error of the proposed method

| No. of patterns | Motion targets | Actual position | Absolute error (%) |
|---|---|---|---|
| 9 | $(0.36, 0.89, 0.34)$ | $(0.3607, 0.8369, 0.3537)$ | 5.28 |
| 21 | $(0.36, 0.89, 0.34)$ | $(0.3385, 0.8725, 0.3444)$ | 2.71 |
| 47 | $(0.36, 0.89, 0.34)$ | $(0.3681, 0.8733, 0.3485)$ | 1.97 |
| 95 | $(0.36, 0.89, 0.34)$ | $(0.3528, 0.8844, 0.3374)$ | 0.92 |
| 143 | $(0.36, 0.89, 0.34)$ | $(0.3575, 0.8835, 0.3345)$ | 0.85 |

## 5    Conclusion and Future Work

In this work, we present the motion control method based on patterns in three-dimensional space, and prove the convergence of the method. To demonstrate its effectiveness, we design a series of experiments. The results show that the control precision can reach more than ninety-nine percent in generating target positions. Our main contribution is extending the motion space from flat to three-dimensional space which has a great practical significance. We do not, however, perform our experiments in the actual platform and we don't have the shoulder's musculoskeletal model by now. Future work will aim to do direct experiments on a practical platform. We will also try to apply deep learning on this issue.

## References

1. Davis, A.M., Beaton, D.E., Hudak, P., Amadio, P., Bombardier, C., Cole, D., Hawker, G., Katz, J.N., Makela, M., Marx, R.G., et al.: Measuring disability of the upper extremity: a rationale supporting the use of a regional outcome measure. J. Hand Ther. **12**(4), 269–274 (1999)
2. De Rugy, A., Loeb, G.E., Carroll, T.J.: Muscle coordination is habitual rather than optimal. J. Neurosci. **32**(21), 7384–7391 (2012)
3. Dieulot, J.-Y., Colas, F.: Robust pid control of a linear mechanical axis: a case study. Mechatronics **19**(2), 269–273 (2009)

4. Holzbaur, K.R., Murray, W.M., Delp, S.L.: A model of the upper extremity for simulating musculoskeletal surgery and analyzing neuromuscular control. Ann. Biomed. Eng. **33**(6), 829–840 (2005)
5. Koker, R., Ferikoglu, A.: Model based intelligent control of a 3-joint robotic manipulator: a simulation study using artificial neural networks. In: Aykanat, C., Dayar, T., Körpeoğlu, İ. (eds.) ISCIS 2004. LNCS, vol. 3280, pp. 31–40. Springer, Heidelberg (2004). doi:10.1007/978-3-540-30182-0_4
6. Lenz, I., Lee, H., Saxena, A.: Deep learning for detecting robotic grasps. Int. J. Robot. Res. **34**(4–5), 705–724 (2015)
7. Liu, N., Yin, Y., Zhang, H.: A fingerprint matching algorithm based on delaunay triangulation net. In The Fifth International Conference on Computer and Information Technology (CIT 2005), pp. 591–595. IEEE (2005)
8. Nagurka, M.L.: Optimal design of robotic manipulator trajectories: a nonlinear programming approach (1987)
9. Nørgård, P.M., Ravn, O., Poulsen, N.K., Hansen, L.K.: Neural Networks for Modelling and Control of Dynamic Systems-A Practitioner's Handbook. Springer, London (2000)
10. Pennestri, E., Stefanelli, R., Valentini, P.P., Vita, L.: Virtual musculo-skeletal model for the biomechanical analysis of the upper limb. J. Biomech. **40**(6), 1350–1361 (2007)
11. Qiao, H., Li, C., Yin, P., Wei, W., Liu, Z.-Y.: Human-inspired motion model of upper-limb with fast response and learning ability-a promising direction for robot system and control. Assem. Autom. **36**(1), 97–107 (2016)
12. Reinbolt, J.A., Seth, A., Delp, S.L.: Simulation of human movement: applications using OpenSim. Procedia IUTAM **2**, 186–198 (2011)
13. Rivas, D., Alvarez, M., Velasco, P., Mamarandi, J., Carrillo-Medina, J.L., Bautista, V., Galarza, O., Reyes, P., Erazo, M., Pérez, M., et al.: BRACON: control system for a robotic arm with 6 degrees of freedom for education systems. In: 2015 6th International Conference on Automation, Robotics and Applications (ICARA), pp. 358–363. IEEE (2015)
14. Schmidt, M., Roux, N.L., Bach, F.R.: Convergence rates of inexact proximal-gradient methods for convex optimization. In: Advances in Neural Information Processing systems, pp. 1458–1466 (2011)
15. Soltanpour, M.R., Khalilpour, J., Soltani, M.: Robust nonlinear control of robot manipulator with uncertainties in kinematics, dynamics and actuator models. Int. J. Innov. Comput. Inf. Control **8**(8), 5487–5498 (2012)
16. Thelen, D.G., Anderson, F.C.: Using computed muscle control to generate forward dynamic simulations of human walking from experimental data. J. Biomech. **39**(6), 1107–1115 (2006)
17. Tondu, B.: Kinematic modelling of anthropomorphic robot upper limb with human-like hands. In: International Conference on Advanced Robotics, ICAR 2009, pp. 1–9. IEEE (2009)
18. Tzvetkova, G.V.: Robonaut 2: mission, technologies, perspectives. J. Theor. Appl. Mech. **44**(1), 97–102 (2014)
19. Zajac, F.E.: Muscle and tendon properties models scaling and application to biomechanics and motor. Critical Rev. Biomed. Eng. **17**(4), 359–411 (1989)

# In-hand Manipulation with Fixed and Spring Support Fingers

Junhu He$^{(\boxtimes)}$, Sicong Pu, and Jianwei Zhang

Department of Computer Science,
Institute of Technical Aspects of Multimodal Systems,
University of Hamburg, Vogt-Koelln-Strasse 30, 22527 Hamburg, Germany
he@informatik.uni-hamburg.de

**Abstract.** In-hand manipulation is one of distinctive skills in anthropomorphic hands. Lots of research has been done, however modeling the process of robotic in-hand manipulations is a challenging topic in robotics. In this paper, a novel in-hand manipulation model is proposed based on push and support fingers. In this model, we consider the in-hand manipulation process as a finger pushing an unknown object to roll onto other fingers, where only one finger is controlled actively to push the in-hand object. This actively controlled finger is called push finger. Moreover the support fingers also play important roles. Two kinds of support fingers are proposed in this model: fixed support finger and spring support finger. The fixed support finger is uncontrolled and fixed as a pivot around which the object rotates. The spring support finger performs as an elastic spring. It can not only press the object against other fingers to ensure the stability of the system but also can help to rotate the object with proper contact force. To achieve the spring-like attribute, a stiffness controller was applied on the spring support finger. At last, in-hand manipulation experiments have been carried out successfully on a real anthropomorphic hand platform to verify the feasibility of our proposed model. Although the object's rotated angle is small in experiments, our proposed method has great potential in perceiving interaction state of the in-hand manipulation system.

**Keywords:** In-hang manipulation · Dexterous manipulation · Compliance control · Anthropomorphic hand · Robotic hand

## 1 Introduction

In last decade, many famous anthropomorphic robotic hands have become available off-the-shelf, such as Shadow Hand [1], Robonaut Hand [2], and DLR/HIT Hand [3]. Extensive research of objects' grasping has been done on them. To date, besides grasping, in-hand manipulations (also named re-grasping or dexterous manipulation) are required by increasing demands on flexible interaction tasks.

This research was funded by Crossmodal Learning DFG and NSFC, TRR-169, and partially supported by CINACS DFG IGK 1247.

© Springer Nature Singapore Pte Ltd. 2017
F. Sun et al. (Eds.): ICCSIP 2016, CCIS 710, pp. 366–381, 2017.
DOI: 10.1007/978-981-10-5230-9_37

According to the research in [4], an in-hand manipulation system is a cooperation of robotic fingers attached to a base, and an object is grasped or manipulated by changing the contact force applied by the fingers. In general grasping and in-hand manipulation research, tasks are achieved based on synthesis models where complete knowledge of robots, target objects and physical laws is modeled explicitly. With this method, one of the most impressive demonstrations is high-speed manipulations [5], in which robot-object interaction models were analyzed explicitly to predict the next state of their system. Obviously, synthetic operations are labor intensive and sensitive to model parameters. Moreover, sometimes planning under contact conditions is impractical due to the computational complexity and the lack of precise and robust dynamic models. Due to the complexity of interaction models, this method is error prone in controlling of fingers' interaction (Fig. 1).

Without precise models, adaptive force control methods offer another way to in-hand manipulation. In robotics, contact force plays an important role in compensating these errors generated by the 'poor' models. In [6], Li and Kao modeled dexterous manipulation with soft contacts and their robotic hand was controlled with a stiffness controller. Biagiotti et al. [7] designed a Cartesian impedance controller for in-hand manipulation. Generally, the contact force is sensitive to the contact state including fingers' relative position, contact area, object's attributes, etc. In the force based in-hand manipulations, all grasping fingers are equipped with force control algorithms. All the fingers have to properly assign the contact force among them. However, it makes the system too complex to be implemented.

**Fig. 1.** In-hand manipulation with spring support fingers.

In this paper, an adaptive in-hand manipulation is proposed to help the robot perceive the interaction state of its in-hand system. In this manipulation, a simple model based on push and support fingers is proposed. In this method, only one finger is actively controlled to push and roll an object onto support fingers. Of these support fingers, one is only passively controlled based on the contact force in the process of manipulation. It is named spring support finger. This spring support finger performs as an elastic spring which keeps pressing the object against other fingers to ensure a stable grasp with proper contact force. Besides, with the help of the spring support finger, it is easier for another finger to push the object forward on the support fingers. Hence our proposed model can dramatically reduces the complexity of in-hand manipulation model.

This paper is organized as follows: In Sect. 2, related works are introduced and the research concept is presented. In Sect. 3, our proposed in-hand manipulation models are introduced. Then in Sect. 4, an in-hand manipulation platform is built for real robotic experiments. Finally, in Sect. 5 in-hand manipulation experiments are carried out to verify our propose model.

## 2    Related Works and Research Concept

In robotic manipulation systems, it is important to model the robot-object interaction properties. Normally, this requires the specific knowledge of the system from precise object-hand models. However, this is a difficult road to take. [8] To avoid building these precise synthesis models, generally, there are two approximate methods: virtual frame and virtual linkage.

### 2.1    Virtual Frame and Virtual Linkage

In [9], instead of using any precise information on the system, virtual data relating to the position and attitude is defined as a virtual frame. The virtual object frame is based at a virtual object position, which is a centroid of a triangle consisting of each center of fingertips, as shown in Fig. 2.

Besides the position, at the object level, the robot hand must assign the grasping force to each contact point under frictional and stability constraints. In order to model the internal force, a concept called virtual linkage is introduced in [10]. The virtual linkage is a mechanism with 6 degrees of freedom in n-grasp manipulation tasks. In [11] Stramigioli introduced a grasping model with the concept of a virtual object considering the net forces applied to the object. In [12] Wimböck, Ott et al. applied an intrinsically passive control (IPC) into Stramigioli's virtual object to realize object motions and grasping force. Its control law takes a desired object frame and desired grasping forces as inputs. Although a lot of work has been done, better and more efficient methods are still required.

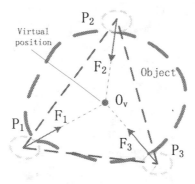

**Fig. 2.** Object virtual frame

## 2.2   Research Concept and In-hand Manipulation Process

In virtual linkage models, all grasping fingers have to carry out force control algorithms to assign the contact force to each other. This makes the system too complex and sometimes even unstable. In this paper, we simplify the force control system by regarding the in-hand manipulation as an action pushing an object to roll onto support fingers. In this process only one push finger is actively controlled according to the manipulation commands, and only one spring support finger is equipped with a force controller to generate compliance behaviors according to the contact on it. Our method is a kind of combination of the virtual frame and virtual linkage methods. On one hand, the object is treated as an object frame (a ball or a triangle); on the other hand fingers are controlled respectively with different controllers. Specially, the spring support finger is as an one dimensional linkage in the manipulation process.

Therefore, in our previous research [13], the object was realized as a ball and the grasping fingers form an elastic surface (elastic fingertip of the fixed support fingers), shown in Fig. 3. Hence for in-hand manipulation, the model is simplified to the thumb pushing a ball to roll onto an elastic surface. However, in our previous work, the elastic surface is uncontrolled; and the push finger is only thumb. Differently, in this paper, the push finger is index finger; and the elastic surface is changed through adding a force controller to one finger.

Furthermore, in this paper we define the grasping fingers with push finger, fixed support finger and spring support finger according to their contributions to manipulations. The push finger is controlled actively to move forward in given directions. According to its action the object is pushed to roll onto the support fingers. The fixed support finger is not controlled. It is fixed as a pivot to keep the position of the object. The spring support finger is controlled passively as a spring, and its position changes only according to the contact force on it. Its function is to press the object with proper contact to the other fingers. With the cooperation among these fingers, an adaptive in-hand manipulation can be achieved easily. Generally, the in-hand manipulation in this paper is conducted

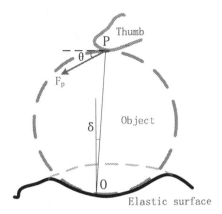

**Fig. 3.** Elastic surface support model.

as follows: the push finger pushes the object to roll onto the fixed support finger with the help of the spring support finger.

Intuitively, any grasping fingers can play the role of support springs around the object. However, too many elastic springs make the interaction more complex and even unpredictable. Hence, in this paper we focus on manipulations with one spring support finger and one fixed support finger.

## 3    Manipulation Model

In this paper, the contact model we adopted is the point contact with friction (PCWF), which is one of the most frequently used contact models in robotic grasping and in-hand manipulation. Thus in our research the following assumptions are considered:

- All robot actions take place within its workspace;
- The manipulating processes are quasi-static (moves with low velocity);
- The fingers and the object are always in physical contact;
- Every grasping finger has only one contact point located in the center of its fingertip.

### 3.1    Spring Support Manipulation Model

We model our in-hand manipulation system with a cooperation of robotic fingers attached to a base, and an object is moved by changing the fingers' position, as shown in Fig. 4.

In this section, we discuss a planar rotation task in 2D space, which is required in opening bottle tasks. As in robotic domestic tasks, to open a bottle is a very common tasks for an anthropomorphic hand. In Fig. 4, the spring support finger is represented with a yellow spring; the fixed support finger is represented with a red pivot. Their contact points on the object are named $A$ and $B$. After applying

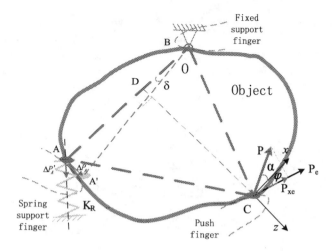

**Fig. 4.** Spring support model. (Color figure online)

a push to the object at the point $C$, the object rotates at an angle $\delta$. In this model, the push frame **C** is defined with its $z$ axis perpendicular to line $AB$ and with its origin locates at contact point $C$ on the object. To spring support frame **A**, its origin locates at contact point $A$ with its $x$ axis parallel to the spring force. Since the spring support frame **A** is not particularly used; it is not plotted in Fig. 4. Therefore, an intuitive finger's movement for the push is

$$\Delta\mathbf{P}_i = \mathbf{R}_i(\delta, g_{conf})\mathbf{P}_i - \mathbf{P}_i, \tag{1}$$

where the $\mathbf{R}_i(\delta, g_{conf})$ is a transformation matrix through which the initial contact point $i$ moves according to the object's rotation. Obviously, the object rotates around the pivot at point $B$. Hence the transformation matrix $\mathbf{R}_i$ depends on the initial grasping configuration $g_{conf}$ (position of the contact points $A$, $B$, and $C$) and the object's rotation angle $\delta$. Term $\mathbf{P}_i$ is the initial position of finger $i$, where $i$ is used to note the fingers and their contact points, $i = A$ or $C$.

In this model, the object rotates around a pivot, as shown in Fig. 5. As virtual frames as in [9] are very suitable here, a virtual triangle object frame is used which is represented by the contact points on the object. As assumed, there is no slippage in this manipulation, thus the dimension of the object triangle frame is constant. From the geometrical relationship, we have

$$\begin{aligned}\|\Delta\mathbf{P}_A\| &= L_A\sqrt{2(1 - cos\delta)}, \\ &\approx L_A\delta,\end{aligned} \tag{2}$$

and

$$\|\Delta\mathbf{P}_C\| \approx L_C\delta, \tag{3}$$

where term $L_A$ is the distance between contact points $B$ and $A$, and term $L_C$ is the distance between contact points $B$ and $C$. In Fig. 4, besides the pivot, the finger on $B$ is controlled as a spring support and the other one is the push finger in the object's counterclockwise manipulation tasks. In fact they are exchangeable. For example, if the manipulation task concerns a clockwise rotation, the finger on $C$ should be controlled as a spring support and the finger on $A$ should act as a push finger relevantly.

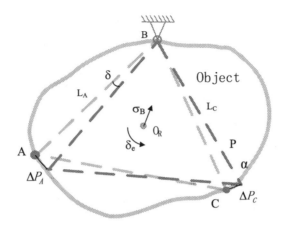

**Fig. 5.** The object rotates around the pivot.

Furthermore, push and spring frames are built as shown in Fig. 4. A push $\mathbf{P}$ is represented by two parameters: push angle $\alpha$ and push distance $P_d$. A push frame is built with its origin at point $C$ and with its $x$ axis perpendicular to line $AB$. In this push frame, the push direction is represented by angle $\alpha$ directly. Obviously, an ideal push is in the direction $P_e$ which is perpendicular to the line $BC$ with the maximum leverage arm. The angle between $P_e$ and axis $x$ is $\varphi$. In this figure, $\varphi$ can be figured out through the geometry information of the frame; however, it is impossible to estimate it directly in real tasks. On one hand, the contact points $A$, $B$, and $C$ are estimated by the center of the fingertips, and the specific contact areas on the fingers are hard to obtain precisely. It makes the dimension of the triangle frame $ABC$ inexact. On the other hand, after a push, there are deformations both on the object and fingers which also change the dimension of the triangle frame slightly. Besides, the errors from the fingers' control make it worse. Since the $\varphi$ is unknown in real tasks, a better way to obtain it is from real experiments with trial and error.

When a push $\mathbf{P}$ is given, it is broken up into two parts. One is in the direction of $\mathbf{P}_e$, named $\mathbf{P}_{xe}$ and the other one is in the direction perpendicular to $\mathbf{P}_e$. Hence we have:

$$P_{xe} = \|\mathbf{P}\|cos(\alpha + \varphi). \tag{4}$$

In a small range, it is approximated to the useful finger movement, $P_{xe} \approx \|\Delta\mathbf{P}_C\|$. According to Eq. 2, we have the relationship between the push and the object's rotation angle:

$$\delta = \frac{P_d cos(\alpha + \varphi)}{L_C}, \tag{5}$$

where $P_d = \|\mathbf{P}\|$ refers to the push distance.

For the spring support finger, since the contact force used in this paper has no direction, a compliance direction is given according to the grasping configuration shown with a black dash line in Fig. 4. Projecting $\Delta\mathbf{P}_A$ (the changed position of $A$) to the spring direction:

$$\Delta P_A^s = \|\Delta\mathbf{P}_A\| cos\gamma, \tag{6}$$

where $\gamma$ refers to the angle between the spring direction and $\Delta\mathbf{P}_A$. Equivalently, we also have:

$$\delta = \frac{\Delta P_A^s}{L_A cos\gamma}. \tag{7}$$

With Eqs. 5 and 7, we have

$$\Delta P_A^s = \frac{L_A P_d cos\gamma cos(\alpha + \varphi)}{L_C}. \tag{8}$$

Hence, a simple way to write Eq. 8 is

$$\Delta P_A^s = K_{rot} P_d cos(\alpha + \varphi), \tag{9}$$

where $K_{rot} = \frac{L_A cos\gamma}{L_C}$ is a constant coefficient, since terms $L_A$, $L_C$, and $\gamma$ are determined by the system structure.

## 3.2 Stiffness Support Fingers

In order to make the spring support finger behave like an elastic spring, we applied stiffness control to the spring support finger. The finger stiffness is

$$f = f_0 + \Delta f,$$
$$\Delta f = \mathbf{K}\Delta P. \tag{10}$$

The term $f$ is the force applied to the fingertip; the $\Delta f$ is the change of force resulting from the change of the position $P$; and the term $\mathbf{K}$ is a stiffness matrix. Combining with Eq. 8, we have

$$\Delta f_C = \frac{L_A K_C cos\gamma P_d cos(\alpha + \varphi)}{L_C}, \tag{11}$$

where $f_C$ refers to the contact force on the spring support finger, and $K_C$ refers to the end stiffness of the spring support finger in its compliance direction.

According to the research in [14], the stiffness matrix $\mathbf{K}$ is set as

$$\mathbf{K} = (\mathbf{C}_s + \mathbf{J}\mathbf{C}_q\mathbf{J}^\mathbf{T})^{-1}, \tag{12}$$

where the $\mathbf{C}_s$ is the structural compliance matrix from the flexible parts of the finger, like the elasticity contact surfaces; the $\mathbf{C}_q$ is the joint compliance diagonal matrix, whose diagonal elements correspond to the stiffness of the joints; and $\mathbf{J}$ is the finger's Jacobian matrix.

The $\mathbf{C}_s$ and $\mathbf{C}_q$ can be set as

$$\begin{aligned} \mathbf{C}_s &= (1/k_{stru})\mathbf{I}, \\ \mathbf{C}_q &= (1/k_{ss})\mathbf{I}, \end{aligned} \tag{13}$$

where the matrix $\mathbf{I}$ is an identity matrix, and the terms $k_{stru}$ and $k_{ss}$ are the structural and the joint stiffness respectively. Hence, for us the structural stiffness $k_{stru}$ is determined by our mechanical system; and the joint stiffness $k_{ss}$ is set by us according to the desired Cartesian stiffness in fingertips. Their effects have been discussed in our previous work. [15] The force control schema is shown in Fig. 6.

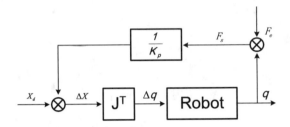

**Fig. 6.** Spring support force control schema.

## 4   In-hand Manipulation System

In order to carry out real in-hand manipulations, a multi-fingered robot hand system is built in this research project.

### 4.1   Anthropomorphic Hand and Contact Sensors

Figure 8 depicts an anthropomorphic robot hand and tactile sensors. The robot hand platform is a shadow hand[1], which takes a truly anthropomorphic approach to robot manipulation, with 19 degrees of freedom.

From the observation of human manipulations, fingertips and distal phalanges are the most used parts in dexterous in-hand manipulations. Therefore in our research only fingertip tactile sensors are adopted. The tactile sensors mounted on our robot hand are BioTac[2]. They have the capabilities of measuring force, vibration and temperature by mimicking human fingers.

---

[1] Shadow dexterous hand: http://www.shadowrobot.com.
[2] Biotac: http://www.syntouchllc.com/.

## 4.2   Vision Tracking System

In order to track the state of the object, the AprilTags system is used in this work. AprilTags is a visual fiducial system [16]. One of its advantages is that it provides a precise 3D position, orientation, and identity of the target object with tags created from an ordinary printer. In Fig. 7, a tag attached to one surface of the object is shown. In in-hand manipulation tasks, the tag faces down; and a normal camera is mounted facing the palm of the hand to make sure the tag is in the field of its vision.

**Fig. 7.** An AprilTag attaches to one surface of the object.

## 5   Experiments

In order to show the feasibility of our proposed method, two manipulation experiments have been carried out on our robot platform. The first one is a push direction experiment, designed to verify the relationship between the push direction and the object's rotation. The second one is a push distance experiment. It is conducted to verify the relationship between the push distance and object's rotation. Besides, the stiffness control performance on the spring support finger is also presented in the push distance experiment.

In these experiments, a stable three fingers grasping is achieved before manipulations. The object is held as shown in Fig. 8. The three grasping fingers are thumb, index finger and ring finger. Specifically, the index finger is conducted as the push finger; the thumb is the fixed support finger; and the ring finger plays the role of the spring support finger. The target object is a foam box with the dimensions of $14.5\,\text{cm} \times 5\,\text{cm} \times 4\,\text{cm}$. The target of our in-hand manipulation is to rotate the object in a horizontal plane. It is worth noting that the horizontal plane in this experiment is defined by the bottom tagged surface of the object after grasping. This renders the hand object system independent of the camera's location. For the spring support finger, the stiffness control frequency is $50\,\text{Hz}$ and the finger stiffness is set to 6.76.

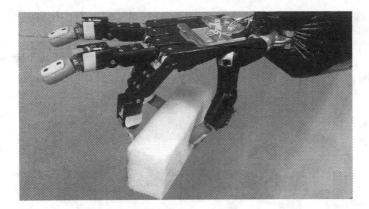

**Fig. 8.** A foam box is grasped with three fingers by the shadow hand.

## 5.1   Push Direction Experiment

In this experiment, the push direction $\alpha$ changes from $-60°$ to $60°$, and the push distance is set to $P_d = 8\,\text{mm}$. In order to facilitate the experiments, the robot moves back to its initial grasping state after each push. Therefore, all the 9 manipulations can be conducted automatically. After that the object is released from the hand. Besides, these manipulation processes are conducted 3 times and their average value is plotted in Fig. 9, where the violet circles are experiment data points. The red line is a regression result with the function of $y = 5.1cos(x - 12.6)$, where $\varphi = -12.6°$. This result fits the Eq. 5.

As a result, the experimental result verifies our proposed model. Furthermore, according to the visual result the best push direction is $\alpha = 12.6°$. It provides us with an optimized push direction for further manipulations.

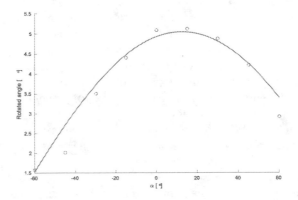

**Fig. 9.** The manipulation result based on different push directions $\alpha$. (Color figure online)

## 5.2   Push Distance Experiment

In this experiment, the push length $P_d$ changes from 4 mm to 10 mm with the step of 1 mm and the push angle is set to $\alpha = 0°$. Equivalently, as we were satisfied with the push direction experiment, these manipulations are carried out 3 times and their average value is used. It is worth noting that the manipulations are evaluated according to the degree of change in the object's position. However, in real tasks, it is almost impossible for the fingers and the object to move within a plane. Therefore the object's rotation is broken down into two directions. One is the direction perpendicular to the horizontal plane, it is the expected rotation in this paper. Hence we adopt it to evaluate the performance of the manipulations. The other direction is in the horizontal plane, it is unexpected movement. Hence it is considered as rotational errors.

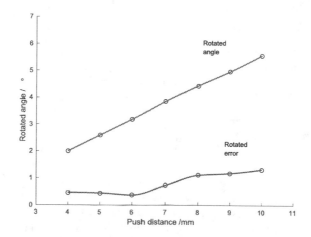

**Fig. 10.** Change in the object's attitude. In this figure, the red line denotes the rotation in the horizontal plane and the gray line refers to the rotation errors. (Color figure online)

The object's rotation is plotted in Fig. 10. In this figure, the red line denotes the rotation angle in the horizontal plane and the gray line refers to the rotational errors. It is easy to find that the rotation angle almost forms a line according to the push distance, which shows a linear relationship between the push distance and the object's rotation. Besides, the rotational errors are small compared to the rotation angle. Unlike the rotation angle, the rotational errors do not exhibit any linear property. Actually, within a small range ($P_d < 6$ mm), they change slowly.

In Fig. 11, the change of the object's position is plotted. Obviously, there is also a linear relationship between the push distance and the change in the object's position. However, its maximum value is 1.2 mm. On one hand, comparing with the change in the object's rotation it is a really small value. On

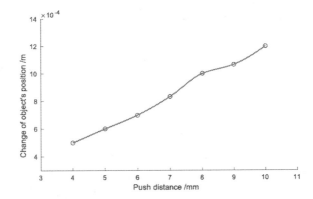

**Fig. 11.** Change in the object's position. It is a distance from the maximum position to the object's initial position in the process of pushes.

the other hand, considering the low control resolution of the finger, it is hard to achieve such a small position change with the robot hand control. Therefore, it can be concluded that it is practical to ignore the position change in our in-hand manipulation method.

### 5.3    Stiffness Control Experiment

The stiffness control performance on the spring support finger is shown in Fig. 12. The dots in this figure are experimental data points; the red solid line denotes the expected stiffness with the function of $y = 6.76x - 7$, where 6.76 is the given stiffness and the 7 is a baseline to compensate the initial grasping force and fingertip position. It is worth noting that the raw data does not lie on the expected stiffness line. This is mainly due to two aspects. Firstly, because of the low resolution of the robot joints which is 1°, the fingers do not move for a small change in the position. Secondly, due to structure compliance, the shadow hand is driven with tendons; even without the force controller the joints still have some compliance attributes that deform them according to the change in external force. Therefore, the fingertip moves when either the direction or the magnitude of the contact force changes.

The contact force is represented with the static pressure value ('PDC' signal in BioTac sensors). Hence, there is no unit for the contact force. In each manipulation, we apply all the contact force to the ground, and record the maximum value for each push.

### 5.4    Discussion

The object rotation angles are very small (7°) in these experiments, due to the joints' limitation of the push finger (index finger). This fits the small range assumption discussed in Sect. 3.1.

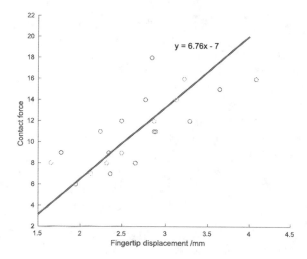

**Fig. 12.** The stiffness of the ring finger. The dots are force position raw data. The red solid line denotes our expected stiffness with the function of $y = 6.76x - 7$. (Color figure online)

**Fig. 13.** Snapshots of one manipulation.

Besides, it is worth noting that even though the in-hand manipulation experiments have been carried out more than 30 times, none of them fails even with intentional disturbances. It shows the robustness of our proposed method. Snapshots of one in-hand manipulation are shown in Fig. 13.

## 6    Conclusions

In this paper, we proposed a novel in-hand manipulation method based on fixed and spring support fingers. In this method, grasping fingers are divided into push finger, fixed support finger and spring support finger. The in-hand manipulation is controlled by having the push finger push the object so that it rolls onto the fixed support fingers with the help of the spring support finger. This method reduces the complexity of in-hand manipulation dramatically.

Finally, real in-hand experiments have been successfully conducted to verify the feasibility of our proposed method. On one hand, the experiments verify the manipulation model presented in Sect. 3.1; on the other hand, the push direction experiment yields the best push direction in the current grasping configuration, which paves the way for our future research. Although the object's rotated angle is small in experiments, our proposed method has great potential in perceiving interaction state of the in-hand manipulation system.

In the future, more experiments will be carried out. With our proposed method, we plan to make the robot explore its in-hand system automatic (push in different directions) to collection sufficient interaction information of its in-hand object. With this collected information, further manipulation tasks can be completed and robotic manipulation skills can be improved.

# References

1. Kochan, A.: Shadow delivers first hand. Ind. Robot Int. J. **32**, 15–16 (2005)
2. Lovchik, C.S., Diftler, M.A.: The robonaut hand: a dexterous robot hand for space. In: IEEE International Conference on Robotics and Automation, pp. 907–912. IEEE, Detroit (1999)
3. Butterfaß, J., Grebenstein, M., Liu, H., Hirzinger, G.: DLR-hand II: next generation of a dexterous robot hand. In: IEEE International Conference on Robotics and Automation, pp. 109–114. IEEE, Seuol (2001)
4. Bicchi, A., Kumar, V.: Robotic grasping and contact: a review. In: IEEE International Conference on Robotics and Automation, pp. 348–353. IEEE, San Francisco (2000)
5. Furukawa, N., Namiki, A., Taku, S., Ishikawa, M.: Dynamic re-grasping using a high-speed multi-fingered hand and a high-speed vision system. In: IEEE International Conference on Robotics and Automation, pp. 181–187. IEEE, Orlando (2006)
6. Li, Y., Kao, I.: A review of modeling of soft-contact fingers and stiffness control for dextrous manipulation in robotics. In: IEEE International Conference on Robotics and Automation, pp. 3055–3060. IEEE, Seuol (2001)
7. Biagiotti, L., Liu, H., Hirzinger, G., Melchiorri, C.: Cartesian impedance control for dexterous manipulation. In: IEEE International Conference on Intelligent Robots and Systems, pp. 3270–3275. IEEE, Las Vegas (2003)
8. Bicchi, A.: Hands for dexterous manipulation and robust grasping: a difficult road toward simplicity. IEEE Trans. Robot. Autom. **16**, 652–662 (2000)
9. Tahara, K., Arimoto, S., Yoshida, M.: Dynamic object manipulation using a virtual frame by a triple soft-fingered robotic hand. In: IEEE International Conference on Robotics and Automation, pp. 4322–4327. IEEE, Alaska (2010)
10. Williams, D., Khatib, O.: The virtual linkage: a model for internal forces in multi-grasp manipulation. In: IEEE International Conference on Robotics and Automation, pp. 1025–1030. IEEE, Atlanta (1993)
11. Stramigioli, S.: Modeling and IPC Control of Interactive Mechanical Systems: A Coordinate-Free Approach. Springer, London (2001)
12. Wimboeck, T., Ott, C., Hirzinger, G.: Passivity-based object-level impedance control for a multifingered hand. In: IEEE International Conference on Intelligent Robots and Systems, pp. 4621–4627. IEEE, Beijing (2006)
13. He, J., Zhang, J.: Push resistance in in-hand manipulation. In: IEEE International Conference on Intelligent Robots and Systems, pp. 2488–2493. IEEE, Chicago (2014)

14. Cutkosky, M.R., Kao, I.: Computing and controlling compliance of a robotic hand. IEEE Trans. Robot. Autom. **5**, 151–165 (1989)
15. He, J., Zhang, J.: In-hand haptic perception in dexterous manipulations. Sci. Chin. Inf. Sci. **57**, 1–11 (2014)
16. ApritTags. http://april.eecs.umich.edu/wiki/index.php/AprilTags

# Cognitive System

# Real-Time Terrain Classification for Rescue Robot Based on Extreme Learning Machine

Yuhua Zhong, Junhao Xiao(✉), Huimin Lu, and Hui Zhang

College of Mechatronics and Automation, National University of Defense
Technology, Changsha 410073, Hunan, China
yuhwachoong@outlook.com, junhao.xiao@ieee.org,
lhmnew@nudt.edu.cn, zhanghui_nudt@126.com

**Abstract.** Full autonomous robots in urban search and rescue (USAR) have to deal with complex terrains. The real-time recognition of terrains in front could effectively improve the ability of pass for rescue robots. This paper presents a real-time terrain classification system by using a 3D LIDAR on a custom designed rescue robot. Firstly, the LIDAR state estimation and point cloud registration are running in parallel to extract the test lane region. Secondly, normal aligned radial feature (NARF) is extracted and downscaled by a distance based weighting method. Finally, an extreme learning machine (ELM) classifier is designed to recognize the types of terrains. Experimental results demonstrate the effectiveness of the proposed system.

**Keywords:** USAR · RoboCup · Real-time · ELM · Terrain classification

## 1 Introduction

Urban search and rescue (USAR) [1] is a branch of rescue tasks concentrates on victim detection and localization from man-made structures, such as collapsed buildings after an earthquake or conflagration. Different from other rescue tasks, such as wilderness rescue which concerns people lost in open spaces, USAR is restricted in highly unstructured closed spaces. Therefore, significant limits are imposed to the size of rescue robots and the types of sensors that can be used.

RoboCup Rescue Robot League (RRL)[1] is an international league of teams that develop and demonstrate advanced robotic capabilities for emergency responders using annual competitions to evaluate and disseminate best-in-class robotic solutions. Standard test methods for rescue robots is offered in RoboCup RRL, which contains 15° and 45° ramps, stairs, inclined planes and others. Considering the ability to pass the complicated terrain, articulated-tracked robot is widely used in RoboCup RRL competitions. Full autonomy rescue mission is a significant part of the competition, in which the rescue robots are required to create maps, plan paths to explore the test lane, search and locate victims.

In order to complete the full autonomy mission, the ability to recognition the terrain in front is essential for rescue robots, which can help the robots to adjust locomotion

---

[1] http://wiki.robocup.org/wiki/Robot_League.

© Springer Nature Singapore Pte Ltd. 2017
F. Sun et al. (Eds.): ICCSIP 2016, CCIS 710, pp. 385–397, 2017.
DOI: 10.1007/978-981-10-5230-9_38

related parameters for better travelability. According to the current RoboCup RRL rules, full autonomy robots should be capable to recognize the 15° and 45° ramp, the ground and the stair, which are shown in Fig. 1.

**Fig. 1.** Four types of terrains in the RoboCup RRL test lane

In this paper, we propose a real-time terrain classification method for rescue robots based on Light Detection and Ranging (LIDAR). It consists of two parts: candidate region extraction and terrain recognition. The experimental results show that the proposed method is able to classify the four types of local terrain online.

The rest of the paper is organized as follow. In Sect. 2, the related works are introduced. In Sect. 3, the experimental system setup is described. In Sect. 4, a LIDAR odometry and mapping (LOAM) [2] based test lane region extraction method is presented in detail. The ELM [3] based online classification terrain classification method is described in Sect. 5. Experimental results and conclusions are presented in Sects. 6 and 7.

Our experimental results can be seen in a publicly available video[2].

## 2   Related Works

The recognition of terrains in front of the rescue robot could be divided into three parts: the test lane region extraction, feature extraction, terrain classification.

For the test lane region extraction, due to the occlusions of single view point, multiple point clouds are required to bring more information of terrains. Therefore, a real-time precise registration method for multiple point clouds is required. As known, the Iterative Closest Point (ICP) algorithm has been widely used for aligning three-dimensional point clouds. However, the ICP algorithm is heavily time-consuming and there are convergence issues. Nuchter et al. [4] presented an ICP-based method to perform simultaneous localization and mapping (SLAM) in a 6-DOF motion

---

[2] http://nubot.trustie.com/videos.

environment. However, the method is high-computational and a coarse pose estimation is necessary which depends on odometry. For the tracked robots, encoder based odometry is inaccurate. Therefore, a straightforward way is to use other sensors for the coarse estimation. For example, Scherer et al. [5] proposed a method to register point clouds by state estimation from visual odometry integrated with an inertial measurement unit (IMU). However, computational issues are more serious if simply using more sensors. Zhang et al. [2] presented a low-drift and real-time SLAM method named LIDAR odometry and mapping (LOAM). The real-time robot state estimation and point cloud registration are done in parallel with low-computational cost by this method.

Researchers have done a lot for the description of point clouds. Features often consist of two parts: the key points and the descriptors. In spatial fields, the key points are usually extracted based on local appearance such as edges or planar patches. Steder et al. [6] proposed a 3D range image feature for object recognition called normal aligned radial feature (NARF). NARF focus on the outer forms of objects and therefore is robust in object recognition. However, the extraction of NARF key points is time-consuming. Lu et al. [7] improved the computational speed using the local coordinate system of scale invariant feature transform (SIFT) key points. Another type of features focus on the local geometry such as fast point feature histograms (FPFH) [8]. FPFH feature describes the local geometry around a point for 3D point cloud. The computational complexity of FPFH is $O(n)$.

Up to now, there have been several machine learning methods applied to improve the recognition performance. Support Vector Machine (SVM) [9] has been widely used for binary classification. And multi-SVM method [10] was proposed to extend for the multi-class classification. GB Huang [3, 11] proposed the extreme learning machine method for exercising a single hidden-layer feedforward neural network with fast training speed, and proved that ELM tends to gain better performance for multiclass classification at fast learning speed.

## 3    System Setup

To facilitate the collection of the test lane LIDAR data, a sensor platform was mounted on a tracked robot. Sensors included a Velodyne VLP-16 LIDAR and an Xsens MTi-10 inertial measurement unit (IMU) for assisting robot pose estimation. The Velodyne VLP-16 LIDAR [12] scans an angular range of 360° in horizontal and 30° in vertical, with a depth range of 100 m, at the frequency of 10 Hz.

As shown in Fig. 2, the Velodyne VLP-16 LIDAR is mounted on the robot horizontally pointing in front. The IMU is attached on the top of the LIDAR. The orientations of IMU and LIDAR are pointing at the same direction.

Two coordinate systems are defined as follows. One is LIDAR coordinate system $\{L\}$, with its origin at the geometric center of the LIDAR, as shown in Fig. 3. The other one is the world coordinate system $\{W\}$, which coincides with $\{L\}$ at the initial pose.

**Fig. 2.** Experimental robot platform

**Fig. 3.** LIDAR coordinate system

## 4 Test Lane Region Extraction

In order to eliminate the disturbance of the walls and audiences outside the test lane, the extraction of test lane region is necessary. Due to the change of the pose of robot on ramps and stairs, simply apply height filter to the point cloud is not enough. Meanwhile, due to the occlusions in a single viewpoint, the registration of multiple point clouds is required.

To overcome these problems, the extraction of test lane region is divided into three stages: the first stage estimates the pose and position of robot with the fusion of point cloud registration and IMU; the second stage registers the point clouds precisely; the final stage filters the test lane region based on prior knowledge.

LIDAR odometry and mapping (LOAM) is proposed by Zhang et al. for real-time low-drift odometry and mapping using a 3D LIDAR moving in 6-DOF. The method achieved both low-drift in motion estimation and low-computational complexity. The key idea of LOAM is to perform odometry algorithm at a higher frequency and mapping algorithm in a lower frequency. The combination of two algorithms allows map creation and pose estimation in real-time. We only used the framework of LOAM, where LIDAR odometry algorithm and LIDAR mapping algorithm are operating in parallel.

### 4.1 Pose Estimation: LIDAR Odometry and IMU Fusion

In the framework of LOAM, an edge and planar feature based fast registration method is applied to get the motion estimation of LIDAR.

We define t as the current time stamp, and $t_k$ as the starting time of the current scan k. Let $T_k^L(t)$ be the LIDAR pose transform between $[t_k, t]$. $T_k^L(t)$ contains the 6-DOF motion of the LIDAR, $T_k^L(t) = \left[\tau_k^L(t), \theta_k^L(t)\right]^T$, where $\tau_k^L = \left[t_x, t_y, t_z\right]^T$ is the translation and $\theta_k^L = \left[\theta_x, \theta_y, \theta_z\right]^T$ is the rotation in $\{L_k\}$. Given $\theta_k^L(t)$, the corresponding rotation matrix can be defined by the Rodrigues formula [13],

$$
R_k^L(t) = e^{\hat{\theta}_k^L(t)} = I + \frac{\hat{\theta}_k^L(t)}{\left\|\theta_k^L(t)\right\|} \sin\left\|\theta_k^L(t)\right\|
$$
$$
+ \left(\frac{\hat{\theta}_k^L(t)}{\left\|\theta_k^L(t)\right\|}\right)^2 \left(1 - \cos\left\|\theta_k^L(t)\right\|\right)
$$

(1)

Where $\hat{\theta}_k^L(t)$ is the skew symmetric matrix of $\theta_k^L(t)$.

Let d be the distances of correspond feature point pairs. Then the LIDAR odometry problem can be defined as the solution of the following equation.

$$
f\left(T_k^L(t)\right) = d, \quad d \to min
$$

(2)

Meanwhile, the integration of IMU data is fused with LIDAR odometry outputs to gain more accurate estimation of motion based on the extended Kalman filter (EKF) [14] method.

### 4.2 Precise Registration: LIDAR Mapping

The mapping algorithm runs at a lower frequency of 1 Hz to reduce the computation. The mapping algorithm matches and registers the point clouds in the world coordinates $\{W\}$. Mapping algorithm is also based on edge and planar feature matching, but extracts 10 times of feature points as in LIDAR odometry algorithm.

The map cloud is downsized by voxel-grid filter each time a new scan is merged with the map in order to distribute the points. The voxel-grid filters average all points in each voxel, leaving an average point in the voxel. Thus the memory usage of the algorithm is limited and the computational speed is ensured. In this paper, we set the voxel leaf size to 2 cm × 2 cm × 2 cm.

### 4.3 Generation of Test Lane Region

To acquire the test lane region, we used the prior knowledge of the test lane. In fact, the test lane region we were interested in is right in front of the robot in the world coordinates. Therefore, the generation of the test lane region is the combination of two steps.

The first step is to fuse the current scan point cloud and the map point cloud. The detail information of surface was lost due to the voxel-grid filter. The fusion of current scan point cloud was the supplement of details. Given the current robot pose and the initial robot pose from the pose estimation, it is easy to transform the current scan point cloud from the LIDAR coordinates $\{L\}$ to the world coordinates $\{W\}$.

The second step is to apply bilateral and height filter to the fused point cloud in the world coordinates $\{W\}$. The size of each square in the test lane is $120\,cm \times 120\,cm$, and the stair is 1.4 m high. In the world coordinates $\{W\}$, the fused point cloud could be easily transformed to the current position without changing the pose. Then the bilateral filter and height filter was applied to the fused point cloud to generate a $240\,cm \times 240\,cm \times 100\,cm$ point cloud, which represents the test lane region in front of the current robot position. The flowchart is shown in Fig. 4, and the sample extracted test lane is shown in Fig. 5.

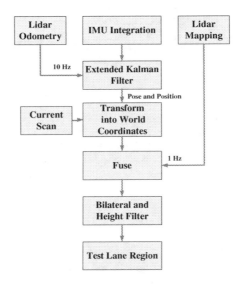

**Fig. 4.** Flow chart of test lane region extraction.

## 5  Recognition of Terrains in Test Lane Region

Once the test lane regions are extracted, the recognition process is initiated. The recognition process is divided into two stages: Feature Extraction and ELM Classifier.

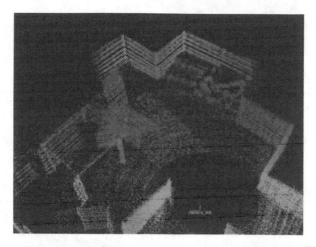

**Fig. 5.** Sample extracted test lane point cloud. The red region is the extracted test lane. (Color figure online)

## 5.1 Feature Extraction

Normal aligned radial feature (NARF) is widely used for object recognition. NARF chose on range images as the way to represent the data to reflect the vision sector of human and focused the outer shapes of objects. Since the main part of the extracted test lane region is the current scan point cloud, which means that the extracted region is a partial view of test lane, NARF is more robust for extraction of key points and descriptor calculation in this situation. In addition, we also extract FPFH features as comparison.

The descriptor of each NARF key points is a 36 dimensional vector. And for each frame of extracted region, there are more than 20 key points selected. Moreover, the same dimension of features in different frame of point clouds is required for classification. Here, we proposed a distance based weighting method to downscale feature into a 36 dimensional vector:

$$F = \sum_{i=1}^{k} \delta_i f_i,$$

$$\delta_i = \frac{1}{2\pi} e^{-\frac{d_i^2}{4}}$$

(3)

Where $d_i$ is the distance between the $i$th key point and the origin of the LIDAR coordinate. According to the Eq. (3), the weighting coefficient of key points comply with normal distribution: $\delta \sim N(0, 2)$. This means that the nearer the key point locates, the larger the weighting coefficient is. We focus more on the terrain close to the robot, which is more significant for security.

## 5.2   ELM Classifier

ELM is a machine learning method with fast training speed and suitable for multi-category classification task. Many research results show that ELM produces comparable or better classification accuracies with implementation computational complexity compared to artificial neural networks and support vector machine methods. In this paper, an ELM classifier is applied to recognize the four types of terrains.

An ELM is a model of the form:

$$f(x) = \sum_{i=1}^{L} h_i(x)\beta_i = h^T(x) \tag{4}$$

Where $h(x) = [h_1(x), \ldots, h_L(x)]^T$ is the ELM feature vector, and $\beta$ represents the vector of expansion coefficients, which means that the ELM is a single hidden layer feedforward neural network. We define the hidden matrix $H = [h(x_1), \ldots, h(x_N)]$, and the output matrix $Y = [y_1, \ldots, y_N]^T$. Hence the optimal vector of expansion coefficients is found by solving:

$$min\|H\beta - Y\|_2^2 \ and \ \|\beta\|_2 \tag{5}$$

Following [15], an improvement version of ELM is adopted by adding a regularization term c, to improve its generalization performance and make the solution more robust.

$$\beta = \left(\frac{1}{c} + H^T H\right)^{-1} H^T Y \tag{6}$$

The classify result of ELM is:

$$f'(x) = \arg\max f_i(x), \ when \ i \in 1, \ldots, M \tag{7}$$

In this paper, the parameters for the ELM are found by cross-validation on an independent portion of the dataset. A sigmoid activation function is used to construct the ELM feature space

$$g(a, x, b) = \frac{1}{1 + e^{-(ax+b)}} \tag{8}$$

And the input and output neuron are set to 36 and 4 respectively, corresponding to the dimensions of the feature and types of output. The optimal parameter c is selected based on the cross validation procedure, and is set to be 0.25. Moreover, the number of hidden nodes is determined by the experiments.

# 6  Experiments

During experiments, the algorithms processing the LIDAR data run on a laptop computer with 2.5 GHz quad cores and 8 GiB memory, on top of the robot operating system (ROS) in Ubuntu 14.04. The software structure is shown in Fig. 6.

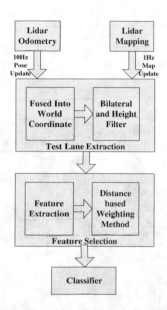

**Fig. 6.** Software structure of the proposed system.

Firstly, the number of hidden nodes could significantly affect the performance of ELM. We set the number of hidden nodes from 1000 to 10000 at 1000 intervals, the average accuracy and classification time of different number of hidden nodes are shown in Fig. 7. From the results, we could find that the performance of ELM is not positive correlation with the number of hidden nodes. Instead, the average accuracy is decreasing when the number of hidden node is over 6000 due to the over-fitting problem. Meanwhile, the classification times of different number of hidden nodes are comparable. Therefore, the number of hidden nodes is set to be 6000 in this paper.

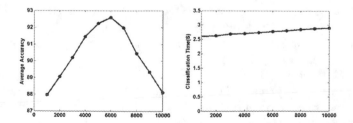

**Fig. 7.** Average accuracy and classification time of different number of hidden nodes of ELM.

The data set is captured from the experimental test lane in our laboratory. We label four types of terrains manually in advance. It is easy to identify the type if there is only ground or stair in a point cloud, but hard to determine the type when in the crossroad. In this paper, we define the intersection-over-ground-truth (IoG) to determine whether a region belongs to a certain type:

$$IoG(x, y) = \frac{point\ number\ in\ the\ intersection\ of\ x\ and\ y}{point\ number\ in\ ground\ truth\ set\ y}$$

The ground truth region is shown in Fig. 8. Th the manually label process could be described as follows:

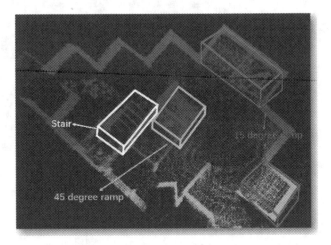

**Fig. 8.** Ground truth of terrains

$$f(x) = \begin{cases} 15°\ Ramp, & if\ IoG(x, I_{R15_1}) + IoG(x, I_{R15_2}) > 0.5 \\ 45°\ Ramp, & if\ IoG(x, I_{R45}) > 0.5 \\ stair, & if\ IoG(x, I_s) > 0.5 \\ ground, & else \end{cases}$$

Where $I_{R15_1}$ and $I_{R15_2}$ are the first and the second ground truth point set of 15° ramp, and $I_{R45}$ stands for the ground truth point set of 45° ramp while $I_s$ is the ground truth point set of stair. The data set contains 4000 sample point clouds of four types, and about 1000 samples per type.

We compare the proposed recognition method (ELM+NARF) with three other recognition methods: (1) multi-SVM classifier+NARF feature; (2) ELM classifier +FPFH feature; (3) multi-SVM classifier+FPFH feature. The same dataset is used to all four recognition methods. The training dataset and the testing dataset are segmented based on 5-fold cross validation method. Due to the randomicity of the ELM, the performance of ELM is the average result of 5 trials.

The comparison accuracy results are shown in Table 1. And the average classification time of each method are presented in Table 2. And typical results of point cloud and real scenario are shown in Fig. 9. In this experiment, all the regularization coefficients are generated by cross validation procedure. The best performance of each type is highlighted in bold. From the results, we could find that the proposed method performs best in two types while performs comparably in the other two types. The proposed method could also get the best performance of average accuracy. For rescue robot in USAR tasks, real-time recognition of local terrains is required, and therefore the classification time is significant to the terrain recognition method. The results show the proposed method performs best in classification time.

**Table 1.** The comparison of recognition accuracy

|  | Ground | Stair | 15° ramp | 45° ramp |
|---|---|---|---|---|
| ELM+NARF | **84.38** | **99.28** | 94.09 | 92.58 |
| Multi-SVM+NARF | 80.29 | 99.08 | 95.06 | 91.36 |
| ELM+FPFH | 79.67 | 98.53 | **95.58** | 92.45 |
| Multi-SVM+FPFH | 80.13 | 97.48 | 94.48 | **93.29** |

**Table 2.** The comparison of classification time

|  | ELM+NARF | Multi-SVM+NARF | ELM+FPFH | Multi-SVM+FPFH |
|---|---|---|---|---|
| Classification time (s) | **0.278** | 0.526 | 0.384 | 0.621 |

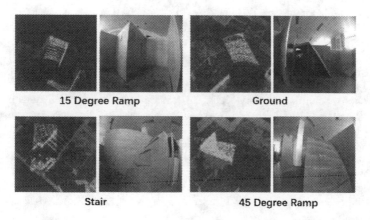

**Fig. 9.** Typical point cloud and real scenario of four types.

# 7  Conclusion

In this paper, we proposed a multi-type terrain recognition system for rescue robot. A map is built using the LOAM algorithm, which serves as a base for test lane region extraction. The NARF and ELM classification method is employed to recognize the types of the local terrain in test lane.

The experimental results of real test lanes show that the proposed system could accurately recognize the terrains in real-time. The proposed algorithm will be used in RoboCup RRL 2016 competitions, during exploring the fully autonomous area.

**Acknowledgements.** Our work is supported by National Science Foundation of China (NO. 61503401 and NO. 61403409), China Postdoctoral Science Foundation (NO. 2014M562648), and graduate school of National University of Defense Technology. All members of the NuBot research group are gratefully acknowledged.

# References

1. Osuka, K., Murphy, R., Schultz, A.C.: USAR competitions for physically situated robots. IEEE Robot. Autom. Mag. **9**, 26–33 (2002)
2. Zhang, J., Singh, S.: Low-drift and real-time LIDAR odometry and mapping. Auton. Robot. **41**, 401–416 (2016)
3. Huang, G.-B., Zhu, Q.-Y., Siew, C.-K.: Extreme learning machine: theory and applications. Neurocomputing **70**, 489–501 (2006)
4. Nüchter, A., Lingemann, K., Hertzberg, J., Surmann, H.: 6D SLAM—3D mapping outdoor environments. J. Field Robot. **24**, 699–722 (2007)
5. Scherer, S., Rehder, J., Achar, S., Cover, H., Chambers, A., Nuske, S., et al.: River mapping from a flying robot: state estimation, river detection, and obstacle mapping. Auton. Robot. **33**, 189–214 (2012)
6. Radu, B.S., Rusu, B., Konolige, K., Burgard, W.: NARF: 3D range image features for object recognition (2012)
7. Lu, Q., Wang, X., Liu, F.: Feature extraction and the description of point cloud image based on S-NARF algorithm. Sci. Technol. Rev. **31**, 45–48 (2013)
8. Rusu, R.B., Blodow, N., Beetz, M.: Fast Point Feature Histograms (FPFH) for 3D registration. In: IEEE International Conference on Robotics and Automation, pp. 3212–3217 (2009)
9. Cristianini, N., Shawe-Taylor, J.: An Introduction to Support Vector Machines: and Other Kernel-Based Learning Methods. Cambridge University Press, Cambridge (1999)
10. Frossyniotis, Dimitrios S., Stafylopatis, A.: A multi-SVM classification system. In: Kittler, J., Roli, F. (eds.) MCS 2001. LNCS, vol. 2096, pp. 198–207. Springer, Heidelberg (2001). doi:10.1007/3-540-48219-9_20
11. Huang, G.B., Zhou, H., Ding, X., Zhang, R.: Extreme learning machine for regression and multiclass classification. IEEE Trans. Syst. Man Cybern. Part B Cybern. **42**, 29–513 (2012). A Publication of the IEEE Systems Man & Cybernetics Society
12. Glennie, C.L., Kusari, A., Facchin, A., Glennie, C.L., Kusari, A., Facchin, A.: Calibration and stability analysis of the VLP-16 laser scanner, vol. XL-3/W4, pp. 55–60 (2016)

13. Murray, B.R., Li, Z., Sastry, S.: Mathematical Introduction to Robotic Manipulation (2015)
14. Sun, S.-L., Deng, Z.-L.: Multi-sensor optimal information fusion Kalman filter. Automatica
    **40**, 1017–1023 (2004)
15. Huang, G.B., Wang, D.H., Lan, Y.: Extreme learning machines: a survey. Int. J. Mach.
    Learn. Cybern. **2**, 107–122 (2011)

# Interaction Force Convex Reduction for Smooth Gait Transitions on Human-Power Augmentation Lower Exoskeletons

Abusabah I.A. Ahmed[1,2]([✉]), Hong Cheng[1], Huaping Liu[3], Xichuan Lin[1],
and Mary Juma Atieno[2]

[1] Center for Robotics, School of Automation Engineering,
University of Electronic Science and Technology of China, Chengdu 611731, China
abusabah22@hotmail.com
[2] Department of Electrical and Computer Engineering,
Karary University, Khartoum 12304, Sudan
[3] Department of Computer Science and Technology,
Tsinghua University, Beijing 100084, China

**Abstract.** Online gait control in human-powered exoskeleton systems is still rich research field and represents a step towards fully autonomous, safe and intelligent navigation. Many Control method performs well and with accepted interaction force between pilot and exoskeleton during system's navigation on level walking, but with large convex when walking speed changed. Adaptive LOcally WEighted Scatterplot Smoothing (ALOESS) is a modification for LOESS regression method that combine multiple regression models for predefined convex threshold. We proposed convex reduction technique for smooth tracking of arbitrary reference trajectories. The large convex resulted during changing gait from flat terrain to stair ascent are studied in this work and the overshoots are reduced to minimize trajectory tracking error. We choose the overshoots to be reduced in this step because the they are larger than undershoots. We demonstrate the proposed control strategy on computer simulations, results show that the proposed strategy can minimize the overshoot by 46%.

**Keywords:** Overshoot reduction · ALOES · Admittance control · Recursive least square estimation · Gait transition · Coupled human-exoskeleton system

## 1 Introduction

The control of lower extremity exoskeletons have gained considerable interests in recent years, especially for human power augmentation applications [1–5]. The Berkeley Lower Extremity Exoskeleton (BLEEX) is the most famous exoskeleton system, which is actuated by hydraulic system. Sensitivity Amplification Control (SAC) algorithm is proposed for BLEEX control which aimed to reduce the sensors complexity [6]. SAC method efficiently controls exoskeleton robot to shadow

© Springer Nature Singapore Pte Ltd. 2017
F. Sun et al. (Eds.): ICCSIP 2016, CCIS 710, pp. 398–407, 2017.
DOI: 10.1007/978-981-10-5230-9_39

human motion but in economic point of view it's so expensive and resource consumer. In other words SAC is expensive for both development and practical applications. Y. Sankai et al. applied impedance control method based Human Intention Estimators (HIE) for human enhancement version of Hybrid Assistive Limb (HAL) [7]. In our last work we proposed a modification for Admitance Controller, which successfully achieved and applied for HUman power Augmentation Lower EXoskeleton (HUALEX) control [8]. The problem of perfect tracking of a known input trajectory without convex is a great deal in human-powered exoskeleton systems. Sudden changing in direction, walking speed or gait type during coupled human-exoskeleton system's navigation will lead to large convex on physical Human Robot Interaction (pHRI). Dahleh M.A. and Pearson J.B. studied the error free controller problem for a restricted class of discrete time tracking systems [9]. They also presented several control applications where positive and negative errors took place. However, their design aim was to minimize $l_1$ norm of positive tracking errors, not the peak values. The pHRI as a result for human mind intention is a cooperative activities between separately human and exoskeleton [10] or close physical interaction [11] are big challenge, but in coupled human-robot system is more challenge because additional issues must considered because coupled human-robot system or exoskeleton robots act directly on the human body. The pressure-sensitive devices are widely used for gait analysis [12].

An Admittance Controller (AC) also called position based impedance controller, uses the end-effector interaction force feedback to estimate the appropriate joint position. The desired joint position and position feedback are used to estimate the appropriate actuators inputs [13]. Since Neville Hogan first introduced impedance controllers [14], they have become well established specially in robotics and coupled human-exoskeleton system. Admittance control extensively utilized in rehabilitation robotics but also was applied to upper limb power augmentation exoskeletons in many researches [15–19], for robot human Quadrocopter [20] and for wheel chair control [21]. The main illness in AC performance is the force convex resulted during gait transitions, which lead to overshoots and undershoots in trajectory tracking. Convex optimization technique has been used in signal processing field which performs efficiently, the application type off-line or on-line describes the optimization restricted.

The paper is organized as follows: Sect. 2 shows the needs for manoeuvrable human-exoskeleton system, and the integration of the system. We validate the performance illness of ordinary admittance control during gait transitions in Sect. 3. Section 4 shows the local regression strategy application on interaction force minimization. The overshoot reduction technique is detailed in Sect. 5. Finally, conclusions and some perspective on future uses and further development of this technique drawn in Sect. 6.

## 2    Maneuverable Human-Exoskeleton Systems

The HUALEX actuated and passively driven DoFs are designed to guarantee the shadow of all expected pilot's maneuvers. As a wearable exoskeleton, the motion

range for each DOF of HUALEX is designed according to human kinematics
with some slight differences due to flexible connections between the exoskeleton
and wearer. In the sagittal plane, the designed ranges of motion at the hip, knee
and ankle joints are $-45°$ to $+45°$, $0°$ to $-135°$ and $-30°$ to $+30°$, respectively.
The recent indoors applications of human-powered exoskeleton systems need to
pay more attention for control to obtain smooth reference trajectories tracking.
The exoskeleton links are made with ideal design (minimum weight and inertia).
The Link lengths are adjustable respect to various pilots. Force sensing technology is also an important feature in human-exoskeleton systems for monitor the
interaction between pilot and exoskeleton and controls these systems. Climbing
stairs requires active knee extension i.e. additional torque must be applied [22].
The degree of knee extension depends on the height of stairs which is stochastic
value. The proper interaction force sensors of HUALEX make successfully investigation of admittance controller, therefore perfect angle correction. The practical measurements of joint angles, encoders on HUALEX and inclinometers on
human limbs beside interaction forces between them are used to investigate the
joint flexions for different stair height. The information from HUALEX's sensors
aimed to obtain the desired change in the input walking trajectory when human
intend to change gait type. It is especially useful when controlling the desired
admittance between the human and HUALEX for transit from flat terrain walking to stair ascent. Since our proposed control strategy for gait transition is a
model-based control strategy, the dynamic model of HUALEX project must be
given.

$$M(\theta)\ddot{\theta} + C(\theta,\dot{\theta})\dot{\theta} + G(\theta) = \tau_{Exo} + \tau_h \tag{1}$$

in which $\theta$ is the vector of each joint angle, $\tau_{Exo}$ and $\tau_h$ represent the input
torques from HUALEX and human wearer, respectively. $M(\theta)$ is the inertia
matrix and a function of $\theta$, $C(\theta,\dot{\theta})$ is the Coriolis matrix and a function of $\theta$
and $\dot{\theta}$, and $G(\theta)$ is a vector of gravitational torques. During human-exoskeleton
system navigation $\tau_h$ is changing according to human intentions.

## 3   The Performance of Ordinary Admittance Control

The admittance of the human leg shank can be given as:

$$Y_h(s) = \frac{1}{Z_h(s)} \tag{2}$$

which characterized by inertia moment$J_h$, damping $B_h$, and stiffness $K_h$. The
desired set of admittance parameters is required to be achieved online so that
the dynamics of human-exoskeleton system interaction behavior controlled and
transferred to appropriate joint flexion correction. The interaction force on
shank is measured as described in details for HUALEX with specified wearer
[3]. Through inverse dynamics the end-effector measured interaction force $f_i$
transferred to joint space interaction torque $\tau_i$. The admittance of the coupled
human-exoskeleton can be described as follows:

$$\Delta\theta(s) = \frac{\tau_i(s)}{Js^2 + Bs + K} \tag{3}$$

where $J$, $B$ and $K$ are systems inertia moment, damping and stiffness respectively. Admittance function determines the joint angular deviation through inverse kinematics. Hence the purpose of the admittance controller is to keep $\Delta\theta$ the difference between $\theta_h$ and $\theta_{Exo}$ as small as possible during system navigation. The resulting new reference position $\theta_d^* = \theta_h + \Delta\theta$ is then fed into PD controller. Experimental simulations are conducted to obtain admittance parameters. The schematic diagram of 1-DOF platform considered in this paper and the admittance model are shown in Fig. 1. During human-exoskeleton system navigation the interaction force in shank strap online transformed to equivalent joint torques at knee joint through trajectory modification. As shown in Fig. 1(b), the inertias of the wearer leg and the exoskeleton are coupled by a damper $B_c$ and spring $K_c$ representing the coupled human and exoskeleton shank brace. The dynamic model of 1-DOF coupled human-exoskeleton system (shank with knee joint) can be represented as in Eq. (4):

$$J\ddot{\theta}(t) + B\dot{\theta}(t) + mgl\sin\theta(t) + C_F \operatorname{sign}\dot{\theta}(t) = \tau(t) + J^T f_i(t) \qquad (4)$$

where $J, B, m, l$ represent inertial moment, viscous friction coefficient, shank mass and length of the one DOF exoskeleton, respectively, $(\theta, \dot{\theta}, \ddot{\theta})$ represent the angle, angular velocity, and angular acceleration of the knee joint, $C_F$ represents Coulomb friction coefficient around knee joint, $\tau(t)$ is actuation torque, $J^T$ is the jacobian transpose of the platform and $f_i(t)$ is the interaction force between human wearer and exoskeleton. We use stiffness $K$, mainly as a linearization of the gravitational torque acting on the shank, such that $mgl\sin\theta \approx K\theta$ [23]. The intention of stairs ascent will lead to overshoot in interaction force, this is the main reason for the overshoot in tracking performance.

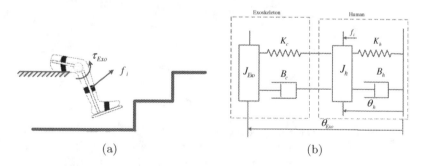

$$\text{(a)} \qquad\qquad\qquad\qquad\qquad \text{(b)}$$

**Fig. 1.** (a) The schematic diagram of single DoF exoskeleton and resulting interaction force with the wearer when going upstairs; (b) The admittance control model of the coupled human-exoskeleton system.

Consider the model of the coupled human-exoskeleton admittance control in Fig. 1(b), we can rewrite Eq. (4) as follows:

$$J_c\ddot{\theta}(t) + B_c\dot{\theta}(t) + K_c\theta(t) + C_F \operatorname{sign}\dot{\theta}(t) = \tau(t) + J^T f_i(t) \qquad (5)$$

The estimation of the dynamic model parameters in Eq. (4) was defined for HUALEX walking speed control by Tran T.H. et al. [3]. In this paper we define it for gait transitions control by ordinary admittance control method (OAC) we keep $C_F = 1.724$ as estimated in [3]. On the system navigation process the interaction force on shank contact is proportional to the wearer intended motion as follows:

$$\Delta\theta(t) = J^T f_i(t) \tag{6}$$

According to the experimental simulation, the resulted tracking control of OAC also indicates performance illness in the gait transition situations. For defining $J, B and K$ in Eq. (6) define the vectors:

$$\begin{aligned} \Phi(t) &= [\ddot{\theta}(t) \quad \dot{\theta}(t) \quad \theta(t)]^T \\ \Psi &= [J \quad B(t) \quad K]^T \end{aligned} \tag{7}$$

Assume relaxed wearer muscles operation i.e. $J^T f_i = 0$, with the definitions in Eq. (12) we can present Eq. (4) in matrix form:

$$\tau(t) = \Phi^T(t)\Psi \tag{8}$$

where, $\Phi^T$ is called the regression vector. The objective is to estimate the unknown parameter vector $\Psi$ from observations of $\tau(t)$ and the regression vector $\Phi(t)$. The best estimate of $\Psi$ can be obtained by minimizing the $L(t)$ least-square criterion which defined as:

$$L(t) = 1/2[\tau(t) - \Phi^T(t)\hat{\Psi}]^T[\tau(t) - \Phi^T(t)\hat{\Psi}] \tag{9}$$

The least-square method is the basic technique for parameters estimation [24]. The minimum of Eq. (9) is our goal for parameter vector estimation:

$$\frac{\partial L(t)}{\partial \Psi} = 0, \qquad \Psi \to \hat{\Psi} \tag{10}$$

We can say $\hat{\Psi}(t)$ is optimal if and only if following condition satisfied:

$$\hat{\Psi}(t)\Phi^T(t)\Phi(t) = \Phi^T(t)\tau(t) \tag{11}$$

The condition in Eq. (11) is called the normal equation. The online best estimation of the parameter vector $\Psi$ based on recursive least-square (RLS) estimation can be achieved when assumed that the matrix $\Phi(t)$ has full rank [24]. Then the least-square estimate of $\hat{\Psi}(t)$ satisfies the recursive equations drawn in Eq. (12)

$$\begin{aligned} \hat{\Psi}(t) &= \hat{\Psi}(t - 1) + K(t)[\tau(t) - \Phi^T(t)\hat{\Psi}(t - 1)] \\ K(t) &= P(t - 1)\Phi^T(t)[1 + \Phi^T(t)P(t - 1)\Phi(t)] \\ P(t) &= 1 - [K(t)\Phi^T(t)]P(t - 1) \end{aligned} \tag{12}$$

From the simulation experimental trails for flat terrain walking, stair ascent 170 mm height and 200 mm height the mean values for 10 trails are drawn in Table 1. Here we just examined the transition from flat terrain walking to stairs

**Table 1.** The estimated parameters of lower shank and knee joint.

| Parameter | Flat terrain walking | Stair ascent(170 mm) | Stair ascent (200 mm) |
|---|---|---|---|
| $J$ (Kgm$^2$) | 0.133 | 0.122 | 0.123 |
| $B$ (Nms/rad) | 6.282 | 7.371 | 7.446 |
| $K$ (Nm/rad) | 33.921 | 31.120 | 29.414 |

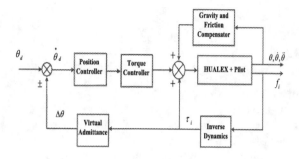

**Fig. 2.** The main block diagram of admittance controller for coupled human-exoskeleton system interaction control.

ascent. In other words, OAC performance faces the problem of rapid change in physical interaction force when human intend to change gait which lead to the performance illness. The dynamic thresholds for overshoot value cutting is the best solution for reliable performance during different heights and obstacles. The OAC block diagram is shown in Fig. 2.

## 4    Local Regression

### 4.1    Locally Weighted Scatterplot Smoothing

Locally weighted scattersite smoothing (LOWESS and LOESS) are strongly related non-parametric regression method that combine multiple regression models in a k-nearest-neighbor-based meta-model. LOESS is a later generalization of LOWESS [25]. LOESS and LOWESS thus build on classical methods, such as linear and nonlinear least squares regression. It does this by fitting simple models to localized subsets of the data to build up a function that describes the deterministic part of the variation in the data, point by point. Statistical methodology and visualization for multivariate fitting was developed by Cleveland and Devlin [26] and the associated LOESS method [27]. The biggest advantage LOESS has over many other methods is the fact that it does not require the specification of a function to fit a model to all of the data in the sample. With two overshoot predictor variables $f_i(t)$ and $f_i(t + \triangle t)$, the local regression model becomes:

$$\hat{f}_i(t) = \mu(f_i(t), f_i(t + \triangle t)) + \varepsilon(t) \tag{13}$$

The bandwidth of LOESS $\triangle t$ has a critical effect on the local regression fit. If $\triangle t$ is too small, insufficient data fall within the smoothing window, and a noisy fit, or large variance, will result. On the other hand, if $\triangle t$ is too large, the local polynomial may not fit the data well within the smoothing window, and important features of the mean function $\mu$ may be distorted or lost completely. LOESS smoothing depends on calculated regression weights using second degree polynomial, $\varepsilon(t)$ is an error term.

$$\omega(t) = (1 - |\frac{\hat{f}_i(t) - f_i(t)}{\triangle t}|^3)^3 \tag{14}$$

## 4.2   Adaptive Locally Weighted Scatterplot Smoothing

Computer simulations are conducted to identify the appropriate thresholds for the feedback signals overshoots and dynamic bandwidth estimation. The relationship between interaction force successive values $\triangle f_i(t)$ is used to decide the treated overshoot value. When $\triangle f_i(t) \geq 40$ the LOESS must applied with fixed bandwidth and dynamic smoothing parameter, depending on the $\triangle f_i(t)$ value. In this application we focus attention on tracking error minimization, consider the minimization of interaction force positive overshoot.

The proposed ALOESS works faster than LOESS method, work when needed is resource saving and efficiency improving in Human-powered Exoskeleton System's control. To insure the efficient performance we identified the working ranges for the proposed feedback signal smoothing technique.

## 5   Overshoot Reduction

The smooth behaviour of feedback signal illustrates the graduated correction of current trajectory which grantee smooth transit from flat terrain walking to stair ascent. For different stairs height (170 mm and 200 mm are examined) we found that the acceptable maximum positive convex is resulted from $\triangle f_i(t) < 40$, consider the given bandwidth (0.02), LOESS smoothing have place above this level. The overshoots happens as a result for pilot intention to change gait type, in order to keep the tracking error as minimum as possible as and without convex we propose overshoot minimization technique. The maximum permitted overshoot value is $\triangle f_i(t) < 40$. We take as inputs for control algorithm the experimentally calculated interaction force convex threshold and the current interaction force value to calculate $\triangle f_i(t)$. The proposed control methodology for AC feedback signal smoothing is achieved for better tracking performance. The performance of proposed method in interaction force minimization for 200 mm stairs height shown in the Fig. 3(a). The achievable interaction force overshoot reduction, under the adaptation restriction that is $\triangle f_i(t) < 40$ and the positive convex value (overshoot) of $f_i(t)$ is reduced to be less than +5 N. The sequence of feedback signal smoothing in the tracking error minimization is noticeable as depicted in Fig. 3(b). From Fig. 3(a) and (b), we can infer from that the convex reduction technique has good control performance in feedback signal smoothing and tracking error minimization.

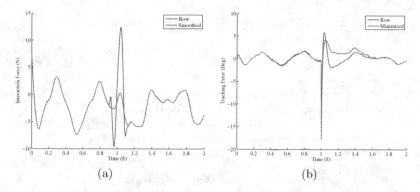

**Fig. 3.** (a) The adaptive LOESS performance on 200 mm stairs height interaction force overshoot reduction; (b) The performance of ALOESS on 200 mm stairs height tracking error minimization.

## 6 Conclusions and Future Works

Our control method minimized the tracking error during gait transition for human-exoskeleton system by reducing the interaction force overshoot. The human intentions on Human-powered Exoskeleton can represents the Exoskeleton brain for autonomous navigation and high level control performance. The proposed feedback signal smoothing scheme for online gait transition control system with limited gait modes (flat terrain walking to stairs ascent) will find a more attentions in future developments forwards fully autonomous HUALEX robotic system. As shown in results the new adaptive LOESS performs well as a resource saving aspect.

The future work will focus on the system response optimization to minimize the transition error, and transition time towards form brain to muscles, then HUALEX can moves freely for more complicated missions. Also we're planning to work in obstacle avoidance in general and adapt to difference stairs height and tread length this will overcome the proposed technique limitations.

**Acknowledgments.** This work was support by NSFC (No. 61503060, 6157021026), Fundamental Research Funds for the Central Universities (ZYGX2014Z009) and SRF for ROCS, SEM.

## References

1. Kazerooni, H., Chu, A., Steger, R.: That which does not stabilize, will only make us stronger. Int. J. Robot. Res. **26**, 75–89 (2007)
2. Zoss, A., Kazerooni, H., Chu, A.: On the mechanical design of the Berkeley lower extremity exoskeleton (BLEEX). In: International Conference on Intelligent Robots and Systems, pp. 3132–3139. IEEE Press, Edmonton (2005)
3. Tran, H.T., Cheng, H., Duong, M.K., Zheng, H.: Fuuzy-based impedance regulation for control of the coupled human-exoskeleton system. In: IEEE International Conference on Robotics and Biomimetics, pp. 986–992. IEEE Press, Bali (2014)

4. Sankai, Y.: HAL: hybrid assistive limb based on cybernics. Robot. Res. **66**, 25–34 (2011)
5. Lee, S., Sankai, Y.: Power assist control for walking aid with HAL-3 based on EMG and impedance adjustment around knee joint. In: International Conference on Intelligent Robots and Systems, pp. 1499–1504. IEEE Press, Switzerland (2002)
6. Kazerooni, H., Racine, J.L., Huang, L., Steger, R.: On the control of the Berkeley lower extremity exoskeleton (BLEEX). In: International Conference of Robotics and Automation, pp. 4353–4360. IEEE Press, Barcelona (2005)
7. Lee, S., Sankai, Y.: Virtual impedance adjustment in unconstrained motion for an exoskeletal robot assisting the lower limb. Adv. Robot. **19**, 773–795 (2005)
8. Abusabah, I.A.A., Hong, C., Lin, X., Huang, R.: Motion planing and control of maneuverable human-powered exoskeleton systems. In: IEEE/RSJ International Conference on Intelligent Robots and Systems (Workshop) (2016)
9. Dahleh, M.A., Pearson, J.B.: L1-optimal compensators for continuous-time systems. IEEE Trans. Autom. Control **32**, 889–895 (1987)
10. Amor, H.B., Neumann, G., Kamthe, S., Kroemer, O., Peters, J.: Interaction primitives for human-robot cooperation tasks. In: IEEE International Conference on Robotics and Automation, pp. 2831–2837. IEEE Press, Hong Kong (2014)
11. Ikemoto, S., Amor, H.B., Minato, T., Jung, B., Ishiguro, H.: Physical human robot interaction mutual learning and adaptation. IEEE Robot. Autom. Mag. **19**, 24–35 (2012)
12. De Rossi, S.M.M., Lenzi, T., Vitiello, N., Donati, M., Persichetti, A., Giovacchini, F., Vecchi, F., Carrozza, M.C.: Development of an in-shoe pressure-sensitive device for gait analysis. In: Annual International Conference of the IEEE Engineering in Medicine and Biology Society, EMBC, pp. 5637–5640. IEEE Press, Massachusetts (2011)
13. Tonietti, G., Schiavi, R., Bicchi, A.: Design and control of a variable stiffness actuator for safe and fast physical human-robot interaction. In: International Conference on Robotics and Automation, pp. 526–531. IEEE Press, Barcelona (2005)
14. Hogan, N.: Impedance control: an approach to manipulation. In: American Control Conference, pp. 304–313. IEEE Press, San Diego (1984)
15. Miller, L.M., Rosen, J.: Comparison of multi-sensor admittance control in joint space and task space for a seven degree of freedom upper limb exoskeleton. In: Proceedings of the 3rd IEEE RAS and EMBS International Conference on Biomedical Robotics and Biomechatronics, pp. 70–75. IEEE Press, Tokyo (2010)
16. Okunev, V., Nierhoff, T., Hirche, S.: Human-preference-based control design: adaptive robot admittance control for physical human-robot interaction. In: The 21st IEEE International Symposium on Robot and Human Interactive Communication, pp. 443–448. IEEE Press, Paris (2012)
17. Carmichael, M.G., Liu, D.: Admittance control scheme for implementing model-based assistance-as-needed on a robot. In: 35th Annual International Conference of the IEEE EMBS, pp. 870–873. IEEE Press, Osaka (2013)
18. Lee, B.K., Lee, H.D., Lee, J.Y., Shin, K., Han, J.S., Han, C.S.: Development of dynamic model-based controller for upper limb exoskeleton robot. In: 2012 IEEE International Conference on Robotics and Automation, pp. 3173–3178. IEEE Press, Saint Paul (2012)
19. Yu, W., Rosen, J., Li, X.: PID admittance control for an upper limb exoskeleton. In: American Control Conference, pp. 1124–1129. IEEE Press, San Francisco (2011)
20. Augugliaro, F., D'Andrea, R.: Admittance control for physical human-quadrocopter interaction. In: European Control Conference, pp. 1805–1810. IEEE Press, Zurich (2013)

21. Oda, M., Zhu, C., Suzuki, M., Luo, X., Watanabe, H., Yan, Y.: Admittance based control of wheelchair typed omnidirectional robot for walking support and power assistance. In: 19th IEEE International Symposium on Robot and Human Interactive Communication, pp. 159–164. IEEE Press, Viareggio (2010)
22. Hoover, C.D., Fulk, G.D., Fite, K.B.: Stair ascent with a powered transfemoral prosthesis under direct myoelectric control. IEEE/ASME Trans. Mechatron. **18**, 1191–1200 (2013)
23. Colgate, J.E., Ollinger, G.A., Peshkin, M.A., Goswami, A.: A 1-DOF assistive exoskeleton with virtual negative damping: effects on the kinematic response of the lower limbs. In: IEEE/RSJ International Conference on Intelligent Robots and Systems, pp. 1938–1944. IEEE Press, San Diego (2007)
24. Astrom, K.J., Wittenmark, B.: Adaptive Control, 2nd edn. Addison Wesley, Reading (1995)
25. Fox, J.: Nonparametric Simple Regression: Smoothing Scatterplots. Sage Publication, London (2000)
26. Cleveland, W.S., Devlin, S.J.: Locally weighted regression: an approach to regression analysis by local fitting. J. Am. Stat. Assoc. **83**, 596–610 (1988)
27. Loader, C.: Local Regression and Likelihood, 3rd edn. Springer, Heidelberg (1999)

# Ensemble One-Class Extreme Learning Machine Based on Overlapping Data Partition

Siqi Wang[1(✉)], Lili Zhao[1], En Zhu[1], Jianping Yin[1], and Heling Yang[2]

[1] College of Computer, National University of Defense Technology,
Changsha 410073, China
405976789@qq.com
[2] Department of Communication Engineering,
Beijing Electronic Science and Technology Institute, Beijing 100070, China

**Abstract.** One-class classification/data description plays a key roles in numerous applications such as anomaly detection. This paper presents a novel ensemble one-class extreme learning machine (EOCELM), which not only yields sound performance but also facilitates the parallel processing of training and testing. Instead of training on the entire training dataset, EOCELM first partitions the training data into overlapping clusters by k-medoids clustering and a simple Minimum Spanning Tree (MST) based heuristic rule. The proposed overlapping data partition makes it possible to describe the sub-structures within one-class training data more precisely without the risk of creating "clutser gap" that may degrade the generalization performance. Besides, the data partition can alleviate the matrix inversion problem of original extreme learning machine (OCELM) when dealing with massive training data. Next, an OCELM is trained for each data cluster as a sub-classifier, which can be implemented in a parallel way. Finally, OCELMs are combined into EOCELM by the simple maximum combining rule. Experiments on synthetic datasets, UCI datasets and MNIST datasets demonstrate the effectiveness of EOCELM when compared with other state-of-the-art one-class learning approaches.

**Keywords:** Extreme learning machine · Non-overlapping data partition · Ensemble

## 1 Introduction

One-class classification (OCC) [1], which is also known as novelty or outlier detection, is an important machine learning topic. Unlike binary or multi-class classification problems, the training dataset of OCC only consists of training data from positive class (or target class), and the training data from negative class (or outlier class) are usually absent. OCC attempts to learn a target data description

S. Wang—This work was supported by the National Natural Science Foundation of China (Project No. 60970034, 61170287, 61232016).

© Springer Nature Singapore Pte Ltd. 2017
F. Sun et al. (Eds.): ICCSIP 2016, CCIS 710, pp. 408–416, 2017.
DOI: 10.1007/978-981-10-5230-9_40

from the target class training data and those data that divert significantly from the description are considered as outliers. Absence of data from negative class renders OCC a more challenging problem and less attention has been given to OCC than other typical classification problems, although OCC is frequently seen in real life and has wide application to realms like anomaly detection [3], machine fault detection [4], document classification [2], etc.

Typically, OCC approaches fall into three categories: *Density based approaches*, such as Mixture of Guassian (MoG) [5] and Parzen density estimation [6]. Approaches in this category relies on estimating the probability density of target class data. Massive training data and a flexible density model are usually required, which are the major limitation of density based approaches. *Reconstruction based approaches*. Reconstruction based approaches, such as auto-encoder [8] and self-organizing maps [7], assume data from target class are subject to some kind of distribution and data from outlier class do not. Therefore, data from target class can be reconstructed with lower error than data from outlier class. *Boundary based approaches*, such as one-class SVM (OCSVM) [9], one-class ELM (OCELM) [10] and Support Vector Data Description (SVDD) [11], aims to learn a compact boundary to enclose training data from target class and considers those data outside the boundary as outliers. Without the need of a large number of training data or any prior assumption on the distribution of target class, OCSVM and SVDD are state-of-the-art approaches in recent OCC research and application due to their flexible descriptive power and sound generalization performance [12–14], and they are shown to be equivalent when Gaussian kernel is used [11]. Based on extreme learning machine (ELM) [15], Leng *et al.* [10] recently propose Gaussian kernel based OCELM as a promising solution to OCC. OCELM can achieve comparable or higher data description performance than OCSVM or SVDD with a significantly faster learning speed. Despite that OCELM provides a very attractive solution for OCC, OCELM has some limitations. One major limitation is that Gaussian kernel based OCELM needs to store all training samples during training and testing for calculating kernel function and matrix inverse. It will be a major computational burden when dealing with massive training data (which will be elaborated in Sec. 2.1). Besides, OCELM and OCSVM attempt to learn a data description with all target data, which may lose the local structural information within target class.

To tackle the above problems, this paper proposes a novel EOCELM. The rest of paper is organized as follows: Sect. 2 reviews OCELM and presents the details of EOCELM. Section 3 presents the experimental results revolving around EOCELM on synthetic datasets, UCI datasets and MNIST dataset to show its superiority over previous methods. Section 4 concludes this paper.

## 2 EOCELM

### 2.1 OCELM

Before we present EOCELM, we briefly review Gaussian kernel based OCELM, which is a simple variant of ELM. ELM is a three-layer feedforward neural network that can be trained efficiently by determining output weights analytically. To be more specific, with the input training samples $\mathbf{X}_{n \times d}$ and $L$ hidden nodes ($n$ and $d$ are the number of training data and the feature dimension), the input features are randomly mapped to a new feature space as the output of hidden layer $\mathbf{H}_{n \times L}$. Then the output weights $\beta$ between hidden layer and output layer is determined by:

$$\beta = \mathbf{H}^T(\frac{\mathbf{I}}{C} + \mathbf{H}\mathbf{H}^T)^{-1}\mathbf{T} \tag{1}$$

where $C$, $\mathbf{T}$ and $\mathbf{I}$ are the regularization coefficient, target output and identity matrix, respectively. The prediction of a new sample $\mathbf{x}$ is given by:

$$f(\mathbf{x}) = h(\mathbf{x})\beta = h(\mathbf{x})\mathbf{H}^T(\frac{\mathbf{I}}{C} + \mathbf{H}\mathbf{H}^T)^{-1}\mathbf{T} \tag{2}$$

where $h(\mathbf{x})$ is the random mapping of $\mathbf{x}$. If the random mapping is unknown, the prediction of $\mathbf{x}$ can be determined by using kernel tricks:

$$f(\mathbf{x}) = \begin{bmatrix} K(\mathbf{x}_1, \mathbf{x}) \\ ... \\ K(\mathbf{x}_n, \mathbf{x}) \end{bmatrix} (\frac{\mathbf{I}}{C} + \mathbf{K}_{train}^T)^{-1}\mathbf{T} = \mathbf{K}_{test}^T(\frac{\mathbf{I}}{C} + \mathbf{K}_{train}^T)^{-1}\mathbf{T} \tag{3}$$

where $(\mathbf{K}_{train})_{n \times n}$ is the kernel matrice formed by the kernel function $K(\mathbf{x}_i, \mathbf{x}_j)$ for each pair of training samples. Modifying an ordinary ELM into a OCELM only needs to fix the target output by $\mathbf{T} = \mathbf{1} \cdot y$, i.e., OCELM tries to map all training samples to a scalar output $y$. Assuming the actual outputs of OCELM for training samples are $y_i$, $i = 1, 2, ...n$, the mapping error of training sample $\mathbf{x}_i$ to the target value $y$ is $d_i = |y_i - y|$. The threshold $d_T$ is chosen to exclude a small fraction of $p$ farthest sampling points ($d_i > d_T$), which can prevent the noise in training set from degrading the boundary. $p$ usually takes small values ($p = 0.1$ for UCI datasets and $p = 0.01$ for MNIST dataset) and $y = 1$.

## 2.2    EOCELM

As shown in Eq. 3, OCELM needs to calculate the $n \times n$ kernel matrice $\mathbf{K}_{train}$ and the persudo inverse $(\frac{\mathbf{I}}{C} + \mathbf{K}_{train}^T)^{-1}$ during training, and the $n \times m$ kernel matrice $\mathbf{K}_{test}$ during testing ($n$ and $m$ are the number of training and testing samples). When $n$ is large, calculating the total $n \times n$ elements in $\mathbf{K}_{train}$ and $n \times m$ elements in $\mathbf{K}_{test}$ will be time-consuming. Besides, calculating the persudo inverse calls for $O(n^3)$ complexity. A natural instinct is to partition the training set $\Omega$ into a few subsets $\{\Omega_1, ...\Omega_k\}$ with the size of subset $n_1, ..., n_k$. An OCELM is trained to describe each subset, and all OCELMs are combined as an ensemble one-class classifier. Since $n_i < n$, the computations of $\mathbf{K}_{train}$, its persudo inverse and $\mathbf{K}_{test}$ will be much less than the original OCELM. Meanwhile, data partition makes it possible to train or test each OCELM in a parallel way with less complexity, which also makes it possible for OCELM to be accelerated when dealing with massive data in OCC. Since there may exist different data distributions within the one-class training set, data partition enables each OCELM to give a more precise description for each local structure of data than the OCELM trained on the entire training set. Due to the above benefits of data partition, we propose an overlapping data partition based EOCELM. For better illustration, we visualize the working steps of EOCELM on a four-banana shape synthetic dataset with different data distributions and densities (see Fig. 1).

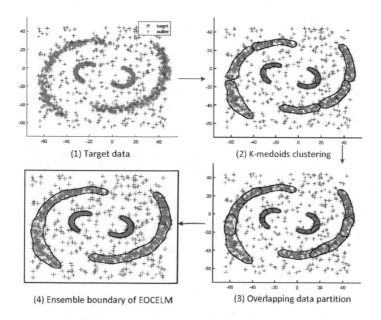

**Fig. 1.** Flowchart of EOCELM.

First of all, we adopt the $k$-medoids clustering (See (2) of Fig. 1) instead of popular $k$-means clustering [16] to create disjoint clusters $\{\Omega_1, ... \Omega_k\}$. The reason is that k-means may create a cluster whose center is outside the cluster, which may degrade the compactness of a data cluster, while k-medoids will not. Another common problem is to determine the number of data clusters $k$ [17]. We discover that in the context of data partition for OCC, this problem is actually not as important as that in data clustering. It should be noted that data partition for OCC does not require a perfect clustering, and a plausible partition will be enough for subsequent data description. Therefore, we simply estimate the cluster number by $k = \lceil \sqrt[3]{n} \rceil$. However, as can be spotted from (2) of Fig. 1, there exist "gaps" between disjoint data clusters created by k-medoids (or any other mainstream clustering algorithm), which actually degrades the generalization performance of ensemble one-class classifier. To bridge the gaps, we for the first time propose to use overlapping partition instead of disjoint partition. The creation of overlapping clusters is explained by Fig. 2: For any two disjoint clusters $i$ and $j$ (black circles), a minimum spanning tree (MST) is

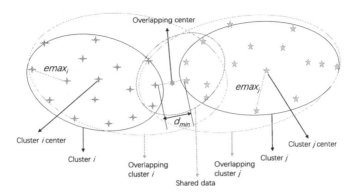

**Fig. 2.** Create overlapping data clusters. (Color figure online)

built within each cluster and the maximum edge length for each MST is found, as $emax_i$ and $emax_j$. Then we calculate the smallest distance $d_{min}$ between cluster members from cluster $i$ and cluster $j$ as inter-cluster distance (which is also referred as "nearest neighbor"). If $d_{min} < \min(emax_i, emax_j)$, we consider that the two clusters should overlap with each other and define the midpoint of nearest neighbor in cluster $i$ and $j$ as the "overlapping center". Afterwards, data points that are closer to the "overlapping center" than two original cluster centers in cluster $i$ and $j$ are set to be "shared data" $\Omega_{ij}$ (red circle). The new overlapping cluster $i$ are constructed by $\Omega'_i = \Omega_i \cup \Omega_{ij}$, and so is cluster $j$ (green circles). As shown in (3) of Fig. 1, overlapping clusters favorably bridge the gap between original clusters. Finally, an OCELM is trained for each cluster and maximum support combining rule [18] is adopted to combine all OCELMs into the EOCELM (See (4) of Fig. 1).

## 3  Experiments

In this section, we demonstrate the effectiveness of the proposed EOCELM by comparing it with two state-of-the-art boundary based OCC approaches, OCSVM and OCELM, on synthetic datasets, UCI datasets and MNIST datasets. In Sect. 3.1, we visualize the decision boundary obtained by three approaches on 2D synthetic datasets from [19] to offer readers a straightforward comparison. In Sects. 3.2 and 3.3, we follow the experimental setting of [16,20] and show the OCC performance of three approaches on UCI datasets and MNIST dataset by calculating the Matthews Correlation Coefficient (MCC):

$$mcc = \frac{TP \cdot TN - FP \cdot FN}{\sqrt{(TP + FP) \cdot (TP + FN) \cdot (TN + FP) \cdot (TN + FN)}} \tag{4}$$

TP, TN, FP and FN denote the number of true positives, true negatives, false positives and false negatives, respectively. The range of MCC is $[-1, 1]$

and larger value indicates better OCC performance. Hyper-parameters (regularization coefficient $C$ and Gaussian kernel width $\sigma$) of three approaches are all selected from $[10^{-6}, ...10^{6}]$ by 5-fold cross-validation. All experiments are carried out under MATLAB 2015b environment on a laptop with i7 4700HQ CPU and 12 GB RAM.

### 3.1 Synthetic Datasets

We generate three 2D synthetic target class datasets for a visual and qualitative comparison. More than one data distribution and densities may be observed within one dataset. It can be easily spooted from Fig. 3 that the proposed EOCELM can yield more compact and accurate boundary than OCELM and OCSVM.

### 3.2 UCI Datasets

For quantitative comparison, we test the proposed EOCELM on 8 commonly used UCI datasets, with sample numbers ranging from 208 to 6598. Since UCI datasets are not specially designed for OCC and no separate testing set is provided, we select the class with largest number of samples as target class while other classes as outlier class for testing, and target class data are randomly partitioned equally into a training and testing set. The experiments are repeated for 10 times and the results (MCC and standard deviation) are shown in Table 1: EOCELM outperforms other approaches on 6 out of 8 datasets.

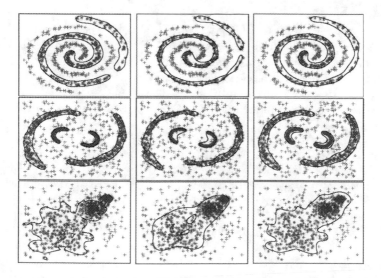

**Fig. 3.** Decision boundaries of EOCELM (left column), OCSVM (middle column), OCELM (right column).

**Table 1.** Performance on UCI datasets.

| Dataset | EOCELM | OCSVM | OCELM |
|---|---|---|---|
| Diabetes | **0.2655**(0.0433) | 0.1296(0.0775) | 0.2038(0.0219) |
| Ionosphere | **0.1417**(0.0504) | −0.2698(0.0384) | 0.1021(0.0987) |
| Abalone | **0.4056**(0.1176) | 0.2406(0.0273) | 0.3186(0.0467) |
| Spambase | **0.3539**(0.0375) | 0.2843(0.0366) | 0.3115(0.0498) |
| Balance | 0.6097(0.1097) | 0.6313(0.1156) | **0.6726**(0.0333) |
| Musk | **0.4351**(0.0942) | 0.2570(0.0212) | 0.3376(0.0326) |
| Vehicle | **0.5051**(0.0491) | 0.3863(0.0133) | 0.4150(0.0377) |
| Sonar | −0.0654(0.0613) | **0.0928**(0.0756) | −0.5580(0.0539) |

**Table 2.** Performance on MNIST datasets.

| Dataset | EOCELM | OCSVM | OCELM |
|---|---|---|---|
| MNIST(0) | **0.5410** | 0.1265 | 0.1657 |
| MNIST(1) | **0.8393** | 0.2247 | 0.3505 |
| MNIST(2) | **0.2061** | 0.1532 | 0.1861 |
| MNIST(3) | **0.3203** | 0.1662 | 0.1712 |
| MNIST(4) | **0.1727** | 0.1249 | 0.1683 |
| MNIST(5) | **0.1631** | 0.1133 | 0.0997 |

### 3.3 MNIST Dataset

We further test the proposed EOCELM on MNIST dataset with a 10000-sample training set and 60000-sample testing set. MNIST consists of 0–9 hand-written digits. Each time training samples of one digit (e.g., 0) are selected to construct an one-class classifier, and the classifier is then tested on the 60000-sample testing set. We test digit 0–5, and the results listed in Table 2 indicates the proposed EOCELM constantly outperform OCELM and OCSVM by evident MCC gain.

## 4  Conclusion

In this paper, we propose a novel EOCELM for OCC. EOCELM builds an ensemble of OCELM classifiers by partitioning the training target data into overlapping clusters, which not only reduce the training and testing complexity of each OCELM but also enables a more delicate description of target data. Compared with other state-of-the-art OCC approaches like OCSVM and OCELM, the proposed EOCELM is easy for parallel processing and shown to have better data description performance. Our future work will be a further investigation into different data partition methods and their relationship with data description performance.

# References

1. Tax, D.M.J.: One-class classification. Ph.D. thesis (2001)
2. Manevitz, L.M., Yousef, M.: One-class SVMs for document classification. J. Mach. Learn. Res. **2**(1), 139–154 (2001)
3. Erfani, S.M., Rajasegarar, S., Karunasekera, S., Leckie, C.: High-dimensional and large-scale anomaly detection using a linear one-class SVM with deep learning. Pattern Recogn. **58**, 121–134 (2016)
4. Shin, H.J., Eom, D.H., Kim, S.S.: One-class support vector machines an application in machine fault detection and classification. Comput. Ind. Eng. **48**(2), 395–408 (2005)
5. Zuo, H., Wu, O., Hu, W., Xu, B.: Recognition of blue movies by fusion of audio and video. In: IEEE International Conference on Multimedia and Expo, pp. 37–40 (2008)
6. Cohen, G., Sax, H., Geissbuhler, A.: Novelty detection using one-class parzen density estimator. An application to surveillance of nosocomial infections. Stud. Health Technol. Inform. **136**, 21–26 (2008)
7. Dasarathy, B.V.: Adaptive local fusion systems for novelty detection and diagnostics in condition monitoring. Proc. SPIE Int. Soc. Opt. Eng. **3376**, 210–218 (1998)
8. Manevitz, L., Yousef, M.: One-class document classification via neural networks. Neurocomputing **70**(7–9), 1466–1481 (2007)
9. Schlkopf, B., Platt, J.C., Shawetaylor, J., Smola, A.J., Williamson, R.C.: Estimating the support of a high-dimensional distribution. Neural Comput. **13**(7), 1443–1471 (2001)
10. Leng, Q., Qi, H., Miao, J., Zhu, W., Su, G.: One-class classification with extreme learning machine. Math. Probl. Eng. **2015**, 1–11 (2015)
11. Tax, D.M.J., Duin, R.P.W.: Support vector data description. Mach. Learn. **54**(1), 45–66 (2004)
12. Rabaoui, A., Davy, M., Rossignol, S., Lachiri, Z., Ellouze, N.: Improved one-class SVM classifier for sounds classification. In: IEEE Conference on Advanced Video and Signal Based Surveillance, AVSS 2007, pp. 117–122. IEEE (2007)
13. Xiao, Y., Wang, H., Zhang, L., Xu, W.: Two methods of selecting Gaussian kernel parameters for one-class SVM and their application to fault detection. Knowl. Based Syst. **59**(2), 75–84 (2014)
14. Lecomte, S., Lengelle, R., Richard, C., Capman, F., Ravera, B.: Abnormal events detection using unsupervised One-Class SVM-Application to audio surveillance and evaluation. In: IEEE International Conference on Advanced Video and Signal-Based Surveillance, pp. 124–129 (2011)
15. Huang, G.B., Zhu, Q.Y., Siew, C.K.: Extreme learning machine: theory and applications. Neurocomputing **70**(1–3), 489–501 (2006)
16. Liu, J., Miao, Q., Sun, Y., Song, J., Quan, Y.: Fast structural ensemble for one-class classification. Pattern Recogn. Lett. **80**, 179–187 (2016)
17. Krawczyk, B., Woniak, M., Cyganek, B.: Clustering-based ensembles for one-class classification. Inf. Sci. **264**(6), 182–195 (2013)

18. Tax, D.M.J., Duin, R.P.W.: Combining one-class classifiers. In: Kittler, J., Roli, F. (eds.) MCS 2001. LNCS, vol. 2096, pp. 299–308. Springer, Heidelberg (2001). doi:10.1007/3-540-48219-9_30
19. Liu, J., Miao, Q., Sun, Y., Song, J., Quan, Y.: Modular ensembles for one-class classification based on density analysis. Neurocomputing **171**(C), 262–276 (2016)
20. Dsir, C., Bernard, S., Petitjean, C., Heutte, L.: One class random forests. Pattern Recogn. **46**(12), 3490–3506 (2013)

# Neural Network Based Dynamic Surface Second Order Sliding Mode Control for AUVs

Kai Zhang[1], Tieshan Li[1(✉)], Zifu Li[2], and C.L. Philip Chen[3]

[1] Navigation College, Dalian Maritime University, Dalian, China
2277493720@qq.com, tieshanli@126.com
[2] Navigation College, Jimei University, Xiamen, China
lzfxmjmul019@163.com
[3] Department of Computer and Information Science,
University of Macau, Macau, China
philip.chen@ieee.org

**Abstract.** In this paper, a novel neural network based dynamic surface second order sliding mode control algorithm is proposed for three-dimensional trajectory tracking control of autonomous underwater vehicles (AUVs) with modeling errors under external disturbances. The controller designed is capable of strengthening robustness of the system and attenuates inherent chattering of classical sliding mode control effectively. An innovative neural network compensator is designed to counteract effects of modeling errors, furthermore, the norm of the ideal weighting vector in neural network system is regarded as the estimated parameter, such that there is only one parameter needs to be adjusted. Meanwhile, the effect of external disturbances is handled by means of hyperbolic tangent function. As a result, the Lyapunov based stability analysis is provided to guarantee semi-global uniform boundedness of all closed-loop signals. Verification of the effectiveness of the proposed algorithm is done through simulation results.

**Keywords:** Autonomous underwater vehicle (AUV) · Trajectory tracking · Dynamic surface control (DSC) · Second order sliding mode control · Neural network (NN) · Hyperbolic tangent function

## 1 Introduction

Today the marine space is a vital competition domain of military and economic powers in the modern world, a large number of nations are energetically developing deep-sea exploration technology [1]. Autonomous underwater vehicles (AUVs) are of great

This work is supported in part by the National Natural Science Foundation of China (Nos. 5117 9019, 61374114), the Fundamental Research Program for Key Laboratory of the Education Department of Liaoning Province (LZ2015006), the Fundamental Research Funds for the Central Universities under Grant 3132016313 and 3132016311, the Hong Kong Research Grants Council under Project no.: CityU113212, Fujian Provincial Department of education Projection (JAJ09148), and The Pan Jinlong project of Jimei University (ZC2012019).

importance for various underwater activities such as underwater rescues, marine science researches, and military purposes, etc.. Therefore, the accurate trajectory tracking control of autonomous underwater vehicles has aroused extensive attention, and so far a large number of robust control methods have been proposed for trajectory tracking of autonomous underwater vehicles. Because of its simplicity, traditional sliding mode control method has been successfully used for position tracking and motion control of underwater vehicles [2, 3], but the discontinuous switching characteristics of the algorithm will cause chattering, which will affect the control accuracy, degrade the system performances and even damage the control units severely. To remove the chattering effect which is inherent in conventional SMC, the second order sliding mode control method was introduced in [4–7]. Recently, to attenuate the influences of the modeling imprecision and external disturbances for the tracking control, a simple adaptive neural network tracking control algorithm was designed for an uncertain autonomous underwater vehicle system in [8].

Motivated by the above-mentioned considerations, in this paper, a novel NN based dynamic surface second order sliding mode control method is proposed for tracking control of autonomous underwater vehicles with modeling errors under external disturbances. The controller, which strengthens robustness of the system, is designed by combining dynamic surface control, second order sliding mode control, radial basis function neural network (RBFNN), and hyperbolic tangent function method. The simulation results of an AUV model illustrate the designed controller suppresses the influence of external disturbances effectively and achieve good control performances for trajectory tracking as well.

## 2   Problem Formulation and Preliminaries

The 6 degrees of freedom nonlinear model of an underwater vehicle motion can be described as [8]

$$M(\eta)\ddot{\eta} + C(v, \eta)\dot{\eta} + g(\eta) + D(v, \eta)\dot{\eta} + \omega + \Delta(v, \eta) = \tau \qquad (1)$$

where, $\eta = [x \quad y \quad z \quad \varphi \quad \theta \quad \psi]^T$ represents position vector and orientation vector with coordinates in earth-fixed reference frame; $M(\eta)$ is the inertia matrix with rigid-body dynamics (including added mass); $v = [u \quad v \quad w \quad p \quad q \quad r]^T$ is the linear and angular vector with respect to the body-fixed reference system; $C(v, \eta)$ represents the matrix of centripetal and Coriolis with added mass forces/moments and rigid-body dynamics. $g(\eta)$ is the vector of gravitational or restoring forces and moments; $D(v, \eta)$ is the hydrodynamic damping coefficients matrix; $\omega$ is an unknown external disturbance vector as a result of waves, wind etc. $\tau$ is the vector of control input forces which is provided by rudders, thrusters or propellers etc. $\Delta(v, \eta)$ is the modeling errors result from parametric errors, system disturbance or non modeling dynamics etc. Under certain conditions, which can have influences on the control performance of a vehicle, especially under the condition of low speed operation.

In this paper, the objective is to achieve a good trace for the desired trajectory $\eta_d$ of AUV with the modeling errors under external disturbances, i.e. $\lim_{t \to \infty} \|\eta - \eta_d\| < \delta, \quad \delta > 0$.

Now, the following notations will be introduced for later use.

Assumption 1: The desired trajectory $\eta_d$ is a fully smooth function of $t$ and $\eta_d$, $\dot{\eta}_d$, $\ddot{\eta}_d$ are bounded, that is, there exists a positive constant $B_0$ satisfy $\eta_d^2 + \dot{\eta}_d^2 + \ddot{\eta}_d^2 \leq B_0$.

Assumption 2: $\omega(t)$ denotes the external environmental disturbances and is bounded, i.e. $|\omega(i)| \leq \omega^*(i) \quad 1 \leq i \leq 6 \quad (\forall \omega^*(i) > 0, \ t \geq 0)$.

Assumption 3: The inertia matrix $M$ is symmetric and positive, and the $M_\eta(\eta) = M_\eta(\eta)^T > 0$ is defined.

Notation1: $\lambda_{\max}(A)$ and $\lambda_{\min}(A)$, respectively, represent the largest and smallest eigenvalues of a square matrix $A$. $\|\cdot\|$ represents Frobenius norm of matrices and Euclidean norm of vectors, i.e., given a matrix $B$ and a vector $Q$, the Frobenius norm and Euclidean norm are given by $\|B\|^2 = tr(B^T B) = \sum_{i,j} b_{ij}^2$ and $\|Q\|^2 = \sum_i q_i^2$.

## 3 Controller Design and Stability Analysis

The detailed design process is described in the next steps.

Choosing $x_1 = \eta; x_2 = \dot{\eta}$, a state space function of 6-DOF dynamic model of AUV can be written as follows.

$$\dot{x}_1 = x_2$$
$$\dot{x}_2 = M^{-1}(\eta)\left(\tau - C(v,\eta)x_2 - D(v,\eta)x_2 - g_\eta - \omega - \Delta(v,\eta)\right) \tag{2}$$

Define the control error surface as follows.

$$z_1 = x_1 - \eta_d \tag{3}$$

$$\dot{z}_1 = x_2 - \dot{\eta}_d \tag{4}$$

The sliding surface $s$ is defined as follows.

$$s = z_2 = \dot{\eta} - \alpha_1 \tag{5}$$

where $\alpha_1$ is the virtual control
$\alpha_1^0$ is defined as follows.

$$\alpha_1^0 = -c_1 z_1 + \dot{\eta}_d \tag{6}$$

$\alpha_1$ can be obtained by introducing a first-order filter with a constant $e_1$ as follows.

$$e_1 \dot{\alpha}_1 + \alpha_1 = \alpha_1^0 \quad \alpha_1(0) = \alpha_1^0(0) \tag{7}$$

The filter error is defined as follows.

$$h_1 = \alpha_1 - \alpha_1^0 \tag{8}$$

Then the proposed control scheme can be designed as follows.

$$\tau = \tau_{st} + \tau_{eq} \tag{9}$$

where $\tau$ is the final controller, $\tau_{st}$ is the super twisting sliding mode control law, and $\tau_{eq}$ is defined as the equivalent control law.

From (9) we can know the final controller consists of the equivalent control which is added with super twisting control. The $\tau_{st}$ is determined as follows.

$$\tau_{st} = \tau_1 + \tau_2 \tag{10}$$

where $\tau_1$ is defined as discontinuous time derivative and $\tau_2$ is in term of continuous function of sliding variable.

$$\dot{\tau}_1 = -p\,\mathrm{sgn}(z_2);\ \tau_2 = -k|z_2|^{0.5}\mathrm{sgn}(z_2) \tag{11}$$

where $p, k$ is control parameter.

$$\dot{s} = \dot{z}_2 = \ddot{\eta} - \dot{\alpha}_1 \tag{12}$$

From (2) we can know

$$\ddot{\eta} = \left(\tau - \left(C_\eta(v,\eta)\dot{\eta} + D_\eta(v,\eta)\dot{\eta} + g_\eta + \omega + \Delta(v,\eta)\right)\right).M_\eta^{-1}(\eta) \tag{13}$$

Given $\dot{s} = 0$, If the $\Delta(v,\eta)$ and $\omega$ are known, then the final equivalent control can be proposed as

$$\tau_{eq}^* = C_\eta\dot{\eta} + D_\eta\dot{\eta} + g_\eta + M_\eta\left(\dot{\alpha}_1 - c_2 z_2 + M_\eta^{-1}\omega + M_\eta^{-1}\Delta(v,\eta)\right) \tag{14}$$

where $c_2 > 0$ is a constant.

Because $\Delta(v,\eta)$ and $\omega$ are unknown, so the RBFNN is used to approximate the $-M^{-1}(\eta)\Delta(v,\eta)$, meanwhile the effect of external disturbances is handled by employing the means of hyperbolic tangent function. we have

$$-M^{-1}(\eta)\Delta(v,\eta) = W_2^{*T}S_2(Z) + \varepsilon_2$$

$$z_2^T W_2^{*T}S_2(Z) + z_2^T\varepsilon_2 \le \frac{\lambda_2^T\|z_2\|^2\|S_2(Z)\|^2}{2b_2^2} + \frac{b_2^2}{2} + \frac{\|z_2\|^2}{2} + \frac{\|\bar{\varepsilon}_2\|^2}{2} \tag{15}$$

where $\lambda_2^T = \|W_2^*\|^2$ is the norm of the ideal weighting vector in a neural network. Since $W_2^*$ is unknown, $\lambda_2^T$ will be replaced by its estimation value in the following design procedure. In this paper, let $\lambda_2 - \hat{\lambda}_2 = \tilde{\lambda}_2$.

Define $d1 = z_2^T M^{-1}(\eta)$, $d2(i) = sign(d1(i))$ and $d = diag(d2)$ $1 \le i \le 6$.
The law of final equation control is proposed as follows.

$$\tau_{eq} = C_\eta \dot{\eta} + D_\eta \dot{\eta} + g_\eta + M(\eta)\left(\dot{\alpha}_1 - c_2 z_2 - \frac{z_2 \hat{\lambda}_2^T \|S_2(Z)\|^2}{2b_2^2} - M^{-1}(\eta)d\omega * \tanh\left(\frac{z_2^T M^{-1}(\eta)d\omega^*}{y}\right)\right) \quad (16)$$

where, $y > 0$ and $\hat{\lambda}_2$ is an adjusted weight vector.
The final proposed controller (9) is transformed as follows.

$$\tau = \left(\int -p\,\mathrm{sgn}(z_2)\right) - k|z_2|^{0.5}\mathrm{sgn}(z_2) + C_\eta \dot{\eta} + D_\eta \dot{\eta} + g_\eta$$
$$+ M(\eta)\left(\dot{\alpha}_1 - c_2 z_2 - \frac{z_2 \hat{\lambda}_2^T \|S_2(Z)\|^2}{2b_2^2} - M^{-1}(\eta)d\omega * \tanh\left(\frac{z_2^T M^{-1}(\eta)d\omega^*}{y}\right)\right) \quad (17)$$

Choose the Lyapunov function candidate

$$V = \frac{1}{2}z_1^T z_1 + \frac{1}{2}z_2^T z_2 + \frac{1}{2}h_1^T h_1 + \frac{1}{2}\tilde{\lambda}_2^T \Gamma_2^{-1}\tilde{\lambda}_2 \quad (18)$$

where $\tilde{\lambda}_2 = \lambda_2 - \hat{\lambda}_2$, $\Gamma_2 = \Gamma_2^T > 0$ is a gain constant matrix, so

$$\dot{V} = z_1^T \dot{z}_1 + z_2^T \dot{z}_2 + h_1^T \dot{h}_1 - \tilde{\lambda}_2^T \Gamma_2^{-1}\dot{\hat{\lambda}}_2 \quad (19)$$

Due to $\dot{z}_2 = \dot{x}_2 - \dot{\alpha}_1$, $\dot{h}_1 = \frac{\alpha_1^0 - \alpha_1}{e_1} - \dot{\alpha}_1^0 = \frac{-h_1}{e_1} + c_1 \dot{z}_1 - \ddot{\eta}_d$, $\dot{\tilde{\lambda}}_2 = -\dot{\hat{\lambda}}_2$ so

$$\dot{V} = z_1^T(z_2 + h_1 + a_1^0 - \dot{\eta}_d) + z_2^T(\dot{x}_2 - \dot{\alpha}_1) + h_1^T(\frac{-h_1}{e_1} + B_2) - \tilde{\lambda}_2^T \Gamma_2^{-1}\dot{\hat{\lambda}}_2 \quad (20)$$

where $B_2 = c_1 \dot{z}_1 - \ddot{\eta}_d$, $B_2(i)$ is a continuous function and has a maximum value $M_2(i)$ i.e. $|B_2(i)| \le M_2(i)$, please refer to [9] for details ($1 \le i \le 6$).
When $p > 0, k > 0$

$$z_2^T M^{-1}(\eta)\left(\int -p\,\mathrm{sgn}(z_2)\right) - k z_2^T M^{-1}(\eta)|z_2|^{0.5}\mathrm{sgn}(z_2) \le 0 \quad (21)$$

Substituting (20) (17) (15) and (12) into (19), we have

$$\dot{V} \le z_1^T(z_2 + h_1 + a_1^0 - \dot{\eta}_d) + \frac{b_2^2}{2} + \frac{\tilde{\lambda}_2^T \|z_2\|^2 \|S_2(Z)\|^2}{2b_2^2} + \frac{\|z_2\|^2}{2} + \frac{\|\bar{\varepsilon}_2\|^2}{2} - c_2\|z_2\|^2$$
$$- z_2^T M^{-1}(\eta)\omega - z_2^T M^{-1}(\eta)d\omega * \tanh\left(\frac{z_2^T M^{-1}(\eta)d\omega^*}{y}\right) + h_1^T(\frac{-h_1}{e} + B_2) - \tilde{\lambda}_2^T \Gamma_2^{-1}\dot{\hat{\lambda}}_2$$
$$(22)$$

It is clear that

$$
\begin{aligned}
-z_2^T M^{-1}(\eta)\omega &\le \left|z_2^T M^{-1}(\eta)\omega\right| \le \left|z_2^T M^{-1}(\eta)d\omega^*\right| \\
\left|z_2^T M^{-1}(\eta)d\omega^*\right| &- z_2^T M^{-1}(\eta)d\omega * \tanh\left(\frac{z_2^T M^{-1}(\eta)d\omega^*}{y}\right) \le 0.2785y
\end{aligned}
\tag{23}
$$

Choose adaptive law

$$
\dot{\hat{\lambda}}_2 = \Gamma_2\left(\frac{\|z_2\|^2\|S_2(Z)\|^2}{2b_2^2} - \sigma_2\left(\hat{\lambda}_2 - \lambda_2^0\right)\right)
\tag{24}
$$

Noting the following fact

$$
\sigma_2\tilde{\lambda}_2^T\left(\hat{\lambda}_2 - \lambda_2^0\right) \le -\frac{\sigma_2\tilde{\lambda}_2^T\tilde{\lambda}_2}{2} + \frac{\sigma_2\left(\lambda_2 - \lambda_2^0\right)^2}{2} \le -a_0\tilde{\lambda}_2^T\Gamma_2^{-1}\tilde{\lambda}_2 + \frac{\sigma_2\left(\lambda_2 - \lambda_2^0\right)^2}{2}
\tag{25}
$$

where, $\frac{\sigma_2}{2\lambda_{max}\left(\Gamma_2^{-1}\right)} \ge a_0$, $\lambda_2^0$ are initial values of $\lambda_2$, $\sigma_2 > 0$, $\lambda_2^0$ and $\sigma_2$ are design constants.

Substituting (25) (24) and (23) into (22), meanwhile choosing $c_1 \ge 1 + a_0, c_2 \ge 1 + a_0, \frac{1}{e_1} \ge \frac{1}{2} + \frac{M_2^2}{2} + a_0$, we have

$$
\begin{aligned}
\dot{V} &\le -a_0\|z_1\|^2 - a_0\|z_2\|^2 - a_0\|h_1\|^2 + \frac{1}{2} + \frac{\|\bar{\varepsilon}\|^2}{2} + \frac{b_2^2}{2} \\
&+ \frac{\sigma_2\left(\lambda_2 - \lambda_2^0\right)^2}{2} - a_0\tilde{\lambda}_2^T\Gamma_2^{-1}\tilde{\lambda}_2 + 0.2785y \le -2a_0 V + D
\end{aligned}
\tag{26}
$$

where,

$$
D = \frac{1}{2} + \frac{\|\bar{\varepsilon}_2\|^2}{2} + \frac{b_2^2}{2} + \frac{\sigma_2\left(\lambda_2 - \lambda_2^0\right)^2}{2} + 0.2785y
$$

From (26), one has

$$
V(t) \le \frac{D}{2a_0} + \left(V(t_0) - \frac{D}{2a_0}\right)e^{-(t-t_0)}
\tag{27}
$$

It follows that, for any $\mu_1 > (D/a_0)^{1/2}$, there is a constant $T > 0$ such that $\|z_1(t)\| \le \mu_1$ for all $t \ge t_0 + T$, and the trajectory tracking errors can be made small if the design parameters are properly selected.

# 4  Simulation Result

In this part, verification of the effectiveness of the proposed control scheme is done through simulation results. The model of the Naval Postgraduate School AUV II [10] is used in this paper.

The reference trajectory is shown as follows.

$$\eta_d = [\,50\sin(t) \quad 20\sin(2t) \quad 20\sin(4t) \quad 3\sin(0.5t) \quad 3\sin(0.5t) \quad 3\sin(0.5t)\,]^T$$

Modeling error is assumed $\Delta(v,\eta) = 6\sin\xi$ $(\xi = z_1 + \dot{z}_1)$. With generality, the external disturbances are defined as a time varying force/moment relies on $\eta$ and $t.\omega = J^T(\eta)f_e(t)$, where $J^T(\eta)$ is the Jacobian transformation matrix.

$$f_e(t) = [\,1+0.5\sin(t) \quad 1+0.4\cos(t) \quad 1+0.5\cos(t) \quad 1+0.4\cos(t) \quad 0.5\cos(t) \quad 1+0.4\cos(t)\,]^T$$

The used parameters of the proposed control algorithm are given as $c_1 = 11$, $c_2 = 16$, $k = 15$, $p = 5$, $e_1 = 0.1$, $y = 0.1$, $\Gamma_2 = diag\{0.5\}$, $\sigma_2 = 0.5$, the original value of $\lambda_2$ is selected as zero. The amount of the nodes in the neural network are selected as $l = 25$, the centres of primary function are evenly distributed in $[-1, 1] \times [-1, 1]$ with the width $\eta_1 = 5$.

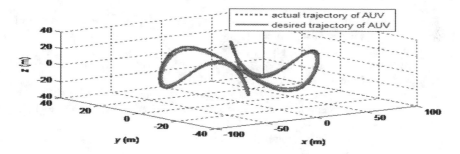

**Fig. 1.** Trajectory of AUV

The results of simulation are shown in Fig. 1, the simulation results illustrate that the trajectory tracking performance of autonomous underwater vehicles is satisfactory by using the proposed controller with modeling errors under external disturbances.

# 5  Conclusion

In this article, by combining dynamic surface control, second order sliding mode control method and neural network algorithm, an adaptive dynamic surface second order sliding mode control method based on neural network is proposed for trajectory tracking control of autonomous underwater vehicles with modeling errors under external disturbances. The method not only attenuates the chatting effect of traditional sliding model control but also reduces the computational burden caused by the neural network which is used for dealing with modeling errors, meanwhile, the external disturbances are handled by employing the quality of hyperbolic tangent function. The results of simulation illustrate the effectiveness of the designed control method.

# References

1. Qi, D., Feng, J.F., Yang, J.: longitudinal motion control of AUV based on fuzzy sliding mode method. J. Control Sci. Eng., 7 pages (2016)
2. Isnail, Z.H., Mokhar, M.B.M., Putranti, V.W.E., Dunnigan, M.W.: A robust dynamic region-based control scheme for an autonomous underwater vehicle. Ocean Eng. **111**, 155–165 (2016)
3. Peng, Y.F.: Robust intelligent sliding model control using necurrent cerebellar model articulation controller for uncertain nonlinear chaotic systems. Chaos, Solitons Fractals **39** (1), 150–167 (2009)
4. Zool, H.I., Vina, W.E.P.: Second order sliding mode control scheme for an autonomous underwater vehicle with dynamic region concept. Math. Prob. Eng., 1–13 (2015)
5. Levant, A.: Higher-order sliding modes differentiation and output-feedback control. Int. J. Control **76**(9–10), 924–941 (2003)
6. Salgado-Jiménez, T., Spiewak, J.-M., Fraisse, P., Jouvencel, B.: A robust control algorithm for AUV: based on a high order sliding mode. In: The MTTS/IEEE Technoocean 2004 (Oceans 2004), Kobe, Japan, pp. 276–281 (2004)
7. Khan, I., Bhatti, A.I., Khan, Q., Ahmad, Q.: Sliding mode control of lateral dynamics of an AUV. In: 9th International Bhurban Conference on Applied Sciences & Technology, Islamabad, Pakistan, pp. 27–31 (2002)
8. Miao, B.B., Li, T.S., Luo, W.L.: NN based a daptive dynamic surface control for fully actuated AUV. Nonlinear Dyn. **84**(2), 1079–1091 (2013)
9. Wang, D., Huang, J.: Neural network-based adaptive dynamic surface control for a class of uncertain nonlinear systems in strict-feedback form. IEEE Trans. Neural Netw. **16**(1), 195–202 (2005)
10. Fossen, T.I.: Guidance and Control of Ocean Vehicles. John Wiley & Sons, New York (1998)

# Vibration Control of a Flexible Robotic Arm by Wave Absorption Based on a Lumped Dynamic Model

Tangwen Yang[1]([⊠]), Yong Qin[2], and Jianda Han[3]

[1] Institute of Information Science, Beijing Jiaotong University,
Beijing 100044, China
twyang@bjtu.edu.cn
[2] State Key Laboratory of Rail Traffic Control and Safety,
Beijing Jiaotong University, Beijing 100044, China
yqin@bjtu.edu.cn
[3] State Key Laboratory of Robotics Shenyang Institute of Automation, CAS,
Shenyang 110016, China
jdh@sia.cn

**Abstract.** A wave absorption control strategy is proposed to suppress vibration at the distal end of a flexible robotic arm while achieving accurate position control. It assumes the flexible arm with an actuator at one end and a load at the other, and interprets the arm's dynamics with a lumped model in terms of mechanical waves entering and leaving the arm at the actuator-arm interface. Control input to the actuator is thus resolved into two superposed waves, which the actuator launches and absorbs simultaneously. From the motion start-up, the launch wave is assigned to the actuator, to which the absorbing wave is added subsequently. The absorbing wave is computed with the delayed tip motion. It absorbs the vibratory energy within the arm, and prevents the wave returning from the arm tip from entering the control system again. The properties of the control scheme proposed are studied throughout. It works very well under uncertainty, and is stable and robust, for tip positioning and trajectory tracking control, as demonstrated in the numerical results.

**Keywords:** Flexible robotic arm · Lumped dynamic model · Vibration control · Wave absorption

## 1 Introduction

Large, flexible robotic systems now feature in many space missions. Not only are they playing a more important role in space station construction and maintenance, and EVA (extravehicular activity) support, but they can also be used to extend and fold the solar arrays on Mars rovers. In addition, large robotic systems find applications in the fields of aircraft and oil tanker clean, and nuclear waste clear-up, where long-reach manipulation is required. Usually, a large robotic system has long and slender arms. For example, the Canadian Mobile Servicing System in the International Space Station is approximately 17 m in length when all the arms are fully extended. Such a robotic

© Springer Nature Singapore Pte Ltd. 2017
F. Sun et al. (Eds.): ICCSIP 2016, CCIS 710, pp. 425–442, 2017.
DOI: 10.1007/978-981-10-5230-9_42

system is far from being stiff, and compared with conventional heavy and bulky industrial robots, it is compliant and safer, and has such advantages as larger work volume, lower energy consumption, etc. But, flexible robotic systems suffer from large deformations and low-frequency vibrations, typically caused by structural flexibility. As a result, issues such as motion planning and dynamic modeling become notoriously difficult, and distal position and force control are more challenging.

Over the past decades, these issues have already received intensive study, with no generic solution to date [1]. Concerning the model of a flexible robotic system, it is frequently derived based on the energy principle with Lagrangian, Hamiltonian or Newton-Euler formulations, and the dynamics equations with infinite vibration modes are usually truncated and remain the first several dominant modes with the assumed-mode method or the finite-element method, as introduced in [2]. In [3–5], lumped systems were used to model flexible-link robots as well. Banerjee and Singhose model a flexible-link robot with a series of rigid beam connected by rotational springs [6]. On the control issue, various approaches such as adaptive control [4], singular perturbation method [7], Lyapunov based controller [8], etc., have been widely investigated. Unfortunately, for these model based controllers, accurate system models are required *a priori*, which have proven difficult to obtain. Dynamics coupling, nonlinearities, parameter variations and uncertainties, etc., contribute to this difficulty. Neurofuzzy appears to be promising to control a flexible manipulator [9], but its learning is time-consuming, and fails to provide fast and accurate response.

Due to the typically light structural damping of a flexible robotic arm, it takes remarkable time for the vibrations at the tip end of the arm to die out after a maneuver. Vibration suppression is a fundamental problem, and thus viable solutions to the problem are required. To the authors' knowledge, the techniques currently used may be generally classified as follows: (a) structure and system design to modify the system dynamics and make the fundamental natural frequency independent of position control [10, 11]; (b) the addition of extra actuators, such as piezoelectric patch actuator to counteract vibration [8]; (c) optimal planning to design suitable actuator motion trajectory [12]; and (d) advanced control algorithms. Of these solutions, control technique is of wide engineering interest and is the focus of this paper as a generic problem. With or without feedback, control attempts to increase the system damping or cancel certain system poles and zeros, which dominate the easily exited vibration modes. As a substantially studied technique, input shaping has been advocated as a feasible solution to reducing vibration of a flexible system [6, 13]. It works by shaping the reference input to the actuator with correctly chosen impulses, but requires knowledge of the flexible system *a priori*, such as the natural frequencies and damping ratios of the first several vibration modes, which however may be uncertain and may vary, and becomes problematic in practice.

From the point of wave motion, the vibration of a flexible structure, such as beam and string, can be interpreted in terms of wave propagating and decaying in waveguide [3, 14–18], and wave based strategies have been introduced to suppress vibration over decades. Matsuda et al. [16] proposed a wave control, in which a compensator formulated as an $H_\infty$ method, is used to minimise the reflective wave to the actuator, for the purpose of vibration control. In [17], a control scheme is developed based on waveform solution of flexible structures, with collocated rate and non-collocated position feedbacks, considering the time delay due to wave motion, and an observer based predictor is introduced to estimate the time-delay of the system state. Besides, some works [18–20] focus on active vibration control with the idea of an imaginary structure, which is used as an absorber to dissipate the wave energy inside the real flexible structure. In [18], an imaginary beam with finite length and distributed damping is assumed to be connected at the free end of a real beam to absorb the vibratory energy of traveling waves. A control scheme for a pendulum system is proposed based on wave absorption [19], where the lateral motion at the pendulum support end satisfies a wave-absorbing condition, and an imaginary counterpart is used to absorb the vibratory energy. In [20], a locally controlled absorber, which comprises of a passive absorber and an internal dynamic feedback, is used for a multi-mass system to tune the vibration characteristics. Wave absorption control needs limited sensing and knowledge of flexible systems. It seems a promising solution to suppress the vibrations at the tip of a flexible arm.

In this paper, a new, practical, wave absorption based control is proposed not only to suppress the vibrations of a flexible arm, but simultaneously position the arm tip precisely. First, a lumped system is used to model the dynamics of the flexible arm, in which damping is neglected. That is, the lumped dynamic model can apply to a worst case of vibratory system. Based on mechanical wave, the motion at the actuator-system interface is interpreted into superposed outward and returning waves. Control input to the actuator is correspondingly resolved into two components, i.e., the launching and absorbing waves. The absorbing wave is applied to restraint the formation of the returning waves, while to absorb the vibratory energy inside the flexible system. It is directly obtained from the measured position at the tip with a specific delay, providing active vibration damping of the overall control system. Finally, numerical results are given to illustrate the effectiveness of the wave control strategy proposed.

## 2  Lumped Dynamic Model of Flexible Robotic Arm

For decades, intensive work has been done to model the dynamics of a flexible robot. Ideally, the model derived is hoped to be accurate and simple enough for the purpose of a real-time control. However, it is actually a quite difficult task. So, approximation is frequently made, as done in the assumed-mode method or the finite element method. Alternatively, lumped mass-spring method is used to model a flexible robotic system. In [5], a flexible beam is modeled by a lumped mass and a weightless linear spring. The model is simple, and computationally efficient, but only one vibration mode is considered. Feliu et al. [4] assumed the mass of a consecutive beam is concentrated in some fixed points, i.e., lumped masses, so that more vibration modes can be taken into account. In [21], a mass-spring model is used to represent a continuous non-linear flexible system, which is lumped- parameter approximation. Since the lumped method is a practical way to derive the dynamic model of flexible structures, it is used below to observe the dynamics of a flexible robotic arm.

To circumvent the effect of gravity, the flexible arm, shown in Fig. 1, is restrained to move in a horizontal plane, and its dynamics behavior is approximated with a lumped system with $n$ mass-spring-damper units. The first mass $m_0$ represents an

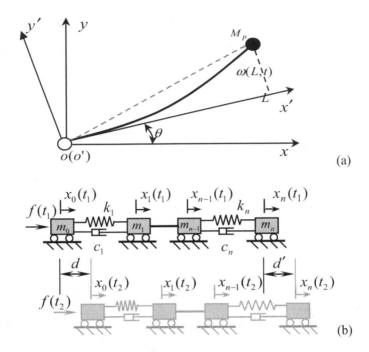

**Fig. 1.** A mass-spring model for a flexible robotic arm: (a) a flexible robotic arm, (b) a lumped mass-spring model

actuator equivalently, and its position is directly controlled by the actuator sub-controller, for the sake of positioning the tip mass $m_n$. Here, the motions of the first and final masses essentially correspond to those of the actuator and of the tip load in the real flexible arm. $x_i(t)$ denotes the displacement of the $i$th mass. $k_i$ and $c_i$ are the spring and damping constants of mass $m_i$ ($i = 1, 2, \cdots, n$), respectively. When an external force $f(t)$ is applied to the first mass, it pushes all masses to move rightwards in sequence.

It is not assumed that the lumped system is uniform. The masses, spring constants and damping coefficients may have different values throughout the system. But, it is required that the vibration modes of the lumped system have a good match with the real flexible arm, and the tip position of the final mass is expected to be

$$x_n(t) = \theta + \omega(L, t)/L \tag{1}$$

where $\theta$ is the rotation angle of the actuator, and presumes that the tip deflection of the flexible arm $\omega(L,t)$ is much less than the arm length $L$.

If there is no deflection and vibration at the tip of the arm, the final mass displacement will be same as the actuator in the lumped system, so will the remained masses. Note that any mass in the middle of the string produces exactly the motion of a point along the arm, and the number of masses indicates the truncated oscillatory frequencies of the arm.

Now, the equations of motion of the lumped system can be derived by virtue of the Newton's law. For the first mass, it yields

$$m_0\ddot{x}_0(t) = f(t) - k_1(x_0(t) - x_1(t)) - c_1(\dot{x}_0(t) - \dot{x}_1(t)) \tag{2}$$

Similarly, for any intermediate mass $i$, the equation of its motion is of the form

$$\begin{aligned} m_i\ddot{x}_i(t) = {} & k_i(x_{i-1}(t) - x_i(t)) - k_{i+1}(x_i(t) - x_{i+1}(t)) \\ & + c_i(\dot{x}_{i-1}(t) - \dot{x}_i(t)) - c_{i+1}(\dot{x}_i(t) - \dot{x}_{i+1}(t)) \end{aligned} \tag{3}$$

$$i = 1, \cdots, n-1$$

and the equation of motion for the final mass can be given by

$$m_n\ddot{x}_n(t) = k_n(x_{n-1}(t) - x_n(t)) + c_n(\dot{x}_{n-1}(t) - \dot{x}_n(t)) \tag{4}$$

Eventually, these equations of motion can be written in a compact state-space form of

$$M_{(n+1)\times(n+1)}\ddot{X} + C_{(n+1)\times(n+1)}\dot{X} + K_{(n+1)\times(n+1)}X = U_{(n+1)\times1} \tag{5}$$

where $M_{(n+1)\times(n+1)} = diag(m_0, m_1, \cdots, m_n)$, $X_{(n+1)\times1} = [x_0\, x_1\, \cdots\, x_n]^T$, $U_{(n+1)\times1} = [f(t)\, 0\, 0\, \cdots\, 0]^T$, and matrices $C$ and $K$ are given by

$$C_{(n+1)\times(n+1)} = \begin{bmatrix} c_1 & -c_1 & 0 & \cdots & 0 & 0 & 0 & 0 & 0 \\ -c_1 & c_1+c_2 & -c_2 & 0 & \cdots & 0 & 0 & 0 & 0 \\ 0 & 0 & 0 & \ddots & 0 & 0 & 0 & 0 & 0 \\ 0 & \cdots & 0 & -c_i & c_i+c_{i+1} & -c_{i+1} & 0 & \cdots & 0 \\ 0 & 0 & 0 & \cdots & 0 & \ddots & 0 & \cdots & 0 \\ 0 & 0 & 0 & 0 & \cdots & 0 & -c_{n-1} & c_{n-1}+c_n & -c_n \\ 0 & 0 & 0 & 0 & 0 & \cdots & 0 & -c_n & c_n \end{bmatrix}$$

$$K_{(n+1)\times(n+1)} = \begin{bmatrix} k_1 & -k_1 & 0 & \cdots & 0 & 0 & 0 & 0 & 0 \\ -k_1 & k_1+k_2 & -k_2 & 0 & \cdots & 0 & 0 & 0 & 0 \\ 0 & 0 & 0 & \ddots & 0 & 0 & 0 & 0 & 0 \\ 0 & \cdots & 0 & -k_i & k_i+k_{i+1} & -k_{i+1} & 0 & \cdots & 0 \\ 0 & 0 & 0 & \cdots & 0 & \ddots & 0 & \cdots & 0 \\ 0 & 0 & 0 & 0 & \cdots & 0 & -k_{n-1} & k_{n-1}+k_n & -k_n \\ 0 & 0 & 0 & 0 & 0 & \cdots & 0 & -k_n & k_n \end{bmatrix}$$

Equation (5) is the dynamic model of the lumped mass-spring-damper system, and used to interpret the dynamic characteristics of the flexible robotic arm. The lumped system may not model the dynamics of a real system precisely. But, its simplicity makes the controller design easy and computationally efficient, and enables to exam the wave behavior of flexible structures.

## 3  Wave Motion in Lumped System

Using these equations above, the motion of each mass in the lumped system can be determined to any input. Figure 2 illustrates the responses of selected masses in a uniform lumped system with 20 masses, to a unit impulse input at the first mass, *i.e.*, $x_0(t) = \delta(t)$, $x_i(0) = 0$, $(i = 1, 2, \cdots, 19)$. A traveling wave propagating rightwards from the first mass can be observed, as it reaches the final mass, a reflected wave returns towards the first mass, superposed on the traveling wave. It is then postulated that the motion of any mass in the lumped system can be obtained by superposing the two waves traveling through that mass, although its motion pattern in space and time is complex. The vibratory motion at the tip of a real flexible manipulator therefore can be viewed as an outcome of two-way waves traveling through all the masses in the equivalent lumped system, and their interaction with the actuator and tip dynamics (*i.e.*, the motions of the first and final masses), which formulate the wave boundary conditions.

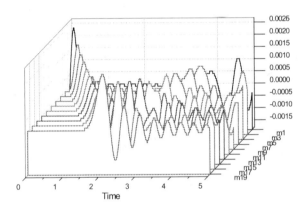

**Fig. 2.** Response of the selected masses to a unit impulse input.

Supposed that the mass-spring system is long enough, and the first mass undergoes a net displacement, the wave launched by that movement will cause the same net displacement at each mass in the string, when it passes that mass. As the launching wave reaches the final mass, it will be reflected, and start to travel back toward the first mass. When this returning wave passes each mass, the augmented displacement is the same as the first. Now, the total net displacement is double the original. Thereafter, the superposed wave motion travels across each mass. This is illustrated in Fig. 3, where the responses are shown for the selected masses in the previous study, to a unit step input, *i.e.*, $x_0(t) = 1$, $x_i(0) = 0$, $(i = 1, 2, \cdots, 19)$. It can be readily seen that when the first mass, *i.e.*, the actuator, launches a wave with a net displacement of one unit, after one reflection, the final mass has undergone a net displacement of two units. All the other masses undergo two-unit net displacements too, as the reflected wave passes each of them. Now if a zero reflection condition can be established at the actuator interface for this returning wave, in other words, the actuator can effectively absorb all the

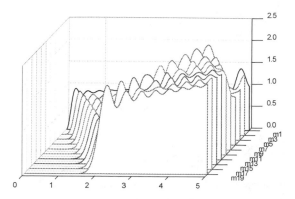

**Fig. 3.** Responses of selected masses to a unit step input.

returning motion, not allowing it to be reflected back into the system again, the entire system will come to rest, having undergone a net displacement of two units. It is this idea which motivates the following controller design.

## 4   Wave Based Control Strategy

### A. Transfer Functions of Dynamic Model

In the control of lumped systems, wave concepts prove fruitful. In [3], the foundation of a wave based control is introduced by exploring the validity and nature of wave concept. Wave is understood as primarily wave front, which propagates vibratory motion as well as DC displacement. In that work, a wave model for an infinite uniform mass-spring system was developed. This model reproduces the lumped system dynamics exactly, while the wave transfer function $G(s)$ of this model is approximated to apply it to a flexible system, since it is transcendental and difficult to work with. This wave transfer function is derived on the basis of a hypothesis, that is, any of the transfer function of two neighbouring masses in the lumped system, is identical to the other, while they are certainly not the same for a finite mass-spring system. Therefore, the transfer function is derived herein from the obtained equation of motion.

Now, back to the equations of motion in Sect. 2, and transform them into the Laplace domain. If the initial state values are zero, the transform of the equation of motion for the first mass is

$$(m_0 s^2 + c_1 s + k_1)x_0(s) - (c_1 s + k_1)x_1(s) = f(s) \tag{6}$$

Similarly, (3) and (4) can be transformed respectively to be

$$(m_i s^2 + c_i s + k_i + c_{i+1} s + k_{i+1})x_i(s) \\ - (c_i s + k_i)x_{i-1}(s) - (c_{i+1} s + k_{i+1})x_{i+1}(s) = 0 \qquad i = 1, \cdots, n-1 \tag{7}$$

and

$$(m_n s^2 + c_n s + k_n)x_n(s) - (c_n s + k_n)x_{n-1}(s) = 0 \tag{8}$$

Equation (8) is rewritten to the form of a transfer function as

$$G_n(s) = \frac{x_n(s)}{x_{n-1}(s)} = \frac{c_n s + k_n}{m_n s^2 + c_n s + k_n} \tag{9}$$

and the transfer functions of all the adjacent mass pairs can be derived, from the second last mass back towards the actuator, with (7), to yield

$$G_i(s) = \frac{x_i(s)}{x_{i-1}(s)} = \frac{c_i s + k_i}{m_i s^2 + c_i s + k_i + (c_{i+1} s + k_{i+1})(1 - G_{i+1})} \tag{10}$$
$$i = n - 1, \cdots, 1$$

and the transfer function $G_0(s)$, between the displacement of the first mass and the applied external force, can be then given by

$$G_0(s) = \frac{x_0(s)}{f(s)} = \frac{1}{m_0 s^2 + (c_1 s + k_1)(1 - G_1)} \tag{11}$$

## B. Launching and Absorbing Motion Definition

Based on wave motion analysis in Sect. 3, the motion of any mass within a lumped system is interpreted as mechanical waves propagating in two directions. These waves within the system are induced by actuator forces or motion, which must also eventually bring the system to rest. Therefore, one of the boundary conditions for these waves can be defined by the actuator motion, the other by the tip or the load end. Enabling the actuator to absorb the waves returning from the final mass, an active vibration control can be achieved essentially.

To move the final mass a desired amount, a controller needs to simultaneously *"push"* the actuator to move half this amount while allowing itself to be *"dragged"* the other half displacement by the returning motion. It means the controller does two jobs, in other words, it gets the actuator to launch and absorb motion at the same time. Launching motion causes the final mass to move half the desired displacement. Absorbing motion counterbalances the waves returning from the tip, and absorbs the vibratory energy out of the system at the actuator, which meanwhile causes another half displacement. A control strategy with this idea elegantly reconciles the potentially conflict of position control and vibration suppression.

To depict the control strategy, the actuator is deliberately isolated from the lumped system, as shown in Fig. 4. The force on its right side is presumed to be made up of two components: launching and returning force waves. This force arises from the

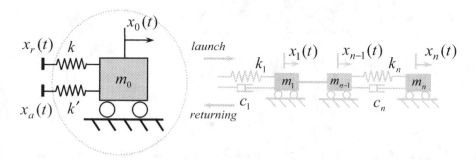

**Fig. 4.** Notional force components.

interaction between the actuator and the other masses in the system. At the same time, the actuator is driven by an external or "input" force, $f(t)$, determined by the controller. The drive force is shown on the left side of the actuator, as if produced by imaginary displacements $x_r(t)$ and $x_a(t)$ acting on two springs with stiffness $k$ and $k'$. The first displacement, $x_r(t)$, is defined as reference input, committed to launch motion and push the system half the target displacement. The second, $x_a(t)$, is absorbing input, designed to counteract the returning wave energy by supplying the right amount of "give" to the actuator when it is pulled by the returning force wave. At steady state, the displacement associated with the absorption process, $x_a(t)$ will then equal the net or total displacement associated with the launch motion, $x_r(t)$. The notional spring $k$ or $k'$ is simply a device to convert $x_r(t)$ or $x_a(t)$ into appropriate input force component to the actuator.

The reference motion $x_r(t)$ could be a step, a ramp, or any trajectory input which is given *a priori*. It launches a wave into the system, and travels down to the final mass where the wave is reflected back towards the actuator. To prevent the reflected wave from returning into the system again, an absorbing input is immediately added to absorb its energy, which is computed from the tip displacement, $x_n(t)$ delayed by a particular time, so that

$$x_a(t) = x_n(t - T_d) \tag{12}$$

where $T_d$ is the time required for the wave to travel from the final mass to the actuator, and is a critical parameter to be determined.

Then, the Laplace transform of (12) is

$$x_a(s) = e^{-T_d s} x_n(s) \tag{13}$$

where $x_n(s)$ can be obtained from the system dynamic model, given by

$$x_n(s) = G_1(s)G_2(s) \cdots G_n(s)x_0(s) = G'(s)x_0(s) \tag{14}$$

where $G'(s)$ is the motion transfer function from the actuator to the final mass.

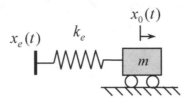

**Fig. 5.** Equivalent input force to the actuator.

Now, the force produced by two notional spring inputs could be merged into an equivalent spring of stiffness $k_e$ with a single input $x_e(t)$, as shown in Fig. 5. This implies that

$$k_e(x_e - x_0) = k(x_r - x_0) + k'(x_a - x_0) \tag{15}$$

Rearranging (15), we have

$$x_e(t) = \frac{k}{k_e}x_r(t) + \frac{k'}{k_e}x_a(t) + x_0(t)\left(1 - \frac{k}{k_e} - \frac{k'}{k_e}\right) \tag{16}$$

Explicitly, the equivalent motion is defined by the reference input, the tip and the actuator motion. Set $k_e = k + k'$, the third term on the right-hand side of (16) will disappear. That is to say, position feedback is not required in the outer loop of the control system (introduced below), and if $k = k'$, we further have

$$x_e(t) = 0.5x_r(t) + 0.5x_a(t) \tag{17}$$

or, in the Laplace domain,

$$x_e(s) = 0.5x_r(s) + 0.5x_a(s) \tag{18}$$

Theoretically, the launch and absorb inputs, $x_r(s)$ and $x_a(s)$, are of the same importance. As to the equivalent motion $x_e(t)$, it is actually the required motion to the actuator, and is the combination of a pre-determined reference motion and a real-time position feedback from the tip.

## C. Control Strategy and Its Properties

Equations (13) and (18) establish the framework of the wave absorption based control, which is illustrated by the block diagram representation of Fig. 6. Overall, the control scheme comprises of inner and outer control loops. The inner is a negative feedback loop for the actuator control, in which the actuator position is fed back and obtained by collocated measurement, and the actuator servo controller could be PID law or other algorithm. In the outer closed loop, the absorbing wave is computed on the basis of the lumped dynamics model, which is used as an observer to estimate the dynamics of the real flexible arm, partly because it is difficult to accurately model the arm dynamics and measure the deflection at the arm tip. Integrated optic sensors (camera, PSD), accelerator, etc., are often used to obtain the deflection and vibration information at the tip of

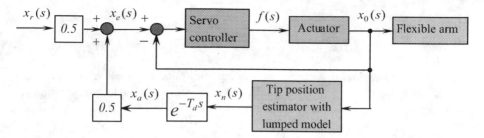

**Fig. 6.** Block diagram of the proposed wave-based control.

a flexible arm, but, these sensor data are unsuitable to compute the tip position because of their slow response time and/or noises.

This control strategy is stable and robust, and works significantly better than simple loop control. Its properties are first analyzed, particularly the steady-state error and stability. Let us presume that a classical PID law $G_c(s)$ is used to control the actuator, written as

$$G_c(s) = k_p + k_d s + k_i \frac{1}{s} \tag{19}$$

where $k_p$, $k_d$ and $k_i$ represent the proportional, derivative and integral constants, respectively.

Now, the transfer function between its input and output motions can be derived, and has the form of

$$G(s) = \frac{x_n(s)}{x_r(s)} = \frac{G_c(s)G_0(s)G'(s)}{2(1 + G_c(s)G_0(s)) - e^{-T_d s}G_c(s)G_0(s)G'(s)} \tag{20}$$

Without loss of generality, the lumped system with one actuator and three masses is taken as an example to investigate these controller properties. Although not necessary, for convenience, the system damping is deliberately neglected herein, and the last three mass-spring pairs are assumed to be identical.

In terms of (9)–(11), the transfer functions in (20) can be given by

$$G_0(s) = \frac{m^3 s^6 + 5km^2 s^4 + 6k^2 m s^2 + k^3}{P(s)}$$

$$G'(s) = \frac{k^3}{m^3 s^6 + 5km^2 s^4 + 6k^2 m s^2 + k^3}$$

thereby obtaining

$$G(s) = \frac{k^3(k_p + k_d s + k_i \frac{1}{s})}{2[P(s) + (k_p + k_d s + k_i \frac{1}{s})(m^3 s^6 + 5km^2 s^4 + 6k^2 m s^2 + k^3)] - e^{-T_d s}(k_p + k_d s + k_i \frac{1}{s})k^3} \tag{21}$$

where

$$P(s) = Mm^3 s^8 + (5km^2 M + km^3)s^6 + (6k^2 mM + 4k^2 m^2)s^4 + (k^3 M + 3k^3 m)s^2$$

and $M$ is the equivalent mass of the real actuator, and $k$ and $m$ are the equivalent spring stiffness and mass values to model the system dynamics of interest. The analytic mass-spring model is lumped-parameter approximation, which is used to virtually represent the continuous flexible robotic arm. The parameters of the lumped model can be experimentally estimated through vibration response analysis of a real flexible arm, as done in [22, 23].

Then, by virtue of the final value theorem, the steady-state error of the control system is given by

$$e_{ss} = \lim_{s \to 0} sE(s) = \lim_{s \to 0} s(x_r(s) - x_n(s)) \tag{22}$$

Using the closed-loop transfer functions derived above, the steady-state error $e_{ss}$ is found to be zero, regardless of the gain values chosen for the PID control law.

Compared with an open-loop case, the addition of the absorption feedback essentially modifies the poles and zeros of the control system. Figure 7 shows the corresponding root loci as $k_p$ and $k_d$ are varied respectively, with the other two control constants fixed. Unfortunately, there exists zeros in the right-half s-plane, which is consistent with the dynamics properties of a non-minimum system, such as a flexible arm. It means that the control system may be not stable for some control gains. As can be seen, a large derivative constant result in poor performance due to the presence of some open-loop zeros on the $j\omega$ axis and in the right-hand half of the s-plane, and it may even cause the whole system unstable. Similarly, from the root locus of the gain $k_p$, it is clear that some care is needed, even though some poles are pushed to move leftwards from the $j\omega$ axis. Because the steady state error of the complete control system is zero, the integrator term in the PID controller is not really necessary, and has been set to zero, making the control algorithm in effect a PD law.

To further analyze the stability of the control strategy, the time-delay term is computed here by a first-order Padé approximation, that is

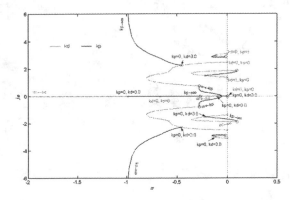

**Fig. 7.** Root contours for the close-loop control system.

$$e^{-T_d s} = \frac{1}{T_d s + 1} \tag{23}$$

and substitute (23) into (21), the characteristic polynomial equation of the closed-loop transfer function can be obtained as follows

$$D(s) = a_1 s^{10} + a_2 s^9 + a_3 s^8 + a_4 s^7 + a_5 s^6 + a_6 s^5 \\ + a_7 s^4 + a_8 s^3 + a_9 s^2 + a_{10} s \tag{24}$$

where

$$a_1 = 2T_d M m^3$$

$$a_2 = 2M m^3 + 2T_d k_d m^3$$

$$a_3 = T_d(10km^2 M + 2km^3) + (2T_d k_p + 2k_d)m^3$$

$$a_4 = 10km^2 M + 2km^3 + 2k_p m^3 + 10km^2 T_d k_d$$

$$a_5 = T_d(12k^2 mM + 8k^2 m) + 10km^2(T_d k_p + k_d)$$

$$a_6 = 12k^2 mM + 8k^2 m + 10km^2 k_p + 12k^2 m T_d k_d$$

$$a_7 = T_d(2k^3 M + 6k^3 m) + 12km^2(T_d k_p + k_d)$$

$$a_8 = 3k^3 M + 6k^3 m + 12k^2 mk_p + 2k^3 T_d k_d$$

$$a_9 = 2k^3 T_d k_p + k^3 k_d$$

$$a_{10} = k^3 k_p$$

Obviously, all the coefficients of the characteristic equation are positive, and it is readily found that the control system has a root at $s = 0$. To this specific case, the system may be marginally stable or marginally unstable, depending on the other roots of the equation. That is, the system stability condition is relevant to the control gains, which determine the location of the roots of the characteristic equation. If all the other roots are in the left-half of the s-plane, the system is stable. The Routh-Hurwitz criterion can be used herein to ascertain whether the system is stable or not. Instead, it tests whether any of the roots lie in the right-half s-plane, without solving the high order polynomial equation. The criterion starts with forming the Routh's tabulation with the coefficients of the equation, and ends the stability analysis by inspecting the signs of the coefficients in the first column of the tabulation. As a result, these coefficients should be positive as well, for the system to be stable. Eventually, the value intervals of the control gains $k_p$ and $k_d$ are found to assure no root in the right-half of the s-plane.

This analysis of a four-mass model can be extended to a system with an arbitrary number of masses, uniform or non-uniform, with same results. The difference is that, as the flexible system changes, the time lag $T_d$, varies with the traveling time for the "wave" to return from the tip to the actuator, which in turn depends on the system flexibility and length. Indeed, when the flexible system is very short or stiff, the delay time is so small that it can be neglected.

## 5   Numerical Simulation

The wave absorption control was previously used to realize a set point control in [24], but it is further tailored here for tip trajectory tracking control as well, and compared to a PD control law. The four-mass lumped model is used in the simulations, and damping in this model is neglected. In fact, any damping presence will help reduce vibrations further, so that the absence of damping in a flexible system becomes a worst case. The parameters of the lumped system are given in Table 1.

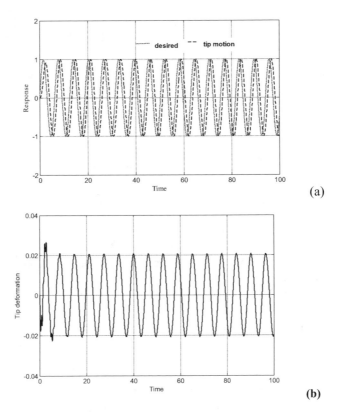

(a)

(b)

**Fig. 8.** The wave-based control results for tip tracking: (a) sine tip trajectories, (b) tip deformation.

Figure 8 shows the responses of the wave based control to a sine reference input. The control gains of the PD law in the inner loop are chosen to be $k_p = 4.0$, and $k_d = 0.5$. Figure 8(a) shows the sine trajectory tracking response at the tip, and (b) the tip vibration. The results of comparative study are given in Figs. 9 and 10, as can be seen the wave absorption strategy nearly does not give rise to vibration at the tip end of this flexible system, whereas the PD law causes large vibrations at the beginning of motion, for both tip tracking and set point control. In the trajectory tracking case, it can be found that there is a response delay time in the wave-based control. Its rise time is apparently longer than that of the PD law, in the set point control. But, the wave absorption approach is much superior to the PD law, from the angle of vibration control, which is the major objective for many flexible systems control.

**Table 1.** Model parameters in the four-mass lumped system

| Parameter symbol | Quantity | Value |
|---|---|---|
| $M$ | Equivalent actuator mass | 1 kg |
| $m$ | Equivalent mass | 0.2 kg |
| $k$ | Equivalent spring stiffness | 50 N/m |
| $T_d$ | Delay time | 1.0 s |

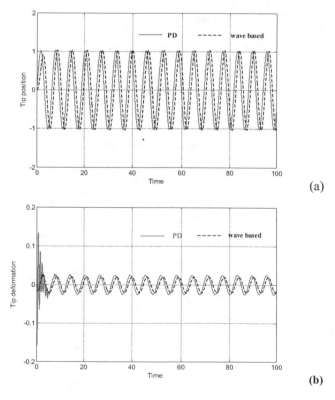

(a)

(b)

**Fig. 9.** Responses of the wave-based and PD controllers for tip tracking.

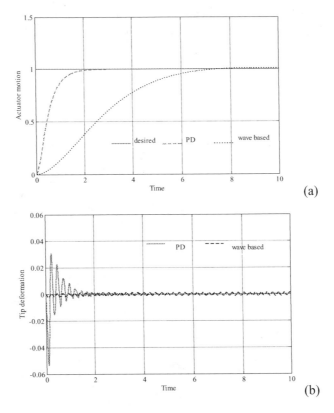

Fig. 10. The set-point control responses: (a) the actuator motion, (b) the vibration at the tip end.

## 6    Conclusion

In this paper, a wave based control is proposed to suppress the vibration at the tip of a flexible robotic arm. The dynamics of the arm is first estimated with a lumped mass-spring system, which could be very flexible, of arbitrary length and with arbitrary component values. The control design is on the basis of interpreting the dynamic behaviour of the flexible system in terms of mechanical waves entering and leaving the system at the actuator-system interface. Therefore, from the motion start-up, a launching motion is assigned to the actuator, to which an absorbing motion is added, to realize active vibration damping and precise motion control, in a single motion. Overall, the control algorithm by virtue of the wave absorption idea is very easy to implement. Numerical simulation results demonstrate that the wave absorption control scheme is stable and robust, for both tip positioning and trajectory tracking control.

# References

1. Robinett III, R.D., Feddema, J., Eisler, G.R., Dohrmann, C., Parker, G.G., Wilson, D.G., Stokes, D.: Flexible Robot Dynamics and Controls. Kluwer Academic/Plenum Publishers, New York (2002)
2. Junkins, J.L., Kim, Y.: Introduction to Dynamics and Control of Flexible Structures. AIAA Education Series, Washington, DC (1993)
3. O'Connor, W.J.: Wave-based analysis and control of lumped-modeled flexible robots. IEEE Trans. Robot. 23(2), 342–352 (2007)
4. Feliu, J.F., Feliu, V., Cerrada, C.: Load adaptive control of a single-link flexible arm based on a new modelling technique. IEEE Trans. Robot. Autom. 15(5), 793–811 (1999)
5. Zhu, G., Ge, S.S., Lee, T.H.: Simulation studies of tip tracking control of a single-link flexible robot based on a lumped model. Robotica 17(1), 71–78 (1999)
6. Banerjee, A.K., Singhose, W.E.: Command shaping in tracking control of a two-link flexible robot. J. Guid. Control Dyn. 21(6), 1012–1015 (1998)
7. Siciliano, B., Book, W.J.: A singular perturbation approach to control of lightweight flexible manipulators. Int. J. Robot. Res. 7(4), 79–90 (1988)
8. Dadfarnia, M., Jalili, N., Xian, B., Dawson, D.M.: A Lyapunov-based piezoelectric controller for flexible Cartesian robot manipulators. ASME J. Dyn. Syst. Meas. Control 126 (2), 347–358 (2004)
9. Caswara, F.M., Unbehauen, H.: A neurofuzzy approach to the control of a flexible-link manipulator. IEEE Trans. Robot. Autom. 18(6), 932–944 (2002)
10. Wang, F.Y., Russell, J.L.: Optimum shape construction of flexible manipulator with total weight constraint. IEEE Trans. Syst. Man Cybern. 25(4), 605–614 (1995)
11. Yang, T.W., Xu, W.L., Han, J.D.: Dynamic compensation control of flexible macro-micro manipulator systems. IEEE Trans. Control Syst. Technol. 18(1), 143–151 (2010)
12. Lambeck, S., Sawodny, O.: Trajectory generation and oscillation damping control for a flexible link robot. In: Proceedings of IECON, Taipei, pp. 2748–2753 (2007)
13. Singhose, W., Vaughan, J.: Reducing vibration by digital filtering and input shaping. IEEE Trans. Control Syst. Technol. 19(6), 1410–1420 (2011)
14. Von Flotow, A.: Traveling wave control for large spacecraft structures. J. Guid. Control Dyn. 9(4), 462–468 (1986)
15. Mei, C., Mace, B.R.: Wave reflection and transmission in Timoshenko beams and wave analysis of Timoshenko beam structures. ASME J. Vibrat. Acoust. 127(4), 282–394 (2005)
16. Matsuda, K., Kanemitsu, Y., Kijimoto, S.: A wave-based controller design for general flexible structures. J. Sound Vibrat. 216(2), 269–279 (1998)
17. Halevi, Y.: Control of flexible structures governed by the wave equation using infinite dimensional transfer functions. ASME J. Dyn. Syst., Meas. Control 127(4), 579–588 (2005)
18. Sawada, Y., Ohsumi, A., Ono, A.: Wave control of a class of flexible beams by an idea of imaginary beam. In: Proceedings of CDC, Kobe, Japan, pp. 4228–4233 (1996)
19. Saigo, M., Tani, K., Usui, H.: Vibration control of a travelling suspended system using absorbing wave control. ASME J. Vibrat. Acoust. 125(3), 343–350 (2003)
20. Filipovic, D., Schroeder, D.: Control of vibrations in multi-mass systems with locally controlled absorber. Automatica 37(2), 213–220 (2001)
21. O'Connor, W.J., McKeown, D.J.: Time-optimal control of flexible robots made robust through wave-based feedback. ASME J. Dyn. Syst. Meas. Control 133(1), 011006:1–6 (2011)

22. Becedas, J., Trapero, J.R., Feliu, V., Sira-Ramirez, H.: Adaptive controller for single-link flexible manipulators based on algebraic identification and generalized proportional integral control. IEEE Trans. Syst. Man Cybern. B Cybern. **39**(3), 735–751 (2009)
23. Yang, T.W.: Vibration suppression and error compensation control for flexible space manipulators - sensing, control and experiments. Ph.D. dissertation, Mechanical Engineering, SEU, Nanjing, China (2001)
24. Yang, T.W., O'Connor, W.J.: Wave theory applied to vibration control of elastic robot arms. In: Proceedings of IASTED-MIC, Innsbruck, Austria, pp. 260–265 (2005)

# Automatic Driving Control Method Based on Time Delay Dynamic Prediction

Jianhui Zhao[1,2], Xinyu Zhang[1(✉)], Ping Shi[3], and Yuchao Liu[4]

[1] Tsinghua University, Beijing, China
xyzhang@tsinghua.edu.cn
[2] Military Transportation University, Tianjin, China
[3] University of Science and Technology, Beijing, China
[4] Institute of Electronic Engineering of China, Beijing, China

**Abstract.** Because of the delay and the front sight distance and other factors in the driving process, self-driving cars can not accurately tracking the path. This paper presents an automatic driving control method based on prediction of the dynamic delay. The vehicle kinematics model to predict the vehicle motion direction and position information of 't' seconds delay time after. And according to deviation value between driving direction and track direction selection the optimal front sight distance. Matlab simulation results show that improved algorithm can track the path at 7 m/s, the average error is controlled within 0.3 M, tracking performance is better than traditional pure pursuit method.

**Keywords:** Automatic driving · Intelligent driving · On-board camera · Complex traffic environment

## 1 Introduction

Autonomous vehicle is an integral part of the future intelligent transportation system [1], and the vehicle automatic steering system in autonomous vehicle control has a very important position. Trajectory tracking control is a basic problems in the process of automatic steering control, which requires the autonomous vehicle to reach the planning trajectory point at the specified time [2, 3]. Because of vehicle is a strong nonlinear, highly coupled and complex system, it is difficult to establish precise dynamics model, the autonomous vehicle trajectory tracking control is always a difficult problem [4–6].

## 2 Related Work

Vehicle automatic navigation technology is a hotspot of many engineering fields. At home and abroad, there are many scholars to study the path tracking control method, which mainly include PID (Proportion integration differentiation) control, fuzzy control, optimal control and pure tracking control method, PID control and Fuzzy control is a kind of does not depend on the specific mathematical model [7, 8], Optimal control and Pure Pursuit control depends on the specific mathematical model [9, 10].

The Pure Pursuit controller is a proportional controller which can convert the lateral deviation of the position and the desired position to the lateral control. This method has

© Springer Nature Singapore Pte Ltd. 2017
F. Sun et al. (Eds.): ICCSIP 2016, CCIS 710, pp. 443–453, 2017.
DOI: 10.1007/978-981-10-5230-9_43

good robustness, and can achieve very good tracking performance even in the large lateral deviation or reference path curvature discontinuity. South Korea Yeu Tae-Kyeong et al. is proposed a tracking algorithm based on vector tracking. The method is realized by using the screw theory, according to the position of the vehicle and the deviation of the course. This method has higher tracking accuracy and stronger adaptability, and it can realize the curve tracking of vehicles in the viscous soil [11]. Kise, M. et al. is proposed based on the minimum turning radius and maximum swing angular rate to path planning, and design two kinds of steering control method, full forward steering and forward - backward - forward steering method using cubic spline function [12]. Chen et al. generates four element state space by a given curve path, in the preview control obtained the vehicles of the future values and target values, by use of optimal control theory to design the tracking controller [13].

All the algorithms mentioned above have high complexity, and the path planning of the three spline function curve is difficult to control. Tracking algorithm based on vector tracking is rather complicated, and is not easy to implement. Chen Jun et al. proposed methods make the design of tracking controller is very complex. The complexity of the algorithm will bring great difficulties to the actual system design, and also easily to reduce the feasibility and stability of the algorithm.

In summary, many scholars have studied the path following control based on the lateral preview error, and have achieved a lot of research results. However, the research on path tracking controller based on the combination of the system delay and preview error model is very little. This paper will focus on the problems exposed in the above research and practice, and establish a set of improved algorithm based on the Pure Pursuit model.

## 3  Pure Pursuit Model

### 3.1  Selecting a Template (Heading 2)

Pure pursuit algorithm (Pursuit Pure) for the study of the robot has many years of history. Many research results show that, as a general tracking algorithm, the pure tracking algorithm shows its great reliability. The algorithm is a geometric calculation method, the purpose is to calculate the vehicle to reach the designated position required to walk through the arc length [14]. The method is simple, intuitive and easy to implement. The key is to determine a suitable visibility distance. The algorithm simulates the vision of the driver in the vehicle and has the bionic characteristics. It has been widely used in the field of path tracking. The algorithm can be expressed in Fig. 1.

$$D + x = R$$

$$D^2 + y^2 = R^2$$

$$x^2 + y^2 = L^2$$

Thus launched: $R = \frac{L^2}{2x}$

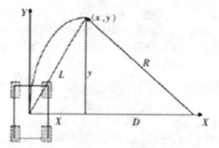

**Fig. 1.** Pure Pursuit geometric analysis

From the point of view of control theory, the four wheel car body is a very complex controlled object, which is related to many factors, such as tire, ground property, slippage, and the implementation of mechanism error. Many researchers have done a lot of work in this area, trying to use mathematical methods to accurately describe such a system. But they are limited by accuracy.

In this paper, a simplified two wheel vehicle kinematics model, which is proposed by A.J. Kelly, is used to consider the tire as a rigid wheel, without considering the lateral slip of the tire and the ground. Based on the calibration test to establish the relationship between vehicle front axle middle position of the rocker arm shaft rotation and steering angle, the actual control of the angle of the front wheels of the object into the front middle position of the virtual steering angle. The kinematics model of the two wheeled vehicle is simplified as shown in Fig. 2. The following relations can be obtained by the kinematic analysis:

$$x'(t) = v(t) \cos \Phi(t)$$

$$y'(t) = v(t) \sin \Phi(t)$$

$$\Phi(t) = v(t) \tan \delta(t)/1$$

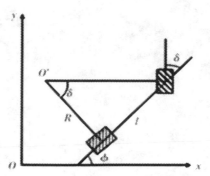

**Fig. 2.** Simplified two wheel vehicle kinematics model

In the formula, 'l' is axial spacing, δ is front wheel angle, Φ is vehicle heading angle. The above equations represent output position (x, y, Φ) and the relationship between the control speed 'v' and the declination of the front wheel δ. Available from Fig. 2:

$$R = 1/\tan\delta$$

In the formula, R is the turning radius, l is wheelbase, and δ is steering angle. By calculating the visibility distance L and deviation of X, we can calculate the turning radius that vehicle to reach the target. Combined with the formula (3), had δ = arctan (2 lx/(L^2)), the formula reflects the relationship between the pure tracking algorithm and the vehicle yaw angle, which lays a theoretical foundation for the establishment of tracking control system. And how to determine the appropriate sight distance has become a key factor influencing the pure pursuit tracking effect.

# 4    Improved of Pure Pursuit Model

## 4.1    Delay Prediction Model

In practice, it is found that there is a delay of 0.2–0.5 s between the steering signal from the vehicle computer and the turning of the steering wheel. And the vehicle is still in the process of motion. This will cause the vehicle to have the very big deviation in the path tracking, if in the high speed situation, will cause the entire vehicle to lose control. It is difficult to reduce or eliminate the delay from the vehicle hardware level. In this paper, we propose a method to eliminate the delay of the system, through the prediction of the position and direction of the vehicle after the delay, so that the vehicle path tracking is more stable.

As shown in Fig. 3, the position of the vehicle at the moment is P (x, y), known as the speed, position, course, wheel rotation. After 't' seconds delay, the vehicle will reach $P'(x', y')$, the model assumes that the time delay of the vehicle is moving at a constant speed, and the wheel rotation angle does not change. 't' seconds after, the expression of the vehicle direction and location is calculated as follows;

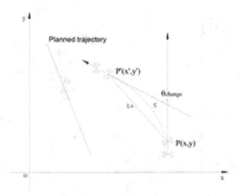

**Fig. 3.** Vehicle motion trajectory in time delay process

The path arc length of the time delay process with constant velocity:

$$S = V \cdot T$$

From Formula (3):

$$R = 1/\tan(\delta)$$

From plane analytic geometry:

$$Ls = 2R\sin\frac{S}{(2R)}$$

By Formula 1 can get the coordinates $p'$ with respect to the point P, the vehicle after t seconds delay after the position relative to the coordinates of the current position of the vehicle:

$$xc = \frac{Ls^2}{2R}$$

$$yc = \sqrt{LS^2 - \frac{Ls^4}{4R^2}}$$

$(x', y')$ is the vehicle position after t seconds delay, the formula is as follows:

$$x' = xc \cdot \cos(\theta - \frac{\pi}{2}) - yc \cdot \sin(\theta - \frac{\pi}{2}) + x;$$

$$y' = xc \cdot \sin(\theta - \frac{\pi}{2}) + yc \cdot \cos(\theta - \frac{\pi}{2}) + y;$$

According to the vehicle kinematics model:

$$\theta change = V \cdot T \cdot \tan(\delta)/1;$$

$\theta$ is Vehicle heading angle, $\theta change$ is the change of course during the time delay, $\theta t$ is the final course angle of vehicle delay.

## 4.2   Preview Point Selection

The traditional way of choosing preview point is in the vehicle as the center of the circle, draw a circle of radius L.L is front sight of the vehicle. But there are some problems in the preview mode, when the vehicle is in the curve of the relatively large curvature, as shown in Fig. 4, the selection of preview points will lead to a large deviation between the vehicle's track and the Target trajectory. This section has been improved on this issue.

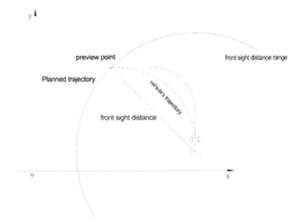

**Fig. 4.** Traditional preview point selection method

As shown in Fig. 5, the first step to find a predetermined trajectory on the nearest point of the vehicle M, and assume that the vehicle in this location. The second step, with P as the starting point to extend the front path to find the LO meter at the O point. O point is the preview point for the vehicle, LO is front sight distance in this model. But in the final calculation of the wheel angle, it is necessary to calculate the linear distance between the vehicle and the preview point L. Finally, the L is brought into the pure pursuit model to calculate the vehicle's trajectory. Compared With the traditional PP model, when the car through the greater curvature curve, the new method is equivalent to reduce the traditional preview model front sight distance. So the vehicle can track the curve track more accurately.

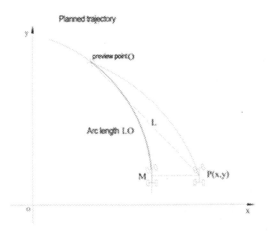

**Fig. 5.** Improved preview selection method

## 4.3  Foresight Selection

Foresight distance in pure pursuit model is a key parameter, the value of the size influence vehicle tracking effect. The larger the foresight distance will make the machine along a small radian arc inching closer to the default path, mechanical tracking does not generate large oscillations in the approximation process. But the time of vehicle approach path will be longer. The smaller the foresight distance will make mechanical along a larger arc path approximation, able to approach the preset path in a short time. But vehicle will oscillate. Based on the analysis of the above two points, the distance is too large or too small is not conducive to vehicle tracking. Numerous studies using a compromise, which gets larger and smaller foresight distance tracking effect by experiment, choose a moderate size of foresight distance. This approach can achieve a better tracking effect in some degree. But because of fixed foresight distance, not based on actual changes and make changes, is not the best. On the other hand, the vehicle speed also affects the tracking effect. The vehicle speed is smaller, the foresight distance becomes short, and the tracking precision is higher. And vice versa, so it is necessary to consider the vehicle speed.

Through the relationship between the long-term experimental data summary and analysis of the foresight distance and speed can be expressed as (Only consider the bend, turn the speed will not exceed 30 km/h):

$$0 < V < 10 \, \text{km/h} \, 2 - 4 \, \text{m}$$

$$10 < V < 20 \, \text{km/h} \, 4 - 5 \, \text{m}$$

$$20 < V < 30 \, \text{km/h} \, 5 - 6 \, \text{m}$$

According to the current vehicle speed feedback to dynamically select the range of preview distance [15], because the speed will not sudden change, so the preview distance will not happen particularly large changes, that can ensure the stability of the vehicle.

Vehicle when driving speed and road curvature has been changing, so foresight distance dynamic regulation is particularly important for the stability control of the car . This section puts forward a method to dynamically adjust the foresight distance. First, using the above method to determine the range of foresight distance according to the speed. And then temporarily freeze the current state of the vehicle, Calculated in the series of steering wheel angle the car to the corresponding to the pre aiming point heading angle, and then the preview Point Road and the direction of the vehicle heading difference, find the heading error minimum value corresponding to the front line of sight and the forward-looking distance that is to determine the final vehicle at the moment of the horizon. By this point by point freezing search to mimic the driver's control behavior, and identify the most appropriate foresight distance, effectively reduce the vehicle tracking the heading error.

## 5   Matlab Simulation Result

Simulation of the impact of vehicle delay on path tracking in Matlab environment. The initial conditions of the simulation are set as follows: The road consists of straight section and curve section. Route length is 100 m, The initial position is (0, 0), the end point is (87.5, −28.6); The starting position of the initial vehicle is the same as the initial position of the road, vehicle heading is 1.85 PI, wheelbase L = 3.05 M, control cycle T = 0.1 s, In the case of speed 7 m/s, Delay t respectively, the value of 0.3 s, 0.4, 0.5 s tracking simulation. Effect of different delay time on vehicle tracking algorithm. The simulation tracking effect is shown in Figs. 6, 7 and 8, and the tracking error results are shown in Table 1.

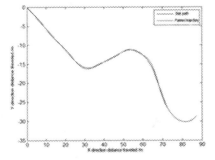

**Fig. 6.** 0.3 s delay tracking effect chart

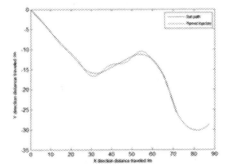

**Fig. 7.** 0.4 s delay tracking effect chart

**Table 1.** Chart lateral error statistics in delay

| [1] Delay/s | [2] Average/m | [3] Maximum/m |
| --- | --- | --- |
| 0.3 | 0.23 | 0.57 |
| 0.4 | 0.37 | 0.83 |
| 0.5 | 1.80 | 7.72 |

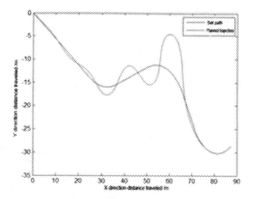

**Fig. 8.** 0.5 s delay tracking effect

The impact of the delay on the vehicle's trajectory tracking is not very large, the average error is 0.23 m, and the maximum error is 0.48 m. In the case of 0.4 s delay, the vehicle has a relatively large tracking error in the corners, and the car has a shock, the average error is 0.37 m, but the maximum deviation is 0.83 m. In the case of 0.5 s delay, the vehicle has lost control, cannot travel along the default path, the average error is 1.8 m, the maximum deviation of 7.7 m.

To improve the simulation of the pure tracking model, the initial conditions do not change, simulation tracking effect as shown in Figs. 9, 10 and 11, tracking error results as shown in Table 2.

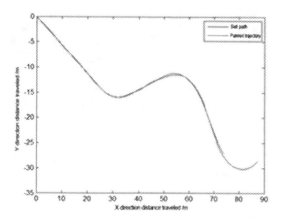

**Fig. 9.** Tracking effect chart after eliminating the 0.3 s delay

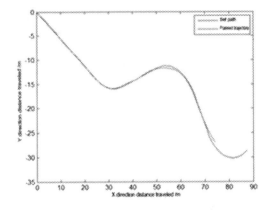

**Fig. 10.** Tracking effect chart after eliminating the 0.4 s delay

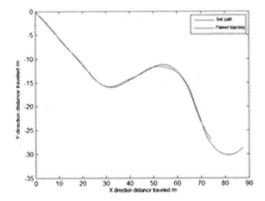

**Fig. 11.** Tracking effect chart after eliminating the 0.5 s delay

**Table 2.** Statistical results of error after eliminating the delay

| Delay/s | Average/m | Maximum/m |
|---------|-----------|-----------|
| 0.3 | 0.19 | 0.41 |
| 0.4 | 0.23 | 0.52 |
| 0.5 | 0.27 | 0.58 |

## 6  Conclusion

For the pure pursuit model tracking error sources of pure pursuit algorithm, the algorithm can calculate more reasonable preview point and eliminate the influence of delay of vehicle path tracking, so that the body in the tracking path planning is in a steady state.

Two kinds of simulation model in the MATLAB environment when travel speed of 7 m/s, delay is 0.5 s, based on dynamic delay prediction model to the average error of the path tracking control in less than 0.3 m, visible algorithm stability.

# References

1. Papadimitratos, P., De La Fortelle, A., Evenssen, K., et al.: Vehicular communication systems: enabling technologies, applications, and future outlook on intelligent transportation. IEEE Commun. Mag. **47**(11), 84–95 (2009)
2. Crawford, D.W, Talamantes, I.D., Emptage, T., et al.: Interactive lean sensor for controlling a vehicle motion system and navigating virtual environments. U.S. Patent 9,120,021, 1 Sep 2015
3. Bella, F.: Driving simulator for speed research on two-lane rural roads. Accid. Anal. Prev. **40** (3), 1078–1087 (2008)
4. Setlur, P., Wagner, J.R., Dawson, D.M., et al.: A trajectory tracking steer-by-wire control system for ground vehicles. IEEE Trans. Veh. Technol. **55**(1), 76–85 (2006)
5. Guo, L., Ge, P.S., Yue, M., et al.: Lane changing trajectory planning and tracking controller design for intelligent vehicle running on curved road. Math. Prob. Eng. **2014**, 9 (2014)
6. Yi, J., Song, D., Zhang, J., et al,: Adaptive trajectory tracking control of skid-steered mobile robots. In: Proceedings of 2007 IEEE International Conference on Robotics and Automation, pp. 2605–2610. IEEE (2007)
7. Li, S., Wei, W., Wang, R.: Study on control structure for the automated guided vehicle base on visual navigation. In: The 27th Chinese Control and Decision Conference (2015 CCDC), pp. 2515–2518. IEEE (2015)
8. Zhang, M., Ma, W., Liu, Z., et al.: Fuzzy-adaptive control method for off-road vehicle guidance system. Math. Comput. Model. **58**(3), 551–555 (2013)
9. Elbanhawi, M., Simic, M., Jazar, R.: Receding horizon lateral vehicle control for pure pursuit path tracking. J. Vibr. Control 1077546316646906 (2016)
10. Enrong, H.K.Z.Z.M., Mingsheng, S.Z.X.B.L.: Joint control method of speed and heading of navigation tractor based on optimal control. Trans. Chin. Soc. Agric. Mach. **2**, 030 (2013)
11. Yeu, T-K., Park, S-J., Hong, S., et al.: Path tracking using vector pursuit algorithm for tracked vehicles vehicles driving on the soft cohesive soil. In: 2006 SICE-ICASE International Joint Conference, pp. 2781–2786 (2006)
12. Kise, M., Noguchi, N., Ishii, K., Terao, H.: Development of the agricultural autonomous tractor with an RTK-GPS and a FOG. In: IFAC: Proceedings of the 4th IFAC Symposium on Intelligent Autonomous Vehicles, pp. 103–106 (2001)
13. Jun, C., Zhongxiang, Z., Ryo, T., et al.: On-tracking control of tractor running a long curved paths. Trans. CSAE **22**(11), 108–111 (2006)
14. Coulter, R.C.: Implementation of the pure pursuit path tracking algorithm. Robotics Institute, Carnegie-Mellon University, Pittsburgh, PA (1992)
15. Kelly, A.J.: A Feedforward Control Approach to Local Navigation Problem for Autonomous Vehicles. CMU Robotics Institute Technical Report (1994)

# Optimal Multiple-Sensor Scheduling for General Scalar Gauss-Markov Systems with the Terminal Error

Jiapeng Xu[1], Chenglin Wen[1(✉)], Daxing Xu[2], and Huiying Chen[3]

[1] School of Automation, Institute of Systems Science and Control Engineering,
Hangzhou Dianzi University, Hangzhou 310018, China
wencl@hdu.edu.cn
[2] College of Electrical and Information Engineering,
Quzhou University, Quzhou 324000, China
[3] School of Engineering, Huzhou University, Huzhou 313000, China

**Abstract.** In this work, we study finite-horizon multiple-sensor scheduling for general scalar Gauss-Markov systems, extending previous results where only a class of systems are considered. The scheduling objective is to minimize the terminal estimation error covariance. Only one sensor can transmit its measurement per time instant and each sensor has limited energy. Through building a comparison function and solving its monotone intervals, an efficient algorithm is designed to construct the optimal schedule.

**Keywords:** Kalman filtering · Multiple-Sensor scheduling · Terminal estimation error covariance

## 1 Introduction

With the development of wireless communication technology, wireless sensor networks (WSNs) have attracted a wide spectrum of applications such as health care, environment monitoring, smart grid [1–3]. In WSNs, a large number of sensor nodes deployed in the area of interest provide various information for observers. However, the available resources such as the sensor energy and communication bandwidth are usually limited in WSNs, which restricts the system performance.

In this context, optimal sensor scheduling problems for remote state estimation have received considerable attention in recent years. The main objective is to minimize cost functions related to the state estimation error. Considering that only one sensor out of a set of sensors can perform a measurement, Huber [4] proposed a information-based pruning algorithm to minimize the estimation error over multiple time steps. Vitus *et al.* [5] considered a similar problem, and provided an optimal and a suboptimal algorithm to prune the search tree of all possible sensor schedules. Joshi and Boyd [6] approximately solved one step sensor scheduling problem based on convex optimization theory. Further,

© Springer Nature Singapore Pte Ltd. 2017
F. Sun et al. (Eds.): ICCSIP 2016, CCIS 710, pp. 454–461, 2017.
DOI: 10.1007/978-981-10-5230-9_44

Mo *et al.* [7] developed a multi-step sensor selection strategy to minimize an objective function related to the estimation error covariance matrix using a relaxed convex form. To achieve the better estimation quality, event-based sensor data scheduling algorithms were proposed in [8–11].

However, there exist the applications in which we focus on the terminal estimation error covariance in practice. Examples include interceptors, standardized tests and other discrete events. Related studies on minimizing terminal estimation error covariance have emerged in past few years. Savage and La Scala [12] firstly presented a set of results in the context of minimizing a terminal cost for a particular class of scalar systems. Further for more general scalar systems, the explicit optimal scheduling policies with the terminal estimation error covariance for single-sensor and multiple-sensor cases respectively were provided in [13,14]. Shi and Xie [15] constructed an optimal sensor power schedule to minimize the expected terminal estimation error covariance over a packet-dropping network.

In this paper, we consider finite-horizon multiple-sensor scheduling for state estimation. The objective is to minimize the terminal estimation error covariance for general scalar Gauss-Markov systems subject to the sensor energy and communication bandwidth constraints. This work extends the previous results by Jia *et al.* did in [14], where the authors showed that when only a subset of the sensors perform the measurements per time instant, a good-sensor-late-broadcast (GSLB) rule performs optimally for a class of scalar Gauss-Markov systems. This paper considers the case of selecting one sensor per time instant. Through building a comparison function and solving its monotone intervals (see Lemma 2), we design an efficient algorithm to construct the optimal schedule for general scalar Gauss-Markov systems.

**Notations.** The positive integer $k$ is the time index. $\mathbb{R}_+$ is the set of non-negative real numbers. For functions $f$, $f_1$, $f_2$ with the appropriate domains, $f_1 f_2(z) := f_1(f_2(z))$ and $f^t(z) := f(f^{t-1}(z))$ with $f^0(z) := z$ and $f^{-1}(z) = (f(z))^{-1}$.

## 2 Problem Setup

Consider the following scalar Gauss-Markov system:

$$x(k+1) = ax(k) + w(k), \qquad y_i(k) = c_i x(k) + v_i(k), \tag{1}$$

where $x(k)$ is the system state, $y_i(k)$ is the measurement taken by sensor $i$ for $i \in \{1, 2, \cdots, M\}$, $w(k)$, $v_i(k)$ and the initial condition $x(0)$ are mutually uncorrelated zero-mean Gaussian random variables with covariances $q > 0$, $r_i > 0$ and $p_0 > 0$, respectively. In addition, $v_i(k)$ and $v_j(k)$ are mutually uncorrelated if $i \neq j$. Define $b_i := c_i^2 / r_i$. Without loss of generality, assume $b_1 < b_2 < \cdots < b_M$. Assume $a, c \neq 0$.

Considering the communication bandwidth constraint, only one sensor can access the communication channel to transmit its measurement per time instant. And consider each sensor has limited energy and assume the energy of all sensors only can send $d$ of the measurements to the remote estimator. Let $J_i > 0$ be the available transmission times of sensor $i$, then $\sum_{i=1}^{M} J_i = d$. Without loss of generality, we assume $T = d$. Thus the sensors are selected according to a schedule $s$ within a time-horizon $T$ denoted as

$$s := [s(1), s(2), \cdots, s(T)], \qquad (2)$$

where $s(k) \in \{1, \cdots, M\}$, indicating the sensor index of the $k$th measurement scheduled within the time-horizon $T$. Assume that $T \geq M$. Let $\gamma_i(k)$ be the indicator function whose value (1 or 0) implies whether sensor $i$ is selected to use the communication channel at time $k$. Thus we have

$$\sum_{i=1}^{M} \gamma_i(k) = 1, k = 1, 2, \cdots, T. \qquad (3)$$

For linear Gaussian systems, the Kalman filter is the best estimator of $x(k)$ in a minimum mean-square sense [16]. For a given schedule $s$, the state estimation error covariance $p(k)$ can be recursively calculated partly in information form

$$p_s(k+1) = \left[ \frac{1}{(a^2 p_s(k) + q)} + b_{s(k+1)} \right]^{-1}. \qquad (4)$$

Taking the limit as $r_i \to \infty$ for $i \in \{1, 2, \cdots, M\}$, the update (4) can be rewritten as

$$p(k+1) = a^2 p(k) + q. \qquad (5)$$

If $|a| \geq 1$, i.e., $a$ is unstable, $p(k)$ in (5) diverges as $k \to \infty$. On the other hand, if $|a| < 1$, i.e., $a$ is stable, $p(k)$ in (5) converges to a steady-state value $\bar{p}$ as $k \to \infty$ and satisfies $\bar{p} = a^2 \bar{p} + q$. Thus we have $\bar{p} = q/1 - a^2$.

Denote $S$ as the set of all possible schedules. In this paper, we wish to find an optimal schedule $s \in S$ to minimize the terminal error covariance subject to the sensor energy and communication bandwidth constraints, i.e.,

*Problem 1.*

$$\min_{s \in S} p_s(T)$$
$$\text{s.t. } \sum_{i=1}^{M} \gamma_i(k) = 1, k = 1, 2, \cdots, T$$
$$\sum_{k=1}^{T} \gamma_i(k) = J_i, i = 1, 2, \cdots, M.$$

## 3    Optimal Schedule

In [14], the authors showed that when $|a| \geq 1$, the optimal scheduling policy to Problem 1 is that good sensors should be scheduled as late as possible. However, they did not present the optimal schedule for the case $|a| < 1$. In this section, we will construct the optimal schedule to Problem 1 for general scalar Gauss-Markov systems.

First define functions $h$, $g_i$, $F_{i,j} : \mathbb{R}_+ \to \mathbb{R}_+$ as follows:

$$h(z) := a^2 z + q, \tag{6}$$

$$g_i(z) := \left(h^{-1}(z) + b_i\right)^{-1}, i = 1, 2, \cdots, M, \tag{7}$$

$$F_{i,j}(z) := g_i g_j(z) - g_j g_i(z), 1 \leq i < j \leq M. \tag{8}$$

Thus $h(z)$ and $g_i(z)$ equate to the time update and measurement update for Kalman filter, respectively. $F_{i,j}(z)$ can be regarded as a comparison function that two different sensors are scheduled with the reverse order in two adjacent time instants for scalar Gauss-Markov systems. Next, we will give three lemmas, which are essential to derive the optimal schedule.

**Lemma 1.** $F_{i,j}(0) > 0$.

**Proof.** From (7), we have $g_i g_j(z) = \left[h^{-1} g_j(z) + b_i\right]^{-1}$, $g_j g_i(z) = \left[h^{-1} g_i(z) + b_j\right]^{-1}$. Define $\varphi_i(z) := h^{-1} g_i(z) + b_j, \varphi_j(z) := h^{-1} g_j(z) + b_i$, then

$$
\begin{aligned}
F_{i,j}(z) &= \varphi_j^{-1}(z) - \varphi_i^{-1}(z) = \frac{\varphi_i(z) - \varphi_j(z)}{\varphi_i(z)\varphi_j(z)} \\
&= \frac{h g_j(z) - h g_i(z) + (b_j - b_i) h g_i(z) h g_j(z)}{\varphi_i(z)\varphi_j(z) h g_i(z) h g_j(z)} \\
&= \frac{b_j - b_i}{\varphi_i(z)\varphi_j(z) h g_i(z) h g_j(z)} \left( \frac{a^4 - a^2 + a^2 q \left(2 h^{-1}(z) + b_i + b_j\right)}{(h^{-1}(z) + b_i)(h^{-1}(z) + b_j)} + q^2 \right).
\end{aligned}
\tag{9}
$$

Straightforward computation shows that $F_{i,j}(0) > 0$. ∎

**Lemma 2.** $F_{i,j}(z)$ have the following two properties:

*(1)* $|a| \geq 1$: $F_{i,j}(z)$ strictly increases on $z \in [0, \infty)$.
*(2)* $|a| < 1$: $F_{i,j}(z)$ is a piecewise monotone function that strictly increases on $z \in [0, \bar{p})$ and strictly decreases on $z \in (\bar{p}, \infty)$.

**Proof.** Considering the derivative of $F_{i,j}(z)$, we have

$$
\frac{dF_{i,j}(z)}{dz} = \frac{dg_i g_j(z)}{dz} - \frac{dg_j g_i(z)}{dz} = \frac{dg_i g_j(z)}{dg_j(z)} \frac{dg_j(z)}{dz} - \frac{dg_i g_j(z)}{dg_i(z)} \frac{dg_i(z)}{dz}.
$$

Since $\frac{dg_i(z)}{dz} = \frac{a^2}{(1 + b_i(a^2 z + q))^2}$, we get

$$
\frac{dg_i g_j(z)}{dg_j(z)} \frac{dg_j(z)}{dz} = \frac{a^2}{(1 + b_i(a^2 g_j(z) + q))^2} \frac{a^2}{(1 + b_j(a^2 z + q))^2} = \frac{a^4}{\psi_{i,j}^2(z)}, \tag{10}
$$

where $\psi_{i,j}(z) = 1 + (b_j + a^2 b_i + b_i b_j q)(a^2 z + q) + b_i q$.

Similarly, we have

$$\frac{dg_j g_i(z)}{dg_i(z)} \frac{dg_i(z)}{dz} = \frac{a^4}{\psi_{j,i}^2(z)}, \tag{11}$$

where $\psi_{j,i}(z) = 1 + (b_i + a^2 b_j + b_i b_j q)(a^2 z + q) + b_j q$.

Therefore,

$$\begin{aligned}
\frac{dF_{i,j}(z)}{dz} &= \frac{a^4(\psi_{j,i}^2(z) - \psi_{i,j}^2(z))}{\psi_{i,j}^2(z)\psi_{j,i}^2(z)} \\
&= \frac{a^6(b_j - b_i)(\psi_{j,i}(z) + \psi_{i,j}(z))((a^2 - 1)z + q)}{\psi_{i,j}^2(z)\psi_{j,i}^2(z)}.
\end{aligned} \tag{12}$$

Case 1: $|a| \geq 1$. Straightforward computation shows that $\frac{dF_{i,j}(z)}{dz} > 0$ for $z \geq 0$ from (12). Therefore $F_{i,j}(z)$ strictly increases on $z \in [0, \infty)$.

Case 2: $|a| < 1$. We can obtain $z = q/(1 - a^2) = \bar{p}$ from $\frac{dF_{i,j}(z)}{dz} = 0$. Thus, we have $\frac{dF(z)}{dz} > 0$ if $0 \leq z < \bar{p}$, and $\frac{dF(z)}{dz} < 0$ if $z > \bar{p}$, i.e., $F(z)$ strictly increases in $z \in [0, \bar{p})$ and strictly decreases in $z \in (\bar{p}, \infty)$.    ∎

**Lemma 3.** *If $|a| < 1$ and $p_0 < \bar{p}$, then $g_i(p_0) < h(p_0) < \bar{p}$. And if $|a| < 1$ and $p_0 > \bar{p}$, then $g_i(p_0) < h(p_0) < p_0$.*

**Proof.** We can verify this lemma straightforwardly from the definitions of $h$, $g_i$ and $\bar{p}$.    ∎

Based on above three lemmas, we are ready to present a important result. Before continuing, we define a few parameters: $\rho(i,j) := a^4 + a^2(b_i q + b_j q - 1) + b_i b_j q^2$, $\sigma(i,j) := (b_i + b_j)q^2 + 2a^2 q$, $\tau(i,j) := \frac{2q^2}{a^2\left(-\sigma(i,j) + \sqrt{\sigma^2(i,j) - 4q^2\rho(i,j)}\right)} - \frac{q}{a^2}$, $\hat{\rho} := \min \rho(i,j) = \rho(1,2)$, $\hat{\tau} := \min \tau(i,j)$, for $i,j \in \{1, 2, \cdots, M\}$, $i \neq j$ to simplify the following notations. For brevity, we will write $\rho(i,j)$, $\sigma(i,j)$ and $\tau(i,j)$ as $\rho$, $\sigma$, $\tau$ when the underlying $i$ and $j$ are clear from the context.

**Theorem 1.** *Let $s_1$ and $s_2$ be two identical sensor schedules except that $s_1(k_1) = s_2(k_2) < s_1(k_2) = s_2(k_1)$ for some $1 \leq k_1 = k_2 - 1 \leq T - 1$. For the following three cases*

**Case 1:**   $|a| \geq 1$, $p_0 > 0$,
**Case 2:**   $|a| < 1$, $\rho(s_1(k_1), s_1(k_2)) \geq 0$, $p_0 > 0$,
**Case 3:**   $|a| < 1$, $\hat{\rho} < 0$, $0 < p_0 < \hat{\tau}$,

*we have $p_{s_1}(T) < p_{s_2}(T)$.*

**Proof.** First we consider Case 1. From Lemma 1 and the first property of Lemma 2, it is easy to verify that

$$g_{s_1(k+1)}g_{s_1(k)}(p_0) < g_{s_1(k)}g_{s_1(k+1)}(p_0), \tag{13}$$

for any $p_0 > 0$. Next, we discuss the case $|a| < 1$. With the observation that

$$\lim_{z \to \infty} F_{i,j}(z) = \lim_{z \to \infty} g_i g_j(z) - \lim_{z \to \infty} g_j g_i(z)$$

$$= \frac{\rho(b_j - b_i)}{(b_j + b_i(a^2 + b_j q))(b_i + b_j(a^2 + b_i q))}, \tag{14}$$

we know $\lim_{z \to \infty} F_{i,j}(z)$ and $\rho$ have the same sign.

Then consider Case 2. When $|a| < 1$ and $\rho(s_1(k_1), s_1(k_2)) \geq 0$, combining Lemma 1 and the second property of Lemma 2, it is clear that (13) still holds.

Thus for Case 1 and 2,

$$p_{s_1}(T) = g_{s_1(T)} \cdots g_{s_1(k+2)} g_{s_1(k+1)} g_{s_1(k)} g_{s_1(k-1)} \cdots g_{s_1(1)}(p_0)$$
$$< g_{s_1(T)} \cdots g_{s_1(k+2)} g_{s_1(k)} g_{s_1(k+1)} g_{s_1(k-1)} \cdots g_{s_1(1)}(p_0) = p_{s_2}(T), \tag{15}$$

where the inequality is from (13) and the fact that $g_i(z)$ is creasing function.

Finally, consider Case 3. Again according to Lemma 1 and the second property of Lemma 2, when $|a| < 1$ and $\hat{\rho} < 0$, we can know that there exists a unique $\bar{z}$ satisfying $F_{i,j}(\bar{z}) = 0$. Then using (9), we can obtain

$$\bar{z} = \frac{2q^2}{a^2 \left(-\sigma + \sqrt{\sigma^2 - 4q^2 \rho}\right)} - \frac{q}{a^2} = \tau. \tag{16}$$

Hence we have $F_{i,j}(z) > 0$ for $0 \leq z < \tau$. Therefore (13) also holds for Case 3. From the fact that $\hat{\tau} > \bar{p}$ and Lemma 3, we get

$$g_i(p_0) < h(p_0) < \hat{\tau}, i = 1, 2, \cdots, M \tag{17}$$

for $0 < p_0 < \hat{\tau}$. Further we obtain $p_s(k) < \hat{\tau}$, $s \in S$ by repeatedly utilizing (17) $k$ times. Therefore, (15) also holds for Case 3. ∎

For given two schedules $s_1$ and $s_2$, Theorem 1 gives the comparative result of $p_{s_1}(T)$ and $p_{s_2}(T)$ when $s_1(k)$ and $s_2(k)$ differ only in two adjacent time instants. From Theorem 1, we can derive the following corollary. The corollary relaxes the requirement that the two time instants are must adjacent in Theorem 1.

**Corollary 1.** *Let $s_1$ and $s_2$ be two identical sensor schedules except that $s_1(k_1) = s_2(k_2) < s_1(k_2) = s_2(k_1)$ for some $1 \leq k_1 < k_2 \leq T$. For the three cases of Theorem 1, we have $p_{s_1}(T) < p_{s_2}(T)$.*

**Proof.** The proof is straightforward and is omitted. ∎

With the previous results, we have the following theorem.

**Theorem 2.** *For the following three cases*

**Case 1:**   $|a| \geq 1$, $p_0 > 0$,
**Case 2:**   $|a| < 1$, $\hat{\rho} \geq 0$, $p_0 > 0$,
**Case 3:**   $|a| < 1$, $\hat{\rho} < 0$, $0 < p_0 < \hat{\tau}$,

*the optimal schedule $s^*$ to Problem 1 is given by*

$$s^* = \left[ \underbrace{1, \cdots, 1}_{J_1}, \underbrace{2, \cdots, 2}_{J_2}, \cdots, \underbrace{M, \cdots, M}_{J_M} \right], \qquad (18)$$

*i.e., good sensors should be scheduled as late as possible within the time-horizon $T$.*

**Proof.** To prove that $s^*$ is the optimal schedule, we need to show that $p_{s^*}(T) < p_s(T)$ for any $s \neq s^*$. Construct a sequence of schedules $\{s_t : t = 1, 2, 3, \cdots\}$ starting from $s$ according to Algorithm 1. It stops after $m \leq \sum_{i=2}^{M} J_i$ iterations and it is clear to see that $s^* = s_m$. By Corollary 1, we get

$$p_s(T) > p_{s_1}(T) > \cdots > p_{s_m}(T) = p_{s^*}(T),$$

for above three cases. Thus $s^*$ is indeed optimal. ∎

---

**Algorithm 1.** Sensor Schedule Iteration

---
1: $t := 0$
2: $s_t := s$
3: $i := M$
4: **while** $i > 1$
5:      $J_{i,M} := \sum_{n=i}^{M} J_n$
6:      **while** $\sum_{k=T+1-J_{i,M}}^{T-J_{i,M}+J_i} \neq i J_i$
7:          $t := t + 1$
8:          $s_t := s_{t-1}$
9:          $k_1 := \max\{k \leq T - J_{i,M}, s_t(k) = i\}$
10:          $k_2 := \max\{k > T - J_{i,M}, s_t(k) < i\}$
11:          $temp := s_t(k_2)$
12:          $s_t(k_1) := temp$
13:          $s_t(k_2) := i$
14:      **end while**
15:      $i := i - 1$
16: **end while**

---

*Remark 1.* The optimal schedule $s^*$ in Theorem 2 is the same as the result of [14] under the case of selecting one sensor. However, [14] only discussed the case $|a| \geq 1$. Theorem 2 covers both the case $|a| < 1$ and $|a| \geq 1$. Most importantly, our proof technique is different from [14], which propels us to gain the result of Theorem 2. In addition, note that for Case 3 in Theorem 2, if the initial condition is violated, an explicit form of the optimal schedule is difficult to be obtained for a general time-horizon $T$ and depends on initial value $p_0$.

## 4    Conclusion

In this paper, we have investigated the multiple-sensor scheduling problem for state estimation of general scalar Gauss-Markov systems subject to the sensor energy and communication bandwidth constraints. Considering the scenario of selecting one sensor per time instant, we construct the explicit optimal schedule and provide its detail deducing process. A interesting problem for future work is extending current results to general high order Gauss-Markov systems.

**Acknowledgments.** This work was supported by the National Natural Science Foundation of China under grant numbers 61333011, 61271144, 61371064 and 61603133.

# References

1. Gungor, V.C., Hancke, G.P.: Industrial wireless sensor networks: challenges, design principles, and technical approaches. IEEE Trans. Ind. Electron. **56**(10), 4258–4265 (2009)
2. Alemdara, H., Ersoy, C.: Wireless sensor networks for healthcare: a survey. Comput. Netw. **54**(15), 2688–2710 (2010)
3. Xu, G., Shen, W., Wang, X.: Applications of wireless sensor networks in marine environment monitoring: a survey. Sensors **14**(9), 16932–16954 (2014)
4. Huber, M.F.: Optimal pruning for multi-step sensor scheduling. IEEE Trans. Autom. Control **57**(5), 1338–1343 (2012)
5. Vitus, M.P., Zhang, W., Abate, A., Hu, J., Tomlin, C.J.: On efficient sensor scheduling for linear dynamical systems. Automatica **48**(10), 2482–2493 (2012)
6. Joshi, S., Boyd, S.: Sensor selection via convex optimization. IEEE Trans. Signal Process. **57**(2), 451–462 (2009)
7. Mo, Y., Ambrosino, R., Sinopoli, B.: Sensor selection strategies for state estimation in energy constrained wireless sensor networks. Automatica **47**(7), 1330–1338 (2011)
8. Wu, J., Jia, Q.S., Johansson, K.H., Shi, L.: Event-based sensor data scheduling: trade-off between communication rate and estimation quality. IEEE Trans. Autom. Control **58**(4), 1041–1046 (2013)
9. You, K., Xie, L.: Kalman filtering with scheduled measurements. IEEE Trans. Signal Process. **61**(6), 1520–1530 (2013)
10. Shi, D., Chen, T., Shi, L.: Event-triggered maximum likelihood state estimation. Automatica **50**(1), 247–254 (2014)
11. Han, D., Mo, Y., Wu, J., Weerakkody, S., Sinopoli, B., Shi, L.: Stochastic event-triggered sensor schedule for remote state estimation. IEEE Trans. Autom. Control **60**(10), 2661–2675 (2015)
12. Savage, C.O., La Scala, B.F.: Optimal scheduling of scalar gauss-markov systems with a terminal cost function. IEEE Trans. Autom. Control **54**(5), 1100–1105 (2009)
13. Yang, C., Shi, L.: Deterministic sensor data scheduling under limited communication resource. IEEE Trans. Signal Process. **59**(10), 5050–5056 (2011)
14. Jia, Q.S., Shi, L.: On optimal partial broadcasting of wireless sensor networks for kalman filtering. IEEE Trans. Autom. Control **57**(3), 715–721 (2012)
15. Shi, L., Xie, L.: Optimal sensor power scheduling for state estimation of Gauss-Markov systems over a packet-dropping network. IEEE Trans. Signal Process. **60**(5), 2701–2705 (2012)
16. Anderson, B., Moore, J.: Optimal Filtering. Prentice-Hall, Englewood Cliffs (1979)

# Simultaneous Calibration of Hand-Eye Relationship, Robot-World Relationship and Robot Geometric Parameters with Stereo Vision

Yuanwei Liu[1], Peijiang Yuan[1(✉)], Dongdong Chen[1], Feng Su[1], and Lei Xue[2]

[1] Robotics Institute, Beihang University, XueYuan Road No. 37, Beijing, China
lywbuaa@126.com, itr@buaa.edu.cn,
winterchen2013@163.com, sfsilence@126.com
[2] Commercial Aircraft Corporation of China Ltd., Shanghai, ChangZhong Road No. 3115, Shanghai, China
xuelei@comac.cc

**Abstract.** Robot-world calibration and hand-eye calibration are fundamental steps for robots equipped with cameras. This problem is described as solving "AX = YB" equation. However, this problem usually interacts with robot calibration, because robot geometric parameters are not very precise. Therefore, we propose a novel calibration method which can calibrate hand-eye relationship, robot-world relationship and robot geometric parameters simultaneously. This method considers hand-eye relationship and robot-world relationship as another two axes of robot arm. Modified D-H convention is used to describe robot position and orientation and stereo cameras are used to measure positioning errors. In order to improve calibration accuracy, least square method is introduced to solve calibration equations. Simulation and implement prove that this overall calibration method is feasible.

**Keywords:** Hand-eye calibration · Robot calibration · Stereo vision · Least square method

## 1 Introduction

In recent years, with the development of Intelligent Manufacture and automatic production, industrial robots with visual feedback become more and more popular. Equipped with cameras, industrial robots can perform pure measurement or perform fundamental jobs, such as drilling, welding or assembly, taking advantage of visual signals. There are two types of robot-camera configurations, "eye-to-hand" configuration and "eye-in-hand" configuration [1]. "Eye-to-hand" means that the camera is fixed on ground and doesn't move with robot. Instead, in "eye-in-hand" configuration, the camera is mounted on robot-arm and moves with the robot. Among them, "eye-in-hand" configuration can avoid the problem of shield by robot-arm and the ability to process

© Springer Nature Singapore Pte Ltd. 2017
F. Sun et al. (Eds.): ICCSIP 2016, CCIS 710, pp. 462–475, 2017.
DOI: 10.1007/978-981-10-5230-9_45

dynamic images has been improved in recent years, so "eye-in-hand" configuration gets widely used in real application.

Aimed at measurement or visual servo, positioning error is a key factor to influence the performance of industrial robots. Calibration is the first and vital step before real work [2]. As for "eye-in-hand" robots, three transformations need to be determined and compensated. First one is the relationship between flange coordinate frame and camera coordinate frame, which is called hand-eye calibration. The second is the relationship between robot coordinate frame and world coordinate frame, which is called robot-world calibration. The last one is the transformation from robot base to robot flange, which is the problem of robot calibration or robot parameters identification.

As for hand-eye calibration problem, many works have been done to solve the equation form like AX = XB. Shiu and Ahmad [3] introduced this problem firstly and solved this problem by separating it into two components. Rotational component meets $R_A R_X = R_X R_B$. Translational component meets $R_A t_X + t_A = R_X t_B + t_X$. They took advantage of the angle-axis formulation of rotation and got the general solution of rotational component $R_X = Rot(k_{A_i}, \beta_i) R_{X_{p_i}}$. Then, with solved $R_X$, translational component $t_X$ could be formulated through least-square method. Later, Tsai and Lenz [4] did some further work and got a better result. What's more, Park and Martin [5] took advantage of Lie group to solve $R_X$. Chou and Kamel [6] applied quaternions to represent the rotational component and Liang [7] introduced the Kronecker product to turn rotational component into a linear system. Except above separable solutions, some simultaneous solutions [8, 9] and iterative solutions [10, 11] were also proposed to solve the problem of AX = XB.

At the same time, the problem of robot-world calibration is usually accompanied with hand-eye calibration problem. This problem was first described by Wang [12] as AX = YB. He solves this problem on the premise that one of the unknown is given, which is a typical separable solution. Besides, there are many simultaneous solutions [13, 14] and iterative solutions [15, 16]. Until now, either "AX = XB" problem or "AX = YB" problem has seemed to be well studied. However, both of them work at the assumption that robot kinematic model or robot transformation is accurate. In fact, because of manufacture and assembly error, robot geometric parameters are not very precise. In this case, the robot transformation (matrix A) is not equal to values which we get or compute from robot controller. Therefore, we need to discuss the third calibration problem, robot calibration.

Robot calibration is a very complicated problem and many studies have focused on calibrating robot geometric parameters with different model or different measurement method. Initially, classical DH convention [17] was used for modelling, but this model is not continuous. Then, researchers added extra parameters or proposed other modelling methods [18–21] to overcome this problem. As for measurement methods, laser tracker [22, 23], laser tracker with IMU [24], other external devices [25, 26] are used to collect data. After calibration, the positioning accuracy of robot can get significant improved. However, these methods always need to use expensive measurement devices and they are not easy to perform.

In order to avoid using expensive external devices, camera can be considered an ideal alternative measurement method [27–30]. However, a contradiction exists.

Hand–eye relationship and robot-world relationship need to be known before measurement with camera, but these two relationships rely on accurate robot geometric model. That is to say, robot calibration and other two calibration are related to each other. Considering that, we propose a novel thought. Since hand-eye relationship and robot-world relationship are both homogeneous transformation matrices, similar form with transformation of each link of robot, it is reasonable to consider hand-eye relationship as 7-th axis of robot and robot-world relationship as 0-th axis (assume robot has 6 axes).

In this paper, we consider hand-eye relationship and robot-world relationship as a part of robot-arm and use modified DH convention and vision measurement technique to fulfill whole calibration. Initial values of hand-eye relationship ($X_0$) and robot-world relationship ($Y_0$) are given by solving equation $AX = YB$ and then X, Y and robot geometric parameters are calibrated and improved simultaneously.

This paper is organized as follow. Section 2 introduces overall calibration method and procedure. Section 3 gives simulation results which verify the feasibility of this method and implement results with UR10. The conclusion is presented in Sect. 4.

## 2    Calibration and Procedure

### 2.1    Initial Values of X and Y by Solving AX = YB

As mentioned above, the relationship between camera and flange and the relationship between robot and workpiece should be given as initial values for robot and hand-eye relationship calibration. This problem is considered as solving "AX = YB" equation, as shown in Fig. 1.

Many methods were proposed to solve this problem, which can be divided into two types. The first type is determining flange-to-camera transformation (matrix X) and robot-to-world transformation (matrix Y) simultaneously. The second one is solving transformation X from equation $CX = XD$, as shown in Fig. 2, and then taking X into equation AX = YB to solve transformation Y. Relatively speaking, the latter is easier to executive in spite of less precise. For the result from AX = YB is just as the initial value of whole calibration and the precision can be compensated in later step, we choose the second method to get initial value of X and Y.

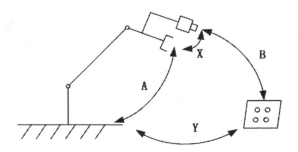

**Fig. 1.**  "AX = YB" problem

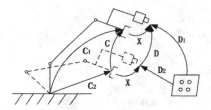

**Fig. 2.** "CX = XD" problem

More specifically, manipulate the robot by teach pendant and make it through two different positions. During this progress, we get the transformation C between two robot positions and the transformation D between two camera positions. Matrix C can be solved by $C = C_2^{-1}C_1$ and matrix D can be solved by $D = D_2^{-1}D_1$. In order to solve "CX = XD" problem, Tsai [4] pointed that at least two nonparallel movements were necessary to solve this equation.

## 2.2 Identification Model

Accurate robot kinematic model is a guarantee of identifying robot geometric parameters. Nowadays, Denavit-Hartenberg convention is a widely accepted method. D-H parameters are composed by joint variable $\theta_i$, link offset $d_i$ from link $i-1$ to link $i$, link twist angle $\alpha_i$ between link $i$ and link $i+1$, and link length $a_i$. According to D-H parameters, the homogenous transformation $_i^{i+1}T$ from link $i$ to link $i+1$ can be described as follow:

$$_i^{i+1}T = Rot(Z_i, \theta_i)Trans(Z_i, d_i)Trans(X_i, a_i)Rot(X_i, \alpha_i) \tag{1}$$

Where $Rot()$ and $Trans()$ are $(4 \times 4)$ homogenous matrices of pure rotation and translation.

In ideal cases, four D-H parameters are enough to describe robot position and orientation. However, there are some shortages in classical D-H convention. In particular, when two consecutive joints are parallel, the offset between them equals to zero in D-H convention. In real cases, however, it is impossible to keep two joints parallel absolutely due to assembly errors. Therefore, small angle errors would lead to huge errors of offset parameter, which means this model is discontinuous in some cases. In order to solve this problem, some modifications of D-H convention are proposed by introducing extra parameters. In this paper, we use the model introduced in [18], which added a parameter $\beta_i$ in classical DH convention. $\beta_i$ represents the twist angle of y axis. When two adjacent joints are not parallel, $\beta_i = 0$, turning the model back to classical DH convention. In this modified model, we get the homogenous transformation as follow:

$$_i^{i+1}T = Rot(Z_i, \theta_i)trans(Z_i, d_i)trans(X_i, a_i)Rot(X_i, \alpha_i)Rot(Y_i, \beta_i) \tag{2}$$

$$A_i = {}_i^{i+1}T = \begin{bmatrix} c\theta_i c\beta_i - s\alpha_i s\theta_i s\beta_i & -c\alpha_i s\theta_i & c\theta_i s\beta_i + s\alpha_i s\theta_i c\beta_i & a_i c\theta_i \\ s\theta_i c\beta_i + s\alpha_i c\theta_i s\beta_i & c\alpha_i c\theta_i & s\theta_i s\beta_i - s\alpha_i c\theta_i c\beta_i & a_i s\theta_i \\ -c\alpha_i s\beta_i & s\alpha_i & c\alpha_i c\beta_i & d_i \\ 0 & 0 & 0 & 1 \end{bmatrix} \quad (3)$$

In this paper, we use UR10 robot produced by Universal Robot company to do simulation and implement. According to modified D-H parameters mentioned above, frame of axes and D-H parameters are listed in Fig. 3 and Table 1. At the same time, we denote the error of D-H parameters as $\delta\alpha_i$, $\delta a_i$, $\delta d_i$, $\delta\theta_i$, $\delta\beta_i$. In next part, we will give the error model that these small D-H parameters errors lead to variations in tool-frame.

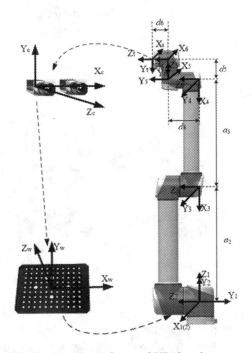

**Fig. 3.** Coordinate frame of UR10 and camera

**Table 1.** MDH paramaters of UR10

| Axis Joint | $\theta$ | $d$(mm) | $a$(mm) | $\alpha$ | $\beta$ |
|---|---|---|---|---|---|
| 1 | 0 | 0 | 0 | $\pi/2$ | – |
| 2 | $-\pi/2$ | 0 | −612 | 0 | 0 |
| 3 | 0 | 0 | −572.3 | 0 | 0 |
| 4 | $-\pi/2$ | 163.9 | 0 | $\pi/2$ | – |
| 5 | 0 | 115.7 | 0 | $-\pi/2$ | – |
| 6 | 0 | 92.2 | 0 | 0 | 0 |

## 2.3 Differential Motion and Error Model

Since we assume errors of D-H parameters and transformation X and Y are very small, we can consider that variations in world-frame caused by these small changes are close to differential motion.

Next, we describe the differential motion produced by D-H parameters error. Let $A_i^N$ and $A_i^R$ denote nominal and actual link transformation of each link and $\Delta_i$ represents differential transformation of current link. Then, the error model can be given as follow:

$$A_i^R = A_i^N + d(A_i^N) = A_i^N \Delta_i = A_i^N Trans(d_x, d_y, d_z) Rot(\mathbf{k}, d\theta) \tag{4}$$

On the one hand, $\Delta_i$ equals to $Trans(d_x, d_y, d_z) \cdot Rot(\mathbf{k}, d\theta)$. And $Trans(d_x, d_y, d_z)$ can be represented as

$$Trans(d_x, d_y, d_z) = \begin{bmatrix} 1 & 0 & 0 & d_x \\ 0 & 1 & 0 & d_y \\ 0 & 0 & 1 & d_z \\ 0 & 0 & 0 & 1 \end{bmatrix} \tag{5}$$

$Rot(\mathbf{k}, d\theta)$ can be represented as

$$Rot(\mathbf{k}, d\theta) = \begin{bmatrix} k_x k_x vers\theta + c\theta & k_y k_x vers\theta - k_z s\theta & k_z k_x vers\theta + k_y s\theta & 0 \\ k_x k_y vers\theta + k_z s\theta & k_y k_y vers\theta + c\theta & k_z k_y vers\theta - k_x s\theta & 0 \\ k_x k_z vers\theta - k_y s\theta & k_y k_z vers\theta + k_x s\theta & k_z k_z vers\theta + c\theta & 0 \\ 0 & 0 & 0 & 1 \end{bmatrix} \tag{6}$$

where $vers\theta = 1 - \cos\theta$.

Since transformation from $A_i^N$ to $A_i^R$ is differential transformation, we have $\lim_{\theta \to 0} \sin\theta = d\theta$, $\lim_{\theta \to 0} \cos\theta = 1$, $\lim_{\theta \to 0} vers\theta = 0$

So,

$$Rot(\mathbf{k}, d\theta) = \begin{bmatrix} 1 & -k_z d\theta & k_y d\theta & 0 \\ k_z d\theta & 1 & -k_x d\theta & 0 \\ -k_y d\theta & k_x d\theta & 1 & 0 \\ 0 & 0 & 0 & 1 \end{bmatrix} \tag{7}$$

Let denote $k_x d\theta = \delta_x$, $k_y d\theta = \delta_y$, $k_z d\theta = \delta_z$, then

$$\Delta_i = \begin{bmatrix} 1 & -\delta_z & \delta_y & d_x \\ \delta_z & 1 & -\delta_x & d_y \\ -\delta_y & \delta_x & 1 & d_z \\ 0 & 0 & 0 & 1 \end{bmatrix} \tag{8}$$

On the other hand, $\Delta_i$ can be solved from Eq. (4) as

$$\Delta_i = (A_i^N)^{-1}[A_i^N + d(A_i^N)] = I + (A_i^N)^{-1}d(A_i^N) \tag{9}$$

$d(A_i^N)$ can be computed from Eq. (3) as

$$d(A_i^N) = \frac{\partial A_i^N}{\partial \alpha_i}\delta\alpha_i + \frac{\partial A_i^N}{\partial a_i}\delta a_i + \frac{\partial A_i^N}{\partial d_i}\delta d_i + \frac{\partial A_i^N}{\partial \theta_i}\delta\theta_i + \frac{\partial A_i^N}{\partial \beta_i}\delta\beta_i \tag{10}$$

Then,

$$\Delta_i = \begin{bmatrix} 1 & -S\beta_i\delta\alpha_i - C\alpha_iC\beta_i\delta\theta_i & S\alpha_i\delta\theta_i + \delta\beta_i & C\beta_i\delta a_i + a_iS\alpha_iS\beta_i\delta\theta_i - C\alpha_iS\beta_i\delta d_1 \\ S\beta_i\delta\alpha_i + C\alpha_iC\beta_i\delta\theta_i & 1 & -C\beta_i\delta\alpha_i + C\alpha_iS\beta_i\delta\theta_i & a_iC\alpha_i\delta\theta_i + S\alpha_i\delta d_i \\ -S\alpha_i\delta\theta_i - \delta\beta_i & C\beta_i\delta\alpha_i - C\alpha_iS\beta_i\delta\theta_i & 1 & S\beta_i\delta a_i - a_iS\alpha_iC\beta_i\delta\theta_i + C\alpha_iC\beta_i\delta d_1 \\ 0 & 0 & 0 & 1 \end{bmatrix} \tag{11}$$

Comparing Eq. (8) with Eq. (11), we have

$$e_i = \begin{bmatrix} d_{ix} \\ d_{iy} \\ d_{iz} \\ \delta_{ix} \\ \delta_{iy} \\ \delta_{iz} \end{bmatrix} = \begin{bmatrix} C\beta_i\delta a_i + a_iS\alpha_iS\beta_i\delta\theta_i - C\alpha_iS\beta_i\delta d_1 \\ a_iC\alpha_i\delta\theta_i + S\alpha_i\delta d_i \\ S\beta_i\delta a_i - a_iS\alpha_iC\beta_i\delta\theta_i + C\alpha_iC\beta_i\delta d_1 \\ C\beta_i\delta\alpha_i - C\alpha_iS\beta_i\delta\theta_i \\ S\alpha_i\delta\theta_i + \delta\beta_i \\ S\beta_i\delta\alpha_i + C\alpha_iC\beta_i\delta\theta_i \end{bmatrix} \tag{12}$$

Hereto, we get the relationship between small error of D-H parameters and differential error in current frame. Besides, we represent the error of transformation X and Y as

$$e_0 = [d_{x0} \quad d_{y0} \quad d_{z0} \quad \delta_{x0} \quad \delta_{y0} \quad \delta_{z0}]' \tag{13}$$

$$e_7 = [d_{x7} \quad d_{y7} \quad d_{z7} \quad \delta_{x7} \quad \delta_{y7} \quad \delta_{z7}]' \tag{14}$$

In calibration process, we measure the error in world-frame. Therefore, $e_i$ should be transformed to tool-frame. Besides, we know that the differential error transformation from one frame to camera frame can be denoted as

$$e_t = \mathbf{J}_i^c e_i \tag{15}$$

Where,

$$\mathbf{J}_i^c = \begin{bmatrix} (\mathbf{R}_i^c)^T & \mathbf{p} \times (\mathbf{R}_i^c)^T \\ 0 & (\mathbf{R}_i^c)^T \end{bmatrix} \tag{16}$$

And

$$\mathbf{T}_i^c = \begin{bmatrix} \mathbf{R}_i^c & \mathbf{p} \\ 0 & 1 \end{bmatrix} = \begin{bmatrix} n_x & o_x & a_x & p_x \\ n_y & o_y & a_y & p_y \\ n_z & o_z & a_z & p_z \\ 0 & 0 & 0 & 1 \end{bmatrix} \tag{17}$$

Here, we summarize the number of variables need to be calibrated. There are 27 variables of DH parameters in robot-arm, 6 variables of differential error in hand-eye relationship and 6 variables of differential error in robot-world relationship. The total error can get by

$$e = \sum_{i=0}^{7} \mathbf{J}_i^c e_i \tag{18}$$

and it has 39 unknown variables to be calibrated.

Equation (18) is our calibration model.

### 2.4 Least Square Method to Identity Robot Geometric Parameters and X and Y

As shown in Fig. 3, real positon of camera can obtained by extrinsic parameter of camera. Extrinsic parameters are determined through camera calibration. With the help of vision measurement, real measurement error is equal to differential transformation from theoretical positon to real measurement position. Take the error back to Eq. (18), each equation can determine 6 unknowns. In order to solve all 39 unknowns, we need at least 7 equations.

However, considering that there exist noises in real measurement, it is necessary to get more equations. Least square method is a good tool to handle redundant equations and gives the best answer. Therefore, we get errors of each section by vison measurement and compensate them further. In next parts, we will verify our calibration method through simulation and real implement.

## 3 Simulation and Implement

### 3.1 Simulation in MATLAB

In simulation, we gave 39 theoretical values which are composed by 6 parameters in robot-world relationship, 27 modified D-H parameters and 6 parameters in hand-eye relationship. 27 modified D-H parameters are given in Table 1 and initial values of Y and X are given as follows:

$$Y_0 = \begin{bmatrix} 1 & 0 & 0 & 800 \\ 0 & 0.9553 & -0.2955 & 0 \\ 0 & 0.2955 & 0.9553 & 200 \\ 0 & 0 & 0 & 1 \end{bmatrix}$$

$$X_0 = \begin{bmatrix} 1 & 0 & 0 & 10 \\ 0 & 0.9801 & -0.1987 & 50 \\ 0 & 0.1987 & 0.9801 & 100 \\ 0 & 0 & 0 & 1 \end{bmatrix}$$

$Y_0$ and $X_0$ can be represented as the combination of rotation axis and translation vector. That is, $\alpha_Y = [0.3, 0, 0]$, $d_Y = [800, 0, 200]$, $\alpha_X = [0.2, 0, 0]$, $d_X = [10, 50, 100]$.

After gave initial parameters values, we added noise value on each parameter which were called *noise parameters*. On the one hand, we computed nominal position and real position in world coordinate system based on initial parameters and noise parameters, which offered us real error between them. On the other hand, position error in world coordinate system could also be measured by differential motion of camera. This differential motion was produced by noise value of each joint and computed by transformation from each joint to world coordinate system. After got real error and differential motion, we constructed calibration equation as mentioned in part 2 and solved noise value with least square method. The noise value of each parameter and calibrated results are listed in Table 2.

**Table 2.** Simulation results

| Joint | No. | Parameter | Noise value | Calibrated results | Error rate |
|-------|-----|-----------|-------------|--------------------|------------|
| 1 | 1 | $\Delta\alpha1$ | 0.001 | 0.001 | 0 |
|   | 2 | $\Delta a1$ | 0.05 | 0.0435 | 13% |
|   | 3 | $\Delta\theta1$ | 0.0015 | 0.0015 | 0 |
|   | 4 | $\Delta d1$ | −0.05 | −0.0560 | 12% |
| 2 | 5 | $\Delta\alpha2$ | 0.0014 | 0.0014 | 0 |
|   | 6 | $\Delta a2$ | −0.2 | −0.1827 | 8.65% |
|   | 7 | $\Delta\beta2$ | 0.002 | 0.0019 | 5% |
|   | 8 | $\Delta\theta2$ | −0.0021 | −0.0021 | 0 |
|   | 9 | $\Delta d2$ | 0.08 | 0.06 | 25% |
| 3 | 10 | $\Delta\alpha3$ | −0.0012 | −0.001 | 1.67% |
|   | 11 | $\Delta a3$ | −0.12 | −0.1421 | 1.84% |
|   | 12 | $\Delta\beta3$ | 0.001 | 0.0011 | 10% |
|   | 13 | $\Delta\theta3$ | 0.0013 | 0.0013 | 0 |
|   | 14 | $\Delta d3$ | −0.06 | −0.04 | 33% |
| 4 | 15 | $\Delta\alpha4$ | 0.0017 | 0.0016 | 5.9% |
|   | 16 | $\Delta a4$ | 0.03 | 0.0581 | 9.37% |
|   | 17 | $\Delta\theta4$ | 0.001 | $9.49 \times 10^{-4}$ | 5.1% |
|   | 18 | $\Delta d4$ | 0.14 | 0.1579 | 12.8% |
| 5 | 19 | $\Delta\alpha5$ | 0.001 | 0.0011 | 10% |
|   | 20 | $\Delta a5$ | 0.07 | 0.0767 | 9.6% |

(*continued*)

**Table 2.** (*continued*)

| Joint | No. | Parameter | Noise value | Calibrated results | Error rate |
|-------|-----|-----------|-------------|--------------------|-----------|
|       | 21  | $\Delta\theta5$ | −0.0016 | −0.0016 | 0 |
|       | 22  | $\Delta d5$ | 0.21 | 0.2141 | 2.0% |
| 6     | 23  | $\Delta\alpha6$ | −0.001 | −0.001 | 0 |
|       | 24  | $\Delta a6$ | −0.04 | −0.0514 | 28.5% |
|       | 25  | $\Delta\beta6$ | 0.001 | 0.000885 | 11.5% |
|       | 26  | $\Delta\theta6$ | 0.001 | 0.0011 | 10% |
|       | 27  | $\Delta d6$ | −0.11 | −0.0963 | 12.5% |
| Y     | 28  | $d_{x0}$ | 0.03 | 0.0286 | 4.7% |
|       | 29  | $d_{y0}$ | 0.5 | 0.712 | 42.4% |
|       | 30  | $d_{z0}$ | −0.04 | −0.053 | 32.5% |
|       | 31  | $\delta_{x0}$ | 0.002 | 0.0021 | 10% |
|       | 32  | $\delta_{y0}$ | −0.0015 | −0.0015 | 0 |
|       | 33  | $\delta_{z0}$ | 0.001 | 0.0011 | 10% |
| X     | 34  | $d_{\times7}$ | 0.03 | 0.021 | 30% |
|       | 35  | $d_{y7}$ | 0.5 | 0.3 | 40% |
|       | 36  | $d_{z7}$ | −0.04 | −0.03 | 25% |
|       | 37  | $\delta_{x7}$ | 0.002 | 0.0018 | 10% |
|       | 38  | $\delta_{y7}$ | −0.0015 | −0.0015 | 0 |
|       | 39  | $\delta_{z7}$ | 0.001 | 0.0009 | 10% |

Units of all angles are *rad* and units of all lengths are *mm*.

Comparing computed values with added noise values, most of error rates are less than 20%. Specific distribution of error rate is shown in Fig. 4. Although error rates in some parameters are comparably high, our calibration model can solve the problem of simultaneous calibration and be applied in real application.

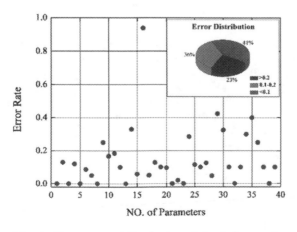

**Fig. 4.** Error rate and distribution of simulation results

## 3.2    Implement with UR10

Figure 5 shows a calibration implement in lab with UR10. Firstly, UR10 was moved through 3 different points, making 2 nonparallel transformations. And then, initial values of X was obtained by solving equation "CX = XD". Next, matrix X was used to solve equation "AX = YB" and we got the initial value of Y. Secondly, with the help of teach pendant, UR10 was moved to 30 different positions or orientations. At each point, the position of flange coordinate system was shown in teach pendant and theoretical position of camera coordinate was computed. At the same time, the extrinsic matrix of stereo camera was recorded and the real position of camera coordinate in world was determined in turn. At last, theoretical positions and real positions of camera coordinate system were used to compute positioning errors. These errors were used to construct calibration equations.

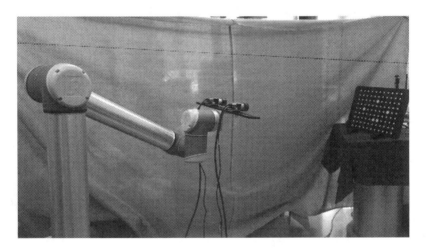

**Fig. 5.** Calibration implement in lab

With least square method, errors of MDH parameters and transformation X and Y were solved and these parameters could be compensated to real values. Compensation results are listed in Table 3.

**Table 3.** Calibration results

| Axis | $\theta$ | $d(mm)$ | $a(mm)$ | $\alpha$ | $\beta$ |
|------|----------|---------|---------|----------|---------|
| 1 | 0 | 0 | 0 | $\pi/2$ | – |
| 2 | $-\pi/2$ | 0.010 | −612.11 | 0 | 0 |
| 3 | 0 | 0 | −572.31 | 0 | 0.002 |
| 4 | $-\pi/2$ | 163.83 | −0.012 | $\pi/2$ | – |
| 5 | 0 | 115.74 | 0 | $-\pi/2$ | – |
| 6 | 0 | 92.10 | 0 | 0 | 0.001 |

Robot-world relationship and hand-eye relationship can be transformed from last 12 parameters and denoted as matrix form.

$$Y = \begin{bmatrix} 0.1105 & -0.9931 & 0.0400 & 1821.83 \\ 0.8547 & 0.0744 & -0.5137 & 965.46 \\ 0.5072 & 0.0909 & 0.8570 & -82.34 \\ 0 & 0 & 0 & 1 \end{bmatrix}$$

$$X = \begin{bmatrix} 0.9998 & -0.0123 & 0.0160 & 14.24 \\ 0.0126 & 0.9997 & -0.0210 & -32.18 \\ -0.0157 & 0.0212 & 0.9801 & 17.63 \\ 0 & 0 & 0 & 1 \end{bmatrix}$$

# 4  Conclusion

This paper proposed a novel calibration method which can overcome the problem that hand-eye and robot-world calibration interacts with robot calibration. Hand-eye relationship and robot-world relationship are considered as one of axes of robot. Errors in parameters of each axis can be transferred to differential motion of camera-frame and real positioning errors can be measured by stereo camera. Least square method can be used to solve calibration equations and errors of all parameters are compensated eventually. Simulation in MATLAB proves the feasibility of this calibration model and algorithm. Calibration accuracy can meet the requirements of practical application. Implement in UR10 gives true value of each parameter.

**Acknowledgment.** The research was performed at the Robotics Institute, Beihang University, under contract with Commercial Aircraft Corporation of China. The authors would like to thank all participants in this research for their contribution and assist.

# References

1. Flandin, G., Chaumette, F., Marchand, E.: Eye-in-hand/eye-to-hand cooperation for visual servoing. In: Proceedings of the IEEE International Conference on Robotics and Automation, ICRA 2000, pp. 2741–2746 (2000)
2. Puskorius, G., Feldkamp, L.: Global calibration of a robot/vision system. In: Proceedings of the 1987 IEEE International Conference on Robotics and Automation, pp. 190–195 (1987)
3. Shiu, Y.C., Ahmad, S.: Calibration of wrist-mounted robotic sensors by solving homogeneous transform equations of the form AX = XB. IEEE Trans. Rob. Autom. **5**, 16–29 (1989)
4. Tsai, R.Y., Lenz, R.K.: A new technique for fully autonomous and efficient 3D robotics hand/eye calibration. IEEE Trans. Robot. Autom. **5**, 345–358 (1989)
5. Park, F.C., Martin, B.J.: Robot sensor calibration: solving AX = XB on the Euclidean group. IEEE Trans. Robot. Autom. **10**, 717–721 (1994)
6. Chou, J.C., Kamel, M.: Finding the position and orientation of a sensor on a robot manipulator using quaternions. Int. J. Rob. Res. **10**, 240–254 (1991)

7. Liang, R.-H., Mao, J.-F.: Hand-eye calibration with a new linear decomposition algorithm. J. Zhejiang Univ. Sci. A **9**, 1363–1368 (2008)
8. Chen, H.H.: A screw motion approach to uniqueness analysis of head-eye geometry. In: Proceedings of the IEEE Computer Society Conference on Computer Vision and Pattern Recognition, CVPR 1991, pp. 145–151 (1991)
9. Daniilidis, K., Bayro-Corrochano, E.: The dual quaternion approach to hand-eye calibration. In: Proceedings of the 13th International Conference on Pattern Recognition, pp. 318–322 (1996)
10. Wei, G.-Q., Arbter, K., Hirzinger, G.: Active self-calibration of robotic eyes and hand-eye relationships with model identification. IEEE Trans. Robot. Autom. **14**, 158–166 (1998)
11. Zuang, H., Shiu, Y.C.: A noise-tolerant algorithm for robotic hand-eye calibration with or without sensor orientation measurement. IEEE Trans. Syst. Man Cybern. **23**, 1168–1175 (1993)
12. Wang, C.-C.: Extrinsic calibration of a vision sensor mounted on a robot. IEEE Trans. Robot. Autom. **8**, 161–175 (1992)
13. Li, A., Wang, L., Wu, D.: Simultaneous robot-world and hand-eye calibration using dual-quaternions and Kronecker product. Int. J. Phys. Sci. **5**, 1530–1536 (2010)
14. Hanqi, Z., Roth, Z.S., Sudhakar, R.: Simultaneous robot/world and tool/flange calibration by solving homogeneous transformation equations of the form AX = YB. IEEE Trans. Robot. Autom. **10**, 549–554 (1994)
15. Hirsh, R.L., DeSouza, G.N., Kak, A.C.: An iterative approach to the hand-eye and base-world calibration problem. In: Proceedings of the 2001 IEEE International Conference on Robotics and Automation, ICRA 2001, pp. 2171–2176 (2001)
16. Kim, S.-J., Jeong, M.-H., Lee, J.-J., Lee, J.-Y., Kim, K.-G., You, B.-J., et al.: Robot head-eye calibration using the minimum variance method. In: 2010 IEEE International Conference on Robotics and Biomimetics (ROBIO), pp. 1446–1451 (2010)
17. Hayati, S., Tso, K., Roston, G.: Robot geometry calibration. In: Proceedings of the 1988 IEEE International Conference on Robotics and Automation, vol. 2, pp. 947–951 (1988)
18. Hayati, S.A.: Robot arm geometric link parameter estimation. In: The 22nd IEEE Conference on Decision and Control, pp. 1477–1483 (1983)
19. Stone, H.W., Sanderson, A.C.: Statistical performance evaluation of the S-model arm signature identification technique. In: Proceedings of the 1988 IEEE International Conference on Robotics and Automation, vol. 2, pp. 939–946 (1988)
20. Zhuang, H., Roth, Z.S., Hamano, F.: A complete and parametrically continuous kinematic model for robot manipulators. In: Proceedings of the 1990 IEEE International Conference on Robotics and Automation, vol. 1, pp. 92–97 (1990)
21. Chen, I.M., Yang, G., Tan, C.T., Yeo, S.H.: Local POE model for robot kinematic calibration. Mech. Mach. Theory **36**, 1215–1239 (2001)
22. Ying, B., Hanqi, Z., Roth, Z.S.: Experiment study of PUMA robot calibration using a laser tracking system. In: Proceedings of the 2003 IEEE International Workshop on Soft Computing in Industrial Applications, SMCia 2003, pp. 139–144 (2003)
23. Nubiola, A., Bonev, I.A.: Absolute calibration of an ABB IRB 1600 robot using a laser tracker. Robot. Comput.-Integr. Manuf. **29**, 236–245 (2013)
24. Wu, Y., Klimchik, A., Caro, S., Furet, B., Pashkevich, A.: Geometric calibration of industrial robots using enhanced partial pose measurements and design of experiments. Robot. Comput.-Integr. Manuf. **35**, 151–168 (2015)
25. Driels, M.R., Swayze, W., Potter, S.: Full-pose calibration of a robot manipulator using a coordinate-measuring machine. Int. J. Adv. Manuf. Technol. **8**, 34–41 (1993)
26. Nubiola, A., Bonev, I.A.: Absolute robot calibration with a single telescoping ballbar. Precis. Eng. **38**, 472–480 (2014)

27. Meng, Y., Zhuang, H.: Autonomous robot calibration using vision technology. Robot. Comput.-Integr. Manuf. **23**, 436–446 (2007)
28. Du, G., Zhang, P.: Online robot calibration based on vision measurement. Robot. Comput.-Integr. Manuf. **29**, 484–492 (2013)
29. Švaco, M., Šekoranja, B., Šuligoj, F., Jerbić, B.: Calibration of an industrial robot using a stereo vision system. Procedia Eng. **69**, 459–463 (2014)
30. Du, G., Zhang, P., Li, D.: Online robot calibration based on hybrid sensors using Kalman Filters. Robot. Comput.-Integr. Manuf. **31**, 91–100 (2015)

# Cognitive Signal Processing

# Indoor Multi Human Target Tracking Based on PIR Sensor Network

Xinyue Sun[1], Meiqin Liu[1(✉)], Weihua Sheng[2], Senlin Zhang[1], and Zhen Fan[1]

[1] College of Electrical Engineering, Zhejiang University, Hangzhou 310027, China
{sxy,liumeiqin,slzhang,fanzhen}@zju.edu.cn
[2] School of Electrical and Computer Engineering, Oklahoma State University,
Stillwater, OK 74078, USA
weihua.sheng@okstate.edu

**Abstract.** In order to solve the problem of human target tracking in smart-home Wireless Sensor Network (WSN) environment, and only based on limited measurement data of Binary PIR sensors, the sensor networks joint likelihood is derived, which proposes the indoor PIR sensor network Binary Auxiliary Particle Filter (Bin-APF) fusion estimate algorithm further more. Meanwhile, as for the problem of multiple human targets measurement classification and trajectory association, combined with PIR's binary measurement, an improved K-Nearest Neighbor algorithm is adopted. And according to parameters of current experimental environment, a simulation is carried out, which contributes to the algorithm proposed. Experiment and Simulation results indicate that the MTT-KNN-Bin-APF algorithm accord well with the expectation of in-home multiple human target localization and tracking in consideration of actual result and error precision. Moreover, the algorithm is in low dependency of sensor network's layout, which is suitable for various type of household arrangement. The method provides a solution to indoor human target tracking and is promising in the field of smart home.

**Keywords:** Wireless Sensor Network · Multi target tracking · K-Nearest Neighbor algorithm · Auxiliary Particle Filter · Information fusion

## 1 Introduction

In recent years, with the development of Internet of Things (IoT) technology and relative industries, more and more different functional sensors are widely applied. Emergence of large amount of Smart-Home products has proposed a challenge of low energy consumption and low manufacturing cost for sensor type selection and adaptation. Indoor human location and tracking is one of the

This work was supported by the National Natural Science Foundation of China under Grant 61328302, the Zhejiang Provincial Natural Science Foundation of China under Grant LY15F030007, and the ASFC under Grant 2015ZC76006.

© Springer Nature Singapore Pte Ltd. 2017
F. Sun et al. (Eds.): ICCSIP 2016, CCIS 710, pp. 479–492, 2017.
DOI: 10.1007/978-981-10-5230-9_46

hot applications of smart home domain based on sensor networks. Pyroelectric infrared sensor (PIR), can sense 7–10 μm infrared wavelength through optical filter materials, while the infrared central wavelength of human radiation is about 9–10 μm. Therefore, PIR may be dedicated for human infrared target detection. As for recent years, it has been studied and applied in some related situations [1–4]. Meanwhile, considering PIR as a binary sensor used for judging whether sensed target, WSN based on PIRs has the benefit of low cost, low power and privacy ensured, and is suitable to be adopted in the household environment. To this end, this paper proposed a novel multi-target tracking algorithm based on PIR sensor network for smart home application. In our environment, the sensor network covers two fundamental part: sensor module and fusion center. The sensor module is consist of PIR as actuator and Arduino as micro-controller. PIR is used to sense information of human activity and Arduino carries out the binary process of the PIR measurement signal, which is sent into the fusion center. After that, fusion center fuses all the sensor data and calculates the target position. It is worth mentioning that the binary measurement provided for the fusion center is carried with observation noise. To solve the problem, we adopt filtering algorithm to estimate the observed human target online. Particle filter estimates target's posterior probability distribution by using discrete random measurements, which can solve the non-linear and non-gaussian problem of tracking procedure [5] and is also becoming a hotspot in recent years. Pitt and Shephard proposed Auxiliary Particle Filter (APF) [6] based on standard particle filter. Compared with the standard one, APF is also built on Sequential Importance Sampling (SIS), but it selects distinct importance density function. And compared with Sampling Importance Resampling (SIR) filter, APF algorithm has the advantage that it samples based on time $k - 1$, together with a reference of measured data of time $k$. So the method can be more close to the target's true state. Furthermore, as for the situation of multi human targets exist at the same time in the monitored room, considering the uncertainty of multi-target measurement source, the problem of data association should be solved. Nearest-Neighbor (NN) data association algorithm is based on decision, and has the advantage of reduced calculation, which is convenience for online processing. Also, it is suit for a high signal-to-noise ratio environment and is applied in the field of pattern classification [7,8]. Although PIR has the benefit of low cost, but the measurement data is still limited during sensing procedure, which will lead to uncertainty of measurement classification. In order to eliminate the disturbance of the indeterminacy, this paper will present a Multi-Target Tracking based on K-Nearest Neighbor (MTT-KNN) algorithm to solve the problem of multi-target trajectory association with passive binary PIR's uncertain measurement source. The proposed method will provide a solution to indoor multi human simultaneous localization.

This paper is organized as follows. Section 2 describes the models of the system including the indoor PIR sensor network model and human kinematical model as well as its observation model. Section 3 derives the tracking method and fusion algorithm of indoor multi human target based on multi PIR sensors in the network. Section 4 gives the result of our simulations. Finally, Sect. 5 presents the conclusion and the future work.

## 2    Models

### 2.1    Indoor PIR Sensor Network Model

In the binary PIR sensor network, PIR depends on heat signal to sense observed body. When the intensity of signal is above the given threshold, current sensor will report to the fusion center that the target is detected, otherwise the signal will be ignored. The detective mode of binary PIR sensor is shown in Fig. 1, the central circle represents a PIR sensor node, and the detection range is within the region of the outer circle. Time $t_0 - t_6$ represents the sample time of human in motion. When human is beyond the signal coverage $(t_0, t_1, t_6)$, PIR node accepts a signal whose intensity is below the given threshold value, and the node will send a "false" measurement to the fusion center; when human steps into the detect range $(t_2, t_3, t_4, t_5)$, PIR node receives a signal with its intensity higher than the threshold, therefore the node will deliver a "true" measurement to the fusion center.

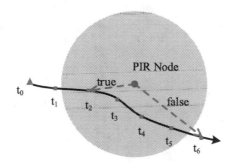

**Fig. 1.** Detective mode of binary PIR sensor

The indoor PIR-WSN consists of $N$ nodes, and is deployed in random, fixed or mixed mode. This article aims at both random and fixed deployment scheme, and presents a simulation analysis. Here, we assume that the fusion center has already known the position data of all the nodes, and also the PIR nodes in the network stay permanent while the tracking process of the human target. The structure of the distributed PIR sensor network is shown in Fig. 2.

### 2.2    Human Kinematical Model and Observation Model

Indoor moving human object is modeled by dynamic equation of discrete time system, as

$$x_k = F_k x_{k-1} + G_k w_k \tag{1}$$

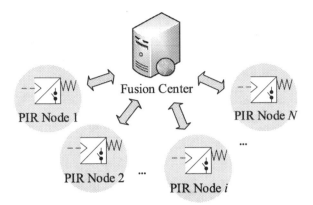

**Fig. 2.** Distributed sensor network structure

where $x_k = [x_{1,k}, \dot{x}_{1,k}, x_{2,k}, \dot{x}_{2,k}]$ is state vector, representing position and velocity of the moving human in the 2-D room coordinate system. $F_k$ is the state transmit matrix, and $G_k$ is the processing noise matrix, as

$$F_k = \begin{bmatrix} 1 & T_s & 0 & 0 \\ 0 & 1 & 0 & 0 \\ 0 & 0 & 1 & T_s \\ 0 & 0 & 0 & 1 \end{bmatrix} \quad G_k = \begin{bmatrix} \frac{T_s^2}{2} & 0 \\ T_s & 0 \\ 0 & \frac{T_s^2}{2} \\ 0 & T_s \end{bmatrix} \tag{2}$$

where $T_s$ is the sampling period of motion process, and $w_k \sim N(0, Q_k)$ is a process noise sequence following the gauss distribution, whose mean value is 0 and covariance is $Q_k = diag(\sigma_{w1}^2, \sigma_{w2}^2)$.

By modeling of the target signal power that PIR sensor receives, the measurement of the $i_{th}$ sensor represents as

$$y_{i,k} = g_i(x_k) + v_{i,k} = \frac{\Psi d_0^\alpha}{\|s_i - r_k\|} + v_{i,k}, i = 1, 2, ..., N \tag{3}$$

where $g_i(\cdot)$ represents the received signal power function model of the $i_{th}$ sensor, and $v_{i,k}$ is the sensor measurement noise of PIR independent of $w_k$. Here, we make two assumptions: (1) The PIR measurement noise is independent of process noise; (2) Measurement noise between PIR sensors is also independent. $s_i$ is the coordinate of the $i_{th}$ PIR sensor in the room, $r_k = [x_{1,k}, x_{2,k}]^T$ is the position of human in time $k$, and $\|s_i - r_k\|$ represents the Euclidean distance of $s_i$ and $r_k$. $\Psi$ represents the human target radiation energy in the reference distance $d_0$. $\alpha$ is a decay factor related to transmission medium, and we assume that it is same and known for all the PIR sensors. In order to apply Particle Filter algorithm, we should know the distribution of $v_{i,k}$: Here, we also assume that $v_{i,k} \sim N(\mu_v, \sigma_v^2)$, where $\mu_v = \sigma^2$, and $\sigma^2$ is a sample of indoor background observation noise. Moreover $\sigma_v^2 = 2\sigma^4/\Sigma$, and $\Sigma$ is the amount of the measurement signal samples that user has obtained [9]. The $i_{th}$ PIR node ($i = 1, 2, ..., N$) receives a human target measurement signal $y_{i,k}$ and then performs a local processing for a binary digital signal, and send to fusion center as follow rules:

- Micro-controller compares the real observation signal intensity with the given threshold $\lambda$. If the value is above $\lambda$, then the detection data will have an impact on the fusion center.
- If the observation signal intensity is below $\lambda$, then the detection data will not act on fusion center.

That is, only if the received signal intensity is enough strong, PIR node in the sensor network can send a valid detection information to fusion center.

The signal model of the $i_{th}$ PIR senor in fusion center is denoted by

$$z_{i,k} = \delta_i q_{i,k} + \xi_{i,k} \tag{4}$$

$$q_{i,k} = \begin{cases} 1 & \text{if } y_{i,k} > \lambda \\ 0 & \text{if } y_{i,k} \leq \lambda \end{cases} \tag{5}$$

where $\delta_i$ is the quantify factor related to the $i_{th}$ sensor, and $\xi_{i,k}$ is measurement noise of fusion center. Similarly, in order to apply Particle Filter algorithm, we would like to know the probability distribution of noise item $\xi_{i,k}$, and thus assume $\xi_{i,k} \sim N(0, \sigma_\xi^2)$.

Hence, as for indoor human target state tracking, we make use of the binary observation sequence $z_{1:k} = \{z_{1,1:k}, z_{2,1:k}, ..., z_{i,1:k}, ..., z_{N,1:k}\}$ to estimate human's motion state sequence $x_{1:k} = \{x_0, x_1, ..., x_k\}$.

## 3   The Tracking Algorithm

### 3.1   Network Fusion Algorithm

According to Bayesian Filter theory, in order to estimate the state $x_k$ of target at time $k$, a Probability Density Function (PDF) $p(x_k|z_{1:k})$ should be obtained. And by two main steps of prediction and update, we can get a posteriori probability, which is helpful to getting the optimal estimation $\hat{x}_k$ [10]. In this experiment, we adopt APF algorithm to estimate the posterior state $p(x_{0:k}|z_{1:k})$. As for APF, when sampling particles at time $k$, we both consider state transition $p(x_k|x_{k-1})$ of time $k-1$ and measurement $p(z_k|x_k)$. As a result, it's a combined process of double sampling and double weight allocation, and the sampled particles are more close to the true state, the estimated value of the filter is more precise [11]. To this end, we sample a particle set $\pi_k$ containing $M$ particles, denoted by $\pi_k = \{x_{0:k}^{(j)}, w_k^{(j)}\}_{j=1}^M$. And then during each sample time $k$, we execute Particle Filter one-step algorithm.

As for the observation noise $\xi_{i,k}$ in Eq. (4), we assume the sensors in our network are independent, then we have

$$p(z_k|x_k^{(j)}) = \prod_{i=1}^{N} p(z_{i,k}|x_k^{(j)}) \tag{6}$$

And then, we denote the factor $p(z_{i,k}|x_k^{(j)})$ of the multiplier by

$$\begin{aligned}
p(z_{i,k}|x_k^{(j)}) &= p(z_{i,k}|q_{i,k} = 0, x_k^{(j)})P(q_{i,k} = 0|x_k^{(j)}) \\
&+ p(z_{i,k}|q_{i,k} = 1, x_k^{(j)})P(q_{i,k} = 1|x_k^{(j)}) \\
&= p(z_{i,k}|q_{i,k} = 0)P(q_{i,k} = 0|x_k^{(j)}) \\
&+ p(z_{i,k}|q_{i,k} = 1)P(q_{i,k} = 1|x_k^{(j)})
\end{aligned} \tag{7}$$

where

$$p(z_{i,k}|q_{i,k}) \sim N(\delta_i q_{i,k}, \sigma_\xi^2) \tag{8}$$

and

$$P(q_{i,k} = 1|x_k^{(j)}) = Q(\frac{\lambda - g_i(x_k^{(j)}) - \mu_v}{\sigma_v}) \tag{9}$$

$$P(q_{i,k} = 0|x_k^{(j)}) = 1 - Q(\frac{\lambda - g_i(x_k^{(j)}) - \mu_v}{\sigma_v}) \tag{10}$$

where the function $Q(\cdot)$ is the complementary cumulative distribution function of the standard normal distribution.

By sampling from the priori state distribution $\varphi(x_0)$, we get an initial particle sample $x_0^{(j)}, j = 1, 2, ..., M$, and the weight of the particles are set to $1/M$. Assume that at sample time $k - 1$, we have already obtained the particle sample set $\pi_{k-1} = {x_{0:k-1}^{(j)}, w_{k-1}^{(j)}}_{j=1}^{M}$, and then following the derivation above, for the next time $k$, a binary PIR sensor network fusion algorithm based on APF is described as:

- Particle state transition: In order to select a max particle probability of particles at time $k$, we use the conditional expectation of $x_k^{(j)}$

$$x_k^{(j)} = E(x_k|x_{k-1}^{(j)}) \tag{11}$$

and the value above can be obtained by the state transition function

$$x_k^{(j)} = F_k x_{k-1}^{(j)} \tag{12}$$

based on which we can then get a sample label set ${i_j}$.

- Particle rebirth: Considering that human state $x_k$ in the room map is combined of 2-D position information and 2-D velocity information, and the human position is related to his velocity, so $x_k^{(j)}$ can be reduced to a 2-D random variable. Therefore, we can get the velocity by joint distribution $p(\dot{x}_{1,k}, \dot{x}_{2,k} | \dot{x}_{1,k-1}, \dot{x}_{2,k-1}, z_k)$ or $p(\dot{x}_{1,k}, \dot{x}_{2,k} | \dot{x}_{1,k-1}, \dot{x}_{2,k-1})$, and then calculate the position value by

$$x_{1,k}^{(j)} = x_{1,k-1}^{(i_j)} + \frac{T_s}{2}(\dot{x}_{1,k}^{(j)} + \dot{x}_{1,k-1}^{(i_j)}) \tag{13}$$

$$x_{2,k}^{(j)} = x_{2,k-1}^{(i_j)} + \frac{T_s}{2}(\dot{x}_{2,k}^{(j)} + \dot{x}_{2,k-1}^{(i_j)}) \tag{14}$$

- Calculation of weight: The fresh particles is allocated a weight by

$$w_k^{(j)} \propto \frac{p(z_k | x_k^{(j)})}{p(z_k | x_k^{(i_j)})} \tag{15}$$

- The estimation: The undetermined state can be estimated according to the particles set after a normalization of the weight. Here we will adopt the form of minimum mean square error (MMSE) to get the target's optimal state estimation

$$x_k = \sum_{j=1}^{M} w_k^{(j)} x_k^{(j)} \tag{16}$$

### 3.2  Multi Human Target Trajectory Association

In the environment of household PIR sensor network, if there is only one person indoor, i.e. only one target exists within the detection range of PIR node, in this case, there is, during each sample time, at most one measure data is from the target among the measurement set obtained by the PIR sensor, while other measure data will be regarded as the background noise in the room. However, when there are two or more people in the room, every man will be a target source, which may be sensed by the PIR sensor. Therefore, it is inevitable to solve the association problem of multi-observation data with multi-target set.

This paper will adopt a modified K-NN classification tracking algorithm, aimed at solving mentioned problem above. The nearest neighbor measured data is classified by category and with the selection of $K$ value, precision of classification will greatly promoted. Therefore the multi-target tracking problem is converted to classify-studying problem, which can solve the indoor multi human target trajectory association problem.

The measurement classification algorithm based on K-NN is described as: if the measured data to be classified contains $K$ most similar measurements, and most of them come from a certain target, then the current measurement data also belongs to the target. The classify regulation is as Fig. 3 shows. The steps of K-NN measurement classification is as follows:

- Calculate the the similarity sequence set $\{S(z_k, Z_1), S(z_k, Z_2), ..., S(z_k, Z_n)\}$ of measurement $z_k$ to be classified with $n$ measurement set $\{Z_1, Z_2, ..., Z_n\}$ that is already classified.
- Sort $\{S(z_k, Z_1), S(z_k, Z_2), ..., S(z_k, Z_n)\}$, and draw the first $K$ measurement data to K-NN set $\Omega_k$.
- According to the "Most Rule" in the set $\Omega_k$, and get the promising source of the measure to be classified.

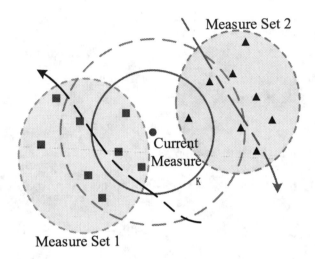

**Fig. 3.** Multi-target measurement K-NN classify

The K-NN measurement classification algorithm is simple and efficient, and is a kind of lazy-learning algorithm. The classifier doesn't need a training set to train the system, thus the time complexity is reduced to zero. Also, the calculation complexity of K-NN classification is in proportion to the amount of the training measurement set, i.e. if the amount of current set is $n$, then the time complexity of K-NN is $O(n)$. Because of the limitation of amount of people in a room, the measured samples' number is limited, and every class of measurements is in average, so the problems that will emerge in sample imbalance situations can be effectively overcome.

Therefore, a specific online Multi Human Target APF algorithm based on PIR wireless sensor network for a smart indoor household environment is thus designed. The flowchart of the algorithm presented is shown in Fig. 4. In this algorithm, the fusion center adopts two working threads during the actual operation. Thread A is used to capture the measurement data of PIR sensors, and conduct finalization and trajectory classification. Thread B, at the same time, is used for generating particles and update states. Human's current state is shown in system output terminal. Moreover, when the man steps on the given point of the room, the algorithm performs initialization as to eliminate the system error online.

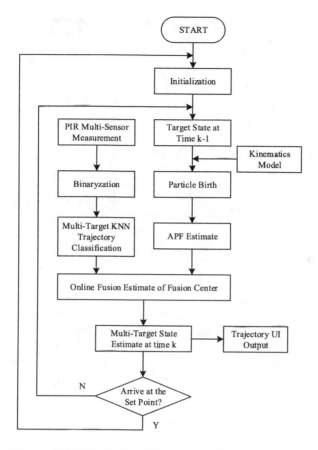

**Fig. 4.** MTT-KNN-Bin-AFP online estimate algorithm

# 4 Simulation

## 4.1 Experimental Environment Description

In our experiment, the indoor environment is covered by the home PIR wireless sensor network, as shown in Fig. 5. Consider that the sensor network consists of $N$ PIR nodes, which are deployed on the ceiling of the experiment room with a size of 5.9 m by 6.8 m.

The decay factor of PIR sensor is set by $\alpha = 2.5$, and at a reference distance of $d_0 = 1.0$ m the corresponding radiation intensity is $\Psi = 20$. The detection threshold of our PIR sensor is $\lambda = 20$. And the motion process noise covariance of person in the room is suppose to be $Q_k = diag(0.01, 0.01)$, while the PIR sensors' measurement noise is given by $\mu = 0.05$ and $\sigma_v = 0.01$. Also, the binary-conversion noise is $\sigma_\xi = 0.01$. The signal-to-noise ratio of the fusion center is regarded as 20 dB. Moreover, the system sample time is $T_s = 1$ s.

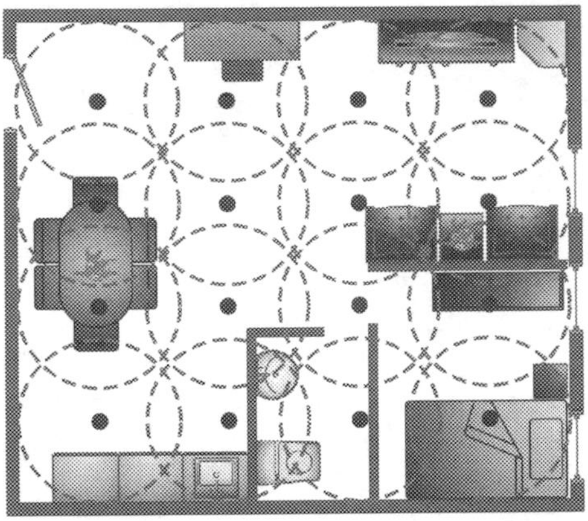

**Fig. 5.** 2D-layout of our experiment room

## 4.2 Single-Target Tracking in PIR-WSN

In the simulation of APF estimation, we sample $M = 500$ particles. And as for the situation of single person indoor, we adopt two methods of fixed-mode and random-mode sensor deployment. The human kinematics model is reduced to constant-velocity (CV) model in a very short period of time. In the network, 16 PIR sensor nodes are both deployed in fixed mode and in random mode. With the tool of MATLAB, simulation results and their RMSE, during 500 times Monte Carlo experiment, are shown in Figs. 6 and 7.

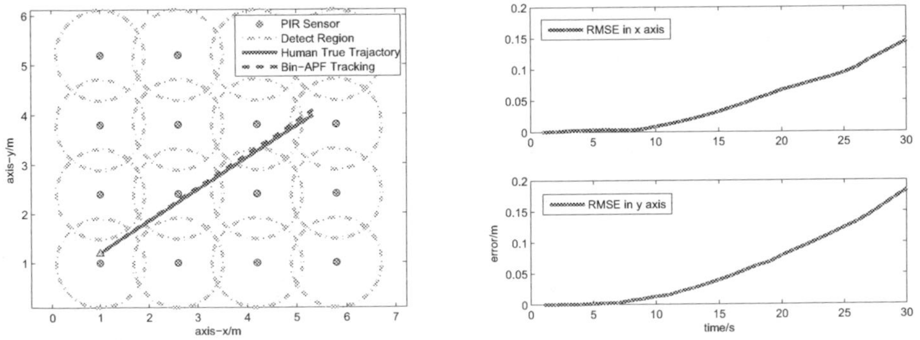


(a) Tracking trajectory (b) RMSE of tracking

**Fig. 6.** Single target tracking with fixed-mode node deployment (N = 16)

In Figs. 6 and 7, as for a PIR sensor network of 16 nodes, whether we adopt a random-mode or a fixed-mode deployment scheme, the Bin-APF estimate and fusion algorithm presented in this paper will achieve a good result in single target

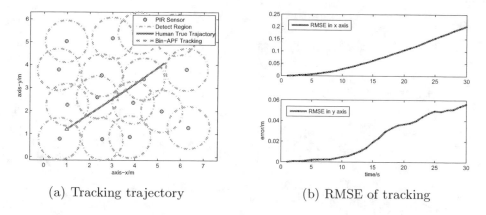

(a) Tracking trajectory                    (b) RMSE of tracking

**Fig. 7.** Single target tracking with random-mode node deployment (N = 16)

indoor tracking. During the first 10 s, the estimation error can be maintained below 0.02 m, and during the time of 10 s – 20 s, the estimation error can be restrained to about 0.05 m, which basically meets the requirement of a household tracking performance. And as we see, the method of random-mode deployment is superior to that of fixed-mode one, by considering the system tracking error. Reason is that the randomness of the system will eliminate the error of a specific point by measurement effectively. However, because that tracking of an indoor human target only depends on nodes with binary data, the amount of system information is obviously limited, so when time goes, the error will increase (after 25 s as the RMSE curves show).

With the purpose of solving this problem, in our practical process, we will adopt an Online-Tracking method. The room will be decorated with some "specific point", and when person steps on the point, the fusion center is supposed to set off an initial procedure. Thus, the error will be reduced online.

Moreover, we realize that the number of PIR nodes in the network is an important factor in the tracking process, so several different numbers of nodes deployed in a random-mode scheme are compared. As Fig. 8 (a)–(d) shows, we tried four different schemes (N = 4, 6, 12, 20). When there are only 4 nodes in the network, tracking divergency will occur after a period of time, however when the node increase to 12 or 20, conditions will improve, especially in the situation of 20 nodes, a relatively accurate trajectory is obtained. Results indicate that more nodes adopted in PIR sensor network can increase tracking precision to some degree. Also, the average calculation time spent in different PIR node number conditions mentioned above during a single Monte Carlo simulation can be found in Table 1. It is also evident that the computing time is basically proportional to the numerical quantity of the PIR nodes in the network. As a result, what we should consider is to find a balanced scheme between tracking accuracy and time consumption.

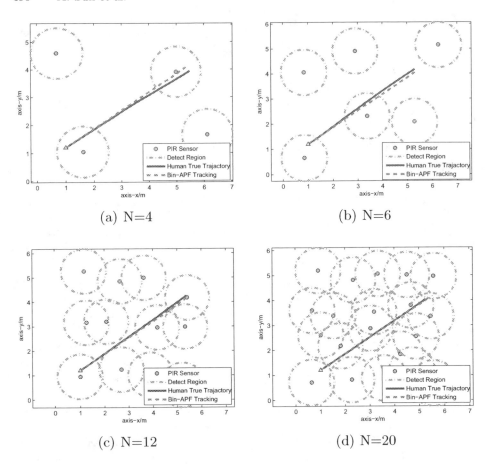

**Fig. 8.** Comparison of tracking results of different node number in the PIR sensor network using random-mode deploy scheme

**Table 1.** Calculation time consumed in different PIR node number conditions

| Number of PIR nodes | N = 4 | N = 6 | N = 12 | N = 16 | N = 20 |
|---|---|---|---|---|---|
| Computing time/s | 0.178921 | 0.246916 | 0.474325 | 0.635975 | 0.761607 |

## 4.3   Multi-target Tracking in PIR-WSN

Based on the effective results in the single-target tracking experiment, we can move forward to the situation of multi human target tracking indoor. By making use of the theory derived in Sect. 3, we also arrange 16 nodes in the room, and regard that the room contains more than one person. The simulation result of the MTT-KNN-Bin-APF presented in this paper is shown in Fig. 9.

In Fig. 9, there are three human targets in the network, which are moving independently, and the PIR sensors observe these targets indiscriminately.

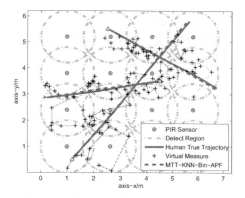

**Fig. 9.** Multi human target tracking in PIR-WSN (N = 16, target = 3)

The three individuals walk towards different directions. And at the very beginning, there is no intersection between them, so the trajectories are relatively accurate, while after the right two targets encountered, the estimate results are influenced to some extent. The reason is that, the same PIR sensor detects different target at the same time, which will lead to an incorrect measurement classification, considering the limit information of binary sensors. However, in general, with a regard to multi target measurement KNN classification result and Bin-APF fusion tracking trajectory, our method can obtain a relatively preferable effect, and evidently it can be applied in the smart home human localization and tracking.

## 5 Conclusion

This paper studies multi human target tracking based on indoor PIR sensor network. Aimed at the drawbacks of the lack of measurement information in the indoor binary PIR-WSN environment, as well as the low adaptability of traditional smart home localization algorithm and severe reliability of household layout, simulation results show that the MTT-KNN-Bin-APF online fusion estimate algorithm achieves the application of binary PIR sensors in smart home and IoT domain, which provides an effective solution to the intelligent service of indoor localization and tracking. Further research will focus on sensor node scheduling and energy consumption, and also, these algorithms based on PIR sensors will be combined with wearable bio-sensors (WBS) to realize more precise indoor human localization and tracking as well as health monitoring.

## References

1. Luo, X., Liu, T., Shen, B., Gao, Q., Luo, X.: Human indoor localization based on ceiling mounted PIR sensor nodes. In: 2016 13th IEEE Annual Consumer Communications Networking Conference (CCNC), pp. 868–874 (2016)

2. Domnech-Asensi, G., Carrillo-Calleja, J.M., Illade-Quinteiro, J., Martnez-Viviente, F., Daz-Madrid, J., Fernndez-Luque, F., Zapata-Prez, J., Ruiz-Merino, R., Domnguez, M.A.: Low-frequency CMOS bandpass filter for PIR sensors in wireless sensor nodes. IEEE Sens. J. **14**, 4085–4094 (2014)
3. Deiana, D., Suijker, E.M., Bolt, R.J., Maas, A.P.M., Vlothuizen, W.J., Kossen, A.S.: Real time indoor presence detection with a novel radar on a chip. In: 2014 International Radar Conference, pp. 1–4 (2014)
4. Sukmana, H.T., Farisi, M.G., Khairani, D.: Prototype utilization of PIR motion sensor for real time surveillance system and web-enabled lamp automation. In: 2015 IEEE Asia Pacific Conference on Wireless and Mobile (APWiMob), pp. 183–187 (2015)
5. Arulampalam, M.S., Maskell, S., Gordon, N., Clapp, T.: A tutorial on particle filters for online nonlinear/non-Gaussian Bayesian tracking. IEEE Trans. Sig. Process. **50**, 174–188 (2002)
6. Pitt, M.K., Shephard, N.: Filtering via simulation: auxiliary particle filters. J. Am. Stat. Assoc. **94**, 590–599 (1999)
7. Padmapriya, K., Sridhar, S.: Low-frequency CMOS bandpass filter for PIR sensors in wireless sensor nodes. In: 2014 International Conference on Information Communication and Embedded Systems (ICICES), pp. 1–5 (2014)
8. Ishii, N., Torii, I., Mukai, N., Kazunori, I., Nakashima, T.: Nonlinear mapping of reducts - nearest neighbor classification. In: 2015 3rd International Conference on Applied Computing and Information Technology/2nd International Conference on Computational Science and Intelligence (ACIT-CSI), pp. 416–421 (2015)
9. Sheng, X., Yu-Hen, H.: Maximum likelihood multiple-source localization using acoustic energy measurements with wireless sensor networks. IEEE Trans. Sig. Process. **53**, 44–53 (2005)
10. Gustafsson, F.: Particle filter theory and practice with positioning applications. IEEE Aerosp. Electron. Syst. Mag. **25**, 53–82 (2010)
11. Bruno, M.G.S.: Sequential Monte Carlo Methods for Nonlinear Discrete-Time Filtering. Morgan & Claypool, San Rafael (2013)

# The Compatibility Study of Reading Halftone Microstructure Information on Mobile Phone

Jianbo Chen, Peng Cao[(✉)], Dazhong Mu, Jianhua Hu, Muming Li, and Jing Wang

Beijing Key Laboratory of Signal and Information Processing
for High-end Printing Equipment, Beijing Institute of Graphic Communication,
Beijing 102600, China
b287619287@163.com, pcaorf2012@163.com

**Abstract.** In the current market, there exists a variety of mobile phone brands whose physical parameters showed on the screen and the parameters of camera resolutions are not exactly the same, which is prone to cause system crashes and compatibility issues in the process of reading halftone microstructural information. To address the problem, the method based on the physical parameters matching is proposed. Meanwhile, it adopts the memory optimization, improving the stability of the system. The experimental results show that it solved the technical bottlenecks in the process of reading halftone microstructural information.

**Keywords:** Halftone · Microstructure · Information hiding · Mobile phone reading · Image matching · Compatibility

## 1 Introduction

Numbers of literature about 2-dimensional code reading on the phone have done and people have a lot of research on it. But in the process of reading halftone microstructure information, it unlike the general two-dimensional code reading requirements which needs demanding imaging. It is necessary to address this issue through the physical bottom and optical imaging macro level. Secondly, a variety of mobile phone brands whose screen resolution and camera resolution cannot match exactly on the hardware platform. This problem caused by phone camera and screen resolution ratio inconsistent and system crash phenomenon.

## 2 Halftone Information Hiding

Halftone information hiding makes use of hidden information features and is applied to the halftone information hiding technology and information security process by some algorithms [1, 2]. The usual halftone screening technology is divided into FM, AM and hybrid screening [3–5]. This paper is based on multi-quadrature amplitude modulation prints encryption security printing technology [5] that the security information is embedded in the microstructure of a halftone image by multi-quadrature amplitude

© Springer Nature Singapore Pte Ltd. 2017
F. Sun et al. (Eds.): ICCSIP 2016, CCIS 710, pp. 493–501, 2017.
DOI: 10.1007/978-981-10-5230-9_47

modulation (QAM). MQAM is a progressive amplitude modulation on two orthogonal carriers and two carriers are orthogonal state. M represents hexadecimal value which has 4,16,32,64,128,256. In 16QAM example, the constellation is as follows: (Fig. 1)

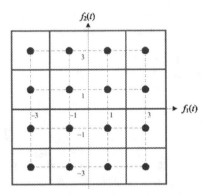

**Fig. 1.** The constellation of 16QAM

Compared to ordinary two-dimensional code, the identification accuracy requires much higher on halftone microstructure information. In the process of two-dimensional code reading, the identification of black and white blocks is easier, while the half-tone microstructural information identification process needs to be accurate to the dot size and dot shape.

By comparing the Table 1 to find, identify common two-dimensional code only needs to identify the smallest black and white pieces which normally occupied 16 to 144 pixel in size. But during reading the halftone micro structural information, we need to read a single micro pixel block structural shape. The comparison found latter reading accuracy requirements higher than the former 10 times or even a hundred times. Thus the obtained image needs to improve for reading in order to get the halftone microstructure information successfully.

## 3   Mobile Phone Screen and Camera

According to a latest market research report from Counterpoint Technology, Android accounted for more than 80% in the mobile device market. Except in front of Samsung, Huawei, Oppo and Xiaomi, a number of unknown android mobile phone brands account for nearly 50% share. They have their own standard hardware configuration resulting in disunity become a common phenomenon. Particularly evident in the 2-dimensional code scanning process, the screen resolution and the camera resolution don't match when we need to get a fixed size image. The scanning software crash and cannot use normally in the process of acquisition of the image information [6]. (Fig. 2)

Resolution is the capability of the sensor to observe or measure the smallest object clearly with distinct boundaries which also known as perceptual clarity by using a higher resolution displaying a clearer image in a smaller area. It can make the image

**Table 1.** The compare of two-dimensional code and halftone image

| Image Type | Ordinary two-dimensional code information | Halftone microstructure information |
|---|---|---|
| Image | | |
| Block | | |
| The smallest unit | 7*7 | 1*1 |
| Identification progression | 1 | 0.0204 |

clearer and "sharp" that usually referred width × height expressing in pixels. Constituted by the pixel value is larger, the more clear image it is. It is an important parameter in the mobile phone hardware configuration. The resolution is mainly composed of screen resolution and camera resolution.

Screen resolution refers to the number of pixels displayed on the screen based on the number of horizontal pixels × the number of vertical pixels generally. The higher the resolution it has, the greater the number of pixels it is, and the more sensitive to the image precision we see. And at the same screen size, the higher resolution you have, the more subtle and delicate display is.

PPI means the number of pixels per inch. It is a standard on description of a screen resolution. Pixels per inch are represented by the number of pixels per inch owned

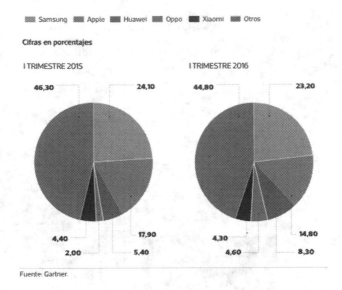

**Fig. 2.** The research on mobile phone market

**Table 2.** Common screen resolution size and PPI values

| Screen size | Screen type | Screen resolution | PPI |
|---|---|---|---|
| 4.0 | HD | 1136 x 640 | 330 |
| 4.5 | HD | 1280 x 720 | 326 |
| 4.5 | FHD | 1920 x 1080 | 490 |
| 5.0 | XGA | 1024 x 768 | 256 |
| 5.0 | FHD | 1920 x 1080 | 441 |
| 5.5 | FHD | 2560 x 1440 | 577 |

(x: the length screen resolution; y: the width of screen resolution; z: the screen size). (Table 2)

$$PPI = \frac{\sqrt{x^2 + y^2}}{Z} \tag{1}$$

Camera resolution refers to the smallest unit of photosensitive sensor on the camera. It commonly refers to as "XXX-megapixel" actually refers to the resolution of the camera. Its value is mainly determined by the size of the camera sensor which contains the points of pixel number. For example 5 million pixel sensor means there are five million pixels. (Table 3)

**Table 3.** Mobile phone camera pixel size and resolution

| Megapixel | Camera resolution | |
|---|---|---|
| | 4:3 | 16:9 |
| 0.7 M | 960 × 720 | |
| 0.8 M | 1024 × 768 | |
| 1 M | 1152 × 864 | 1366 × 768 |
| 1.2 M | 1280 × 960 | |
| 3.2 M | 2048 × 1536 | |
| 4 M | 2304 × 1728 | 2560 × 1440 |

# 4    Adaptability Between Camera and Screen

We choose eclipse as the test platform to get a plurality of mobile phone screen resolution and camera configuration during the 2-dimensional code scanning process, the resolution results and compare in the following table (Cr.x is equal to the length of camera resolution, Cr.y is equal to the width of camera resolution and same as the screen resolution). (Table 4)

**Table 4.** The log on some mobile phone brands

| Mobile phone style | Cr.x | Cr.y | Sr.x | Sr.y | Cr.x/Sr.x | Cr.y/Sr.y |
|---|---|---|---|---|---|---|
| Samsung S6 | 1920 | 1080 | 2560 | 1440 | 0.75 | 0.75 |
| Huawei mate7 | 1920 | 1080 | 1812 | 1080 | 1.06 | 1.00 |
| Huawei honor6 | 1920 | 1080 | 1920 | 1080 | 1.00 | 1.00 |
| Baidu Cloud | 1280 | 720 | 1184 | 720 | 1.08 | 1.00 |
| LG nexus 5 | 1920 | 1080 | 1772 | 1080 | 1.08 | 1.00 |
| Samsung S5 | 1920 | 1080 | 1920 | 1080 | 1.00 | 1.00 |
| Xiaomi 4 | 1920 | 1080 | 1920 | 1080 | 1.00 | 1.00 |

From the above table we observed, mobile phone camera resolution returns to the screen self-adapting by and large. Camera resolution is determined by screen resolution when the matrix size can exactly match the screen size and returns the corresponding size. Such as Samsung S5 and Xiaomi 4, the camera and the screen x, y values are the same. If they cannot an exact match, return to the default value. Such as Samsung S6 screen resolution is 2560 * 1440 and the camera cannot return to the matrix size of this parameter. The default returns 1920 * 1080. In the table, some of the phone's screen-x is slightly smaller than the value of x value returned by the camera. The Huawei mate7 screen-x = 1812 which less than 1920. The LG and Baidu cloud also appears the same phenomenon. The analysis showed that the mobile phone is integrated into the function keys on the touch screen resulting in a small part of the display portion is occupied. And the phenomenon of missing is shown below. (Fig. 3)

The region A is a scanning frame and system cut the corresponding position from the camera pixel matrix information according to the size of the region A on screen.

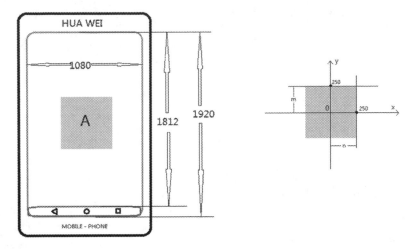

**Fig. 3.** The resolution and the region A

When it needs to get a fixed-size area image information in A, this paper presents a relative ratio algorithm to obtain A's pixel information.

$$A_{pixel}.left = A_{srceen}.left \cdot \frac{camera.x}{screen.x} \tag{2}$$

$$A_{pixel}.top = A_{srceen}.top \cdot \frac{camera.y}{screen.y} \tag{3}$$

$$A_{pixel}.right = A_{srceen}.right \cdot \frac{camera.x}{screen.x} \tag{4}$$

$$A_{pixel}.buttom = A_{srceen}.buttom \cdot \frac{camera.y}{screen.y} \tag{5}$$

Supposed we need 500 * 500 pixel matrix, and the first set x and y of screen is 500. The screen matrix size meets the requirements. Assuming camera resolution and the screen resolution ratio of 1: 1 then using 500 * 500 screen sizes to cut camera pixels, still obtain 500 * 500. But if the ratio is not 1: 1, the intercept matrix of pixels from camera is not equal to 500 * 500. It led to the crash on the phone when 2-dimensional code scanner running.

In response to this problem, in order to meet the different hardware parameters and improve the adaptability on Android phone, this paper positions the center point coordinate to obtain the fixed pixels. Firstly, we get the 0 point position coordinates (x, y). Secondly, through the x + 250, x − 250, y + 250, y − 250 method it may be obtained 500 * 500 matrix of pixels. This algorithm can solve the situation which camera resolution and screen resolution's ratio is not equal to 1.

$$A_{pixel}.x = \frac{1}{2}(A_{pixel}.left + A_{pixel}.right) \tag{6}$$

$$A_{pixel}.y = \frac{1}{2}(A_{pixel}.top + A_{pixel}.buttom) \tag{7}$$

$$A_{pixel}.left = A_{pixel}.x - 250 \tag{8}$$

$$A_{pixel}.right = A_{pixel}.x + 250 \tag{9}$$

$$A_{pixel}.top = A_{pixel}.y - 250 \tag{10}$$

$$A_{pixel}.buttom = A_{pixel}.y + 250 \tag{11}$$

## 5 Memory Optimization

In the process of halftone microstructural information scanning software development, there are a lot of image acquisition and image processing. And these processes, the system have used a large number of bitmap resources and two bit array. If not timely release of memory, the software is prone to excessive memory usage, system crashes phenomenon while continuous scanning. Optimize memory has five main ways: reckon, reduce, reuse, recycle, and review [7].

In the optimization process, we found that the main role of memory consumption is bitmap, and the vast majority system crashes are in the operating bitmap. The bitmap operations include: image display, image pixel processing. Another reason is the irrational use of the array which also leading memory consumption especially during image processing. For example, system create excessive static array that failed to create in memory after the release causing the program to run after the segment and memory usage rate of over 100% resulting in a crash at last. So we generally use the way to create a dynamic array and try to define the variable matching memory it used [8].

## 6 Experiment

In the APP development process, we contrast and found that, the development software named Xcode can show the memory usage directly. So in the course of the experiment, we choose Xcode as the tool to visually display the experimental operation.

From the lower side of in the Fig. 4 coordinate graphs observed in each of the scanning process, the left part are steep rise by the flat portion to the peak, get back again gently after the end of the scan, and. In a scanning process, there is one frame and one frame on the image acquisition and image processing, so the memory will be significantly improved just like the peak. However, the development trend of the entire volatility curve, we find that the APP memory is increasing during running with a time of scanning process and finally crashed when the memory occupancy rate of around 13%. By this time the number of continuous scanning is generally about 50 to 60 times. If we release the bitmap image and array after use timely, carve shows a trend of fluctuation curve to the right which the flat part of the memory status is always up and down in the vicinity of a certain level fluctuations. We have not found a program crash phenomenon in the multi-scanning process.

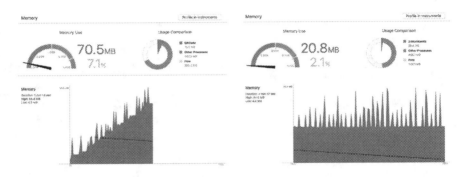

**Fig. 4.** Memory usage situation before and after optimization

# 7   Conclusion

In the process of halftone microstructure information reading, this paper solve the system crashes phenomenon directed against the screen and camera resolution inconsistent. And a method by relative ratio to obtain coordinates of the center point of the target pixel matrix is put to obtain information of fixed size. In the course of the experiment, the release of bitmap and array on image processing achieves the purpose of optimizing memory while observing the memory usage status in scanning process. The experiments solve the key technology on the characteristic information reading and improve the compatibility and stability of the scanning APP.

**Acknowledgments.** This paper is supported by the National Natural Science Foundation of China (No. 61370140).

# References

1. Zhe-can, L., Peng, C.: Halftone screening and information hiding algorithm based on the location of dots. J. Beijing Inf. Sci. Technol. Univ. **12**(28), 25–28 (2013)
2. Zhe-can, L.: Research on Information Hiding Algorithm Based on Halftone Screening. Beijing Institute of Graphic Communication, Beijing (2014)
3. Peng, C.: The encryption security printing technology of pseudo random signal modulation FM network printing spatial position, 200910235265.9.2009-10-20, China

4. Peng, C.: The encryption security printing technology based multi-quadrature amplitude modulation prints, 201010115306.3.2010-03-01, China
5. Peng, C.: The encryption security printing technology on binary encryption AM signal modulation printed dot shape, 201110093006.4.2011-04-14, China
6. Yongju, Z., Jingxin, Z.: Smartphone market research: brand around the user selects. Commun. World **33**, 15–16 (2010)
7. Jiade, Z.: The Android optimization Cheats. Consum. Electron. **15**, 46–50 (2015)
8. Bangqin, C., Hao, X.: The optimization of methods that Bitmap occupies the memories to avoid OOM in Android. J. Hennan Inst. Eng. (Nat. Sci. Edn.) **26**(2), 60–62 (2014)

# Gender Identification Based on Human Structural MRI with a Multi-layers-vote Algorithm

Longfei Zhao, Xue Wei, Xingjie Wu, Hui Shen, and Dewen Hu[(✉)]

National University of Defense Technology, Changsha, Hunan, China
dwhu@nudt.edu.cn

**Abstract.** Gender difference is a factor that cannot be ignored for scientific research. Taking into account of the diversity of the samples, we often select the samples that have statistically matched gender proportions and the same size of the experimental group and the control group, so as to eliminate the influence of the gender. This impact should be especially considered in the process of brain science research. In this paper, we proposed a kind of multi-layer-vote (MLV) algorithm based on Support Vector Machine (SVM) to achieve gender classification of the human brain structural MRI data. The data was selected from Human Connectome Project (HCP). First, from top-down the initial data generate different layers of sub data according to certain rules, and then from bottom-up, the classification of the mother samples is obtained by the way of sub sample voting. W found that the brains of female and male are different with a mean classification accuracy of 98%.

**Keywords:** Gender identification · HCP · Structural MRI · Multi-layers-vote · SVM

## 1 Introduction

As is known to all, there are many differences between men and women in behavior. For example, men generally perform better in space imagination [1] whereas women tend to outperform batter in emotion and language [2–4]. These observations motivated the study of gender classification based on the image of human structural MRI. As a noninvasive procedure, magnetic resonance imaging (MRI) is a powerful tool in the investigation of brain structure and function [5]. Determining gender by examining the human brain is not a simple task, due to the complex spatial structure of the human brain and large dimension of MRI data. Moreover, there is no obvious sex difference in anatomical structure of the brain that can be seen by the visual inspection. Although sex-specific brain activation has been well documented, the possible sex-related differences in brain structure are largely unexplored.

Compared with previous methods, multivariate pattern analysis (MVPA) methods have been used to extract spatial and/or temporal patterns in neuroimaging data. For example Wang et al. [6] employed a principal component analysis (PCA) approach to identify the complex patterns of gender differences in brain structure in a group of 140

© Springer Nature Singapore Pte Ltd. 2017
F. Sun et al. (Eds.): ICCSIP 2016, CCIS 710, pp. 502–508, 2017.
DOI: 10.1007/978-981-10-5230-9_48

healthy young individuals. When using gray matter (GM) alone, the PCA approach obtains an accuracy of approximately 88%.

In this paper, we proposed a multi-layers-vote (MLV) algorithm based on Support Vector Machine (SVM). This algorithm included top-down and bottom-up procedures. Firstly, the initial data generate different layers of sub data according to certain rules. Then, these sub data as the mother data generate the next sub data until the layer number of setting. Finally, the classification of every layer mother samples is obtained by the way of sub sample voting from bottom-up. As a very good dimension reduction method, MLV algorithm can reduce the high dimensional data to a simple and effective low dimensional data. The experimental results showed that the accuracy of classification can be improved by voting of layer by layer.

## 2   Materials and Methods

### 2.1   Subject and Preprocessing

The data was obtained from the Human Connectome Project 500 subjects [7]. We selected 400 out of them as experimental data which include 200 female samples and 200 male samples.

The data was processed by SPM8 software and VBM8 package. Figure 1 shows the flowchart of data preprocessing. Firstly, the skull of the T1 data was stripped. Secondly, by using the free segmentation program of the 'Estimate and write' toolbox in VBM8, the data was segmented into white matter, cerebrospinal fluid, gray matter. Thirdly, the data was normalized to the standard Montreal Neurological Institute (MNI) space. Then, the gray matter was normalization by VBM8. Finally, using the "Smooth" toolbox in SPM8, the gray matter data was smoothed with a Gaussian with an 8 mm full-width half-maximum kernel.

### 2.2   Methods

Ten-fold cross-validation strategy was used to evaluate the generalization performance of the MLV classifier. Every fold has 360 training samples and 40 test samples.

In this paper, the MLV algorithm adopts three layers of voting method. Figure 2 shows the algorithm flow chart. Firstly, we divided the initial samples into three groups according to different angles of view: left data set, mid data set, right data set. The samples of the initial layer are the mother sample of the second layer samples. The third layer samples were generated by the second layer samples. For the left data set and right data set, each sample generated 121 sub samples. And each mid data sample can generate 145 sub samples. Similarly, the samples of the second layer are the mother sample of the third layer samples. The representation of initial 3D data is (121, 145, 121). The 3 sets of third layer sub sample are two-dimensional data, represented by (x, 145, 121), (121, y, 121), (121, 145, z).

For convenience, we take the mid data set as an example to describe the process of voting. The initial data size is 121*145*121, and each initial sample is divided into 145 sub-sample with size of 121 * 121. Figuratively, in third layer each set of sub sample is

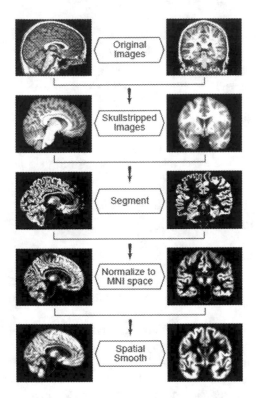

**Fig. 1.** The flowchart of the structural MRI preprocessing [8].

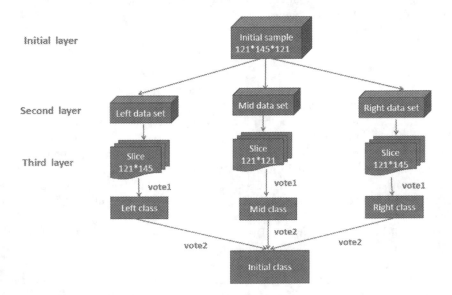

**Fig. 2.** The flow chart of MLV algorithm

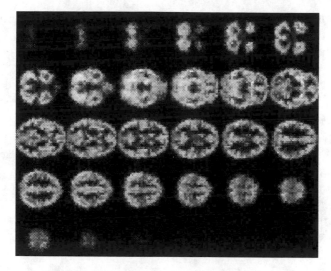

**Fig. 3.** The slices of mid brain data set

equivalent to a brain cut into a lot of pieces according to a certain direction. The slices of mid brain data set is shown in Fig. 3.

For the initial layer, the number of the initial training data is 360, while the test data is 40. In the third layer, each initial brain is cut into 145 slice. In the following process, our research object is the slice of the brain. For the initial brains, each slice of the brain has 360 training data and 40 test data. In order to get the correct rate of every slice of the brain, we proposed cross-validation on 360 slices training data. The SVM method was used to calculate the correct rate of male and female classification for each slice of the brain.

By this way, we can get the accuracy of each slice of the different brain data set. We selected $N$ (odd number) of the slices as the vote representatives whose accuracy is the top $N$ of all slices. In the test set, we selected the same slices as the test data. So each mother sample has $N$ slice representatives. The class of mother sample can be got by voting of the vote representatives. Note that, for different data set we can select different $N$.

For each mother sample, we can get a judgment vector containing N elements donated P2. For class one, if the number of votes is more than (N-1)/2, we assumed the class of the mother sample is one, and the element value of judgment vector is one, otherwise the element value is zero. Besides for all test set, we can get a correct rate donated B in this voting.

The left data set and right date set are handled in the same way as the mid data set. Then we can get judgment vector p1, correct rate A of left data set, and judgment vector p3, correct rate C of right data set.

For each initial sample, the class is determined by corresponding element in the judgment vector P1, P2, P3. If more than one judgment vector whose element is one, then we suppose this initial sample to be class one.

To quantify the performance of our algorithm, we defined Sensitivity (SS), Specificity (SC), and Generalization rate (GR).

$$SS = TP/(TP + FN) \tag{1}$$

$$SC = TN/(TN + FP) \tag{2}$$

$$GR = (TP + TN)/(TP + FN + TN + FP) \tag{3}$$

TP is the number of male which was predicted correct. FN is the number of male classified wrong. TN is the number of female which was predicted correct. FP is the number of female classified wrong. Sensitivity is the proportion of male subjects which were predicted correct. Specificity is the proportion of female subjects which were predicted correct. Generalization rate is the overall proportion of subjects which were predicted correct.

## 3 Result

For the issue of binary classification about female and male, the third layer data obtain an average of correct rate about classification of female and male after 10 fold computation. Figure 4 shows each slice accuracy of the three set data.

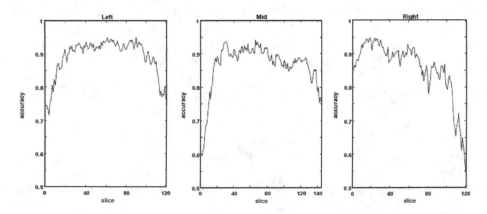

**Fig. 4.** The accuracy of each slice on three data set

From the figure, there is a considerable part of sub samples, in which correct rate is between 0.5 and 0.7. We supposed that these brain slices are invalid and have no impact on the accuracy of the classification. Most slices accuracy is between 0.85 and 0.9. We selected N sub samples whose correct rate is top N as the third layer vote representatives of each data set.

After some times calculate with different N, we got different accuracy of the data. In this paper, we selected N = 19 as the vote representative number of left data set,

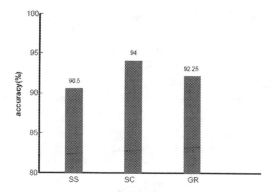

**Fig. 5.** The accuracy of classification on the initial data

N = 19 for mid data set, and N = 19 for right data set. Figure 5 shows the value of SS SC GR on the initial data. It was found that female has a high distinction than male on gender.

Figure 6 shows the classification accuracy on different layer. The mean accuracy of the third layer is 93.67%, and the mean accuracy of the second layer is 97%, while the accuracy of the initial layer is 98%. It can be found that the accuracy is increased with the number of layer increase.

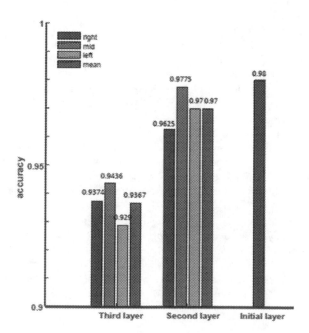

**Fig. 6.** The accuracy of three data layers

## 4   Conclusion

In this paper, we have proposed a multi-layer-vote algorithm based on SVM for the classification of female and male brains. This algorithm has very good results for reducing the dimension of the sample and the elimination of redundant information.

On HCP data, the correct rate of classification about female and male reaches 98%, suggesting reliable gender differences in the brain. Besides, it can be found that the correct rate continues to increase, with the increase of the number of layers. These results highlighted potential impact of gender as a non-negligible factor in analyses of the structural brain.

**Acknowledgement.** This work is supported by National Natural Science Foundation of China (Grant No. 61375034).

## References

1. Rizk-Jackson, A.M., Acevedo, S.F., Inman, D., Howieson, D., Benice, T.S., Raber, J.: Effects of sex on object recognition and spatial navigation in humans. Behav. BrainRes. **173**, 181–190 (2006)
2. Hyde, J.S., Linn, M.C.: Gender differences in verbal ability: a meta analysis. Psychol. Bull. **104**, 53–69 (1988)
3. Rahman, Q., Wilson, G.D., Abrahams, S.: Sex, sexual orientation, and identification of positive and negative facial affect. Brain Cogn. **54**, 179–185 (2004)
4. Canli, T., Desmond, J.E., Zhao, Z., Gabrieli, J.D.: Sex differences in the neural basis of emotional memories. Proc. Natl. Acad. Sci. U. S. A. **99**, 10789–10794 (2002)
5. Biswal, B.B., Mennes, M., Zuo, X.N., Gohel, S., Kelly, C., Smith, S.M., Beckmann, C.F., Adelstein, J.S., Buckner, R.L., Colcombe, S., Dogonowski, A.M., Ernst, M., Fair, D., Hampson, M., Hoptman, M.J., Hyde, J.S., Kiviniemi, V.J., Kotter, R., Li, S.J., Lin, C.P., Lowe, M.J., Mackay, C., Madden, D.J., Madsen, K.H., Margulies, D.S., Mayberg, H.S., McMahon, K., Monk, C.S., Mostofsky, S.H., Nagel, B.J., Pekar, J.J., Peltier, S.J., Petersen, S. E., Riedl, V., Rombouts, S.A., Rypma, B., Schlaggar, B.L., Schmidt, S., Seidler, R.D., Siegle, G.J., Sorg, C., Teng, G.J., Veijola, J., Villringer, A., Walter, M., Wang, L., Weng, X.C., Whitfield-Gabrieli, S., Williamson, P., Windischberger, C., Zang, Y.F., Zhang, H.Y., Catellanos, F.X., Milham, M.P.: Toward discovery science of human brain function. Proc. Nat. Acad. Sci. USA **107**, 4734–4739 (2010)
6. Wang, L.B., Shen, H., Tang, F., Zeng, Y.F., Hu, D.W.: Combined structural and resting-state functional MRI analysisi of sexual dimorphism in the young adult human brain: an MVPA approach. NeuroImage **6**, 931–940 (2012)
7. The Human ConnectomeProject. http://www.humanconnectomeproject.org
8. Yuan, L., Chen, F., Zeng, L., et al.: Gender identification of human brain image with a novel 3D descriptor. IEEE/ACM Trans. Comput. Biol. Bioinf. (2015) (In press)

# Airborne Self-adaptive Multi-sensor Management

Meiqin Liu$^{(\boxtimes)}$, Yue Zhang, Zhen Fan, Yan He, and Senlin Zhang

College of Electrical Engineering, Zhejiang University, Hangzhou 310027, China
{liumeiqin,zhang_yue,fanzhen,heyan,slzhang}@zju.edu.cn

**Abstract.** Sensor management plays an important role in data fusion system, the airborne multi-sensor system typically operates under resource constraints that prevents the simultaneous use of all resources all of the time. Considered the multi-sensor management, this paper presents an algorithm of modified efficiency function which synthetically considers the environmental factors, mission requirements, target statements and sensor characteristics to make it self-adaptive and suitable for multi-sensor management in resource limited area. It could realize the self-adaptive scheduling on tracking accuracy under environmental and resource constraints. The simulation on PAR, IRST and ESM show that the algorithm is reasonable and effective.

**Keywords:** Sensor management · Target priority · Sensor-target pairing · Modified efficiency function · Airborne · Measurement precision

## 1 Introduction

Multi-sensor data fusion is a system which could obtain, coordinate and complement information from multi-sensors. The airborne multi-sensor management is an important preposition module of it. The sensor management is able to provide assistant decision by using limited sensor resources in order to gain optimal measurement values of all specified characteristics, and the core issue of which is to make a certain decision on selecting type of sensor, mode of operating and parameter of work.

A comprehensive management under airborne tasks depends on both the information of data fusion and manual input. In order to control the sensor, criterions should be defined firstly, which should be quantified to measure the sensor allocation. The criterions ranging over some quantifiable parameters, such as: the identification of friend or foe, the detection probability of a new target, the precision of state estimation and the measurement precision. These parameters are selectively applied to the objective function to meet different needs.

This work was supported by the Aeronautical Science Foundation of China under Grant 2015ZC76006, and the Zhejiang Provincial Natural Science Foundation of China under Grant LY15F030007.

© Springer Nature Singapore Pte Ltd. 2017
F. Sun et al. (Eds.): ICCSIP 2016, CCIS 710, pp. 509–520, 2017.
DOI: 10.1007/978-981-10-5230-9_49

To make a definition of the objective function, scholars have put forward some sensor management principles. References [1–3] presented a method of sensor management based on the tracking process covariance matrix, which is a target to be valid in accuracy control. However, the battlefield environment is complex that accuracy only is not enough. Reference [4] presented a method to judge the threat degree of tracking target, which can be used as a reference for the environment. Reference [5] presented a method based on prediction of sensor nodes. It can be assumed that prediction of benefit can be used in management. The objective function can be set based on the method of linear programming [6], dynamic programming [7], information entropy [8] and statistical methods. The optimization method can be selected from synthesis method [9], genetic algorithms and information theory methods [10]. Reference [11] presented a method based on function of efficiency and waste. The efficiency function can meet the requirements of distribution while the waste function is redundant in judging the weight of priority and pairing, and the pairing coefficient is not quantitative and the function is inapplicable in adaption. The method presented in this paper provides some modification of the efficiency function to make it suitable for airborne environment. First, the precision of target state estimation and the measurement precision of the sensor are associated with the function, which makes it possible to quantify the relationship between sensor and target. Then, the covariance of the permissible error is led up to the function to ensure that the manual intervention to sensors. In addition, the objective function is time-varying so that the management is self-adaptive, which can for a wide use in dynamic environment.

## 2    Assignment of Sensor Resources Based on Modified Efficiency Function

The process of tracking can be seen in Fig. 1, and the process of management module can be seen in Fig. 2. Suppose that our aircraft equips with a data fusion system in multi-target tracking, and there are three sensors included: Phased Array Radar (PAR), Infrared Search and Track (IRST) and Electronic Support Measure (ESM). Measurement of ESM and estimation from the state fusion module are the entries of management module. Elements in Fig. 2 will be introduced in the following section. In this section, the target priority and sensor-target pairing are recommended, the conversion of the measurement precision is defined, the modified function of efficiency is established, and the assignment algorithm of sensor management is solved with the constraint.

### 2.1    Target Priority

This paper is a study of observation and management of multiple sensors in one airplane for multiple targets. Therefore, the function of target priority should be established in an autonomous mode. There are many factors which can affect the target priority, and they change in different specified tasks. In this paper the following factors would be considered:

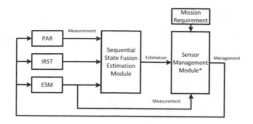

**Fig. 1.** The tracking system scheme

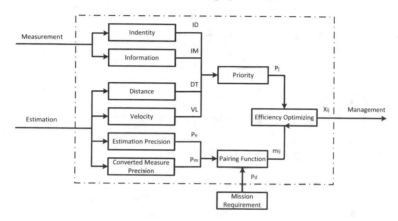

**Fig. 2.** The management module scheme

- Identity ($ID$): Identity is the individual characteristics (foe or friend) of the target, $ID = 1$ means a foe, and $ID = 0$ means a friend.
- Information ($IM$): Information is the knowledge acquired through observation from the target, which can reflect the threat degree. The value depends on the type of the target and it is determined in advance.
- Distance ($DT$): Distance means the range from target to sensor. The shorter the distance is, the greater the priority level is. The value depends on the reciprocal of relative distance.
- Velocity ($VL$): Velocity means the speed of the target relative to the sensor. The faster the airplane is, the greater the velocity value is. The value depends on the magnitude of the velocity vector.

Based on the above factors, it could be defined that $p_j(ID, IM, DT, VL)$ is a priority value of target $j$. Its value is determined by appropriate calculation of factors listed above, and ranges from 0 to 1. When a manual intervention is added to the target $j$, its priority is upmost, $i.e.$, $p_j(\ ) = 1$. The specific expression of $p_j(\ )$ is not only a mathematical problem but also a question of practical experience. A simple and practical expression of $p_j(\ )$ is the linear weighted summation of the above four parameters.

$$p_j = \alpha \times ID + \beta \times IM + \gamma \times DT + \delta \times VL \qquad (1)$$

The value of $ID, IM$ is determined at the first scan by ESM (electronic support measure). $VL_j = f(j, VL'_{1 \sim n_t})$, $DT_j = f(j, DT'_{1 \sim n_t})$ $(j = 1, 2, \cdots, n_t)$, while $n_t$ is the number of targets, $VL'_j$ is the relative velocity of target $j$, $DT'_j$ is the reciprocal of relative distance from the target $j$ to sensor. Function of $f(\ )$ is a normalized function which defined by (2). The weighted coefficient $\alpha, \beta, \gamma$ and $\delta$ should be determined in real cases, which are positive numbers and should meet the requirement $\alpha + \beta + \gamma + \delta = 1$.

$$f(j, A_{1 \sim n_t}) = \frac{A_j - \min\{A_1, A_2, \cdots, A_{n_t}\}}{\max\{A_1, A_2, \cdots, A_{n_t}\} - \min\{A_1, A_2, \cdots, A_{n_t}\}}, j = 1, 2, \cdots, n_t \quad (2)$$

## 2.2  Sensor - Target Pairing

Define $m_{ij}$ $(i = 1, 2, \cdots, n_s, \ j = 1, 2, \cdots, n_t)$ ($n_t$ is the number of targets, $n_s$ is the number of sensors) as a pairing coefficient of sensor $i$ and target $j$, and ranges from 0 to 1. The pairing coefficient consists of two parts, one for "quality factors" of sensor and the other for "probability values" of target data.

The "Quality factors" denote the different monitoring abilities of specific sensors for targets, which changes according to different requirements. These sorts of parameter reflect the observation efficiency of the sensor for the target in estimation. The "probability values" denote the information gained by preliminary or previous measurement. These sorts of parameter reflect the observation efficiency at present [11].

The $m_{ij}$ is hard to denote by a mathematical expression for wide use because the "Quality factors" varies from different requirement. However, it can be quantified for special needs. In this paper, the accuracy is the main goal to be satisfied, so the accuracy factors could be used to build the pairing function.

There are three factors to be considered:

- Estimation precision $(Pe)$: Estimation precision is the state covariance estimate, which is always calculated by filtering and expressed under Cartesian coordinates.
- Desired precision $(Pd)$: Desired precision is the desired estimation precision to be reached for targets. It is defined under Cartesian coordinates by system in this paper.
- Measurement precision $(Pm)$: Measurement precision refers to the deviation degree of the measurement, which is usually expressed as a covariance of the measurement error. The $Pm$ is under spherical coordinates, which should be translated into Cartesian coordinates before comparing with the $Pe$ and $Pd$. The translations will be discussed in Sect. 2.3.

To denote the different monitoring abilities of specific sensors for targets, a distance function $g(A, B)$ is defined to judge the difference between matrix $A$ and $B$. Considering the nature of the covariance matrix, suppose that $A, B \in R^{n \times n}$ and they are positive semi-definite. Define the difference $D = A - B$, then

$D = D^T$. If $d_{ii} < 0$, which means the covariance $a_{ii}$ is more accurate than $b_{ii}$, and in this paper which means the estimation precision has met the requirement or the sensor $i$ is not so helpful to improve the tracking precision of target $j$, so the $d_{ii}$ will be set 0.

$$g(A, B) = \sum_{i=1}^{n} (d'_{ii}), \quad i = 1, 2, \cdots, n \tag{3}$$

$$d'_{ii} = \begin{cases} d_{ii}, & \text{if } d_{ii} \geq 0, \\ 0, & \text{if } d_{ii} < 0. \end{cases} \tag{4}$$

Considering $g(Pe_j, Pm'_{ij})$ and $g(Pe_j, Pd_j)$ $(i = 1, 2, \cdots, n_s, j = 1, 2, \cdots, n_t)$. $Pm'_{ij}$ is the conversion of $Pm_i$ from spherical coordinates to Cartesian coordinates. These two distance functions should be translated by normalized function (2) to form its value from 0 to 1 firstly. Then the normalized distance functions $\tilde{g}(Pe_j, Pm'_{ij})$ and $\tilde{g}(Pe_j, Pd_j)$ can be used to build the pairing function (5). The weighted coefficient $\eta$ and $\zeta$ should be determined in real cases, and they should meet the requirement $\eta + \zeta = 1, \eta > 0, \zeta > 0$.

$$m_{ij} = \eta \times \tilde{g}\left(Pe_j, Pm'_{ij}\right) + \zeta \times \tilde{g}(Pe_j, Pd_j) \\ i = 1, 2, \cdots, n_s, \ j = 1, 2, \cdots, n_t \tag{5}$$

As the function shows, the less the sensor is further required for tracking target, the less value of function $m_{ij}$ be.

## 2.3    Conversion of the Measurement Covariance

To compare the three factors $Pm, Pe$ and $Pd$, the $Pm$ should be translated into Cartesian coordinates. The translation function is presented [12].

The observations are:

$$\theta_{ij}^m = \theta_j + \nu_{\theta,i}; \quad \phi_{ij}^m = \phi_j + \nu_{\phi,i}; \quad r_{ij}^m = r_j + \nu_{r,i} \tag{6}$$

Where $\theta_j$, $\phi_j$, and $r_j$, are the true azimuth, elevation angles and range of the target $j$, $\theta_{ij}^m$, $\phi_{ij}^m$, and $r_{ij}^m$ are the measurement of the target $j$ by the sensor $i$, $\nu_{\theta,i}$, $\nu_{\phi,i}$, and $\nu_{r,i}$ are independent zero-mean noise with the standard covariance $\sigma_{\theta,i}^2$, $\sigma_{\phi,i}^2$, and $\sigma_{r,i}^2$. Considering $Pm_i = \text{diag}[\sigma_{\theta,i}^2, \sigma_{\phi,i}^2, \sigma_{r,i}^2]$, the direct conversion of $Pm_i$ is $Pm'_{ij}$

$$Pm'_{ij} = \begin{bmatrix} R_{ij}^{11} & R_{ij}^{12} & R_{ij}^{13} \\ R_{ij}^{12} & R_{ij}^{22} & R_{ij}^{23} \\ R_{ij}^{13} & R_{ij}^{23} & R_{ij}^{33} \end{bmatrix} \tag{7}$$

The elements to be used in (5) are given by

$$R_{ij}^{11} = \text{var}(\tilde{x}_{ij} \mid \theta_j, \phi_j, r_j) \\ = -r_j^2 \cos^2 \phi_j \cos^2 \theta_j e^{(-\sigma_{\theta,i}^2 - \sigma_{\phi,i}^2)} + \tfrac{1}{4}(r_j^2 + \sigma_{r,i}^2)(\cos 2\phi_j \cos 2\theta_j \\ e^{(-2\sigma_{\theta,i}^2 - 2\sigma_{\phi,i}^2)} + \cos 2\phi_j e^{-2\sigma_{\phi,i}^2} + \cos 2\theta_j e^{-2\sigma_{\theta,i}^2} + 1) \tag{8}$$

$$R_{ij}^{22} = \text{var}(\tilde{y}_{ij} \,|\, \theta_j, \phi_j, r_j)$$
$$= -r_j^2 \cos^2 \phi_j \sin^2 \theta_j e^{(-\sigma_{\theta,i}^2 - \sigma_{\phi,i}^2)} - \tfrac{1}{4}(r_j^2 + \sigma_{r,i}^2)(\cos 2\phi_j \cos 2\theta_j \qquad (9)$$
$$e^{(-2\sigma_{\theta,i}^2 - 2\sigma_{\phi,i}^2)} - \cos 2\phi_j e^{-2\sigma_{\phi,i}^2} + \cos 2\theta_j e^{-2\sigma_{\theta,i}^2} - 1)$$

$$R_{ij}^{33} = \text{var}(\tilde{z}_{ij} \,|\, \theta_j, \phi_j, r_j) \qquad (10)$$
$$= -r_j^2 \sin^2 \phi_j e^{-\sigma_{\phi,i}^2} - \tfrac{1}{2}(r_j^2 + \sigma_{r,i}^2)(\cos 2\phi_j e^{-2\sigma_{\phi,i}^2} - 1)$$

When the true values are unknown, the state estimation could be used as the approximation of $\theta_j$, $\phi_j$, and $r_j$.

## 2.4    Modified Function of Efficiency

Once having functions $p_j(\ )$ and $m_{ij}(\ )$, one can define a modified function of efficiency $e_{ij}(\ )$ ($i = 1, 2, \cdots, n_s$, $j = 1, 2, \cdots, n_t$) based on Ref. [11], which expresses the pairing efficiency of sensor $i$ and target $j$.

$$e_{ij}(p_j, m_{ij}) = \varpi \times p_j(\ ) + \xi \times m_{ij}(\ ) \qquad (11)$$

Where $\varpi$ and $\xi$ are two weighing values, which denote the different impact of priority and pairing coefficients, and $\varpi + \xi = 1, \varpi > 0, \xi > 0$. The maximum value of functions $p_j(\ )$ and $m_{ij}(\ )$ are all 1, so $0 < e_{ij}(\ ) \le 1$. There is a basic principle that priority has stronger impact than pairing [13].

## 2.5    Assignment Algorithm of Sensor Management

Suppose that there are $m$ single sensors, $n_s - m$ sensor combinations and $n_t$ targets ($n_s = 2^m - 1$). The matrix composed of $e_{ij}(\ )$ is a $n_s \times n_t$ matrix. Suppose that $X$ is a solution matrix, where $x_{ij} = 1$ denotes that sensor (or combination) $i$ is assigned to target $j$ while $x_{ij} = 0$ denotes that sensor (or combination) $i$ is not assigned to target $j$.

The optimal rule is that synthesis efficiency is maximized, i.e.

$$E(X) = \sum_{i=1}^{n_s} \sum_{j=1}^{n_t} (e_{ij} \times x_{ij}), \quad \overline{X} = \arg\max(E(X)) \qquad (12)$$

One sensor can be assigned to many targets, and the number is constrained by sensor tracking power $t_J (J = 1, 2, \ldots, m)$ which denotes the number of targets scanned once by a sensor. Suppose $D(J)$ is a collection of sensor combinations who contains the single sensor $J$. One target can also be scanned by many sensors, at least one sensor should be guaranteed. Therefore, the optimal solution matrix $\overline{X}$ should be limited by constraints as follows. And the method of mathematical programming is used for optimization.

Constraints of maximum tracking power of sensors are

$$\sum_{i \in D(J)} \sum_{j=1}^{n_t} x_{ij} = t_J \qquad (13)$$

Constraints of targets scanned by sensors are

$$\sum_{i=1}^{n_s} x_{ij} \geq 1, \quad j = 1, 2, \cdots, n_t \tag{14}$$

# 3   Sequential Fusion Estimation

Suppose the discrete state equation of target $j$ is:

$$x^j(k) = F^j(T_k)x^j(k-1) + G^j(T_k)w^j(k-1), \quad j = 1, 2, \cdots, n_t \tag{15}$$

The measurement equation of sensor $i$ is:

$$z_i^j(k) = h_i[x^j(k)] + v_i^j(k), \quad i = 1, 2, \cdots, n_s \tag{16}$$

Where $x^j(k)$ represents the true state of target $j$ at time $t$, $F^j$ and $G^j$ are system matrixes. $w^j(k-1)$ and $v_i^j(k)$ are process noise and observation noise, and they are vector-valued zero-mean white Gaussian noise sequence with covariance $Q^j(k-1)$ and $Pm_{ij}(k)$. $T_k$ is the sampling interval. $z_i^j(k)$ represents the measurement data of target $j$ by sensor $i$, $h_i(\ )$ is the observation equation. When the sensor combination who consisted of $K$ single sensors is tracking target $j$. The algorithms are as follows ($S = 2, \ldots, K$) [14]:

The status update equation

$$\begin{aligned}
[x^j(k|k)]^1 &= x^j(k|k-1) + [K^j(k)]^1 \{z_1^j(k) - h_1[x^j(k|k-1)]\} \\
[x^j(k|k)]^S &= [x^j(k|k)]^{S-1} + [K^j(k)]^S \{z_S^j(k) - h_S[x^j(k|k-1)]\} \\
x^j(k|k) &= [x^j(k|k)]^K
\end{aligned} \tag{17}$$

The linearization of observation equation

$$H_{ij}(k) = \frac{\partial h_i}{\partial x}\Big|_{x=x^j(k|k-1)} \tag{18}$$

The Kalman filter gain

$$\begin{aligned}
[K^j(k)]^1 &= P_i^j(k|k-1)H_{1j}^T(k)\{H_{1j}(k)P_i^j(k|k-1)H_{1j}^T(k) \\
&\quad + Pm_{1j}(k)\}^{-1} \\
[K^j(k)]^S &= [P_i^j(k|k)]^{S-1}H_{Sj}^T(k)\{H_{Sj}(k)[P_i^j(k|k)]^{S-1}H_{Sj}^T(k) \\
&\quad + Pm_{Sj}(k)\}^{-1}
\end{aligned} \tag{19}$$

The covariance of state estimation

$$\begin{aligned}
[P_i^j(k|k)]^1 &= \{I - [[K^j(k)]^1 H_{1j}(k)]\}P_i^j(k|k-1) \\
[P_i^j(k|k)]^S &= \{I - [[K^j(k)]^S H_{1j}(k)]\}[P_i^j(k|k)]^S - 1 \\
P_i^j(k|k) &= [P_i^j(k|k)]^K
\end{aligned} \tag{20}$$

$[\bullet]^S$ means the data has been disposed by $S$ sensors.

## 4    Simulation

The validity of algorithm is tested, and the simulation goal is tracking four targets with three sensors.

### 4.1    Setting of Task

Our aircraft is operating at a constant velocity. From some time, Three targets (Where A and B for foe planes, C for friend aircraft) come into our airspace, and the flight time is 0~40 s. Then target D appears into the airspace, and our aircraft keep moving at a constant velocity after changing direction at time 41~100 s. Suppose that all the targets and our aircraft are operating at a constant altitude of 500 m. Target A, B and C are in motion of constant velocity, while target D is in motion of constant acceleration. The trajectories of these movements are shown in Fig. 3, and the relative positions are shown in Fig. 4. The process noise covariance matrix of four targets are: $Q^1 = Q^2 = Q^3 = Q^4 = \mathrm{diag}(0.1, 0.1, 0.1, 0.1)$, and each sensor is: $Q^s = \mathrm{diag}(0.1, 0.1, 0.1, 0.1)$.

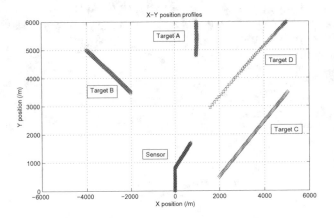

**Fig. 3.** The movement of targets and sensor

The three sensors concluded in fusion system are of different properties. PAR does well in distance measurement, IRST does well in angle measurement, and ESM does well in recognition. The standard deviation of measuring error and tracking power of three sensors are listed in Table 1. To simplify the calculation, the standard deviation (SD) of measuring error of the sensor combination would be figured out by (21) and (22).

$$\sigma_{\theta_{a,b}} = \sqrt{\frac{\sigma_{\theta_a^2}\sigma_{\theta_b^2}}{\sigma_{\theta_a^2} + \sigma_{\theta_b^2}}}, \sigma_{\phi_{a,b}} = \sqrt{\frac{\phi_{\theta_a^2}\phi_{\theta_b^2}}{\sigma_{\phi_a^2} + \sigma_{\phi_b^2}}}, \sigma_{r_{a,b}} = \sqrt{\frac{\sigma_{r_a^2}\sigma_{r_b^2}}{\sigma_{r_a^2} + \sigma_{r_b^2}}} \qquad (21)$$

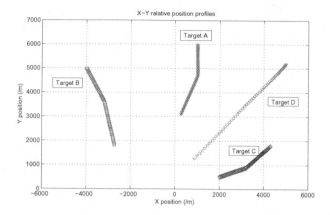

**Fig. 4.** The relative positions of targets and sensor

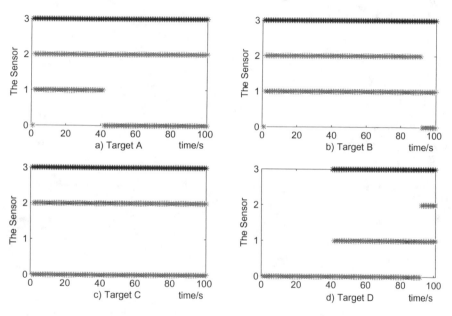

**Fig. 5.** The sensor assignment for targets

$$\sigma_{\theta_{a,b,c}} = \sqrt{\frac{\sigma_{\theta_a^2}\sigma_{\theta_b^2}\sigma_{\theta_c^2}}{\sigma_{\theta_a^2}\sigma_{\theta_b^2}+\sigma_{\theta_b^2}\sigma_{\theta_c^2}+\sigma_{\theta_a^2}\sigma_{\theta_c^2}}},$$

$$\sigma_{\phi_{a,b,c}} = \sqrt{\frac{\sigma_{\phi_a^2}\sigma_{\phi_b^2}\sigma_{\phi_c^2}}{\sigma_{\phi_a^2}\sigma_{\phi_b^2}+\sigma_{\phi_b^2}\sigma_{\phi_c^2}+\sigma_{\phi_a^2}\sigma_{\phi_c^2}}}, \qquad (22)$$

$$\sigma_{r_{a,b,c}} = \sqrt{\frac{\sigma_{r_a^2}\sigma_{r_b^2}\sigma_{r_c^2}}{\sigma_{r_a^2}\sigma_{r_b^2}+\sigma_{r_b^2}\sigma_{r_c^2}+\sigma_{r_a^2}\sigma_{r_c^2}}}$$

The desired precisions of four targets in 0~40 s are $Pd_1 = Pd_2 = Pd_3 =$ diag$(30, 30, 30)$, and the desired precisions of four targets in 41~100 s are $Pd_1 =$ diag$(30, 30, 30)$, $Pd_2 =$ diag$(10, 10, 10)$, $Pd_3 =$ diag$(30, 30, 30)$, and $Pd_4 =$ diag$(10, 10, 10)$. Considering the mission requirements, the weighting coefficients could be set $\alpha = \frac{1}{4}, \beta = \frac{1}{4}, \gamma = \frac{1}{4}, \delta = \frac{1}{4}, \eta = \frac{1}{2}, \zeta = \frac{1}{2}, \varpi = \frac{2}{3}$ and $\xi = \frac{1}{3}$.

## 4.2   Simulation Result

Figure 5 is the sensor assignment of simulation, different number represents the different sensor is assigned to target. Number 0 means there is no sensor assigned to target, number 1 means sensor PAR is assigned to target, number 2 means sensor IRST is assigned to target, number 3 means sensor ESM is assigned to target (the serial number can be looked up in Table 1). Figure 6 is the number of

**Table 1.** Measuring ability of sensors

| Sensor | SD of azimuth $\sigma_\theta$/rad | SD of elevation $\sigma_\phi$/rad | SD of range $\sigma_r$/m | Tracking power $t_J$ |
|---|---|---|---|---|
| PAR (1) | 0.010 | 0.010 | 5 | 2 |
| IRST (2) | 0.002 | 0.002 | 20 | 3 |
| ESM (3) | 0.020 | 0.020 | 30 | 4 |

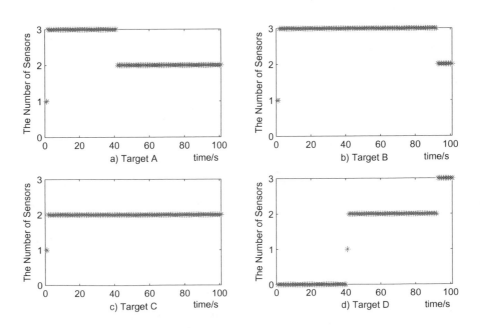

**Fig. 6.** The number of sensors for each target

sensors that each target is distributed. It can be seen from the Fig. 5 that three
targets are detected and recognized by ESM at first scan. And next the sensors
were distributed to three targets stably in 0~40 s. Target C is a friend plane
so that the fewer sensor was assigned. Then target D appears and be tracked
by ESM, the PAR was dispatched from target A to target D on account of
the desired precisions in 41~91 s. Finally, in 92~100 s, the last management is a
dispatch from target B to target D because the target D is too close to the sensor
so that it needs more attention. It can be also seen from Fig. 6 that all sensors has
been used to the greatest extent in order to guarantee the measurement accuracy
except for the first scan. The sensor management simulation is conformed to the
requirements.

## 5  Conclusion

This paper focuses on the management of multi-sensor multi-target tracking
system under the airborne environment. The method of this paper synthetically considers the distribution problem of sensor resources (which exists in target detection, observation accuracy and tracking power), the priority of targets
(which concludes identification, traveling direction and relative distance) and
the self-adaptive ability while tracking. The function of efficiency is able to realize the sensor distribution, and the modified efficiency function proposed in this
paper introduced the distance function of covariance so that it can satisfy both
manual intervention and automatic update of the pairing and priority functions.
Simulation results demonstrate that the algorithm is able to allocate sensors
under limited resources and adjust adaptively under the changing priority. This
algorithm for management is reasonable and effective.

## References

1. Ratton, L.: Radar scheduling with emission constraints. Acquis. Track. Pointing
   **16**, 4714 (2002)
2. Hestilow, T.J., Wei, T., Huang, Y.: Sensor scheduling and target tracking using
   expectation propagation. In: 2005 IEEE/SP Workshop on Statistical Signal
   Processing, pp. 1232–1237. IEEE (2005)
3. Katsilieris, F., Driessen, H., Yarovoy, A.: Threat-based sensor management for
   target tracking. IEEE Trans. Aerosp. Electron. Syst. **51**(4), 2772–2785 (2015)
4. Zhi, J., Liu, J., Fu, C.: Evaluation of aerial target threat degree based on improved
   grey interrelated analysis method. In: IEEE International Conference on Grey Systems and Intelligent Services, pp. 740–744 (2009)
5. Yan, D.: Sensor scheduling in target tracking. In: 2014 11th World Congress on
   IEEE Intelligent Control and Automation (WCICA), pp. 2023–2025 (2015)
6. Chen, H., Chen, G., Shen, D.: Orbital evasive target tracking and sensor management. In: Hirsch, M.J., Pardalos, P.M., Murphey, R. (eds.) Dynamics of Information Systems, pp. 233–255. Springer, New York (2010)
7. Dong, H.H.: The application of auto disturbance-rejection controller in a servo
   tracking equipment. Ind. Control Appl. **26**(9), 60–62 (2007)

8. Moran, B., Howard, S.D., Cochran, D.: An information-geometric approach to sensor management, pp. 5261–5264 (2012)
9. Huang, H.P., Wu, L.Q., Han, J.Q.: A new synthesis method for unit coordinated control system in thermal power plant-ADRC control scheme. In: International Conference on Power System Technology, pp. 133–138 (2004)
10. Ruan, J.H., Yang, F.G., Song, R.: Study on ADRC-based intelligent vehicle lateral locomotion control. In: Proceedings of the 7th World Congress on Intelligent Control and Automation, pp. 2619–2624 (2008)
11. Liu, X.X., Pan, Q., Zhang, H.C., Dai, G.Z.: Study on algorithm of sensor management based on fucntions of efficiency and waste. Chin. J. Aeronaut. 13(1), 39–44 (2000)
12. Longbin, M., Xiaoquan, S., Yiyu, Z., Bar-Shalom, Y.: Unbiased converted measurements for tracking. IEEE Transs. Aerosp. Electron. Syst. 34(3), 1023–1027 (1998)
13. Yongfei, H., Lin, D., Jianping, Z.: Algorithm of multisensor management with the waste function. J. North Univ. Chin. 26(5), 345–347 (2005)
14. Qiang, G., Harris, C.J.: Comparison of two measurement fusion methods for Kalman-filter-based multisensor data fusion. IEEE Trans. Aerosp. Electron. Syst. 37(1), 273–280 (2001)

# Linear Dynamical Systems Modeling for EEG-Based Motor Imagery Brain-Computer Interface

Wenchang Zhang[1,2], Fuchun Sun[1,2(✉)], Chuanqi Tan[1,2], and Shaobo Liu[1,2]

[1] The State Key Laboratory of Intelligent Technology and Systems,
Computer Science and Technology School, Tsinghua University,
FIT Building, Beijing 100084, China
fcsun@mail.tsinghua.edu.cn
[2] Institute of Medical Equipment, Wandong Road, Hedong District, Tianjin, China

**Abstract.** Motor imagery-based Brain Computer Interfaces (MI-BCI) has attracted more and more attention due to its effectivity for stroke and spinal cord injury patients' rehabilitation. Common Spatial Pattern (CSP) and other spatio-spectral feature extraction methods become the most effective and principle successful solutions for MI-BCI pattern recognition in the recent few years. This paper applies Linear dynamical systems (LDS) referring to control field for EEG signals feature extraction and classification. Compared to other state-of-the-art methods, this model has lots of obvious advantages, such as simultaneous generation spatial and temporal feature matrix, without complex preprocessing or post-processing, ease of use, and low cost. A study is shown to program by computer and assess the performance of feature selection and classification algorithms for use with the LDS. Extensive experimental results are presented on public dataset from 'BCI Competition III Data Sets IVa'. The results show that LDS, using Martin Distance and k-Nearest Neighbors classification algorithm, yields higher accuracies compared to prevailing approaches.

**Keywords:** BCI · MI · EEG · LDS · Feature extraction

## 1 Introduction

EEG-based BCI has become a hot research topic in recent few years because of the advent of simpler brain rhythm sampling and powerful low-cost computer equipment. Programs developing new augmentative communication and control external equipment based on EEG-BCI brings promising hope to those with severe neuromuscular disabled, such as amyotrophic lateral sclerosis, brainstem stroke and spinal cord injury. [1] Especially in the field of stroke rehabilitation, Motor Imagery (MI) represents a new approach to access the motor system and rehabilitation at all stages of stroke recovery and enables people with severe motor disabilities to use EEG-BCI for communication, control, and

F. Sun et al. (Eds.): ICCSIP 2016, CCIS 710, pp. 521–528, 2017.
DOI: 10.1007/978-981-10-5230-9_50

even to restore their motor disabilities. [2, 3] Therefore, there are an increasing number of researches that reported methodology studies on MI-BCI for stroke patient rehabilitation [4, 5].

Among various EEG signals, certain neurophysiological patterns can be recognized and used to determine the user intentions, such as visual evoked potentials (VEPs), P300 evoked potentials, slow cortical potentials (SCPs), and sensorimotor rhythms. MI-BCI concentrates on sensorimotor $\mu-$ or $\beta-$rhythms, which exists phenomenon known as event-related synchronization (ERS) or event-related desynchronization (ERD). So there are obvious feature diversities in EEG during MI. However, it is a challenge in MI recognition due to the low signal-to-noise ratio. For these reasons, more and more digital signal processing (DSP) methods and machine learning algorithms are applied for the deployment of MI-BCI analysis. Unlike static signal such as image, semantic, and so on, EEG is dynamic, which has spatio-temporal feature space. A great variety of features extraction focus in Power Spectral Density (PSD) values [6, 7], AutoRegressive (AR) parameters [8, 9], and Time-frequency features [10]. For MI-BCI pattern recognition, there are mainly three methods: AutoRegressive Components ($AR$) [11], Wavelet Transform (WT) [12, 13], CSP [14, 15]. Due to power in extracting spatial features, CSP becomes one of the most effective and principle success-ful solutions for MI-BCI analysis, according to winners' methods analysis of 'BCI Competition III Data Sets IVa' [16] and 'BCI Competition IV database 1' [17]. Therefore, more and more researchers devote to improving the original CSP method for better performance: Common Spatio-Spectral Pattern (CSSP) [18], Common Sparse Spectral Spatial Pattern (CSSSP) [19] Sub-Band Common Spatial Pattern (SBCSP) [20] Filter Bank Common Spatial Pattern (FBCSP) [21], Wavelet Common Spatial Pattern (WCSP) [22], and Separable Common SpatioSpectral Patterns (SCSSP) [23]. Most of them improved CSP methods aim to fuse spectral characteristics in view of spatio-spectral feature space and achieve success by compared experiments.

Despite its effectivity in extracting features of MI-BCI, CSP related work needs a lot of preprocessing and post-processing, such as filtering, de-mean, spatio-spectral feature fusion, which influence classification accuracy easily and sensitively. In this paper, a novel machine learning model called LDS is pro-posed for processing EEG signals in MI-BCI. Although LDS succeed in the field of control and is applied widely, to our best knowledge, this model is merely tried in EEG analysis. Compared to CSP method, LDS has the following advan-tages: first, LDS can simultaneously generate spatio-spectral dual-feature matrix; second, no need any signals preprocessing or post-processing, raw data can be directly input to the model; Third, ease of use and low cost; Last, the extracted features by LDS are much more available and effective for classification. Our best contribution is applying and programming LDS model to solve the MI-BCI pattern recognition problem and presenting the better performance by compared experiments.

The rest of this paper is organized as follows: Sect. 2 provides LDS model and introduces how to apply LDS model used throughout this paper to realize

EEG analysis. Section 3 studies the performance of LDS method in different experimental setups and compares to other approaches. Finally, the summary and conclusion are presented in Sect. 4.

## 2    LDS Modeling

LDS, also known as linear Gaussian state-space models, have been used extensively in engineering to model and control dynamical systems. In recent few years, more and more problems, extending to Computer Vision [24,25], Speech Recognition [26], Tactile Perception [27], are solved successful by LDS. It is easy to see that EEG signals are sequences of brain electron sampling which have typical dynamic textures. We present a characterization of EEG dynamic textures by LDS modeling and apply machine learning (ML) algorithms to capture the essence of dynamic textures for classification.

### 2.1    Feature Extraction

Let $Y(t)_{t=1...\tau}, Y(t) \in \Re^m$, be a sequence of $\tau$ EEG signal sample at each instant of time $t$. If there is a set of $n$ spatial filters $\phi_\alpha : \Re \to \Re^m, \alpha = 1...n$, we have $x(t) = \sum_{i=1}^k A_i x(t-i) + Bv(t)$ with $A_i \in \Re^{n \times n}, B \in \Re^{n \times n_v}$, independent and identically distributed realization item $v(t) \in \Re^{n_v}$ ,and suppose that sequence of observed variables $Y(t)$ can be represented approximately by function of dimensional hidden state $x(t)$, $y(t) = \phi(x(t)) + \omega(t)$, where $\omega(t) \in \Re^m$ is an independent and identically distributed sequence drawn from a known distribution resulting in a positive measured sequence. we redefine the hidden state of $x(t)$ to be $[x(t)^T \ x(t-1)^T \ ... \ x(t-k)^T]^T$ and consider a linear dynamic system as an auto-regressive moving average process without firm input distribution.

$$\begin{cases} x(t+1) = Ax(t) + Bv(t) & x(0) = x_0 \\ y(t) = \phi(x(t)) + \omega(t) \end{cases} \tag{1}$$

With $\nu(t), \phi(x(t))$ distribution unknown, however.

In order to solve the above problem, we can regard as a white and zero-mean Gaussian noise linear dynamical system and propose a simplified and closed-form solution

$$\begin{cases} x(t+1) = Ax(t) + Bv(t) & \nu(t) \backsim N(0,Q), \quad x(0) = x_0 \\ y(t) = Cx(t) + \omega(t) + \bar{y} & \omega(t) \backsim N(0,R), \end{cases} \tag{2}$$

where $A \in \Re^{n \times n}$ is the transition matrix that describes the dynamics property, $C \in \Re^{m \times n}$ is the measurement matrix that describes the spatial appearance, $\bar{y} \in \Re^m$ is the mean of $y(t)$, $\nu(t)$ and $\omega(t)$ are noise components. We should estimate the model parameters $A, C, Q, R$ from the measurements $y(t), \ldots, y(\tau)$ and transform into the maximum-likelihood solution:

$$\hat{A}(\tau), \hat{C}(\tau), \hat{Q}(\tau), \hat{R}(\tau) = \underset{A,C,Q,R}{\arg \max} \ p(y(1), \ldots, y(\tau)) \tag{3}$$

However, optimal solutions of this problem bring computational complex. We apply matrix decomposition to simplify computation by the closed-form solution. The singular value decomposition (SVD) is the best estimate of C in the sense of Frobenius:

$$\hat{C}(\tau), \hat{X}(\tau) = \arg\min_{C,X} \|W(\tau)\|_F$$

$$\text{subject to}\ \ Y(\tau) = CX(\tau) + W(\tau);\ \ \ C^T C = I. \tag{4}$$

So let $Y = U\sum V^T$, we get the parameter estimate of $\hat{C}, \hat{X}$

$$\begin{cases} \hat{C} = U \\ \hat{X} = \sum V^T \end{cases} \tag{5}$$

Where $\hat{X} = [X(1), X(2), \ldots, X(\tau)]$. $\hat{A}$ can be determined by Frobenius:

$$\hat{A}(\tau) = \arg\min_A \|X_2(\tau) - AX_1(\tau - 1)\|_F \tag{6}$$

Where $X_2(\tau) = [X(2), X(3), \ldots, X(\tau)]$. So the solution is in closed-form using the state estimated

$$\hat{A}(\tau) = [X(:,2)X(:,3)\ldots X(:,\tau)][X(:,1)X(:,2)\ldots X(:,\tau-1)]^\dagger \tag{7}$$

where † denotes matrix pseudoinverse. Finally, we can obtain $[A, C]$, a couple of spatio-temporal feature matrix that can be realized by Algorithm 1.

*Algorithm 1 LDS function*

```
program LDS(A,C,B)
  {Input: Y(t), EEG signal sample; h, hidden parameter;
  nor, iteration coefficient
  Output: A,temporal matrix;C,spatial matrix;B,noise;};
  begin
  Ymean = mean(Y,2)        % get mean of Y(t)
  [U,S,V] = svd(Y-Ymean) % singular value decomposition
  C=U(:,1:h)               % C is the first h terms of U
  X = S(1:h,1:h)*V(:,1:h)'
  A=[X(:,2)X(:,3)...X(:,m)]*pinv[X(:,1)X(:,2)...X(:,m-1)]
                           % pinv is matrix pseudoinverse
  A = A/nor                % normalization and iteration
  V=[X(:,2)X(:,3)...X(:,m)]-A[X(:,1)X(:,2)...X(:,m-1)]
  [Uv,Sv,~] = svd(V)       % singular value decomposition of V
  B= Uv(:,1)               % Compute B
  end
```

## 2.2  Classification

We extract features by above LDS model and get two feature matrix A,C. Unfortunately, A,C have different modal properties and dimensionalities and can't represent by a feature vector. Riemannian geometry metric for the space of LDS is hard to determine and needs to satisfy several constraints. Common classifiers, such as Nearest Neighbors (NNs), Linear Discriminant Analysis (LDA), Support Vector Machines (SVM) and so on, can't classify features in matrix form. The feature matrix must map to vector space. We propose Martin Distance [28,29], which is based on the principal angles between two subspaces of the extended observability matrices, as kernel to present distance of different LDS feature matrix. It can be defined as

$$D^2(\Theta_a, \Theta_b) = -2 \sum_{i=1}^{n} \log \lambda_i \tag{8}$$

Where $\Theta_a = C_a, A_a, \Theta_b = C_b, A_b$. $\lambda_i$ is the eigenvalue solving as following equation:

$$\begin{bmatrix} 0 & o_{ab} \\ o_{ab}^T & 0 \end{bmatrix} \begin{bmatrix} x \\ y \end{bmatrix} = \lambda \begin{bmatrix} o_{aa} & 0 \\ 0 & o_{bb} \end{bmatrix} \begin{bmatrix} x \\ y \end{bmatrix} \quad s.t. \quad x^T o_{aa} x = 1, y^T o_{bb} y = 1 \tag{9}$$

Where the extended observability matrices $o_a = [C_a^T, A_a^T C_a^T, \ldots, (A_a^T)^n C_a^T]$, $o_b = [C_b^T, A_b^T C_b^T, \ldots, (A_b^T)^n C_b^T], o_{ab} = (O_a)^T o_b$.

We can classify EEG signals by comparing Martin Distance between training data and testing data. Nearest two samples mean that they maybe same class. Therefore, the forecast label and predict accuracy can be calculated by k-Nearest Neighbor (KNN) algorithm.

# 3    Experimental Evaluation

## 3.1    Data Acquisition and Preprocessing

We use Dataset IVa from BCI competition III, which is recorded from five healthy subjects, labeled $'aa'$, $'al'$, $'av'$, $'aw'$ and $'ay'$, with Visual cues indicated for 3.5 s performing right hand and foot motor imagery. The EEG signal has 118 channels and markers that indicate the time points of 280 cues for each subject, band-pass filtered between 0.05 and 200 Hz, and down-sampled to 100 Hz.

Before feature extracting for compared experiment, the raw data needs some Preprocessing. Firstly, we extract a time segment located from 0.5 to 3 s and employed FastICA to remove artifacts arising from eye and muscle movements. Secondly, we chose 21 channels over the motor cortex (CP6, CP4, CP2, C6, C4, C2, FC6, FC4, FC2, CPZ, CZ, FCZ, CP1, CP3, CP5, C1, C3, C5, FC1, FC3, FC5) that related to motor imagery.

## 3.2    Solution by CSP

Bandpass filter design is critical for CSP algorithm due to it is very sensitive to frequency band. We apply Butterworth filter to bandpass filter EEG signals within a specific frequency band between 8 and 30 Hz (Fig. 1), which encompasses both the $\alpha$ rhythm (8–13 Hz) and the $\beta$ rhythm (14–30 Hz).

We program CSP code by MATLAB for getting spatial filter parameters and feature vectors by variance. Finally, a LDA classifier is applied to find a separating hyperplane of the feature vectors of all trials.

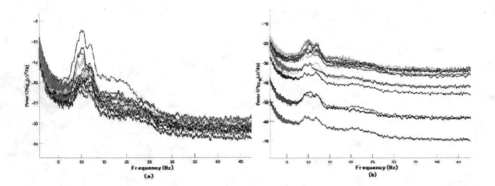

**Fig. 1.** Spectrograph of dataset IVa al (a) before filtering (b) after filtering by butterworth bandpass filter between 8 and 30 Hz.

**Table 1.** Experimental accuracy results (%) obtained from each subject in BCI competition III dataset IVa for CSP, CSSP and our proposed algorithm (LDS)

| Subject | aa | al | av | aw | ay | mean |
|---------|-------|-------|-------|-------|-------|-------|
| CSP | 71.43 | 94.64 | 61.22 | 89.28 | 73.02 | 77.92 |
| CSSP | 77.68 | **96.43** | 63.27 | **90.63** | 79.37 | 81.48 |
| LDS | **78.57** | 96.43 | **69.89** | 90.18 | **79.76** | **82.97** |

### 3.3   Results

From Table 1, It is clearly to see that the classification accuracies are much different from subjects and algorithms. The black bold figures present the best performance results, and LDS is in the majority. The last row show that the mean of LDS classification accuracy is much better than CSP and a little higher than CSSP, although our model is raw and has not further improved yet. Another important observation is that CSSP and LDS perform better than CSP due to their both spatial and temporal features extraction.

## 4   Conclusion

CSP has gain much success in past MI-BCI research. However, it is reported that CSP is only a spatial-filter and sensitive to frequency band and needs prior knowledge to choose channels and frequency bands. Without preprocessing, the result of classification accuracy maybe poor. LDS can overcome these problems by extracting both spatial and temporal features simultaneously for improving the classification performance. The success of LDS comparing to CSP algorithm is demonstrated on BCI Competition III datasets experiment. The major contribution of our work is that realizing LDS model for MI-BCI and achieving a better accuracy than CSP.

**Acknowledgment.** This work was supported by the National Natural Science Foundation of China (Grant Nos. 91420302 and 91520201).

# References

1. Wolpaw, J.R., Birbaumer, N., McFarland, D.J., Pfurtscheller, G., Vaughan, T.M.: Brain-computer interfaces for communication and control. Clin. Neurophysiol. **113**, 767–791 (2002)
2. Ang, K.K., Guan, C.: Brain-computer interface in stroke rehabilitation. J. Comput. Sci. Eng. **7**(2), 139–146 (2013)
3. Sharma, N., Pomeroy, V.M., Baron, J.C.: Motor imagery: a backdoor to the motor system after stroke? Stroke **37**(7), 1941–1952 (2006)
4. Silvoni, S., Ramos-Murguialday, A., Cavinato, M., Volpato, C., Cisotto, G., Turolla, A., Piccione, F., Birbaumer, N.: Brain-computer interface in stroke: a review of progress. Clin. EEG Neurosci. **42**(4), 245–252 (2011)
5. Bai, O., Lin, P., Vorbach, S., Floeter, M.K., Hattori, N., Hallett, M.: A high performance sensorimotor beta rhythmbased brain-computer interface associated with human natural motor behavior. J. Neural Eng. **5**(1), 24–35 (2008)
6. Chiappa, S., Bengio, S.: HMM and IOHMM modeling of EEG rhythms for asynchronous BCI systems. In: European Symposium on Artificial Neural Networks, ESANN (2004)
7. Millan, J.R., Mourino, J.: Asynchronous BCI and local neural classifiers: an overview of the Adaptive Brain Interface project. IEEE Trans. Neural Syst. Rehabil. Eng. **11**(2), 159–161 (2003). Special Issue on Brain-Computer Interface Technology
8. Penny, W.D., Roberts, S.J., Curran, E.A., Stokes, M.J.: Eeg-based communication: a pattern recognition approach. IEEE Trans. Rehabil. Eng. **8**(2), 214–215 (2000)
9. Pfurtscheller, G., Neuper, C., Schlogl, A., Lugger, K.: Separability of EEG signals recorded during right and left motor imagery using adaptive autoregressive parameters. IEEE Trans. Rehabil. Eng. **6**(3), 316–325 (1998)
10. Wang, T., Deng, J., He, B.: Classifying eeg-based motor imagery tasks by means of timefrequency synthesized spatial patterns. Clin. Neurophysiol. **115**(12), 2744–2753 (2004)
11. Krusienski, D.J., McFarland, D.J., Wolpaw, J.R.: An evaluation of autoregressive spectral estimation model order for brain-computer interface applications. In: Proceedings of the 28th Annual International Conference of the IEEE Engineering in Medicine and Biology Society (EMBS 2006), New York, NY, USA, pp. 1323–1326, September 2006
12. Demiralp, T., Yordanova, J., Kolev, V., Ademoglu, A., Devrim, M., Samar, V.J.: Time-frequency analysis of single-sweep event-related potentials by means of fast wavelet transform. Brain Lang. **66**, 129–145 (1999)

13. Farina, D., de Nascimento, O.F., Lucas, M.F., Doncarli, C.: Optimization of wavelets for classification of movement-related cortical potentials generated by variation of force-related parameters. J. Neurosci. Methods **162**, 357–363 (2007)
14. Ramoser, H., Muller-Gerking, J., Pfurtscheller, G.: Optimal spatial filtering of single trial EEG during imagined hand movement. IEEE Trans. Rehabil. Eng. **8**, 441–446 (2000)
15. Grosse-Wentrup, M., Buss, M.: Multiclass common spatial patterns and information theoretic feature extraction. IEEE Trans. Biomed. Eng. **55**, 1991–2000 (2008)
16. Blankertz, B., et al.: The BCI competition III: Validating alternative approaches to actual BCI problems. IEEE Trans. Neural Syst. Rehabil. Eng. **14**(2), 153–159 (2006)
17. Tangermann, M., et al.: Review of the BCI competition IV. Front. Neurosci., July 2012
18. Lemm, S., Blankertz, B., Curio, G., Muller, K.R.: Spatio-spectral filters for improving the classification of single trial EEG. IEEE Trans. Biomed. Eng. **52**, 1541–1548 (2005)
19. Dornhege, G., Blankertz, B., Krauledat, M., Losch, F., Curio, G., Muller, K.R.: Combined optimization of spatial and temporal filters for improving brain-computer interfacing. IEEE Trans. Biomed. Eng. **53**, 2274–2281 (2006)
20. Novi, Q., Guan, C., Dat, T.H., Xue, P.: Sub-band Common Spatial Pattern (SBCSP) for brain-computer interface. In: 3rd International IEEE/EMBS Conference on Neural Engineering, CNE 2007, pp. 204–207 (2007)
21. Ang, K.K., Chin, Z.Y., Zhang, H., Guan, C.: Filter Bank Common Spatial Pattern (FBCSP) in brain-computer interface. In: International Joint Conference on Neural Networks (IJCNN 2008) (2008)
22. Mousavi, E.A., Maller, J.J., Fitzgerald, P.B., Lithgow, B.J.: Wavelet common spatial pattern in asynchronous offline brain computer interfaces. Biomed. Sig. Process. Control **6**, 121–128 (2011)
23. Aghaei, A.S., Mahanta, M.S., Plataniotis, K.N.: Separable common spatio-spectral patterns for motor imagery BCI systems. IEEE Trans. Biomed. Eng. **63**(1), 15–29 (2016)
24. Saisan, P., Doretto, G., Wu, Y.N., Soatto, S.: Dynamic texture recognition. In: IEEE Computer Society Conference on Computer Vision and Pattern Recognition (CVPR), vol. 2, p. II-58. IEEE (2001)
25. Doretto, G., Chiuso, A., Wu, Y.N., Soatto, S.: Dynamic textures. Int. J. Comput. Vis. (IJCV) **51**(2), 91–109 (2003)
26. Mesot, B., Barber, D.: Switching linear dynamical systems for noise robust speech recognition. IEEE Trans. Audio Speech Lang. Process. **15**(6), 1850–1858 (2007)
27. Ma, R., Liu, H., Sun, F., Yang, Q., Meng, G.: Linear dynamic system method for tactile object classification. Sci. China: Inf. Sci. **57**, 120205(11) (2014)
28. Martin, R.J.: A metric for ARMA processes. IEEE Trans. Sig. Process. **48**(4), 1164–1170 (2000)
29. Chan, A.B., Vasconcelos, N.: Classifying video with kernel dynamic textures. In: IEEE Conference on Computer Vision and Pattern Recognition (CVPR), pp. 1–6. IEEE (2007)

# Study and Construction for the Compressed Sensing Measurement Matrix Which is Easy to Hardware Implementation

Yanming Fan, Licheng Wu, and Xiali Li[✉]

MinZu University of China, Beijing, China
wulicheng@tsinghua.edu.cn, xiaer_li@163.com

**Abstract.** In the compressed sensing process, measurement matrix plays a significant role in signal sampling and signal reconstruction. Therefore, to construct measurement matrix which is simply-structured, has small memory and is easy to be implemented into hardware is the key to put the compressed sensing theory into application. On the basis of study on Partial Hadamard measurement matrix and Pseudo-Random Sequence, this paper brings up two measurement matrixes which are easy to put into hardware, namely sequence partial Hadamard measurement matrix and circulant pseudo-random sequence measurement matrix, in which the latter consists of the circulantm sequence and circulant gold sequence measurement matrix. It further proves that measurement matrix constructed by pseudo-random sequence complies with the RIP principle. To test the performance of the two measurement matrixes, the paper tries to simulate the two-dimensional image signal. It is found that, under low sampling, the reconstruction of the sequence Partial Hadamard measurement matrix is optimal with the premise that the length of the sampling signal must be $2^k$. Though it is inferior to the sequence Partial Hadamard measurement matrix, the reconstruction of the circulant pseudo-random sequence measurement matrix excels Gaussian random measurement matrix, and also overcomes the sequence Partial Hadamard measurement matrix's $2^k$-length limitation. In a word, the two kinds of measurement matrix are easy to be implied into hardware, can avoid the uncertainty of the random matrix and also overcome the wasting storage of random matrix. Therefore, they have good practical application values.

**Keywords:** Compressed sensing · Measurement matrix · Sequence partial hadamard · Pseudo-random sequence

## 1 Introduction

Compressed Sensing (CS) [1–3] as a new sampling theory, which uses sparse signal characteristic and obtain discrete samples of signals by means of random sample under the condition of far less than Nyquist sampling rate, then reconstructs original signal perfectly by the nonlinear reconstruction algorithm. Compressed Sensing theory characteristics- "light encoding and heavy decoding", which makes it is a reasonable choice to apply compressive sensing theory to the hardware system of low power wireless transmission. Compressed Sensing mainly solves three problems, which are

© Springer Nature Singapore Pte Ltd. 2017
F. Sun et al. (Eds.): ICCSIP 2016, CCIS 710, pp. 529–540, 2017.
DOI: 10.1007/978-981-10-5230-9_51

signal sparse representation, structure measurement matrix and reconstruction algorithm design [4], the merits of measurement matrix performance is directly related to whether the original data can be reconstructed accurately. Therefore, measurement matrix plays a significant role in signal sampling and signal reconstruction.

At present, measurement matrix, which is analyzed from measurement matrix elements, can be divided into two categories, the first category is random measurement matrix, such as Gauss, Bernoulli, and so on, the matrix elements are independent, and their incoherence to sparse matrix is stronger, so they can satisfy RIP [5] condition at large probability, however, the larger computation consumption and the disadvantages of large memory capacity make random measurement matrix is difficult to implement on hardware. The second category is deterministic measurement matrix, such as Toeplitz matrix, polynomial matrix and so on [6, 7], their elements are certain and structure is fixing, which is suitable for hardware implementation, but reconstruction result is not good. Besides, there is some measurement matrix for designated signal (partial Hadamard measurement matrix [8], convolution observation matrix for radar signal [9], measurement matrix for speech signal [10]), although they are better than Gaussian random measurement matrix in certain conditions, they do not possess universality, for example, partial Hadamard measurement matrix sample data length must be 2k. At present, there are scholars construct the measurement matrix based on pseudo random sequence [11, 12] and verify the performance of pseudo random sequence is better than Gaussian random matrix, but the construction method to correlation measurement matrix is more complicated. Therefore, it is important to study measurement matrix which is easy to hardware implement, simple structure and better reconstruction effect, and its research has important value for compressed sensing theory to practical application.

Based on the in-depth study deterministic measurement matrix, this paper focuses on the measurement matrix which is easy to hardware implementation and has good reconstruction effect. First, an improved structure is proposed for partial Hadamard measurement matrix, that is select Hadamard matrix row vector sequentially to construct the measurement matrix, through simulation verification, it is verified that using the simple structure can obtain better signal reconstruction results under the same reconstruction algorithm. Then, this paper brings up simple structure measurement matrix- circulant m sequence and circulant gold sequence measurement matrix. Finally, the simulation results show that the proposed two kinds of measurement matrix possess good adaptability and practicability.

## 2  Improvement and Construction to Measurement Matrix

At present, embedded hardware system faces the main problems are: energy limitation and weak computing power, memory constrained. So, design measurement matrix that easy to implement to hardware should conform to the following principles: (1) measurement matrix occupies less memory, simple elements; (2) the operation try to involve only addition and subtraction, elements must be real Numbers; (3) the measurement matrix and sparse matrix incoherence is stronger; (4) fast sampling and reconstruction. Deterministic observation matrix such as toeplitz, Hadamard, their elements are made up of $\pm 1$ or $(0, 1)$, matrix operation involves only addition and subtraction operations without complicated multiplication, therefore, these advantages of deterministic measurement matrix can be the starting point of constructing easy hardware implementation measurement matrix.

## 2.1    Sequence Partial Hadamard Measurement Matrix Construction

Partial Hadamard measurement matrix has excellent performance, it can reconstruct original signal under less sampling data, and under the same sampling rate, the reconstruction effect of signal is better than the other measurement matrix. Hadamard matrix elements are composed of $+1$ and $-1$, its construction process is as follows:

$$H_1 = [1] \tag{1}$$

$$H_2 = \begin{bmatrix} 1 & 1 \\ 1 & -1 \end{bmatrix} \tag{2}$$

$$H_4 = \begin{bmatrix} H_2 & H_2 \\ H_2 & -H_2 \end{bmatrix} = \begin{bmatrix} 1 & 1 & 1 & 1 \\ 1 & -1 & 1 & -1 \\ 1 & 1 & -1 & -1 \\ 1 & -1 & -1 & 1 \end{bmatrix} \tag{3}$$

$$H_N = H_{2^n} = H_2 \otimes H_{2^{n-1}} = \begin{bmatrix} H_{2^{n-1}} & H_{2^{n-1}} \\ H_{2^{n-1}} & -H_{2^{n-1}} \end{bmatrix} = \begin{bmatrix} H_{\frac{N}{2}} & H_{\frac{N}{2}} \\ H_{\frac{N}{2}} & -H_{\frac{N}{2}} \end{bmatrix} \tag{4}$$

according to the construction process, it is found that the construction method is create a Hadamard orthogonal matrix, whose size is $N * N$, $N = 2^k$, $k = 1, 2, 3 \ldots$, then select $M$ lines row vector randomly to create $M * N$ partial Hadamard measurement matrix, but its incoherence to sparse matrix will be weak. After analysis on Hadamard measurement matrix, this paper proposes a simplified construction method, that is when select row vector, not randomly, but sequentially, for example, this paper select $1 : M$ or $N - M + 1 : N$ vector to construct measurement matrix, which can better maintain Hadamard matrix orthogonality and incoherence and has the advantages of simple construction way and easy to hardware implementation. The simulation results show that this construction method can achieve a better reconstruction results, and the simulation results are shown in Sect. 4.1. This paper names in order select row vector to construct measurement matrix as sequence partial Hadamard measurement matrix.

## 2.2    Circulant Pseudo-random Sequence Measurement Matrix Construction

Partial Hadamard measurement matrix can reconstruct original signal accurately under less sampling data, but signal length must $2^K$, so its scope of application range has been limit. Is there a deterministic measurement matrix that can break through the limitation of signal length and satisfy the RIP condition and the principle of incoherence? First, it is further studied that the conditions needed to construct measurement matrix, it has been proved [13] that if the measurement matrix elements content expression (5) and (6), it can satisfy the RIP condition. Such as partial Hadamard measurement matrix, which meets expression (5), in which the elements of $\pm 1$ each accounted for 1/2.

$$\varphi_{i,j} \begin{cases} -1 & p = 1/2 \\ +1 & p = 1/2 \end{cases} \tag{5}$$

$$\varphi_{i,j} \begin{cases} -1/\sqrt{3} & p = 1/6 \\ 0 & p = 1/3 \\ +1/\sqrt{3} & p = 1/6 \end{cases} \tag{6}$$

This paper will consider pseudorandom sequence—m sequence and gold sequence to be compressed sensing measurement matrix construction breakthrough and propose a simple m sequence and gold sequence to construct measurement matrix manner.

If a sequence, on the one hand, it can be determined in advance and can be product and reproduce repeatedly; on the other hand, it has a kind of random sequence's random characteristics (statistical properties), this sequence is called pseudorandom sequence. Pseudo random sequence is also known as the pseudo noise sequence, that is PN code, it has the following three characteristics:

(1)  In the sequence, elements are close to equal probability appear, that is the number of elements 0 and 1 appear to differ by no more than 1;
(2)  In the sequence, consecutive same elements are called run, in the same length of run, the number of "0" and "1" are substantially equal.
(3)  It has a similar white noise autocorrelation properties。

M sequences and gold sequences belong to pseudo-random sequence, which meet pseudo-random sequence characteristics. m sequence is the longest linear shift register sequence, the linear shift register is generated by the shift register and the feedback coefficient, as Fig. 1, once the feedback coefficient $c_i$ is determined, m sequence is determined. Generated m sequence is varied according to the feedback coefficients, the length of the sequence is related to linear shift registers (feedback coefficients) rank, that is $len = 2^n - 1$. Each rank N has a corresponding polynomial (7):

$$f(x) = \sum_{1}^{n} c_i x^i \tag{7}$$

The polynomial is the primitive polynomial of rank $n$, that is feedback coefficient. The sequences discussed in this paper are composed of (0,1) or (−1, +1), this paper select (−1, +1). According to the properties of m sequence, generated sequence element +1 than −1 only one more, it can be considered that each element is accounted for 1/2, therefore, it can be inferred that the measurement matrix composed of m sequence can accurately reconstruct the original signal. Gold sequence is similar to m sequence, so gold sequence also can be measurement matrix. The method of constructing measurement matrix with m sequence and gold sequence is introduced in detail.

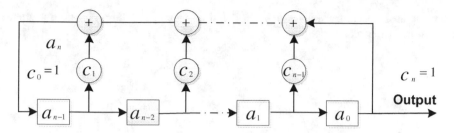

**Fig. 1.** n bit linear feedback shift register structure

The way to construct m sequence measurement matrix mainly uses the idea of circulant matrix, it make generation m sequence right cycle shift one bit each time to form N columns. Finally, select M lines to constitute measurement matrix.

(1) First, generate m sequence, whose periodic is $L = 2^n - 1$, where $L > N$ (original signal length), and it will be as the first column of measurement matrix;

(2) Let m sequence element right cycle shift one bit to generate a new sequence, it will be as the second column of measurement matrix;

(3) Let previous column m sequence right shift one bit to generate a new sequence, it will be the next column of measurement matrix;

(4) Repeat the above (step 3) until generate N columns, then constitute a $L*N$ matrix;

(5) In order select $1:M$ rows vector to construct measurement matrix $\mathbf{Mx}$.

Generated matrix form as expression (8), this paper call it circulant m sequence measurement matrix.

$$Mx = \begin{pmatrix} m_1 & m_n & \cdots & m_n \\ m_2 & m_1 & \cdots & m_{n-1} \\ \cdot & \cdot & \cdot & \cdot \\ \cdot & \cdot & \cdot & \cdot \\ m_n & m_{n-1} & \cdots & m_1 \end{pmatrix} \tag{8}$$

The construction method of gold sequence measurement matrix is similar to circulant m sequence measurement matrix, it also use the idea of circulant matrix of gold sequence is generated by using the idea of circular matrix to construct measurement matrix.

(1) First, generate gold sequence (elements are $\pm 1$), whose periodic is $L = 2^n - 1$, where $L > N$ (original signal length), gold sequence is the optimal pair of two m sequences, and it will be as the first column of measurement matrix;

(2) Let gold sequence element right cycle shift one bit to generate a new sequence, it will be as the second column of measurement matrix;

(3) Other step see the way to construct circulant m sequence measurement matrix.

Generated matrix form as expression (9), this paper call it circulant gold sequence measurement matrix.

$$Gx = \begin{pmatrix} g_1 & g_n & \cdots & g_n \\ g_2 & g_1 & \cdots & g_{n-1} \\ \vdots & \ddots & \ddots & \vdots \\ g_n & g_{n-1} & \cdots & g_1 \end{pmatrix} \tag{9}$$

The reason why this paper select $M$ row vectors in order to construct measurement matrix is consider about computing power, after all, embedded system hardware computing power is weak, randomly selected computing will increase consumption.

## 3 Relevant Evidence to Pseudo-random Sequence Measurement Matrix

M sequences and gold sequences are pseudo-random sequence, emergence probability about element +1 and −1 is about 1/2, and Pseudo random sequence is considered to be the binary sequence, therefore, measurement matrix which is constructed by pseudo-random sequence elements are even-distributed, the last chapter has shown that when measurement matrix satisfies expression (1), it will satisfy the RIP condition with great probability. This paper can divide a matrix which is distributed as expression (5) into two random binary matrix:

$$\Phi_s = \Phi_a - \Phi_b \tag{10}$$

Compressed sensing measurement process:

$$y = \Phi x \tag{11}$$

It is equivalent to the following form:

$$y_i = \langle x, \varphi_i \rangle \ i = 1, 2, \ldots n \tag{12}$$

Then for each measurement value:

$$y_i(x, \Phi_s) = y_i(x, \Phi_b) - y_i(x, \Phi_b) 1 \leq i \leq n \tag{13}$$

It can be known from expression (13) that When $\Phi_s$ obtain all the information of original signal x, $\Phi_a$ just get part information. Suppose amount of information which is obtained by $\Phi_s$ is 1, then when $n$ is large enough, the amount of information will be obtained by probability:

$$1 - (1/2)^n = 1 - 2^{-n} \tag{14}$$

Its final amount of information is also close to 1. According to the paper [14, 15], it can be concluded: $\Phi_a$ is a $n*N$ matrix obeying random binary distribution, given $n$, $N$, $\delta \in (0, 1)$ and $k \leq cn/log(N/k)$, existence $c_1, c_2 > 0$, when there is a corresponding random uniform distribution matrix $\Phi_s$ obeying expression (5) with probability $p \geq 1 - 2exp(-nc_2)$ to meet the RIP, random binary matrix $\Phi_a$ can make the compressible signal with probability $p \geq [1 - 2exp(-nc_2)](1 - 2^{-n})$ reconstruction exactly. Where:

$$c_2 \leq (3\delta^2 - \delta^3)/48 - c_1[1 + \log(12/\delta)/\log(N/k)] \qquad (15)$$

In expression (15), k is the signal sparsity. From the view of constructing measurement matrix, circulant m sequence and circulant gold sequence measurement matrix has good cross-correlation characteristics and just coincides with incoherence condition, due to the constructed measurement matrix satisfy certain linear stochastic independence, these characteristics are consistent with the requirements of compressive sensing for measurement matrix.

# 4 Simulation Verification and Analysis

This paper constructs sequence partial Hadamard measurement matrix through improving partial Hadamard measurement matrix construction method; by using the characteristic of m sequence and gold sequence in the pseudo-random sequence, the paper constructs circulant m sequence and circulant gold sequence measurement matrix, and give a simple mathematical proof that the pseudo random sequence can be used as the measurement matrix. Next to verify the performance constructed measurement matrix by simulation. First, the paper compare sequence partial Hadamard measurement matrix with partial Hadamard measurement matrix; then, verify the constructed circulant pseudo-random sequence measurement matrix availability and compare with other measurement matrix; Final, the comparative analysis of the constructed measurement matrix apply in commonly reconstruction algorithm will be conducted.

In this paper, the simulation uses a two-dimensional Lena gray image to conduct block compression sampling and reconstruction, the block size is 8 * 8, sparse transform is discrete cosine transform (DCT), the sampling rate is 0.25, 0.5 and 0.75 respectively.

## 4.1 Simulation Analysis to Sequence Partial Hadamard Measurement Matrix

Simulation analysis to sequence partial Hadamard measurement matrix, reconstruction algorithm is orthogonal matching pursuit (OMP) algorithm, the simulation results are shown in Table 1.

It can be known from Table 1, when the sampling rate is low, sequence partial Hadamard measurement matrix reconstruction image PSNR value is nearly 5 dB

Table 1. Reconstructed image PSNR value (dB)

| Partial Hadamard | 0.25 | 0.5 | 0.75 |
|---|---|---|---|
| Sequence 1 : M | 25.10 | 29.82 | 29.92 |
| Sequence N – M + 1 : N | 25.06 | 29.82 | 29.92 |
| Randomly selected | 20.07 | 24.92 | 29.37 |

higher than that of partial Hadamard matrix randomly selected, when the sampling rate is high, the gap between two is not obvious, the sequence partial Hadamard matrix structure is fixed, without multiple measurements, it can achieve good reconstruction effect at lower sampling rate. In addition, Hadamard measurement matrix exist Butterfly fast algorithm, which is very suitable for hardware system and reduce system power consumption, it provides better support for hardware to realize compressed sensing principle.

## 4.2  Usability Verification to Circulant Pseudo-random Sequence Measurement Matrix

This paper simply proves circulant pseudo-random sequence can be used as measurement matrix theory probability, next to verify the suitability and practicality of constructed measurement matrix. Lists comparison result with Gaussian Random measurement matrix, Toeplitz measurement matrix, sequence partial Hadamard measurement matrix, the reconstruction algorithm is the OMP. Table 2 shows reconstructed images PSNR values at different sampling rate 2. Figure 2 shows image simulation results using different measurement matrix at the sampling rate of 0.25.

Table 2. Different measurement matrix reconstruction PSNR value (dB)

| Sampling rate | Gaussian Random | Toeplitz | Sequence partial Hadamard | Circulant m sequence | Circulant gold sequence |
|---|---|---|---|---|---|
| 0.25 | 16.31 | 20.91 | 25.10 | 20.56 | 20.09 |
| 0.50 | 23.56 | 24.30 | 29.82 | 24.98 | 24.66 |
| 0.75 | 27.76 | 28.40 | 29.97 | 29.69 | 29.17 |

It can be known from Table 2 and Fig. 2 that the measurement result of sequence partial Hadamard is best, which is higher about 9 dB than Gaussian Random, the other deterministic measurement matrix is also higher about 4 dB than Gaussian Random. When sampling rate up to 0.5, sequence partial Hadamard is higher about 6 dB, others are higher 1 dB. With sampling rate up to 0.75, the reconstruction effects gap between each measurement matrix is close. It can be shown from simulation results that deterministic measurement matrix reconstruction effect is better, in which improved sequence partial Hadamard matrix sampling effect is best, and constructed circulant pseudo-random sequence (circulant m sequence and circulant gold sequence) measurement matrix also obtain good sampling effect.

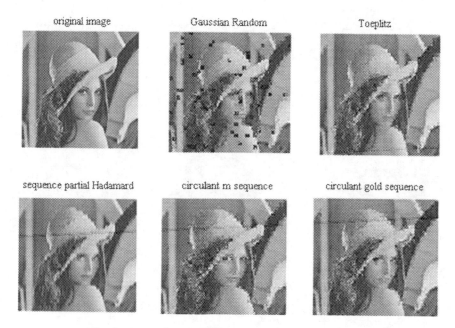

**Fig. 2.** Simulation results when the sampling rate is 0.25

## 4.3 Comparative Analysis to Measurement Matrix Apply in Common Reconstruction Algorithm

Simulation experiments still use the above conditions, test image is 256 * 256 Lena grey image, reconstruction algorithm is solving the minimum $l_0$-norm BP algorithm and solving the minimum $l_1$-norm OMP algorithm and OMP algorithm and its improve algorithm Segmentation Orthogonal Matching Pursuit algorithm (StOMP). Comparable measurement matrix includes Gaussian Random, sequence partial Hadamard, circulant m sequence and circulant gold sequence matrix, m sequence use 7 level feedback coefficient, the chosen primitive polynomial is $f(x) = x^7 + x^6 + x^3 + x^1$, that is the initial status of each register is [1 1 0 0 1 0 1].

This simulation difference with the above is that sparse basis is sparse wavelet transform, each time process 256 pixels, the sampling rate vary from 0.2 to 0.8, step is 0.05. Gaussian random measurement matrix, sequence partial Hadamard measurement matrix, circulant m sequence and circulant gold sequence measurement matrix under different reconstruction algorithms PSNR simulation results as shown in Fig. 3.

It can be known from Fig. 3, sequence partial Hadamard measurement matrix reconstruction effect is best, it is higher 2 dB than Gaussian Random, three kinds of measurement matrix reconstruction effect overall trend is same in the BP algorithm and OMP algorithm, which are all increase with the increase of sampling rate. Sequence partial Hadamard measurement matrix reconstruction effect is bouncing Changing in StOMP algorithm, while the other two kinds of measurement matrix's reconstruction result are similar. Circulant pseudo-random sequence (circulant m sequence and

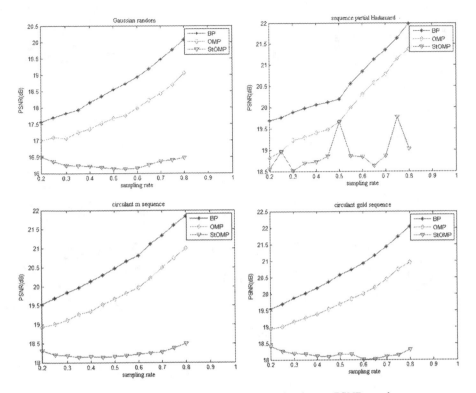

**Fig. 3.** Measurement matrix reconstruction image PSNR result

circulant gold sequence) measurement matrix reconstruction result is better than Gaussian Random.

In addition, this paper conducts comparative analysis to three kinds of measurement matrix in reconstruction time, it is as shown in Table 3, which is a record of the sampling rate of 0.6.

**Table 3.** Measurement matrix reconstruction time table (units:s)

| Name | BP | OMP | StOMP |
|---|---|---|---|
| Gaussian Random | 33.5 | 4.4 | 3.2 |
| Sequence partial Hadamard | 19.8 | 2.7 | 2.6 |
| Circulant m sequence | 28.4 | 3.6 | 2.8 |
| Circulant gold sequence | 28.8 | 3.7 | 2.9 |

It can be known from Table 3 that under the same conditions, sequence partial Hadamard measurement matrix and circulant pseudo-random sequence (circulant m sequence and circulant gold sequence) measurement matrix reconstruction operation time is less than the Gaussian Random. It can be validated that the performance of sequence partial Hadamard measurement matrix and circulant pseudo-random sequence measurement matrix are better than Gaussian Random measurement matrix.

# 5 Conclusions

For embedded hardware system with limited energy, less storage, poor computing power, this paper proposes two kind of measurement matrix: sequence partial Hadamard measurement matrix and circulant pseudo-random sequence (circulant m sequence and circulant gold sequence) measurement matrix, which are easy to hardware implementation and memory saving. The two kinds of measurement matrix are better than Gaussian Random measurement matrix in reconstruction effect through simulation analysis. What's more, the two kinds of measurement matrix is relatively sample in construction, recursion property, easy to be implied into hardware, it can also avoid the uncertainty of the random matrix and also overcome the wasting storage of Random matrix, save a lot of memory space, circulant pseudo-random sequence measurement matrix also overcomes the sequence partial Hadamard measurement matrix's $2^k$-length limitation, The constructed measurement matrix not only has theoretical significance, but also provides a new way for the hardware to realize the compressed sensing measurement matrix, therefore, they have good practical application values.

# References

1. Candes, E.J., Romberg, J.: Robust signal recovery from incomplete observations. In: Proceedings / ICIP International Conference on Image Processing, pp. 1281–1284 (2006)
2. Candes, E.J., Tao, T.: Decoding by linear programming. IEEE Trans. Inf. Theory **34**(4), 435–443 (2004)
3. Donoho, D.L.: Compressed sensing. IEEE Trans. Inf. Theory, **52**(4), 1289–1306 (2006)
4. Dai Qiong-hai, F.C., Xiang-Yang, J.: Research on compressed sensing. Chin. J. Comput. **34** (3), 425–434 (2011)
5. Candes, E.J., Tao, T.: Near-optimal signal recovery from random projections: universal encoding strategies. IEEE Trans. Inf. Theory **52**(12), 5406–5425 (2007)
6. Haupt, J., Bajwa, W.U., Raz, G., et al.: Toeplitz compressed sensing matrices with applications to sparse channel estimation. IEEE Trans. Inf. Theory **56**(11), 5862–5875 (2010)
7. Devore, R.A.: Deterministic constructions of compressed sensing matrices. J. Complex. **23** (4–6), 918–925 (2007)
8. Jiang, L., Huang, T., Shen, H., et al.: Orthogonal multi matching pursuit algorithm based on local randomized Hadamard matrix. Syst. Eng. Electron. **35**(5), 914–919 (2013)
9. Liu, J.H., Xu, S., Gao, X., et al.: Compressed sensing radar imaging based on random convolution. Syst. Eng. Electron. **33**(7), 1485–1490 (2011)
10. Haobo, X.U., Fengqin, Y.U.: Speech compressed sensing based on sparse pre-treatment and circulant measurement. Comput. Eng. Appl. **50**(23), 220–224 (2014)
11. Dang, K., Ma, L., Tian, Y., et al.: Construction of the compressive sensing measurement matrix based on m sequences. Xian Dianzi Keji Daxue Xuebao/J. Xidian Univ. **42**(2), 186–192 (2015)
12. Wang, X., Cui, G., Wang, L., et al.: Construction of measurement matrix in compressed sensing based on balanced Gold sequence. Yi Qi Yi Biao Xue Bao/Chin. J. Scientific Instrum. **35**(1), 97–102 (2014)

13. Baraniuk, R., Davenport, M., Devore, R., et al.: A simple proof of the restricted isometry property for random matrices. Constructive Approximation **28**(3), 253–263 (2008)
14. Zhang, G., Jiao, S., Xu, X., et al.: Compressed sensing and reconstruction with bernoulli matrices. In: 2010 IEEE International Conference on Information and Automation (ICIA), pp. 455–460. IEEE (2010)
15. Zhang, G., Jiao, S., Xu, X.: Compressed sensing and reconstruction with Semi-Hadamard matrices. In: 2010 2nd International Conference on Signal Processing Systems (ICSPS), pp. V1-194–V1-197. IEEE (2010)

# Hemispheric Asymmetry of the Functional Brain Connectome

Wei Shang[1], Ting Li[1], Jie Xiang[1], Rui Cao[1], Bin Wang[1,2(✉)],
Jinglong Wu[3], and Hui Zhang[2]

[1] College of Computer Science and Technology, Taiyuan University
of Technology, No. 79 Yingze West Street, Taiyuan 030024, China
wangbin01@tyut.edu.cn
[2] Department of Radiology, First Hospital of Shanxi Medical University,
Taiyuan, China
[3] Graduate School of Natural Science and Technology, Okayama University,
Okayama, Japan

**Abstract.** Researches of neuroimaging have revealed that there are many differences between left hemisphere and right hemisphere both in anatomical structure and in cognitive function. However, little is known about the topological organization of the functional networks of the two hemispheres. In the present study, we used functional magnetic resonance imaging to examine the topological organization and hemispheric differences in the functional networks in the two hemispheres. Analysis of asymmetry on functional networks was performed on a group of 192 healthy right-handed Chinese subjects. It revealed that both left and right hemisphere showed small-worldness features. We also found a significant rightward asymmetry on clustering coefficients and characteristic path length, a significant leftward asymmetry on global efficiency. In addition, the right hemisphere shows a stronger tendency of organizational modularity. These results may explain some differences in behaviors and cognition.

**Keywords:** Hemispheric asymmetry · Functional brain connectome · Resting-state fMRI

## 1 Introduction

The human brain is asymmetric in both structure and function [1]. For example, leftward volume asymmetries have been consistently observed in brain regions specialized for language [1]. The right hemisphere is dominant for attention [2], and there is evidence that right hemispheric also play a dominant role in visuospatial attention [3].

Graph theoretical analysis is an admirable tool to explore the topological organization of complex networks, and it has been proved that the method is sensitive to the human brain research [4]. Importantly, it has been applied to the study of human brain networks in healthy people and patients [5].

Recently, a few studies have reported hemisphere-related differences in the anatomical topological organization of brain networks, by using of white matter (WM) structural networks and diffusion-weighted MR networks [6, 7]. Researches of the differences in

© Springer Nature Singapore Pte Ltd. 2017
F. Sun et al. (Eds.): ICCSIP 2016, CCIS 710, pp. 541–547, 2017.
DOI: 10.1007/978-981-10-5230-9_52

functional networks were not enough clear. In this study, we analyzed the differences in global properties of brain networks between the two hemispheres.

## 2     Materials and Methods

### 2.1     Subjects

All the subjects in this study were selected from the 1000 Functional Connectomes (http://fcon_1000.projects.nitrc.org/). We selected 192 right-handed subjects from the database of Beijing, whose age ranged from 18 to 26 (female/male, 118:74).

### 2.2     Image Acquisition

All subjects were scanned on a 3.0-Tesla MRI scanner. Resting-state functional images were obtained with the following parameters: 235 time points; repetition time (TR) = 2000 ms; number of slices = 33.

### 2.3     Symmetrical Template and Regions of Interest

In order to remove the influence of asymmetric template T1 image to the results, we made a symmetrical T1 template for normalization, by flipping the original T1 template and then averaged the original T1 template and the flipped template.

The regions of interest (ROIs) were defined according to the Automated Anatomical Labeling (AAL) template. First, the AAL template was flipped, and then symmetric mask was created by getting the intersection of LR-flipped mask and the original mask.

### 2.4     Imaging Preprocessing

All preprocessing was performed in Matlab2009b using the Data Processing Assistant for Resting-State fMRI (DPARSF, Yan and Zang, 2010, http://www.restfmri.net). The process had the following steps: removed first 10 time points; slice timing; realign; covariates regression (6 head motion parameters as well as parameters for the white matter signal, global mean signal, and cerebrospinal fluid signal); normalized by using the symmetrical T1 template and then resampled them into 3 mm $\times$ 3 mm $\times$ 3 mm cubic voxels; smoothed with a Gaussian kernel of $4 \times 4 \times 4$ mm$^3$; band-pass filtered with a range from 0.01 Hz to 0.08 Hz.

### 2.5     Network Construction

As shown in Fig. 1, we extracted ROI time courses, selected the time courses of 45 regions in left and right brain, Pearson Correlation was used to get correlation matrixes. Finally, correlation matrixes transformed into binary matrixes by using sparsity. We

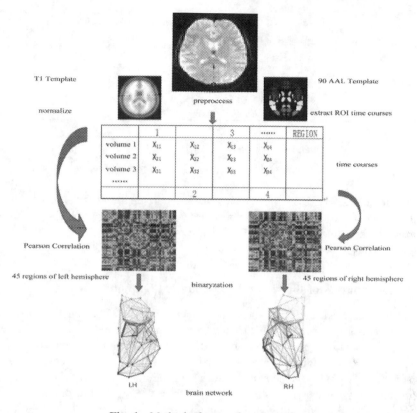

**Fig. 1.** Method of network construction

selected a sparsity from 18% to 40%, this sparsity value could ensure that the networks were fully connected while minimizing the number of false-positive paths [8, 9].

## 2.6  Network Analysis

Graph theory can be used to analyze the brain functional networks quantitatively. Clustering coefficient (C), characteristic path length (L), normalized clustering coefficient ($\gamma$), normalized characteristic path length ($\lambda$), the ratio of Gamma and Lambda ($\sigma$), global efficiency (Egl), local efficiency (Eloc), modularity and number of module were used to characterize the global topological properties of brain networks.

# 3  Results

## 3.1  Small-World Properties of Cortical Networks

Studies demonstrated that functional brain networks exhibited small-world features. The small-world properties were shown in Fig. 2. The left and right networks had the

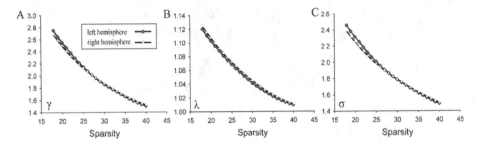

**Fig. 2.** Small-world properties in left and right hemisphere

similar characters, for example, characteristic path length ($\lambda \approx 1$) and clustering coefficients ($\gamma > 1$). All the networks showed $\gamma > 1$, $\lambda \approx 1$ and $\sigma > 1$. As the values of the sparsity thresholds increased, the $\gamma$ values decreased rapidly and the $\lambda$ values changed slightly.

## 3.2   Measurements of the Networks in Different Sparsity

Paired t-tests revealed the global network properties (C, L, Eloc and Egl) had significant differences between left hemisphere and right hemisphere, results showed in Fig. 3. Differences of global network properties appeared in a ranger which labeled by the stars ($p < 0.01$). Ignored a few sparsity values, the differences between left hemisphere and right hemisphere in the clustering coefficients and local efficiency were significant at higher sparsity values (S = 26%, S = 28%), but the differences in the characteristic path length and global efficiency were significant in the whole range.

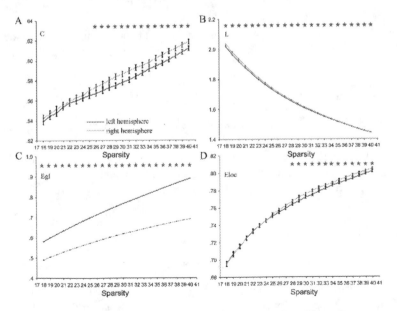

**Fig. 3.** Global network properties over a range of sparsity values

### 3.3   Measurements of the Networks with AUC

In order to evaluate the features in the whole sparsity, paired t-tests were performed for AUC of the left and right hemisphere. Results showed in Fig. 4. The AUC of C and L in the right hemisphere were significant greater than the left hemisphere ($p < 0.01$). The AUC of Eloc in the right hemisphere showed marginal significance greater than the left hemisphere ($p < 0.05$). However, the AUC of Egl in the left hemisphere were significant greater than the right hemisphere ($p < 0.01$).

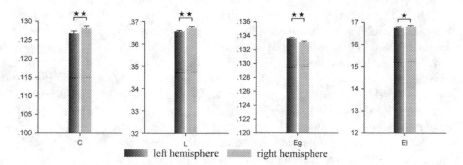

**Fig. 4.** AUC of left and right hemisphere in clustering coefficients, characteristic path length, global efficiency and local efficiency

### 3.4   Measurements of Organizational Modularity

To further explore the inter-hemisphere organizational feature, we calculated number of module and modularity for each hemisphere. The number of module in each hemisphere was almost the same. The significant difference of modularity began at a high sparsity value ($S = 34\%$), showed a significant rightward asymmetry (Fig. 5).

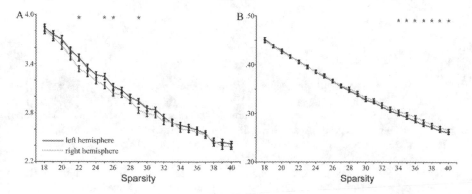

**Fig. 5.** Number of module (A) and modularity (B) for each hemisphere in sparsity range

## 4 Discussion

In this study, we constructed functional networks based on separated hemispheres rather than on the whole brain. We found that the normalized clustering coefficients $\gamma$ were greater than 1 and the normalized characteristic path length $\lambda$ were close to 1 for hemispheric networks of 192 subjects. When evaluating the global network properties using a summary parameter "small-worldness" $\sigma = \gamma/\lambda$, we also observed that $\sigma$ was greater than 1. In a word, these hemispheric networks exhibited a typically small-world feature, in keeping with previous hemispheric network studies [10].

A significant rightward asymmetry on clustering coefficients and characteristic path length was found, the result agreed with a previous studies which reported that right hemisphere showed higher values of small-worldness [6].

A significant leftward asymmetry on global efficiency was found. Left hemisphere showed increased efficiency at global levels, suggesting that the brain regions in the left hemisphere interconnect in better integration compared to the right hemisphere [11].

A significant rightward asymmetry on modularity was found. Modularity represents the compact degree of module [12]. It indicated that connection between each region in right hemisphere was less than left hemisphere. This phenomenon was in agreement with the result of leftward asymmetry on global efficiency.

## 5 Conclusion

In summary, we have demonstrated differences of global properties in each hemisphere by analyzing resting state fMRI. Critically, this study demonstrated a significant rightward asymmetry on clustering coefficients, characteristic path length and modularity but a significant leftward asymmetry on global efficiency.

**Acknowledgments.** This work was supported by the National Natural Science Foundation of China (61503272, 61373101) and Postdoctoral Science Foundation of Shanxi Medical University.

## References

1. Toga, A.W., Thompson, P.M.: Mapping brain asymmetry. Nat. Rev. Neurosci. **4**, 37–48 (2003)
2. Smith, D.V., Clithero, J.A., Rorden, C., Karnath, H.O.: Decoding the anatomical network of spatial attention. Proc. Nat. Acad. Sci. USA **110**, 1518–1523 (2013)
3. Halligan, P.W., Fink, G.R., Marshall, J.C., Vallar, G.: Spatial cognition: evidence from visual neglect. Trends Cogn. Sci. **7**, 125–133 (2003)
4. Reijneveld, J.C., Ponten, S.C., Berendse, H.W., Stam, C.J.: The application of graph theoretical analysis to complex networks in the brain. Clin. Neurophysiol. **118**, 2317–2331 (2007)
5. He, Y., Evans, A.: Graph theoretical modeling of brain connectivity. Curr. Opin. Neurol. **23**, 341–350 (2010)

6. Li, M., Chen, H., Wang, J., Liu, F., Long, Z., Wang, Y., Iturria-Medina, Y., Zhang, J., Yu, C., Chen, H.: Handedness-and hemisphere-related differences in small-world brain networks: a diffusion tensor imaging tractography study. Brain Connectivity **4**, 145–156 (2014)
7. Iturria-Medina, Y., Perez Fernandez, A., Morris, D.M., Canales-Rodriguez, E.J., Haroon, H.A., Garcia Penton, L., Augath, M., Galan Garcia, L., Logothetis, N., Parker, G.J., Melie-Garcia, L.: Brain hemispheric structural efficiency and interconnectivity rightward asymmetry in human and nonhuman primates. Cereb. Cortex **21**, 56–67 (2011)
8. Bassett, D.S., Meyer-Lindenberg, A., Achard, S., Duke, T., Bullmore, E.: Adaptive reconfiguration of fractal small-world human brain functional networks. Proc. Nat. Acad. Sci. USA **103**, 19518–19523 (2006)
9. He, Y., Chen, Z., Evans, A.: Structural insights into aberrant topological patterns of large-scale cortical networks in Alzheimer's disease. J. Neurosci. **28**, 4756–4766 (2008)
10. Tian, L., Wang, J., Yan, C., He, Y.: Hemisphere-and gender-related differences in small-world brain networks: a resting-state functional MRI study. Neuroimage **54**, 191–202 (2011)
11. Caeyenberghs, K., Leemans, A.: Hemispheric lateralization of topological organization in structural brain networks. Hum. Brain Mapp. **35**, 4944–4957 (2014)
12. Newman, M.E., Girvan, M.: Finding and evaluating community structure in networks. Phys. Rev. E: Stat., Nonlin, Soft Matter Phys. **69**, 026113 (2004)

# Nonlinear Filtering for Emission Source Tracking Using Biased RSS Measurements

Xianqing Li and Zhansheng Duan[✉]

Center for Information Engineering Science Research,
College of Electronics and Information Engineering,
Xi'an Jiaotong University, Xi'an 710049, Shaanxi, China
lixianqing@stu.xjtu.edu.cn, zduan@uno.edu

**Abstract.** Under indoor environments, positioning and tracking using GPS and radar measurements are very scarce. Comparatively, positioning and tracking using received signal strength (RSS) measurements from wireless sensor networks are gaining more and more attention. However, so far all localization or tracking algorithms did not take systematic sensor biases into account. If the biases are not corrected, they will lead to degradation in tracking performance. In this paper, we propose a framework to jointly estimate the dynamic source state and static sensor biases using nonlinear filters such as Extended Kalman filter (EKF) and Unscented Kalman Filter (UKF). Numerical examples show that this framework can estimate both source state and sensor biases very well.

**Keywords:** RSS · Source tracking · Bias estimation · Nonlinear filtering

## 1 Introduction

Target positioning and tracking technology plays a key role in many applications, e.g., intelligence reconnaissance, intelligent transportation system, intelligent homing, logistics, smart agriculture, and smart cities. Due to the advantages of small volume, low price, low power consumption, simple layout, scalability, etc., wireless sensor networks based target positioning and tracking using received signal strength (RSS) measurements are becoming more and more popular [1].

RSS-based positioning methods can be roughly divided into two classes. The first class is model free. Although this type of methods are more accurate, their operating processes are also more complex. For example, for the fingerprint method [2], during the offline stage, the location area of interest is first divided into multiple grids and then the received signal strength of each grid is associated with that grid to build the RSS database. During the online stage, the signal

Z. Duan—Research supported in part by National 973 project of China through grant 2013CB329405, National Natural Science Foundation of China through grant 61673317, and the Fundamental Research Funds for the Central Universities of China.

F. Sun et al. (Eds.): ICCSIP 2016, CCIS 710, pp. 548–555, 2017.
DOI: 10.1007/978-981-10-5230-9_53

strength received by the sensor is compared with the RSS database and then the target location associated with the closest received signal strength is selected as the location estimate. The second class is model based. Hing Cheung So [3] proposed two linear least squares (LLS) estimators for RSS-based positioning. In both LLS estimators, unbiased estimates of the square of the distance between the target and the sensor is obtained first. Then weighted least squares (WLS) estimation using different weighting matrices are applied to estimate the target location. Angelo Coluccia [4] proposed an iterative least squares (ILS) estimator that regards the ranging phase as a Bayesian problem and estimates the distances via empirical Bayesian paradigm. Another WLS method was proposed by Paula Tarrio [5], in which the weighting matrix is composed of the variance of the maximum likelihood estimate of the square of the distance between the target and the sensor.

RSS measurements were also used for target tracking. The widely used tracking filters using RSS measurements include Extended Kalman Filter [6], Unscented Kalman Filter [7]. Also [8,9] proposed to enhance the tracking performance using either Particle Filter (PF) or its variants. Kung-Chung Lee [10] made a comparison between UKF and PF for RSS-based tracking. It was concluded that the UKF underperforms the PF in two practical scenarios and UKF is not robust in practice.

The above positioning and tracking algorithms did not take into account the systematic sensor biases. However, due to system aging, faults and even failures, systematic sensor biases are inevitable. For practical applications, neglecting physically existing systematic sensor biases will lead to the degradation of positioning and tracking performance. This necessitates sensor registration for positioning and tracking using RSS measurements.

In this paper, a framework of jointly estimating the dynamic emission source state and static sensor biases is proposed. To deal with sensor biases, we augment the biases onto the state vector and then estimate them together using nonlinear filters such as EKF and UKF.

The rest of this paper is organized as follows. The source dynamic model and the path loss model are introduced in Sect. 2. Section 3 details the nonlinear filtering framework for joint source tracking and bias estimation. Section 4 illustrates the joint estimation performance using numerical examples. Conclusions are given in Sect. 5.

## 2    System Model and Problem Formulation

### 2.1    Kinematic Model

The kinematic model of the emission source is represented by the following discrete-time dynamic system

$$X_{k+1} = F_k X_k + G_k w_k \tag{1}$$

For simplicity, we assume that the source moves in a 2D plane and the state vector is $X_k = [x_k, \dot{x}_k, y_k, \dot{y}_k]^T$. Also, the process noise $w_k$ is assumed to be zero-mean white Gaussian and $w_k \backsim N(0, Q)$.

When the source takes a constant velocity (CV) motion, we have

$$F_k = \text{diag}\left(\begin{bmatrix} 1 & T \\ 0 & 1 \end{bmatrix}, \begin{bmatrix} 1 & T \\ 0 & 1 \end{bmatrix}\right), G_k = \text{diag}\left(\begin{bmatrix} T^2/2 \\ T \end{bmatrix}, \begin{bmatrix} T^2/2 \\ T \end{bmatrix}\right) \tag{2}$$

When the source takes a coordinated turn (CT) motion, we have

$$F_k = \begin{bmatrix} 1 & \frac{\sin \omega T}{\omega} & 0 & -\frac{1-\cos \omega T}{\omega} \\ 0 & \cos \omega T & 0 & -\sin \omega T \\ 0 & \frac{1-\cos \omega T}{\omega} & 1 & \frac{\sin \omega T}{\omega} \\ 0 & \sin \omega T & 0 & \cos \omega T \end{bmatrix}, G_k = \begin{bmatrix} T^2/2 & 0 \\ T & 0 \\ 0 & T^2/2 \\ 0 & T \end{bmatrix} \tag{3}$$

where $T$ is the sampling interval, and $\omega$ is the turning rate.

## 2.2  Path Loss Measurement Model

The RSS measurement received by sensor $i$ located at $(x^{(i)}, y^{(i)})$ can be modeled by the following log-normal shadowing model [11]:

$$P_k^{(i)} = P^{(0)} - 10\alpha \log_{10}(d_k^{(i)}/d^{(0)}) + v_k^{(i)} \tag{4}$$

where $P_k^{(i)}$ is the sensor received strength in dBm at a distance of $d_k^{(i)} = \sqrt{(x_k - x^{(i)})^2 + (y_k - y^{(i)})^2}$ from sensor $i$ to the source at time $k$, $P^{(0)}$ is the received strength in dBm at a distance of $d^{(0)}$, $\alpha$ is the path loss exponent, $v_k^{(i)}$ is a zero-mean white Gaussian noise representing log-normal shadow fading effects, and $i = 1, \cdots, N$.

## 2.3  Problem Formulation

Furthermore we assume that the measurement of sensor $i$ is subject to a systematic bias $\Delta P^{(i)}$. Then the path loss measurement model can be rewritten as:

$$P_k^{(i)} = P^{(0)} - 10\alpha \log_{10}(d_k^{(i)}/d^{(0)}) + \Delta P^{(i)} + v_k^{(i)} \tag{5}$$

Correspondingly the measurement equation at the fusion center is:

$$z_k = [P_k^{(1)}, P_k^{(2)}, \cdots, P_k^{(N)}]^T = h(X_k, \Delta P) + v_k \tag{6}$$

where

$$h(X_k, \Delta P) = \begin{bmatrix} P^{(0)} - 10\alpha \log_{10}(d_k^{(1)}/d_0) + \Delta P^{(1)} \\ P^{(0)} - 10\alpha \log_{10}(d_k^{(2)}/d_0) + \Delta P^{(2)} \\ \vdots \\ P^{(0)} - 10\alpha \log_{10}(d_k^{(N)}/d_0) + \Delta P^{(N)} \end{bmatrix}, v_k = \begin{bmatrix} v_k^{(1)} \\ v_k^{(2)} \\ \vdots \\ v_k^{(N)} \end{bmatrix}, \Delta P = \begin{bmatrix} \Delta P^{(1)} \\ \Delta P^{(2)} \\ \vdots \\ \Delta P^{(N)} \end{bmatrix}$$

$v_k$ is the zero-mean white Gaussian measurement noise and $v_k \backsim N(0, R)$. Denote the measurement sequence as $Z_{1:k} = \{z_1, z_2, \cdots, z_k\}$. Given the measurement sequence, our goal is to estimate the source motion state sequence $X_{1:k} = \{X_1, X_2, \cdots, X_k\}$ and the sensor bias vector $\Delta P$ simultaneously.

# 3 Joint State and Bias Estimation

To simultaneously estimate the source state and sensor bias, a very natural idea is to extend the source state $X_k$ with the sensor bias $\Delta P$ to form an augmented state $X_k^a = [X_k^T, \Delta P^T]^T$. Then the augmented dynamic system is:

$$X_{k+1}^a = F_k^a X_k^a + G_k^a w_k^a \tag{7}$$

where

$$F_k^a = \begin{bmatrix} F_k & 0 \\ 0 & I_{N \times N} \end{bmatrix}, G_k^a = \begin{bmatrix} G_k & 0 \\ 0 & G_{\Delta P} \end{bmatrix}, w_k^a = [w_{x,k}^T, w_{\Delta P,k}^T]^T$$

$w_{\Delta P,k}$ is the process noise associated with sensor bias, $w_{\Delta P,k} \backsim N(0, Q_{\Delta P})$, and $G_{\Delta P}$ is its gain matrix. Since the RSS measurements are nonlinear functions of the augmented state, we can use nonlinear filters, e.g., Extended Kalman filter (EKF) and Unscented Kalman Filter (UKF), to jointly estimate the source state and system bias.

## 3.1 Augmented Extended Kalman Filter

The Extended Kalman filter [12] linearizes nonlinear state equation and measurement equation using the first-order Taylor series expansion. Thus the framework of the standard Kalman filter can be used to estimate the system state. For the augmented dynamic system (7) and measurement equation (6), the Augmented Extended Kalman filter (AEKF) to simultaneously estimate the source state and sensor bias can be summarized as in Table 1.

**Table 1.** AEKF for emission source tracking using biased RSS measurements

| Prediction |
|---|
| $\hat{X}_{k+1|k}^a = F_k^a \hat{X}_{k|k}^a$ |
| $P_{k+1|k}^a = F_k^a P_{k|k}^a (F_k^a)^T + G_k^a Q_a (G_k^a)^T$ |
| $\hat{z}_{k+1|k} = H_{k+1} \hat{X}_{k+1|k}^a$ |
| $S_{k+1} = H_{k+1} P_{k+1|k}^a H_{k+1}^T + R$ |
| $H_{k+1} = \left. \frac{\partial h(X_{k+1}, \Delta P)}{\partial X_{k+1}^a} \right|_{X_{k+1}^a = \hat{X}_{k+1|k}^a}$ |
| **Update** |
| $K_{k+1} = P_{k+1|k}^a H_{k+1}^T S_{k+1}^{-1}$ |
| $\hat{X}_{k+1|k+1}^a = \hat{X}_{k+1|k}^a + K_{k+1}(z_{k+1} - \hat{z}_{k+1|k})$ |
| $P_{k+1|k+1}^a = P_{k+1|k}^a - K_{k+1} S_{k+1} K_{k+1}^T$ |

## 3.2  Augmented Unscented Kalman Filter

The Unscented Kalman filter uses the Unscented Transform (UT) [13,14] to approximate the first two moments of nonlinear transforms used in LMMSE estimation. For the augmented dynamic system (7) and measurement Eq. (6), the Augmented Unscented Kalman filter (AUKF) to simultaneously estimate the source state and sensor bias can be summarized as in Table 2.

**Table 2.** AUKF for emission source tracking using biased RSS measurements

For a given $\hat{X}^a_{k-1|k-1}$ and $P^a_{k-1|k-1}$, sigma points $\chi^i_{k-1|k-1}$ and their associated weights $\omega^c_i$, $\omega^m_i$, $i = 0, 1, 2, \cdots 2n$ are

$$\begin{cases} \chi^i_{k-1|k-1} = \hat{X}^a_{k-1|k-1}, i = 0 \\ \chi^i_{k-1|k-1} = \hat{X}^a_{k-1|k-1} + \left( \sqrt{(n+\lambda) P^a_{k-1|k-1}} \right)_i, \\ i = 1, 2, \cdots, n \\ \chi^i_{k-1|k-1} = \hat{X}^a_{k-1|k-1} - \left( \sqrt{(n+\lambda) P^a_{k-1|k-1}} \right)_{i-n}, \\ i = n+1, n+2, \cdots, 2n \end{cases}$$

$$\begin{cases} \omega^m_i = \lambda/(n+\lambda), i = 0 \\ \omega^c_i = \lambda/(n+\lambda) + (1 - \alpha^2 + \beta), i = 0 \\ \omega^m_i = \omega^c_i = 0.5/(n+\lambda), i = 1, 2, \cdots 2n \end{cases}$$

Prediction

$$\begin{cases} \chi^i_{k|k-1} = F^a_k \chi^i_{k-1|k-1}, i = 0, 1, 2, \cdots, 2n \\ \hat{X}^a_{k|k-1} = \sum_{i=0}^{2n} \omega^m_i \chi^i_{k|k-1} \\ P^a_{k|k-1} = \sum_{i=0}^{2n} \omega^c_i (\chi^i_{k|k-1} - \hat{X}^a_{k|k-1})(\chi^i_{k|k-1} - \hat{X}^a_{k|k-1})^T + G^a_k Q_a (G^a_k)^T \end{cases}$$

$$\begin{cases} z^i_{k|k-1} = h\left( \chi^i_{k|k-1} \right), i = 0, 1, 2, \cdots, 2n \\ \hat{z}_{k|k-1} = \sum_{i=0}^{2n} \omega^m_i z^i_{k|k-1} \\ P_{zz,k|k-1} = \sum_{i=0}^{2n} \omega^c_i (z^i_{k|k-1} - \hat{z}_{k|k-1})(z^i_{k|k-1} - \hat{z}_{k|k-1})^T + R \\ P_{xz,k|k-1} = \sum_{i=0}^{2n} \omega^c_i (\chi^i_{k|k-1} - \hat{X}^a_{k|k-1})(z^i_{k|k-1} - \hat{z}_{k|k-1})^T \end{cases}$$

Update

$$\begin{cases} K_k = P_{xz,k|k-1} P^{-1}_{zz,k|k-1} \\ \hat{X}^a_{k|k} = \hat{X}^a_{k|k-1} + K_k \left( z_k - \hat{z}_{k|k-1} \right) \\ P^a_{k|k} = P^a_{k|k-1} - K_k P_{zz,k|k-1} K^T_k \end{cases}$$

where $\lambda = \alpha^2(n + \kappa) - n$, $n$ is the dimension of $X^a_k$ and $n = 4 + N$ in this work, $\alpha$ usually takes a very small value, e.g. 0.01, the best $\kappa$ for Gaussian case is zero, the optimal value of $\beta$ for Gaussian case is 2, $(\sqrt{(n+\lambda) P^a_{k-1|k-1}})_i$ is the $i^{th}$ column of the square root of matrix $(n + \lambda)P^a_{k-1|k-1}$.

## 4 Illustrative Examples

In a two-dimensional $60 \times 60$ $m^2$ rectangular region, four RSS sensors are deployed at the four corners to track a common emission source simultaneously. One run of the source trajectory (CV first and then CT) and the deployment of the sensors are shown in Fig. 1. The relevant parameter settings are summarized in Table 3.

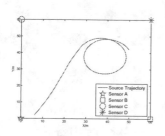

**Fig. 1.** Trajectory of one run

**Table 3.** Parameters settings

| Symbol | Value |
|---|---|
| $\bar{X}_0$ | $[8\,\text{m}, 0.2\,\text{m/s}, 4\,\text{m}, 0.3\,\text{m/s}]$ |
| $Q$ | $diag\,[0.000004, 0.000007]$ |
| $R$ | $diag\,[3.5^2, 3.5^2, 3.5^2, 3.5^2]$ |
| $\eta$ | $[3\,\text{dBm}, 4\,\text{dBm}, 5\,\text{dBm}, 6\,\text{dBm}]$ |
| $\omega$ | $-2\pi/180$ |
| $T$ | $0.5$ |
| $d^{(0)}$ | $1\,\text{m}$ |
| $P^{(0)}$ | $-40.2\,\text{dBm}$ |
| $\alpha$ | $3$ |

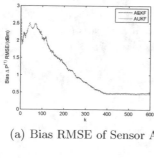

(a) Bias RMSE of Sensor A

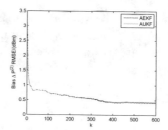

(b) Bias RMSE of Sensor B

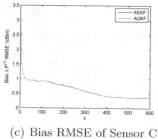

(c) Bias RMSE of Sensor C

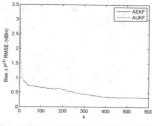

(d) Bias RMSE of Sensor D

**Fig. 2.** Bias RMSE

We use AEKF and AUKF to jointly estimate the source state and the systematic biases over 100 Monte-Carlo runs. Figure 2(a) to (d) show the comparison results of 4 sensor biases estimation RMSE of the two filters. We can see that the RMSE curves of the four sensor biases all converge and the estimation accuracy is one order less than the bias in terms of magnitude. Figure 3 show the source tracking RMSE, from which it can be seen that the tracking performance gradually gets better with the increase of time. In addition, the performance of AUKF is slightly better than AEKF in terms of bias estimation and tracking accuracy but the difference is almost negligible.

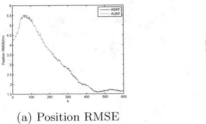

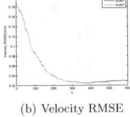

(a) Position RMSE                    (b) Velocity RMSE

**Fig. 3.** Tracking RMSE

## 5    Conclusion

In this paper, we consider the problem of emission source tracking using biased RSS measurements in WSN. The main idea to deal with this problem is to extend the source state with the systematic sensor biases to form an augmented system state and then use nonlinear filters, e.g., EKF and UKF, to jointly estimate the source state and systematic sensor biases. Numerical examples show that the framework works pretty well.

## References

1. Kuriakose, J., Amruth, V., Nandhini, N.S.: A survey on localization of wireless sensor nodes. In: Proceedings of 2014 International Conference on Information Communication and Embedded Systems, Chennai, India, pp. 1–6 (2014)
2. Bshara, M., Orguner, U., Gustafsson, F., et al.: Fingerprinting localization in wireless networks based on received-signal-strength measurements: a case study on WiMAX networks. IEEE Trans. Veh. Technol. **59**, 283–294 (2010)
3. So, H.C., Lin, L.X.: Linear least squares approach for accurate received signal strength based source localization. IEEE Trans. Signal Process. **59**(8), 4035–4040 (2011)
4. Coluccia, A., Ricciato, F.: RSS-based localization via bayesian ranging and iterative least squares positioning. IEEE Commun. Lett. **18**, 873–876 (2014)

5. Tarrio, P., Bernardos, A.M., Besada, J.A., et al.: A new positioning technique for RSS-based localization based on a weighted least squares estimator. In: Proceedings of 2008 IEEE International Symposium on Wireless Communication Systems, Reykjavik, Iceland, pp. 633–637 (2008)
6. Lategahn, J., Muller, M.: TDOA and RSS based extended Kalman filter indoor person localization. In: Rohrig, C. (ed.) Vehicular Technology Conference (VTC Fall), Las Vegas, NV, pp. 1–5 (2013)
7. Khalil, L., Jung, P.: Scaled unscented Kalman filter for RSSI-based indoor positioning and tracking. In: 2015 9th International Conference on Next Generation Mobile Applications, Services and Technologies, Cambridge, pp. 132–137 (2015)
8. Wang, Z., Zhao, Z., Qian, X.: The analysis of localization algorithm of unscented particle filter based on RSS for linear wireless sensor networks. In: 2013 32nd Chinese Control Conference (CCC), China, Xi'an, pp. 7499–7504 (2013)
9. Song, Y., Hongyi, Y.: A RSS based indoor tracking algorithm using particle filters. In: Global Mobile Congress 2009, Shanghai, pp. 1–4 (2009)
10. Lee, K.-C., Oka, A., Pollakis, E., Lampe, L.: A comparison between unscented Kalman filtering and particle filtering for RSSI-based tracking. In: 2010 7th Workshop on Positioning Navigation and Communication (WPNC), Dresden, pp. 157–163 (2010)
11. Sarkar, T.K., Ji, Z., Kim, K., Medouri, A., Salazar-palma, M.: A survey of various propagation models for mobile communication. IEEE Antennas Propag. Mag. 45(3), 51–82 (2003)
12. Jaazwinski, A.H.: Stochastic Processes and Filtering Theory. Academic Press, New York (1970)
13. Julier, S.J., Uhlmann, J.K., Durrant-Whyte, H.F.: A new approach for filtering nonlinear systems. In: Proceedings of the 1995 American Control Conference, vol. 3, pp. 1628–1632. IEEE Press, Seattle (1995)
14. Julier, S.J., Uhlmann, J.K., Durrant-Whyte, H.F.: A new method for the nonlinear transformation of means and covariances in filters and estimatiors. IEEE Trans. Autom. Control 45(3), 472–482 (2000)

# A New EEG Signal Processing Method Based on Low-Rank and Sparse Decomposition

Wanzeng Kong[1(✉)], Yan Liu[1], Bei Jiang[1], Guojun Dai[1], and Lin Xu[2]

[1] Key Laboratory of Complex Systems Modeling and Simulation
of Ministry of Education, Hangzhou Dianzi University, Hangzhou, China
kongwanzeng@hdu.edu.cn
[2] School of Humanities and Law, Hangzhou Dianzi University,
Hangzhou, China
xl@hdu.edu.cn

**Abstract.** Electroencephalography (EEG) signal processing is one of the critical parts in Brain-Computer Interface (BCI) applications. In this paper, we propose a hypothesis that EEG signal is composed by spontaneous background signals and mental task signals. Then, we introduce a new EEG signal processing method based on low rank and sparse decomposition. EEG signals can be decomposed as the sum of a low-rank signal matrix and a sparse signal matrix. BCI competition dataset of motor imagery is applied to compare the accuracy of the sparse EEG signal and the original EEG signal. The results show that the sparse part outperforms original data and the accuracy is improved by 3% to 5%.

**Keywords:** EEG · Signal processing · Motor imagery · Low-rank and sparse decomposition

## 1 Introduction

Electroencephalograms (EEG) record rich cortex information related to nervous system produced by the brain. The analysis of EEG is the main basis for Brain Computer Interface (BCI) applications. The EEG signal usually has very low amplitude and strong background noises. It is difficult to extract useful information from it. Therefore, signal processing for EEG is a great item which is valuable in research.

With the development of signal processing technology, more and more methods are applied in EEG processing. Most methods were proposed by analyzing the signal from the view of source. They are constrained to produce uncorrelated components and find linear transformations of the original data. Two appealing representatives are Independent Component Analysis (ICA) [1] and Canonical Correlation Analysis (CCA) [2]. ICA is a feature extraction method that can blindly separate the mixed source signal into statistical independent components. ICA seeks to perform a linear transform, and this linear transform can make the resulting variables as statistically independent from each other as possible. CCA is a multivariate statistical analysis method that seeks to identify and quantify the related linear relationships between two variables. All

© Springer Nature Singapore Pte Ltd. 2017
F. Sun et al. (Eds.): ICCSIP 2016, CCIS 710, pp. 556–564, 2017.
DOI: 10.1007/978-981-10-5230-9_54

methods mentioned above are applied as a Blind Source Separation (BSS) technique [3]. The BSS focuses on extracting the underlying information from a set of source signal linear mixtures.

Numerous studies have now shown that neural system has a fundamental property which is the presence of ongoing spontaneous variability [4–9]. This variability is usually considered to be noisy and ignored. A research indicates that brain has a normal level of "background noise" which is an electrical activity patterns fluctuate across the brain, and decisions could be predicted before it was made [10]. Based on these works, we hypothesized that EEG signal is superposed by a background signal and a mental tasks signal.

Here, we introduce a new method for EEG signal processing based on low-rank and sparse matrix decomposition. Different from the traditional methods, this method analyses the information from the part of the signal. It uses low-rank and sparse decomposition to process the EEG signal, and the EEG signal can be divided into a low-rank matrix and a sparse matrix. We propose a model based on reasonable experimental assumption that EEG signal is superposed by a spontaneous background signal and a mental tasks signal. To do so, we assess the utility of this method on BCI competition datasets.

## 2 Low-Rank and Sparse Decomposition

### 2.1 Low-Rank and Sparse Matrix Decomposition Model

Low-rank and sparse matrix decomposition was also known as low-rank matrix recovery, robust principle component analysis (RPCA) [11], rank-sparsity incoherence [12] and so on. It aims to increase the performance of PCA in the presence of outliers. Low-rank and sparse decomposition assumes to decompose a data matrix $X$ into $L + S$, where $L$ is a basis matrix of low-rank and $S$ is the associated sparse error. It seeks to recover the matrices $L$ and $S$ by solving the following convex optimization problem [11, 12]:

$$\min_{L,S} \|L\|_* + \lambda \|S\|_1 \quad s.t. X = L + S \tag{1}$$

In (1), the nuclear norm $\|L\|_*$ is the sum of the singular values in matrix $L$, and the $\ell_1$-norm $\|S\|_1$ is the sum of the absolute values of entries in $S$. This convex optimization problem is called Principal Component Pursuit (PCP). To solve the problem of (1), some popular algorithms have been applied such as inexact augmented Lagrange multipliers (ALM) [13], accelerated projected gradient method [14] and so on.

Full SVD as a costly subroutine is repeatedly used in solving the above problem. In real world applications this model does not always exist for the data observations which are often corrupted by noise. Therefore, a more adaptive model is proposed.

$$X = L + S + G \tag{2}$$

Where $L + S$ approximates $X$ and $G$ is the noise. Such model has attracted increasing attention including stable PCP [15], GoDec [16] and DRMF [17].

The decomposition problem stated in (2) can be solved by minimizing the loss function [16] :

$$\min_{L,S} \|X - L - S\|_F^2$$
$$s.t. \ rank(L) \leq r, \tag{3}$$
$$card(S) \leq k.$$

where $r$ is constrained rank of $L$, $k$ is the cardinality of $S$.

## 2.2    EEG Signal Decomposition

We assume that EEG signal is superposed by spontaneous background signals and mental task signals (Fig. 1). The inherent background signal is relatively steady signals, and the mental tasks signal is generated by corresponding cortical neurons in certain missions. Under real-world conditions, the collected EEG is sums of above both and the noise.

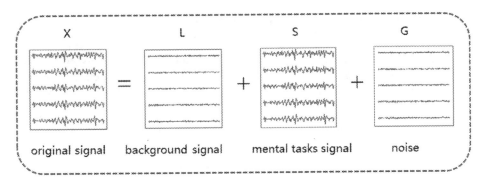

**Fig. 1.**  The hypothesis of EEG signal decomposition.

In order to separate out the signals, we apply GoDec algorithm [16] to extract inherent background signal and mental tasks signal from EEG. Then we use those parts for motor imagery experiment.

For a section of continuous pretreatment EEG signal, we stack each trial as a column of original data matrix $X$. Based on (3), we decompose the signal $X$ into a low-rank part $L$ and a sparse part $S$.

The problem of (3) can be solved by solving the following two subproblems until convergence:

$$\begin{cases} L_t = \arg\min_{rank(L) \le r} \|X - L - S_{t-1}\|_F^2 \\ S_t = \arg\min_{card(S) \le k} \|X - L_t - S\|_F^2 \end{cases} \tag{4}$$

A dense matrix X's bilateral random projections [18] with closed form $Y_1$ and $Y_2$ is used to obtain the low-rank approximation of $X$ with rank $r$.

$$Y_1 = XA_1, \quad Y_2 = X^T Y_1 \tag{5}$$

Where $A_1$ is a $n \times r$ random matrix. Then we calculate the QR decomposition of $Y_2$.

$$Y_2 = Q_2 R_2 \tag{6}$$

For a matrix $X = L + S + G$, the low-rank part $L$ is built as $L = AB$, wherein both $A$ and $B$ are $n \times r$ standard Gaussian matrices. Algorithm 1 summarize the procedure of low-rank and sparse decomposition for EEG.

---

**Algorithm 1** Low-Rank and Sparse Decomposition [16]

---

**Input:** EEG signal matrix $X$, rank $r$, card $k$, tolerance $\varepsilon$
**Initialize:** $L_0 := X$, $S_0 := 0$, $t := 0$
**while** $\|X - L_t - S_t\|_F^2 / \|X\|_F^2 > \varepsilon$ **do**
   $t := t + 1$;
   $\tilde{L} = X - S_{t-1}$;
   $Y_1 = \tilde{L}A_1$, $Y_2 = \tilde{L}^T Y_1 = Q_2 R_2$;
   $L_t = (\tilde{L}Q_2)Q_2^T$
   $S_t = P_\Omega(X - L_t)$, $\Omega$ is an nonzero subset of the first $k$ largest entries of $|X - L_t|$;
**end while**
**Output:** low-rank matrix $L$, sparse matrix $S$

---

The value of $k$ is constrained the sparsity of part $S$, and it is hard to determine. $\hat{k}$ is the proportion of element number in matrix $X$. $\hat{k}$ is used to replace the value of $k$.

## 3 Experiment

### 3.1 EEG Datasets

We innovatively apply low-rank and sparse decomposition method to decompose the EEG signal into background signal and the mental task signals. In order to assess and compare the different part presented here, we used motor imagery EEG data of 9 subjects, from 2 public datasets of BCI competitions. They are described as follows.

1. Dataset 1 comes from BCI competition III Data set IIIa. The cued motor imagery EEG signal was made with 60 electrodes. The EEG was sampled with 250 Hz. It contains EEG signals from 3 subjects with 4 classes (left hand, right hand, foot and tongue). For the purpose of this study, only EEG signals corresponding to left and right hand were used.

2. Dataset 2 is derived from BCI competition III Data set IVa: This data set was recorded from 5 healthy subjects, who performed right hand and foot motor imagery. The signals were recorded using 118 electrodes at a sampling rate of 100 Hz. For each subject there are 280 trials and the time positions of the 280 cues are also provided.

### 3.2   Data Processing

In this work, for each subject Algorithm 1 is used to decompose training dataset and test dataset into three parts, individually. Matrix $X$ is the original data, part $L$ is the low rank part, and part $S$ is the sparse part. Then the part $S$ are used as new training dataset and new test dataset. Matrix $X$ is used similar feature extraction method and classification method for comparison.

For all the datasets, we used the Common Spatial Patterns (CSP) algorithm to extract features from time segment located from 0.5 s to 2.5 s after the cue [19]. The CSP algorithm is a feature extraction method which can learn spatial filters maximizing the discriminability of two class [20, 21]. Each trial was filtered in 8–30 Hz by a $5^{th}$ order Butterworth band-pass filter [21]. And we used 3 pairs of filters for feature extraction [20]. Then an Linear discriminant analysis (LDA) is used to classify [22].

### 3.3   Results and Summary

Here, we explore the accuracy of sparse part for EEG. As shown in Fig. 2, the image on the left is the accuracy of sparse part $S$ when $\hat{k}$ is fixed as 0.6 and $r$ changes from 1 to 40 on dataset 1. There is decreasing relationship among the rank of data and classification accuracy. The smaller rank, the accuracy is higher. The right one shows the accuracy when $r$ is fixed as 1 and $\hat{k}$ changes from 0.1 to 1. From Fig. 2 (b), we can conclude that there is a good result when $\hat{k}$ between 0.6 and 1.

For each subject of dataset 1, Table 1 reports the average classification accuracies of 10 times obtained on the test sets. As shown in Table 1, the result of part $S$ is better than original data $X$ for subject 1. For subject 2, when $r = 3$, $\hat{k} = 0.8$ the algorithm gives the best result of part $S$. For the third subject, we can found when $r = 3$, $\hat{k} = 1$, part $S$ produces the best result. And when $1 \leq r \leq 5$, $\hat{k} = 1$, the result of $S$ is also better than $X$.

Dataset 2 is repeated for 10 times to get the average accuracies. The classification results of original data $X$ and sparse part $S$ in the proposed method are given in Table 2. We can find the result of part $S$ is generally better than $X$.

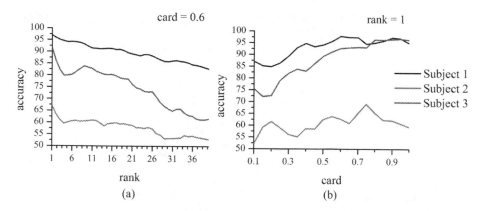

**Fig. 2.** The result of sparse part $S$ dataset 1. (a) The accuracy of $S$ when $\hat{k} = 0.6, 1 \leq r \leq 40$. (b) The accuracy of $S$ when $0.1 \leq \hat{k} \leq 1, r = 1$.

**Table 1.** Average accuracies of dataset 1

| Subject | Rank ($r$) | Card ($\hat{k}$) | X | S |
|---------|------------|------------------|-------|-------|
| 1 | 1 | 0.6 | 95.56 | 97.11 |
| | 2 | 0.8 | 95.56 | 96.89 |
| | 3 | 0.8 | 95.56 | 96 |
| 2 | 1 | 0.6 | 61.67 | 65 |
| | 2 | 0.9 | 61.67 | 63.67 |
| | 3 | 0.8 | 61.67 | 66.83 |
| 3 | 1 | 0.9 | 93.33 | 95.33 |
| | 2 | 0.9 | 93.33 | 95.5 |
| | 3 | 1 | 93.33 | 95.83 |

Figure 3 shows the topography of the first and the last eigenvector of CSP filters obtained from different parts for subject 1 on dataset 1. The part $S$ is generally smoother and physiologically more relevant than original data $X$. And part $L$ is almost irrelevant with motor imagery tasks.

Overall, we use the algorithm to decompose the original EEG signal into low rank part $L$, sparse part $S$ and noise $G$. Then we compare the classification result of $S$ and $X$ based on the same method. We can found that part $S$ has better accuracies than X when there is appropriate value of rank and cardinality. The results of the experiment confirmed that sparse part of EEG data contains important information of motor imagery. In other word, part $S$ contains the mental task signal of subject. Furthermore, the experiment result shows the accuracy of part $L$ is correct about 50%, which means that part $L$ is classified as random. Thus, we infer the low-rank part is the background signal of brain. This confirms the predictions of our hypothesis.

**Table 2.** Average accuracies of dataset 2

| Subject | Rank ($r$) | Card ($\hat{k}$) | $X$ | $S$ |
|---|---|---|---|---|
| 1 | 1 | 0.6 | 66.07 | 71.34 |
|   | 2 | 0.6 | 66.07 | 72.32 |
|   | 3 | 0.7 | 66.07 | 70.18 |
| 2 | 1 | 0.6 | 96.43 | 97.5 |
|   | 2 | 0.9 | 96.43 | 96.43 |
|   | 3 | 0.9 | 96.43 | 96.6 |
| 3 | 1 | 0.8 | 47.45 | 48.72 |
|   | 2 | 1 | 47.45 | 50.92 |
|   | 3 | 0.9 | 47.45 | 50.41 |
| 4 | 1 | 0.8 | 71.88 | 71.16 |
|   | 2 | 1 | 71.88 | 71.47 |
|   | 3 | 1 | 71.88 | 75.36 |
| 5 | 1 | 0.6 | 49.6 | 51.43 |
|   | 2 | 0.6 | 49.6 | 50.63 |
|   | 3 | 0.7 | 49.6 | 53.53 |

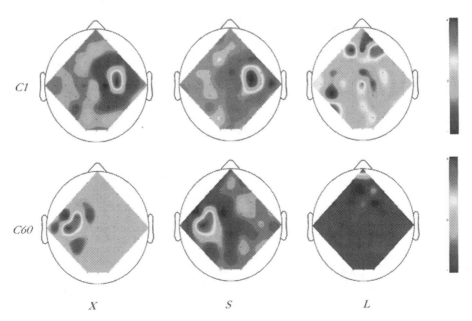

**Fig. 3.** Electrode weights for corresponding filters obtained from different part $(X, S, L)$, for subject 1 on dataset 1.

# 4   Conclusion

In this paper, we introduce a new method for EEG signal processing based on low-rank and sparse matrix decomposition, which decomposes EEG data $X$ into the sum of three matrices: a low-rank matrix $L$ which corresponds to the background signal, a sparse matrix $S$ representing the mental task signal and a noise matrix $G$. Then, we applied each part to classifying the motor imagery tasks.

We explored the rank $r$ of low-rank part $L$ and cardinality $\hat{k}$ of sparse part $S$. The experimental results are shown that part $S$ is better than $X$ to classify the motor imagery tasks when there is appropriate value of rank and cardinality. Thus, we can conclude the sparse part correlate with mental task signals. The pre-defined cardinality and rank were changed, so the results were also changed. When we choose the appropriate $r$ and $\hat{k}$, the good result is obtained.

Overall, low-rank and sparse matrix decomposition method provided a novel point of view and analysis framework for EEG signal processing. But this method still has some limitations. For example, the method has characteristics of randomness. Owing to the algorithm of initialization, using the same $r$ and $k$ after each run may lead to difference result in the application of classification of the motor imagery task signals. Thus, an important direction for future investigation is to develop algorithm that perform more robust, and can find an effective rank and cardinality of EEG easily.

**Acknowledgments.** This work was supported by National Natural Science Foundation of China (Grant No. 6167010376 and 61102028), International Science & Technology Cooperation Program of China (Grant No. 2014DFG12570), Project funded by China Postdoctoral Science Foundation (Grant No.2015M571878), and Zhejiang Provincial Natural Science Foundation of China (Grant No. LQ12G03001).

# References

1. Wang, X., Paliwal, K.K.: Feature extraction and dimensionality reduction algorithms and their applications in vowel recognition. Pattern Recogn. **36**(10), 2429–2439 (2003)
2. De Clercq, W., Vergult, A., Vanrumste, B., Van Paesschen, W., Van Huffel, S.: Canonical correlation analysis applied to remove muscle artifacts from the electroencephalogram. IEEE Trans. Biomed. Eng. **53**(12), 2583–2587 (2006)
3. Friman, O., Borga, M., Lundberg, P., Knutsson, H.: Exploratory fMRI analysis by autocorrelation maximization. NeuroImage **16**(2), 454–464 (2002)
4. Arieli, A., Sterkin, A., Grinvald, A., Aertsen, A.: Dynamics of ongoing activity: explanation of the large variability in evoked cortical responses. Science **273**(5283), 1868–1871 (1996)
5. Cohen, M.R., Maunsell, J.H.: When attention wanders: how uncontrolled fluctuations in attention affect performance. J. Neurosci. **31**(44), 15802–15806 (2011)
6. Goldstein, M.H., King, A.P., West, M.J.: Social interaction shapes babbling: testing parallels between birdsong and speech. Proc. Nat. Acad. Sci. **100**(13), 8030–8035 (2003)

7. Nir, Y., Mukamel, R., Dinstein, I., Privman, E., Harel, M., Fisch, L., Gelbard-Sagiv, H., Kipervasser, S., Andelman, F., Neufeld, M.Y.: Interhemispheric correlations of slow spontaneous neuronal fluctuations revealed in human sensory cortex. Nat. Neurosci. **11**(9), 1100–1108 (2008)

8. Romei, V., Brodbeck, V., Michel, C., Amedi, A., Pascual-Leone, A., Thut, G.: Spontaneous fluctuations in posterior α-band EEG activity reflect variability in excitability of human visual areas. Cereb. Cortex **18**(9), 2010–2018 (2008)

9. Tsodyks, M., Kenet, T., Grinvald, A., Arieli, A.: Linking spontaneous activity of single cortical neurons and the underlying functional architecture. Science **286**(5446), 1943–1946 (1999)

10. Bengson, J.J., Kelley, T.A., Zhang, X., Wang, J.-L., Mangun, G.R.: Spontaneous neural fluctuations predict decisions to attend. J. Cogn. Neurosci. **26**, 2578–2584 (2014)

11. Candès, E.J., Li, X., Ma, Y., Wright, J.: Robust principal component analysis? J. ACM (JACM) **58**(3), 11 (2011)

12. Chandrasekaran, V., Sanghavi, S., Parrilo, P.A., Willsky, A.S.: Rank-sparsity incoherence for matrix decomposition. SIAM J. Optim. **21**(2), 572–596 (2011)

13. Lin, Z., Chen, M., Ma, Y.: The augmented lagrange multiplier method for exact recovery of corrupted low-rank matrices, UIUC Technical report UILU-ENG-09-2214 (2010)

14. Chen, J., Liu, J., Ye, J.: Learning incoherent sparse and low-rank patterns from multiple tasks. ACM Trans. Knowl. Discov. Data (TKDD) **5**(4), 22 (2012)

15. Zhou, Z., Li, X., Wright, J., Candes, E., Ma, Y.: Stable principal component pursuit. In: 2010 IEEE International Symposium on Information Theory Proceedings (ISIT), pp. 1518–1522. IEEE (2010)

16. Zhou, T., Tao, D.: Godec: randomized low-rank & sparse matrix decomposition in noisy case. In: International Conference on Machine Learning, vol. 3, p. 2 (2011)

17. Xiong, L., Chen, X., Schneider, J.: Direct robust matrix factorizatoin for anomaly detection. In: 2011 IEEE 11th International Conference on Data Mining (ICDM), pp. 844–853. IEEE (2011)

18. Zhou, T., Tao, D.: Bilateral random projections. In: 2012 IEEE International Symposium on Information Theory Proceedings (ISIT), pp. 1286–1290. IEEE (2012)

19. Lotte, F., Guan, C.: Regularizing common spatial patterns to improve BCI designs: unified theory and new algorithms. IEEE Trans. Biomed. Eng. **58**(2), 355–362 (2011)

20. Blankertz, B., Tomioka, R., Lemm, S., Kawanabe, M., Muller, K.-R.: Optimizing spatial filters for robust EEG single-trial analysis. IEEE Sig. Process. Mag. **25**(1), 41–56 (2008)

21. Ramoser, H., Muller-Gerking, J., Pfurtscheller, G.: Optimal spatial filtering of single trial EEG during imagined hand movement. IEEE Trans. Rehabil. Eng. **8**(4), 441–446 (2000)

22. Lotte, F., Congedo, M., Lécuyer, A., Lamarche, F., Arnaldi, B.: A review of classification algorithms for EEG-based brain–computer interfaces. J. Neural Eng. **4**(2), R1 (2007)

# The Neural Activation in Fusiform Face Area for Object Perception in Wide Visual Field

Jiayue Guo[1], Bin Wang[2], Jinglong Wu[1(✉)], Seiichiro Ohno[3],
and Susumu Kanazawa[4]

[1] Graduate School of Natural Science and Technology,
Okayama University, 3-1-1 Tsushima-Naka, Okayama, Japan
wu@mech.okayama-u.ac.jp
[2] College of Computer Science and Technology,
Taiyuan University of Technology, Taiyuan, China
[3] Department of Radiology, Okayama University Hospital,
Okayama University, Okayama, Japan
[4] Graduate School of Medicine, Dentistry, Pharmaceutical Sciences,
Okayama University, Okayama, Japan

**Abstract.** The fusiform face area (FFA) is thought to be preferentially involved in the processing of faces, and its neural responses exhibit category biases to objects presented in the central visual field. Differences neural activities in FFA for objects categories aligning in the central and peripheral visual field were measured. We using a wide-view (about 120°) visual presentation system developed for vision research and functional magnetic resonance imaging (fMRI), the subject were presented with objects, which were presented at a range of viewpoints in 6 level of eccentricity degree. We investigated the BLOD response to stimuli in the FFA. The result suggests face had much bigger neural activation than other objects in the FFA areas and exhibited significant differences in the neural responses to object categories at eccentricity positions of 0° and 11°, but we not find this the neural response character in the peripheral visual field.

**Keywords:** Fusiform Face Area · Object category · fMRI · Wide-view visual field

## 1 Introduction

Functional magnetic resonance imaging (fMRI) has been used for over a decade to study early cortical retinotopic maps in the human brain [1–4]. The visual field is mapped in each area along two orthogonal axes: polar angle and eccentricity [1–4]. In higher areas, visual areas are smaller and receptive fields of neurons are larger [5]. Neurons with large receptive fields are sometimes mistakenly considered unsuitable candidates for encoding spatial location. The parcellation of these areas is difficult because they are largely non-retinotopic and different types of objects activate slightly different regions. The higher visual regions in the human occipitotemporal cortex are involved in the recognition of objects and faces. These regions comprise a large

© Springer Nature Singapore Pte Ltd. 2017
F. Sun et al. (Eds.): ICCSIP 2016, CCIS 710, pp. 565–575, 2017.
DOI: 10.1007/978-981-10-5230-9_55

constellation of areas in both the ventral and dorsal visual pathways that lie anterior and lateral to early retinotopic cortex [6, 7]. These regions contain a variety of response profiles. In the ventral visual cortex, the fusiform face area (FFA) [6, 8] has been shown to respond preferentially to scenes and buildings. And humans have the ability to recognize faces quickly and efficiently over a large proportion of the visual field without needing to make eye movements.

Central-peripheral organization of the face-selective areas is discovered in the human visual cortex. The center/periphery organization, that is, eccentricity mapping, is one of the most striking and robust organizational principles in the primate visual cortex. However, object representations are arranged according to a central versus peripheral visual field bias [9–11]. In the ventral visual cortex, the lateral regions, FFA represent foveal eccentricities and the medial regions. For instance, FFA shows a greater magnitude neural response to lower field images than to upper field images [12–14]. These differences in the FFA, face-selective areas imply uniform processing of face at these different positions. While, there was another hypothesis is uniform processing of objects at different eccentricity, that the decay in activity as eccentricity increasing was same for objects (faces, houses, animals, and cars) in FFA areas.

In previous, much work has been done to characterize the location or category selectivity of FFA region [9–11, 14, 15]. However, these studies main focus the central or pre-central $(0 - 12°)$ field side. No studies to date have systematically tested for eccentricity biases in higher-level category-selective areas within a wide vision field. Therefore, we compared mean response magnitude in FFA for object at wide eccentricities up to $60°$.

In the present study, we used fMRI and a wide-view presentation system [16, 17] to further tested the differences between object category and eccentric effects by performing a series of object experiments in which we presented different object categories (faces, house, animals, cars) at different eccentric positions in a block design. During the MRI scanning, the subject was asked to view stimuli from four object categories (faces, houses, animals, and cars) that were arrayed in rings at six eccentricity levels within a visual field with $60°$ of eccentricity (Fig. 1). The subjects were asked to categorize the images while maintaining fixation. We used functional localizer experiment for identifying face-selective regions of interest, and four scanning sessions for the block-design positions experiment to compare the neural response to object at the six levels of eccentricity. We investigated the neural activation maps and neural response magnitudes to object categories at different eccentricity positions in FFA.

## 2   Experimental Procedures

*Subjects.* Ten subjects participated in the study (11males, 2 females), ages 21–29 years, mean age 24 years. All subjects were right-handed and had normal vision. MR imaging was performed at the hospital of Okayama University. The experiments were undertaken with the written consent of each subject, and approved by the Ethics Committee of Hospital of Okayama University.

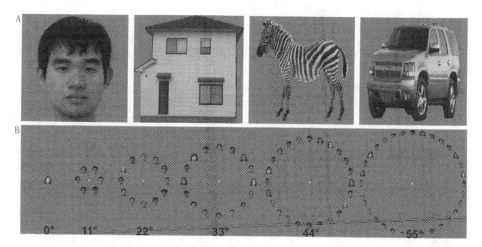

**Fig. 1.** Sample stimulus images used in the experiment. (A) Sample image for each of the four object categories. The image of the face shown here does not depict the actual stimulus and is only intended to be an example. (B) Shows the positions and the size of the presented images.

*Stimuli.* Stimuli were projected on a wide-view visual presentation system [18, 19]. Subjects viewed the stimulus on a sphere of 52 mm. The mean distance between subjects' eyes and the screen was 30 mm. The subjects wore contact lenses to focus on the stimulus, and the visual field of the stimulus was 120° horizontal × 120° vertical.

*Localizer Experiment.* The localizer experiment was used to define the face-selective area (FFA). Each subject participated in one localizer scan to define the selected area for face, house, animal and car. The stimuli were 30 grayscale images of faces, houses, animals, cars and objects respectively. Control nonsense patterns were 30 phase-scrambled images of the intact objects. Each scan began and ended with 12 s of rest and contained 20 stimulus blocks of 10-s duration, five for each category, separated by 10-s intervals of rest. For each block of the localizer scan, 10 images from a stimulus class were presented centrally and subtended 20°. Two or three images in each block were repeated, and subjects were asked to perform a 'one-back' matching task, while fixating on a central fixation presented in the center of each image.

*Position Experiments.* The objects position experiments utilized grayscale images of human faces, houses, animals and cars. Objects were presented at a range of view-points, and gray-grounds (see Fig. 1A). Each experiment utilized 192 unique images from each category. The inside to the outside of concentric ring images with a width 10° of visual angle displayed in each position. The gap of each concentric ring is 1° visual angle. We chose to use a constant image size because the magnification factors in face, house, animal and car selected area were unknown, and the magnifications of central and periphery were quite different. We wanted to compare neural activation for face, house animal and car in different position through central and periphery visual field. Images were presented in equally spaced positions on the display screen, totally six positions. The images were centered at the fixation point (foveal) to centered 60°. (See Fig. 1B).

The object experiment contained 4 runs of a block-design experiment. In each 8-s block different images from one category (face, house, animal and car) were shown at a specific position. Images were shown at a rate of 1 Hz (800 ms per image, with a 200 ms interstimulus interval). Image blocks were interleaved with baseline blocks (grayscale screen with fixation point) lasting 8 s. Each run contained one block for each position and category combination; thus the session contained 24 blocks per run (4 categories × 6 positions). During scanning, subjects were instructed to categorize each image, while maintaining fixation on a red fixation point (which was always present through the experiment, and which a red disk with 1.8° diam). Behavioral responses were collected during scanning using a magnet-compatible button box connected to the stimulus computer.

*Image Acquisition.* Imaging was performed using a 3-Tesla MR scanner (Siemens Allegra, Erlangen, Germany). For the functional series we continuously acquired images with 30 slices using a standard T2 weighted echo-planar imaging (EPI) sequence (TR = 2 s; TE = 35 ms; flip angle = 85°; 6 4 × 6 4 matrices; inplane resolution: 2.3 × 2.3 mm; slice thickness: 2 mm, with gap of 0.3 mm). The slices were manually aligned approximately perpen-dicular to the calcarine sulcus to cover most of occipital, posterior parietal, and posterior temporal cortex. After the function scans, high-resolution sagittal T1-weighted images were acquired using a magnetization prepared rapid gradient echo sequence (MP-RAGE; TR = 1800 ms; TE = 2.3 ms; matrix 256 × 256 × 224; 1 mm isotropic voxel size) to obtain a 3D structural scan.

*The Data Preprocessing.* Anatomical and functional images were analyzed using BrainVoyager QX 2.11 (Brain Innovation, Maastricht, The Netherlands). Anatomical scans were segmented for identification of the white/gray matter boundaries and were then used for cortical surface reconstruction and inflating [20–22]. The functional data were correcting correction, three-dimensional motion correction motion, high-pass temporal filtering (0.01 Hz) before statistical analysis [20]. Spatial Smoothing with a full width half maximum Gaussian kernel of 4 mm were applied for localizer scans and face, building position scans, and no spatial Smoothing retinotopic mapping scans. The functional data were transformed into the conventional Talairach space, yielding a 4D data representation [23].

*General Linear Model.* We applied a general linear model (GLM) to position experiments and localizer experiment data on a voxel-by-voxel basis. This boxcar function was convolved with a double-gamma hemodynamic response function to account for hemodynamic effects [24]. To combine the 6 runs of position experiments for each individual, a second-level analysis was performed using a fixed effects model to estimate BOLD response amplitudes for each stimulus condition with a fixated effects ANOVA. All statistical analyses used the statistical threshold of $p < 0.01$ corrected with the false discovery rate (FDR) and a cluster threshold of 20 mm$^3$. The response maps were rendered on a cortical surface from a high-resolution structural MRI scan of a standard brain based on Talairach coordinates.

*Region of Interest Analysis.* Localizer data were used to identify areas selective for faces in the ventral cortex. Using the contrast threshold of $P < 0.01$ corrected with the FDR and spatial extent of at least 20 contiguous voxels, the face-selective FFA was defined as a region that responded more strongly to faces than houses, common objects and textures [6, 8, 25]. FFA ROIs were defined in the right hemisphere for all of the subjects and in the hemisphere for one of the subjects (See Fig. 2). We extracted the response magnitude of the neural activities to faces in FFA for each position condition. Then, the neural response magnitudes underwent data analysis using SPSS software (version 16.0; SPSS Inc, Chicago, Ill).

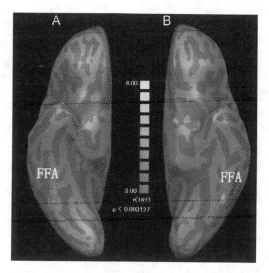

**Fig. 2.** The ventral view of the inflated cortex shows the locations of FFA. The face-selective area is shown by the red-yellow color. (A) Shows the FFA ROIs were defined in the right hemisphere. (B) Shows the FFA ROIs were defined in the left hemisphere (Color figure online).

## 3   Result

*Behaviors result.* The response time and accuracy of the participants' recognition of the stimuli as belonging to one of the four categories at each retinal position are listed in Table 1. The constant (no scaling) image size used in the main experiment made it difficult for the participants to categorize the stimuli when they were presented at the far peripheral positions. At eccentricities of 0–33°, the behavioral performance was good; the subjects could recognize image presented in the peripheral visual field but failed to recognize images at the more extreme peripheral positions (eccentricities of 44° and 55°). Some subjects had no or weak responses to the images of faces and houses when they were presented at the most peripheral positions, which resulted in missed responses. Linear mixed models for repeated measures with factors of eccentricity and category $(6 \times 4)$ were applied. Accuracy was significantly affected by stimulus eccentricity [$F (5, 34) = 61.3$, $p < 0.001$] and category [$F(3,44) = 27.9$, $p < 0.001$]. In addition, there was a significant interaction between category and eccentricity [$F (15, 23) = 7.18$, $p < 0.001$], indicating that the discrimination accuracy for each object category was influenced by eccentricity. For example, the accuracy of face image

**Table 1.** Behavioral results of the position experiment.

| | Category | Eccentricity of stimulus position | | | | | |
|---|---|---|---|---|---|---|---|
| | | 0° | 11° | 22° | 33° | 440 | 55° |
| Accuracy(%) | Face | 0.84 ± 0.05 | 0.96 ± n.02 | 0.95 ± 0.04 | 0.98 ± 0.02 | 0.86 ± 0.04 | 0.77 ± 0.06 |
| | House | 0.86 ± 0.06 | 0.93 ± 0.04 | 0.93 ± 0.04 | 0.64 ± 0.07 | 0.63 ± 0.12 | 0.25 ± 0.08 |
| | Animal | 0.77 ± 0.07 | 0.96 ± 0.02 | 0.84 ± 0.07 | 0.79 ± 0.1 | 0.27 ± 0.07 | 0.14 ± 0.07 |
| | Car | 0.79 ± 0.08 | 0.95 ± 0.03 | 0.96 ± 0.02 | 0.82 ± 0.04 | 0.50 ± 0.09 | 0.16 ± 0.1 |
| Reaction Time(ms) | Face | 684 ± 21 | 621 ± 28 | 586 ± 43 | 580 ± 43 | 673 ± 38 | 669 ± 41 |
| | House | 725 ± 43 | 645 ± 39 | 644 ± 15 | 715 ± 37 | 709 ± 48 | 701 ± 35 |
| | Animal | 724 ± 44 | 643 ± 26 | 622 ± 41 | 643 ± 35 | 680 ± 58 | 785 ± 25 |
| | Car | 762 ± 29 | 615 ± 33 | 595 ± 46 | 651 ± 45 | 683 ± 49 | 777 ± 60 |

*Note: the values are shown as the mean ± SEM.*

recognition was substantially higher than that for the other image categories at the far peripheral positions (eccentricity of 33–55°), although at an eccentricity of 33°, the accuracy of discriminating houses was less than that for faces and cars. The response time was significantly affected by stimulus eccentricity [$F(5,15) = 2.6$, $p = 0.01$], whereas there was no main effect of category [$F(3,29) = 2.5$, $p = 0.08$]. A pairwise comparison showed that for animal images, response times were shorter for stimuli presented at an eccentricity of 22° than for an eccentricity of 0°.

*The location of FFA.* The localizer data were used to identify bilateral extrastriate regions selective for faces, houses, cars animals and objects. Subjects displayed high levels of accuracy (approximately 90%) during the 'one-back' task. The face-selective area (FFA) was identified with a region that responds more strongly to faces compared to textures [8, 9, 26] (Fig. 2). All areas were defined by using an uncorrected contrast threshold of $P < 0.005$.

*Neural Activities to Face in Wide Fields.* The neural responses in the FFA showed a significant main effect of eccentricity [$F(5, 83) = 158.19$, $p < 0.001$] and a significant interaction between eccentricity and category [$F(15, 53) = 4.34$, $p < 0.001$] (Fig. 3). Pairwise comparisons revealed that significant differences between object categories were mainly found at eccentricities of 0°and 22 ($p < 0.05$). In particular, the neural responses to face images were larger than those to other objects image at eccentricity of 0°and 11°. However, the different neural responses to objects images were not find after 22° eccentricity.

*Activation Maps of Eccentric Object in Ventral Face-selective Area.* We identified the activation maps in ventral face-selective area (FFA) at six levels of eccentricities via comparison with the fixation baseline. Figure 4 shows the mean activation maps from all subjects. The fusiform face area (FFA) had intense neural activities across the 6 levels of eccentricity. The neural activation maps across the eccentricity levels had similar neural activation maps among each object category (face, house, animal and car). As predicted, the neural activities demonstrated eccentricity effects. The neural activations were intense in the central visual field and monotonically decreased with an increase in the eccentricity level. Moreover, among the 6 levels of eccentricity, the activation maps substantially overlapped. The objects at the central position had the

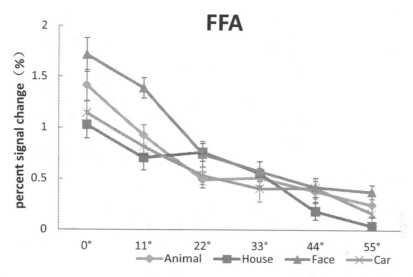

**Fig. 3.** Mean response amplitude to the four categories in FFA. In general, the relationships between eccentricity and the neural responses in FFA differed significantly, demonstrating that this region contain eccentricity information.

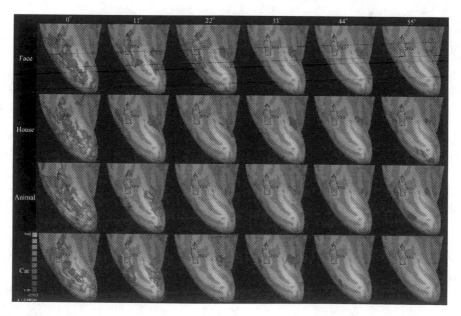

**Fig. 4.** Mean activation maps in the visual cortex. Face (A), house (B), animal (C), and car (D) had the strongest neural activities at the central position and became weaker farther away from the visual center.

strongest neural activities, and the activation maps covered most of the lateral visual cortex, which also included the cortex that showed the peripheral visual field. The peripheral objects had weak neural activities, and the activation maps covered the anterior part of the lateral visual cortex, which mainly showed the peripheral visual field. Though comparisons among the four categories, we identified additional differences in neural activities. At an eccentricity of $0° 11°$, the face image had the strongest neural activities compared with the other objects images (house, animal and car) in the FFA (Fig. 4).

## 4   Discussion

Our study provides a broad-based survey of position information in FFA (See Fig. 2) located in the visual cortex. We measured the mean response amplitudes in positions at 6 level with in a wide field up to $60°$. In this study, we combined of retinotopic mapping and object picture, that allowed us to identify retinotopic property responsive to object in FFA, and those actively used during spatial attention. We well found the neural activities of the object perception of FFA in wide view field.

*Object Discrimination in the Peripheral Visual Field.* Evidence from behavior performance and neural activities indicates the visual system has the ability to discriminate and identify objects with decreasing robustness as the eccentricity increases [15, 27, 28]. The variance in these abilities is thought to be related to the larger receptive field size in the peripheral visual cortex; thus, the visual system represents central stimuli with a fair degree of fidelity, but it more crudely encodes stimuli in the peripheral field. In the present study, using stimuli in a wider field of view, we also demonstrated the object discrimination performances became worse in the more peripheral visual field, especially the positions of $44°$ to $55°$ eccentricities (Table 1). More importantly, in the peripheral visual field, the discrimination accuracies of the object categories were quite different; the face had substantially increased accuracies compared with the other categories at the peripheral position. This increased accuracy is likely to be related to the neural activities in the FFA and the increased ratio relative to response magnitudes in the V1 (RRV1) [29]. The discrimination abilities for peripheral objects exhibit eccentric biases, which provide an advantage in the study of object processing in the visual cortex. In the present study, we investigated the retinotopic representations in the lateral visual cortex using the wide-view stimulus presentation system.

*Different neural processing in eccentricity.* Human vision was divided into central and peripheral vision [30]. Peripheral vision has mostly been characterized in terms of the reductions in resolution or contrast sensitivity as eccentricity increases. The ability of humans to detect movement is better in peripheral vision than in foveal vision, but color discrimination is markedly worse [31, 32]. From the mean response magnitudes in FFA (Fig. 3), the neural activities decreased as the visual stimuli (images of faces, houses, animals and cars) were presented at progressively greater distances from the vision center. These results confirmed the central/peripheral organization in the primate visual cortex.

*Differences in Neural Activities to Objects Category in FFA.* In addition to the eccentric effect, the FFA also exhibits differences between neural activities to objects categories. In the present study, we demonstrated the responses to object category in the FFA were significantly different at the most eccentric position, especially at the eccentricities of 0° and 11° (Fig. 3). In another study [15], only slightly higher responses were identified when driven by animate categories (body parts, animals, and faces) compared with inanimate categories (cars, sculptures, and houses). The different behavior performances in discrimination and memory peripheral object [28] and the response accuracy in the present study also supported our proposing. These found were related to the central representation in face- and peripheral representations in house-selective areas [10, 11]. Thus, we proposed that the FFA exhibited eccentricity biases in processing object category in the center position. The FFA also had a role link between object processing in the lower-level and higher-level visual areas.

The differences between object categories become minimal in the far peripheral field with eccentricities smaller for 22° (Fig. 3). In these far than eccentricities of 22° positions, the ability to discriminate and identify objects became substantially weaker. The neural response to these object categories were also substantially weaker compared with the neural response in the center positions. The absence of a difference in categories may be because of the weak neural response in far peripheral positions.

## 5   Conclusion

In conclusion, we used a wide-view visual presentation system and functional magnetic resonance imaging (fMRI), to measure the neural response in fusiform face areas to the faces, houses, animals and cars in 6 levels of eccentricity degree. We demonstrated these regions had an intensity effect of eccentricity for retinotopic representation and neural response to objects in FFA areas. Moreover, face had much bigger neural activation than other objects in the FFA areas and exhibited significant differences in the neural responses to object categories at eccentricity positions of 0° and 11°. We proposed that the fusiform face areas had eccentricity biases for object processing smaller for the eccentricity position of 22°.

**Acknowledgment.** This work was supported by JAPAN SOCIETY FOR THE PROMOTION OF SCIENCE (JSPS) KAKENHI grant numbers 25249026, 25303013 and 16K18052, a Grant-in-Sid for Strategic Research Promotion from Okayama University. We thank the subjects who participated in this study and the staff of the Okayama University Hospital for their assistance with data collection.

## References

1. Sereno, M.I., et al.: Borders of multiple visual areas in humans revealed by functional magnetic resonance imaging. Science **268**(5212), 889–893 (1995)
2. Rajimehr, R., Tootell, R.B.H.: Does retinotopy influence cortical folding in primate visual cortex? J. Neurosci. **29**(36), 11149–11152 (2009)

3. Wandell, B.A., Dumoulin, S.O., Brewer, A.A.: Visual field maps in human cortex. Neuron **56**(2), 366–383 (2007)
4. Brewer, A.A., et al.: Visual field maps and stimulus selectivity in human ventral occipital cortex. Nat. Neurosci. **8**(8), 1102–1109 (2005)
5. Serences, J.T., Yantis, S.: Spatially selective representations of voluntary and stimulus-driven attentional priority in human occipital, parietal, and frontal cortex. Cereb. Cortex **17**(2), 284–293 (2007)
6. Grill-Spector, K.: The neural basis of object perception. Curr. Opin. Neurobiol. **13**(2), 159–166 (2003)
7. Schwarzlose, R.F., et al.: The distribution of category and location information across object-selective regions in human visual cortex. Proc. Nat. Acad. Sci. **105**(11), 4447–4452 (2008)
8. Kanwisher, N., McDermott, J., Chun, M.M.: The fusiform face area: a module in human extrastriate cortex specialized for face perception. J. Neurosci. **17**(11), 4302–4311 (1997)
9. Kanwisher, N.: Faces and places: of central (and peripheral) interest. Nat. Neurosci. **4**(5), 455–456 (2001)
10. Levy, I., et al.: Center-periphery organization of human object areas. Nat. Neurosci. **4**(5), 533–539 (2001)
11. Hasson, U., et al.: Eccentricity bias as an organizing principle for human high-order object areas. Neuron **34**(3), 479–490 (2002)
12. Stephan, K.E., et al.: Interhemispheric integration of visual processing during task-driven lateralization. J. Neurosci. **27**(13), 3512–3522 (2007)
13. Schwarzlose, R.F., et al.: The distribution of category and location information across object-selective regions in human visual cortex. Proc. Nat. Acad. Sci. USA **105**(11), 4447–4452 (2008)
14. Yue, X.M., et al.: Lower-level stimulus features strongly influence responses in the fusiform face area. Cereb. Cortex **21**(1), 35–47 (2011)
15. Sayres, R., Grill-Spector, K.: Relating retinotopic and object-selective responses in human lateral occipital cortex. J. Neurophysiol. **100**(1), 249–267 (2008)
16. Wu, J.L., et al.: Development of a method to present wide-view visual stimuli in MRI for peripheral visual studies. J. Neurosci. Methods **214**(2), 126–136 (2013)
17. Wang, B., et al.: Visual field maps of the human visual cortex for central and peripheral vision. Neurosci. Biomed. Eng. **1**(2), 102–110 (2013)
18. Wu, J., et al.: Retinotopic mapping of the peripheral visual field to human visual cortex by functional magnetic resonance imaging. Hum. Brain Mapp. **33**, 1727–1740 (2011)
19. Yan, T., et al.: Development of a wide-view visual presentation system for visual retinotopic mapping during functional MRI. J. Magn. Reson. Imaging **33**(2), 441–447 (2011)
20. Goebel, R., Esposito, F., Formisano, E.: Analysis of functional image analysis contest (FIAC) data with brainvoyager QX: from single-subject to cortically aligned group general linear model analysis and self-organizing group independent component analysis. Hum. Brain Mapp. **27**(5), 392–401 (2006)
21. Dale, A.M., Fischl, B., Sereno, M.I.: Cortical surface-based analysis – I. Segmentation and surface reconstruction. Neuroimage **9**(2), 179–194 (1999)
22. Fischl, B., Sereno, M.I., Dale, A.M.: Cortical surface-based analysis - II: inflation, flattening, and a surface-based coordinate system. Neuroimage **9**(2), 195–207 (1999)
23. Talairach, J., Tournoux, P., Musolino, A.: Anatomical stereotaxic studies of the frontal-lobe in the management of the epilepsies. Epilepsia **29**(2), 205 (1988)
24. Friston, K.J., et al.: Event-related fMRI: characterizing differential responses. Neuroimage **7**(1), 30–40 (1998)

25. Grill-Spector, K., Kourtzi, Z., Kanwisher, N.: The lateral occipital complex and its role in object recognition. Vis. Res. **41**(10–11), 1409–1422 (2001)
26. Grill-Spector, K.: The neural basis of object perception. Curr. Opin. Neurobiol. **13**, 159 (2003). **13**(3): 399
27. Yao, J.G., et al.: Field of attention for instantaneous object recognition. PLoS ONE **6**(1), e16343 (2011)
28. Yoo, S.A., Chong, S.C.: Eccentricity biases of object categories are evident in visual working memory. Vis. Cogn. **20**(3), 233–243 (2012)
29. Wang, B., et al.: Regional neural response differences in the determination of faces or houses positioned in a wide visual field. PLoS ONE **8**(8), e72728 (2013)
30. Martin, P.R., et al.: Chromatic sensitivity of ganglion cells in the peripheral primate retina. Nature **410**(6831), 933–936 (2001)
31. Noorlander, C., et al.: Sensitivity to spatiotemporal colour contrast in the peripheral visual field. Vis. Res. **23**(1), 1–11 (1983)
32. Mullen, K.T.: Colour vision as a post-receptoral specialization of the central visual field. Vis. Res. **31**(1), 119–130 (1991)

# Global Optimal Locally Weighted Learning-Based Identification Modeling for Azimuth Stern Drive Tug Manoeuvring

Weiwei Bai[1], Junsheng Ren[1(✉)], Chuan Che[2], Tieshan Li[1], and C.L. Philip Chen[1,3]

[1] Navigation College, Dalian Maritime University, Dalian, China
jsren@dlmu.edu.cn
[2] Second Clinical College, Dalian Medical University, Dalian, China
[3] Faculty of Science and Technology, Computer and Information Science, University of Macau, Macau, China

**Abstract.** This paper presents a black-box modeling approach, locally weighted learning (LWL), for tug handling simulator. Concerned with the problem of parameter drifting and unmodeled dynamics in the conventional mechanism modeling, LWL is proposed for Delta Linda tug to learn the mapping between the input and output directly and employs the empirical regression model instead of the real physical model. Compared with BPNN prediction, the validity and usefulness of the algorithm are illustrated with a 3 degree-of-freedom of Delta Linda tug and LWL is proved to be an accurate manoeuvring modeling tool.

**Keywords:** Locally Weighted Learning (LWL) · Identification modeling · Azimuth stern drive tug · Global optimal

## 1 Introduction

Tug handling simulator, one of the most important training platforms, has been more studied recently [1]. Generally, the quality of tug handling simulator is tightly interrelated with mathematical model.

As is well known, the tug mathematical model is usually on the basis of mechanism modeling. The tug motion function is established on Newtonian law of motion first. Then the hydrodynamic derivatives in the hydrodynamic model are mostly being solved by databases or empirical formulas, captive model tests, theoretical and numerical calculation et al. [2,3]. However, many terms are

J. Ren—This work was supported by the National 863 project, No. 2015AA016404; National Natural Science Foundation of China, No. 51109020, 51179019, 61374114; Basic Research Project of China Transport Department, No. 2014329225370; The Fundamental Research Program for Key Laboratory of the Education Department of Liaoning Province, No. LZ2015006; The Fundamental Research Funds for the Central Universities, No. 3132016310, 3132016311, 3132016313.

© Springer Nature Singapore Pte Ltd. 2017
F. Sun et al. (Eds.): ICCSIP 2016, CCIS 710, pp. 576–583, 2017.
DOI: 10.1007/978-981-10-5230-9_56

neglected in parametric model during the calculation phase, which would result in not only the unmolded dynamic but also the parameter drifting. In addition, on account of the azimuth stern drive tug form which differs with conventional vessel, many databases and empirical formulas are inapplicable. In this study, an applicable approach is proposed to solve these problems.

Locally Weighted Learning (LWL), a classical nonparametric learning method for black-box identification, was firstly proposed by William S. Cleveland in 1979 [4]. As such, it is firmly grounded in the framework of nonparametric learning theory, which has been developed for almost half hundred years by Sethu Vijayakumar [5] and Stefan Schaal [6]. In a nutshell, LWL characterizes properties of fitting enable themselves to fit the highly nonlinear function [7].

## 2    Problem Formulation

### 2.1    Distance

The relevance of the training points and the query point are determined by distance. There are numerous distance functions including Euclidean distance, Mahalanobis distance and so on. In this study, we will adopt the Mahalanobis distance,

$$d(x, q) = \sum_j (x_j - q_j)^2 = (x - q)^{\mathrm{T}}(x - q). \tag{1}$$

where $x$ is the sample, $q$ is the query point, $j$ is the dimensional of the sample point.

### 2.2    Gaussian Kernel

LWL determines the number of regression samples by adjusting the size of the neighborhood. Essentially, it establishes a linear local model for a query point. The parameters of the local model and the size of the neighborhood are determined by kernel function, and Gaussian Kernel is one of the most common used kernel functions.

$$K(d) = \exp(-d^2). \tag{2}$$

LWL usual adjusts the size of the neighborhood by the distance metric. There are two forms of the distance metric. One is the internal form which takes the form of a matrix exists in the distance matrix. Another is the external form $h$, for instance,

$$K(d) = \exp(-(1/2h^2)d^2). \tag{3}$$

where $h$ is distance metric.

## 2.3   Objective Function

In order to train the distance metric, a global objective function can be defined as:

$$J = \sum_{i=1} (\hat{y}_i - y_i)^2. \tag{4}$$

The training stops when the value of objective function reaches the minimum value, and the optimal global distance metric is obtained.

**Table 1.** The test data form the zigzag test

| | |
|---|---|
| Displacement | $710\,\text{m}^3$ |
| Length between perpendicular | $26.36\,\text{m}$ |
| Length overall | $32.9\,\text{m}$ |
| Breadth moulded | $10.36\,\text{m}$ |
| Draught fore/aft | $3.94/4.95\,\text{m}$ |
| Type of thruster | Azimuthing thrusters |
| Shaft power (ahead) total | $21619\,\text{kw}$ |

## 2.4   Mathematical Model of Delta Linda Tug

Delta Linda tug, a typical high power ASD tug, was built by MARCO shipyard in 1999. In this study, the model of Delta Linda tug was established on the basis of MMG model (Mathematical Model Group) which was proposed by Japan Mathematical Model Group [8]. The characters of Delta Linda tug are shown in Table 1. The ASD tug has two azimuthing thrusters, and the maximum rudder angle is $180°$. The body-fixed coordinate origin is supposed at midship, and the ship motion function will be shown as below,

$$\begin{cases} (m + m_x)\dot{u} - (m + m_y)vr = X_\text{H} \\ (m + m_y)\dot{v} + (m + m_x)ur = Y_\text{H} \\ (I_\text{ZZ} + J_\text{ZZ})\dot{r} = N_\text{H} - Y_\text{H}x_\text{G} \end{cases}. \tag{5}$$

where $m$ is the ship's mass; $m_x$, $m_y$ are added mass in the $x$, $y$ direction, respectively; $I_\text{ZZ}$ and $J_\text{ZZ}$ are mass moment of inertia and added mass moment of inertia by body rotating $Z$ axis, respectively; $x_\text{G}$ is the longitudinal coordinate of ship's center of gravity in the body-fixed coordinate system; $u$, $v$, $r$ are the surge speed, sway speed and yaw speed, respectively; $X_\text{H}$, $Y_\text{H}$ are the hydrodynamic force, act on the hull, in the direction of $X$-axis and $Y$-axis direction, respectively; $Z_\text{H}$ is the hydrodynamic moment, act on the hull, rotating $Z$-axis direction.

The tug handling simulator mathematical model of Dalian Maritime University has high accuracy. The mathematical model is introduced from DMI who has a great deal of experience in modeling. However, the study on this physical mathematical model is far from enough, and there is little knowledge about this model working principles and parameters. Additionally, every introduced model needs a license from DMI, and economic burden has significantly increased. Therefore, it is of great significance to know more about this mathematical model by the identification modeling.

## 3 LWL Algorithm

The fitting goal is to obtain the potential relationship between the input and output. In this study, the input states include current rudder angle, ship motion last states and last accelerations, while the output states include the current ship motion states and accelerations. One of methods is to train a global function. However, for highly nonlinearity, it is very difficult to apply. Another method is to find some local models replacing the global model. LWL is a classic local fitting approach. Since the data is always stored in computer, LWL is also called memory based learning method. The key process is to approximate a global function using a piecewise linear model. Calculating the neighborhood and fitting the local model are the two important issues of LWL.

In this section, we focus on calculating the regression parameters $b$ and $b_0$ of local model.

$$y = \boldsymbol{X}^{\mathrm{T}} b + b_0 = \bar{\boldsymbol{X}}^{\mathrm{T}} \beta. \tag{6}$$

where $\bar{\boldsymbol{X}} = [\boldsymbol{X}^{\mathrm{T}}, 1]^{\mathrm{T}}$ is the sample extended metric. Then the regression model is,

$$\hat{y} = \boldsymbol{X}_q^{\mathrm{T}} \beta. \tag{7}$$

At the beginning, the query point subtracts samples and calculates the distance between query point and sample point. Then the sample weight is calculated,

$$w_i = K(d(x_i, q)). \tag{8}$$

The weight function adopts the Eqs. (2) and (4). The weight is positive and less than one, and its magnitude will decrease when the distance between the query point and sample increases. In addition, the weight is also related to the distance metric. A small distance metric is assigned to kernel at the beginning phase. Many samples which are far from query point have been given up by the distance metric, and then a neighborhood around the query point is constructed. The sample input matrix $X$ and output matrix $y$ are multiplied by the relative weight,

$$\begin{cases} z_i = w_i x_i \\ v_i = w_i y_i \end{cases}. \tag{9}$$

$$\begin{cases} \boldsymbol{Z} = \boldsymbol{W} \boldsymbol{X} \\ \boldsymbol{v} = \boldsymbol{W} \boldsymbol{y} \end{cases}. \tag{10}$$

where $\boldsymbol{W} = \mathtt{diag}(w_1, w_2, \cdots, w_j)$. It can be obtained by the least square method.

$$\begin{cases} (\boldsymbol{Z}^\mathrm{T}\boldsymbol{Z})\beta = \boldsymbol{Z}^\mathrm{T}\boldsymbol{v} \\ \beta = (\boldsymbol{Z}^\mathrm{T}\boldsymbol{Z})^{-1}\boldsymbol{Z}^\mathrm{T}\boldsymbol{v} \end{cases}. \tag{11}$$

The prediction of query point is presented as follows,

$$\hat{y}_q = \boldsymbol{q}\beta = \boldsymbol{q}(\boldsymbol{Z}^\mathrm{T}\boldsymbol{Z})^{-1}\boldsymbol{Z}^\mathrm{T}\boldsymbol{v}. \tag{12}$$

where $q$ is the input vector of query point. Usually, the magnitude of ship acceleration is very small, which will cause $(\boldsymbol{Z}^\mathrm{T}\boldsymbol{Z})^{-1}$ singularity. A smaller design parameter metric $\boldsymbol{\Lambda}$ is applied to solve this problem. For this diagonal matrix has smaller eigenvalue, it has little influence on the eigenvalue of $(\boldsymbol{Z}^\mathrm{T}\boldsymbol{Z})^{-1}$.

$$\hat{y}_q = \boldsymbol{q}\beta = \boldsymbol{q}(\boldsymbol{Z}^\mathrm{T}\boldsymbol{Z} + \boldsymbol{\Lambda})^{-1}\boldsymbol{Z}^\mathrm{T}\boldsymbol{v}. \tag{13}$$

Next, it will train the distance metric $h$ based on the prediction residual error,

$$J = \sum_{i=1} (\hat{y}_i - y_i)^2. \tag{14}$$

Distance metric is learned as follows,

$$h(k) = h_{\max} - \mathtt{exp}(\mathtt{log}(((h_{\max} - h_{\min} + 1)/s)k)). \tag{15}$$

where $s$ is a designing parameter. $k$ is the iterative step.

## 4    LWL Modeling for Delta Linda Tug

### 4.1    Experiments Designing

In this paper, the propeller initial rotation is steadily fixed at 258 $\mathtt{rpm}$, and its change does not take into consider. In order to stimulate the characteristics of ship motion adequately, we design a series of training experiments. The first one is figure-of-eight experiment which first plays the rudder to starboard side, when the ship heading turned $360°$, then plays a same magnitude rudder angle to portside, after that, the same rudder is played similar with the first step when ship heading turned $360°$. Finally, the experiment is finished after the ship heading turned $360°$ and the data for $\delta$, $u$, $v$, $r$, $\dot{u}$, $\dot{v}$, $\dot{r}$ are recorded. In consideration of the computation burden, the interval time of 0.5 s is selected for training data and test data. Table 2 depicts the record of experiments.

To further stimulate the tug motion characteristics, we will add the zig-zags test data to the training data set. The record of experiments is shown in Table 3.

The test experiment is made up of $22°$ zigzags test and $13°$ turning test. As shown in Tables 4 and 5.

**Table 2.** The training data from figure 8 test

| Num. | Magnitude of rudder angle | Samples num. |
|------|---------------------------|--------------|
| 1 | 10° | 358 |
| 2 | 15° | 317 |
| 3 | 20° | 276 |
| 4 | 25° | 243 |
| 5 | 30° | 230 |

**Table 3.** The training data from zigzag test

| Num. | Magnitude of rudder angle | Samples Num. |
|------|---------------------------|--------------|
| 6 | 10° | 106 |
| 7 | 15° | 123 |
| 8 | 20° | 130 |
| 9 | 25° | 134 |
| 10 | 30° | 141 |

**Table 4.** The test data from zigzags test

| Num. | Magnitude of rudder angle | Samples num. |
|------|---------------------------|--------------|
| 1 | 22° | 131 |

**Table 5.** The test data from turning test

| Num. | Magnitude of rudder angle | Samples num. |
|------|---------------------------|--------------|
| 2 | 13° | 116 |

## 4.2  Simulation Results of Ship Manoeuvring

In this section, the simulator of Dalian Maritime University is studied. In order to show the superiority of the proposed algorithm, BPNN prediction algorithm would be implemented for comparison. In the several experiments below, sway and yaw speed adopt the same distance metric to weaken computation burden. The parameters of the proposed algorithm are $h_{max} = 100$, $h_{min} = 10$, $\Lambda = \texttt{diag}[0.001 \cdots 0.001]_{2048 \times 2048}$, $s = 30$. 3-layer BPNN is applied in which the number of nodes in the first, second and third layer are 15, 20 and 10, respectively.

Figures 1, 2 and 3 indicate the prediction results of test experiment num. 1 which is 22° zigzag. From the comparison between the identification of the proposed scheme and BPNN algorithm, we can see that the prediction data is

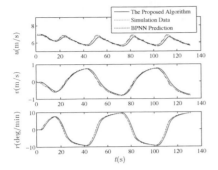

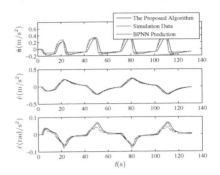

**Fig. 1.** Surge, sway and yaw speed

**Fig. 2.** Surge, sway and yaw acceleration

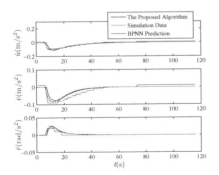

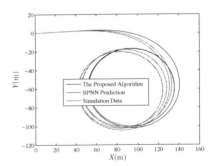

**Fig. 3.** Zigzag manoeuvring result

**Fig. 4.** The trajectory of text experiment num. 2

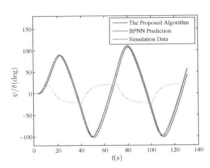

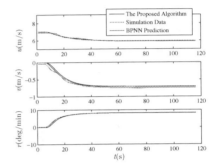

**Fig. 5.** Geometrical relationship

**Fig. 6.** The $F_s$ under ND control

almost similar with the simulation data. Figures 1 and 2 indicate the speed states and acceleration states. Figure 3 shows the zigzag manoeuvring results. All the above comparison indicate the proposed algorithm has a high performance and accuracy.

In the following, Figs. 4, 5 and 6 indicate turning test experiments num. 2. Figures 5 and 6 present the speed and acceleration states. Figure 4 shows the turning test trajectory.

What can be concluded from the above simulation results is that LWL is an effective learning method for modeling of Delta Linda tug maneuvers. The predictions of the training zigzag tests and turning circle tests show great accuracy. The trained LWL has learned the character of tug maneuvers.

## 5   Conclusions

In this paper, an identification modeling of tug maneuvers algorithm is proposed. This approach is based on the training data set in memory and the Leave-One-Out cross validation is applied to train the distance metric in the training phase. Nevertheless, due to the great inertia, and the relationship between input and output is one to many mapping, the ASD tug motion states shows more particular. As is well known, one to many mapping is not a function, and there is the non-separable problem in the ship motion state. Hence, it is not reliable to use common fitting methods. However, LWL can cope with these difficulties by raising the input dimension, and parameter drift and unmolded dynamics are effectively settled simultaneously. According to the simulation results, LWL is proved to be an accurate tug maneuvers modeling tool.

## References

1. Gong, M., Nie, L.X.: Nonlinear modeling and virtual scene simulation of the z-propeller tug. Adv. Mater. Res. **902**, 392–397 (2014)
2. Wang, X., Zou, Z., Hou, X., Xu, F.: System identification modeling of ship manoeuvring motion based on support vector regression. J. Hydrodyn. **27**(4), 502–512 (2015)
3. Sutulo, S., Guedes, S.: An algorithm for offine identification of ship manoeuvring mathematical models from free-running tests. Ocean Eng. **79**, 10–25 (2014)
4. William, S.: Robust locally weighted regression and smoothing scatterplots. J. Am. Stat. Assoc. **74**(368), 829–836 (1979)
5. Sethu, V., Stefan, S.: Local dimensionality reduction for locally weighted learning. In: IEEE International Symposium on Computational Intelligence in Robotics and Automation, pp. 220–225. IEEE Press, New York (1997)
6. Stefan, S., Christopher, G.: Robot juggling: an implementation of memory-based learning. Control Syst. Mag. **14**(1), 57–71 (1994)
7. Ma, J., Jonathan, C., Frank, C.: Robust locally weighted regression for superresolution enhancement of multi-angle remote sensing imagery. IEEE J. Sel. Topics Appl. Earth Obs. Remote Sens. **7**(4), 1357–1371 (2014)
8. Nakato, M., Kose, K., Saeki, T.: Experimental study on accelerating and decelerating ship motions on manoeuvrability. J. Soc. Naval Archit. Japan **144**, 50–56 (1978)

# A Spiking Neural Network Model
# for Sound Recognition

Rong Xiao[1], Rui Yan[1], Huajin Tang[1(✉)], and Kay Chen Tan[2]

[1] Neuromorphic Computing Research Center, College of Computer Science,
Sichuan University, Chengdu, China
rxiao@stu.scu.edu.cn, {ryan,htang}@scu.edu.cn
[2] Department of Computer Science, City University of Hong Kong,
Kowloon Tong, Hong Kong
kaytan@cityu.edu.hk

**Abstract.** This paper presents a spiking neural network (SNN) model
of leaky integrate-and-fire (LIF) neurons for sound recognition, which
provides a way to simulate the brain processes. Neural coding and learning by processing external stimulus and recognizing different patterns
are important parts in SNN model. Based on features extracted from
the time-frequency representation of sound, we present a time-frequency
encoding method which can retain the adequate information of original sound and generate spikes from represented features. The generated
spikes are further used to train the SNN model with plausible supervised
synaptic learning rule to efficiently perform various classification tasks.
By testing the encoding and learning methods in RWCP database, experiments demonstrate that the proposed SNN model can achieve the robust
performance for sound recognition across a variety of noise conditions.

**Keywords:** Temporal coding · Temporal learning · Time-frequency
information · Spiking neural network · Sound recognition

## 1 Introduction

For decades, neuroscientists have been trying to understand how human brains
work. In the meantime, neural network models have been designed by engineers
to mimic our brains and solve practical problems. Among them, spiking neural
network as the third generation of neural network is considered to have greater
computational power and more biological realism [1–4] by incorporating spikes
into the computation model. Although how information is represented in the
brain still remains unclear, there are strong reasons to believe that pulses are
the optimal way of encoding information for transmission. Experimental observations show that the spike makes sense in visual [5], auditory [6], olfactory
[7] pathways and hippocampus [8] in different neuronal systems [9]. In recent

This work was supported by the National Natural Science Foundation of China under
grant number 61673283.

F. Sun et al. (Eds.): ICCSIP 2016, CCIS 710, pp. 584–594, 2017.
DOI: 10.1007/978-981-10-5230-9_57

years, some spiking neuron models have been proposed, such as the Hodgkin-Huxley-type model [10], the Izhikevich model [11], the leaky integrateand-fire (LIF) model, and the spike response model (SRM) model [12]. Meanwhile, various novel encoding methods have been proposed for converting the external stimulus information into the corresponding spiking trains, including the rate coding [13], temporal coding [14,15] and population coding scheme [16,17].

Training an SNN is a non-trivial task. Various learning rules based on spike times have been proposed. In neuroscience, Spike-timing-dependent plasticity (STDP) is found as an unsupervised learning rule [18], which can adjust the efficacy of synapses connections based on the relative timing of pre- and postsynaptic spikes. Researchers have come up with different temporal learning rules according to STDP mechanism, like the Tempotron [19], ReSuMe [20] and PSD rule [21]. SNN has achieved promising performance in various pattern recognition problems [22–25]. A recent study has further demonstrated the computational power of spiking neurons over perceptrons for processing spatiotemporal patterns, and illustrated their computational benefits to process both visual and auditory sensory signals [26]. These methods are mainly focused on the image related tasks, however, it is under explored about the application in the field of sound recognition. Sound recognition in noisy environments is a challenging problem in the field of audio processing [27]. Previous works on acoustic event classification mostly followed speech recognition approaches, which investigated acoustic characteristics (such as Discrete Wavelet Transform (DWT), Perceptual Linear Prediction (PLP) and the Mel-Frequency Cepstral Coefficients (MFCCs)) by using Self-organising maps (SOM), vector quantization (VQ), hidden Markov models (HMM) and other classification techniques [28,29]. Research found that the techniques traditionally can not get good results for environmental sound recognition [30,31]. The reason for this is that they are less biologically plausible compared to the spiking-time-involved rules, which motivates us to investigate computational models for rapid and robust pattern recognition from a biological point of view. Inspired by biological findings, researchers have come up with different theories of encoding and learning. For example, Gammatone wavelet filterbanks have been explored for feature extraction process in [32], which achieved a good recognition performance at low signal-to-noise ratio (SNR). Dennis et al. [33] developed a spiking neural network model with temporal learning for robust sound classification and achieved relatively high correct classification rate.

Inspired by the work [33], we propose a novel feed-forward spiking neural network approach for sound recognition with temporal learning rule. The classification system includes two parts: robust acoustic feature extraction and recognition with SNN. Since the local time-frequency information contributes greatly to human auditory, we convert the representative sound characteristic (local time-frequency information) into a spiking train by a simple mapping rather than the SOM. Then these temporal patterns are learnt via the SNN using temporal learning rules for recognition. As a result, our method is able to outperform the LSF-SNN method. Compared with conventional audio processing methods, our method by utilizing SNN for biologically inspire to deal with the sound pattern recognition also demonstrates the robustness.

## 2    A Spiking Neural Network Model

Human ears can extract useful sound information in a complex environment so that we can recognize it in real world. Thus, the first step in almost all auditory patter recognition tasks is to extract more representative features, such as the MFCCs. However, the way does not effectively simulate the form of our brain that use the analog data as input to recognize the sound. In SNN, the data is transformed to spike trains for further computation by encoding neurons, where the proper encoding methods are needed to generate spatiotemporal spike patterns. Once the spike is obtained, we can use the learning algorithm to train the feed-forward spiking neural network, so as to correctly recognise the types of sound.

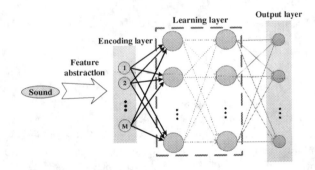

**Fig. 1.** A schematic of the feedforward computational model for pattern recognition. The feature extracted from the sound file is converted into spatiotemporal spikes by the encoding neurons. This spiking pattern is passed to the next layer for learning. The final decision is represented by the output neurons.

In this paper, the whole framework of the proposed feedforward spiking neural network contains three functional parts: feature abstracting and encoding layer, learning layer and output layer (see Fig. 1), each part performs different functional roles. Since sound signals have more distinctive time-frequency characteristics unlike speech signal, we utilize temporal coding scheme to generate spatiotemporal spikes based on the time-frequency information. Then the Tempotron rule [19] is used to train the system. In the learning layer, the precise spike timings are computed. When the membrane potential exceeds a constant threshold, it can generate spikes. After training, the recognition memory is stored by the synaptic weights, which could be modified based on the relative timing difference between pre- and postsynaptic spikes. After the learning procedure, the learning neurons send spikes to the output neurons. The input pattern will be considered as the class associated with the firing neurons. In this paper, the input pattern will be labeled by the neuron that produces the closest spike train to the desired spike train. Below is the details of the first two layers used in the proposed spiking neural network.

## 2.1 Feature Extracting and Temporal Coding

External stimuli can be encoded by spatio-temporal spikes in the brain. In [33], the authors utilized the Best Matching Unit (BMU) of SOM to generate the temporal coding. In our system, we propose a temporal coding model based on the actual time-frequency information. Figure 2 provides a general structure for sounds recognition with the process of feature extraction and temporal coding.

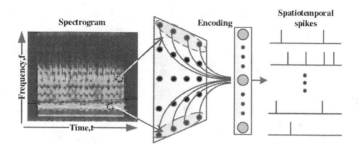

**Fig. 2.** Architecture of the encoding model. A spectrogram (as the stimuli) is presented to the encoding layer. The time-frequency information is obtained based on the keypoints. Each time information would fire a spike. These spikes are transmitted to the next layer as the spatiotemporal pattern.

Firstly, the sound is converted from its original domain to a representation in the frequency domain by Fast Fourier Transform (FFT) over several windows. Then, an one-dimensional order filter is used in the feature extracting phase with selecting the local maximum value as keypoint, $K_i = [f_i, t_i, s_i]$. This is applied to get a series of index numbers separately across time $(t_i)$ and frequency $(f_i)$, and $s_i = s(f_i, t_i)$ is the spectral value at the keypoint. We utilize the difference between the spectral value $(s_i)$ and the mean of the patch $(u_i)$ [33] for further making noise source separation. The patch of dimension $p \times p$ from the two-dimensional region surrounding each keypoint, where $p = 5$. We represent the patch information as follows:

$$patch(i) = [s_i(t + p, f), ...s_i(t, f + p)] \tag{1}$$

Since some keypoints do not represent the sparse signal information, which belong to background. We define a discriminant:

$$C = s_i - u(i), \ for \ u(i) = mean(patch(i)) \tag{2}$$

$C$ is the difference, and we take the threshold to 4 dB. When the difference exceeds the constant threshold, the time-frequency information of keypoint is reserved as a representation of sparse signal information.

In this paper, temporal coding scheme is used to generate spatiotemporal spikes based the actual time-frequency information. This is because that temporal coding scheme can offer significant computational advantages based on the precise timing spikes. We generate the spike pattern, $P_f(t_i)$, over all the keypoints reserved in the spectrogram, which can be defined as follows:

$$P_f(t_i) = \begin{cases} 1, for\ C > 4 \\ 0, otherwise. \end{cases} \tag{3}$$

As a result, the time which belongs to the same frequency point will be grouped into a single neuron. Thus, it can be seen that a neuron generates a plurality of pulses in response to the external stimuli. These spatiotemporal spikes are transmitted to the next layer for computation.

## 2.2   Temporal Learning Rule

In [19], the Tempotron rule can optimize the synaptic weights through minimization of potential difference between the firing threshold and the actual membrane voltage. And it has only two output results: firing or not firing. The firing state is used to respond to a class $(P^+)$, while no firing state is presented with a pattern corresponding to another class $(P^-)$. According to the LIF model, the postsynaptic neurons receive spikes from different presynaptic neurons, which produced different levels of stimulation or inhibition by different synaptic weights. The membrane potential of the neuron is the weighted sum of all the inputs:

$$V(t) = \sum_i w_i \sum_{t_i} K(t - t_i) + V_{rest} \tag{4}$$

where $w_i$ and $t_i$ are the synaptic efficacy and the firing time of the $i^{th}$ afferent. $V_{rest}$ is the rest potential of the neuron. $K(t - t_i)$ denotes the normalized PSP kernel: $K(t - t_i) = V_0(\exp[-(t - t_i)/\tau_m] - \exp[-(t - t_i)/\tau_s])$, where $\tau_m$ and $\tau_s$ denote decay time constants of membrane integration and synaptic currents. $V_0$ normalizes PSP so that the maximum value of the kernel is 1. And $K(t - t_i)$ is a causal filter that only considers spikes $t_i \leq t$. when the membrane potential $V(t)$ crosses the firing threshold, the neuron emits a spike, after which the potential is reset to $V_{rest}$.

The Tempotron rule will modify the synaptic weights $(w_i)$ whenever an error is present, which applies the gradient descent method to minimize the cost. The learning rule is as follows:

$$\Delta w_i = \lambda \sum_{t_i < t_{max}} K(t_{max} - t_i) \tag{5}$$

where $t_{max}$ denotes the time at which the neuron reaches its maximum potential value in the time domain. $\lambda$ is a constant representing the learning rate. It denotes the maximum change on the synaptic efficacy. In this learning rule, if on output spike is elicited on a $P^+$ pattern, each synaptic efficacy is increased $(\lambda > 0)$. If the neuron erroneously fired a spike on a $P^-$ pattern, each synaptic efficacy is decreased $(\lambda < 0)$.

# 3    Simulation Results

## 3.1    Sound Database

This experiment is conducted using RWCP (Real World Computing Partnership) Sound Scene Database. The database is available from [34]. We evaluate the proposed sound classification method using the database, and select the following ten sound classes: horn, bells5, bottle1, buzzer, cymbals, kara, metal15, phone4, whistle1 and whistle3, in which sound files are recorded at 16 kHz sampling rate with low SNR and sparse frequency spectrum. To evaluate the robustness of the method, the following noises are added: "Speech Babble", "Destroyer Control Room", "Factory Floor 2" and "Volvo" extracted from the NOISEX92 database. In addition, we extract all features from 10 classes of sounds corrupted with 20 to 0 dB SNR. For each of the experiment, the classification accuracy is investigated in mismatched conditions using only clean samples, noise free, for training.

## 3.2    Sound Encoding

The encoding focuses on converting sounds into particular form of spikes patterns by the encoding neurons. A good encoding method should retain adequate information of the original sounds, so as to facilitate the later learning process. In this section, we encode information into spike trains based on time, frequency and time-frequency characteristics to explore one of the most suitable encoding methods. This coding mechanism is a continuous encoding with time and frequency characteristics, respectively. They choose input values for each encoding neuron in one-to-one approach. The minimum value for the first encoding neuron, and the next value for the second encoding neuron, and so on. The discontinuous encoding chooses input values for each encoding neuron by the coding strategy discussed previously with time-frequency characteristics. As a result, the time which belongs to the same frequency point will be grouped into a single neuron (many-to-one relationship) (see Fig. 3). After selection, the encoding neurons convert the input values to spike trains and combine the temporal learning rules to calculate the output pulse time.

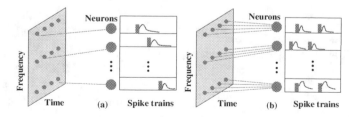

**Fig. 3.** A schematic of encoding. (a) one-to-one relationship: continuous encoding with time and frequency characteristics, respectively. (b) many-to-one relationship: discontinuous encoding with time-frequency characteristics.

Consider the local sparsity measure, the keypoint information will generate spiking trains when the difference exceeds threshold, whereas others will be discarded since such keypoints are more likely to belong to background. Then each feature point is regarded as a spike received by the neuron of brain. The feature points are mapped into a predefined encoding time window and a specific neuron.

### 3.3    Sound Recognition

Our model shows the procedure that the feature values are extracted and are encoded to a spatiotemporal spiking pattern. To simply compare these three encoding ways, we perform the recognition task on the small database from the RWCP using the Tempotron rule. And we choose 10 neurons as the readout. Each learning neuron corresponds to one category. The neurons are trained for 100 epochs. In each training epoch, a training data set of 300 samples is formed. There are 30 samples for each sound. After training, the neurons are tested on different noise levels. On each noise level, 30 noise patterns are generated for each sound.

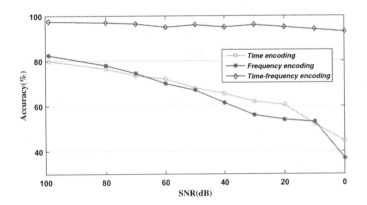

**Fig. 4.** Recognition results of sounds by different encoding methods when face with different noises.

Through simulation for recognition, we find the time-frequency encoding method is better than the other methods in convergent speed and in correct rate under the same condition (see Fig. 4). This is because the encoding method converts the time-frequency values into firing times of spikes, which retains adequate information of the original incoming sound. And using this local sparse information to generate the spiking pattern would be compatible with biological observations. In addition, it is quite important to correctly identify the type of sound, and can tolerate a certain noise in sound recognition. Thus, the combine system should hold some level of robustness. To assess the robustness of the combine system, we train the neuron with a number of patterns. Then we test the performance of the neuron with the discontinuous encoding method when face with different noise. Through several iterations of training and testing, the network could recognize all the patterns in this database.

Table 1. The correct rate of recognition in noise conditions

| Noise type | Noise level | | | |
|---|---|---|---|---|
| | 99 | 20 | 10 | 0 |
| Speech Babble | 97.50 | 95.00 | 97.00 | 94.00 |
| Destroyer Control Room | 97.50 | 97.00 | 95.00 | 94.00 |
| Factory Floor 2 | 96.00 | 96.00 | 95.50 | 93.50 |
| Volvo | 98.00 | 98.50 | 98.50 | 96.00 |

Table 1 shows the correct rate of recognition in different noise conditions. Even under challenging 0 dB SNR condition, it achieves more than 90.00%. This indicates that our system has good robustness. To see the ability of our system on the recognition task, the average performance is reported in clean and at 20, 10 and 0 dB SNR. In Table 2, the performance of correct recognition decreases with increasing noise. But it can also maintain a high correct rate (around 94.00%) in the challenging 0 dB SNR condition. This indicates that the learning rule is robust to the presence of temporal noise to some extent.

Table 2. Classification performance

| Percentage | Tempotron rule | LSF-SNN | MFCC-HMM |
|---|---|---|---|
| Clean | 97.50 | 97.30 | 99.00 |
| 20 dB | 97.00 | 97.30 | 62.10 |
| 10 dB | 95.50 | 95.30 | 34.40 |
| 0 dB | 94.00 | 90.2 | 21.80 |
| Average | 96.00 | 95.03 | 54.33 |

Meanwhile, the methods LSF-SNN and MFCC-HMM are also evaluated [33]. We set the same classification condition on the training and testing database for different methods. According to results shown in Table 2, proposed scheme achieves favorable classification accuracy for all noise conditions and significantly outperforms the LSF-SNN method. Compared with the conventional methods such as MFCC-HMM method, the proposed temporal encoding with spiking neurons is better and obtains an average accuracy of 96.00%.

## 4    Discussion and Conclusion

In this paper, a biologically plausible SNN model for sound recognition is presented. This model contains two functional parts: feature extraction with temporal coding and sound recognition with temporal learning rule. From the result that accepted signals in brain can be transmitted in the form of a pulse [35], the local time-frequency information is sparsely represented in precise timing of spikes. For the temporal learning rules, the synaptic weights are adjusted based on the relative timing difference between pre- and post-synaptic spikes.

Comparing with speech signals, sound signals include more distinctive time-frequency characteristics. In order to fully use the time-frequency features and better simulate the sound process in the brain, how to find a suitable encoding method in SNN model to generate spikes from this time information is very important. In [33], Dennis et al. have utilized the self-organizing map (SOM) to create topographically ordered spatial representations of Local Spectrogram Features (LSF) information for generating temporal coding. In this paper, we utilized the local time-frequency information of keypoints in the spectrogram to obtain spikes in the temporal coding, where all time points corresponding to one frequency value were grouped into one single neuron. Different from the encoding method in [33] which need a unsupervised learning to get sound spikes, our presented temporal coding method can easily generate spikes only by a simple mapping. Tempotron learning in SNN model has been widely applied to realize the image and object recognition due to simply training process and effective recognition results [23,36]. In this paper, we focused on exploring the effectiveness of Tempotron learning rules for sound spikes. By combining the temporal coding and Tempotron learning into SNN model, the sound recognition system has been constructed.

By simulating a few different noises into the chosen sound signals from RWCP database, experimental results demonstrated that the proposed SNN model can achieve better classification accuracy for different noise conditions comparing with LSF-SNN and MFCC-HMM model.

## References

1. Mouel, C., Harris, K.D., Yger, P.: Supervised learning with decision margins in pools of spiking neurons. J. Comput. Neurosci. **37**(2), 333–344 (2014)
2. Indiveri, G., Liu, S.C.: Memory and information processing in neuromorphic systems. Proc. IEEE **103**(8), 1379–1397 (2015)
3. Bohte, S.M.: The evidence for neural information processing with precise spike-times: a survey. Nat. Comput. **3**(2), 195–206 (2004)
4. Benchenane, K., Peyrache, A., Khamassi, M., Tierney, P.L., Gioanni, Y., Battaglia, F.P., Wiener, S.I.: Coherent theta oscillations and reorganization of spike timing in the hippocampal- prefrontal network upon learning. Neuron **66**(6), 921–936 (2010)
5. Meister, M., Berry II, M.J.: The neural code of the retina. Neuron **22**(3), 435–450 (1999)
6. Heil, P.: Auditory cortical onset responses revisited. I. First-spike timing. J. Neurophysiol. **77**(5), 2616–2641 (1997)

7. Perez-Orive, J., Mazor, O., Turner, G.C., Cassenaer, S., Wilson, R.I., Laurent, G.: Oscillations and sparsening of odor representations in the mushroom body. Science **297**(5580), 359–365 (2002)
8. Mehta, M.R., Lee, A.K., Wilson, M.A.: Role of experience and oscillations in transforming a rate code into a temporal coding. Nature **417**(417), 741–746 (2002)
9. Vanrullen, R., Guyonneau, R., Thorpe, S.J.: Spike times make sense. Trends Neurosci. **28**(1), 1–4 (2005)
10. Hodgkin, A.L., Huxley, A.F.: A quantitative description of membrane current and its application to conduction and excitation in nerve. J. Physiol. **117**(4), 500–544 (1952)
11. Izhikevich, E.M.: Simple model of spiking neurons. IEEE Trans. Neural Netw. **14**(6), 1569–1572 (2003)
12. Gerstner, W., Kistler, W.M.: Spiking Neuron Models: Single Neurons, Populations, Plasticity . Cambridge University Press, Cambridge (2002)
13. Panzeri, S., Brunel, N., Logothetis, N.K., Kayser, C.: Sensory neural codes using multiplexed temporal scales. Trends Neurosci. **33**(3), 111–120 (2010)
14. Tiesinga, P., Fellous, J.M., Sejnowski, T.J.: Regulation of spike timing in visual cortical circuits. Nat. Rev. Neurosci. **9**(2), 97–107 (2008)
15. Gutig, R.: To spike, or when to spike? Curr. Opin. Neurobiol. **25**, 134–139 (2014)
16. Natarajan, R., Huys, Q.J., Dayan, P., Zemel, R.S.: Encoding and decoding spikes for dynamic stimuli. Neural Comput. **20**(20), 2325–2360 (2008)
17. Leutgeb, S., Leutgeb, J.K., Moser, M.B., Moser, E.I.: Place cells, spatial maps and the population code for memory. Curr. Opin. Neurobiol. **15**(6), 738–746 (2006)
18. Masquelier, T., Guyonneau, R., Thorpe, S.J.: Competitive STDP-based spike pattern learning. Neural Comput. **21**(5), 1259–1276 (2009)
19. Gütig, R., Sompolinsky, H., Tempotron, T.: A neuron that learns spike timing-based decisions. Nat. Neurosci. **9**(3), 420–428 (2006)
20. Ponulak, F., Kasiński, A.: Supervised learning in spiking neural networks with ReSuMe: sequence learning, classification, and spike shifting. Neural Comput. **22**(2), 467–510 (2010)
21. Yu, Q., Tang, H., Tan, K.C., Li, H.: Precise-spike-driven synaptic plasticity: learning hetero-association of spatiotemporal spike patterns. PLoS ONE **8**(11), e78318 (2013)
22. Orchard, G., Meyer, C., Etienne-Cummings, R., Posch, C., Thakor, N., Benosman, R.: Hfirst: a temporal approach to object recognition. IEEE Trans. Pattern Anal. Mach. Intell. **37**(10), 2028–2040 (2015)
23. Zhao, B., Ding, R., Chen, S., Linares-Barranco, B., Tang, H.: Feedforward categorization on aer motion events using cortex-like features in a spiking neural network. IEEE Trans. Neural Netw. Learn. Syst. **26**(9), 24–31 (2015)
24. Hu, J., Tang, H., Tan, K.C., Li, H., Shi, L.: A spike-timing-based integrated model for pattern recognition. Neural Comput. **25**(2), 450–472 (2013)
25. Brody, C.D., Hopfield, J.J.: Simple networks for spike-timing-based computation, with application to olfactory processing. Neuron **37**(5), 843–852 (2003)
26. Yu, Q., Yan, R., Tang, H., Tan, K.C., Li, H.: A spiking neural network system for robust sequence recognition. IEEE Trans. Neural Netw. Learn. Syst. **27**(3), 621–635 (2016)
27. O'Shaughnessy, D.: Automatic speech recognition: history, methods and challenges. Pattern Recogn. **41**(10), 2965–2979 (2008)
28. Cowling, M., Sitte, R.: Comparison of techniques for environmental sound recognition. Pattern Recogn. Lett. **24**(15), 2895–2907 (2003)

29. Woodard, J.P.: Modeling and classification of natural sounds by product code hidden markov models. IEEE Trans. Signal Process. **40**(7), 1833–1835 (1992)

30. Goldhor, R.S.: Recognition of environmental sounds. In: 1993 IEEE International Conference on Acoustics, Speech and Signal Processing (ICASSP), vol. 1, pp. 149–152 (1993)

31. Liu, L.: Ground vehicle acoustic signal processing based on biological hearing models. Masters Thesis, University of Maryland, College Park (1999)

32. Valero, X., Alias, F.: Gammatone cepstral coefficients: biologically inspired features for non-speech audio classification. IEEE Trans. Multimedia **14**(6), 1684–1689 (2012)

33. Dennis, J., Yu, Q., Tang, H., Li, H.: Temporal coding of local spectrogram features for robust sound recognition. In: 2013 IEEE International Conference on Acoustics, Speech and Signal Processing (ICASSP), pp. 803–807 (2013)

34. Real World Computing Partnership, "RWCP Sound Scene Database". http://tosa.mri.co.jp/sounddb/index.htm

35. Nguyen, V.A., Starzyk, J.A., Goh, W.-B., Jachyra, D.: Neural network structure for spatio-temporal long-term memory. IEEE Trans. Neural Netw. Learn. Syst. **23**(6), 971–983 (2012)

36. Hu, J., Tang, H., Tan, K.C., Li, H.: How the brain formulates memory: a spatio-temporal model research frontier. IEEE Comput. Intell. Mag. **11**(2), 56–68 (2016)

# A Non-uniform Quantization Filter Based on Adaptive Quantization Interval in WSNs

Chenglin Wen[1(✉)], Chaoyang Zhu[1], Daxing Xu[1], and Lidi Quan[2]

[1] Institute of Systems Science and Control Engineering,
Hangzhou Dianzi University, Hangzhou 310018, China
wencl@hdu.edu.cn
[2] Collage of Engineering, Huzhou University, Huzhou 313000, China

**Abstract.** Wireless sensor networks (WSNs) fusion systems are usually faced with the communication bandwidth constraints, so it is necessary to adopt quantization. The existing quantization is usually under the assumption of known distribution function of data. However, obtaining the accurate distribution function of data is impossible. Therefore, in this paper, based on the obtained measurements, a kind of non-uniform quantization strategy under the principle of least square sum of quantization error is proposed firstly. Then, the solving method of non-uniform quantizing points based on adaptive quantization interval is presented. Next, we further provide a recursive updating method of quantizing points which include semi real-time update and real-time update. Finally, on the basis of the new method, we establish the Kalman Filter based on the new idea of Non-uniform Quantization and give some analysis of performance, which includes the theoretical part and experiment simulation.

**Keywords:** Non-uniform quantization filter · Sensor network · Adaptive quantization interval · Bandwidth-constrained · Updating of non-uniform quantizing point

## 1 Introduction

[1]Multi-sensor information fusion has got a rapid development and has been applied in many fields, such as, military affairs, national defense, high-tech and so on [1]. Among many kinds of sensor fusion systems, WSNs is developing fast in recent years. As one of important estimation methods, Kalman filtering is usually used in multisensor fusion system. In addition, comparing with Wiener filtering, Kalman filtering is not only suitable for stationary random process, but also for non-stationary random process. It is precisely due to the so many excellent characteristics of Kalman filtering, the extended Kalman filtering, unscented Kalman filtering are developed one after another. However, the above filtering theory is only taking into the form of original measurements account, but not considering the form with transmitted information.

In practical, it is necessary that we transmit measurements from sensors to data processing center through wireless or wired transmission channel. The communication

---

[1] This work was supported by the National Natural Science Foundation of China under grant numbers 61371064, 61304258, 61304186 and 61271144.

F. Sun et al. (Eds.): ICCSIP 2016, CCIS 710, pp. 595–605, 2017.
DOI: 10.1007/978-981-10-5230-9_58

capability of WSNs depends on the bandwidth of each transmission channel and the bandwidth determines the code length of transmitted message. Moreover, the code length expressing the transmission information determines the number of measurements which is transmitted. Generally speaking, the measurements collected by the sensors are bounded and the number of measurements is far beyond the carrying capacity of bandwidth. In order to solve this problem, quantizing these measurements should be one of reasonable ways to reduce the types of transmission measurements. The quantizing points similar to clustering center will only be transmitted. Thus, It is inevitable to bring about round-off error with quantization strategy adopted. Round-off error of quantization has direct impact upon filtering accuracy. Therefore, it has been a hot research topic that how to reduce the round-off error and further reduce the influence on filtering [2–5].

From the above, adopting quantitative methods in the transmission channel is necessary. The performance of filtering based on quantitative measurements depends on quantization error. Therefore, designing a new quantitative method to improve the filtering performance has attracted people's attention.

There are some commonly used quantitative methods, which can be roughly classified according to the different method of partition data interval. When the data is subject to uniform distribution, we usually divides the interval evenly, that is, uniform quantization. S.L. Sun and C.L. Wen proposed Kalman filters based on both quantized measurements (KFQM) and quantized innovations (KFQI), and they divided the measurement interval or innovation interval evenly and transmited the quantized information [10, 11]. K. Alexey adopted uniform quantization strategy to transmit a finite number of bits to fusion center, and decentralized estimator was required to have a MSE that is within a constant factor to that of the best linear unbiased estimator [20]. A. Ribeiro proposed recursive algorithms for distributed state estimation based on the sign of innovations (SOI), where the transmission from each sensor to fusion center must be a 1-bit message [12, 13]. M. Eric broaden the scope of [12, 13] by addressing the middle ground between estimators based on severely quantized (1-bit) data and those based on original data, and proposed two novel decentralized Kalman filtering estimators based on quantized measurements and innovations. In essence, these methods based on SOI still belong to the category of uniform quantization. B. Taha reduced the MSE of the distribution estimation by exploiting the correlation between observations and transmit the quantized prediction errors to FC rather than the quantized measurements [8]. A.S. Leong considered state estimation of a discrete time linear system using multiple sensors, where the sensors quantized their individual innovations and proved the stability of the estimation scheme [7]. X. Shen derieved a fixed-point-type necessary condition for sensor quantization rules and linear estimation fusion rule [6]. L. Di established a quantized gossip-based interactive Kalman filtering algorithm in a WSN, where the sensors exchanged their quantized states with neighbors via inter-sensor communications and proved the weak convergence when the quantization alphabet is finite [9]. All the above are mainly about uniform quantization to measurements and innovations. In pratical, most of data is not subject to uniform distribution, which gives rise to the limitation of this method in practical application.

As for non-uniform distribution of data, N. Elia and S.K. Mitter proposed logarithmic quantization and gave the corresponding analysis [17, 18]. M.Y. Fu extended the idea in [18] to MIMO systems [19]. Logarithmic quantization is usually used in feedback control system and plays a role of enlarging small signal. Llord S.P adopted the Lloyd-Max quantizer [15]. J. Chen proposed the corresponding online update scheme to a dynamic quantizer, and the recursive quantized Kalman filter was derived based on the Bayesian principles [16]. The all above methods are under the assumption of known measurements distribution function. However, it is difficult to obtain the approximate distribution function of measurements for a class of systems, let alone the exact distribution function. Though there could be so many operating times in industrial system and civil aviation flight, we still cannot obtain the exact distribution function due to the uncertain factors in each run and limited operating times. Therefore, the research of quantitative methods which depends on actual measurements obtained has attracted people's attention.

Summarizing the discussions made so far, it is of both theoretical significance and practical importance to design a non-uniform quantization filter with adaptive quantization interval. This appears to be a challenging task with two essential difficulties identified as follows: (1) how to establish an objective function based on the obtained measurements and solve it. (2) how to establish an iterative updating strategy to reduce the computation of the data.

The rest of this paper is organized as follows. System description and problem statement are in Sect. 2. In Sect. 3, we give the strategy of non-uniform quantization, and further provide an update method of quantizing points. The effectiveness of three algorithms is illustrated via computer simulation in Sect. 4. The final section concludes this paper.

## 2 Problem Description

Consider a class of discrete time stochastic systems proposed by the following model

$$x(k+1) = A(k)x(k) + \Gamma(k)w(k) \tag{1}$$

$$z(k) = C(k)x(k) + v(k) \tag{2}$$

where $k$ is the discrete time index. $x(k) \in R^{n \times 1}$ is the system state, $z(k) \in R^{1 \times 1}$ denotes the measurement. $A(k) \in R^{n \times n}$ is state transition matrix and $C(k) \in R^{1 \times n}$ is measurement matrix. $\Gamma(k) \in R^{n \times f}$ denotes the coefficient matrix of state noise. $w(k) \in R^{f \times 1}$ and $v(k) \in R^{1 \times 1}$ are noise input, which are zero-mean Gaussian with covariance $Q(k)$ and $R(k)$, respectively.

**Assumption 1.** $w(k)$ and $v(k)$ are white noises satisfying

$$E\{[w^T(k), v^T(k)][w^T(k_1), v^T(k_1)]^T\} = \delta_{kk_1} diag\{Q(k), R(k)\} \tag{3}$$

**Assumption 2.** The initial state $x(0)$ is independent of $w(k)$ and $v(k)$ and has the following statistical properties

$$E\{x(0)\} = \bar{x}(0), \ E\{[x(0) - \bar{x}(0)][x(0) - \bar{x}(0)]\} = p(0) \qquad (4)$$

Considering the limited communication bandwidth, the measurement $x(k)$ must be quantized as message value $m(k)$ and then be transmitted. We have the formulation as follows

$$m_i(k) = z(k) + h_i(k), i = 0, 1, 2 \qquad (5)$$

Where $h_i(k) \in R^{1 \times 1}$ is the quantization error or round-off error. While $i = 0$, $h_0(k) = 0$ and it is obvious that $m_0(k) = z(k)$. While $i = 1$, $h_1(k)$ denotes the message value of the uniform quantization error and while $i = 2$, $h_2(k)$ is to the non-uniform quantization error.

Then the formula (2) can be rewritten as follows

$$m_i(k) = C(k)x(k) + \theta_i(k), i = 0, 1, 2 \qquad (6)$$

where $\theta_i(k) = v(k) + h_i(k), i = 0, 1, 2$ is called as pseudo measurement noise and corresponding noise covariance is $R_{\theta_i}(k)$. $R_{\theta_0}(k) = R(k)$ denotes noise error of the original measurements. $R_{\theta_1}(k)$ denotes the pseudo noise covariance of measurement with uniform quantization. Similarly, $R_{\theta_2}(k)$ is for non-uniform quantization. We have Kalman filter according to (1) and (6)

$$\hat{x}_i(k|k - 1) = A(k - 1)\hat{x}_i(k - 1|k - 1) \qquad (7)$$

$$P_i(k|k - 1) = A(k - 1)P_i(k - 1|k - 1)A^T(k - 1) + \Gamma(k - 1)Q(k - 1)\Gamma^T(k - 1) \qquad (8)$$

$$K_i(k) = P_i(k|k - 1)C^T(k)[C(k)P_i(k|k - 1)C^T(k) + R_{\theta_i}(k)]^{-1} \qquad (9)$$

$$\hat{x}_i(k|k) = \hat{x}_i(k|k - 1) + K_i(k)[m_i(k) - C(k)x_i(k|k - 1)] \qquad (10)$$

$$P_i(k|k) = [I - K_i(k)C(k)]P_i(k|k - 1) \qquad (11)$$

where $i = 0$ is corresponding to Kalman filter based on the original measurements (KFOM), $i = 1$ is to Kalman filter based on the uniform measurements (KFUM), $i = 2$ is to Kalman filter based on the non-uniform measurements (KFNM). The rest we will mainly discuss the methods of non-uniform quantization and corresponding filter in this paper.

For the convenience of description, we rewrite such a set of message as quantizing points $q^0(s), q^1(s), \ldots, q^T(s)$, $T$ is quantitative copy number and $s$ denotes update time. Suppose that we need to update the quantizing points every time while we obtain $M$ measurements. The first group of measurements are $(z(1), z(2), \ldots, z(M))$ and the next group of quantizing points are denoted as $q^0(s + 1), q^1(s + 1), \ldots, q^T(s + 1)$. Therefore, we have following update formula

$$\{q^0(s+1), q^1(s+1), \ldots, q^T(s+1)\} = F(q^0(s), q^1(s), \ldots, q^T(s); z(sM+1), z(sM+2), \ldots, z(sM+M))$$

(12)

**Remark 1:** $F$ is update function, and $(z(sM+1), z(sM+2), \ldots, z(sM+M))$ denote $(s+1)th$ batch of measurements. Obviously, (12) indicates that the quantizing points to calculate are related to the last batch of quantizing points and current batch of measurements. At a particular condition, (12) will be degenerated into a kind of real-time update strategy only if $M = 1$, that is, quantization interval is adaptive. While $s = 0$, the initial quantizing points $q^0(0), q^1(0), \ldots, q^T(0)$ are known and uniform. As for $q^0(1), q^1(1), \ldots, q^T(1)$, there are two methods to compute. Except the method (12), we present a more accurate method, where $q^0(1), q^1(1), \ldots, q^T(1)$ are called the initial non-uniform quantizing points. In the rest of this paper, we will introduce how to obtain the initial non-uniform quantizing points and then do the iterative calculation according to the formula (12).

## 3   Non-uniform Quantization Strategy

**Assumption 3.** All measurements are bounded, as follows

$$z(k) \in [a, b], a < b$$

(13)

where $z(k)$ are the measurements. $a$ and $b$ are known constants. Suppose that $T$ denotes the maximum quantization copy number under bandwidth constrained condition. According to (13)

$$\bigcup_{j=0}^{T-1} [q^j(s), q^{j+1}(s)] \in [a, b]$$

(14)

The relationship of all quantizing points can be expressed as follows

$$a \leq q^0(s) < q^1(s) < \ldots < q^T(s) \leq b$$

(15)

We define $\Delta_{\max}(s) = \max\{\Delta^1(s), \ldots, \Delta^{T-1}(s)\}$ and according to (15), $\Delta^j(s) = q^{j+1}(s) - q^j(s)$. Suppose the maximum interval meet some restriction

$$\Delta_{\max}(s) < \frac{3(b-a)}{T} (T > 3)$$

(16)

**Remark 2:** It is worthwhile to note that the distance $\Delta^j(s) = q^{j+1}(s) - q^j(s)$ between any two quantizing points may be equal or unequal. When any two $\Delta^j(s)$ are equal to each other, it will be degenerated into the uniform quantization. In this paper, the distribution function of measurements is unknown and the aim is to find quantizing points with limited number of measurements. Generally speaking, the quantizing points will be not evenly scattered over a bounded interval. With the constraint condition (16), the biggest quantization interval $\Delta_{max}(s)$ has an upper bound on the set in case of some extreme situation, such as the biggest interval is constant with increase of number of measurements. As is seen in (16), the biggest interval is set to three times of the uniform quantization interval under the same constraint condition.

Under assumption 3, unevenly divide $[a, b]$ into intervals with uncertain length, and round the observation $z(k)$ to one of two neighboring interval endpoints in a probabilistic manner

$$u^j(k) = q^{j+1}(s) - z(k), \ p^j(k) = \frac{z(k) - q^j(s)}{\Delta^j(s)} \tag{17}$$

then the noise variance of non-uniform quantization is computed as

$$\sigma_2^2(s) = E\{[m_2(k) - z(k)]^2\} = (\Delta^j(s) - u^j(k))^2(1 - p^j(k)) + (u^j(k))^2 p^j(k)$$
$$= (\Delta^j(s))^2 p^j(k)[1 - p^j(k)] \leq \frac{(\Delta^j(s))^2}{4} = R_2(s) \tag{18}$$

hence, combing (6), we can compute pseudo measurement noise covariance

$$\sigma_{\theta_2}(k) = E\{\theta_2(k)\theta_2^T(k)\} \leq diag\{R_{\theta_0}(k) + R_2(s)\} = R_{\theta_2}(k) \tag{19}$$

Subsequently, we will introduce how to compute the initial non-uniform quantizing points. For the first $M$ measurements $z(1), z(2), \ldots, z(M)$, under the condition of known two boundaries, uniform quantization strategy is necessary. After we obtained the first batch of measurements, we should find $(T + 1)$ non-uniform quantizing points under the principle of least square sum of quantization error with obtained measurements, then it is necessary to quantify next batch of measurements by obtained quantizing points. In fact, what we should do is to find $(T - 1)$ quantizing points $q^1(1), \ldots, q^{T-1}(1)$. So we have following optimal formula

$$\{q^{0*}(s), q^{1*}(s), \ldots, q^{T*}(s)\} = \arg \min_{\{q^{1*}, q^{2*}, \ldots, q^{(T-1)*}\}} \sum_{k=1}^{M} |z(k) - q^{j*}|^2 \tag{20}$$
$$s.t.\{a < q^{j*} < b, j \in [1, T-1]; q^{j*} = a, j = 0; q^{j*} = b, j = T$$

**Remark 3:** Obviously, $s = 1$ denotes the first group of non-uniform quantizing points and $q^{j*}$ denotes the optimal solution. However, we can't solve the equation actually due to infinite points in the interval, so. Assuming that $\varepsilon^*$ indicates global minimum sum of square quantization error.

$$\varepsilon^*(s) = \sum_{k=1}^{M} |z(k) - q^{j*}(s)|^2, j \in [0, T] \tag{21}$$

Next we provide a sub-optimal method to find the non-uniform quantizing points. Because the analytical expression of non-uniform quantizing points can't be easily obtained and the points in $[a, b]$ is infinite, first of all, we take $(L+1)(L \gg T)$ equidistant discrete points over the quantization interval $[a(r), b(r)]$ in order to facilitate the realization of digital computer, and these discrete points are signed as $d^0(s), d^1(s), \ldots, d^L(s)$, which satisfy the following relationship

$$a = d^0(s) < d^1(s) < \ldots < d^T(s) < \ldots < d^{L-1}(s) < d^L(s) = b(r) \tag{22}$$

Then taking (15) and (22) into account, it reduces to

$$q^0(s) = a = d^0(s), \quad q^T(s) = b = d^L(s) \tag{23}$$

hence, combing (23), the problem is transformed into a search for $(T-1)$ non-uniform quantizing points from $(L-1)$ discrete points. So the sub-optimal method to solve the problem is described

$$\{q^0(s), q^1(s), \ldots, q^T(s)\} = \arg \min_{\{q^1, q^2, \ldots, q^{T-1}\}} \sum_{k=1}^{M} |z(k) - q^j|^2 \tag{24}$$

$$s.t. \{q^j \in \{d^1(s), \ldots, d^{L-1}(s)\}, j \in [1, L-1]; q^j = a, j = 0; q^j = b, j = T$$

**Remark 4:** That is to say, let the $(T-1)$ non-uniform quantizing points traverse discrete points $d^1(s), d^2(s), \ldots, d^{L-1}(s)$ to find the optimal solution. It is obvious that the accuracy of quantizing points is related to the number of discrete points. Suppose that the minimum sum of square quantization error is denoted as $\varepsilon(s)$ when we just take $(L+1)$ discrete points. We have

$$\varepsilon(s) = \sum_{k=1}^{M} |z(k) - q^j(s)|^2, j \in [0, T] \tag{25}$$

Under same constrained condition, when the number of discrete points tends to infinity. Then

$$\varepsilon^*(s) = \lim_{L(r) \to \infty} \varepsilon(s) \tag{26}$$

hence, (25) will be turned into (21). Thus, the initial non-uniform quantizing points are obtained.

Next, the process to solve the formula (12) will be introduced. As estimation fusion is proceeding all the time, it is improper to quantize all subsequent batches of measurements with the first group of quantizing points, for there must be some change to the distribution function of measurements. Thus, updating the non-uniform quantizing points is necessary. Generally speaking, the global distribution of measurements will tends to be stable if $s \to \infty$. The amount of computation will be large if we still use (20), (24) to find quantizing points. For each batch of $M$ measurements, the distribution function of measurements will not be same. By means of analysis, optimal quantizing point $q^{j*}(s+1)$ will be in the vicinity of last quantizing point $q^{j*}(s)$. We have

$$q^{j*}(s) - \lambda^j(s) < q^{j*}(s+1) < q^{j*}(s) + \lambda^j(s)$$
$$s.t. : j \in [1, T-1] \tag{27}$$

Thus, we can use current group of quantizing points and next batch of measurements to update quantizing points. So we have

$$\{q^{0*}(s+1), q^{1*}(s+1), \ldots, q^{T*}(s+1)\} = \arg \min_{\{q^{1*}, q^{2*}, \ldots, q^{(T-1)*}\}} \sum_{u=1}^{M} |z(sM+u) - q^{j*}|^2$$
$$s.t. \{q^{j*} = q^{0*}(s+1) = q^{0*}(s), j = 0; q^{j*} = q^{T*}(s+1) = q^{T*}(s), j = T; (27)$$
$$\tag{28}$$

**Remark 5:** $\lambda^j(s)$ is suitable and small enough. Obviously, $s > 1$ and the points in interval $[q^j(s) - \lambda^j(s), q^j(s) + \lambda^j(s)]$ are infinite so we can't find solution of (28). But we can use the same method in (24) to find the sub-optimal solution. We take a series of equidistant discrete points in the interval $[q^j(s) - \lambda^j(s), q^j(s) + \lambda^j(s)]$. It can greatly reduce the algorithm complexity to find the quantizing points according to the latest batch of measurements other than the all obtained measurements. So formula (12) is solved.

## 4   Simulations and Performance Analysis

In this section, a simulation is illustrated to compare the estimate accuracy among KFOM, KFUQ and KFNQ. Considering a bandwidth constrained sensor networks presented in Sect. 2

$$\begin{cases} x(k+1) = \begin{bmatrix} 0.6333 - 0.0672 \\ 2.0570 \quad 0.6082 \end{bmatrix} x(k) + \begin{bmatrix} -0.0653 \\ 1.4462 \end{bmatrix} w(k) \\ z(k) = [-0.7568 \quad 1.2493] x(k) + v(k) \end{cases}, \bar{x}(0) = [0.1 \, 0.2]^T, p(0) = \begin{bmatrix} 0.10 \\ 00.6 \end{bmatrix} \tag{29}$$

Where $w(k)$, $v(k)$ are uncorrelated zero-mean white noises with covariance $Q = 0.05$, $R = 0.05$, respectively. We choose each batch of measurements $M = 200$, and the uniform quantization copy number and non-uniform quantization copy number are 6 all the time. That is to say, the number of quantizing points is 7. The number of discrete points $L = 26$.

Then, the simulation procedure is described as follows: At first, we can obtain the endpoints of measurements by priori information. Then, we choose KFOM and KFUQ to deal with the first batch of measurements. Second, we find the sub-optimal non-uniform quantizing points according to (24). At last step, we use KFOM, KFUQ and KFNQ to deal with the second batch of measurements. The whole simulation is divided into three parallel processes, which is shown in Table 1.

The simulation are all based on the second batch of measurements and the average of 50 Monte-Carlo simulations. Simulation results are shown in Figs. 1 and 2, and Tables 2 and 3.

**Table 1.** Three kinds of simulation processes

| Algorithm | First batch of measurements | Second batch of measurements |
| --- | --- | --- |
| Process 1 | KFOM | KFOM |
| Process 2 | KFUQ | KFUQ |
| Process 3 | KFUQ | KFNQ |

It can be seen from Fig. 1 that the comparison of quantization error between KFUQ and KFNQ is illustrated, corresponding numerical results in Table 2. From Fig. 2 that the state estimation curves among KFOM, KFUQ and KFNQ are showed, corresponding numerical results in Table 3. It can be seen that the covariance of KFNQ no matter the first state component or second is less than that of KFUQ under same condition and the KFOM which do not adopt quantitative strategy has the least covariance, that is best precision. Moreover, the quantization error of KFNQ (0.1265) is much less than that of KFUQ (0.1787) according to Fig. 1.

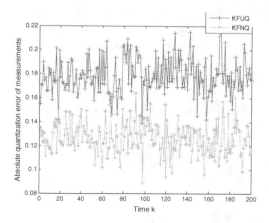

**Fig. 1.** Quantization error of KFUQ and KFNQ

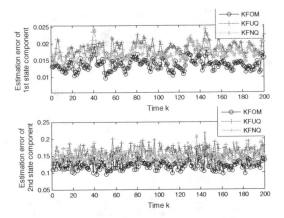

**Fig. 2.** Estimation error curves of three algorithms

**Table 2.** Mean absolute quantization error of measurements

| Algorithm | KFUQ | KFNQ |
|---|---|---|
| Mean absolute error | 0.1787 | 0.1265 |

**Table 3.** Mean absolute error of estimation

| Algorithm | | KFOM | KFUQ | KFNQ |
|---|---|---|---|---|
| Mean absolute error | 1st state component | 0.0138 | 0.0186 | 0.0172 |
| | 2nd state component | 0.1235 | 0.1592 | 0.1472 |

## 5  Conclusion

In this paper, the non-uniform quantization filtering based on adaptive quantization interval has been investigated for a class of networks multi-sensor fusion systems with communication bandwidth constraints when the distribution of measurements is not uniform. The KFNQ based on adaptive quantization interval is proposed and the algorithm of finding quantizing points, updating of quantizing points are further put forward. In addition, we analyze the upper bound of the quantization noise variance which is related to the quantization copy number and the number of discrete points. At the same time, the simulation results verify the validity of analysis.

## References

1. Chen, B., Zhang, W.A., Yu, L., et al.: Distributed fusion estimation with communication bandwidth constraints. IEEE Trans. Autom. Control **60**(5), 1398–1403 (2015)
2. Chen, B., Zhang, W.A., Yu, L.: Distributed fusion estimation with missing measurements, random transmission delays and packet dropouts. IEEE Trans. Autom. Control **59**(7), 1961–1967 (2013)

3. Akyildiz, I.F., Su, W., Sankarasubramaniam, Y., et al.: Wireless sensor networks: a survey. Comput. Netw. **38**(4), 393–422 (2002)
4. Gubner, J.A.: Distributed estimation and quantization. IEEE Trans. Inf. Theory **39**(4), 1456–1459 (1993)
5. Marano, S., Matta, V., Willett, P.: Distributed estimation in large wireless sensor networks via a locally optimum approach. IEEE Trans. Signal Process. **56**(2), 748–756 (2008)
6. Shen, X., Zhu, Y., You, Z.: An efficient sensor quantization algorithm for decentralized estimation fusion. Automatica **47**(5), 1053–1059 (2011)
7. Leong, A.S., Dey, S., Nair, G.N.: Quantized filtering schemes for multi-sensor linear state estimation: stability and performance under high rate quantization. IEEE Trans. Signal Process. **61**(15), 3852–3856 (2013)
8. Bouchoucha, T., Ahmed, M.F., Al-Naffouri, T.Y., Alouini, M.S.: Distributed estimation based on observations prediction in wireless sensor networks. IEEE Signal Process. Lett. **22**(10), 1530–1533 (2015)
9. Li, D., Kar, S., Alsaadi, A.E., et al.: Distributed Kalman filtering with quantized sensing state. IEEE Trans. Signal Process. **63**(19), 5180–5193 (2015)
10. Sun, S., Lin, J., Xie, L., et al.: Quantized Kalman filtering. In: IEEE 22nd International Symposium on Intelligent Control, pp. 7–12 (2007)
11. Wen, C., Ge, Q., Tang, X.: Kalman filtering in a bandwidth constrained sensor network. Chin. J. Electron. **18**(4), 713–718 (2009)
12. Ribeiro, A., Giannakis, G.B.: Bandwidth-constrained distributed estimation for wireless sensor networks-partI: Gaussian case. IEEE Trans. Signal Process. **54**(3), 1131–1143 (2006)
13. Ribeiro, A., Giannakis, G.B.: Bandwidth-constrained distributed estimation for wireless sensor networks-partII: unknown probability density function. IEEE Trans. Signal Process. **54**(7), 2784–2796 (2006)
14. Msechu, E.J., Roumeliotis, S.I., Ribeiro, A., Giannakis, G.B.: Decentralized quantized Kalman filtering with scalable communication cost. IEEE Trans. Signal Process. **56**(8), 3727–3741 (2008)
15. Lloyd, S.P.: Least squares quantization in PCM. IEEE Trans. Inf. Theory **28**(2), 129–137 (1982)
16. Chen, J., Wu, Y., Qi, T.: Distributed quantized Kalman filtering for wireless sensor networks. Control Theor. Appl. **28**(12), 1729–1739 (2011)
17. Elia, N., Mitter, S.K.: Quantization of linear systems. In: Proceeding of IEEE Conference on Decision and Control, pp. 3428–3433 (1999)
18. Elia, N., Mitter, S.K.: Stabilization of linear systems with limited information. IEEE Trans. Autom. Control **46**(9), 1384–1400 (2001)
19. Fu, M.Y., Xie, L.H.: The sector bound approach to quantized feedback control. IEEE Trans. Autom. Control **50**(11), 1698–1711 (2005)
20. Krasnopeev, A., Xiao, J.J., Luo, Z.Q.: Minimum energy decentralized estimation in a wireless sensor network with correlated sensor noises. Eurasip J. Wirel. Commun. Netw. **4**, 473–482 (2005)

# Ambulanceye – The Future of Medical Rescues

Wenfeng Wang[1], Xi Chen[1(⊠)], Huaying Zhou[2], Hongwei Zheng[1(⊠)],
Dandan Sun[3], and Jing Qian[4(⊠)]

[1] State Key Laboratory of Desert and Oasis Ecology,
Xinjiang Institute of Ecology and Geography,
Chinese Academy of Sciences, Urumqi 830011, Xinjiang, China
{chenxi,hzheng}@ms.xjb.ac.cn
[2] Department of Electronic Engineering,
Yantai Automobile Engineering Professional College, Yantai 265500, China
[3] The Second Surgical Department,
Zouping Hospital of Traditional Chinese Medicine, Zouping 256200, China
[4] Center for Geo-Spatial Information,
Shenzhen Institutes of Advanced Technology,
Chinese Academy of Sciences, Shenzhen 518055, China
jing.qian@siat.ac.cn

**Abstract.** This study advances the concept of "ambulanceye" as a conjecture on the future of medical rescues, assuming that the advanced driver assistant systems (ADAS) can be equipped in ambulances and contribute to driving security through timely danger caution. Recognition of the danger is based on detecting and tracking of eigenobjects (defined as the potential dangerous objects in the video). Simulated performances shown that ambulanceye can overcome ocular restriction resulted from weathering extremes and other accidents that can cause sights blurred. Nevertheless, considerable uncertainties still remain in real-time analyses and characterization of eigenobjects trace. A next research priority is to develop an ADAS system for efficient eigenobjects recognition and tracking.

**Keywords:** Blind area · Ambulanceye · Medical rescues

## 1 Introduction

Intelligent monitoring system has been installed over the streets in the major cities and studies on the algorithms for the intelligent video recognition have attracted much attention [1–5]. Recognition of video bigdata has become one key direction associated with cities security and has been rapidly developed in the past decade, especially after its combination with geographic information, which further produced some new technologies - mainly including rapid and exact acquirement of geographic data, real-time information processing for 3D-reconstuction and behavior recognition [6–10].

This encourage us to offer a new blueprint for the future medical rescues - how to save driving time of ambulances with high speed and meanwhile ensure driving safety [11]. Considering rapid development of video recognition and its getting wider applications in the advanced driver assistant systems (ADAS), more and more attention

© Springer Nature Singapore Pte Ltd. 2017
F. Sun et al. (Eds.): ICCSIP 2016, CCIS 710, pp. 606–615, 2017.
DOI: 10.1007/978-981-10-5230-9_59

are paid to the Self- and peer-assessments of ambulance drivers' performance in recent years [12–15]. Meanwhile, intelligent monitoring system with efficient facilities have been put into use in smart hospitals towards efficient medical rescues [16, 17].

Nevertheless, significance of ADAS to ambulances employed for medical rescues still has not attracted enough attention. Since the intelligent monitoring systems have been widely applied in smart hospitals [18–20], it is feasible to expand their applications to ambulances for medical rescues to strengthen the security of doctors, nurses, patients, drivers and the safety of other people and mobiles along the way to the scene of medical rescues. This study a simple first approach is worthy of attempt and the future research priority must be timely highlighted [21–26].

Objectives of this study are (1) to advance the concept of "ambulanceye" as a conjecture on the future medical rescues - assuming that ADAS can be equipped in ambulances and make contributions to driving security through timely danger recognition and caution, and (2) to present evidences for feasibility of such an emerging technology and suggest it as a future research priority for ADAS researchers.

## 2 Materials and Methods

### 2.1 Data Sources

In order to make it more challenging and convincing, geospatial videos are collected from the Hetian Region during sampling days under poor atmospheric visibility. Hetian Region is located in the southernmost part of the Xinjiang Province, China, while the Xinjiang Province locates in the northwestern border of China, which is the largest administrative in China division and the 8th largest country subdivision in the world,

**Fig. 1.** Location of the study site.

with an arid climate, spanning over 1.6 million km$^2$ from the east border to the northwestern border along the famous Silk Road running (Fig. 1).

## 2.2   Algorithms

Evaluations of the future performance of ADAS in applications to ambulances for medical rescues are established using the data set of geospatial videos collected in a driving vehicle. Danger recognition and caution are based on detecting and tracking of eigenobjects (defined as the potential dangerous objects in the video), which are carried out through a set of algorithms - such as optical flow method, compressive sensing tracking and deep learning [27–40], which are employed to realize video recognition for validating feasibility of dangers recognition and caution. A first sketch of eigenobjects is presented in Fig. 2, with the pre-cognition difficulty represented by the circles size and early-warning level represented by the arrows color. As well-known, in medical rescues ambulances can go through a red light, which caused a series of accidents, some of which are avoidable if utilizing early-warning by ambulanceye. Therefore, red light can also be included as an eigenobject. Overall, this first sketch includes 12 eigenobjects to indicate potential dangers. It must be pointed out that this is not the whole story - any subsequent revision and expansion of the sketch of eigenobjects are certainly valuable.

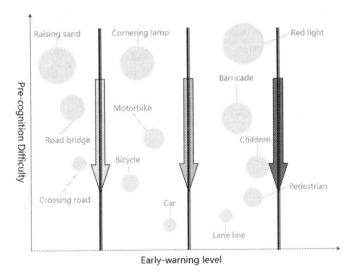

**Fig. 2.** A first sketch of eigenobjects.

# 3   Results and Discussions

## 3.1   Necessity to Introduce 'Ambulanceye'

As well-known, any vehicle has a blind area and ambulances are no exception. Exactly, a series of accidents have happened when ambulances were going to the scene of accidents. Nobody can deny the necessity to introduce "ambulanceye" unless they present another efficient way to avoid such unfortunate accidents. Furthermore, the importance of ADAS shall be largely recognized since treatments of additional accidents cost much time. The basic idea in practical applications of ambulanceye can be very simple - dangers recognition and caution. A full screen of drivers' blind area is characterized in Fig. 3, integrating the widely-recognized insights. It is easy to see that the vast majority of blind areas are in the lack of realization by the ambulance drivers, because that the medical rescues are always emergent and their time maybe insufficient - they might cannot arrive the scene of medical rescues in time and great loss of people's lives and property would be subsequently produced since too much time had been spent in artificially finding dangers.

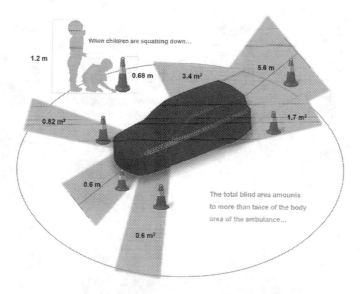

**Fig. 3.** Description of driver blind area.

Consequently, ambulanceye is very important for improving the efficiency of the future medical rescues and an ADAS system of eigenobjects recognition is suggested to be employed in ambulances to reduce additional unfortunate accidents. A first perspective concept of ambulanceye is shown in Fig. 4.

Alternatively, ambulanceye as an emerging technology for monitoring ambulance driving safety in the future medical rescues can also be taken as a further combination of intelligent recognition and real-time tracking with geographic information to timely detect and caution the potential dangers within the blind area.

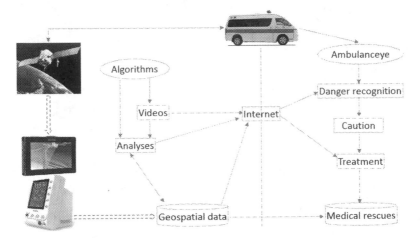

**Fig. 4.** Concept of ambulanceye.

**Fig. 5.** Examples of eigenobjects detecting and tracking.

## 3.2    Feasibility of Danger Recognition and Caution

Examples of eigenobjects detecting and tracking indicate that ambulanceye can even overcome the ocular restriction when facing weathering extremes (Fig. 5). However, it is also necessary to point out that videos collected by vehicle-tachograph need a 'debouncing' treatment.

To further explain how to find the dangers and make a precaution for drivers, one most simple example - the performance of ambulanceye in applications to detecting and warning potential dangers are validated by the lane-departure detecting for timely danger caution. Similar to the performance in eigenobjects detecting and tracking, dangers recognition and caution in ambulances driving also can overcome restriction of accidents that causes sights blurred, providing that ambulanceye is employed (Fig. 6). This certainly enhance the security experience of the doctors, nurses, patients and drivers and in turn improve work efficiency in the future medical rescues.

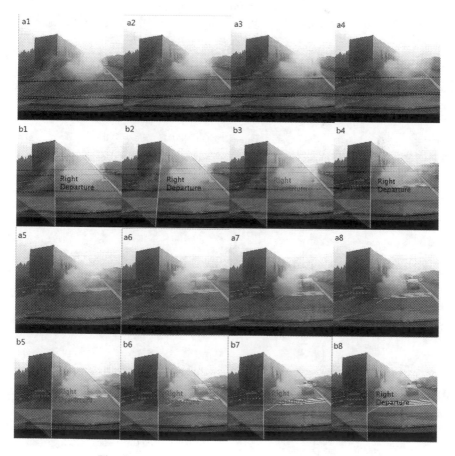

**Fig. 6.** Lane departure detecting for danger caution.

### 3.3    Framework of Future Medical Rescues

For a theoretical illustration of the significance to introduce ambulanceye for the future medical rescues, a simple yet efficient mathematical model of working time in one medical rescue can be formulated as follows

$$t = b - c * x\%$$

where t is the practically working time in this medical rescue, b is the basic time, c is the technically condensed time by ambulanceye and x% is the ambulanceye-working efficiency in danger recognition and caution.

Obviously, efficiency of future medical rescues is largely determined by the coefficient c, which majorly depends on the efficiency x%. Ambulanceye indicates more efficient way to reduce unfortunate accidents when ambulances are going to the scene of accidents. Furthermore, ambulanceye can also help to improve efficiency of the future medical rescues and build reputation of medical rescues - to help the people understand how the functions of ambulances are carried out wholly under the premise of ensuring safety - people can evaluate it by quantitative indices (e.g., c and x).

Concept of ambulanceye can be further developed and make help in future medical rescues. A next research priority is to find an optimal method for robust and real-time analyzing and mining the history and personnel movement trace. A first framework of the future medical rescues is shown in Fig. 7.

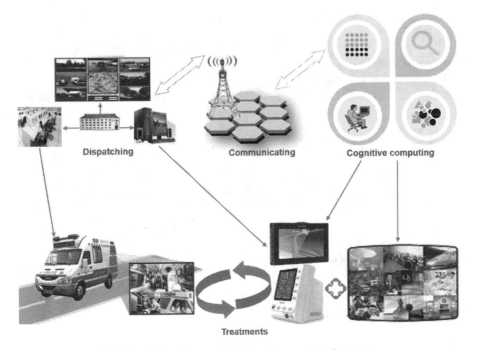

**Fig. 7.** A first framework of the future medical rescues.

# 4  Concluding Remarks

Ambulanceye as an emerging technology can detect and track eigenobjects and help to break through the major restriction on the overall operating efficiency of ambulances for medical rescues imposed by driver blind areas. It facilitates the visualization of potential dangers even when facing special weathering accidents and other accidents that causes sights blurred. Ambulanceye not only link doctors, nurses, drivers and archival data of local information or danger recognition and caution along the way to the scene of medical rescues, but also expands the applications of ADAS and in turn motivates medical incorporation with the time of big data.

**Competing Interests**
None declared.

**Acknowledgments.**  This research was financially supported by the CAS 'Light of West China' Program (XBBS-2014-16), the Shenzhen Basic Research Project (JCYJ20150630114942260), the "Thousand Talents" plan (Y474161) and the National High Technology Research and Development Program (2013AA122302).

# References

1. Kovar, L., Gleicher, M.: Automated extraction and parameterization of motions in large data sets. ACM Trans. Graph. **23**(3), 559–568 (2004)
2. Philip Chen, C.L., Zhang, C.Y.: Data-intensive applications, challenges, techniques and technologies: a survey on big data. Inf. Sci. **275**(11), 314–347 (2014)
3. Marx, V.: The big challenges of big data. Nat. **498**(7453), 255–260 (2013)
4. Richtárik, P., Takáč, M.: Parallel coordinate descent methods for big data optimization. Math. Prog. **156**(1), 1–52 (2016)
5. Vazhkudai, S., Schopf, J.M.: Using regression techniques to predict large data transfers. Int. J. High Perform. Comput. Appl. **17**(3), 249–268 (2003)
6. Waldrop, M.: Big data: wikiomics. Nat. **455**(7209), 22–25 (2008)
7. Kim, G.H., Trimi, S., Chung, J.H.: Big-data applications in the government sector. Commun. ACM **57**(3), 78–85 (2014)
8. Mervis, J.: Agencies rally to tackle big data. Sci. **336**(6077), 22–22 (2012)
9. Wigan, M.R., Clarke, R.: Big data's big unintended consequences. Comput. **46**(6), 46–53 (2013)
10. Talia, D.: Clouds for scalable big data analytics. Comput. **46**(5), 98–101 (2013)
11. Westgate, B.S., Woodard, D.B., Matteson, D.S., Henderson, S.G.: Large-network travel time distribution estimation for ambulances. Eur. J. Oper. Res. **252**(1), 322–333 (2016)
12. Shin, D.M., Yoon, B.G., Han, Y.T.: Analysis of ambulance traffic accident during driving. vol. 30(1), pp. 130–137 (2016)
13. Shin, D.M., Kim, S.Y., Han, Y.T.: A study on the comparative analysis of fire-fighting ambulances about the aspects of safety and efficiency using the question investigation. vol. 29(2), pp. 44–53 (2015)

14. Ambrose, J.: Emergency response driving education within UK ambulance services. J. Paramedic Pract. **5**(6), 351–353 (2013)
15. Sundström, A., Albertsson, P.: Self- and peer-assessments of ambulance drivers' driving performance. Iatss Res. **36**(1), 40–47 (2012)
16. Raaber, N., Duvald, I., Riddervold, I., Christensen, E.F., Kirkegaard, H.: Geographic information system data from ambulances applied in the emergency department: effects on patient reception. Scand. J. Trauma Resuscitation Emerg. Med. **24**(1), 1–9 (2016)
17. Fu, Q., Li, B., Yang, L., Wu, Z., Zhang, X.: Ecosystem services evaluation and its spatial characteristics in central Asia's arid regions: a case study in Altay prefecture, china. Sustain. **7**(7), 8335–8353 (2015)
18. Xie, Z., Liu, G.: Blood perfusion construction for infrared face recognition based on bio-heat transfer. Bio-Med. Mater. Eng. **24**(6), 2733–2742 (2014)
19. Jin, L., Niu, Q., Jiang, Y., Xian, H., Qin, Y., Xu, M.: Driver sleepiness detection system based on eye movements variables. Adv. Mech. Eng. **2013**(5), 1–7 (2013)
20. Wang, T., Dong, J., Sun, X., Zhang, S., Wang, S.: Automatic recognition of facial movement for paralyzed face. Bio-Med. Mater. Eng. **24**(6), 2751–2760 (2014)
21. Vithya, G., Sundaram, B.V.: Inpatient critical stage monitoring in smart hospitals by contextual Fuzzy based QoS routing for WBMS network nurse call system. Wirel. Pers. Commun. **94**, 1–16 (2016)
22. Nandyala, C.S., Kim, H.K.: From cloud to Fog and IoT-based real-time U-healthcare monitoring for smart homes and hospitals. Int. J. Smart Home **10**(2), 187–196 (2016)
23. Chen, X., Wang, L., Ding, J., et al.: Patient flow scheduling and capacity planning in a smart hospital environment. IEEE Access **4**, 135–148 (2016)
24. Al-Refaie, A., Chen, T., Judeh, M.: Optimal operating room scheduling for normal and unexpected events in a smart hospital. Oper. Res. pp. 1–24 (2016)
25. Vecchia, G.D., Gallo, L., Esposito, M., et al.: An infrastructure for smart hospitals. Multimed. Tools Appl. **59**(1), 341–362 (2012)
26. Yao, W., Chu, C.H., Li, Z.: Leveraging complex event processing for smart hospitals using RFID. J. Netw. Comput. Appl. **34**(3), 799–810 (2011)
27. Fang, Y.L., Zhang, A., Wang, H., Li, H., Zhang, Z.W., Chen, S.X., Luan, L.Y.: Health risk assessment of trace elements in Chinese raisins produced in Xinjiang province. Food Control **21**(5), 732–739 (2010)
28. Jing, L.: Incremental learning for robust visual tracking. Int. J. Comput. Vis. **77**(1–3), 125–141 (2008)
29. Dewan, M.A.A., Granger, E., Marcialis, G.L., et al.: Adaptive appearance model tracking for still-to-video face recognition. Pattern Recogn. **49**(C), 129–151 (2016)
30. Babenko, B., Yang, M.H., Belongie, S.: Robust object tracking with online multiple instance learning. IEEE Trans. Pattern Anal. Mach. Intell. **33**(8), 1619–1632 (2011)
31. Wu, Y., Jia, N., Sun, J.: Real-time multi-scale tracking based on compressive sensing. Vis. Comput. Int. J. Comput. Graph. **31**(4), 471–484 (2015)
32. Mei, X., Ling, H.: Robust visual tracking and vehicle classification via sparse representation. IEEE Trans. Softw. Eng. **33**(11), 2259–2272 (2011)
33. Yamins, D.L.K., Dicarlo, J.J.: Using goal-driven deep learning models to understand sensory cortex. Nat. Neurosci. **19**(3), 356–365 (2016)
34. Chen, L., Qu, H., Zhao, J., Principe, J.C.: Efficient and robust deep learning with Correntropy- induced loss function. Neural Comput. Appl. **27**(4), 1019–1031 (2016)
35. Ghesu, F.C., Krubasik, E., Georgescu, B., Singh, V.: Marginal space deep learning: efficient architecture for volumetric image parsing. IEEE Trans. Med. Imaging **35**(5), 1217–1228 (2016)

36. Erfani, S.M., Rajasegarar, S., Karunasekera, S., Leckie, C.: High-dimensional and large-scale anomaly detection using a linear one-class SVM with deep learning. Pattern Recogn. **58**, 121–134 (2016)
37. Greenspan, H., Ginneken, B.V., Summers, R.M.: Guest editorial deep learning in medical imaging: overview and future promise of an exciting new technique. IEEE Trans. Med. Imaging **35**(5), 1153–1159 (2016)
38. Wang, Y., Luo, Z., Jodoin, P.M.: Interactive deep learning method for segmenting moving objects. Pattern Recogn. Lett. (2016). doi:10.1016/j.patrec.2016.09.014
39. Ngo, T.A., Lu, Z., Carneiro, G.: Combining deep learning and level set for the automated segmentation of the left ventricle of the heart from cardiac cine magnetic resonance. Med. Image Anal. **35**, 159–171 (2016)
40. Leng, J., Jiang, P.: A deep learning approach for relationship extraction from interaction context in social manufacturing paradigm. Knowl.-Based Syst. **100**(C), 188–199 (2016)

# Author Index

Printed in the United States
By Bookmasters